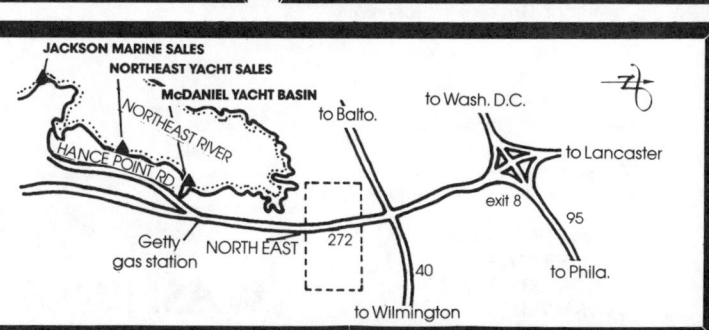

HOW TO USE

Chesapeake Bay Magazine Guide to Cruising the Chesapeake Bay

Guide To Cruising The Chesapeake Bay is designed to be useful as a planning reference, as well as a ready guide for up-to-date information to be used in conjunction with navigational charts. The drawings and NOAA charts in this *Guide* are not for use in navigation; they are intended to show the general location of the various areas.

Mariners seeking complete coverage of all changes in navigational aids on the Bay should subscribe to the U.S. Coast Guard's "Local Notices to Mariners," Dept. of Trans., U.S. Coast Guard Commander, Fifth Coast Guard District, 431 Crawford St., Portsmouth, VA 23705 (804)398-6225.

At the front of the *Guide* are several feature articles with cruising and galley tips; information on weather, first aid, marine radio use, annual events, museums on Chesapeake Bay, etc.

The *Guide* has been divided into three geographic regions:

Upper Bay: C&D Canal to Chesapeake Bay Bridge

Middle Bay: Chesapeake Bay Bridge to Potomac River

Lower Bay: Smith and Tangier Islands to Cape Charles

Within each section are cruises also geographically arranged north to south, from the mouth of a river, proceeding upriver, and hopscotching from western to eastern shores.

At the back of the *Guide* is a distance chart, a foldout five-mile grid, tide tables, etc. Also at the back of the *Guide* is a listing of approximately 450 restaurants and marinas on the Bay. The information supplied for each establishment was compiled from questionnaires filled out by personnel of the establishment. Restaurants and marinas wishing to be included in the listing should call (301)263-2662 for details.

An important part of the *Guide* is the detailed index which alphabetically lists rivers, creeks, anchorages and points of interest.

We would appreciate hearing from those who use the Guide concerning any additions or corrections you think would improve it. Send these to: Editor, *Guide to Cruising the Chesapeake Bay*, 1819 Bay Ridge Ave., Annapolis, MD 21403.

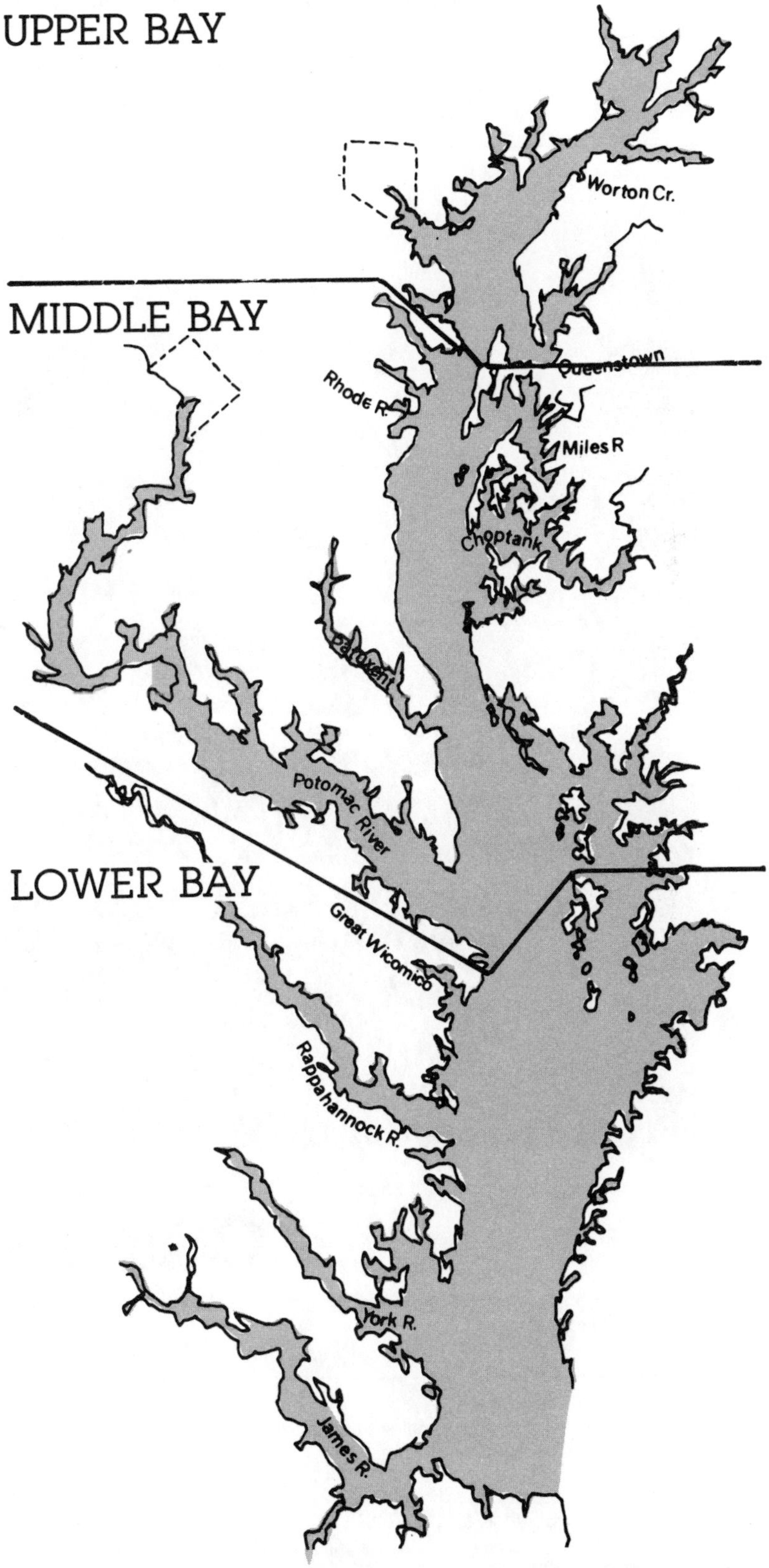

Businesses wishing to sell the Guide are encouraged to call for our wholesale rates, (301) 263-2662 or D.C. 261-1323.
Cruise art & photographs by Richard C. Goetemiller, unless otherwise stated
Cover photo by Bob Grieser

1987

GUIDE TO CRUISING THE

CHESAPEAKE BAY

CONTENTS

FEATURES 7

UPPER BAY: C&D CANAL TO CHESAPEAKE BAY BRIDGE 32

MIDDLE BAY: CHESAPEAKE BAY BRIDGE TO POTOMAC RIVER 110

LOWER BAY: SMITH AND TANGIER ISLANDS TO CAPE CHARLES 232

MEET OUR CONTRIBUTING EDITORS
...AND SHARE THEIR FAVORITE GALLEY RECIPES

The *Guide to Cruising the Chesapeake Bay* relies on input from contributing authors in many areas of the Bay to bring you the most up-to-date information possible. To help you become better acquainted with them, we bring you these short biographies. To enhance your cruising days, we asked them to pass along their favorite sandwich recipes.

STEPHEN BLOCH

Stephen Bloch is an attorney serving on active duty with the Navy in Norfolk. He has cruised the Chesapeake extensively and, a few summers ago made a single-handed cruise to Maine. Other notable sailing adventures have been serving as Executive Officer on a three-week Naval sail training cruise from Norfolk to New England and back and crewing on a 48-foot yawl from Puerto Rico to Norfolk. His combined expertise in sailing, writing and law has found its way into magazine articles and a chapter on wills in the book *Managing Your Escape.*

"Maybe tastes change when circumstances change," he comments when asked to describe his favorite sandwich to eat while cruising (recipe follows). "This one's actually quite good, especially when you're out on the water." Does this imply that it's less edible ashore? Try it and judge for yourself.

Bloch's Braunschweiger on Bread for Cruising

Braunschweiger
Sliced onions
Dijon mustard
Wholewheat bread

Place first three ingredients on fourth in amounts and order to taste.

LARRY EWAN

Larry Ewan is a Commander in the United States Navy. He and his wife Sherry cruise the Chesapeake in their Hunter 31 *Zephyr* with their children Jennifer and Gregory and their basset hound Cupcake. Larry's expertise extends far beyond the area around Poquoson, Va., where *Zephyr* is home-ported. He became acquainted with the Bay as captain of a Naval vessel which cruised between the C and D Canal and Hampton Roads from 1977 and 1979. Before the advent of air cushion vehicles, his ship held the speed record of 4 hours and 15 minutes from Baltimore to Norfolk.

"Eating (or munching) is a sound heard regularly on *Zephyr*", Larry says, "so Sherry keeps a well-stocked galley. Our favorite sandwich evolved gradually over a period of time as we pursued the ever elusive "taste." We found that by changing the order of how ingredients were placed in the sandwich we could change the flavor. The final result is the best blend, to be savored with salt air and a cold, refreshing beverage. Be aware that these sandwiches are habit-forming!"

Ewan's Best Blend

Rye or pumpernickel bread, or kaiser roll
Butter/margarine
Mayonnaise/salad dressing
Mustard (spicy)
Salt and pepper
Ripe tomato
Crunchy lettuce
Very thinly sliced meats (need at least two, e.g. ham, turkey, roast beef, corned beef, etc.)
Kosher dill pickle
Dehydrated onion bits or bacon bits (gives crunch)
Swiss, provalone or other cheese very thinly sliced

Delicately apply margarine to both pieces of bread or roll. On one side apply mayo, to the other side a layer of spicy mustard. Sprinkle onion/bacon bits over mayo side. Cover mayo and onion bits with your selection of cheese and smother the pickle side with your chosen meats layering them alternately. Atop the cheese arrange crisp lettuce leaves and ripe tomato slices. Salt and pepper to taste. Admire your creation, then put halves together. Slicing is suggested. (In this way you can continue to admire it while you eat it.) Use two hands, close eyes, open mouth and enjoy.

DICK GOERTEMILLER

Long-time Bay country residents Dick and his wife Dixie now call Reedville, Va., their home port. They have been boating on Cheasapeake Bay since 1966, at present sailing their Pearson 35 *Moon Song II.*

Utilizing Dick's background as an advertising agency art director, in 1971 they founded *Chesapeake Bay Magazine.* Their "Cruise of the Month" articles have provided the concept for *Guide to Cruising the Chesapeake Bay.*

Dick and Dixie are also goodwill ambassadors for *Chesapeake Bay Magazine*, making a slide presentation to groups interested in hearing about "The Charm of the Chesapeake Bay." Dick also pursues his career as a marine artist, specializing in watercolors capturing the essence of life on the water around the Chesapeake Bay.

Goertemiller's Multi-Purpose Hummus

As a sandwich filling, hummus is great in pita bread or any good, subtantial whole-grain bread. Nice additions include cucumber slices, sprouts, shredded carrots and lettuce or other greens. As a dip, hummus is super with assorted raw vegetables. Those who want to cut calories or fat intake can use the lesser amount of tahini. Hummus is an inexpensive change from the usual high fat, high salt, high calorie junk food munchies.

2 c. cooked chick peas (garbanzos) or 1-16 oz. can, drained
1 clove garlic
2-6 T. tahini (sesame seed butter)
3 T. lemon juice
Dash of cayenne pepper

Puree chick peas and garlic in blender; add small amount of cooking water, as needed, till smooth, dip-able consistency. Add tahini, lemon juice and pepper. Blend to combine.

HARRIET HAZLETON

Harriet Hazleton and her husband Lloyd have been cruising aboard *Chinook*, their 41-foot Hatteras, since 1963. During that time *Chinook* has visited ports throughout the Chesapeake and along the East Coast from Cape May to Florida and in the Bahamas. Harriet compiled the listings of museums which appears in this book and writes the "Marina Hop" column for *Chesapeake Bay Magazine.* Many of the "cruising know-how" tips which are sprinkled throughout this book are her contributions. Together with Anne Hays, Harriet authored *Chesapeake Kaleidoscope.* Harriet and Lloyd are long-time active members of the Northern Virginia Power Squadron, which Harriet most recently served as Public Relations officer.

When asked about a favorite sandwich recipe, Lloyd asked for clarification. Do you want the one we like the best or the one we have most often? Whichever—Harriet serves her sandwiches in a basket since finding that they tend to slide off a plate in a seaway or blow off the plate on the way up to the fly bridge.

STEPHEN KNOX

Stephen Knox holds a BS degree in Nuclear Engineering and is a member of the Society of Naval Architects and Marine Engineers and the American Society of Naval Engineers. A former officer in the U.S. Navy, he is now a general superintendent at the ANA Shipyard and lives in Portsmouth, Va. His hobbies of sailing and photography are both utilized in his articles for *Guide to Cruising the Chesapeake Bay* and *Chesapeake Bay Magazine*. He and his wife, Annette Wilkins, and daughter Jenny sail the creeks and rivers of the lower Bay in their O'Day 30 *Rosinante III*. Steve gives Annette credit for editing, proof reading and "generally improving everything I write." He also gives her credit for being in charge of the galley.

"Food seems to take on an added dimension on our weekend cruises. Sailing always seems to increase the appetite. Our meals are sometimes rushed during the busy work week. When planning our trips I try to include extra touches that I do not usually have time to include," Annette said when she sent these recipes.

Chicken Salad Pita

4 cooked chicken breasts
¾ c. raisins
½ c. coarsely chopped English walnuts
½ c. diced celery
2 coarsely chopped hard boiled eggs
Salt and pepper
Mayonnaise
Shredded lettuce

Debone and chop chicken, add remaining ingredients, with salt, pepper and mayonnaise to taste. Chill. Serve in pita bread lined with lettuce.

ERICA LOWERY

Erica Lowery and her husband Dick have owned a boat and cruised for about 20 years. Based on those years of providing food afloat for a family of four, Erica began collecting taste-tested recipes some of which have appeared during the past six years in both *Guide to Cruising the Chesapeake Bay* and *Chesapeake Bay Magazine*'s "Galley Time" column. She is presently editing a boating cookbook.

Erica and Dick presently sail a Southern Cross 35. Their son races a Laser and their daughter a Snipe. "They don't cook aboard their boats but do take sandwiches," Erica says and here are some of the family favorites.

Califorina Special

8 oz. cream cheese
1 avocado
½ t. lemon juice
Salt and pepper to taste
1 c. alfalfa sprouts
1 large sliced tomato
Optional: raisins, onions, bacon, chopped nuts, green pepper rings

Soften cream cheese at room temperature. In a mixing bowl, mash avocado with a fork. Add softened cream cheese. Blend in lemon juice and seasonings. (If mixture is too thick to spread, moisten with a little mayonnaise.) Spread mix on sprouted wheat bread, or your favorite bread, add sprouts, tomato slices and any or all other optionals. Serves 2-3.

Steak Sandwich, Philly Style

4 thin sandwich steaks (1 lb.)
2 t. margarine or cooking oil
1 thinly sliced large onion
1 seeded and sliced green pepper
⅛ t. garlic powder
2 t. steak sauce
Optional: 4 slices cheese, Mozzarella or Provolone.

Slice each steak into strips, about ½ inch wide. Melt margarine in a skillet; add steak strips and saute for 2-3 mintues, until just cooked. Remove meat from pan and set aside. Add onion, green pepper and garlic powder to pan. Saute until crisp but not crunchy! Add steak sauce and meat. When heated through, remove and serve on sub rolls. Cheese may be heated by adding it to pan for 1 minute before removing meat and vegetables. Serves 4.

ANDI MANCHESTER

Andi Manchester says she met boating when she met Joe, her husband, and has been hooked on both ever since. Andi and Joe cruise the Chesapeake with their three children in an aluminum 37-foot Marinette sedan cruiser they affectionately call *C.T.C. (Classy Tin Can).*

The Manchesters enjoy exploring the towns around the Bay and, while exploring, have often found it difficult to find the things they wanted and needed to find. Recognizing that others must have similar problems, Andi created the "Walking Tour" series for *Chesapeake Bay Magazine* and *Guide to Cruising the Chesapeake Bay.*

Andi fulfills a multi-faceted role as housewife, entreprenuer, and freelance writer. She and a partner run two businesses (The Paper Link and Graphic Whimsies) and she and Joe buy houses in need of repair to either resell or rent.

If you've read the Walking Tours, you will know that Andi is an authority on where to find the best ice cream. She claims, however, that her talents do not include making sandwiches.

CHERYL MANDALA

Cheryl Mandala is executive editor of Mortgage Commentary Publications. She writes *Chesapeake Bay Magazine*'s "Galley Time" column and has been a contributor to the magazine for several years. She has been cruising on the Chesapeake with her husband and children on their 52′ Chris Craft Constellation since 1970.

"You should know that my husband always says his favorite sandwich is Beef Wellington, but a freshly-made crab cake on a soft bun is always welcome with our crew."

Cheryl's Crab Cakes

1 lb. crab meat well picked-over
1 well beaten egg
½ c. cracker crumbs
2 T. dijon mustard
½ t. Worcestershire sauce
4 T. mayonnaise
1/3 c. minced fresh parsley
Butter

Combine all ingredients except butter and mix until blended. Make into patties. Saute in butter until brown. Serve on soft rolls or buns.

BILL MCMENAMIN

Bill McMenamin has been a United Press correspondent; a newspaper reporter; State Department foreign affairs analyst; and U.S. Information Agency writer, editor, and chief of press and publications for East Asia and the Pacific. He served 30 years in the Naval Reserve and retired a full Commander after serving as P.T. boat skipper and aboard a variety of other ships, including destroyers, cruisers and flat tops around the world, ashore and afloat. Now, in addition to freelancing for magazines, Bill is working on a book about cruising.

He has sailed the Atlantic Coast from Nova Scotia to the tip of Florida and the Gulf Coast. He singlehanded his 25-foot sailboat *Seacapade* to Florida and the Bahamas. He and his wife, Pearl, have two children and two grandchildren.

Barnacle Bill McMenamin's Special Crab Salad

1 cup backfin crab meat
½ c. chopped celery
½ c. sweet yellow or green pepper
1 chopped hard boiled egg
1 T. sweet pickle relish
Pinch of salt and pepper
Dash of Tabasco sauce
1 t. French's yellow mustard
2 T. mayonnaise
Lettuce leaves
Seeded sandwich rolls

Carefully check the crab meat and remove any shell. Combine in a bowl with mayonnaise, celery, egg, pepper and pickle relish and flavor with lemon juice, mustard, Tabasco, salt and pepper. Mix well, place in covered container and cool in refrigerator until ready to serve. Heap on rolls and garnish with lettuce.

DR. ROBERT MONTGOMERY

Bob Montgomery, a retired cardiologist, and his wife, Carol, live aboard their 30-foot ketch, *Porpoise*, in Solomons, Md. Bob began his sailing career as a teenager in Knockabouts and has been cruising on the Chesapeake for the past 25 years. He holds a U.S. Coast Guard license for Inland Operator-Sail. He has written for professional journals and is the author of the "Shipboard First Aid" column for *Chesapeake Bay Magazine*.

Anything With Sprouts

"Our favorite sanwich is sprouts—anything with sprouts. They go with ham, cheese, tomato, peanut butter, or even baked beans. The sprouts may be mung bean, radish, alfalfa (my favorite) or a mixture often sold as "salad sprouts." They're so easy to grow that we nearly always have ajar going, whether we're ashore or afloat. We use a jar we bought in a sprout-growing outfit, but any quart jar would be just as good. Put a double layer of seeds on the bottom and cover with water. Twelve hours later, pour the water off through a cheesecloth cover held in place with a rubber band. Rinse the sprouts twice a day, shaking them vigorously before pouring the water off through the cheesecloth. In four to five days you'll have one of the prettiest, tastiest and most nutritious sandwich garnishes going."

DR. HYMAN RUDOFF

Dr. Hyman Rudoff claims 60 years of interest in ships and boats. He sailed for 20 years, half of that in the Chesapeake and half in the Great Lakes and abroad. His boat is a Pearson Vanguard sloop named *Hanoah*. He is a Past Commander of the Cambridge Power Squadron. A Power Squadron Junior Navigator, he has taught and written on navigation and piloting.

In professional life an industrial chemist specializing in plastics, in private life he maintains a shop where he makes gadgets, gilhickies and dinguses.

AUDREY SCHARMEN

Audrey Scharmen was born on the Kansas prairie. As an Air Force wife, she lived in the arid southwest until her husband's final assignment in the service brought them to Washington, D.C. Once exposed to Chesapeake Bay, they fell in love with the water and boats and retired to Drum Point, on Mill Creek, near Solomons. They do their boating in a 1970 20-foot Orlando Clipper named *Hosy Baby*. For the past ten years they have been members of Flotilla 15-4 of the U.S. Coast Guard Auxiliary. Audrey writes regularly for the *Calvert Independent* newspaper and for Coast Guard Auxiliary publications as well as *Chesapeake Bay Magazine*. She makes her favorite sandwich in an electric frying pan aboard their boat.

Chesapeake Quesadilla

The variations are endless—any kind of chopped cooked meat and/or vegetables may be used, but we like to make them with fresh Maryland blue crab meat.

For each quesadilla you need 1 large flour tortilla
4 heaping T. crabmeat
1 chopped green onion
1 strip of canned whole green chile
1 strip of mozarella cheese

Spread each ingredient, layering in order listed, down the middle of the tortilla and fold as you would an eggroll. Fry in pan in small amount of hot oil until golden brown on each side. Serve with a bottled Mexican sauce for dipping—piquante, green salsa or taco sauce.

DR. FRANCIS SHEILD

Dr. Francis Sheild's acquaintance with Chesapeake Bay goes back to his boyhood in Hampton, when he used to ride along on the "pound boats" just for fun. For two years while he was in high school he worked at the Virginia Fisheries Lab and earned a Coast Guard license with the time he spent aboard the lab's 65-foot research vessel. In his spare time he was sailing Hampton One Designs and Penguins. When he got older he crewed aboard larger boats, two of which earned High Point awards while he served them as navigator. From 1973 to 1979 he raced frequently offshore, navigating boats in the Annapolis to Newport Race and several other races to Bermuda, and in the Hatteras and New York/Cape Cod areas.

His taste in sandwiches is cosmopolitan. "I like them all, from PBJ's to NY delis," he says. He sent us this "old standby."

Sheild's Mix and Match

Sliced French bread
Butter
Mustard
Mayonnaise
Swiss Cheese
Sliced roast beef and/or turkey
Liverwurst
Lettuce
Sliced tomatoes
Sliced onions
Salt and pepper

Lightly butter bread, spread mustard on one slice and mayonnaise on the other. Heap on layers of sliced swiss cheese, roast beef and/or turkey and a good spread of liverwurst. Add lettuce, sliced tomatoes, a big fat slice of sweet onion and salt and pepper to taste.

DEE SMITH

Dee Smith comes from a boating family and has had her own boat since she was 13. The first one was a 14-foot outboard; her present boat is a 25-foot Owens Sea Skiff in which she has ventured as far north as Trenton, N.J., and as far south as Savannah, Ga. Dee's literary credits include being creator, writer and editor of a weekly trade association publication for the Delaware Valley Health Care Industry and Editorial Associate for the book "Norman Rockwell and The Saturday Evening Post. She has contributed articles to *Chesapeake Bay Magazine* for more than 11 years and currently writes the northern Bay "Cruise of the Month."

Dee says she has the dubious reputation of being able to burn water and that her favorite sandwich is anything prepared for her aboard her boat by her guests! Failing that, she recommends peanut butter and jelly in a pinch. "On more than one disastrous occasion (stove malfunction, storm), I have been sustained by the unimaginative old peanut butter and jelly. It doesn't go bad and it keeps you going."

GENE WHICKER

Gene Whicker is a real estate broker in Colonial Beach and is our expert in that area. He and his wife Cora Lee and their two sons began taking boating vacations on the Chesapeake in 1967 and have been exploring the Bay and its tributaries in their leisure time ever since. Their boat is the *Nauti Lady*, a 35-foot wooden double-planked Owens powerboat which they have owned since 1975. You can recognize the *Nauti Lady* readily by the mermaid on the transom.

"She's an old boat, but very comfortable. We like to relax on the boat. We don't rush anywhere. And we don't eat sandwiches. We try to eat things that lower both weight and blood pressure—low calorie and low salt—and that usually turns out to be a salad." Gene says their favorites are crab and shrimp.

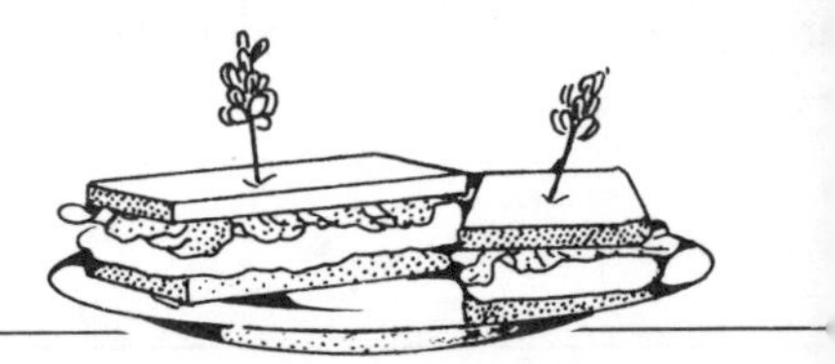

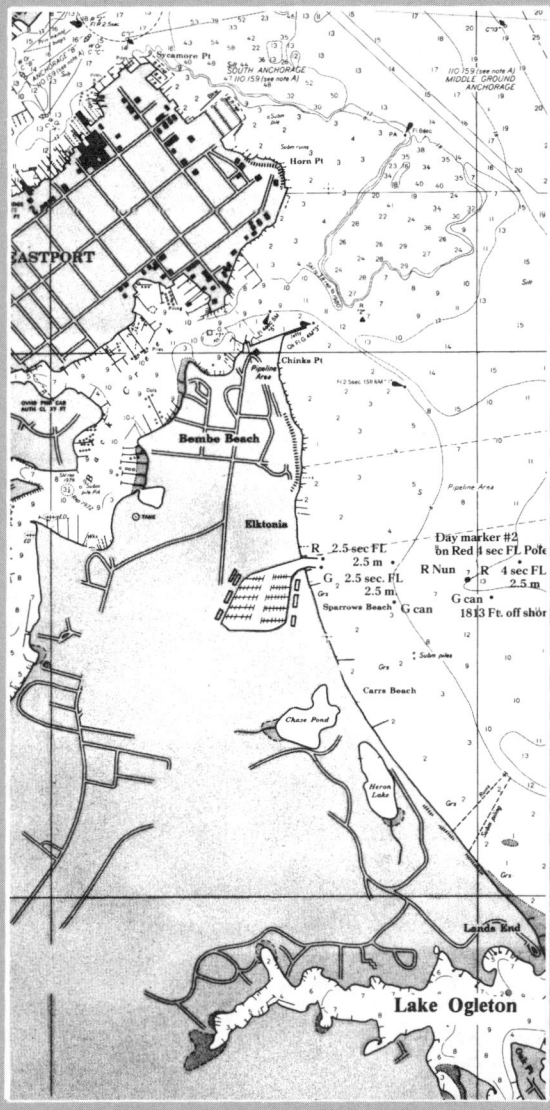

ANNUAL CHESAPEAKE BAY EVENTS

MAY

Salisbury Dogwood Festival
Salisbury, Md. (301)749-0144

Mayfest
Calvert County, Md. (301)257-6696

May Day Weekend
St. Mary's City, Md. (301)862-1634

Spring Festival
Havre de Grace, Md. (301)939-2299

Havre de Grace Decoy Festival
Havre de Grace, Md. (301)939-3833

Fairmount Academy's "1800's Festival"
Fairmount, Md. (301)651-0351

Chestertown Tea Party
Chestertown, Md. (301)778-2936

Chincoteague Seafood Festival
Chincoteague, Va. (804)787-2460

Jamestown Festival Day
Jamestown Festival Park, Jamestown, Va.
(804)229-1607

Water Festival on the Pocomoke
Snow Hill, Md. (301)632-2080

Commissioning Week at the
U.S. Naval Academy
Annapolis, Md.

Rock Hall Boat Show
Rock Hall, Md. (301)639-7241

Pocomoke Pear Tree Festival
Pocomoke City, Md. (301)957-3222

Blessing of the Fleet
St. Michaels, Md. (301)745-2916

Strawberry Festival
Salisbury, Md. (301)749-1905

Annual Sea Explorer Regatta
Patuxent River, Md. (301)326-4291

Salisbury Festival
Salisbury, Md. (301)749-0144

Annual Ghent Arts Festival
Norfolk, Va. (804)446-4759

JUNE

Harborfest
Norfolk, Va. (804)627-5329

Red Cross Waterfront Festival
Alexandria, Va. (703)549-8300

Potomac River Festival
Colonial Beach, Va. (804)224-7531

Strawberry Festival
Cambridge, Md. (301)228-4770

Hoopers Island Fishing Tournament
Hoopers Island, Md. (301)397-3131

Pocomoke Cypress Festival
Pocomoke City, Md. (301)957-1919

Charter Days Weekend
St. Mary's City, Md. (301)862-1634

Salisbury Seafood Festival
Salisbury, Md. (301)749-0101

Alexandria Waterfront Festival
Alexandria, Va. (703)549-0205

Annual Portsmouth Seawall Festival
Portsmouth, Va. (804)397-3453

Human Flag Ceremonies
Fort McHenry, Baltimore, Md. (301)563-FLAG

Flag Day Ceremony
Annapolis, Md. (301)839-3329

National Flag Day Celebration
Fort McHenry, Baltimore, Md. (301)563-FLAG

Annapolis Arts Festival
Annapolis, Md. (301)268-8687

Annual Boston Whaler Fishing Tournament
Mears Point Marina
Kent Narrows, Md. (301)822-8105

Harborlights Music Festival
Baltimore, Md. (301)727-5580

Great Rappahannock River White Water
Canoe Race, Fredericksburg, Va.
(703)371-5085

Delmarva Chicken Festival
(301)228-3234

Queen Anne's County Boat Races
Grasonville, Md.
(301)643-5857

Seafood Festival
Tilghman, Md. (301)745-5530

JULY

Fourth of July Weekend Celebration
Rock Hall, Md. (301)778-0416

Fish Fry
Rock Hall, Md. (301)778-0416

Rock Hall Regatta
Rock Hall, Md. (301)639-7968

Kent Co. Waterman's Association
Boat Docking
Rock Hall, Md. (301)639-2176

International Maritime Festival
Inner Harbor, Baltimore, Md.
(301)837-0862

Jamestown Maritime Heritage Festival
Williamsburg, Va. (804)229-1607

North East Water Festival
North East, Md. (301)287-5718

Chester River Yacht and
Country Club Regatta
Chestertown, Md. (301)778-5521

Blessing of the Fleet
St. Clements Island, Md. (301)769-3878

Peach Festival
Salisbury, Md. (301)749-1905

J. Millard Tawes Crab & Clam Bake
Crisfield, Md. (301)968-2500

Maryland Pride in Tobacco Festival
Leonardtown, Md. (301)475-2798

Cambridge Power Boat Regatta
Cambridge, Md. (301)228-4146

Sail Regatta
Cambridge, Md. (301)228-2141

Talbot County Fair
Easton, Md. (301)822-1244

Chincoteague Pony Swim
Chincoteague, Va. (804)336-6519

Canal Day Celebration
South Chesapeake City, Md. (301)885-5089

FIREWORKS DISPLAYS

Please call the appropriate phone number to verify dates and times.

Baltimore Harbor, Md.
Harborplace, Patapsco River
(301)387-4636

Annapolis Harbor
Severn River, Md.
(301)263-7958

Washington, D.C.
Tidal Basin near Washington Monument
(202)426-6700

Cambridge, Md.
Long Wharf on the Harbor
(301)228-4020

Chesapeake City, Md.
C&D Canal
(301)885-2326

Havre de Grace, Md.
Susquehanna River
(301)272-5594

Fireworks, cont.

Chestertown, Md.
Chester River
(301)778-0500

Miles River Yacht Club
Near Martingham, Miles River
(301)745-9511

Oxford, Md.
Tred Avon Yacht Club
(301)226-5269

Cambridge, Md.
Near Choptank River Bridge
(301)228-4031

Chesapeake Beach, Md.
Rod 'N Reel Restaurant
On the Bay
(301)257-2735

Solomons, Md.
Near Thomas Johnson Bridge
Patuxent River
(301)535-1013

Colonial Beach, Va.
Potomac River
(804)224-7181

Windmill Point, Va.
Windmill Point Marine Resort
Rappahannock River
(804)435-1166

Yorktown, Va.
York River
(804)898-3400

Norfolk, Va.
Waterside
(804)627-7809

AUGUST

Colonial Beach Boardwalk Art & Craft Show
Colonial Beach, Va. (804)224-7531

Betterton Day
Betterton, Md. (301)778-4302

Havre de Grace Arts and Crafts Show
Havre de Grace, Md. (301)939-2296

Portsmouth Seafood Festival
Portsmouth, Va. (804)397-3453

Summer Candlelight Tour
Londontown Publik House
Edgewater, Md. (301)956-4900

Calvert County Jousting Tournament
Port Republic, Md. (301)586-0565

Seafood Festival
Havre de Grace, Md. (301)836-8986

Cambridge Seafood Festival
Cambridge, Md. (301)228-3575

Governor's Cup Yacht Race
Annapolis to St. Mary's City
(301)863-7100

Ocean City Blue Marlin Tournament
Ocean City, Md. (301)289-6363

Queen Anne's County Fair
Centreville, Md. (301)758-1779

Hydroplane Races on the Susquehanna
Havre de Grace, Md. (301)939-3184

Dorchester Seafood Feast-i-val
Cambridge, Md. (301)228-3234

Bayfest
Calvert County, Md. (301)855-6681

Maryland Governor's Cup
Powerboat Regatta
Essex, Md. (301)686-8610

Ocean City Saltwater Festival
(Labor Day Weekend)
Ocean City, Md. (301)289-8311

National Hard Crab Derby
Crisfield, Md. (301)968-2500

SEPTEMBER

Cape Charles Day
Cape Charles, Va. (804)331-1488

Virginia Beach Neptune Festival
Virginia Beach, Va. (804)490-1221

Maryland Seafood Festival
Annapolis, Md. (301)268-7682

Sunfest in Ocean City, Md.
(301)289-2800

Candlelight Walking Tour
Chestertown, Md. (301)778-3499

St. Mary's County Fair
Leonardtown, Md. (301)475-8434

Fall Harvest Festival
Havre de Grace, Md. (301)939-2299

Labor Day Skipjack Races
Deal Island, Md. (301)784-2428

Annual Hampton Bay Days
Hampton, Va. (804)727-6108

Classic Wooden Boat Show
Alexandria, Va. (703)549-7078

Traditional Sailboat Races
St. Michaels, Md. (301)749-2916

Pork Festival
Salisbury, Md. (301)749-6141

Point Lookout State Park Bathtub Races
Scotland, Md. (301)872-5688

OCTOBER

U.S. Sailboat Show
Annapolis, Md. (301)268-8828

U.S. Powerboat Show
Annapolis, Md. (301)268-8828

Olde Princess Anne Days
Princess Anne, Md. (301)651-1705

Somerset County Antiques Show & Sale
Princess Anne, Md. (301)651-3152

Wildfowl Carving & Art Exhibition
Salisbury, Md. (301)742-4988

Chincoteague Oyster Festival
Chincoteague, Va. (804)336-6161

Uppershore Decoy Festival
North East, Md. (301)287-5718

Mid-Atlantic Small Craft Festival V
Chesapeake Bay Maritime Museum
St. Michaels, Md. (301)749-2916

Oktoberfest
St. Michaels, Md. (301)749-2916

Annual Crab Carnival
West Point, Va. (804)843-2289

Chestertown Wildlife Show and Sale
Chestertown, Md. (301)348-5231

Chincoteague Oyster Festival
Chincoteague, Va. (804)336-6161

Patuxent River Appreciation Days
Solomons, Md. (301)326-2042

St. Mary's Oyster Festival
Leonardtown, Md. (301)872-5040

Chesapeake Appreciation Days
November 1-2
Sandy Point State Park, Annapolis, Md.
(301)647-4747

ETHNIC FESTIVALS

ETHNIC FESTIVALS
INNER HARBOR, BALTIMORE, MD.
(301)837-4636

JUNE

Lithuanian Festival
Festival Hall

Greek Festival
St. Nicholas Church

Polish Festival
Canton Lots

Asian Festival
Hopkins Plaza

JULY

Italian Festival
Hopkins Plaza

AUGUST

AfrAm Festival
Festival Hall

German Festival
Canton Lots

India Days Festival
Hopkins Plaza

Hispanic Festival
Hopkins Plaza

American Indian Festival
Festival Hall

Jewish/American Festival
Hopkins Plaza

SEPTEMBER

Ukranian Festival
Hopkins Plaza

Irish Festival
Festival Hall

Korean Festival
Hopkins Plaza

NOTE: The Festival Hall and Hopkins Plaza are within walking distance of the Inner Harbor. St. Nicholas Church and Canton Lots, however, require a taxi ride.

MUSEUMS
on the Chesapeake Bay

Around the Chesapeake Bay there are more than 20 maritime museums, plus numerous other collections covering a wide variety of interests. Museums that can be reached from marinas, either by foot or public transit (or taxi cab if available), are the only ones listed. If you want additional information, phone on weekdays to Maryland's Office of Tourist Development (301)269-3517, Virginia Division of Tourism (804)786-2051 or Washington D.C.'s Convention and Tourism Bureau (202)789-2000. The following Bay area museums are listed in geographical order: Upper, Middle and Lower Bay.

Upper Bay Museums

Old Lock Pump House, C&D Canal, South Chesapeake City, Md. (301)885-5621. Interpretive museum and original pump house with huge 30-ft. water wheel. Monday-Saturday 1-4:15; Sunday 10-6. Free.

Turner's Creek Museum, near Kent County Landing on Turner's Creek, Sassafras River. Old buildings moved to form reconstructed village, plus old farming equipment.

Steppingstone Museum, Havre de Grace, Md. (301)939-2299. Stone farmhouse, shops of artisans such as leather worker, blacksmith. May-September, Saturday, Sunday 1-5. Admission.

Susquehanna Museum, Havre de Grace (301)939-1800. Furnished as 1840 lock house on old canal. June through August, Sunday 1-5.

Rock Hall Museum, Municipal Bldg., Rock Hall, Md. (301)758-2300. Indian artifacts, replica of vanished 18th-century town, nautical relics. Friday-Sunday 2-4. Free.

Baltimore has many museums including Museum of Art, B&O Railroad Museum, Maryland Science Center. Phone (301)752-8632 for additional information.

Radcliffe Maritime Museum, Maryland Historical Society, Baltimore. (301)685-3750. See rigged ship models, decorative carvings and items illustrating Maryland's maritime heritage. Tuesday-Saturday, 11-4; Sunday 1-5. Summer hours subject to change. Free.

U.S. Frigate Constellation, Inner Harbor, Baltimore. (301)539-1797. Working restoration of first of six frigates designed and built for U.S. Navy. May 15-October 15, 10-5:45; different winter hours. Admission.

William Paca House, Annapolis. Photo by Celia Pearson.

Baltimore Seaport and Baltimore Maritime Museums, Pier 4, Pratt St., Baltimore. (301) 837-1776. See *U.S.S. Torsk*, last U.S. submarine to sink enemy shipping in World War II, plus other displays. June 21-Labor Day 10-5; different winter hours. Admission.

Chestertown, Md. Call Chamber of Commerce (301)778-0416. See 1750 tavern, 1730 Customs House, more.

Middle Bay Museums

Banneker-Douglass Museum of Afro-American Life and History, 84 Franklin St., Annapolis. (301)269-3955. View exhibits on contemporary artists, Afro-American experience in Md.

Historic Annapolis, Inc., Annapolis waterfront. (301)267-8149, call tour office for details. Includes William Paca House, Tobacco Prise House, Victualling House. Admission.

U.S. Naval Academy Museum, Annapolis, (301)267-2108. Two galleries of indoor historical exhibits, Naval Academy Chapel, crypt of John Paul Jones, etc. Tuesday-Saturday, 9-5; Sunday 11-5. Closed Monday and winter holidays. Free.

London Town Publik House and Gardens, Edgewater, Md. on South River. (301)956-4900. Old brick mansion, former county almshouse and last remaining building of once flourishing town of 1700's. Tuesday-Saturday 10-5; Sunday 12-4. Admission.

Chesapeake Beach Railway Museum, Chesapeake Beach, Md. (301)257-3892. Old railway station with exhibits of once famous resort started in 1890's. June-August, Thursday-Sunday 1-4. Free.

Chesapeake Bay Maritime Museum, St. Michaels, Md. (301)745-2916. Shows Chesapeake maritime history, restored smallcraft of area. Includes antique marine engines, navigating instruments, cottage lighthouse. Waterfowling exhibit. May 1-October 31, daily 10-5. Shorter winter hours, closed Monday. Admission.

Oxford Museum, Morris and Market St., Oxford, Md. Depicts 19th-century maritime history. Also remarkable 1707 map of Oxford. Summers Friday, Saturday, Sunday. Free.

Spocott Windmill and Museum, Lloyds, Md. (301)228-7090. Use dinghy to reach head of Gary Creek, Little Choptank River or 6 miles west of Cambridge. Post windmill reconstruction of an earlier Dutch type mill similar to those built in Dorchester County in colonial times. Visible at all times. Free.

Brannock Maritime Museum, 210 Talbot Avenue, Cambridge, Md. (301)228-6938. Small, privately funded museum featuring area shipbuilding and memorabilia from this part of the Chesapeake.

Dorchester Heritage Museum, Horn Point, Cambridge. (301)228-6172. Maritime aircraft, farming, Indian exhibits in working museum. Saturday-Sunday 1-4:30. Free.

Calvert Marine Museum, Solomons, Md. (301)326-2042. Local maritime history, estuarine natural history, paleontology, Drum Point Lighthouse, salt marsh boardwalk. Commercial fisheries exhibit in historic Lore Oyster House nearby (admission). May-October 10-5, Monday-Saturday; Sunday 12-5. Different winter hours. Free.

Historic St. Mary's City, St. Mary's City, Md. (301)862-9880. See Maryland *Dove*, near replica of ship which brought settlers in 1634, also archaeological sites, 1676 State House reconstruction and more. Visitor center open daily 10-5 for film and some exhibits. Other sites March-December Wednesday-Sunday 10-5. Admission.

Harry Lundeberg School of Seamanship, Piney Point, Md. (301)994-0010. Training school of Merchant Marine. Several vessels ncluding yacht *Manitou* sailed by the late ›res. John F. Kennedy. First Sunday of each nonth 9-5. Free.

St. Clements Island Potomac River Auseum, Colton Pt. on Potomac River 301)769-2222. Highlights archaeological emains in Potomac River area. Limited to ife in Southern Md. Open weekdays 9-4, veekends Memorial Day to Labor Day oon-8. Free.

Smithsonian Institution, 14th and Con-titution Ave. N.W., Washington, D.C. For naritime interests, visit Hall of American Aaritime Enterprise and Hall of the Armed orces. Also models and graphics showing levelopment of colonial commerce, inland vaterways and various other exhibits. Daily 0-5:30. Free.

Truxtun-Decatur Naval Museum, 1610 I St. N.W., Washington, D.C. (202)433-651. Housed in carriage house of historical Decatur House on Lafayette Square. Has rints, photographs, ship models and other nemorabilia relating to naval personalities. Open daily at 10:30. Free.

U.S. Navy Memorial Museum, Washington Javy Yard, 9th and M St. S.E., Washington. 202)433-2651. Naval history in 19th century Breech Mechanism Shop of old Naval Gun actory. See relics, weapons, paintings, aval documents, more. Free.

Marine Corps Museum, Navy Yard, Vashington (202)433-3840. Depicts over 200 ears of Marine Corps history, presenting its lose association with the Navy. See exhibits f uniforms, flags, musical instruments, art tc. Monday-Saturday 10-4; Sunday 12-5. ree.

Washington Dolls House and Toy Museum, 236 44th St. N.W. (202)244-0024. See miniature xotic houses, Victorian doll houses, Edwardian earoom, etc.

Explorers' Hall of National Geographic ociety, 1145 17th St. N.W. (202)857-7588. Has vorld's largest unmounted globe, plus changing xhibits; also educational film series. Free.

Lincoln Museum at Ford's Theater, 511 10th St. N.W. (202)426-6927. Has pistol of Lincoln's ssassin, also painting of Lincoln being carried rom Ford's Theater where he was shot.

National Archives, Constitution Ave. & 8th St. N.W. (202)523-3000. Constitution of U.S. lus other significant exhibits. Free.

Lower Bay Museums

J. Millard Tawes Museum, Somers Cove, Crisfield. (301)968-2500. Collection f photographs, paintings and much more rom life of late Crisfield resident and ormer Maryland governor. Open daily 10-. Admission.

Lem Ward Museum, City Dock, Crisfield 301)968-2500. Famed waterfowl artists, teve and Lem Ward's memorabilia. Daily -5. Admission.

Crisfield Historical Museum, Main St. 301)968-2390. Depicts area life from Indian imes to present. Open Monday-Saturday, 0:30-12:15 and 1:30-5. Free.

Julia A. Purnell Museum, Snow Hill, Md. on Pocomoke River. (301)632-0515. See Vorcester County lore depicted from Indian times and colonial period and through Victorian period. Daily 11-5; Sunday 1-5. Admission.

Calvert Marine Museum, Solomons. Photo by Bob Grieser.

Hopkins & Bro. Store, Onancock, Va. (804)787-8220. Architectural museum with original furnishings. Marine general store dating back to 1842. June 1-Labor Day 8:30 A.M.-9 P.M.; shorter hours in other months. Free.

Watermen's Museum, Yorktown, Va. (804)887-2641. Waterfront near highway bridge. Story of Virginia's working watermen from Indian times to present told in exhibits, paintings, photographs, displays. April-Labor Day, Thursday-Saturday 10-4; Sunday 1-4. Free.

Yorktown Victory Center, Yorktown, Va. (804)887-1776. Explore living museum with multi-media exhibits, sights and sounds of Revolutionary War. Daily 9-5 except Christmas, New Year's. Admission.

National Americana Museum, Water St., Yorktown (804)898-6789. Social history depicts 200 years of national memories, original U.S. flags, Bicentennial paintings and more. Wednesday-Saturday, noon-8 P.M., Sunday 2-8. Admission.

Colonial National Historical Park, Jamestown and Yorktown. (804)898-3400. Exhibits and films at both sites, plus much more. Admission.

Colonial Williamsburg, Williamsburg, Va. Accessible to boaters although not on water. Call toll-free 1-800-582-8976.

Syms-Eaton Museum and Kecoughtan Indian Village, Hampton (804)727-6248. History of Hampton, oldest continuous English-speaking settlement in America plus village showing early Indian life.

Casemate Museum, Fort Monroe, Hampton, Va. (804)727-3391. Depicts history of old Fort Monroe and Coast Artillery Corps. Free.

Hampton University Museum, Hampton (804)727-5308. See ethnic art, artifacts from sub-Saharan, African and American Indian cultures, works by black artists. Free.

Portsmouth Naval Shipyard Museum, 2 High St., Portsmouth, Va. (804)393-8591. See large ship models and history of Portsmouth in photos and models. Tuesday-Saturday 10-5; Sunday 2-5. Free.

War Memorial Museum, 9285 Warwick Blvd., Newport News. (804)247-8523. Documents America's wars from 1775 to the present. Monday-Saturday 9-5; Sunday 1-5, closed some holidays. Admission.

The Mariners' Museum, Newport News Va. (804)595-0368. Trace man's involvement with the sea. See figureheads, half models, many examples of decorative art. Smallcraft from around the world. Monday-Saturday 9-5; Sunday 12-5. Admission.

Virginia Museum of Marine Sciences, Virginia Beach, Va. Call toll-free 1-800-446-8038 for more details. Visitors can experience Virginia's four marine habitats: Coastal plains river, salt marsh, Chesapeake Bay and Atlantic Ocean floor just beyond the Continental Shelf. Also Man and the Marine Environment.

Maritime Historical Museum in Old Seatack Coast Guard Station, Virginia Beach, Va. Same phone as above. Built in 1903 and now a historic landmark, the station has nautical artifacts, scrimshaw, photographs and *Norwegian Lady* exhibit.

—Harriet R. Hazleton

MARINE VHF RADIO OPERATIONS

The marine VHF radio service provides the medium for safety, navigation, and personal communications to all vessels afloat. Most recreational boaters use the marine radio properly; a small percentage deliberately abuse it, and another small percentage, through ignorance, use poor operating procedures or are cited for an equipment malfunction or rules violation. Let's review the rules.

The FCC rules now permit operating a marine VHF radio without a Restricted Radiotelephone License in U.S. waters. The license is required if you operate in international waters. A station license is still required for all marine VHF radio stations.

When operating the radio, before starting a call, be sure of the name of the vessel or shore station you intend to call. Use a normal tone of voice. Shouting does not increase the range of the radio. Listen before you transmit. Don't talk over other callers. Do not call a station for more than 30 seconds. If you do not get a reply, wait at least 5 minutes before calling again.

Call other boats on Channel 16. Call on ship-to-ship working channels (such as 68, 69) when you know the boat you are calling is listening there. After contact is made, immediately change to a clear working channel for the type of communication you intend to conduct. No exceptions! (See Channel selection guide.) Identify your station by callsign at the beginning and end of each contact.

Use the one-watt position first. Switch to the 25-watt position if you are unable to maintain communications with one watt. Monitor Channel 16 when your radio is on and not being used for another purpose.

HOW TO CALL ANOTHER BOAT

1) Make sure the radio is on.
2) Press the microphone button and call the boat you wish to contact followed by "THIS IS" (use name of your boat and radio callsign). For example, "*FOXY LADY, FOXY LADY*, THIS IS *SUNSET*, WHISKEY ROMEO ROMEO TWO—TWO—FOUR TWO, OVER."
3) If you don't get a reply immediately, try again but don't call longer than 30 seconds. If no reply the second time, try it again in 5 minutes.
4) When contact is made on Channel 16, switch immediately to a working channel. Say, "*FOXY LADY*, GO TO CHANNEL 68, THIS IS *SUNSET*, WRR 2242, OUT."

HOW TO CALL MARINE OPERATOR

1) Make sure your radio is on.
2)Select the Marine Operator channel in your area (see list opposite). Listen to be sure it is not being used.
3) Press the microphone button and say, "MARINE OPERATOR, THIS IS (name of boat and radio callsign.)"
4) When the operator replies, say, "MARINE OPERATOR, THIS IS (boat name) PLACING A CALL TO (city and telephone number)."

Also, inform the operator of how you are going to pay for the call. Either collect, credit card or through a billing arrangement such as a Marine Identification Number or MIN. The MIN provides a billing arrangement for both local and long distance VHF calls. The MIN is an alternative to a calling card number and eliminates the possibility of a radio listener using your number to charge land-based calls. The MIN is exclusively yours. It can not be used by any other boat or on land.

To obtain such a number, contact your local business office by dialing the changes in service number listed on your phone bill. You will need to provide your FCC number, the call number assigned to your VHF radio and the name of your boat.

There is a $16.00 processing charge to obtain your MIN, in addition to the regular marine call charges. The rate for a one minute local call is $2.91 and $3.27 for three minutes. Long distance rates depend on your location and the area code and first three digits of the number you are calling.

HOW TO MAKE AN EMERGENCY CALL

In an emergency situation, it is important that you remain calm and give pertinent and concise information so rescue boats or aircraft can be dispatched without delay. Vague information such as, "I AM ABOUT THREE MILES OR SO FROM A BIG BRIDGE," must be avoided. Before you call for help, look around for a landmark on shore, or the number of a nearby buoy or day marker, or anything that you can accurately describe in relation to your position.

You should also have accurate knowledge of your own boat. It is amazing how many boaters do not know the color or length of their boat; the type of fuel it uses (gas or diesel) or the capacity of fuel tanks.

THE MARINE DISTRESS PROCEDURE

Speak slowly, clearly and calmly.
1) Make sure radio is on.
2) Select VHF Channel 16 (156.8 MHz)
3) Press microphone button and say: "MAYDAY—MAYDAY—MAYDAY. THIS IS (your boat name and radio callsign), MAYDAY.
4) Tell where you are and state the nature of your emergency.
5) Give the number of persons aboard and condition of any who are injured.
6) Estimate the present seaworthiness of your boat.
7) Briefly describe your boat: (length, color and type).
8) Say: "I AM LISTENING ON CHANNEL 16."
9) End your message by saying: "THIS IS (boat name and radio callsign), OVER."

Release the mike button and listen. If no one replies, repeat the MAYDAY procedure starting at item No. 3.

If you have questions about the operation of your marine radio, or would like a copy of the FCC booklet titled "How to Use Your VHF Marine Radio," call or write the Baltimore Bureau of the FCC, 1017 Federal Building, Baltimore, MD 2120[illegible] (301)962-2728. Their booklet fulfills the requirement for knowing the current rules.

If you want more detailed information, you can buy a copy of the 97-page "Marine Radiotelephone Users Handbook" prepared by the Radio Technical Commission for Marine Services ($7.95) P.O. Box 19087, Washington, D.C. 20036 ☐

Ed Ant[illegible]

EMERGENCY OPERATING SIGNALS

The three spoken international emergency signals are:

MAYDAY. This distress signal indicates that a station is threatened by grave and imminent danger and requests immediate assistance. Mayday has priority over all other communications.

PAN PAN. The urgency signal PAN (pronounced Pahn) is used when the safety of the vessel or person is in jeopardy.

SECURITY. This safety signal is used for messages about the safety of navigation or important weather warnings.

You must give any messages beginning with one of these signals priority over routine messages.

MARINE RADIO CHANNEL USE

	AUTHORIZED USE
6 (156.3 MHz)	Use for safety purposes only, such as search and rescue, etc.
9 (156.450 MHz)	Use for contacting commercial marinas and other commercial or non-commercial vessels.
12 (156.6 MHz)	This is a backup channel for the Coast Guard.
13 (156.650 MHz)	Use for bridge information and monitoring intentions of shipping in approach situations.
14, 20, 65A, 66A, 73, 74	This is a port operations channel.
16 (156.8 MHz)	This is the original calling channel before switching to 9, 68, 69, 71, 72, 78A or Coast Guard 22A or 12. You cannot get the marine operator on this channel.
22A (157.1 MHz)	Coast Guard Channel. After initial contact with Coast Guard on channel 16, you are advised to switch to channel 22.
24, 25, 26, 27 and 28	Use to contact the Marine Radio Telephone Operators.
68, 69, 71, 72, 78A	This is the general working channel for non-commercial vessels.

CHESAPEAKE BAY MARINE OPERATORS

MARINE OPERATORS	*CHANNEL*	*SERVICE AREA*	*CALL SIGN*	*TELEPHONE COMPANY*
Baltimore	25 (157.250 MHz) & 26 (157.3 MHz)	Chesapeake Bay	KGD518	C&P Telephone
Cambridge	28 (157.4 MHz)	Chesapeake Bay	KRS907	C&P
Prince Frederick	27 (157.350 MHz)	Chesapeake Bay	KSK209	Radio Communications
Point Lookout	26 (157.3 MHz)	Potomac/Bay	KAQ383	C&P
Washington	28 (157.4 MHz)	Potomac/Washington	KTA453	Radio Communications
Norfolk	25, 26 & 27 (see above)	Norfolk/Hampton	KIC631	C&P

SHIPBOARD FIRST AID KIT

How much first aid gear does your boat need? There is no short answer because each crew's special requirements will alter the list. Some general guidelines, though, will help you provide the essentials without stocking unnecessary extras.

Our lists are designed for two levels of first aid care: first, "home treatment" of minor problems which don't warrant calling a doctor; and, second, emergency management of a sick or injured person so he will survive the delay in getting to a doctor without becoming worse. The potential length of that delay is a major factor in determining the requirements for each kit.

DAYSAILER: This boat is only two to four hours from its own berth or from another marina with nearby ambulance service.

•ACE bandage (2)—excellent all-around bandage for stopping bleeding, binding sprains, etc.
•Betadine—a good cleansing agent for any wound or scrape.
•Sterile gauze pads—one of these can help keep a wound clean until you get home.
•Adhesive tape
•Bandaids
•Aspirin or Tylenol
•Seasick remedy—many are available, including Dramamine, Bonine, Transderm Scop* (the patch behind the ear), and my favorite, ephedrine* with Phenergan*.
•Sunburn lotion—use it for prevention, at least #8, since prevention beats any treatment.
•Meat tenderizer—for jellyfish stings.
•Eye patch—to prevent further damage to an injured eye until you can get to an emergency room.

OVERNIGHTER: This boat is no more than 12 hours from its own berth and sometimes is even closer to another source of medical care.

•Everything listed for a daysailer plus:
•Tweezers—good ones are worth the expense.
•Extra ACE bandage
•Burn ointment—such as Silvadene*—for severe burns.
•Eye ointment—such as Neosporin*.
•Anbesol or oil of clove—either can ease the pain of toothache remarkably.
•Stronger pain killer—such as aspirin with codeine*.
•Antihistamine—such as Benadryl* or Sominex (chemically identical).
•Hydrocortisone cream—such as Cortaid—for painful sunburn, poison ivy, etc.

CRUISER: This boat will cruise for several days or more but will be in or near the Bay, hence no more than a day or two from medical care.

•Everything in the overnighter plus:
•Gauze bandage, 2″, two rolls—sometimes easier to use than an ACE bandage.
•Adhesive tape, extra roll.
•Sharp scissors—these have many uses in addition to cutting bandage and tape, like trimming a torn nail or cutting hair away from a scalp wound.
•Alcohol swabs
•Thermometer
•Diarrhea medicine—such as Kaopectate or Pepto Bismol. Add Pedialyte if infants will be aboard.
•Antacid—such as Mylanta or Maalox
•Ipecac syrup—if young children will be aboard.
•Cold medicine—such as Coricidin.
•Anakit* or EpiPen*—both contain adrenalin for injection in case of a sudden overwhelming allergic reaction to insect stings.
•Suppositories—such as Anusol for hemorrhoids.
•Emetrol—to control vomiting.
•Gatorade—for heat illness.

*These medications require a doctor's prescription.

Extra items may be dictated by your own experience or by individual needs. For example, you might include nitroglycerine tablets if a crew member has coronary heart disease, or sugar cubes for a diabetic who takes insulin.

Your first aid kit doesn't require a special container. I use plastic food storage boxes which won't rust, keep their contents dry, and fit into odd nooks and crannies.

A review of the first aid kit ought to be part of each spring's maintenance. As you check it for completeness, be sure to replace any dated items that have expired. Then, at the end of the season, take home the liquid items. You wouldn't believe the mess we found after a cold snap last year—frozen Pepto Bismol had thawed out. □

—Robert R. Montgomery, M.D.

SUN SENSE

While enjoying the sun out on the Bay, we need to give some attention to protecting ourselves from its potentially unhealthy effects. These especially involve the skin and eyes as well as the body as a whole.

SKIN CARE

Skin care includes protection against both short-term effects of overexposure—sunburn—and long-term damage—skin cancer. Using an effective sunburn lotion or cream and wearing a hat will go a long way toward achieving both ends. Modern sunburn preventatives are numbered according to their effectiveness. Those numbers indicate how much longer it takes the user to burn than if he used none at all. For example, if you know that your skin begins to burn in 20 minutes without protection, using a number 6 should allow you to stay out 6 times as long: 2 hours. The greatest protection—15—lets you stay out 15 times as long (300 minutes, 5 hours, in our example). These numbers are only estimates, though, and it makes sense to be conservative in relying on them, especially if you burn easily.

How about a good tan; doesn't it help protect your skin? Only partly. It will allow its owner to stay out longer without burning, but it has some drawbacks, too. Years of gorgeous tans can "age" the skin, especially the face, much too fast. And a "leathery" face is not too great. Furthermore, years of sun exposure as the tans accumulate will significantly increase the risk of skin cancer.

Wearing a hat is the best protection against facial skin cancer. This may seem ridiculous when you're 20, but it's a different story 20 years or so later when the dermatologist gets ready to operate on your face. Be on the lookout, too, for any new moles and for any change in old ones. Either could be a sign of melanoma, another kind of skin cancer that is more common after years of sun exposure.

If you do get sunburned, try a cool, moist towel on the skin and take two aspirin if it hurts a lot. If these measures are inadequate, try a cream with hydrocortisone or fluorinated steroids. The various "----caine" lotions and creams may be comforting, but they cause sensitivity reactions in enough patients that most doctors no longer recommend them.

EYES

The eyes need special sun protection, especially for boatmen. The brilliance of both the direct light and that reflected off the water prompts most of us to wear sunglasses simply to be more comfortable. But we should be discriminating in choosing those sunglasses. They should be dark and preferably gray or brown. (Yellow ones are fine for "cutting" haze, but they don't block out enough light for general use.) The darker they are, the more glare they will cut out, the more comfortable you will be, and the better you will see.

Sunglasses also need to protect the eyes from the effects of the sun's ultraviolet rays. This portion of sunlight is particularly harmful to the retina, the membrane in the back of the eye that receives visual images, and after several years can injure the retina severely enough to cause visual loss that cannot be corrected. This damage can be prevented by wearing sunglasses that filter out those rays. Sunglasses made of glass do a good job, but plastic lenses need to be specially treated to filter ultraviolet adequately. Such a filter is included in some of the better plastic models when they are made, but it can be added later to any of the other. An optician with the proper equipment can test lenses to see how effectively they block ultraviolet light, then add the filter if it is needed.

Leaving your sunglasses off once in a while will not doom you to irreparable retinal damage, because the lens of the eye blocks out some of the ultraviolet rays before they reach the retina. But when the lens is removed because of cataracts, even that protection is lost; so people who have undergone that operation need to be extremely careful to choose good sunglasses and to wear them. Although some of the newer lenses implanted at cataract surgery contain an ultraviolet filter which lessens the risk of retinal injury, it's safer to wear good, ultraviolet-filtering sunglasses.

BODY

The body as a whole also needs to be protected from the effects of the summer sun to prevent heat illness. This occurs when the body gets low on the water it needs to make sweat, the mainstay of defense against overheating. As sweat evaporates, it cools the body; but if the water stores run low, sweating slows down and the body temperature begins to rise. Here's where danger begins, the onset of heat exhaustion. This form of heat illness is so common that most of us have had at least a mild form of it. It's the feeling of being simply "too tired". For instance, the last bluefish of the day might seem like just too much effort to bring in. Prevention—and treatment—is easy: drink lots of fluids, mostly water and fruit juice. Drinks with electrolytes in them, such as Gatorade, are fine, but avoid taking a lot of extra salt. It will not help and might even make the situation worse.

If heat exhaustion is ignored, the body's heat builds up as its water supplies continue to dwindle, and heat stroke may develop. In this very severe, sometimes fatal form of heat illness, the victim stops sweating altogether. The body temperature then rises unchecked and may reach a level so high that the vital organs cannot function any more. This is a true emergency, so try to get medical help. Meanwhile, get the victim out of the sun, preferrably into an air-conditioned area. Try to bring the body temperature down with wet towels cooled in ice water and encourage him to drink cool liquids. Fortunately, heat stroke is not common and can be prevented by drinking plenty of liquids and avoiding long hours of vigorous activity in very hot summer sun.

Enjoy the Chesapeake summer, but with a measure of respect for its heat and sun and a fair ration of protection for yourself. □

—Robert R. Montgomery, M.D.

CHESAPEAKE WEATHER

Prudent boatmen, planning an outing on the Bay, should begin monitoring marine weather forecasts at least 12 to 24 hours in advance of their planned departure. Mariners should make mental, or even written, notes of the basic weather conditions during this time frame. This will help one achieve a sense of developing weather patterns that are likely to be experienced while on the Bay. A respect for vagaries of Bay weather by boaters and a knowledge of its general weather conditions are imperative for boating safety and enjoyment.

NATIONAL WEATHER SERVICE FORECASTS & WARNINGS

The National Weather Service provides weather forecasts and warnings for the Chesapeake Bay around the clock. Forecasts are issued four times daily at 5 a.m., 11 a.m., 5 p.m. and 11 p.m. with amended forecasts issued whenever conditions differ considerably from those forecasted. The forecasts and the warning system are not infallible. It is imperative that boaters know the characteristics of their craft under the various wind and wave conditions that might be encountered on the Bay. They must realize that local thunderstorms can produce dangerously strong winds over small areas which escape detection by the National Weather Service radar and observational system. Therefore, it is necessary that boaters remain aware of weather conditions and be prepared *and able* to reach safety under threatening weather conditions.

SMALL CRAFT ADVISORIES

These advisories are issued when winds and seas become a problem for small craft. The key words in the small craft advisories are *small* and *advisories.* Although the term small craft has never been defined, it is considered to pertain to boats up to approximately 24 feet in length. In giving this *advice,* the National Weather Service must assume that a boater knows the capabilities of his individual boat and his own abilities, and can judge whether it is safe to venture out in his particular area. The small craft advisory (SCA) is issued when winds of at least 20 knots prevail, which can produce three-foot waves. During the colder months, (December thru March), the minimum criteria are 25 knots and 4 foot waves.

SPECIAL MARINE WARNINGS

Special marine *warnings* are issued for winds of 34 knots or higher and waterspout sightings, severe thunderstorm warnings for winds of 50 knots or higher and tornado warnings for tornado winds when there is good evidence that these conditions will occur within one hour. A *watch* may be issued in advance of any warning, to indicate a potential for storm development in a given area.

It is important to remember that forecasters generally have limited information concerning the actual strength of the winds in severe thunderstorms or the specific area of the Bay that will be affected. Because of this, all boaters in the warned area should immediately seek protected waters. In seeking a lee shore, remember that the strong gusty winds associated with thunderstorms will come from the *southwest* to *northwest* direction in nearly every instance on the Bay.

GALE, STORM AND HURRICANE WARNINGS

Gale warnings are issued when winds are expected between 34 and 47 knots. Only the largest boats should attempt to sail when gale warnings are in effect.

Storm warnings are issued when speeds range between 48 and 63 knots. All boats and even ocean going ships should seek harbor when storm warnings are issued.

Hurricane warnings are issued when wind speeds are expected to be 64 knots or more. Every vessel should be securely moored when this warning is issued.

OBTAINING WEATHER INFORMATION

The most complete and current weather forecasts and warnings for the Chesapeake Bay are taped and broadcast over VHF-FM channels by the National Weather Service every three to five minutes around the clock. They include the latest marine forecasts, observations, special weather statements and warnings. Forecasts are updated at the issuance times indicated previously and amended as needed.

The National Weather Service VHF-FM transmitters have an approximate line of site range of 40 to 60 miles depending on location and sensitivity of individual receivers. Some of the more expensive portable weather radio units carry an alarm tone that is automatically sounded when a weather warning is issued. The transmitter locations are as follows:

CONTINUOUS WEATHER BROADCAST STATIONS NATIONAL WEATHER SERVICE

Location	Call Sign	Frequency		Station
Washington, DC	KHB-36	162.55	MHz	Weather 1
Baltimore, MD	KEC-83	162.40	MHz	Weather 2
Salisbury, MD	KEC-92	162.475	MHz	Weather 3
Heathsville, VA	WXM-57	162.40	MHz	Weather 2
Richmond, VA	WXK-65	162.475	MHz	Weather 3
Norfolk, VA	KHB-37	162.55	MHz	Weather 1

In 1981, Baltimore Washington International Airport's weather station started **"Bay Nowcasts."** The coverage utilizes periodic reports from volunteer private citizens living on the Bay front in conjunction with other more traditional information from satellites, radar, etc. The volunteer information for the upper Bay reports come from the following areas: Chesapeake City, Thomas Point, Calvert Cliffs, Cove Point, Naval Research Lab at Chesapeake Beach, North Point, Tilghman Island, Gibson Island, Kent Island, Point Lookout, and Taylors Island, Hart & Miller Island, Plum Point, and North Beach. A similar Bay Nowcast for the lower Bay originates from the Norfolk station (162.55 MHz). The Baltimore station (162.40 MHz) originates the upper Bay Nowcast. Bay Nowcasts are updated every three hours from 6 a.m. to 6 p.m., using whatever reports are available.

A number of commercial AM & FM radio stations broadcast marine forecasts as part of their regular news programs. A few may supply observations or even weather reports from boats on the Bay. Because of inherent delays in communications, forecasts and warnings may not always be up to date.

The Coast Guard maintains radio stations which broadcast weather information and warnings from National Weather Service forecasts. The Baltimore Coast Guard broadcasts on station NMX at 157.1 MHz (Channel 22) as does Hampton Roads. All Coast Guard stations will broadcast severe emergency weather warnings on 156.8 MHz or Channel 16. □

Fred Davis

This article was prepared by Mr. Fred Davis, a meteorologist with the National Oceanic & Atmospheric Administration (NOAA). The article was excerpted and adapted from "The Chesapeake: A Boating Guide to Weather" by Jon Lucy, Terry Ritter, and Jerry LaRue. This publication is available for $1.00 from the Sea Grant Communication Office, Virginia Institute of Marine Science, Gloucester Point, VA 23062, and is highly recommended by the editors.

Notes

PHOTO BY BOB GRIESER

TELEPHONE CONTACT NUMBERS FOR DRAWBRIDGES

The following is a list of telephone contact numbers for drawbridges in the Fifth Coast Guard District whereby mariners can obtain specific information on a bridge or its opening schedule or, when required, request a bridge opening in advance.

Waterway & Location — Maryland	Mile No.	Telephone
Bohemia River, US 213, Cayots	4.0	(301) 398-1565
Cambridge Harbor (Creek), SH 342, Cambridge	0.1	228-8311
Chester River, US 213, Chestertown	26.8	778-0810
Choptank River, US 50, Cambridge	15.6	228-3668
Choptank River, SH 404, Dover	50.4	479-0297
Fishing Creek, RT 335, Hooper Island, Honga	1.0	397-3627
Kent Narrows, US 50, Narrows	1.0	643-5963
Knapps Narrows, SH 33, Tilghman Island	0.4	886-2588
Marshyhope Creek, Brookview	5.8	742-2101
Miles River, SH 370, Easton	10.0	822-3565
Nanticoke River, RT 313, Sharptown	30.0	883-3150
Nanticoke River, US 50, Vienna	22.2	376-3449
Patuxent River, SH 231, Benedict	24.4	535-1740
Pocomoke River, RT 675, Pocomoke City	15.6	957-2980
Pocomoke River, RT 12, Snow Hill	29.9	742-2101
Potomac River, I-495, Alexandria	103.8	638-2078
Sassafras River, US 213, Georgetown	10.0	275-8105
Severn River, SH 450, Annapolis	3.0	269-3800
Sinepuxent Bay, US 50, Ocean City	0.5	289-7126
South River, SH 2, Edgewater	5.7	269-3809
Spa Creek, SH 181, Annapolis	0.4	269-3840
Stoney Creek, SH 173, Riviera Beach	0.9	215-6630
Weems Creek, SH 436, Annapolis	0.7	269-3815
Wicomico River, Main Street, Salisbury	22.4	742-7888
Wicomico River, US 50, Salisbury	22.4	742-8965

Waterway & Location — Virginia	Mile No.	Telephone
Chickahominy River, RT 5, Barrets Ferry	1.5	(804) 253-4835
Chuckatuck Creek, US 17, Suffolk	1.0	238-2215
James River, US 17 258, Newport News	5.0	244-3607
James River, SH 156, Hopewell	65.0	541-8282
Nansemond River, SH 125, Holiday Pt.	7.7	255-4730
Pamunkey River, SH 33, West Point	1.0	843-3242
So. Br. Elizabeth River, I-64, Chesapeake	7.1	545-8656
York River, US 17, Yorktown	7.0	Not manned toll house on shore 627-6207

Chesapeake Bay Hurricane Holes

LOWER BAY (south to north)

Western Shore

1. Linkhorn Bay, off Lynnhaven Bay above Cape Henry; both the south and east branches.
2. Hampton River, north shore inside Hampton Roads; up Sunset Creek; do not anchor in the Hampton River channel.
3. Perrin R.; Sarah Creek, York R.
4. East River, off Mobjack Bay.
5. Corrotoman River, lower Rappahannock River, north shore.
6. Dividing Creek, north of Fleets Bay, about midway between Rappahannock and Potomac Rivers.
7. Horn Harbour, about 5 miles up Great Wicomico River.

Eastern Shore

8. Cape Charles Harbor, located nine miles north of the Cape.

9-10. Occohannock and Nandua Creeks.

11-12. Pungoteague and Onancock Creeks.

13. Saxis, upper Pocomoke Sound.

MIDDLE BAY (south to north)

Western Shore

14. St. Mary's River, lower Potomac, north shore.
15. Mill Creek, Patuxent River, north shore at Solomons.
16. Mill Creek, Patuxent River above bridge, western shore.
17. Patuxent River, above the Potomac River.

Eastern Shore

18. Crisfield, Tangier Sound.
19. Nanticoke River, Tangier Sound, behind Bloodsworth Island.

UPPER BAY (south to north)

Western Shore

20. Rhode River, south of Annapolis between West and South Rivers between High Island and steep south shore or go up Sellman Creek.
21. Little Round Bay, up Severn River, off Round Bay.
22. Stony Creek, off Patapsco River, south shore between Sloop Cove and Long Cove or in Nabbs Creek.
23. Frog Mortar Creek off Middle River, north shore.

Eastern Shore

24. Dun Cove, off Harris Creek, behind Tilghman Island.
25. Tred Avon River, north of entrance to Choptank River, above Oxford.
26. Miles River, behind Tilghman Point, in Leeds or Hunting Creeks.
27. Wye River, north of Miles River.
28. Chester River, north of Kent I land, Reed Creek or Chestertow
29. Sassafras River, head of the Ba Turner Creek.
30. Cove to port just above entrance to La Trappe Creek. Courtesy: Hymar Rudoff.

Here are some of the many Chesapeake Bay hurricane holes providing good vessel anchorages during periods of high winds.

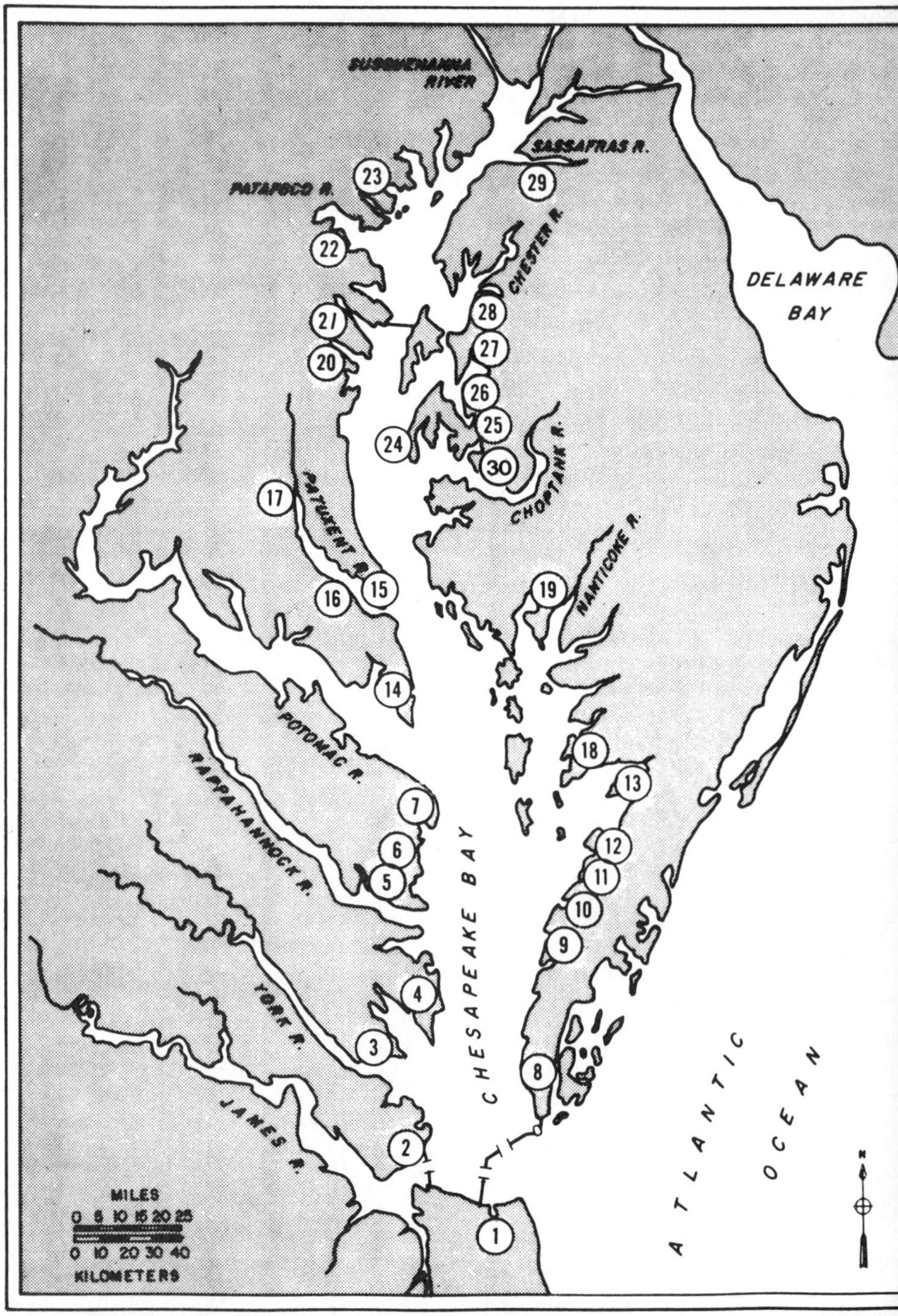

1-29. Courtesy: Virginia Institute of Marine Science, The Chesapeake: A Boating Guide to Weather.

FLOAT PLAN

The Coast Guard encourages you to fill in a Float Plan similar to the one which appears on this page. Then leave it with friends or relatives to whom you can report your safe arrival. Should your friends or relatives fail to receive information on your arrival when due, or within a reasonable amount of time thereafter, they should notify the nearest Coast Guard facility. The information contained on the plan will be valuable to the Coast Guard in case a search is required.

1. NAME OF PERSON AND TELEPHONE NUMBER

____

2. DESCRIPTION OF BOAT/TYPE ______________

COLOR______________TRIM______________

REGISTRATION NO.______________

LENGTH__________NAME__________MAKE__________

OTHER INFO. ______________

3. PERSONS ABOARD ______________

NAME______________AGE______

ADDRESS & TELE. NO. ______________

NAME______________AGE______

ADDRESS & TELE. NO. ______________

NAME______________AGE______

ADDRESS & TELE. NO. ______________

4. ENGINE TYPE______________H.P.______

NO. OF ENGINES__________FUEL CAPACITY__________

5. RADIO YES/NO TYPE__________FREQS.__________

6. SURVIVAL EQUIPMENT: (CHECK AS APPROPRIATE)

☐PFD'S ☐FLARES ☐MIRROR ☐SMOKE SIGNALS

☐FLASHLIGHT ☐FOOD ☐PADDLES ☐WATER ☐OTHER

7. TRIP EXPECTATIONS: LEAVE AT __________(TIME)

FROM ______________

GOING TO ______________

EXPECT TO RETURN BY__________ (TIME) AND IN

NO EVENT LATER THAN______________

8. ANY OTHER PERTINENT INFO. ______________

____

9. AUTOMOBILE LICENSE__________TYPE__________

TRAILER LICENSE __________COLOR AND MAKE OF

AUTO ______________

WHERE PARKED ______________

10. IF NOT RETURNED BY __________ (TIME) CALL THE

COAST GUARD, OR__________(LOCAL AUTHORITY)

TELEPHONE NUMBERS ______________

TELEPHONE NUMBERS ______________

ADDITIONAL NOTES: ______________________________

____

____

PLANNING A WEEK'S CRUISE ON THE NORTHERN BAY

One of the many pleasures of boating on the Chesapeake Bay is extended cruising. No other body of water in the world is so suited to this pleasurable activity. There are hundreds of miles of shoreline holding innumerable creeks, coves, and protected anchorages for boating families. It remains only for us to discover it.

A week seems to be a comfortable time span for extended cruising. In planning a week's cruise, there are a few guidelines I like to follow. First off, I try to make sure that each leg is of reasonable length. No sense in long grueling days, one right after another. Therefore, most legs of this cruise are only about 25 to 30 miles. Second, we try to plan the cruise so that most stopovers are near supplies, fuel and repairs. And third, I like to have variety. Harbors and marinas are desirable sometimes, but occasionally it's nice to find a deserted cove or creek for some quiet time.

You will find that the following itinerary has an open day as well. Use it whenever you like. If the weather is stormy, you may choose to tie up at a marina and go ashore for the day.

The point is, don't let an itinerary "lock" you into a schedule. Tight schedules are one of the things we'd like to get away from! Mileages will be approximate, as well as compass courses. As to charts, most times I use NOAA charts. For this cruise you will find useful charts #12270, 12267 and 12264. Another good set of charts available is in the "Guide for Cruising Maryland's Waters," and there are other chart books to choose from, as well.

First Day: Annapolis to St. Michaels
Distance: Approximately 24 miles, NOAA chart #12270

St. Michaels is one of the most popular cruising spots on the Chesapeake Bay. The harbor is large enough to accommodate a dozen or more boats at anchor, and there are three marinas that have some transient facilities available. If you want to consider being on the hook, come early in the afternoon to assure yourself a spot.

From Annapolis, the Severn River main channel marks will lead you almost directly to black bell #77. From there a course of 171° will bring you to Bloody Point Light, a tall red light tower at the foot of Kent Island. This course will take you diagonally through the main ship channel. If you are experiencing heavy freighter traffic, it might be wise to cut directly across the channel, spending as little time in it as possible. Then follow the Kent Island coastline south to Bloody Point.

At the lighthouse, you may be tempted to head directly up Eastern Bay. Don't! Shoaling spots have been reported in some areas south of Kent Point, so it's best to honor the black bell #1 a little over a mile away on course 137°. From there, course 065° will take you to the red 4-second flasher north of Tilghman. Then course 161° will bring you almost to the mouth of St. Michaels harbor. Of course, be wary of the large shoal area off the mouth of the Wye River. Although it is well marked, you should check your charts against the marks as you spot them.

As you turn to enter St. Michaels harbor, you will first spot the cottage-style lighthouse on Navy Point. The main harbor is to port, and a secondary—and frequently crowded anchorage—is on the north side of the light.

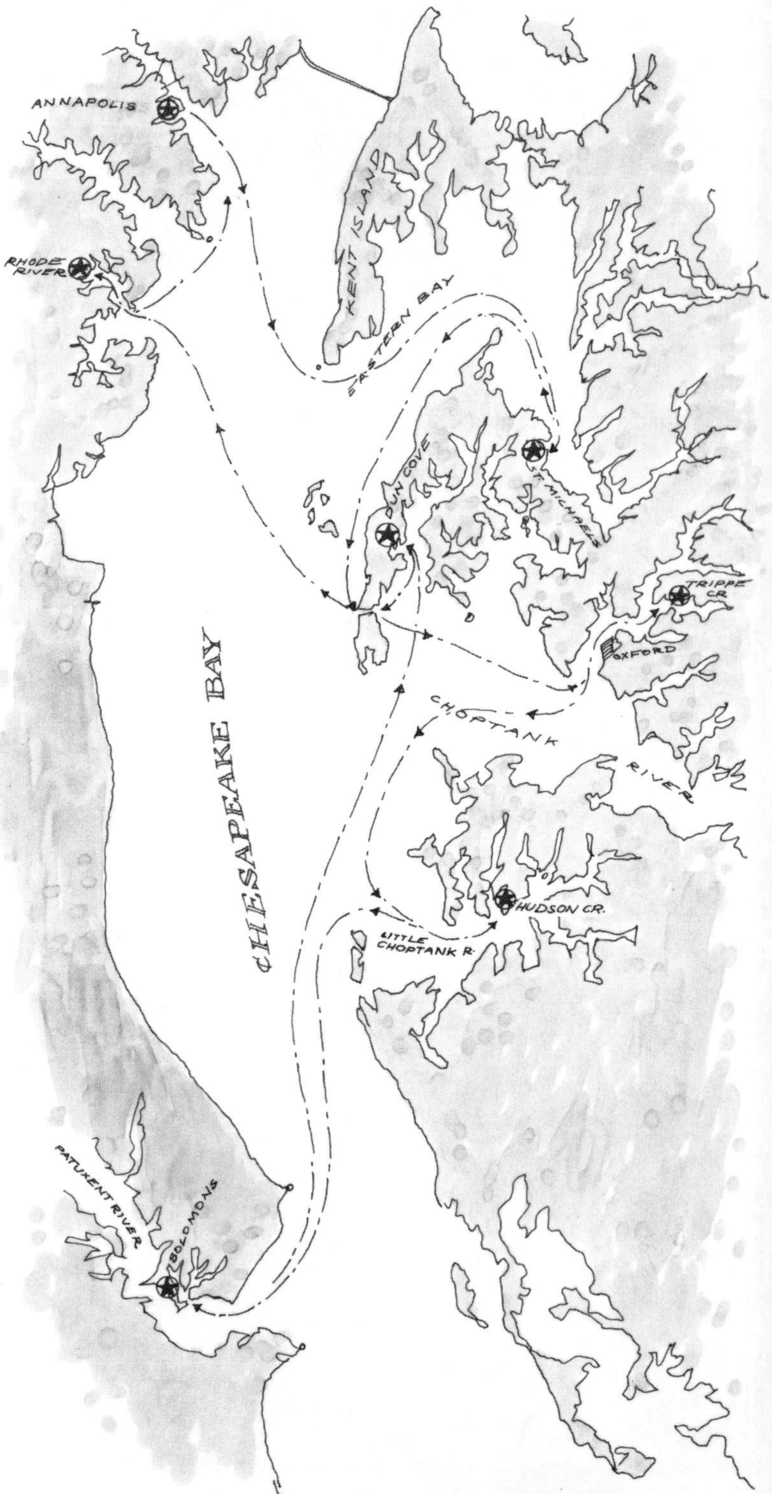

A popular destination in St. Michaels. Photo by Bob Grieser.

If you decide to anchor in the harbor, there are several launch services available to carry you to nearby restaurants, most of which also have either dock space or a dinghy dock. There are plenty of interesting things to do ashore; for more details, see the St. Michaels cruise and walking tour.

By the way, if you want to spend the first night away from civilization, you may choose to skip St. Michaels and turn off into the Wye River. The most popular anchorage is Shaw Bay, just above the river's entrance. If you're looking for more seclusion, both branches of this popular river offer any number of cozy creeks and coves. Enjoy!

Second Day: St. Michaels to Trippe Creek, above Oxford on the Tred Avon River

Distance: Approximately 30 miles, NOAA chart #12267

On this leg of our cruise, we retrace our steps around Tilghman Point and down Eastern Bay. However, instead of heading for Kent Point, we hug the port shore, cut between Poplar Island and the mainland, and head for Knapps Narrows. A word of caution: As you transit Poplar Island Narrows, exercise caution to avoid the numerous crab floats there. Although attempts are being made to keep floats out of the fairway, there are many "drifters."

Just south of Poplar Island Narrows you will find a shortcut through Tilghman Island into the Choptank. This route is four or five miles shorter than going around Black Walnut Point. Knapps Narrows is a busy waterway, and the entrance channel can look a little "hairy." But don't let it scare you. There's plenty of water if you keep in the channel. The drawbridge is quick to respond to your horn, and should be an interesting experience for first-timers. Note: East of the bridge the marks become red to port—as if you are leaving the harbor.

The Choptank will provide a scenic and interesting leg of your trip. To port are Harris and Broad Creeks with good harbors in case of storms. As you round up into the Tred Avon, you will most likely find yourself in the midst of crowds of boats since Oxford is another of those favorite centers for boating families. Here, on Town Creek, you will find several good marinas, boatyards and restaurants. Crossing the Tred Avon you will see one of the few free-running ferries on the East Coast.

The Tred Avon is well buoyed, and finding Trippe Creek a mile and a half upstream of Oxford is easy and the scenery beautiful. On Trippe Creek we have two favorite anchoring spots. Snug Harbor on the north shore will give you protection from northerlies, and on the south shore just around Deepwater Point, and as far south into the cove as your draft will permit, is good in a southerly. It was while swimming here that we discovered some extremely cool underwater currents—perhaps a spring or two.

Third Day: Trippe Creek to Hudson Creek on the Little Choptank

Distance: 22 miles (approx.), NOAA charts #12267 and 12264

From Trippe Creek retrace your steps to the mouth of the Tred Avon and from there follow the red buoys to the mouth of the Choptank River. At red buoy #10, follow course 198° to the B/W nun off the mouth of the Little Choptank. This will keep you well clear of the large shoal just south of the Sharp's Island Light. You will note that this area is crowded with crab pots, and their floats are everywhere.

The Little Choptank River is rather straight-forward. Pay attention to the marks off Ragged Point—they stand far offshore and blend into the background. Hudson Creek is the second creek to port, just after Brook's Creek. As you turn upstream on Hudson Creek, just curl around the #1 daymark and anchor in the hook of Casson Point. The beach is sandy and inviting, but numerous "No Trespassing" signs warn boatmen off.

Hudson Creek and the Little Choptank afford an uninhabited setting for the boating family. If you want supplies, try Slaughter Creek or Madison Bay, where there is a marina and restaurant.

Fourth Day: Hudson Creek to Solomons on the Patuxent River

Distance: 24 miles (approx.), NOAA chart #12264

Here's a leg where you'll have a chance to do a little open Bay sailing. As you clear the mouth of the Little Choptank, keep well north of James Island. Once again, have a lookout posted to warn of crab floats. From #1 red flasher take course 258° to the red nun #2 out in the Bay, and from there it's nine miles to Cove Point. On this leg of your cruise a careful lookout must be kept for freighters. You'll be crossing the main ship channel, and these big ships travel at a good rate of speed.

Once past Cove Point you can follow the shoreline into Drum Point. There are several fish traps off Little Cove Point, so you'll keep to seaward of them. Once again, the area between Cove Point and Drum Point is crowded with crab floats; and if you wish to avoid them, head further offshore to deeper water.

Annapolis Harbor. Photo by Bob Grieser

Once past Drum Point, you will notice on your chart a large one- and two-foot shoal called "The Flats." You have the choice of staying in mid-Patuxent and skirting these shallows or taking the inside passage. Both ways are well buoyed and safe, so suit yourself.

The harbor of Solomons, Maryland, is active and interesting. There are marinas along the shore and upstream on Back Creek, along with plenty of restaurants catering to a variety of tastes and pocketbooks. Most have a courtesy pier for boating families. The Calvert Marine Museum up Back Creek displays the old Drum Point Lighthouse and has a courtesy pier. It's well worth the visit. See the Solomons cruise for more details.

Fifth Day: Solomons to Dun Cove on Harris Creek

Distance: 30 miles (approx.), NOAA charts #12264 and 12267

Once again you will find your course from the Patuxent River will take you right up the middle of the Bay. This should present no problems if a "freighter watch" is kept by your crew. However, a more cautious boater could simply follow the western shoreline past the Calvert Cliffs nuclear power plant, all the way up to Plum Point and from there cut directly across the Bay north of the leaning Sharp's Island Light. This will add a few miles over the direct route from Cove Point, skirting east of the Sharp's Island shoal.

Either way, when you arrive at Blackwalnut Point, you're almost there. Leave Blackwalnut Point to port and follow Harris Creek north, past Knapps Narrows to Dun Cove two miles beyond. Check the Dun Cove cruise for more details. The most important point is don't turn into the cove until you're sure you'll miss the shoal that projects from the south side of its entrance. Dun Cove is loved for its quiet pastoral setting. An attractive farm borders most of its shoreline, and boats from all over the Bay make this a regular stop.

Sixth Day: Dun Cove to Rhode River

Distance: 19 miles (approx.), NOAA charts #12267 and 12270

On this leg, retrace your steps through Knapps Narrows and head out into the Bay on a course that will take you south of Poplar Island. Once clear of its shoals, head due north about eight miles until you pick up the black bell #73 off the Rhode River entrance. As you turn west from there, look carefully for each buoy since many of the daymarks will disappear into the shoreline. However, once you are at #1 daymark, the others are easy to spot. There's plenty of deep water on the Rhode River, and your only problem will be in choosing from the several anchorages. There are three islands which are quite attractive and provide some protection.

The Rhode River is close enough to West River to entice the boater to one of the good restaurants there. There's nothing better than enjoying a fine meal and then motoring carefully up to the Rhode River to spend the night.

And what a perfect way to end your week's cruise; Annapolis our starting point, is only twelve miles away—an easy sail which should give you time to unload your boat and gather your memories.

This short cruise has, due to time constraints, seemed to ignore many fine creeks and anchorages. If you're an old cruising hand, this itinerary may not suit you because it includes too many old favorites. To the experienced hand, I say, perhaps you are beyond the need of a suggested cruise. But for the new cruising family I have tried to lay out some of the favorite spots—those which have made boaters so enthusiastic about the Chesapeake.□

—Richard C. Goertemiller

PLANNING A WEEK'S CRUISE ON THE SOUTHERN BAY

The southern part of the Chesapeake Bay is a cruising paradise yet to be discovered by the majority of Bay boaters. If you're looking for something different this season, some new anchorages, a change of pace, there's over sixty miles length of Bay here that many Bay boaters never see. And although the area is known for its quiet, secluded creeks and anchorages, the boating hereabouts need not be primitive. There are ample yachting facilities close at hand, if that suits your boating style.

If the southern Bay seems a bit far off by boat, consider that a reasonable drive from anyplace in the Bay area will bring you to the docks of one of many capable and professional charter companies here. But whether you charter or bring your own boat, there's lots to do and a wide variety of places to visit.

What follows is, for us, an ideal week's cruise.

I've tried to keep several things in mind as I planned this cruise. First, each leg of the cruise is a reasonable distance; most are under thirty miles. Second, you will find a blend of quiet, secluded anchorages and harbors with marinas and restaurants. Third, some days will offer a bit of challenge; two days will take you (briefly) out of sight of land. This can be a bit of an adventure if you do most of your regular boating where the Bay is not this wide.

I am aware that there are many fine anchorages not included in this cruise. This is the result of the limits imposed by time considerations, certainly not any prejudice on my part. Feel free to alter the itinerary as you like.

As with other cruises, mileages and compass courses are approximate. I have arbitrarily selected the Rappahannock River Bridge as a starting place. Geographically, this puts you right in the middle of this area's boating centers, which are Deltaville, Carter Creek, the Corrotoman, and Urbanna. If you are coming into the area from the north, you'd make Grog Island your first anchorage. If you came up from the Norfolk end, perhaps it would make more sense to you to start at Mobjack Bay, which is day 5. Our start on the Rappahannock is near many of the lower Bay's charter fleets in case you plan to drive in and charter a boat for a week.

But, enough preliminaries. I can smell the salt breeze already, so let's get started.

First Day: Rappahannock River Bridge to Grog Island on Dymer Creek.

Distance: Approximately 16 miles, NOAA chart #12235.

The Northern Neck of Virginia (bordered on the north by the Potomac River and on the south by the Rappahannock River) offers an impressive array of delightful rivers and creeks. There are, in fact, seven to choose from, starting on the north end with Cockrell Creek, the Great Wicomico River, Mill Creek, Dividing Creek, Indian Creek, Dymer Creek, and Antipoison Creek.

For convenience sake, I'm recommending Grog Island, both because it is among the closest anchorages for your first night out and because the island has an attractive sandy beach which is perfect for picnics or beach parties. Just to the north Indian Creek has a marina at its headwaters, and partway up on the north shore is Rappahannock Seafood in case you may have need of some left-behind supplies.

When transiting the Rappahannock, be sure to honor the lighted spar off Mosquito Point. On a hazy morning there's a possibility that this mark could get lost in the mist. From there the Windmill Point Light is not easily seen, but a course of 103° M should take you right to it. From this light (an iron platform with lighted beacon driven in beside it) you'll have to follow the gentle curve of Fleets Island. A course of 330° M will keep you off the shoal, but just barely, so don't permit too much westward drift.

In a little under five miles you will come to "N" (Fl 4 sec 18 ft 5 M) at the northern end of Fleets Island. When the light is abeam, you will probably be able to pick out the Dymer Creek marks, a series of four lighted beacons. Don't become confused by the Indian Creek marks which are nearby. If you take a course of 284° M, the channel to Dymer Creek will open up to you.

As you pass the fourth mark, "7" (Fl G 4 sec), Grog Island will be to starboard. The island from this side resembles a left-handed "L". The foot, which is a long, submerged sandbar, points westward. Give this shoal a wide berth as you skirt the western side of the island. The deeper water is at the northwest end; but wherever you anchor, it'll be a short dinghy ride to the beach. In case of rough weather, there's a well protected harbor in Ashley Cove across Dymer and about a half mile upstream.

Second Day: Grog Island to Onancock on Onancock Creek (the eastern shore)

Distance: Approximately 29 miles, NOAA charts #12235 and #12228

This day should be fun and provide a bit of challenge. There's about 25 miles of open water between Grog Island and the mouth of Onancock Creek. And once you're in sight of the Eastern Shore, the creeks all seem to look alike till you get close in.

As you leave the last of Dymer Creek's entrance marks, "2" (Fl R 4 sec 15 ft 4 M), set a course of 086° M. This will bring you to red bell "2" (Fl R 4 sec) off Onancock Creek. This leg is a little over 21 miles long, so be sure you compensate for wind and tidal drift. You can check your speed and course by the B/W nuns marking the entrance to Fleets Bay. B/W N "C 69" is on the rhumb line approximately six miles offshore.

From red bell "2" the Onancock Creek channel marks are a little over three miles off on a course of 104° M. A pair of B/W nuns will guide you. The channel itself is well marked and easy to follow. The trip upstream to Onancock, five miles distant, is attractive and inviting. At the town there are slips and bulkhead for tie-ups on a first-come, first-served basis. There are supplies and fuel available also. The holding ground in the harbor is good should you choose to anchor out. For more details, see the Onancock cruise.

Third Day: Onancock to Tangier Island

Distance: Approximately 17 miles, NOAA chart #12228

This should be an easy day. Tangier Island is only 17 miles or so distant, so you can sleep late if you like. Or perhaps a brief detour might prove interesting. Watts Island, which lies 4½ miles away, on a course of 334° M, is reported to have a sandy beach, ideal for swimming and exploring. There is little there other than some wild goats and chickens and a graveyard.

The waters north of Watts Island are littered with unmarked shoals, so it is advisable to leave by way of its southern end, where the shallows are marked.

There is a main channel that cuts across Tangier Island from the Bay on the west to Tangier Sound on the east. The major obstruction is an overhead power cable with a clearance of 50 feet. If your boat will clear this cable, then perhaps you'll enjoy entering from the Sound and exiting at the the Bay's side. That way you'll see more of the island's waterfront. From Watts Island Rocks Qk Fl take a course of 324° M to C "3" off Tangier Island's east side, and about half a mile beyond that you'll pick up the channel markers.

If you choose to enter Tangier Island from the Bay, you'll skirt the southern end of the island looking for Tangier Sound Light, an automated light on a platform. About a mile northwest of the light is a white and orange day beacon bearing 304° M. From here you can begin to follow the shoreline, being careful to stay offshore far enough to avoid the shallows. A mile and a half to the west are some of the Navy's target ships. Stay well clear of the target area since Naval aircraft conduct bombing exercises fairly regularly.

A little over two miles from the W/Or "A" beacon is the outside mark for Tangier Island's western entrance channel, "1" (Fl 2½ sec 15 ft 5 M). The depth into the harbor on Tangier is six feet, and the markers are easy to follow. To starboard are workboat docks, and just beyond are some visitor slips. Make inquiry about where to tie up and room will usually be found, even if the docks are crowded.

Tangier is an interesting island with unusual people and customs and a famous restaurant. For more details, see the cruise to Smith and Tangier Islands.

Fourth Day: Tangier Island to Deltaville

Distance: Approximately 26½ miles, NOAA charts #12228 and #12235

This day of our cruise will test your navigational skills. Because of the target areas around Tangier Island, we won't be able to take the "straight line" rhumb line course. Instead, when you leave the Tangier channel marker "1" (Fl 2½ sec 15 ft 5 M), head south on course 186° M for about 3½ miles to C "1". From there take a course of 210° M for a little over ten miles to a pair of lighted buoys in the Rappahannock Channel, "41" (Fl G 4 sec) and R "42" (Fl R 4 sec). This slight dogleg course will skirt around the currently used target ships as well as the wreck of the *San Marcos* (where live shells and unexploded bombs still present a hazard).

From this pair of buoys change course to 257° M for seven miles, which will bring you to "1" (Fl G 2½ sec), the outermost mark into the Piankatank River. At this point just follow the markers to R "6" (Fl R 6 sec), and from there a course of 328° M will take you to the markers into Jackson Creek.

This channel into Jackson Creek is deceptive. Although well marked, its extreme left-turn dogleg has lured boaters into shortcutting across the shoal. Be sure to follow all the marks in proper sequence, even when it looks as though you're going to go onto the beach at "4". If you honor all the marks, you won't have any trouble.

When you get to R "10", the creek divides. There are good anchorages in each branch, but on the right-hand branch is a large marina where you can get fuel and repairs. The nearby town of Deltaville, although small, has ample groceries and a good restaurant. It makes a pleasant walk from the marina.

Fifth Day: Deltaville to Put In Creek, Mobjack Bay

Distance: Approximately 29 miles, NOAA charts #12235 and #12238

Mobjack Bay has been called the "Best-kept secret of the Chesapeake Bay." It's a Bay-within-a-Bay. The route to Mobjack is fairly straightforward. As you leave the mouth of the Piankatank, simply follow the curve of Gwynn Island and then head south toward Wolf Trap Light. The light is easy to spot—an iron caisson with a brick structure on top, painted red. Here, as the story goes, a British merchant ship, the *Wolfe*, ran aground and after nearly three months was finally refloated. The shoal was named Wolf's Trap, and consequently the light bears that name.

Seven miles southwest of Wolf Trap Light is New Point Comfort with its historic sandstone light tower. This light, built in 1804, stands on the north side of the entrance to Mobjack Bay, a fairly large body of water with four major tributaries which provide enough diversity for a week's worth of cruising. For purposes of this cruise, I have selected East River and its branch, Put In Creek.

Mobjack has broad areas designated for fishtraps, so when traversing the bay, keep well in the fairway. If you follow the buoys, you should have no trouble finding East River. Approximately two miles upstream is Put In Creek. As you motor up East River, you may see the last standing tide mill on the Chesapeake. It is said that this mill ground grain for George Washington's army during the seige of Yorktown. For more details, see the cruise to the East River.

Sixth Day: Mobjack Bay to Healy Creek, Piankatank River

Distance: Approximately 32 miles, NOAA charts #12238 and #12235

Much of this day's course is retracing the previous day's cruise. When you enter the Piankatank, however, you will proceed upstream instead of heading for Jackson Creek.

As you round Gwynn Island, Stove Point Neck is due west; and its mile-long shoal runs off southeast from its southernmost tip to "8" (Fl R 2½ sec). Be sure you honor this mark, and beware that adjacent to it is a floating temporary mark designating shoaling. From here you will turn upstream toward the tip of Stove Point Neck. Note that shoaling has occured here at "10" (Fl R 4 sec 15 ft 4 M), so give this mark a wide berth.

Upstream 1¾ miles is "13" (Fl G 4 sec) which appears to be a starboard mark because it seems so close to the north shore. Keep this mark to port, though; and Healy Creek marks will be just ahead, to starboard. The entrance marks appear homemade, but don't hesitate. There's plenty of water inside. This is one of the Chesapeake's really beautiful creeks. For more details, see the cruise to Healy Creek.

Seventh Day: Healy Creek to Rappahannock River Bridge

Distance: Approximately 18 miles, NOAA chart #12235

On purpose, this is to be a short day. This should give you time to clean up and unload your boat. This route is, again, straightforward, keeping within sight of land in well marked channels. As you leave the Piankatank you'll want to follow the marked channel until Stingray Point Light is abeam to avoid the prominent shoal there. This light is composed of the base of the original cottage-style lighthouse with an automated light replacing the cottage.

The Rappahannock presents no hazards as you can see, and that's just as well. In the time it takes to travel the eight miles to the bridge and a nearby home port, you'll have a chance to mull over your memories of this cruise. If you've never cruised this area, I guarantee you'll not soon forget the experience. If you're an oldtimer to these waters, I'm sure this cruise won't be boring. As with the rest of the Bay, even the familiar is fascinating; and each day holds new discoveries. □

—Richard C. Goertemiller

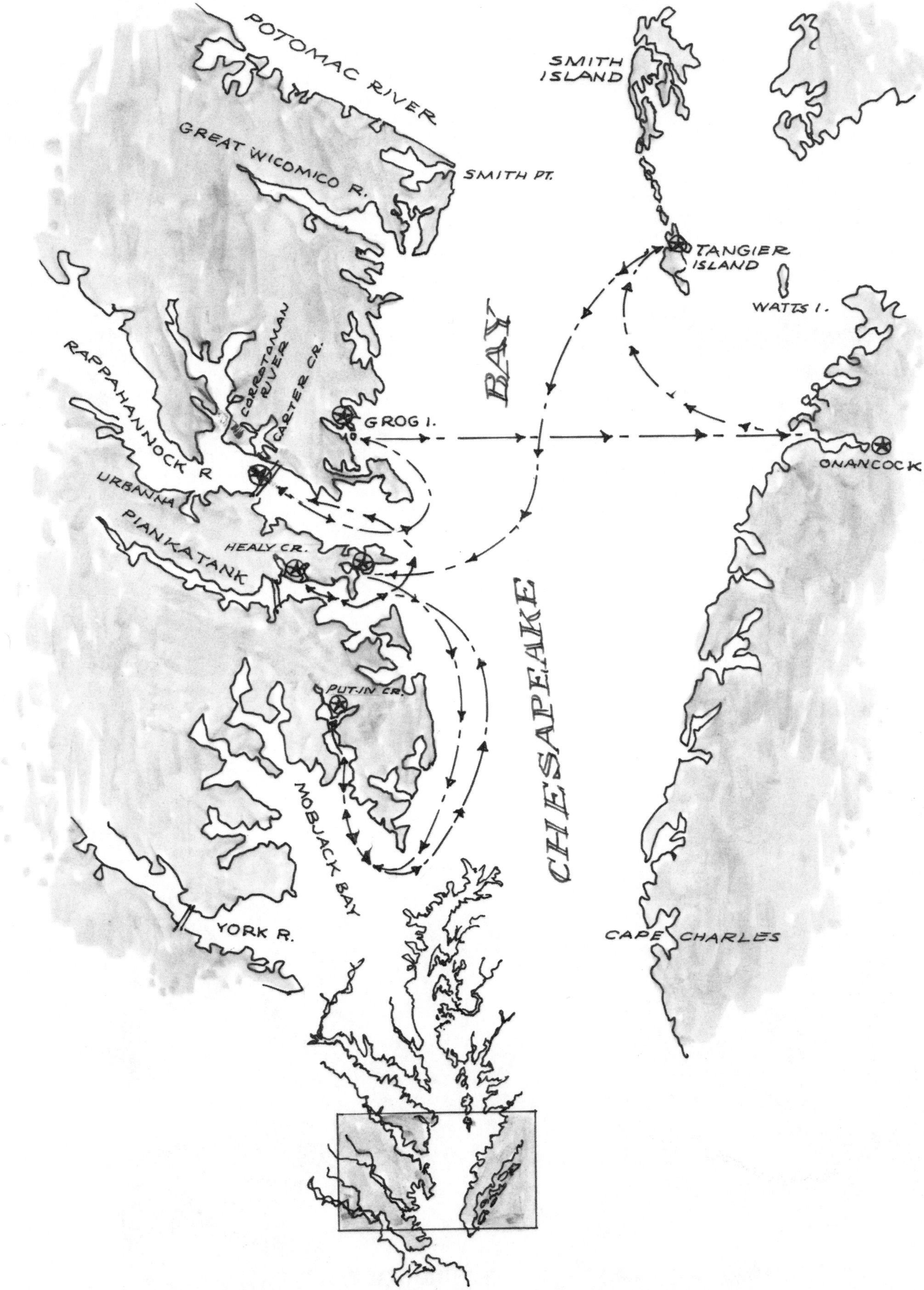
POTOMAC RIVER
SMITH ISLAND
GREAT WICOMICO R.
SMITH PT.
TANGIER ISLAND
WATTS I.
BAY
RAPPAHANNOCK R.
CORROTOMAN RIVER
CARTER CR.
GROG I.
ONANCOCK
URBANNA
PIANKATANK
HEALY CR.
PUT-IN CR.
CHESAPEAKE
MOBJACK BAY
YORK R.
CAPE CHARLES

UPPER BAY:

C&D CANAL TO CHESAPEAKE BAY BRIDGE

Bordered by the Chesapeake and Delaware Canal to the north and the Chesapeake Bay Bridges to the south, this section of the Bay is truly where it all begins.

Millions of years ago there was no Bay, only a river flowing slowly from its source (in what is now New York state) to the sea. In time the land at the mouth of this river sank until it was so low that sea water ran in and flooded it, cutting off all tributaries and, in fact, drowning the river. That river is known to us today as the Susquehanna and its "drowning" gave us the Chesapeake Bay. And in the course of time, the Bay and its many tributaries have played a significant role in the beginnings of our country.

Today, cruising yachtsmen, many unaware of these happenings millions of years ago, are able to enjoy the quiet coves and creeks of the Upper Bay's rivers. The quiet, picturesque Elk, Bohemia, Sassafras, Susquehanna and Northeast rivers are a beautiful introduction to Bay cruising. The facilities at Havre de Grace and Georgetown also make it a convenient area to cruise.

Each section of Chesapeake Bay has its own peculiar personality, beauty and charm. The Upper Bay is no exception and offers a variety of cruising fare, from tranquil coves to modern suburbia.

From these quiet Upper Bay rivers, the cruiser is then treated to the small towns of Rock Hall and Gratitude on the Eastern Shore. And then the cruiser is gradually brought to the busy, inhabited creeks of the Magothy and Patapsco and the commercial port of Baltimore City on the Western Shore.

After crossing back to the Chester River the cruiser will discover many creeks, rivers and beautiful anchorages leading all the way up to the historic and distinctive Chestertown.

Upper Bay Charts:

12260	12277
12272	12278
12273	12279
12274	12281
12275	12282

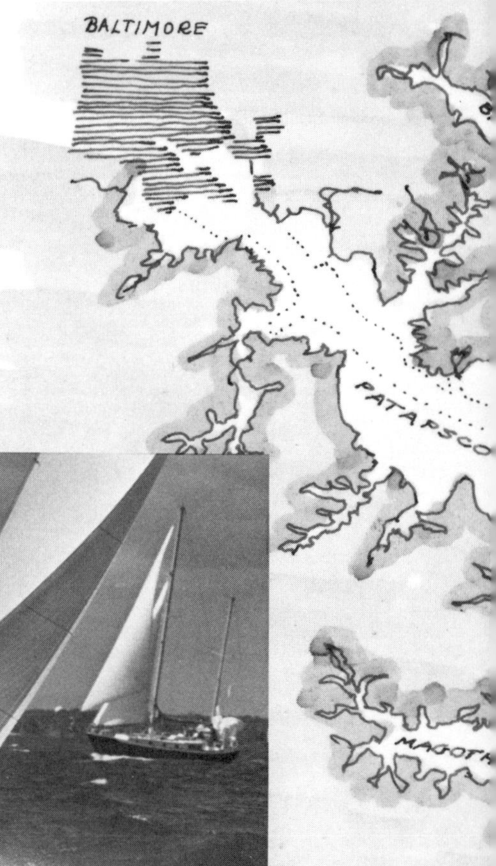

PHOTOS BY BOB GRIESER

SUSQUEHANNA R.
NORTHEAST R.
C&D CANAL
ELK RIVER
BOHEMIA R.
BUSH R.
GUNPOWDER R.
SASSAFRAS R.
STILLPOND CR.
WORTON CR
FAIRLEE CR
HART-MILLER I.
CHESAPEAKE BAY
CHESTERTOWN
ROCK HALL
CHESTER RIVER
CORSICA R.
BRIDGE
KENT NARROWS
N

CHESAPEAKE AND DELAWARE CANAL, CHESAPEAKE CITY

off the Elk River

As you slip between the protective jetties which mark its unpretentious entrance from the Delaware or enter Back Creek from the Elk, there is little to indicate the magnitude of effort which was and is the Chesapeake and Delaware Canal.

The original Chesapeake and Delaware Canal was first opened for business in 1829. At that time it was 13 miles long with a waterline width of 66 feet, a bottom width of 36 feet, and a depth of 10 feet.

In 1927 the Army Engineers completed a face lifting which eliminated locks, built bridges, widened the canal to 90 feet, and deepened it to 12 feet.

The present channel with a minimum of 29 feet is to be deepened to 35 feet under a long-term improvement program, although this plan is now under careful scrutiny by environmentalists.

The canal is government-owned and toll free, a vital link of the Intracoastal Waterway that connects the Chesapeake and Delaware Bays. From Reedy Point on the Delaware Bay to Chesapeake City it is 12 miles. Five bridges now cross the canal. Four are high level, fixed bridges with a minimum clearance of 135 feet. The remaining bridge, the Penn Central Railroad Bridge located at Canal Station, has a vertical lift span with a clearance of 45 feet down and 133 feet up. This span will open in response to one long and one short blast from your ship's horn.

Once you have entered the C & D Canal do not be lulled into a false sense of security, either by the gently swaying reeds at the Delaware entrance or the tranquility of Back Creek, for the canal demands your constant attention. You must be careful of the debris washed in from the Delaware, the freighters, and the tugs with their barges in tow.

Above all, be mindful of the current. Be sure to use the Tidal Current Tables. Although official publications list the current velocity at 2 to 2.6 knots, anyone who has eve watched boats leaving the anchorage basin at Chesapeak City and being swept sideways down the canal knows that a times the current reaches 6 knots.

The channel is marked with buoys and lights from eac entrance and the buoyage system reverses itself at Chesapeak City. Between the Delaware Bay entrance and Chesapeak City, even numbers and flashing red lights are on the nort side and odd numbers and flashing white lights are on th south side. As you enter from the Elk River, even number and flashing red lights are on the south side and odd number and flashing white or green lights are on the north side.

Traffic control lights are located at Old Town Point Whar in Maryland and at Reedy Point, Delaware. A green ligh indicates the canal is open to traffic, a red light that it is closed TV cameras which monitor traffic through the canal are als located at these two points. A third camera, which would b located in the waterway, is under consideration.

When navigating the C & D Canal, it is wise to stay out o the middle, just in case of an emergency—perhaps a larg ship looming around the next bend, which could neither sto nor maneuver around an incapacitated craft.

The canal is under the supervision of the Distric Engineer,Corps of Army Engineers, Philadelphia, anc because of conditions peculiar to this waterway, certair restrictions are enforced. Transiting the canal under sai between Reedy Point and Welch Point is not permitted Water-skiing between these two points is also prohibited. As ir most cases, all vessels proceeding with the current have the right-of-way. However, here all small pleasure craft relinquish the right-of-way to deeper draft vessels having limitec maneuverability. At night, the canal is lighted with mercury vapor lights located approximately 140 feet from the edge o the channel. In case of an emergency, the dispatcher a Chesapeake City monitors VHF Channel 16.

For yachtsmen heading south through the C & D Canal the Chesapeake Bay begins at Chesapeake City. Chesapeake City was established to facilitate running the canal as well a to serve the thousands of small craft making the passage every

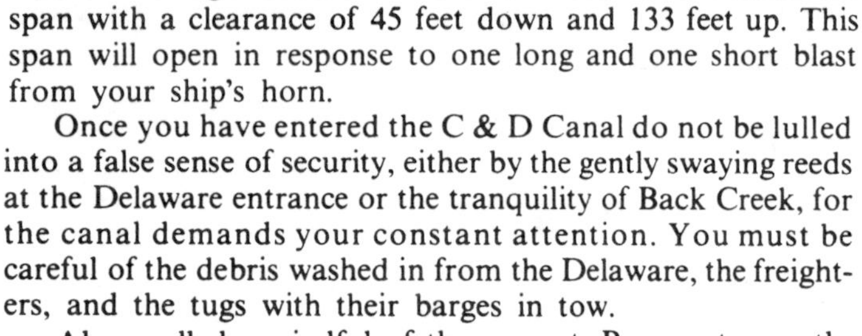

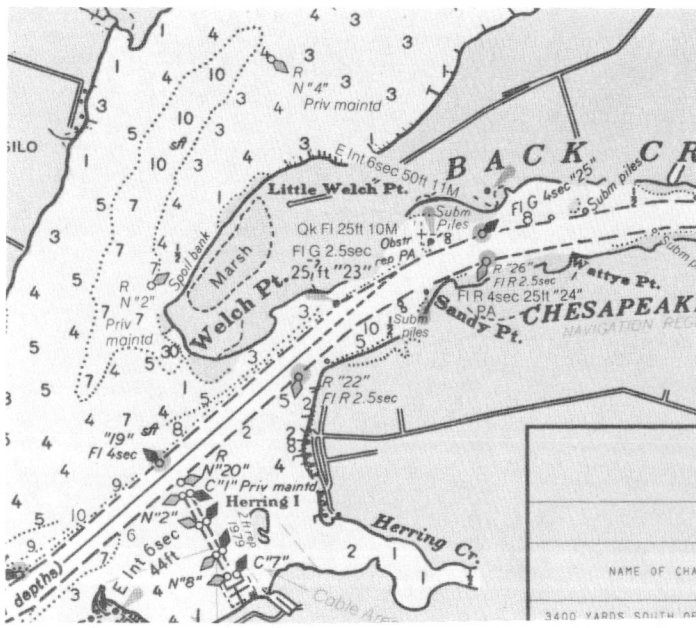

From NOAA Chart 12274—not to be used for navigation.

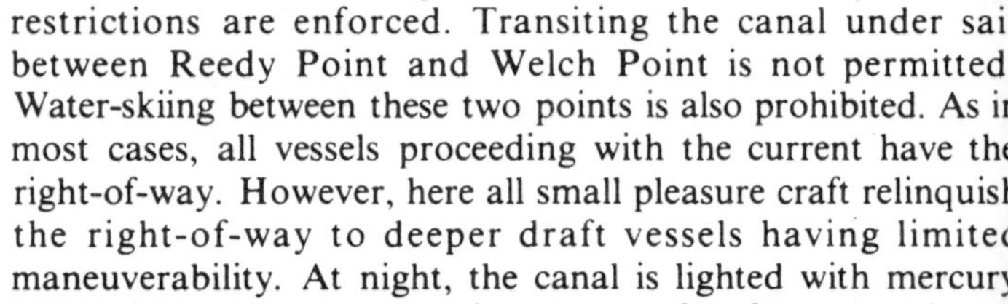

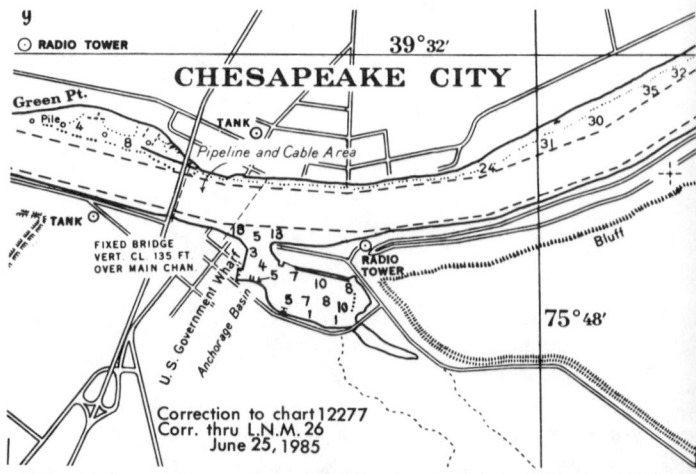

Correction to NOAA chart 12277—not to be used for navigation.

PHOTO BY BOB GRIESER

year. At Chesapeake City you can find berths, gasoline, diesel fuel, some marine supplies and restaurant facilities. If you should attempt to dock against the current, be sure to maintain a healthy speed to make headway; be careful the tricky current does not cut out at the last moment. When you get close to shore the current seems to "let go"—so be prepared to go into strong reverse at the last minute.

On the north shore just east of the high bridge is Schaefer's Canal House Restaurant, with adjacent fuel docks and grocery supplies. The restaurant has large canal-view windows that allow you to enjoy your meal and watch canal traffic at the same time. And when a large freighter or tanker passes, the maitre d' will announce the vessel's name, displacement, ports of call, and destination, as well as any other item that might be of interest.

For your anchorage take your boat directly across the canal to the public anchorage basin, which is large enough to accommodate a number of cruising boats.

When you enter the basin, Dockside Restaurant and Yacht Club will be dead ahead. The restaurant has a good view of the Canal and offers free dockage while dining. There is, however, a charge for overnight slips. Formerly, with the permission of the Canal Dispatcher, you could tie up free of charge at the government wharf on the west side of the basin. In a recent conversation with one of the dispatchers he informed me there are generally several Corps of Engineers boats using the dock, and tying up is usually permitted in emergencies only.

Be aware that there is more current than one might expect in the basin. Allow swinging room when anchoring.

When you visit South Chesapeake City, you must make it a point to visit the C & D Museum. This building houses the oldest and largest steam engine on the original foundation in the United States. The machinery operated from 1851 to 1927, with only one breakdown. A huge wooden waterwheel, 38 feet in diameter and 10 feet wide, capable of lifting 1,200,000 gallons of water into the lock every hour, is also in the museum. The museum is open Sundays, Easter through Thanksgiving 10 A.M. to 5:30 P.M.; major non-religious holidays 8 A.M. to 4:15 P.M.; Monday through Saturday 8 A.M. to 4:15 P.M.

Other points of interest in Chesapeake City include the Harriott Hotel of 1835 vintage. Turning from the canal, the largest building you will see on the left is Franklin Hall which houses the Chesapeake City Library. The windows are beautifully draped and the tables and chairs are exquisite hand-crafted Shaker reproductions. A handsome wooden staircase leads to what will eventually be a meeting room and museum. The library is staffed from 2 to 4:30 P.M. Tuesdays and Thursdays and from 10 A.M. to noon on Saturdays by volunteers of the Women for Federal Restoration.

What is it that seems different about this town? Why does it impart such a feeling of timelessness? As we marvel at the ornate intricacies of the Victorian architecture, scarcely paying heed to the "average" homes interspersed, we realize what it is! We are not walking through some re-created village of the past. This is the real thing. Chesapeake City is a now town—a living, working, playing reality. The new and the old stand side by side, and we are experiencing a living history. □

NOTE: Shoaling reported to a depth of 2.8′ MLW in the middle of the entrance to the Anchorage Basin at Chesapeake City. Water depth is 9.6′ MLW on the west side of the entrance and 5.6′ MLW on the east side.

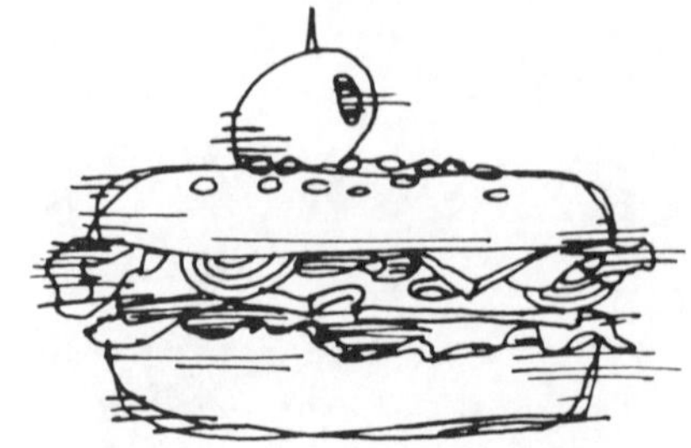

GALLEY TIPS

Stock your galley with plastic tumblers or mugs that come with reusable or disposable lids. A cover-up is handy if the cry of "jibe-ho" comes immediately after the drinks are poured.

Prepare lunch before you cast off in the morning. If heavy seas are anticipated, stow assembled lunch items in a small cooler or ice chest in the cockpit rather than in main refrigerator. Much easier to serve quickly than to do a juggling act in the galley with refrigerator contents cascading about.

Carry lunches, drinks, or other items topside on a serving tray or baskets with an edge at least an inch deep.

Collect a set of reusable plastic bottles in a size or sizes to carry items used most often on your boat. You'll like the no-spill, no-break (and no-cost) features for such oft-used items as salad oil, vinegar and catsup, and liquid soap. Label well, of course!

Install a strap that hooks in place quickly that you can lean on for balance while working in the galley. Make sure the strap and fittings are strong enough for the job. Easy to install if your galley is "L" or "U" shaped.

Sling a string hammock for fruit storage near the companionway. The fruit won't get squashed or bruised there, and it will be close at hand for snacking. If your lockers sometimes get wet, a hammock is also a good dry place to keep bread, cereal, crackers, chips and the like.

Behold the lovely cabbage! It survives well without refrigeration and can substitute for more perishable lettuce. Shred for use in sandwiches and salads. Saute or steam shredded cabbage for a tantalizing hot vegetable dinner.

BOATKEEPING TIPS

Seal some spare matches in a small plastic bag to insure having dry ones in an emergency. "Burp-top" plastic containers or band-aid boxes can also be used for this purpose.

Never use metal hangers on a boat. They will eventually leave a rust stain on your clothes. So buy yourself some strong, plastic hangers in assorted colors. Then assure that look-alike foul weather gear is easy to find quickly by assigning everyone his own or her own color of hanger.

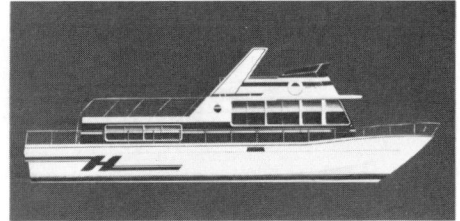

A Walking Tour of:
CHESAPEAKE CITY

Chesapeake City is well-known as an overnight stop to cruising boaters. On our first visit we were headed to Ocean City, Maryland, on our maiden voyage out of the Chesapeake Bay. Not only were we excited about our upcoming vacation, but we were fascinated by just being in the C&D Canal. This man-made project has had a tremendous impact on maritime commerce, for although it is only 14 miles long, it trims 286 miles off the trip between Baltimore and Philadelphia! Its opening in 1829 marked the beginning of a bustling era for Chesapeake City.

Now it was our scheduled stop. Choosing an in-town marina was easy; Schaefer's Canal House Marina is the only one. Its one long dock parallels the canal and caters exclusively to transients on a first come/first serve basis. You don't have to be a seasoned sailor to tie up here, but you need to be an adept boat handler. Since the average current runs at over 2 knots, even the fixed bridge (linking this half of town with its southern complement) has a wake! Be sure your provisions include a long extension cord, patience, and a sense of humor. On a busy summer weekend you may have to play "outlet roulette," or understand that there is just so much electricity to be shared by all.

Schaefer's is a complex of indulgences and conveniences that now is a canal institution. Among its various eating places is Schaefer's Canal House Restaurant. The dining room, serving three meals daily, overlooks the canal giving its patrons a beautiful view of the pleasure craft and freighters passing by.

Curious about the town, we asked a store clerk about what to see and do. She paused for a moment and said, "Nothing in particular that I can think of." Unconvinced, we set out to explore. In the area of town near the marina we found Town Hall, a fire house, and quiet residential neighborhoods. Most of the evening traffic seemed to be heading in two directions—to and from Schaefer's. Aside from being very pleasant to walk around, the clerk was right about what we found. Since it was late and we wanted an early start the next morning, we decided to skip the southern part of town.

A year later we headed to New Jersey and again stopped in Chesapeake City. Schaefer's still had a monopoly on transient dockage and offered the same amenities as before. Commercial traffic through the canal was a bit heavier this time and we discovered "freighter watching." When one of these floating warehouses goes by you have a front row seat not only to their passage, but occasionally to the transfer of pilots. (After watching this daring procedure I concluded that pilots are part captain and part aerial artist!) Again, we skipped the southern side of town.

This past summer we were in Chesapeake City for the third time and found everything the same as before. Well acquainted with the northern shore, our curiosity had grown about the south side. We were determined to see and judge it for ourselves.

We began our tour at the Canal Museum. While it is convenient to tie up at the adjacent Corps of Engineers' dock, it's ideal only if your boat fits in the spaces between its large pilings. The dock itself was not in the best repair when we were there and boards extending beyond the pilings as possible boarding platforms looked to be of questionable value. We tied up "creatively" and carefully climbed across the tops of pilings to disembark. Our kids loved it but other boaters might prefer a less athletic approach. One alternative is to tie up at the public wharf located on your starboard as you enter the basin. (Either way, have your fenders ready; between current and bulkhead conditions they'll come in handy.) Or, you could anchor in the protected basin and dinghy to the dock.

Once ashore, it's a short walk to the old pumphouse which now serves as the canal museum; its waterwheel, 40 feet in diameter, is on display at the rear. Exhibits and a working model explain the canal's history and mechanics. Four locks and 6 mule teams were the backbone of the system, essential because the original canal was 10 feet above sea level. Since 1919, when the federal government purchased it for $2.5 million, a $25 million progression of modernizing improvements has lowered, widened and deepened the canal to accommodate today's commercial and defense vessels.

Chesapeake City's vibrance has been directly related to the canal. From its inception, the canal transformed this agricultural village into a viable port. When the federal government converted the lock system to an uninterrupted through passage, Chesapeake City began to decline. No longer needing to stop, vessels didn't. Widening the canal resulted in the loss of commercial waterfront properties, adding to the town's economic woes. In 1942, when the lift bridge was destroyed by a passing freighter and replaced with a ferry crossing, traffic into town became deliberate, planned, and sparse. Six years later the present bridge opened, but it bypassed the business district and allowed traffic to skirt over the heart of town. However, Chesapeake City didn't die, it hibernated. Today, like Snow White kissed by the handsome prince, the town is reawakening. Local resources are being channeled into restoring Chesapeake City to its bygone glory. All the old charm is still there, it just needs polishing, which is exactly what the townfolk are doing.

A good place to start a walking tour of south Chesapeake City is at the public wharf, at the foot of Bohemia Avenue. There, along the canal, are the Canal Grill and Old Wharf Gifts. The former is a snack stand where you can treat yourself to barbecued hot dogs, chicken, and hamburgers cooked on a huge stone grill. Although tempted, we weren't hungry enough for anything very substantial—but there's always room for ice cream! They serve the three standard flavors—chocolate, vanilla, and strawberry—not much variety but delicious none-the-less. Old Wharf

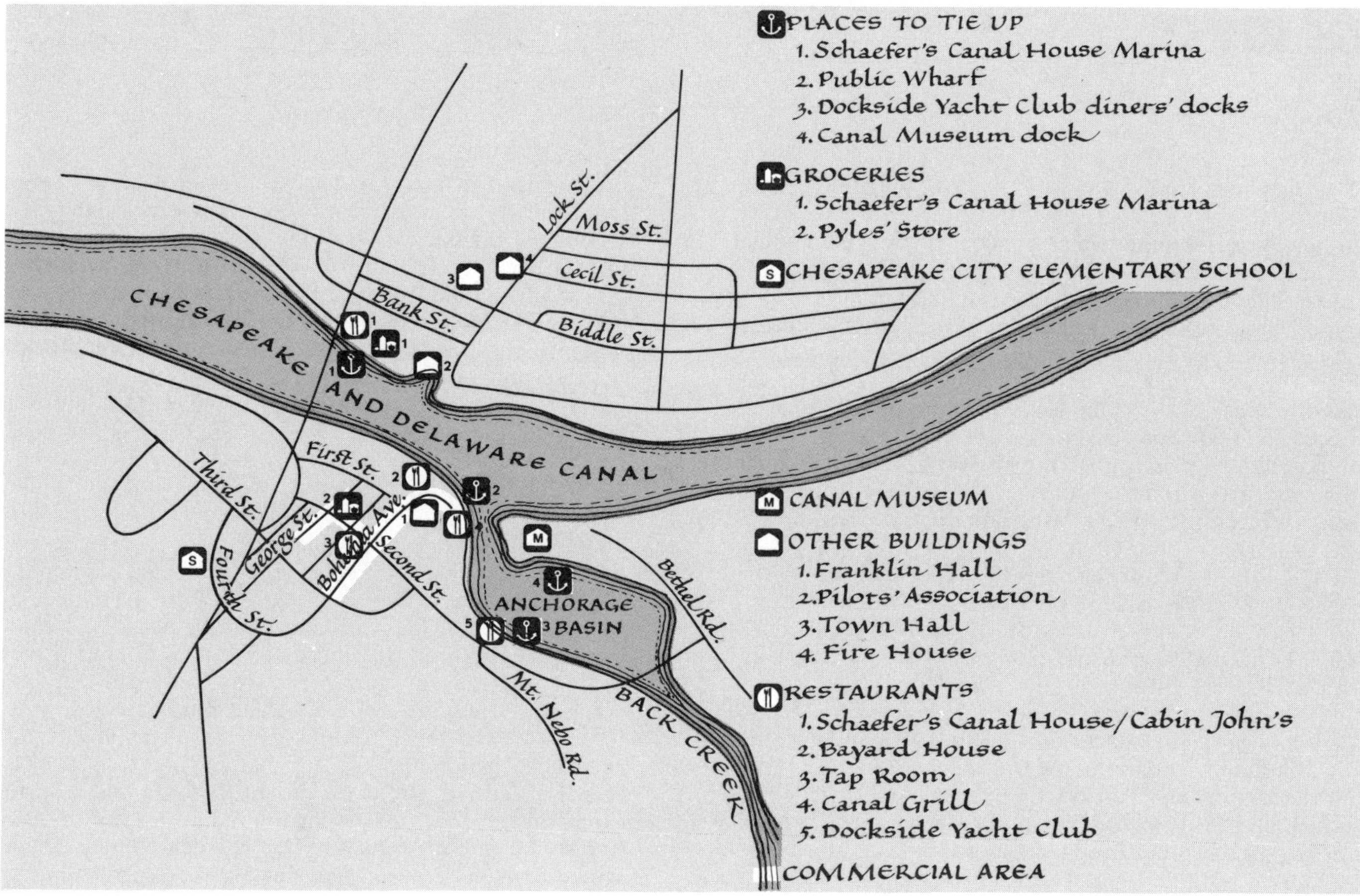

Gifts, in a cozy waterfront cottage, sells a potpourri of items from handcrafted dolls to small decorating accessories.

Stretching up Bohemia Ave. to First St., is a row of restored 19th century houses, each with a plaque giving date and ownership identification. Closest to the water is the Bayard House, believed to be the oldest building in town. Known variously as the Back Creek House, Bayard House, and Harriot Hotel with The-Hole-in-the-Wall Bar, it was restored as a restaurant in 1983 and specializes in regional cuisine. Though this charming inn looks elegant, you can dress informally. (Lunch and dinner served daily.) Across the street from the Bayard House is Franklin Hall, a tall brick structure surrounded by a lovely park. It has been a hardware store, dry goods store, public room, Masonic Lodge, and now houses a branch of the Cecil County Library and the Cecil County Arts Council. The Arts Council sponsors rotating multi-media exhibits by area artists and is open to the public Monday-Friday, 9 A.M. to 5 P.M.

Continuing up Bohemia Avenue you'll find the Back Creek General Store, handsomely restored. Inside is a treasure of handcrafted items including soaps, quilts, stenciled baskets, Christmas stockings, even corn meal and popcorn. A short distance farther is the well-stocked Dennis' Antique Store. It would take the combined heirlooms and attic artifacts of many families to begin to equal its inventory. Among several other shops around town are an art gallery, clothing and plant boutiques, and we saw signs of more businesses to open soon. Most stores are open Wednesday through Sunday.

Food is another area in which Chesapeake City is very accommodating. If you are dining out, two more restaurants complete your options. The Tap Room, on Bohemia Ave. at Second St., serves seafood, homemade Italian specialties, and was recommended to us by several local residents as having the best steamed crabs around. Back at the waterfront is the Dockside Yacht Club (courtesy dockage to diners). Open Wednesday through Sunday, April through October, their lunch and dinner menus include seafood, veal, and mesquite grilling. If you are dining in and need to reprovision, try Pyles Store at the corner of Second and George Streets. Unlike a supermarket, this neighborhood store doesn't offer a large variety of brands of any one item, but the stock is complete enough to supply any galley. Fresh meats and cheeses are augmented by live or steamed crabs. (Open 7 days a week.)

Together, both sides of Chesapeake City host Canal Day, held annually around the 4th of July. A true celebration, it has something for everyone. A parade with bands, floats, V.I.P.'s and antique cars leaves the north side and makes its way across the bridge into the southern half of town. All kinds of food tempt the taste buds and the diet while artisans and craft people display their work. Rain or shine, the celebration goes on and as long as the weather cooperates fireworks provide the festive finale to the day.

A walking tour of Chesapeake City's historic area is available as is a guided tour ($2.50 per person by appointment only, it includes a slide presentation and entry into restored homes). For more information contact the Chesapeake City District Civic Association, Inc. at 301-885-5233 or the Cecil County Office of Planning and Economic Development at 301-398-0200, ext. 144. □

—Andi Manchester

ELK RIVER

The light on Turkey Point (Fl 6 sec 129 Ft. 6M) marks the end of the Bay and the beginning of the Elk River. Although there is ample water outside the buoyed channel, sometimes dredge buoys, barges, cables, etc., are found in the area. Therefore, unless you are familiar with the river, it is a good practice to stay within the buoyed area. Ships can come down on you quickly, however sailboaters should keep a sharp eye when tacking, and motorboaters would be wise to ride the edges of the channel ready to get out of the way if necessary or if trouble develops.

The Elk River is a glistening silvery ribbon of water which separates the mountains to the west and the gently rolling countryside to the east. The view on this river is nothing short of spectacular.

It is 1.8 miles from flashing "5" (Fl 4 sec) off Turkey Point to R "8" (Fl R 2.5 sec) off **Cabin John Creek.** There is a good beach on the south side of the creek and many boaters, reluctant to expose themselves to the wider Elk and Bohemia Rivers, "duck into" Cabin John Creek for the night. They do not "duck in" too far, however, since the creek is navigable for only a short distance. If you do venture into Cabin John, let caution be the watchword; take care to avoid the "mysterious" obstruction somewhere at the creek's mouth. I have heard conflicting reports as to whether it is or is not still there. One thing is for certain. Over the years I have known both sailboaters and powerboaters who have come in unhappy contact with it and, in at least one instance, a sinking occurred.

The obstruction, believed to be a rock, is just inside the mouth of Cabin John Creek almost directly in the middle and is not visible even at low water. It is not noted on some of the newer charts, but most area boaters doubt it has been removed. With this in mind, it's a good idea to be a little extra cautious when entering Cabin John Creek.

On previous trips to Cabin John I have visited people who have a home near the head of the creek, and although my boat has a draft of only about a foot (when going very slowly), I had to watch the tide in order not to be stranded there. In fact, on one occasion I didn't leave a minute too soon, churning up mud for several hundred feet. To local sailboaters the tide is a real factor in their boating lives.

Another anchorage can be found on the northwest side of the Elk. It is just above Turkey Point, opposite the trailer park.

Across from Cabin John Creek you will find a boating facility at **Rogues Harbor in Elk Neck State Park.** The depths in Rogues Harbor are from three to five feet. Although the charts show three feet near the southwest shore, I would not venture too close to shore at any point. The few times I have visited the cove, I noticed that most of the boats anchor well out from the sandy beach.

High on one of the bluffs surrounding the cove we could see campers in Elk Neck State Park. The park accommodates both tents and tent-trailers. Housekeeping cabins are available from early June to early September. Other facilities offered by the park include four launching ramps, boat and motor rentals, a pier and concession building with gas, tackle, bait and other supplies. An extensive, protected beach can be found on the Northeast River side of the neck. Motorists may reach the park by taking Route 272 from the town of North East. Rogues Harbor is located approximately 10 miles from North East by car.

Rogues Harbor provides excellent protection from blows from the north, northeast and northwest. However, some sections of the harbor are vulnerable to winds from the south and southwest. It is a beautiful daytime anchorage. I, personally, would prefer not to spend the night here—mainly because of its proximity to the heavily-traveled shipping lanes on the Elk River. I feel Cabin John Creek is a more suitable anchorage for overnight.

Continuing up the Elk, across from Old Town Point Wharf on the starboard, **Piney Creek Cove** lies to port. The mouth of Piney Creek Cove, from Oldfield Pt. to Hylands Pt. is 1.2 miles wide, narrowing to approximately 1 mile while maintaining depths of 4 to 6 feet except along the northern shores which are very shallow.

Once you enter the cove proper you are sheltered from wind from almost any direction, except perhaps a strong southerly blow. This is a good place to pause and enjoy the beauty of the high headlands of Elk Neck and the gently rolling countryside across the way, and you can swim in nettle-free water, safely out of the busy channel.

Despite the quiet countryside, there was always activity here, even before the C&D Canal. At one time, a ferry ran between Oldfield Point on the north shore and Courthouse Point on the south, transporting troops during the Revolutionary War. On August 27, 1777, a detachment of General Howe's troops crossed here on their way to Philadelphia.

Upstream, keeping buoy "19" to starboard, we round Welch Point and head up the section of Elk River known to local boaters as the **Little Elk**. Take a look at your charts. Notice anything strange? It would seem that any relationship between channel markers and deep water is purely coincidental. Perhaps this accounts for the fact that while running right between the markers, I usually manage to churn up mud. This probably also accounts for the fact that more people seem to be running out of the marked channel than are running in it.

Why, you ask, would you want to cruise a river with such problems? The answer is obvious when you look around you. The scenery is some of the very finest on the Bay. For this reason, we'll proceed as far as we safely can and use other means for more indepth exploring.

Running 0.5 of a mile past buoy "19", we pick up N "2" and 1.5 miles from N "2" to starboard is a delightful anchorage called **"Paddy Piddles Cove"** (one can only wonder). If there is enough water for your boat (pay particular attention to your depth sounder, lead line or whatever) and if you decide to proceed, you will find marinas on either side of the river 1.3 miles farther up stream, and you will be able to find: berths, electricity, hull and motor

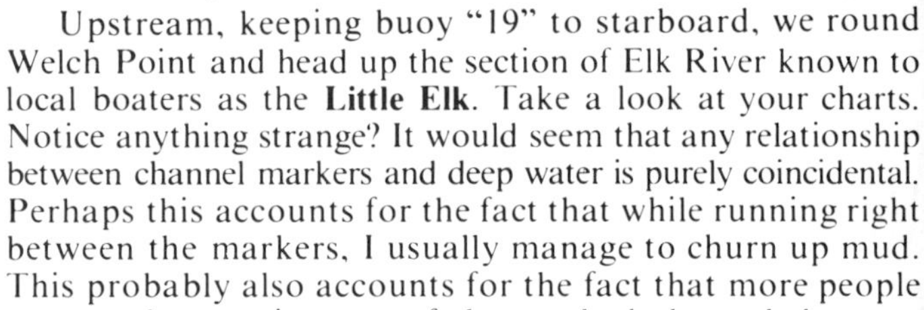

PHOTO BY BOB GRIESER

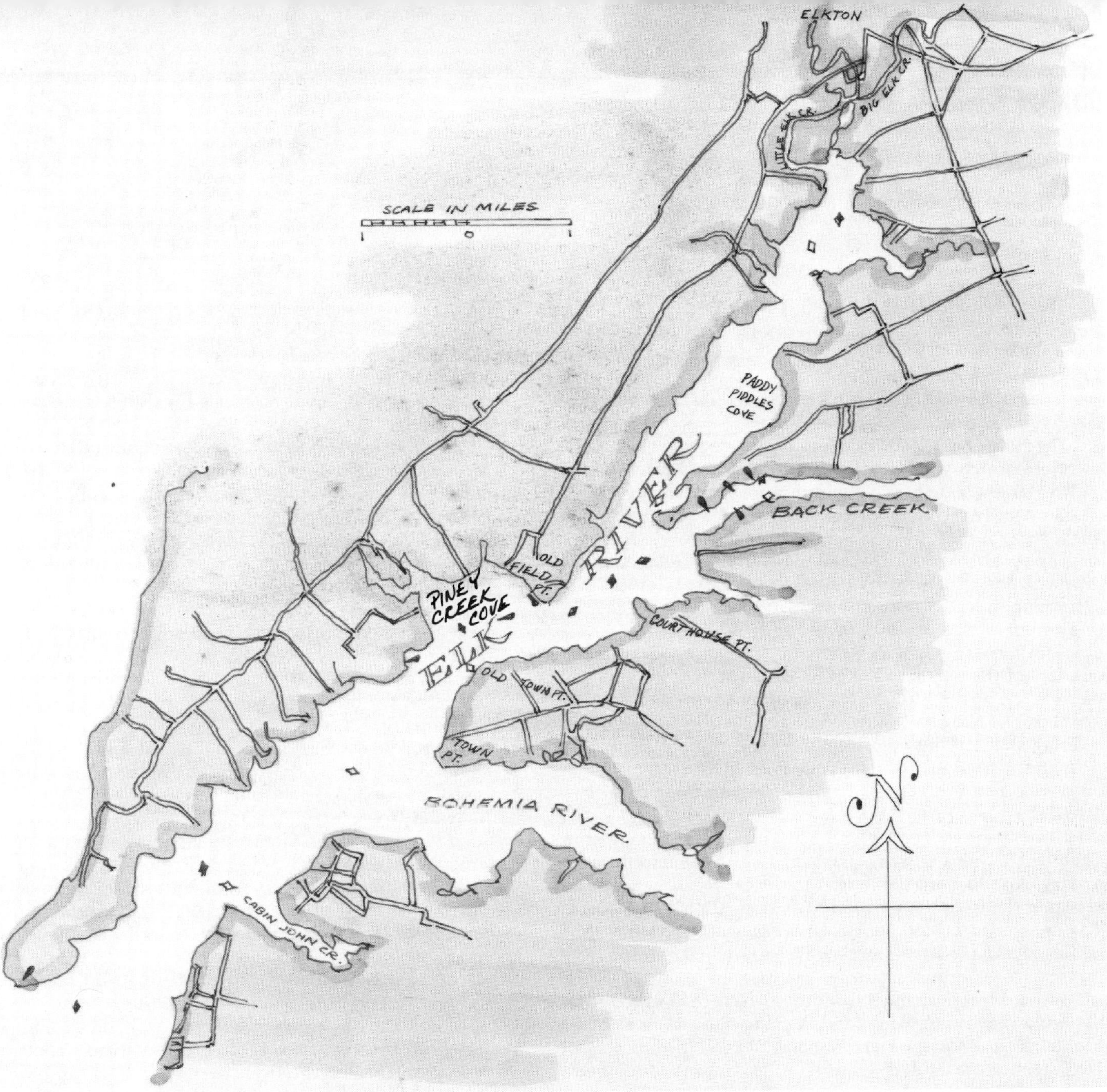

repairs, lift-out facilities, hardware, groceries, and toilet and shower facilities. The channel is marked to the junction of **Big and Little Elk Creeks.**

My advice would be to anchor at Paddy Piddles Cove and use your dinghy to explore further. There is a 2.3 foot tidal range and a current velocity of 0.6 knots in this area.

At one time, the river must have been quite deep because Frenchtown was a major embarkation point for ports along the Chesapeake Bay. Continental soldiers, on their way to victory at Yorktown, embarked here. Don't spend any time looking for Frenchtown, however, because it is not there. It was burned by Admiral Cockburn in 1813.

From the junction of Big Elk Creek and Little Elk Creek, there is reported to be depths of 3 feet to the fixed highway bridges 0.6 and 0.4 miles above their mouths. The channels in these creeks are narrow and crooked and contain numerous snags and unmarked shoals.

Above the junction of Big Elk Creek and Little Elk Creek is the City of Elkton, originally Head of Elk. It is said that Captain John Smith named the Elk River because he saw a resemblance to the horns of an elk in the two Elk Creeks which join to form the river at Elk Landing.

Elkton was founded early in the eighteenth century and at that time was quite a "cross roads" town. The county seat of Cecil County was moved from Charlestown to Head of Elk in 1786 and the town began to grow. Elkton escaped the fate of Frenchtown in the War of 1812 when the guns of Fort Defiance, about a mile down the river, drove the British away. Originally, the river came quite close to the town and ships unloaded their wares behind the buildings on Main Street.

In more recent times, Elkton was the place to go for quick marriages. Maryland required no waiting period and Elkton was the closest town across the Delaware State Line. Marriages became big business and wedding chapels lined Main Street. Couples lined up by the hundreds for weddings assembly-line style. Everyone prospered until, alas, in 1938 a 48-hour waiting period was initiated and business subsided. Today, probably more for tradition than anything else, many people still come to Elkton to be married. □

The three miles from R"6" off Turkey Point to R "10" at the mouth of the Bohemia River are three of the most beautiful miles in all of Bay country. I'll be honest with you, this is *Makani Kai's* home port, and it will be hard not to be prejudiced. However, after this cruise I think you'll agree I have good reason.

The Bohemia is wide with 7-to 10-foot depths at its mouth; therefore no buoyage is necessary. It is wise, however, to give Town Point a wide berth. One mile above the river's entrance on the southwest side is **Veazey Cove,** which is a popular anchorage for local boaters because there are no jellyfish here.

The cove's only drawback is that there is no direct sunset view. Otherwise, it provides excellent protection from everything except a northerly wind. Veazey Cove has depths of 5 to 6 feet, and is a mile wide at its opening. If you have a deep-draft boat, it is wise to stay in the middle, about three-quarters of the way into the cove. On a summer weekend, all manner of power, house, and centerboard sailboats are anchored in the shallow waters, sterns close to the beach insuring that less intrepid swimmers can stand if they wish. Although a good many boats will remain in the cove overnight on a summer weekend, at dusk their number begins to dwindle.

However, in calm weather or southerly winds, many of us prefer anchoring along the high banks which extend west from Veazey Cove to Ford Landing. The scenery is better, and there is a fine sandy bottom with a very gradually sloping beach. The only inconvenience here is an occasional wash from a tug or freighter in the Elk. However, the substantial distance from the ships usually minimizes the swells.

The Bohemia's channel is wide and averages 7 to 8 feet for two miles upstream, where red flashing buoy "2" marks the beginning of a narrower and winding channel with depths of 16-20 feet to the bridge, some 3.1 miles from the Bohemia's mouth. Tidal range on the river is 2.1-2.2 feet. There are marine facilities on both the north and south shores. However, some entrance channels are shallow.

One-half mile past buoy "2" to port, a lovely manor house comes into view. This is a replica of the home of one of the most important figures in early Maryland and Eastern Shore history, Augustine Herman *(Chesapeake Bay Magazine,* September 1977). Herman was born in Bohemia (now Czechoslovakia). He became an agent of a Dutch commercial house and in the early 1600's was a leading citizen of the Dutch colony of New Amsterdam, and a close associate of Peter Stuyvesant. When a dispute arose between the Dutch and the Marylanders, Stuyvesant dispatched Herman to see the Governor of Maryland. It was on this journey that Herman got his first glimpse of his beloved Bohemia and the land of pleasant living of the gentleman farmer. Herman sided with the Marylanders, making a map depicting their interests rather than those of the Dutch. In payment for this map, Herman obtained a grant of Bohemia Manor, and in 1666, a decree of naturalization was issued. This decree was believed to be the first instance of naturalization within the limits of the United States.

The original Bohemia Manor comprised some 20,000 acres—bounded on the north by Back Creek, on the west by the Elk and Bohemia Rivers, and on the south by the Bohemia River and Great Bohemia Creek. The eastern boundary was not clear, but probably coincided with the western border of Delaware.

There are many picturesque descriptions of life at Bohemia Manor (the ruins of which you will see just beyond the next cluster of trees)—lavish hospitality, blazing fires, formal gardens, a deer park, Herman's coach and four, his collections of paintings. Today, it is hard to envision the ships which sailed up the shallow river to load and unload at the plantation's wharves.

You are now approaching the draw bridge. If you need more than the clearance indicated on the pilings, and you wish to continue upstream, you have two choices. You can contact the bridge tender and have the bridge raised (instructions posted on the bridge) or you can explore the upper reaches in your dinghy. I would suggest you use your dinghy or perhaps rent a rowboat from one of the two facilities on Scotchman Creek, since above the bridge the channel is winding and sometimes shoaling. In a smaller boat, you may take the **Great Bohemia Creek** which meanders lazily through gently rolling horse country. This picturesque setting is the home of the famous race horse Kelso. Depending on the tide and the size of your boat, you may be able to venture for three miles on this quiet, sequestered stream. Quiet, that is, except in the fall when it becomes one of the main flyways of the chattering Canada geese.

The **Little Bohemia Creek,** while wider and deeper, is navigable for only a mile above the bridge. If you are fortunate enough to anchor here overnight in late June or early July, you will see the high, dark banks come alive as millions of fireflies nestle here.

Just above the headwaters of the Bohemia River is "Old Bohemia," St. Francis Xavier Jesuit Mission, established in 1704. This mission served the Catholic population of the entire Delmarva Peninsula and southeastern Pennsylvania (and was

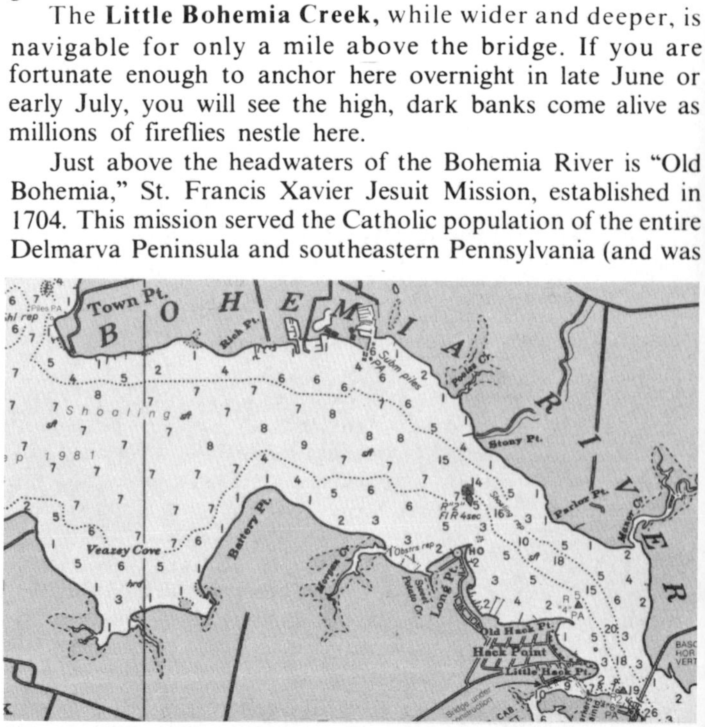

From NOAA Chart 12274—not to be used for navigation.

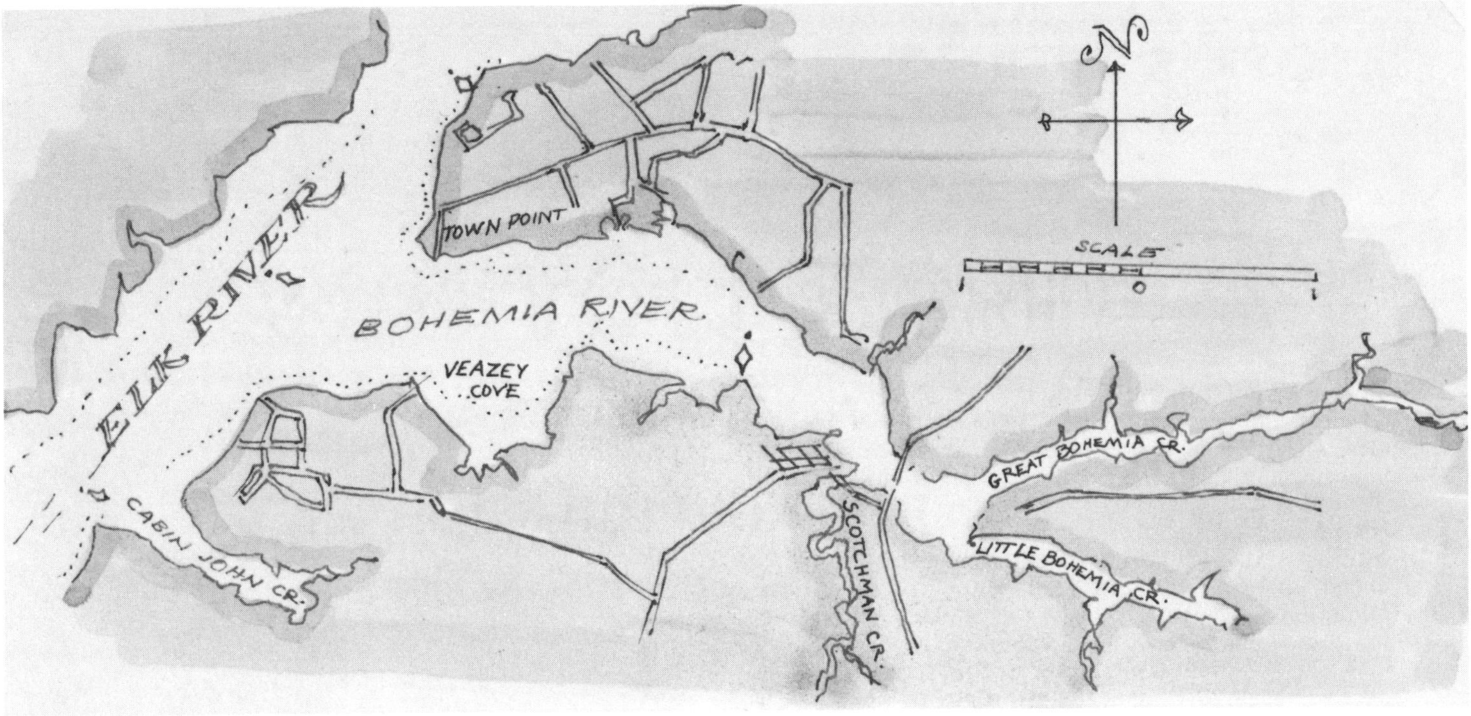

PHOTO BY BOB GRIESER

the haven to which Michener's Rosalind brought her two sons in his novel *Chesapeake).* Bohemia Academy was founded in 1745, and was the Jesuits' immediate predecessor of Georgetown University in Washington, D.C.

Another interesting side trip on the Bohemia is **Scotchman Creek,** 0.2 of a mile below the bridge. Again, it will be necessary to use a small boat, because of the long, low fixed bridge at the creek's entrance. Once you pass the facilities just under the bridge, the narrow creek winds its way for miles through a wilderness, pungent with the scent of wood and disturbed only occasionally by the rustling of leaves, the flapping of an egret's wings, or the shrill cry of a gull.

Back on the Bohemia proper, I would suggest that you anchor **just above buoy "2" across from Long Point,** to enjoy dinner. Here you can look down the entire length of this beautiful river and watch as the sun disappears beyond the mountains on Elk Neck. Then the river itself puts on a spectacular display, beginning with vivid fiery tones, dimming gradually—ever so gradually—to pink and finally purple hues. Time seems to stand still for a few moments—an eternity!

Notes

The Sassafras River was my introduction to Chesapeake Bay boating, and its beauty is still a source of exhilaration to me. Gently rolling emerald hills, with an occasional splash of golden wheat, blend majestically with steep wooded banks rising to heights of 80 feet above the winding river. Around each bend is a new and exciting panorama.

The Sassafras is a river which should be explored on a weekday, if at all possible. If you travel this river on a weekend, chances are you will encounter a "wall" of boats coming at you. Negotiating the wakes can sometimes be more trouble than negotiating a summer Bay squall. But no matter, the Sassafras is definitely worth the effort.

We will begin this trip at RG "A" (QR), 1.2 miles west by south of Turkey Point. From this buoy to "1" (Qk Fl Bell) off Grove Point, the distance is 2.7 miles. The mouth of the Sassafras from Grove Point to Howell Point is 3.4 miles wide, and the water is navigable all the way across (not cutting the points too closely). We have often heard it said "the winds are stronger on the Sassafras," and we have found this to be true.

BETTERTON

The distance from Bell "1" to Betterton, on the river's south shore, is 1.7 miles; from Grove Point to Betterton 1.4; and from Howell Point to Betterton 2.3. The mean range of the tide at Betterton is 1.7 feet.

Many people have relatives who remember going to this summer resort. At one point, an amusement barge was anchored between the town's two docks and, although this seems incredible to me, I am assured by local residents that there was even a roller skating rink on the barge!

In the past, the **Port Welcome** used to bring passengers from Baltimore to enjoy the beach and this picturesque town. However, the cruise from Baltimore to Betterton has been dropped from the schedule. Chesapeake storms have taken their toll on the town's piers, but it is heartening to see that after all these years, Betterton is undergoing a gigantic facelift. The county has acquired much of the waterfront area and is improving the beach, building a bathhouse, picnic pavilion and stone fishing jetties and restoring the boardwalk. After years of relative slumber, on or about July 4, 1986, Betterton will awaken to a new era.

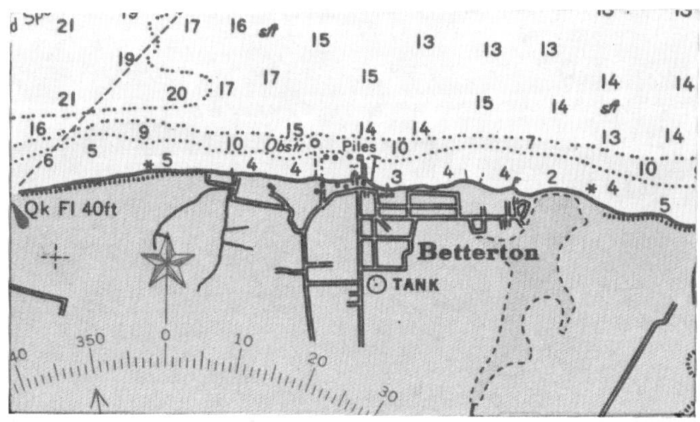

From NOAA Chart 12274—not to be used for navigatio

Because of its exposure to the Bay, Betterton is not a good place to tie up overnight, or in fact to tie up at all until the new pier, to be completed before the summer of 1987, is built. Fuel is not available.

LLOYD'S CREEK

Lloyd's Creek is on the south side of the river, 2.0 miles from Betterton, but it is extremely difficult to find since a low spit of land runs for almost a mile across its mouth, leaving a very narrow opening at the east end. Once you have felt your way in carefully, you are in an anchorage protected from winds from every direction. There is even a tiny, wooded island in the lagoon. There has been some shoaling reported, and I would not advise venturing into Lloyd's Creek without taking soundings or paying careful attention to your depth sounder. Deep draft sailboats should not attempt to go into Lloyd's Creek.

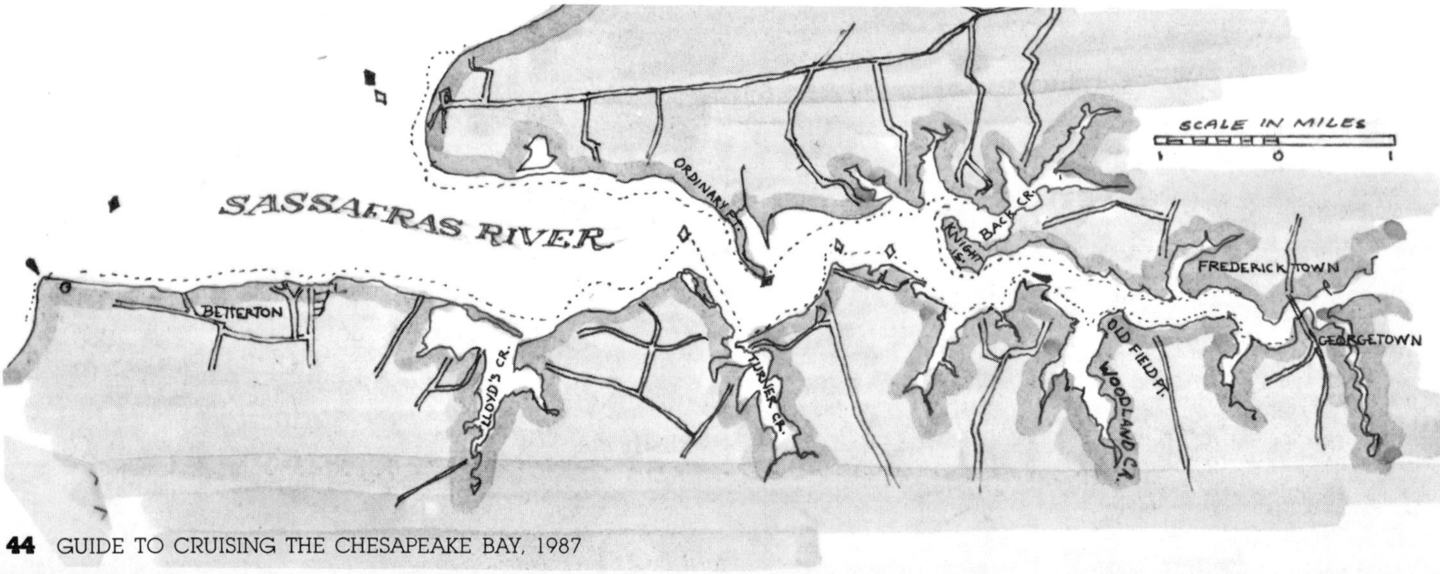

PHOTO BY BOB GRIESER

It is 3.2 miles from Betteron to R "2" (Fl R 4 sec), the first buoy in the river. To port, C "3" some 0.6 of a mile away is visible and C "5" (Fl G 6 sec) appears off Ordinary Point. **Ordinary Point** was so named because there was at one time a tavern or ordinary here which was run in conjunction with a ferry. The point has also been known as Ornery Point and has appeared on some charts with that name, probably because sailors had so much trouble weathering it in a head wind. (Or possibly Ornery was just the local pronunciation of Ordinary, much as Baltimore condenses to "Bal'mer—Ed.) Behind Ordinary Point is a popular anchorage, with a sandy bottom. The best way to anchor here is with your stern facing the beach and your stern anchor set firmly on the beach. Passing boats can sometimes make this a rough anchorage as can a strong easterly wind.

TURNER CREEK

Proceeding on to Turner Creek, you will find it directly across from Ordinary Point (to starboard traveling up river). The creek has a deep but narrow and unmarked entrance. Keep slightly to starboard of the center of the creek to avoid the sand spit to port, since a good portion of it is covered at high tide. Care must be taken not to drift too far to starboard because there are pilings in a tiny cove (indentation really) to starboard across from the spit. If you are not familiar with Turner Creek, it's a good idea to feel your way in slowly. One-tenth of a mile past the sand spit, or where your depth sounder registers 11 feet, turn hard to port and you are in the Turner Creek anchorage.

The county park's bulkhead is to starboard upon entering the anchorage, with 6-8 feet depths alongside. The park has a large pavilion, suitable for cruise picnics, and several brick barbecues. A deposit is required for use of the pavilion, returnable when the caretaker is satisfied it is being left in good condition. The park has a volleyball court, a launch ramp and access to a beach. The restrooms are located in the basement of what was once an old trading post (1700 vintage) perched high upon the hill. They are, however, locked in the evening. You may tie up at the bulkhead for as long as you like, but there are no electricity or other facilities.

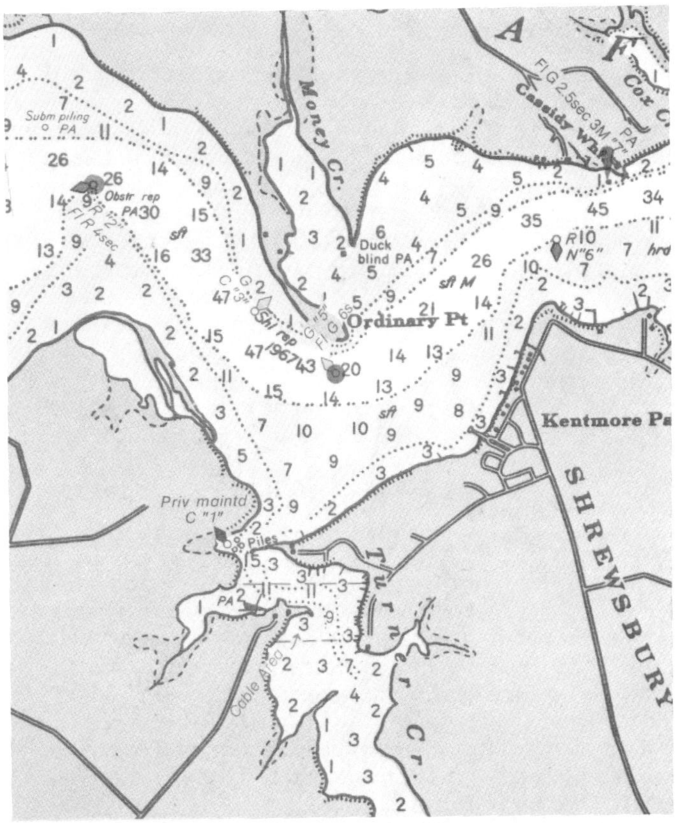

From NOAA Chart 12274—not to be used for navigation.

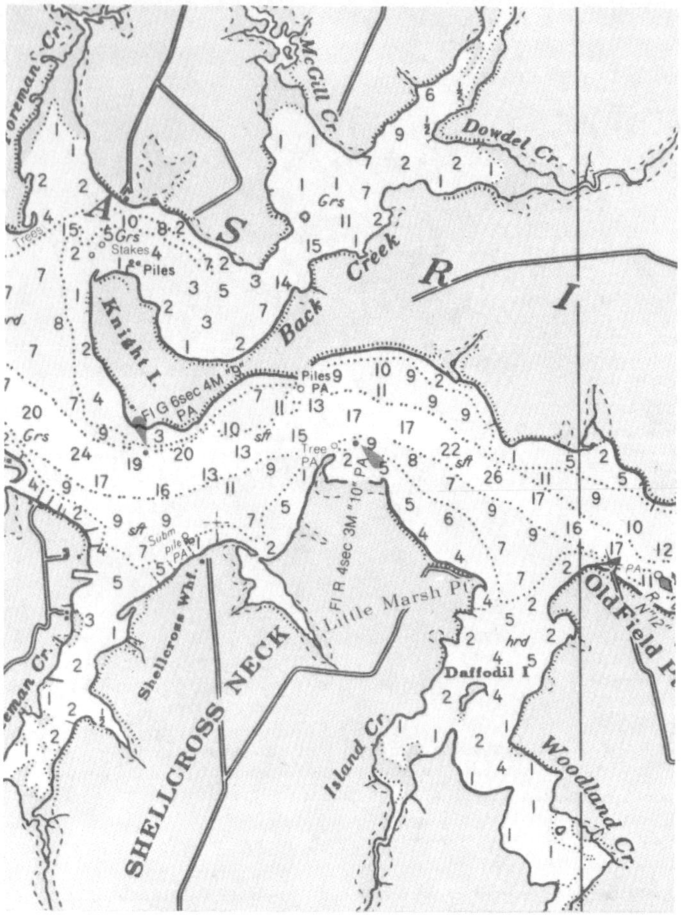

From NOAA Chart 12274—not to be used for navigation.

BACK CREEK

Another fine anchorage on the Sassafras is behind **Knight Island on Back Creek**. The distance from Ordinary Point to the entrance of Back Creek is 1.6 miles. After passing N "6," you should see the tip of Knight Island dead ahead. Between N "6" and N "8," the channel veers to starboard, therefore between these two buoys, begin easing to port and head to the entrance of Back Creek, careful to give Knight Island a good berth by favoring the north bank of the river until you have cleared the entrance of the creek. This can be a good quiet anchorage, since the water skiing usually ceases at dusk. We favor the north shore where the charts indicate 5 to 10 feet of water. On a previous trip to Back Creek, we anchored just inside the point of the island. However, this time we played it safe and headed farther in, anchoring in over 7 feet of water.

WOODLAND CREEK

Three miles from Ordinary Point, between buoys R "10" and R "12" to starboard is Woodland Creek. However, on our first trip up the Sassafras we were totally unaware of the anchorage and proceeded toward the Granary to get a slip for the night.

Since it was early and the weather hot, we asked the attendant if there was a good place to swim, and he told us about Woodland Creek, approximately 1.5 miles down the river off Old Field Point.

Tired and warm we made our way back to the anchorage. Just inside Old Field Point on the east shore of Woodland Creek is a beautiful sandy beach and this is where the majority of the boats anchor. Farther into the creek is Daffodil Island with four feet of water near its east shore. However if you get there early enough on a weekend to get a spot on the east shore of the creek the sandy beach is worth it. Since this was a weekday, we opted for the beach, and almost immediately after dropping the hook were all enjoying the refreshing water. All, that is, except my poor German sheperd. Since we had no way to get her back aboard, Tammy was relegated to being cooled down with buckets of water. (Actually, I think she preferred this.)

After a long and varied journey, we felt as if we were in another world, and indeed we were. There were no cars, no ships, no tugs—just tranquility and beauty. So this is what Chesapeake Bay boating is like. I was converted immediately.

GEORGETOWN

Georgetown, on the south bank of the Sassafras in Kent County, and Fredericktown, on the north bank of the Sassafras in Cecil County, are named for two sons of George II. The area encompassed by the two villages, linked by the Route 213 bridge, is commonly all referred to as Georgetown. There are a number of marinas here and they provide boaters with just about everything, including chartering of house and sail boats. It would be easier to list what is not available. To my knowledge, there is no rental of rowboats nor are there any camping facilities. The tidal range here is 2 feet. On shore, excellent facilities are provided by several good restaurants. At Georgetown, there is additional anchorage available among the moored boats.

By far, the area's most famous individual was Miss Kitty Knight of Georgetown. Kitty Knight was credited with saving the town of Georgetown from being burned by Admiral Cockburn during the War of 1812. Her home now serves as a restaurant and lounge.

The highway bridge at Georgetown has a 40-foot bascule span with a clearance of 4 feet. One mile above the bridge is a marina which provides many services. However, you will find it difficult to restock the galley in Georgetown.

Beyond the marina the channel runs in the middle of the river. There is fairly good water for 0.6 mile. Past this point, unless you have a good local knowledge of the river, I would do the rest of my exploring by dinghy. □

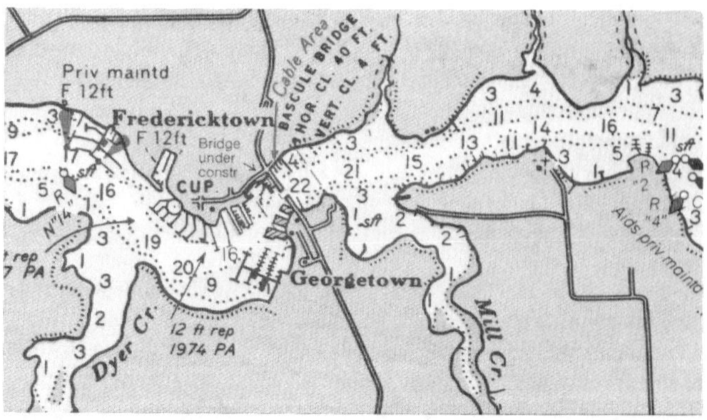

From NOAA Chart 12274—not to be used for navigation.

Anchoring Tips

1. Equip your boat with at least two anchors—three is ideal—and make sure at least one of them is a digging type that will hold in soft mud.
2. Have plenty of extra line available, should you need to let out more rode than you have on your anchor. Letting out more rode gives your anchor a better "bite" on the bottom.
3. If in any doubt about the holding ground or weather conditions, set two anchors.
4. Try to avoid a crowded anchorage.
5. If you can't avoid a crowded anchorage, set a Bahamian Moor as follows: Approach your anchorage spot slowly (at about two knots); take the engine out of gear and drop an anchor over the stern with plenty of rode. Allow the line to take up until your anchor is set and stops the forward motion of the boat. At this point, have your mate drop the bow anchor, once again with plenty of extra rode. Then disengage the anchor line from the stern and walk it around to the bow, where you feed it through the same chock as the bow line. Tighten up on this stern line until the bow rode is taut, and then secure it. You will swing with a wind or current shift, but only within a radius roughly equivalent to the length of your vessel. **Note:** In larger boats (over 40 feet), or in strong current or wind conditions, this method of setting a Bahamian Moor is unsatisfactory because of the weight of the vessel.

Wayne Thompson
Terry McChrystal

UNITED STATES POWER SQUADRONS

SAFE BOATING SUGGESTIONS

Bow riding is a hazard to life and limb. Wearing a life jacket does not insure against amputation or death.

Go through a check list of equipment and operating procedures before starting out for a day on the water.

Check your entire fuel system for signs of leaks, cracks or aging in general.

Check the current weather reports before you set sail for a day on the water and watch the sky for the appearance of sudden storms so you can get back to port safely.

Don't stand up in a small boat or allow your passengers to do so. If it becomes necessary to move around while underway, do so with caution.

If your boat should capsize or swamp don't try to swim for shore. Stay with your boat. Quite often the person who swims for help drowns. The person who stays with the boat is rescued and survives.

Observe the Federal regulations for Personal Flotation Devices (life jackets, etc.) that apply to your boat's size.

SUSQUEHANNA RIVER

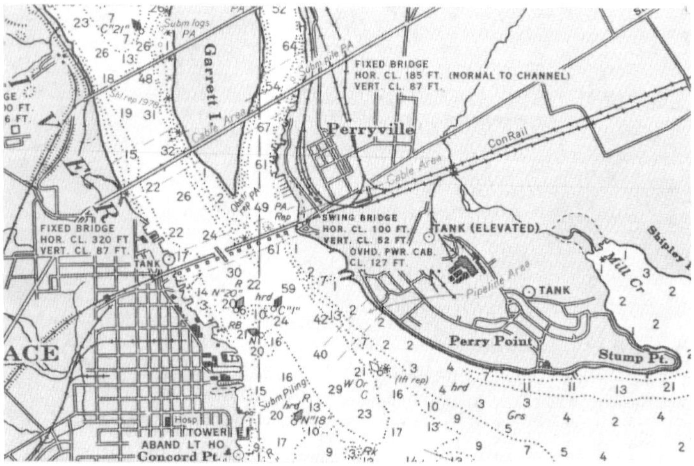

Chesapeake Bay is the drowned river valley of the Susquehanna. To understand the term "drowned river," envision perhaps a million years ago when there was no Bay—only level land, across which a river flowed slowly from the north to the sea. The river flowed some 450 miles from its source in what is now New York State, draining an area on the Atlantic coast second in size only to the St. Lawrence.

According to geologists, in the course of time, Maryland's Eastern Shore sank beneath the sea—not once, but four times. The first time the land emerged (according to theory) the Susquehanna river, finding itself blocked by a great shoal or bank of detritus, was diverted to the south for 150 miles before finding an outlet to the sea. Gradually, the land at the mouth of the river sank until it was so low the sea water ran in and flooded it, cutting off all the tributaries from the main river and, in fact, drowning the Susquehanna.

Coming from a different age and from a different direction, we shall explore this mighty river which takes its name from an equally mighty people, the Susquehannocks.

We will begin our exploration at the mouth of the Susquehanna by picking up red and black midchannel buoy "A" RG QR 1.2 miles west by south of Turkey Point. It is 1.3 nautical miles from "A" to C "1" in the river proper. To port, Spesutie Island, prominent in the early history of the Bay, is now a part of the Aberdeen Proving Grounds, with prohibited land areas and restricted and dangerous adjacent waters. At night when firing is in progress, a flashing red light is shown on Mulberry Point on the west side of Spesuite Narrows. Chart 12274 clearly shows the limits of the danger area.

It is 0.6 mile from C "1" to N "2," and then the channel veers to port in the 0.8 mile between N "2" and C "3". It is *imperative* you stay between the buoys, for the channel here is very narrow as it threads its way through the extremely shallow Susquehanna Flats. The Flats abound with wildlife and are a favorite seasonal haunt of hunters and crabbers.

To starboard, Fishing Battery Light (Fl 6 sec., 38 F, 4M) comes into view, 1.2 miles distant from C "3." From C "3" to N "18" off Havre de Grace it is 4.3 miles.

There are several marinas at **Havre de Grace**, and here the transient can find: berths and electricity; hull, radio and motor repairs; lift and railroad facilities; charts; water, ice, hardware, groceries; toilet and shower facilities; food, camping facilities; row and motor boat rentals; bait and tackle; gasoline and diesel fuel. The city offers transient slips at 25¢ per ft./per night ($5 minimum) at Tydings Memorial Park Marina. Transients are advised to call (301)939-1800 (City Hall) to ascertain if a slip will be available there and to make reservations. The municipal park is within walking distance of the business district. The mean tidal range in this area is 1.7 feet.

Besides the marinas, there are several places at Havre de Grace that make good anchorages. One is on the west side of the channel, just beyond Tidewater Marina, and the other is just before the railroad bridge.

We were delighted to find that everything we needed could be found less than two blocks away. Supplies secured, we set off to investigate the town named by General Lafayette. In 1782, the General was enroute from Mt. Vernon to Philadelphia, a route which took him through this town which was then known as Lower Susquehanna Ferry. He admired the beauty of the spot and was told that a countryman of his, upon first seeing the place, exclaimed, "C'est Le Havre de Grace!" General Lafayette replied, "It is indeed much like Le Havre. In this new free country, it may be fittingly called Le Havre de Grace." Lafayette's suggestion was accepted and in 1785 the town was officially given the name of Havre de Grace, Harbor of Mercy.

There is a new point of interest in Havre de Grace—the restored lock house of the old Susquehanna and Tidewater Canal. This historic building was opened to the public after two years of careful and faithful reconstruction under the aegis of the Susquehanna Museum of Havre de Grace, Inc. It is located at the northern end of Havre de Grace on the riverfront property adjacent to the Havre de Grace Marina, south of the Susquehanna River Bridge. The museum is open Sundays from 1 to 5 P.M. Tours at other times may be arranged by calling (301)939-3947.

Sidewalk sales were taking place as we strolled the streets lined with unusual buildings. When we returned to the boat we had lunch and proceeded on a leisurely cruise up the Susquehanna to see the sights.

Across the river from Havre de Grace, **Perryville's** marinas offer: berths and electricity; lift facilities; food; camping and lodging; toilet, shower and laundry facilities; water, ice, groceries, hardware; bait and tackle; and gasoline fuel. Here, as at Havre de Grace, the tidal range is 1.7 feet.

From N "18" to C "21" west of Garrett Island, it is 1.6 miles, and it is here that you will see the rocks which make the Susquehanna different from all other rivers of the Bay. Pay particular attention to navigation aids, since running aground here could mean more than a bent shaft, prop, or damaged keel. Garrett Island, which cuts the river in half at this point, is to starboard. Originally known as Palmer's Island, the now deserted, heavily-wooded island was once envisioned as a picturesque area for the campus of the first university in the Northern Hemisphere. Unfortunately, Edward Palmer died in

1625, only three years after he acquired the island. For a short time, the island was known as Watson's Island, then the name was changed to Garrett's Island in honor of a railroad president who administered the Baltimore and Ohio Railroad during the Civil War.

At the north end of Garrett Island, we pick up the red and black midchannel nun buoy. Here the channel runs along the east side of the river and you should bear to starboard. Keeping the red and black buoy dead astern, there is plenty of deep water to Port Deposit, 2.1 miles from the buoy. The total distance from RB "A" at the mouth of the Susquehanna to Port Deposit is 10.7 miles.

Port Deposit's marinas provide: berths and electricity; hull and motor repairs; lift facilities; water, ice, groceries, hardware; food; row and motor boat rentals; bait and tackle; toilet and pump out facilities; and diesel and gas fuel. The mean range of the tide here is 2.1 feet.

The lower half of the town was laid out into streets and building lots, which appeared on a plat dated October 21, 1812. The name of the town on the plat was Cresswell's Ferry, but at the next winter's session of the legislature, the name was changed to Port Deposit—supposedly because it was a port of deposit for lumber. There is also reason to believe that at one time the town had been called Rock Run.

The Susquehanna Canal, completed in 1805 and enlarged in 1810, seems to have given great impetus to the growth of Port Deposit. The opening of a granite quarry near the town in 1829 added to its prosperity.

Port Deposit is about as far as the Chesapeake boater can cruise on the Susquehanna, and a glance upstream will reveal the reason—rocks. Captain John Smith who explored the river in 1608, named this portion of it "Smith's Fales."

For a time the white man was content to use the Susquehanna as did the Indian with his farming, traveling, hunting and fishing centered about it. Later, he used it for his lumbering operations and built canals along it. However, he had long lived with a dream of harnessing its mighty power to serve his needs even further. This was finally accomplished under the charter of the Susquehanna Power Company, a Maryland Corporation and a subsidary of Philadelphia Electric.

In March, 1926, construction of the great hydroelectric project, second in size only to Niagara, commenced. The dam itself was only one of the many major engineering feats connected with the project. The Columbia and Port Deposit Railroad was speedily relocated. This involved the construction of nearly 16 miles of double-track roadbed over rugged terrain. The Conowingo Bridge was demolished and the Baltimore Pike carried over the river on the top of the dam, making it necessary to relocate eight miles of state highway.

On November 16, 1927, the new highway across the dam opened to the public, and on March 1, 1928, just two years after construction began, power from Conowingo was transmitted!

Behind the dam is a lake 14 square miles in area and 14 miles long. Owners of trailerable boats can launch them at facilities on the east side of the lake above the dam. The scenery on the lake is exquisite and the fishing is reported to be good.

The mighty Susquehanna alone is responsible for half of the Bay's supply of fresh water. Conversely, in times of heavy rains, the Susquehanna sends a tremendous burden of silt, sewage and debris into the Bay. The hurricanes of 1972 and 1975 sent just such torrents down, creating havoc with the Bay's oyster and clam industries.

It seems that periodically the great river must assert itself—must remind us all who was here first. □

PHOTO BY BOB GRIESER

COMFORT TIPS

Wear an old, white, long-sleeved shirt for no-cost, cover-up cool protection from the sun.

Keep a cool boat on a muggy night. Anchor by the stern instead of the bow and let the open end of your cabin catch the breeze. Open a forward hatch for maximum air flow-thru. This scheme works in light or moderate seas, with the current running with the wind.

Make your own insect screens: Buy velcro tape and inexpensive mosquito netting. Cut the netting to fit your hatches and sew the hook side of the tape around the edges. Glue the other side of the tape (fuzzy side out) around the edges of the hatchways. Easy to put in place, these screens roll or fold up for easy storage.

Burn citronella candles after sunset. Whether you're in a mosquito control area or not, a little old-fashioned discouragement to these varmints is worthwhile. Besides, there's nothing like candlelight to provide a romantic "sundowner" setting.

A Walking Tour of:

HAVRE DE GRACE

"Havre de Grace?" Tell people you are going to Baltimore's Inner Harbor or St. Michaels and they say, "Nice. Enjoy. Great!" Tell them you are going to Havre de Grace and they ask, "Why?" We reasoned that at worst we'd find the kind of place that inspires visitors to alter course and head for Baltimore or St. Michaels. Or, we could discover a fascinating town and a new atmosphere in which to enjoy one of life's small pleasures: ice cream.

Every cruise needs a specific destination, in our case a marina. Havre de Grace offers four, all at different parts of town. Having no idea what "town" was, we chose the most centrally located—Tidewater Marina. We later discovered that "town" is not that big and each marina is within walking distance of everything (some walks are just longer than others).

Tidewater lies at the foot of Bourbon Street where it intersects with Market Street. Since Market parallels the water and borders the town it seemed as good a place as any to begin our exploration. The plan was to turn left (south) on Market and keep walking until we ran out of street, town, or energy.

Two blocks later, on the corner of Girard and Market, is Bomboy's, a yellow and white house where we succumbed to one of Havre de Grace's tasty temptations—homemade chocolates. There are five of us so of course we *had* to try five different chocolate creations. Delicious—one and all.

Sticky fingers licked (you can't waste chocolate), we resumed our excursion. A block farther, at Revolution Street, and extending to Lafayette Street, the town nudges its way closer to the water. At Lafayette we detoured left to Concord Point Lighthouse. Built of granite and standing 26 feet high, it served as an aid to navigation for 155 years before being decommissioned in 1975. Today it is a registered historic landmark. Though closed when we were there, it is open to visitors Sundays from 1-5 P.M. We walked behind it and found a grassy area with a commemorative cannon dedicated to John O'Neill, its first keeper. Mr. O'Neill was a hero in the War of 1812, leading the defense when the British attacked. Unfortunately, the local militia was not as stout-hearted as their leader and left, allowing the British to land on May 13, 1813. After ransacking the town and taking furniture and even an elegant coach as souvenirs, the British burned 40 of the 60 existing homes.

Our quest to find the end of Market Street and/or the town was rewarded two blocks past Lafayette Street at the Bayou Hotel, *the* nightlife spot in the '20s. (It is now being reborn as an apartment building.) After lingering a minute to enjoy the view (children are not long lingerers) we turned right, onto Commerce Street.

Here, nestled into the shoreline of the Chesapeake Bay, is the Havre de Grace Yacht Basin. Adjacent to and sharing its parking lot is the Millard F. Tydings Park. This park is host to a variety of annual festivals including the 4th of July carnival, parade and fireworks display; the Seafood Festival held the second weekend in August; and the Art Show held the third weekend in August. (Boaters attending city events are warmly welcomed with complimentary dockage. Of course, space at the yacht basin is limited but the city will do its best to accommodate visiting yachtsmen.) This is not a run-of-the-mill, grass-and-shade-tree park; it has tennis courts, picnic tables, barbecue grills, benches, and last but not least, a playground.

Continuing west, the core downtown aura is replaced with more modern homes, small developments, and an area of beautiful larger homes which back up to the water. To stay downtown and in the area suggested for a general walking tour by the Chamber of Commerce you have to turn right off Commerce Street at the park and head north on either South Union Avenue or Washington Street.

Congress Avenue almost splits the town in half. In the southern half are modest, well-cared-for homes on quiet, tree-lined streets. There is two-way

The Lockhouse Museum.

Concord Point Lighthouse. Photos by Joe Manchester.

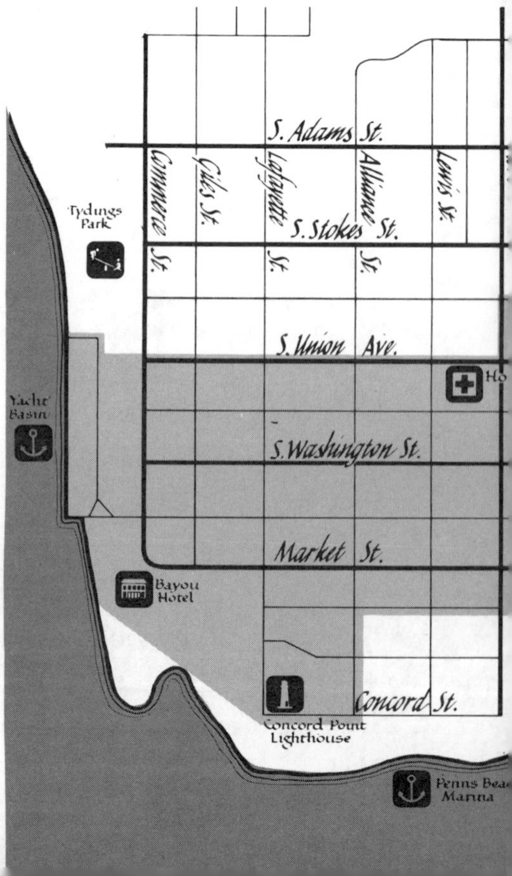

traffic on most of these streets but sidewalks on at least one side eliminate the traffic danger.

About two houses before Congress on Washington, painted a cheerful green, is a restaurant called The Galley (open daily for breakfast and lunch). This marks the beginning of the commercial district.

From Congress Avenue to the railroad bridge, from North Union Avenue to the Susquehanna River is the greater business district with N. Washington and St. John's Streets commercially densest. There is a potpourri of most every kind of business (from antique stores to a laundromat) and almost all are local endeavors (except for a Western Auto and an A&P we didn't notice any chain stores). We found no fast food eateries, no bike rentals (visitors who want transportation other than feet can have a rental car delivered to their marina from Aberdeen) and no movie theaters. For boat-based visitors desirous of eating their evening meal in a nice yet informal atmosphere (where nothing rocks and someone else does the dishes) two restaurants were suggested to us (though we ate at neither)—the Crazy Swede and the Tugboat Landing and Bay Steamer.

We window shopped late on Saturday afternoon and made several discoveries. First, a few stores closed earlier than their posted closing times. Second, the majority of businesses are closed Sundays. Third, "River City" is in the name of several businesses. At first we were taken aback—we were still in Havre de Grace but where is "River City"? It turns out that "River City" is a nickname, bestowed on the town by journalists, that has stuck. Havre de Grace comes by this nickname honestly, as its origins were closely tied to the river (some of its early bricks were even made from the riverbed).

To aid automobile traffic there is an island at the intersection where N. Union, St. John and Water Streets merge. A statue of General Lafayette (of Revolutionary fame) graces it for the town has a kinship with the general—it owes its name to him. Originally this city was a ferry terminal where travelers on the main route from Virginia and points south crossed the Susquehanna River en route to Philadelphia and points north. During the early 1780's Lafayette, making this journey, was so smitten by the beauty of the area (it reminded several French travelers of the port city of Le Havre) that he suggested it be called Le Havre de Grace, Harbor of Mercy. When the settlement of Lower Susquehanna Ferry officially became a town it took the name "Havre de Grace" for its own.

Due north is the old Penn Central Railroad bridge, still in use today. Among the sites beyond the bridge are the Havre de Grace Marina, North Park (not as large or elaborate as Tydings Park but host to annual powerboat races held the first weekend in August) and the Lockhouse.

Havre de Grace was once the southern entrance to the Susquehanna & Tidewater Canal, an inland trade route carrying commerce from Philadelphia and Baltimore 45 miles to landlocked central Pennsylvania. Except for the Lockhouse and restored lock bridge, vestiges of the canal have all but disappeared. In 1970 a group of volunteers formed a non-profit organization to restore this structure to its mid-1800's self. Now a museum, it is open Sunday afternoons from 1-5.

Exploring complete, we backtracked to the corner of Congress and Washington and the kind of emporium we are always on the lookout for—an ice cream parlor (and this one is old-fashioned at that). The River City Ice Jam serves sandwiches and desserts but we had our hearts set on ice cream. We walked up to the counter, placed our order, and sat down at one of the round tables to enjoy both the cones and the atmosphere. (They even offer child-sized versions of both cones and seating for young patrons.)

Maps, a general walking tour, a historic walking tour (profiling eighteen 19th century buildings), brochures about specific points of interest, etc. are all available through the Chamber of Commerce and various businesses (including A. J. Fair Realty and the Ice Jam), while the marinas usually have maps of the town on hand for visitors. Havre de Grace is also the site of summer concerts and sailboat races. For further information contact the Chamber of Commerce (301-939-3303). □

—Andi Manchester

ering of author's map by Joan Machinchick

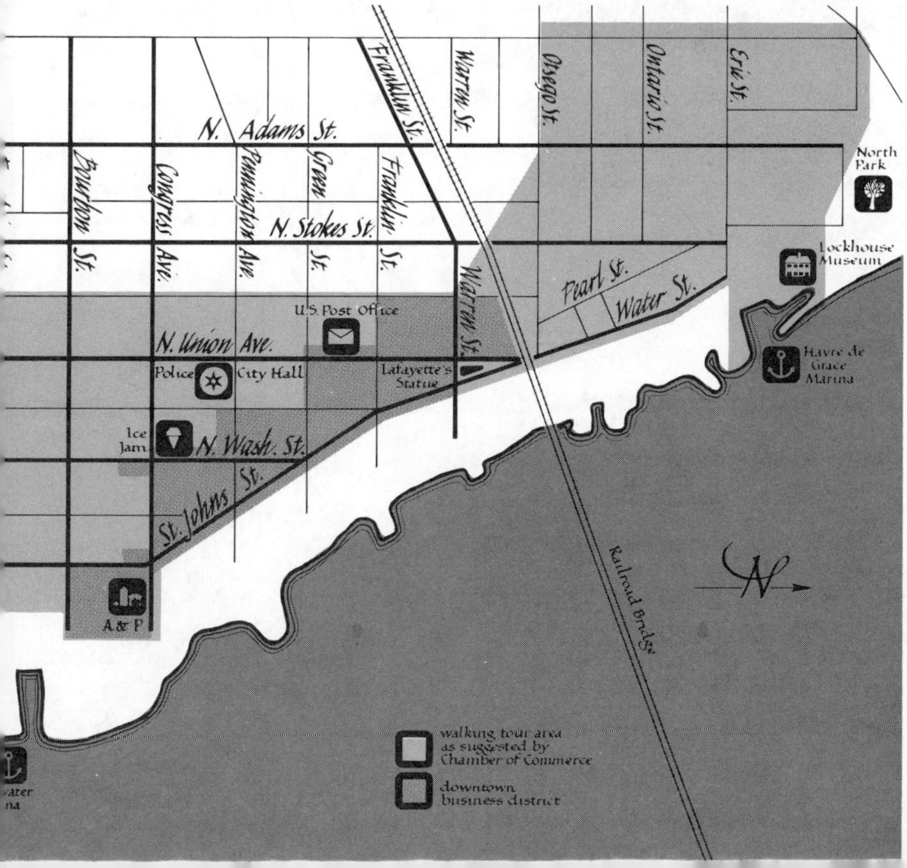

NORTHEAST RIVER

Almost anytime is a perfect time to explore the Northeast River. However, on weekends the wash from boats coming from the extensive facilities up river can make this particular stretch quite uncomfortable. As we reach Turkey Point, we have our first glimpse of what many consider to be the true "top of the Bay," Turkey Point Light (Fl 6 sec 129 feet, 6M). This can be one of the roughest spots in the entire Chesapeake, since the Elk, Sassafras and the Susquehanna Rivers all join forces with the Bay here. There is an unwritten rule for boaters in the upper Bay here—a take-off on Murphy's Law. "If anything is going to go wrong, you can bet it will go wrong off Turkey Point—and nine times out of ten, there will be a storm on its way."

When you round the point, give it a good berth and head up the approach to the Northeast River. You should be able to sight R "2", some 2.5 miles ahead. Nine-tenths of a mile from the Point, during the months of May through October, you will come across a measured one-half nautical mile. Once you have safely rounded Turkey Point, take time to admire the scenery. There is something about this stretch of water that seems to stimulate the imagination. The succession of high wooded bluffs to starboard always remind me of a family of huge whales dozing serenely on top of the water.

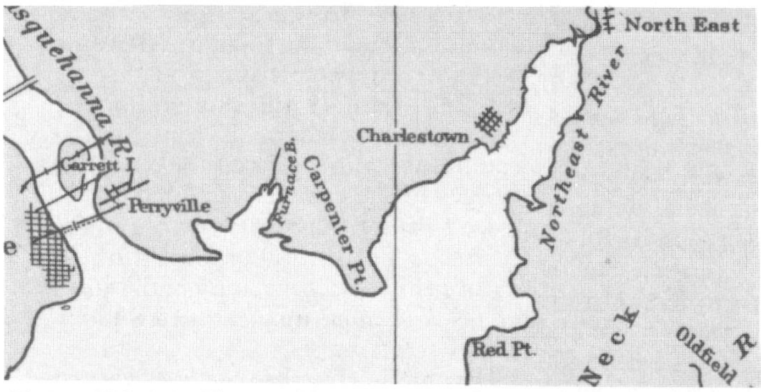

From NOAA Chart 12260—not to be used for navigation.

To starboard we see one of **Elk Neck State Park's** [(301) 287-5333] beaches. At one time, this entire area was inhabited by tribes of Iroquois Indian stock, primarily the powerful Susquehannocks, and thousands of Indian artifacts have been found along the banks of the Elk and Northeast Rivers. This further enhances the already popular pastime of beachcombing for driftwood along these shores.

In 1936, Dr. William L. Abbott willed 368 acres of his estate, including his home, to the State of Maryland to be used for recreation, and thus Elk Neck State Park was established. Over the years, the park has acquired additional land, until it now consists of more than 1,700 acres. The topography of Elk Neck State Park is so varied that it allows one to go from sandy beaches and marshlands to heavily-wooded bluffs, rising more than 100 feet above the Northeast River.

Campgrounds in the park accommodate either tent or tent-trailer, and at least one heated washroom is open for year-round use. Housekeeping cabins are available from the second week in June to the second week in September. There is an extensive, protected beach on the Northeast River side of the Neck, with a picnic area and pavilion. Boaters may take advantage of the launching facilities on the Elk River side of the park either by renting a boat or launching their own. There is fishing in both the Elk and Northeast Rivers, and crabbing is popular

on the Susquehanna flats.

Two and seven-tenths miles from R "2" (Fl 4 sec), R "6" (Fl 4 sec) rests off Red Point, the mouth of the Northeast River. I am sure I was not alone in thinking the river began at Turkey Point. Actually it does not, the Turkey Point area is still Chesapeake Bay.

Cara Cove (listed on some charts as Carrott Cove) is just off R "6" to starboard. The cove is approximately one-half mile wide and a half-mile long, and provides excellent protection for blows from every direction except north and northwest. Depths are 4-5 feet, with a tidal range of 1.9 feet. Most of the cove's shoreline is private property and the residents "don't want to lose their privacy." Therefore, beachcombing and exercising pets on the shore of the cove is frowned upon. There are, however, cottages for rent from mid-May to mid-September, with boat-launching facilities available to the occupants.

From the mouth of the river proper at Red Point, it is 2.4 miles to day marker "12" off **Charlestown**. The tidal range in the river is 1.9 feet.

Charles Town was established in September, 1742 as a shipping center for the head of Chesapeake Bay. It was precisely laid out with 200 lots as well as a common area to be enjoyed by all of the town's inhabitants.

Charles Town and Baltimore had their beginnings at approximately the same time, and the two ports were rivals until the Revolutionary War when Charles Town had to bow to Baltimore's superior facilities and location. Another blow to the port of Charles Town was the hurricane of 1786. Prior to this, all ships had to navigate a precarious channel to Havre de Grace by way of Charles Town. The hurricane cut the Locust Point Channel, which made Havre de Grace an easily accessible deep-water port. Finally, in 1780 the Cecil County seat was moved from Charles Town to Elkton and despite its fascinating history, which included visits by George Washington, the town gradually lost hope of becoming a city of importance.

The town of **North East** lies 1.7 miles beyond Charlestown. Outside the town proper is an anchorage basin with an adjoining public park.

Each year on a weekend in mid-July the Northeast River is transformed into a gigantic, living, undulating stage, as throngs gather along its banks to watch and be a part of a very special kind of festival. Some of the water events include: a Bay craft boat parade; sculling contests; retriever demonstrations; double oar rowing heats; boat docking contest; net demonstrations; gunning rigs; sink boxes; net mending; a new boat parade; radio controlled sailboats; water ski show; drag boat demonstrations; and a bathtub race. The Water Festival spills over onto the land with: an art show; flea market; street parade; parachute demonstration team; decoy carving and a host of other events. The annual North East Water Festival is the fruition of months of work and preparation by a coalition of business, church, civic and school related organizations who joined forces "to promote the historic and recreational aspects of North East and the surrounding area."

Also enhancing the historical preservation part of this area is the new Upper Bay Museum, which houses the largest public display of upper Chesapeake Bay historic artifacts in the world. The museum is located on the water at North East in the former H.L. Harvey Fish House and focuses on the cultural heritage of the Chesapeake. □

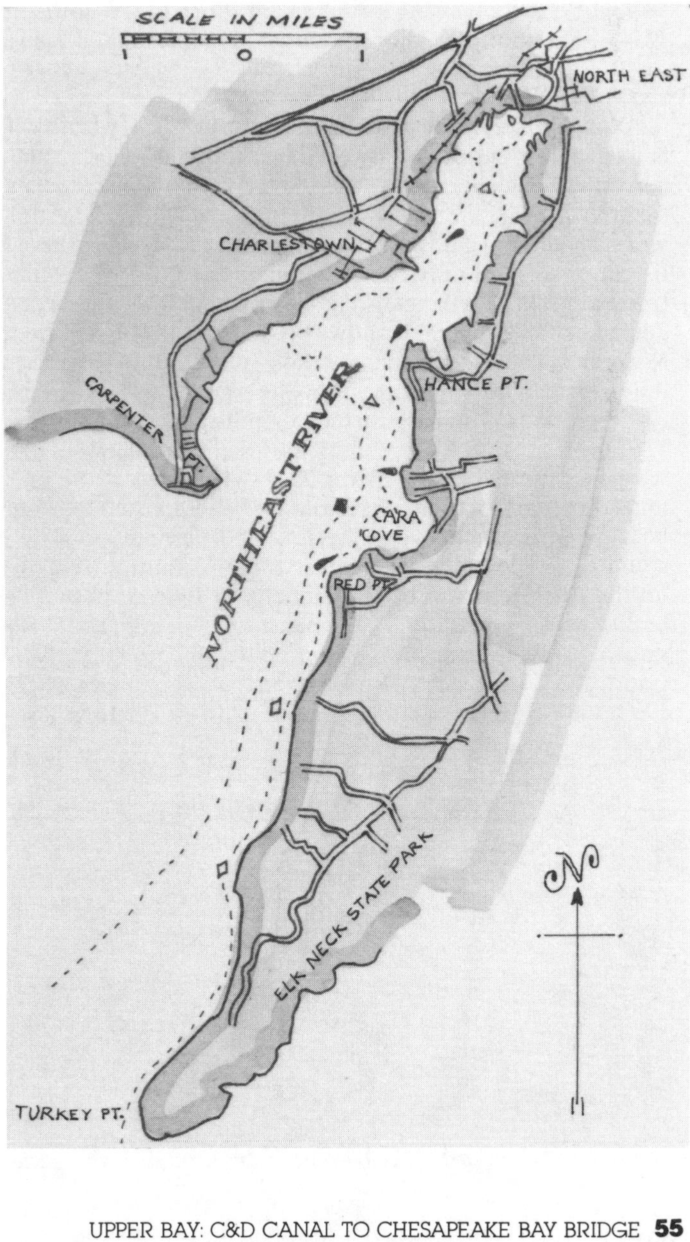

BUSH RIVER

If you have been as intimidated by "Restricted Areas" as I, then I suppose you also have been missing a very special treat, the Bush or, if you will, Captain John Smith's "Willowbyes Flu" River. For years I have discounted this scenic river as just another part of the Aberdeen Proving Grounds. Not so! Although we will get into the official restrictions later, the only *real* restriction is the 12-foot vertical clearance at the railroad bridge, some 6.7 miles upstream. However, for those who can make arrangements through the Bush River Yacht Club for a bridge opening, or those who have smaller or trailerable craft (there are three surfaced ramps above the bridge), you will be in for an unexpected surprise.

Starting at Q Fl G "1" off Grove Point, it is 4.1 miles to Buoy "35" off Howell Point. From this buoy, a course of 254° M should put you right on N "2" some 5.2 miles away at the mouth of the Bush River and in the Susquehanna National Wildlife Refuge.

Now then, regarding the restrictions: On days when firing is in progress (usually on weekdays from 8:00 a.m. — 3:30 p.m.) there will be a patrol boat off Worton Point and one located upriver in the area off Chilbury Point. The boats will stop you until it is safe to proceed. Locals tell us there is usually a delay of only twenty minutes or so. If there is to be firing at night, it will be on Tuesday or Thursday nights only and a flashing red light is shown off Worton Point, Stillpond Neck and Pond Point on the east side of Bush River (3.5 miles above the mouth). However, going ashore in the restricted area is **strictly forbidden** and carries a heavy fine.

From N "2" to Fl G 2.5 sec. "3" the distance is 1.4 miles and to starboard we pass Bush River Neck where one of the most important early settlements in the area once existed, perhaps because of the richness of the soil, and perhaps because it could easily be defended against Indians. Baltimore Town on the Bush predates the present city of Baltimore by over half a century, yet by 1773, Baltimore on the Bush was known only by tradition. Another town known only by tradition is Harford Town on Bush, where on March 22, 1774, the first term of court was held. Also at Harford Town

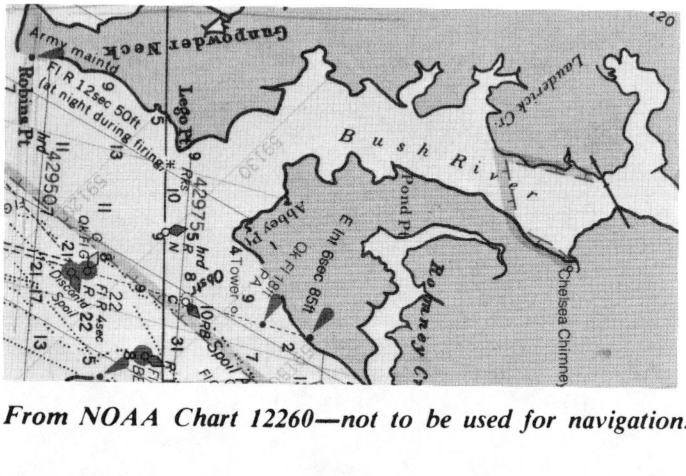

From NOAA Chart 12260—not to be used for navigation.

on Bush, the French troops of Count de Rochambeau camped on their way to the north from the victory at Yorktown.

Aberdeen Proving Ground, which extends to both sides of the river, was established in 1917 after the original Ordnance Proving Ground at Sandy Hook, New Jersey became inadequate. However, the establishment of Aberdeen heralded the demise of one of the oldest and most historic playgrounds in the nation. From early Colonial times, the Susquehanna River flats and the Bush and Gunpowder River Necks had been famous for duck and goose hunting and fishing. Many elaborate club houses were built to accommodate sportsmen who came from all parts of the country to shoot canvasbacks, redheads and other species of duck. Congressmen and other prominent individuals could be counted among the enthusiasts.

Now, in sharp contrast, the Aberdeen Proving Grounds are the hub of all ordnance activities for the army in research, development and testing of arms, ammunition, tanks and combat vehicles as well as motorized transportation. Even the hunters' outlawed "big" guns of the past would pale before the mighty blasts which now shake the earth for miles around.

As noted earlier, the total distance from N "2" at the river's mouth to the bridge is 6.7 miles, with minimum depths of seven feet.

The bridge is a bascule span with a horizontal clearance of 35 feet, and a vertical clearance of 12 feet; arrangements for opening can be made only through the Bush River Yacht Club (301)676-1122.

Beyond the bridge is the treat I promised. The river gives the appearance of a gigantic lake mirroring the gently rolling mountains which dip into the tranquil depths. To port five-tenths of a mile above the railroad bridge, **Otter Point Creek** has depths of three feet for one mile above the entrance.

Marinas on Otter Point Creek and on the eastern shore of the Bush River provide: surfaced ramps, hull and motor repairs, marine railways, lift-out facilities, berths, electricity, food, toilet facilities, showers, water, ice, groceries, hardware, bait and tackle, gas, diesel and charts.

Straight ahead is the water tower at the Bata Shoe Company in Belcamp. It is about 1.5 miles from the bridge (depth 5′-6′) to Bush and Church Points, directly opposite each other. Although **Church Creek** ahead to starboard has some fairly deep water at its entrance, depths run only 2 to 3 feet from Church Point to the mouth of Church Creek. Someday, I hope to return and explore this creek by dinghy. I am sure it would be a very interesting trip.

The Proving Grounds and the bridge have kept the area relatively sequestered and, although the people there go out of their way to be friendly, somehow you get the feeling that deep down, they don't mind their solitude a bit. □

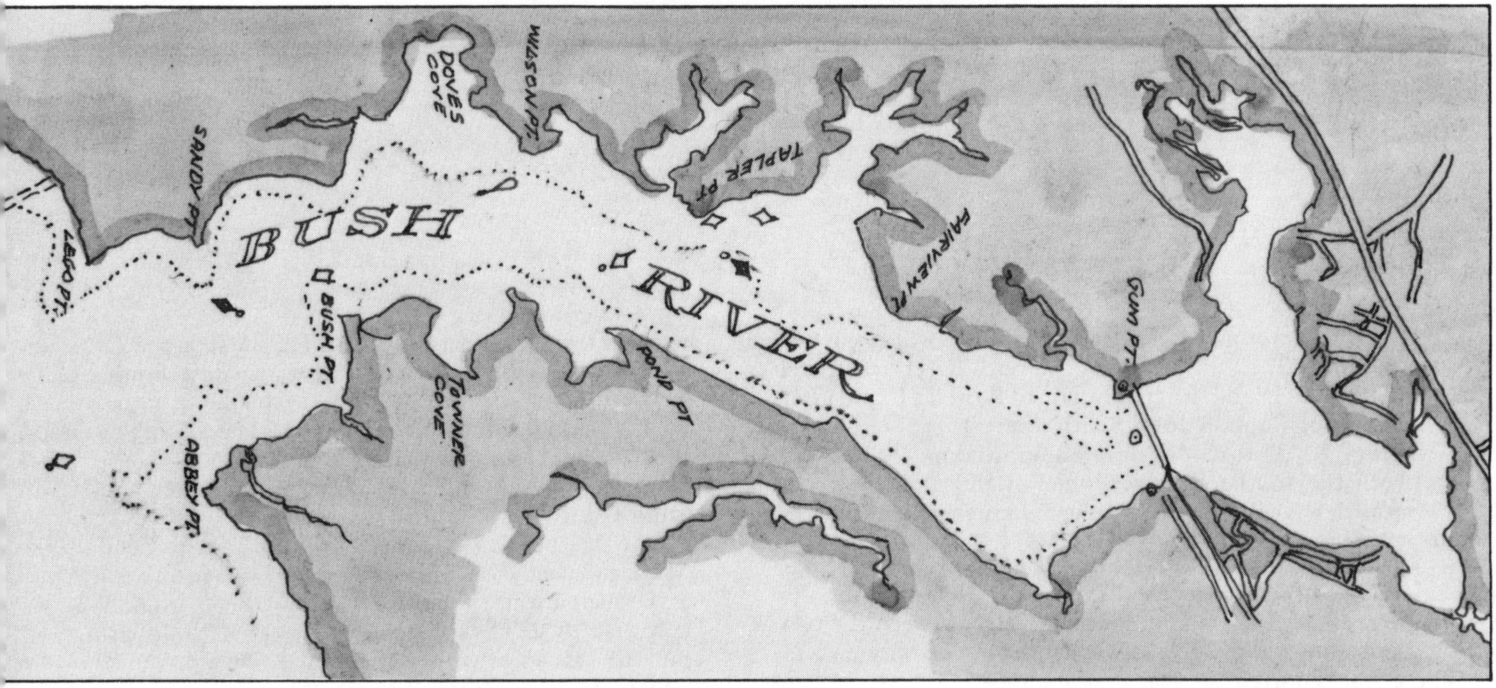

SAFETY TIPS

Make plans to protect your boat if you go aground and cannot get off right away. Bay storms can come up quickly. Set several anchors and use plenty of chafing gear; canvas and tape will suffice. Above all, plan for the possibility that the boat will be pounding; and if so, think of ways to minimize the damage.

Plug a hole with a bunch of rags if you strike something and begin to take on water. If you have a wooden boat, you should carry a plywood board and foam to nail to the hull. With fiberglass, a rag stuffed with foam should stop most leaks until help and a pump arrive.

Carry two anchors. You'll enjoy having a small "lunch hook" that is easily lowered and raised and is perfectly adequate for fair weather situations. But every boat should have a heavier anchor too, to put down when the wind and seas are up.

Use nylon line, not dacron, for anchoring. Experienced boatmen note that the stretch in nylon takes the strain out of the anchor and your boat.

Let out your anchor line according to the weather. The rougher the weather, the more line you should let out. The scope, or length of line let out, determines the holding power. Normal conditions call for a rode of 7 to 8 times the water depth.

Explain to EVERYONE the man overboard procedure: Whoever sees the action must yell "Man overboard" *and keep him in view*. Next, the helmsman brings the boat about as the observer continues to keep a constant watch on the person in the water. This is very important as he can be hard to spot if any sea is running.

Tying up properly is the secret to comfortable rafting. First, breast lines fore and aft. Then spring lines diagonally from your aft cleat to your neighbor's fore cleat. Now, repeat a diagonal in the opposite direction. *Be sure all lines are really tight!* The whole idea is that the boats should move together as one unit; then they will not bounce against one another.

Make sure everyone who is aboard your boat knows how to run it, both under power and/or sail. They should have a basic knowledge of how to use all equipment aboard. Don't wait for an emergency.

Ranking right up there with "red right returning" and "red sun at night, sailor's delight," here's a handy saying to help you to remember which way to turn a valve to close it before you leave your boat or to open it when you are preparing to leave the dock. "Right-y-tight-y. Left-y-loose-y.

GUNPOWDER RIVER

If firing is not in progress in the area, we will begin our trip from N "2" at the mouth of the Bush River and travel behind Pooles Island (originally named Powell's Island after a member of Captain John Smith's party).

From N "2" to C "1," located approximately halfway between the southern tip of Pooles Island and the tip of Gunpowder Neck, the distance is 3.9 miles on a course of about 230°.

From C "1" to R "4" at the mouth of the Gunpowder it is 2.5 miles. Do not try to cut directly to R "6" farther up the river, because Spry Island Shoal, directly between the two markers, has submerged logs with depths of only two to three feet reported.

If firing is in progress, begin your trip up the Gunpowder at Pooles Island Light (Fl 2 sec. 27 Ft. 7 M) which is out of the restricted area.

Although locals tell us that the Gunpowder River has not been closed in twelve years, when firing is in progress patrol boats will patrol the area during the day. At night flashing red lights are shown on Robins Point at the south end of Gunpowder Neck and on Maxwell Point on the east side of the Gunpowder River, 3.5 miles above the river's mouth. Going ashore in the restricted area is strictly prohibited, since there may be unexploded ordnance in the area. However, water skiing is permitted when the water area is open for use by the general public, provided that no water skier touches any dry or subaqueous land and comes no closer than 200 meters (say 650 ft.) to any shoreline. Other outside the boat activities, such as swimming, scuba diving, etc., are also in violation of the regulations governing the restricted area.

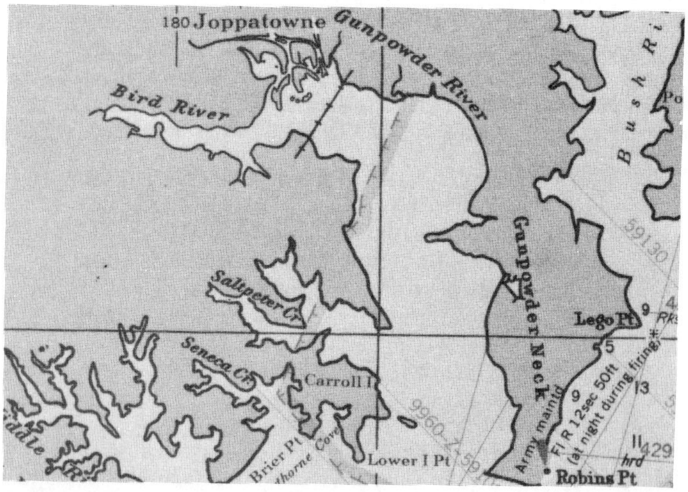

From NOAA Chart 12260—not to be used for navigation.

If you do begin your trip at Pooles Island Light, a course of 307° (approx.) will bring you to B/W N "41B," 1.6 miles from the light. Another 1.6 miles on this same course will bring you to R "4" at the river's mouth.

At this point, you must be careful not to head up the Middle River. This area can be very confusing, since you make such a wide swing to get to buoy R "4." At buoy R "4," a course of 023° (approx.) to R "6," 0.7 mile away, will put the stacks of what I presume to be a power plant on Seneca Creek to port. If these stacks remain to starboard after you pass R "4," you will know you have not made the proper course adjustment.

From R "6" to R "8", the distance is 0.8 mile on a course of 070°. To port the wide and basically uninhabited Gunpowder River stretches before you.

At C "9" (Fl green 4 secs.) 0.4 mile distance, a course of 349° (approx.) will line you up with the buoys to run upriver.

Off buoy #11, to port is **Saltpeter Creek.** The charts show some depths of five to seven feet. However, it is not buoyed and since there are also some two-foot depths, I would avoid this creek unless you know the area well.

Just below the fixed railroad bridge (19 feet horizontal clearance, 11 feet vertical clearance), 7 miles above the mouth of the river, you will see a line of buoys, beginning with C "1" and N "2," which mark the dredged channel below Joppatown.

In negotiating the bridge, you must pay attention, not only to the vertical clearance, but also to the depth of the water. Low water, of course, will provide more clearance. Those who operate larger boats out of Joppatown become very proficient in their study of the tides on the Gunpowder.

At **Joppatown,** there is a marina with 300 slips which has accommodations for transients. There are also marine supplies and haul out facilities as well. Joppatown is a beautiful suburban community, and several stores are within walking distance of the marina.

Just past the railroad bridge to port, the **Bird River** is buoyed for 2.5 miles, with depths of two or three feet.

In all, the Gunpowder River channel has depths of 11 feet for two miles, six feet to eight feet for 3.5 miles and about five feet in the dredged section below Joppatown. □

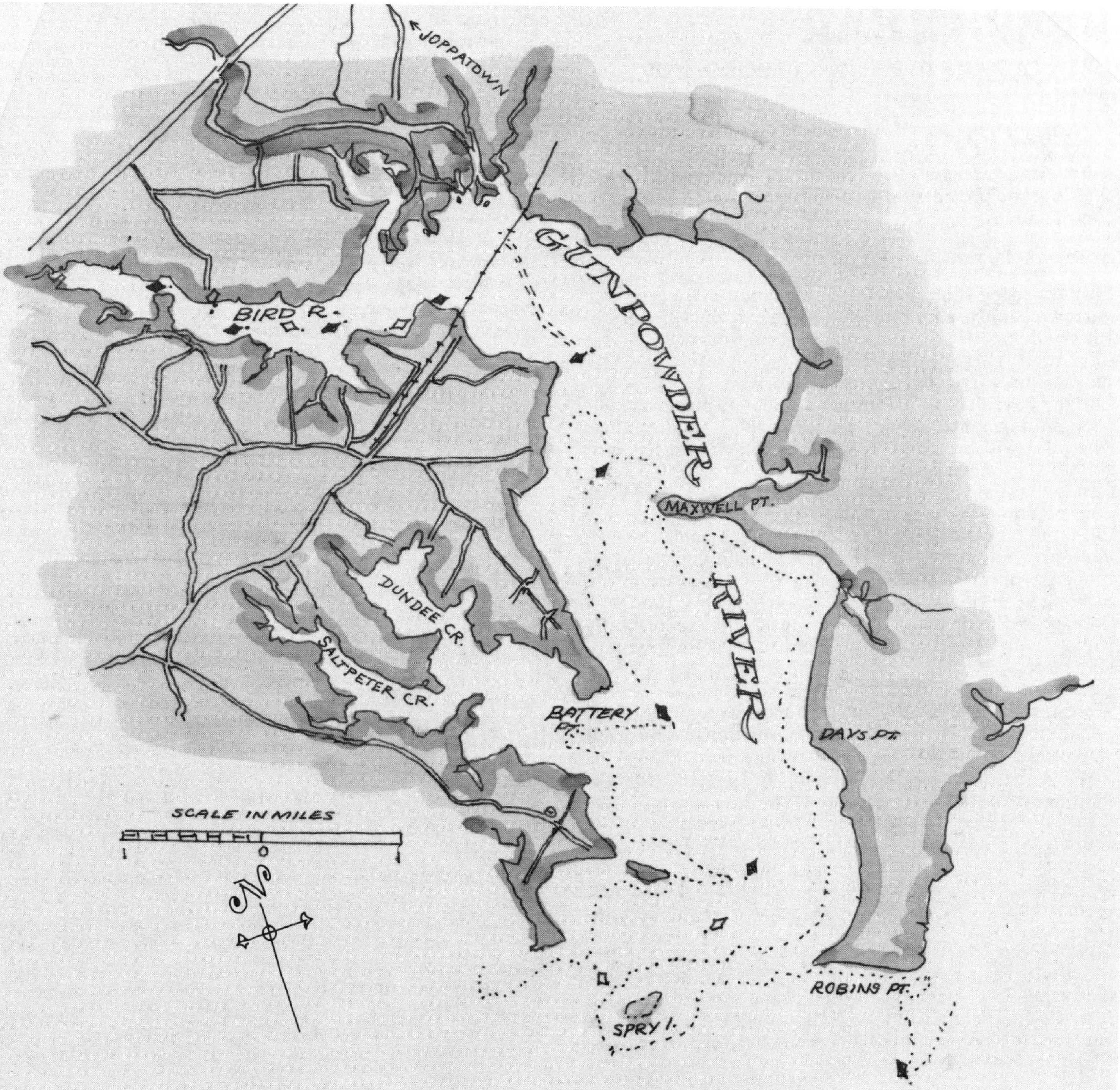
JOPPATOWN
GUNPOWDER
RIVER
BIRD R.
MAXWELL PT.
DUNDEE CR.
SALTPETER CR.
BATTERY PT.
DAYS PT.
SCALE IN MILES
ROBINS PT.
SPRY I.
N

Notes

KEEP CLEAR

Big Ships in the Chesapeake Bay

A major shipping channel runs the length of the Chesapeake Bay, and here pass tons of cargo borne by the big ships. An awareness of the constraints under which these ships operate provides the best protection against dangerous confrontations.

Some facts you should know.

☐Unlike many small boats, big ships must often keep to a narrow channel, and Rule 9 of the newly revised rules of the road specifically states that small craft "shall not impede the passage of a vessel which can safely navigate only within a narrow channel or fairway."

☐In the Bay, all of the commercial ships you meet will have U.S. pilots aboard, regardless of the vessel's nationality. The pilot will be monitoring VHF radio channel 13 for ship-to-ship messages.

☐In low visibility, ships navigate by radar and small craft **may** or **may not** be detected.

☐It often takes less than 10 minutes for a fast ship to reach you once you spot it in clear weather, and in hazy weather it takes a lot less. At 10 knots, a ship goes 1 nautical mile in 6 minutes; at 15 knots, it can be on you in 4 minutes.

☐Large, difficult-to-maneuver ships cannot successfully avoid smaller craft in narrow channels. It is up to you to **stay clear.**

☐A ship that is slowing down does not steer very well; it needs the propeller's action on the rudder to respond. If the pilot feels that a turn will save the situation, he may not slow down.

☐When the ship's engines are put "full astern," **there is nothing more the pilot can do.** He may lose control of the ship, but the reversing action will in most cases swing the ship's bow to starboard. Therefore, if you have a choice, try to escape on his port side. Keeping these things in mind will give you a better chance. *Remember that it takes 4 to 6 minutes and 2,000 to 4,000 feet for a ship to stop* ***after*** *its engines are reversed.*

☐Watch out for tugs towing barges, especially at night, when poorly lit barges may remain invisible. Remember that a partially submerged towing cable can cut a boat in two. Commercial fishing vessels, though more maneuverable, may pose a problem when hauling large nets, which may be deceptively long.

What can you do?

☐**Keep a constant lookout,** especially astern. The safe sailor has a roving eye (when he is on the water).

☐**Stay out of the way.** This does not mean that the ocean "belongs" to the big ships and you have no rights. Avoid sailing or traveling in the ship channels when you can, especially if visibility is poor because of fog, rain or darkness.

☐**Do not underestimate the speed of a large vessel.** If your boat is slow, a sailboat for example, you might not be able to take effective evasive action if you find yourself on a collision course with a large ship in visibility of a quarter-mile or less—the speed differential is simply too great.

☐**Be visible.** At night, make sure that your navigation lights are bright and are not obscured by sails, flags or dinghies in davits. If you see the running lights of a vessel and you don't think you have been seen, begin to get out of the way, using flashlights on sails, a spotlight, flash bulbs, or a white flare to indicate your position (a strobelight should be reserved as distress signal only). Carry a radar reflector as high on the boat as you can.

In the time it took you to read to this point, a ship going at 15 knots would have traveled one nautical mile.

☐**Keep watch at night.** Even on a clear night you will have difficulty seeing a big ship approach. You might see it first as a black shadow against a background of shore lights, or as a shadow moving rapidly across still water—at that point you are not far apart. Remember that your lights will **not** be easily spotted from the ship.

☐**Watch the ship's lights.** If you want to determine whether you are in the path of a ship, pay attention to the sidelights as well as the masthead lights. If you see only one sidelight, or if one is much brighter than the other, you can be fairly sure you are not in the direct path of the ship. This also gives an indication of which way to move in order to get clear altogether. If you see both sidelights, you're dead ahead—MOVE OUT FAST. Also learn to recognize the mastlights of a tug towing one or more barges and of a commercial fishing vessel towing a net.

☐**Know whistle signals,** used only when vessels are in sight of one another. The pilot of a ship will frequently **not** use the "port" or "starboard" whistle signals when passing small boats because he is afraid the signals will not be understood and might lead to erratic changes in course. If you hear five or more short blasts on the whistle, it is the "danger" signal. Check and see if it is for you—and if it is, make way fast.

☐**Use your radio.** If you have a VHF radio aboard, remember that while channel 16 is the calling/distress frequency, you may call directly on channel 13 without going through channel 16 first for bridge-to-bridge communications related to safe meeting and passing between ships and other watercraft.

☐**Choose safe anchorages.** Each year commercial ships and fishing vessels ram and sink a few boats anchored in navigation channels or tied to marker buoys. Coast Guard buoys tell ships "here is where you must pass," and it is illegal as well as unsafe, to tie up to them.

☐**Use binoculars.** At night, especially, they can help you determine ships' lights and direction with greater accuracy.

☐**Carry a radar reflector.** Though no guarantee that a ship will spot you, a radar reflector at least improves your chances.

Navigating in Baltimore Harbor

When navigating small craft in Baltimore Harbor remember:

☐Be particularly cautious around commercial cargo piers. Ships, tugs or barges may be maneuvering in the vicinity and sudden propeller wash or wakes generated by these vessels can be extremely dangerous to small craft.

☐Stay out of the main ship channel if your draft permits.

☐Maintain a monitor aboard your boat to keep watch.

☐Don't pass close to ships leaving piers—you don't know what's on the other side of them, and their turbulence can cause you problems.

☐Don't forget harbor speed limits—you're responsible for your wake.

Information courtesy of University of Maryland Cooperative Extension Service. Pamphlets are available by writing to U. of Md., CES, Rm. 1214 Symons Hall, College Park, MD 20742.

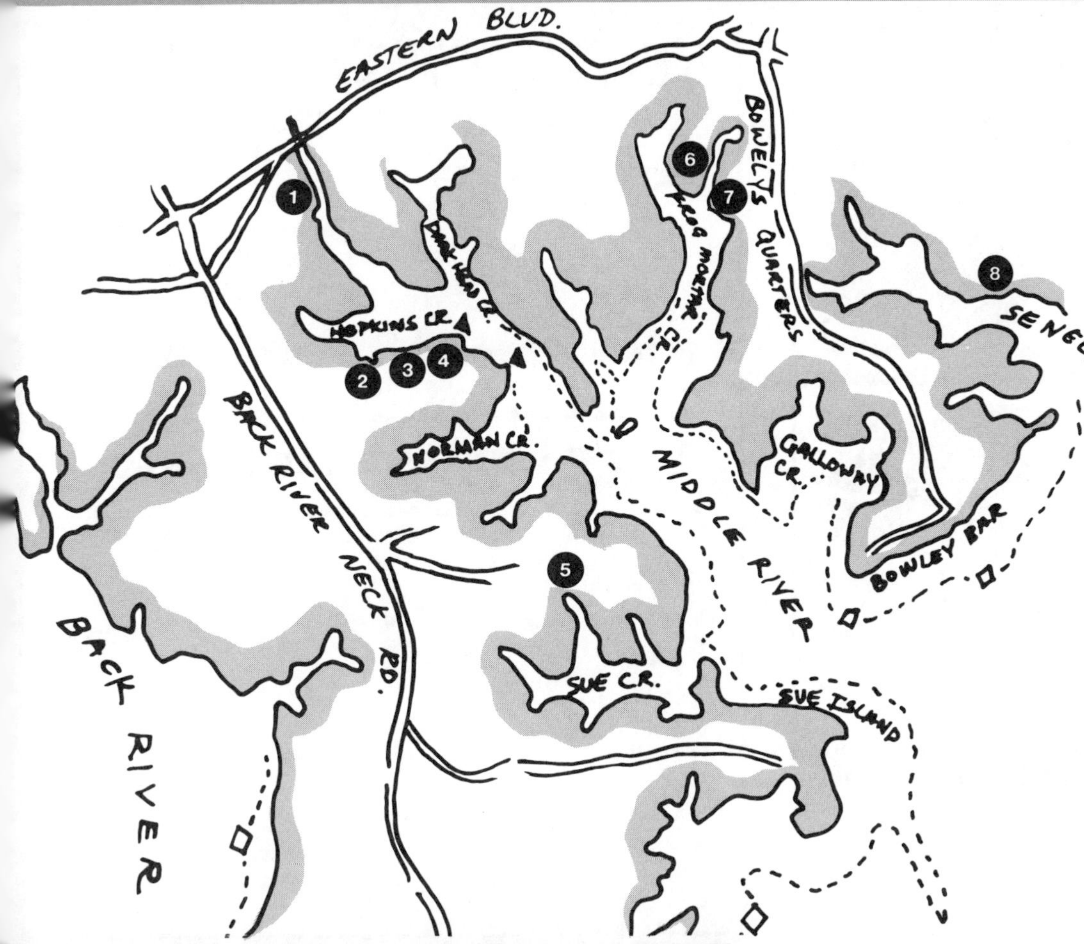

1. Buedel's Marina
2. Deckelman's Boatyard
3. River Watch Restaurant & Marina
4. Anchor Bay Marina Sales & Ships Store
5. Boating Center of Baltimore
6. New Tradewinds *On Armstrong Creek*
7. Maryland Marina
8. Porter's Seneca Marina

Cruise the waters of Middle River and find the best marine and restaurant facilities anywhere on the Bay. Whether you need service, supplies, an overnight slip, a delicious meal, or even a new cruising boat, it can be found in the Middle River area.

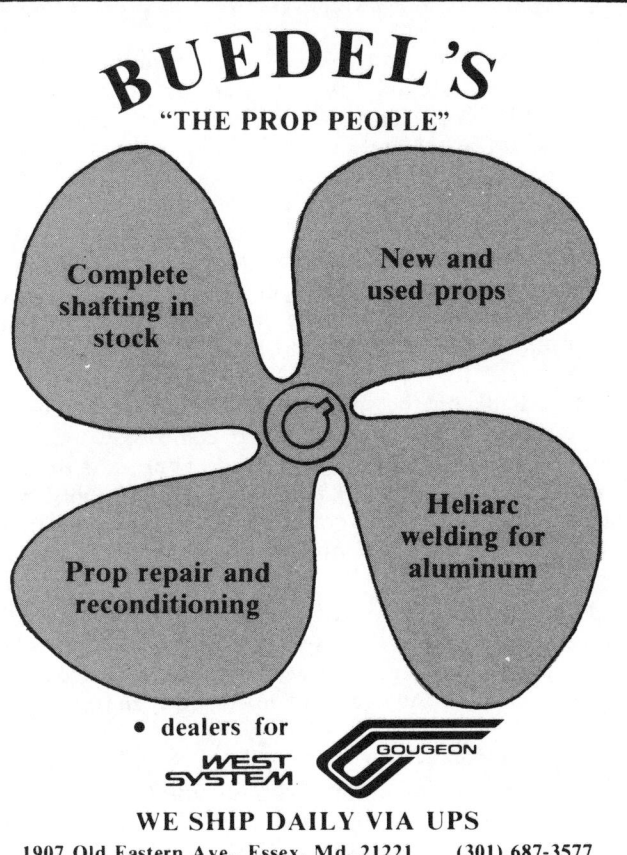

MIDDLE RIVER

The Middle River, easily accessible to Baltimore and Central Pennsylvania, is an extremely popular Bay boating area. Over 20 marinas located on the river and its tributaries run the gamut from very small, simple boatyards to gigantic, sophisticated operations and touch on everything in between. Here the boater can find just about everything he requires, including berths; moorings; hull, motor and radio repairs; marine railways and lifts; food; lodging; marine head pump out stations; hardware and nautical charts. In addition to these extensive facilities, the Baltimore Yacht Club is located on Sue Island to port (entering) off buoy R "4" at the river's entrance.

To reach the Middle River, pick up Pooles Island Light (Fl 2.5 sec. 27 Ft. 7 M visibility—horn 9/15-6/1), located 0.8 of a mile south of Pooles Island. A course of 299° will put you on target for R "4" (Qk. Fl.) (5.4 miles away) just inside the entrance of the river. Three and two-tenths miles from Pooles Island Light, you will be abreast of buoy R "4" (Fl. 4 sec.), marking the entrance to the Gunpowder River to starboard. Three and nine-tenths miles from Pooles Island Light, C "3" (Fl. G 4 sec.) will be directly to port.

The Middle River has an 8½-foot dredged channel leading to an anchorage basin at the head of **Dark Head Creek** (east fork of the river), 3.2 miles above the river's entrance. The west fork of the river has depths of 6-7 feet for approximately one mile.

As we proceed upstream, let's check out some of the Middle River's tributaries.

Seneca Creek to starboard, marked by buoy C "WRI" off Bowley Bar, has depths of 5-8 feet for 2.4 miles.

The entrance to **Sue Creek,** to port, is marked by a 14-foot marker (Fl. G 2.5 secs. 5 M visibility). On our visit to Sue Creek we noticed a shoal just east of the Baltimore Yacht Club

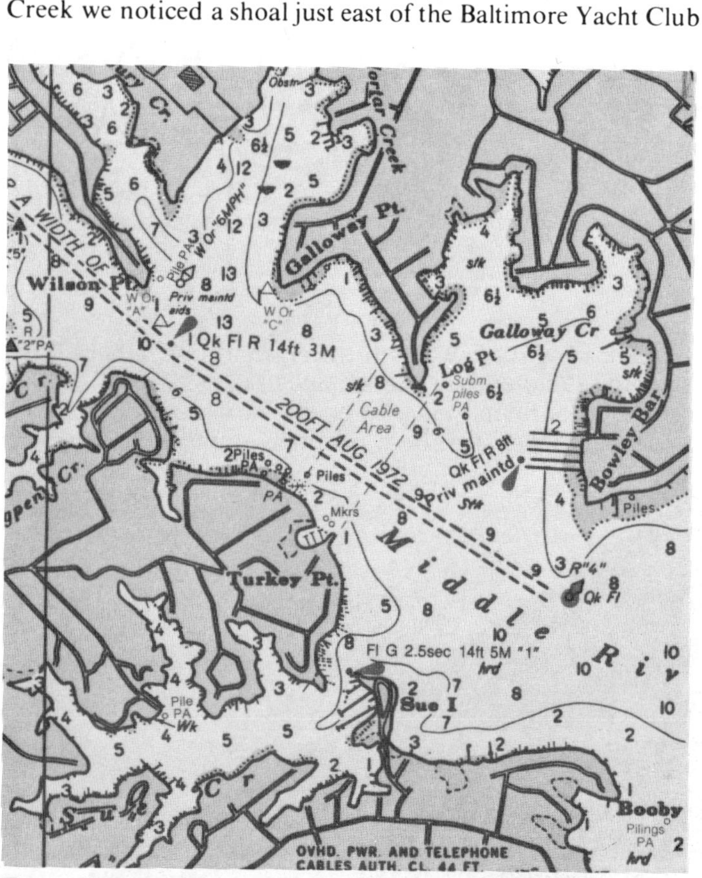

From NOAA Chart 12278—not to be used for navigation.

on Sue Island. And, on the west side, the shoal off Turkey Point is reported to extend further than the charts show. We motored in till the red buoy #4 was abeam, then turned for the green flasher #1 at the entrance of Sue Creek, keeping the red #4 dead astern.

Once you pass the docks at the yacht club, take the main branch of the creek, west of the club. Don't turn too soon, however. There's a bothersome shoal on the starboard point, where we went aground. It took only a few minutes to kedge off, and a friendly boater on the club piers called out that deep water would be found on the port side.

We motored slowly upstream and anchored under the lee of the high bank on the south shore (about where the "Cr." shows on chart #12273). The bank here is mostly wooded, and the holding ground is good, soft mud. There was only one house on the side of the creek near us, and a few lights shown on the opposite shore. We were in about six feet of water, and after a refreshing swim, spent a delightful evening here with ample privacy.

Galloway Creek, the next creek to starboard, is in reality nothing more than a broad cove, with depths of 5-6½ feet. However, don't cut Log Point too closely or venture too far into the creek without excellent up-to-date charts or local knowledge.

Frog Mortar Creek to starboard of the 14 ft. marker (I. Qk. Fl. R 3 M visibility) has depths from 5-12 feet for 1.5 miles.

Norman Creek, also to port, above the marker has depths of 5-7 feet for approximately 0.5 of a mile.

Hopkins Creek, the next creek to port, has depths of 5-8 feet for a mile on its west branch and 6½-8 feet for 0.5 of a mile on its east branch. The west fork of Hopkins Creek is an ideal spot for anchoring. As you proceed upstream, the best place is on the port side just before the docks of the condominium ashore. There you will also find a path that leads from the water to a residential street, at the end of which you will find supermarkets, fast food outlets, a liquor store, etc., etc. It is a modest walk (about 1/3 mile). On busy summer weekends, when everyone is heading for the Eastern Shore, you will find this location peaceful, uncrowded and relatively secluded.

In sharp contrast to the present bustling boat scene, the myriad of homes apartments and marinas lining the river and its tributaries and the crowded streets and highways, this area has a rather placid history. In former times, even the Indians—the Yeocomicos, Nanticokes and Mattawas—were docile. However, the Susquehannocks, as Susquehannocks were known to do, occassionally stopped by to stir things up a little. Except for these occasional disturbances, the quiet farming area meandered lazily through time, escaping involvement in both the War of 1812 and the Civil War.

The pace picked up a bit in 1895 with the building of Hollywood Park, at the east end of Back River Bridge. The park provided amusements for the children while the adults refreshed themselves. Hollywood Park, which burned down in 1912, owed a great deal of its success to Baltimore's Sunday closing laws.

When the rest of the country plunged into the Depression in 1929, the Middle River area's economy was bolstered by the building of the Glen L. Martin aircraft plant. The site was picked because of its proximity to Washington and the labor supply which could be provided from Baltimore. Also taken into consideration were the year-round good flying conditions.

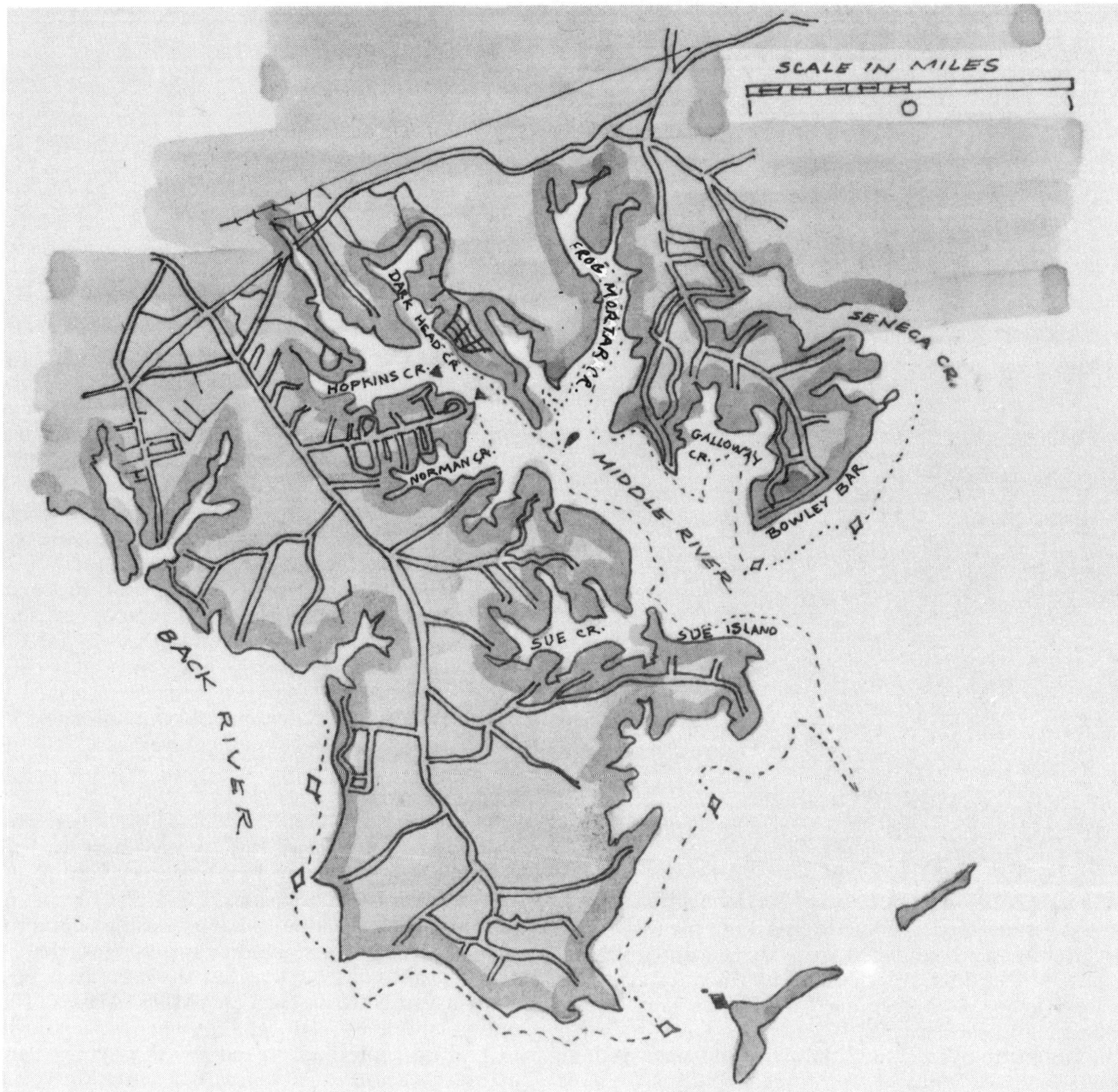

The first planes turned out by the plant were the BM-2 dive bomber for the Army and the PM-1 Navy patrol flying boat.

Among the famous visitors to the Martin Company were Charles A. Lindbergh, Amelia Earhart, FDR, and Carl Sandburg.

Although the Martin Company is no longer a part of the Middle River scene, there is a huge industrial park here now, and the Glen L. Martin State Airport is still a reminder of the important part this area played in aviation history. □

Notes

HART AND MILLER ISLANDS

South of the Middle River

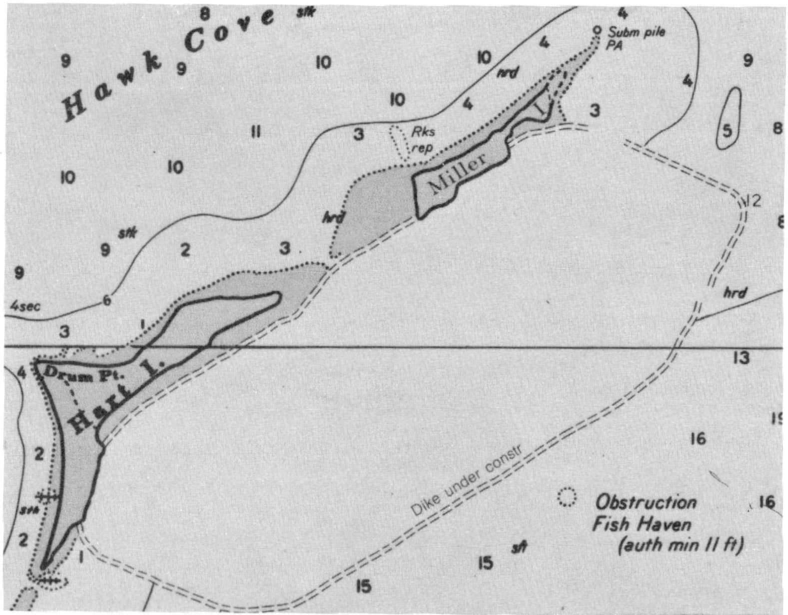

From NOAA Chart 12278—not to be used for navigation.

For some time readers have been asking for an update on Hart and Miller Islands. Most of them want to know, "Are the islands completely ruined by the depositing of Baltimore Harbor dredge spoils?" and "Can you still go ashore and enjoy the beaches?"

Well, quite frankly, we didn't know the answers to these questions. We hadn't been there ourselves in six years or more, and a lot can change in that time.

I do remember there was a lot of concern when it was announced that the Hart-Miller Island site was where a lot of the dredged material would be dumped. Caused quite a controversy, as I recall. It's been years since I heard anything further.

Recently we visited Hart and Miller Islands and were encouraged with what we found. Our course brought us from Seven-Foot Knoll Light right up through the middle of the Craighill Channel Range. The wind was fifteen knots and gusting. We were guests aboard *Summer Wind,* a 34-foot Tartan sloop. All day long the wind had blown and, at first, I had thoughts of coming into Back River by way of the narrow cut-through at Cuckold Point. Our chart warned of shoaling, however, so we continued northeast, along the eastern side of Hart and Miller.

The amount of construction that has taken place is amazing! A long bulkheaded retaining wall has been constructed extending from the south end of Hart Island along the entire length of Miller Island, curving around to terminate at the island's tip. There are several work barges with their mooring cables presently anchored along the Bay-side of the bulkhead (the charts call it a dike), so this would be an unhealthy place for the boater to explore or anchor.

On the Hawk Cove, or western, side it's a different matter. We were broad reaching north till we reached the black bell #1 off the northern tip of Miller Island. Giving the shoals off the island plenty of room, we jibed to a port-side reach and cut across toward the red nun #2 off Wells Point.

Hawk Cove lay open to us as we sheeted in and beat our way toward Drum Point. Miller Island looked the same as always along its western shore. The sandy hillocks that formed its bulk were sprouting thick bunches of wild grasses and, here and there, was an occasional thicket of scrub brush. If you choose, you can get fairly close to anchor and go ashore. But this is not the real attraction.

Further south is Hart Island. Here is the favored anchorage. The island curves westward to a longish shoal at Drum Point, where a black bell marks the way into Back River. Hart Island is a handsome body of land with some good-sized trees along its central and western part that huddle protectively around a couple of sandy beaches. Many picnics and beach parties have been enjoyed here. It is also a chance to take a brief walk in the woods. What a way to end a hot day on the Bay!

Hart's eastern end is less desirable. There you will find a considerable area of flat, grassy marsh. I am told the mosquitoes and flies will all but carry you off if the wind is easterly. On these occasions, our friends have anchored east of Hart; but with all of the bulk-heading equipment, barges, and mooring cables, I don't recommend that.

Our old charts corrected through June 23, 1984, still show a gap between Hart and Miller Islands. The water was only a couple of feet deep, but when we felt daring, we used to pull up centerboards and slip through, out into the Bay, using this shortcut. I remember watching as a larger boat tried to imitate us. He almost made it, but he suddenly stopped in his tracks. We all got out and waded over to him and helped push him back into Hawk Cove.

The bulkheading company has deposited a huge amount of sand which now fills in the gap. This has created a very nice beach area which can be enjoyed by visitors. I understand there are even a couple of Parks Department personnel there in the summer to keep the area safe and clean.

Hawk Cove is a considerable body of water; if the wind is strong, out of the north or northwest, you might be in for a rough night. There is quite a fetch and things can get choppy. On the other hand, if the wind is out of the south, or southeast, as is usually the case in the summer, the islands give fine protection.

As *Summer Wind* beat her way down to Drum Point, we could see the graceful lines of several pleasure boats anchored just offshore. On the beach a dinghy was pulled up, and a cheery fire illuminated a small group of people. We passed the anchored boats and envied them, since we had not planned to spend the night here and were just passing through. *Summer Wind* jibed once more and headed north, toward Middle River. As we went, I could look back at this snug harbor and in the gathering dusk see the twinkle of anchor lights beckoning to us. "Don't worry," I thought to myself. "We'll be back, and it will be just like the old days — only better." □

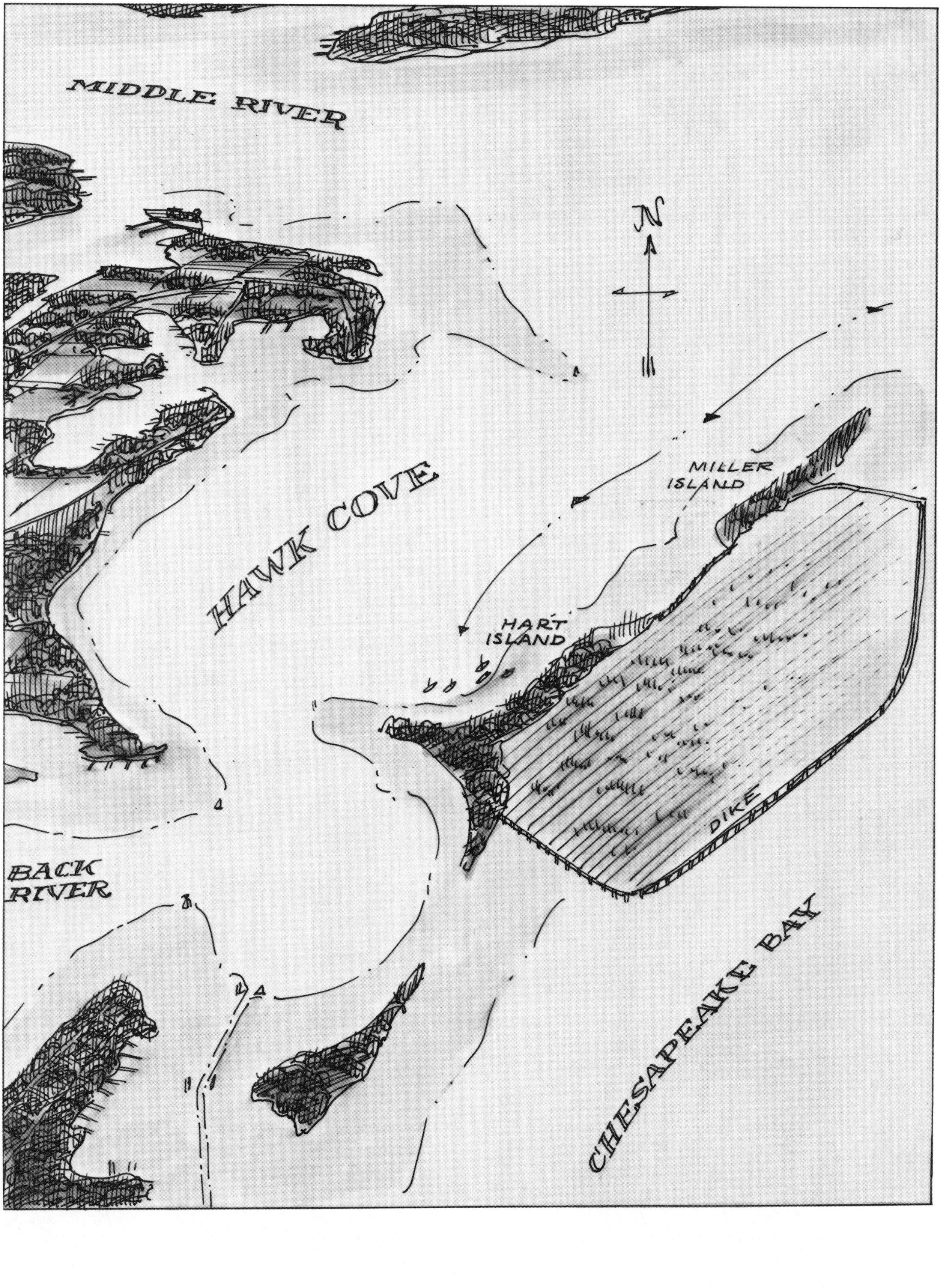
MIDDLE RIVER
N
HAWK COVE
MILLER ISLAND
HART ISLAND
DIKE
BACK RIVER
CHESAPEAKE BAY

STILLPOND

south of the Sassafras River

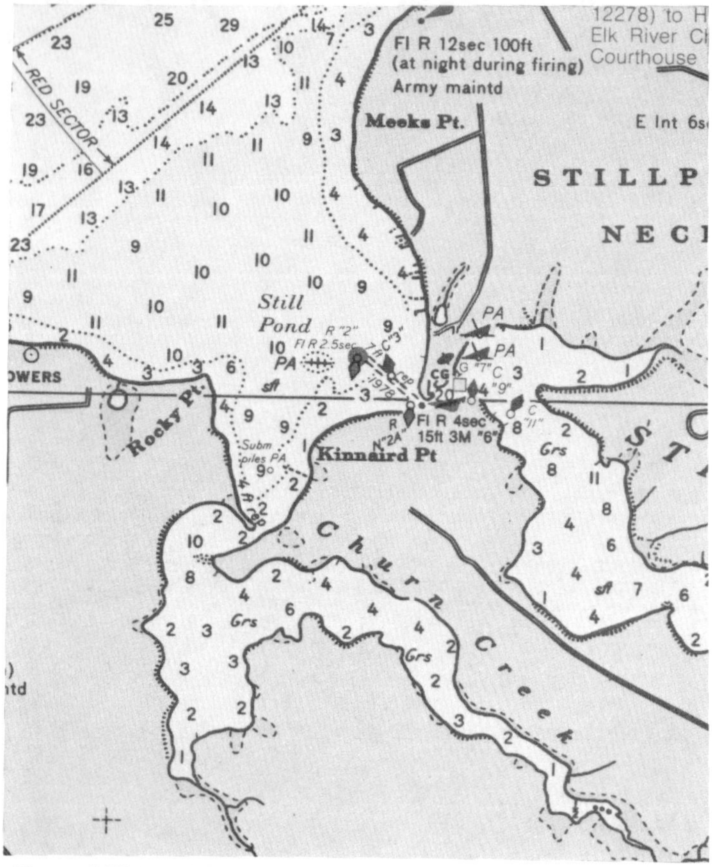

From NOAA Chart 12274—not to be used for navigation.

One of the most popular anchorages on the northern Eastern Shore is Still Pond. At times anything but—I always wondered where the name originated. I finally discovered that the name Still Pond is a corruption of the former name "Steel's Pond." Another explanation suggests the name was supposed to have been "Steele's Pone." In Elizabethan English "pone" means favorite. In any event, either of these names would have been more appropriate and less misleading.

Still Pond is one of the most easily accessible anchorages from the Bay. It's located two nautical miles south of Howell Point on the Sassafras River and two miles north of Worton Point at the entrance to Worton Creek.

Still Pond is a small bay scooped out of the shoreline with another short arm of water that extends south from Rocky Point and Kinnaird Point. There is little protection from northwesterlies, but in mid-summer, wind from the south is shielded by land. Best side of the anchorage is the west shore where deep water reaches almost to its sandy beach.

Any summer weekend will find boats lined along the entire length of this mile-wide indentation or "bay" as some call it. Swimming, fishing, crabbing and shelling are popular pastimes for the gunkholers who take full advantage of Still Pond's 9- to 11-foot depths. The anchorage is protected from southerly or easterly winds, but in a northerly or westerly blow, those who know the area well head up Stillpond or Churn Creeks.

The first time I entered Stillpond Creek, we literally felt our way in with a boat hook. Now the channel is well marked and judging from the size of the sailboats rafted in the creek, the entrance doesn't seem to be the problem it once was. However, caution is advised in the narrow entrance channel. Once in the creek proper, there are depths of 4-9 feet for

approximately 2 miles—and for those who trailer their craft, a surfaced ramp is located near the head of the creek.

A U.S. Coast Guard Station is located to port just inside the entrance of Stillpond Creek. The facility, opened in 1969, is a search and rescue operation center for the upper Chesapeake. The station is responsible for the area from the mouth of the Patapsco River to the Delaware River end of the C & D Canal. Visitors are welcome.

On entering Stillpond Creek, I was overwhelmed by its serenity. Just a few yards away was the bustle of a very active anchorage and a little farther beyond that, the Bay's main shipping lanes, but an amazing transformation to a world of tranquility is made as you enter the creek.

There have been reports of some shoaling at the entrance to Churn Creek on the south side of Still Pond, and indeed if you check your charts you will see depths of two feet listed. However, if you can "feel" your way past this sand bar, particularly at high water, the creek has depths of 3-10 feet for about a mile. Locals have been known to keep the entrance "dredged" by blasting through in their workboats.

Still Pond is located across from the Aberdeen Proving Grounds and a flashing red light is shown on Meeks Point on the north side of Still Pond at night when firing is in progress within the restricted waters of the Grounds (FL. R 12 Sec., 100 feet).

The sleepy town of Still Pond, a few miles from the creek was the scene of an event which seems entirely out of character. It was the first town in Maryland where women voted. The town was incorporated in 1908, and the incorporation provided that "the legal voters of Still Pond, female included, who pay taxes, had resided there six months, and were twenty-one years of age," could vote. The historic election took place on the 1st Saturday in May, 1908. Three commissioners were elected and three women (refusing offers from the men to let them write their tickets) voted independently.

That was a long time ago. However, from its physical appearance, I don't believe the town could have changed very much in all those years. You can be sure the terrain has not. Still Pond remains a perfect place to pursue all the delights of Bay boating—or a place to just relax and enjoy. □

NOTE: Shoaling reported across the creek from Channel B "10" WSW to DBN "7"—3.5 ft at MLW.

WORTON CREEK

south of the Sassafras River

The very first overnight cruise our family went on was to Worton Creek. Those of you who can remember your first cruise know our fears and worries as we loaded our tiny boat with grocery bags full of supplies and gear. More recently we went up the Bay to visit this old cruising spot.

If you are heading north, pick up BW N "60B" off Rock Hall and follow the line of black and white buoys running along the Eastern Shore, just starboard of the main shipping lanes. Northeast of Pooles Island at BW buoy N "42B," a course of 114-115° should bring you right into the mouth of Worton Creek, 1.8 miles away, and far enough off Handy's Pt. to avoid the shallows just north of it.

If you're heading south, Worton Creek is approximately 5 miles south of Howell Point at the mouth of the Sassafras River. If you stay just to port of the main shipping channel, there is plenty of water. At Worton Point, you can continue on to BW N "42B," approximately one mile off the point, or you can round the point (giving it a wide berth), pick up R "2" and begin heading in.

As you enter Worton Creek and round the long sand spit to starboard, you'll see many boats with their bows resting on the beach. The beach drops off so sharply here that even sailboats can pull their bows into the sand and still have adequate water under their keels. Before proceeding, you might want to anchor here and enjoy a refreshing, nettle-free swim. It is only on rare occasions, such as an extended drought, that a sea nettle ever finds its way this far north.

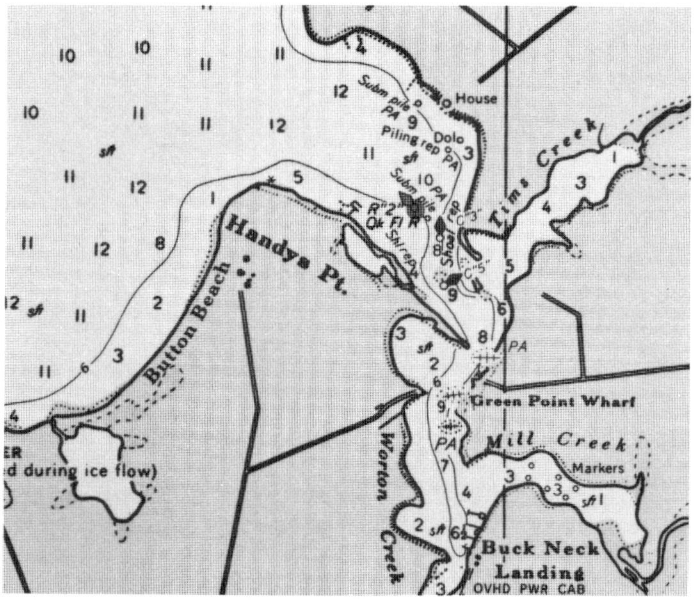

From NOAA Chart 12278—not to be used for navigation.

The number of large sailboats moored in the creek attest to its good depth, 6-9 feet, and the marina here has recently been dredged to insure good water in the slips.

One of the most convenient, full-service marinas to Chesapeake Bay traffic is in Worton Creek. Located 0.9 of a mile past R "2" at the creek's entrance, Worton Creek Marina provides just about anything the yachtsman could want. Transients are welcome, and although the marina owners try not to turn anyone away, Saturday nights are particularly busy and it is better to play it safe with reservations.

The Harbor House Restaurant and Bar is located high on the hill overlooking the marina. It is open May 1 through October 31, serving dinner only and is closed on Tuesdays.

Our memories of Worton Creek were of a tranquil anchorage with easy access to the Bay. On our most recent visit we found wall-to-wall moored boats. We couldn't even find a place to anchor. We then examined the entrance to Tim's Creek; but the charts showed a narrow and tricky channel. So we went to the red bell at the entrance of Worton and turned to the north shore where a few other boats were anchored.

Some boats anchor in the outer Bay, near the north shore just before entering Worton Creek. The creek offers adequate protection in winds from the north, east and south.

The gentle curve of the land to the north was bright with the setting sun, and the sandy beach invited us for a stroll. At various points along the beach were sections of huge timbers, some bolted together, suggesting a shipwreck many years ago. A most delightful feature was the river bottom here. Standing neck deep, I was walking on sand, not slimy mud. What a pleasant place to spend the night; only a strong westerly will give you problems here. □

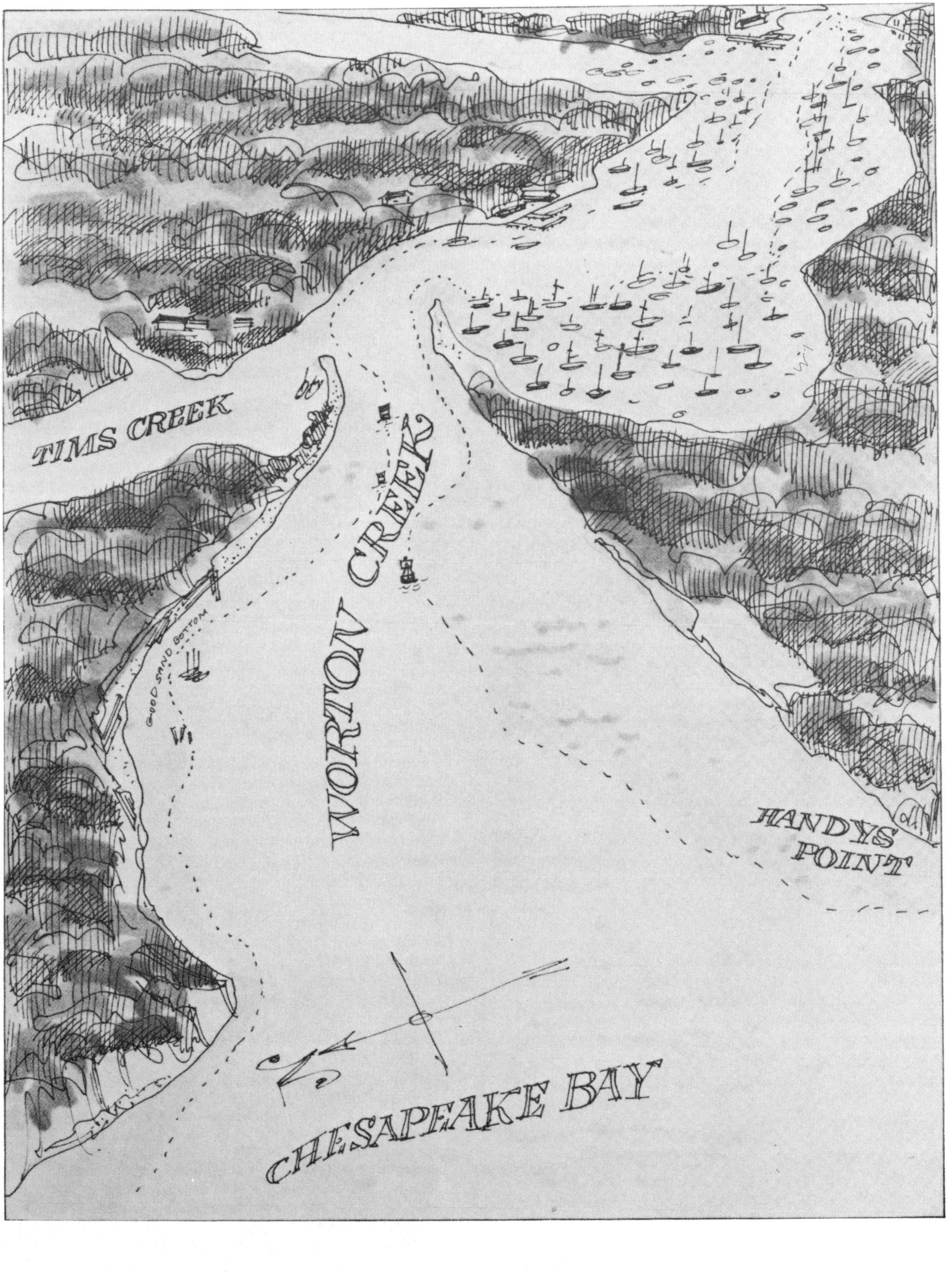
TIMS CREEK
WORTON CREEK
GOOD SAND BOTTOM
HANDYS POINT
CHESAPEAKE BAY
N

FAIRLEE CREEK

south of the Sassafras River

Even threatening skies could not dampen our enthusiasm for the cruise that lay ahead. This was the first time I had ever planned to travel with any other boats. I had always shied away from organized cruises, simply because to me they represented all the formality I came to the Bay to avoid.

However, this was to be a very casual Fourth of July three-day weekend cruise to Fairlee Creek. It was about 11 A.M. when we finally left the Bohemia River. Our destination, Fairlee Creek, was 22.3 nautical miles away. Until we reached Howell Point we stayed pretty much on the edge of the shipping channel, since I consider this the most direct route. At Howell Point the channel comes in very close to shore (0.3 of a mile off) and from this point it begins to veer to starboard. I knew there was enough water to stay to port of the markers—careful, of course, to give Worton Point a wide berth and careful also to avoid the many crab pots here. We ran well inside BW "42B" which appears on the chart off Worton Creek. I say "appears" because, frankly, I did not see it, but then I wasn't looking for it either. My attention was focused on our destination and the crab pots, so aptly pointed out by our crew. Of course, if you do find yourself at "42B", a course of 189°M will bring you to R "2" (Gp Fl R (2) 5 sec). The shallowest point on this course is about 7 feet. Although the weather continued to look threatening, the Bay was calm, and in less than two hours we arrived at buoy R "2" (Gp Fl R (2) 5 sec), marking the entrance of Fairlee Creek.

At Fairlee, it is **imperative** that you follow the markers—and believe them! C "3" is practically on the beach as is N "6", and you must snake your way between C "3", C "5" and N "6".

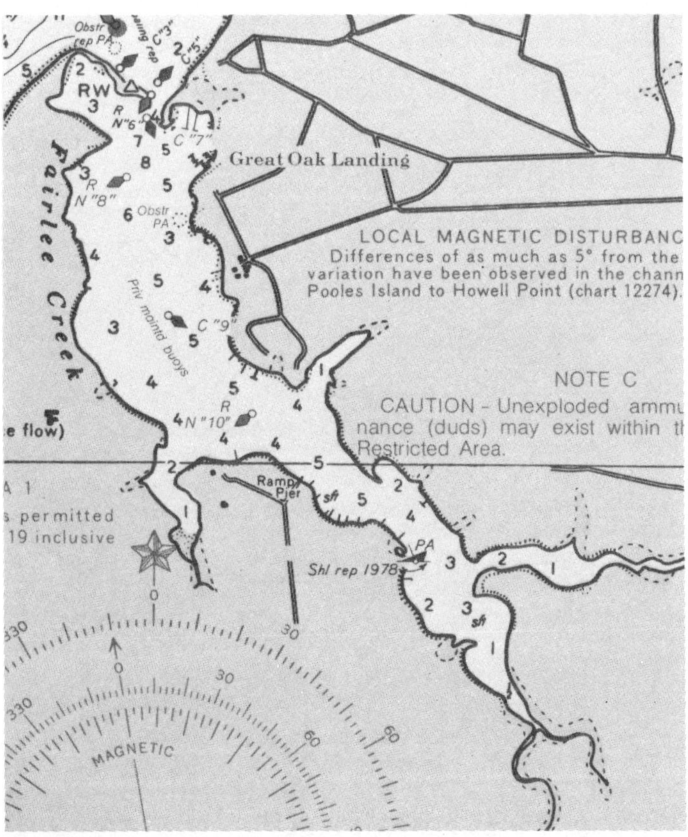

From NOAA Chart 12278—not to be used for navigation.

Although not presently shown on the chart, two sets of range markers painted yellow and obviously privately placed, help keep you in the narrow channel. This comes startlingly close to the shore—just before you have to turn ninety degrees to starboard in about as much room as a ten-cent piece. a fairly strong tidal current at the turning point adds a little challenge to the maneuver.

Coming into Fairlee Creek is always an experience, but on a Fourth of July weekend it was even more so. The tide was rushing in with us, and the sharp turn around the spit of land was tricky to negotiate. The small boats crisscrossing the channel didn't do much to help the situation either. I found I had to gun the engine to get steerage around the spit and into the creek. Other cruisers found it necessary to go into reverse briefly or, in the case of those with twin screws, to play one engine against the other.

Once past the spit, there is plenty of water as evidenced by the size of the boats in the creek. This is a popular spot for cruising yachtsmen making the Intracoastal run. As is the case in Worton Creek, there is a good anchorage behind the sand spit. Fairlee Creek itself is a good anchorage and although too broad for protection on cold winter days, would be quite welcome on hot summer nights when the open water encourages a cooling breeze.

Once inside the creek, Great Oak Landing is to port. Although it used to be a private club, this facility is now open to the general public. The marina offers: berths and electricity, toilets, showers, water, ice, groceries, diesel and gas. On shore, the resort complex offers dining, cocktails, a 32-unit motel, a pool and beach, golf, small sailboat rentals, and miniature golf. Horseback riding and tennis are located nearby.

On our Fourth of July cruise we pulled over to the beach behind the spit and rafted up. When we decided to use our inflatable to go ashore and explore Greak Oak, we encountered some trouble. The inflatable was the wrong type of boat to attempt to cross the fast-moving channel current. Once safely on the farther shore, we vowed to return by a safer route upstream. □

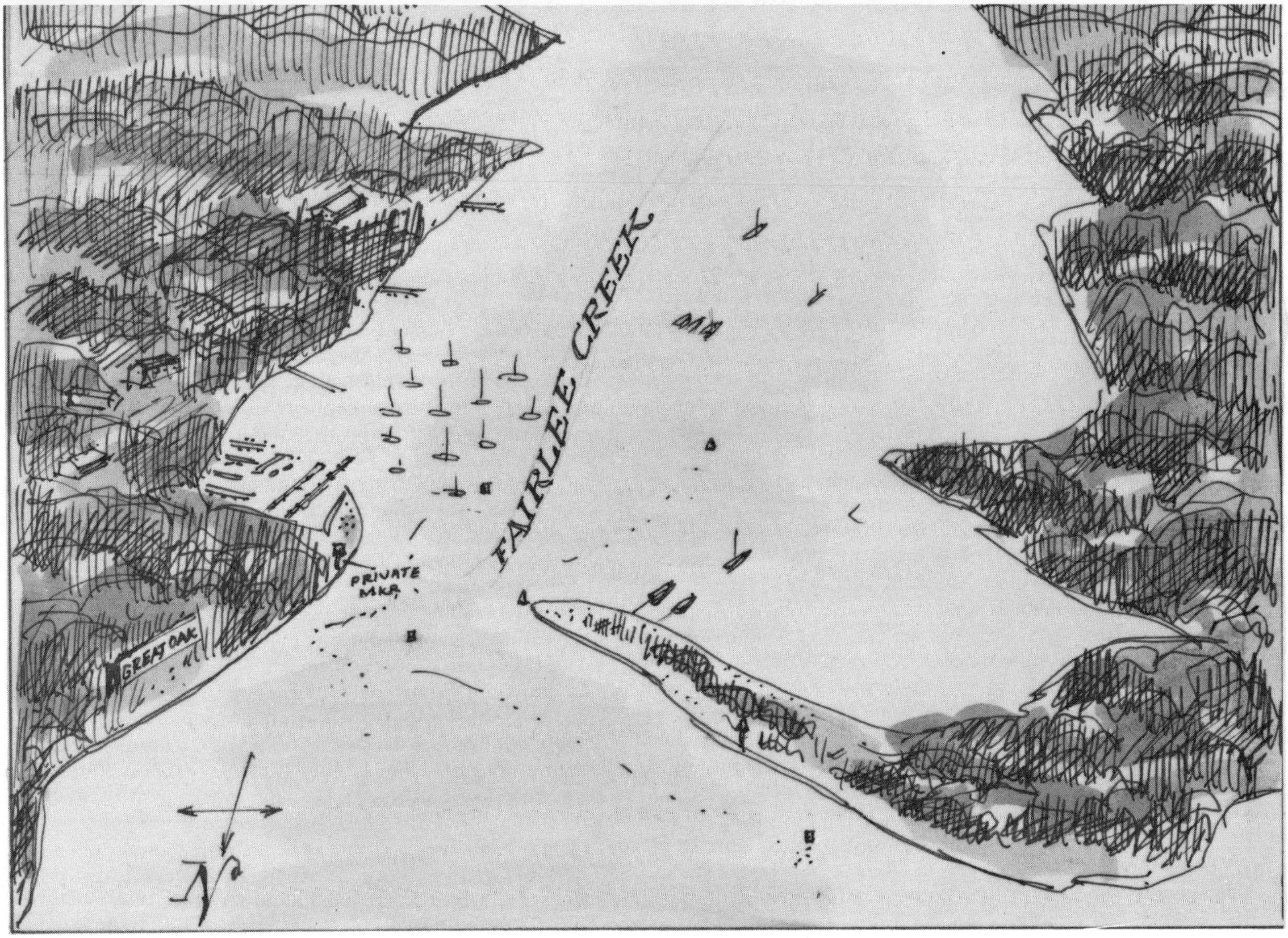

Notes

SWAN CREEK

north of the Chester River

Swan Creek has long been a favorite destination for cruisers because of its rural beauty. It is protected by a long shoal, the Swan Point Bar, which hangs down like an arm, for almost four miles from Swan Point. This shoal shows depth of five feet and less. If you are approaching Swan Creek from the upper Bay, pick up R "20" off Tolchester and take a course of about 220° to R "6," southwest of Swan Point. This course roughly follows the line of buoys marking the Tolchester Channel until it is about 0.7 miles inshore of "7" which marks the southern end of the channel. Buoy "6" is about a mile farther along the course. (If you want to be extra careful, bias your course a little to starboard—i.e. toward the channel—from R "16" to R "12.") An alternative, somewhat longer but easier, is simply to follow the line of buoys to "7." From there "6" bears about 190°. Having reached "6," you will see to port a quick flashing, 30-foot structure 2.3 miles away. If your boat draws 4½ feet or less, you can cross the bar here. A course of 098° will bring you to the light, with Can "5" just ahead to port.

If you have a deep draft boat or are approaching from the south, pick up green buoy "1". A course of 358° from green buoy "1" will take you to the red flasher off Huntingfield Point. Continuing on this course, keep Can "5" to port and Nun "6" to starboard.

Just beyond Nun "6" you will see Gratitude Marina on the right. The facility has lift and repair facilities, a small store and snack bar, very clean restrooms and a warm welcome.

The welcome to strangers would no doubt have been less hospitable back in the 1880's during the Oyster Wars between the dredgers and tongers. New regulations were supposed to keep dredgers off certain bars, which were reserved for tongers. But the dredgers did not want to give up the bars, and would often shoot at the tongers who dared to challenge them. To retaliate, the tongers set up a cannon at Gratitude to protect their oyster bar. But one night, the dredgers came ashore and stole the cannon.

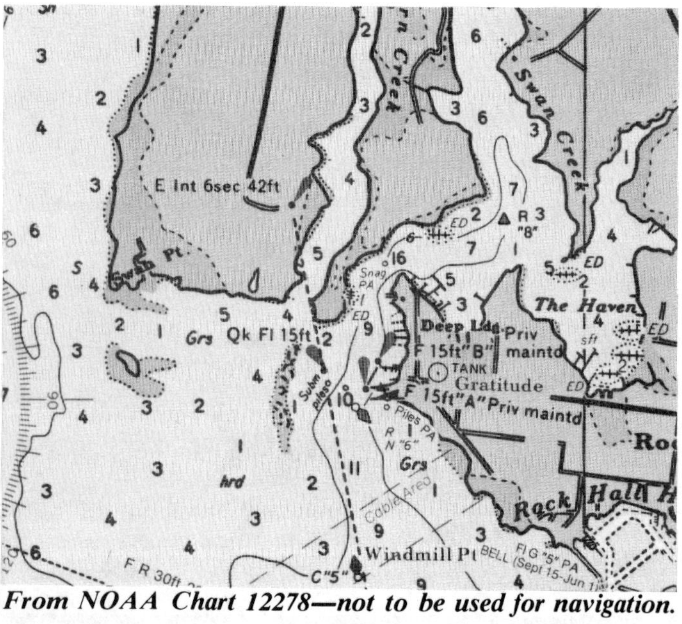

From NOAA Chart 12278—not to be used for navigation.

The dredgers later got their come-uppance from Capt. Howard of the Oyster Navy, who sank a boat that was illegally dredging one day by ramming it with his steam-powered vessel. And then he sank a second one, while the others fled or surrendered.

Many towns with interesting and unusual names often have interesting and unusual explanations for those names, and Gratitude is no exception. One explanation is that the town was named for the ferry boat *Gratitude* which used to dock there. Another version of the name's origin, and one readily identifiable with Bay boaters, is that many years ago some sailors were caught in a fierce Bay storm. After battling the elements for what must have seemed an eternity, they finally made land. They promptly named their landfall, Gratitude.

If you continue up the creek, around the point into the cove called Deep Landing, you'll find Swan Creek Marina. A lot of boats are moored in the cove opposite the marina, so if you fail to find comfortable room to swing on an anchor there, proceed up the north branch of Swan Creek, but watch your chart for depths compatible with your boat's draft.

Shoaling has been reported off daymarker R "8." Don't run too close to the marker, but do keep it to starboard. Locals say that in many instances boats that have gone aground here have been trying to pass the marker to starboard. There are reports that the Army Engineers plan to dredge here, but to date dredging has not begun.

Continuing past R "8" to the next cove, The Haven, you'll come to another marina, The Haven Harbour. The channel into The Haven has been marked by the marina and will handle 5- to 6-foot draft boats. A swimming pool and indoor/outdoor recreation areas are available to patrons.

If you choose to eat ashore, you will find a seasonal restaurant, Swan Creek Pub, adjoining Gratitude Marina. Or, a few blocks down the road, several year-round establishments serve home-style food.

Swan Creek is beautiful at any time of the year, but many people say their favorite time to cruise there is in the fall, when geese, ducks and swans darken the sunset sky and are your companions on the water for the night. □

Note: If you are farther offshore to start with, say, for instance, bound southward from Poole's Island Light, be aware that tugs with tows don't necessarily stick to the channels, and may often cut across the angle between the Brewerton Channel and the Tolchester Channel.

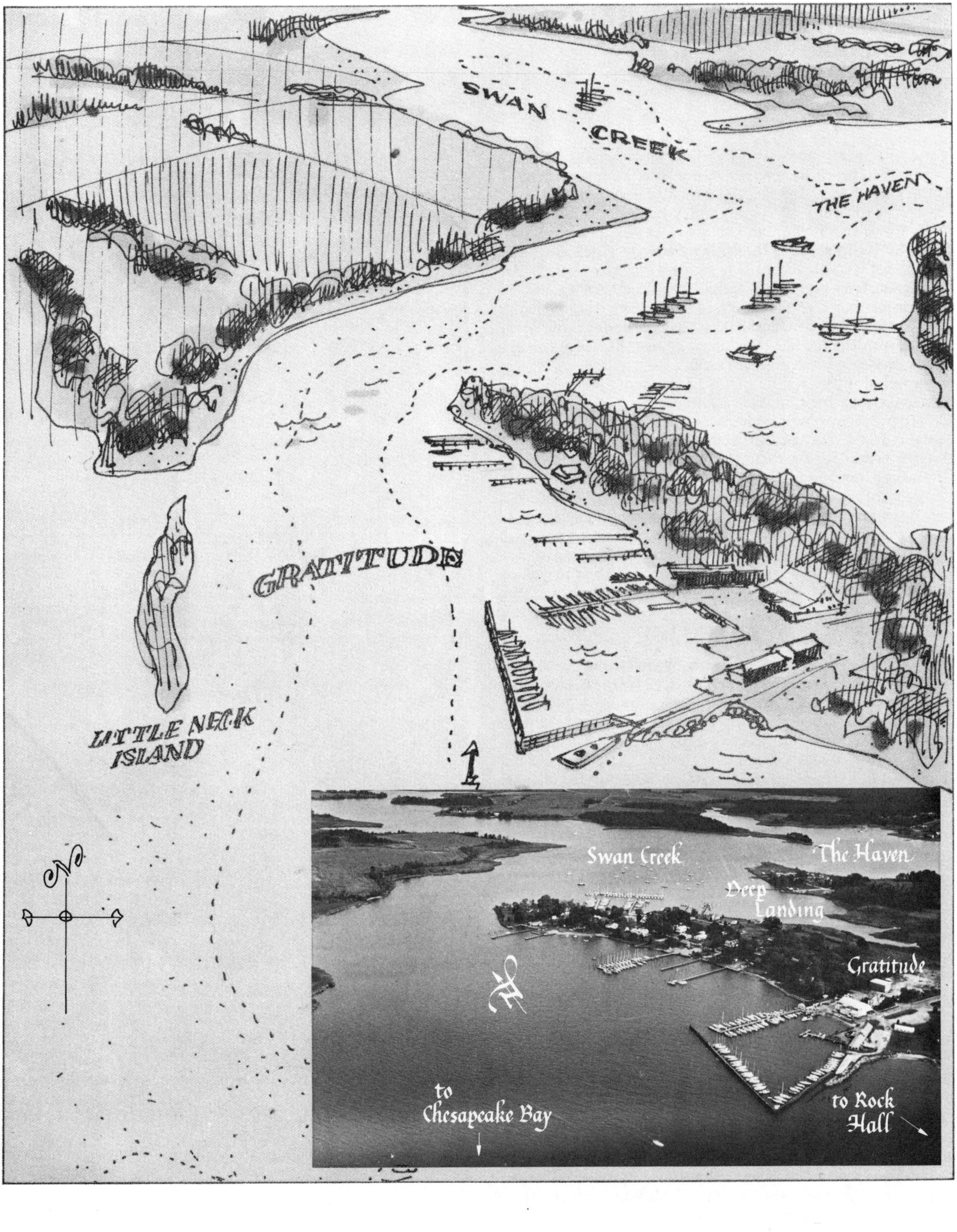

PHOTO BY BOB GRIESER

ROCK HALL

north of the Chester River

In Colonial times, George Washington, Thomas Jefferson, James Madison, Tench Tilghman and many others often eased the arduous overland journey between Philadelphia, New York and Boston and southern centers of population such as Williamsburg by sailing between Rock Hall and Annapolis.

Sailing ferries no longer operate from Rock Hall's protected harbor just north of the mouth of the Chester River, close by the open waters of Chesapeake Bay. Nowadays, the main business in the harbor is fishing, just as it has been for 250 years. But new and remodeled facilities and a dredging project completed in the spring of 1982 have made Rock Hall an attractive port for cruising yachtsmen.

To get there, navigate the Swan Point Bar as you would to enter Swan Creek, except from the Huntingfield Point red flasher head 050° past Can "1" and through the lighted entrance, or from Can "5" head 120° to Can "1" before turning to pass through the stone jetties.

Be aware that the harbor entrance and the channels inside have changed over the past several years. The stone jetties which protect the harbor from the northwest and west have been raised and their orientation changed slightly to reduce the surge in the harbor when the winds from those directions are strong, as they often are in fall and winter. And the north jetty has been given a dogleg, to shelter the opening into the harbor.

The preferred channel is now the north channel which has been dredged to a depth of 7 feet. Once inside the new opening you can proceed on a heading of 010°, honoring daymarks around the fringe of the harbor and passing a succession of marine facilities offering repair capabilities, marine stores, slips, gas, diesel and ice until you come to the docks and red buildings of The Sailing Emporium, at the end of the channel on the south side. Bay cruisers inform us of an unmarked shoal near this area. Sources advise that after the last red marker, stay close to port until the gas dock is to starboard, and then make your approach.

Or you can use the old channel, now marked with daymarks 2E through 6E, by proceeding from the opening of the jetties toward the Mobil sign on Hubbard's dock.

If you have a yen for some fresh fish, crabs or oysters (depending on the season), tie up and head for either Hubbard's or Rock Hall Seafood. If you have time to order a few hours ahead, Mr. Cain at Cain's Crab House, steams especially well-seasoned crabs.

The only rocks in Rock Hall are those brought in to build the jetties. The origin of the town's name is lost in history. This does not discourage most people from giving you an "explanation," however. One is that "rock" referred to oyster shells. Great numbers were brought in by the watermen, and when the shells were piled up in front of a particular building, it became known as Rock Hall, which then gave its name to the town. I'm told that hearing this reasoning causes some townspeople great merriment. These people insist the town is named after the rock fish harvested by Rock Hall fishermen. But this idea makes some people laugh, too. ☐

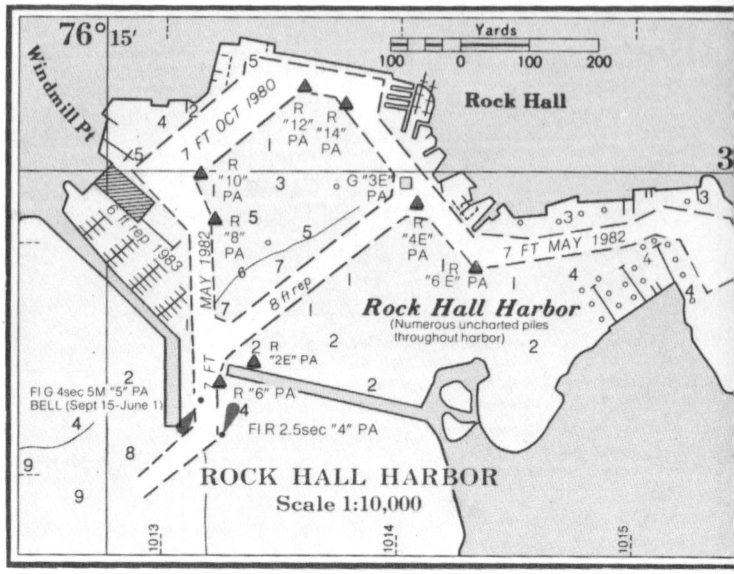

From NOAA Chart 12278—not to be used for navigation.

Notes

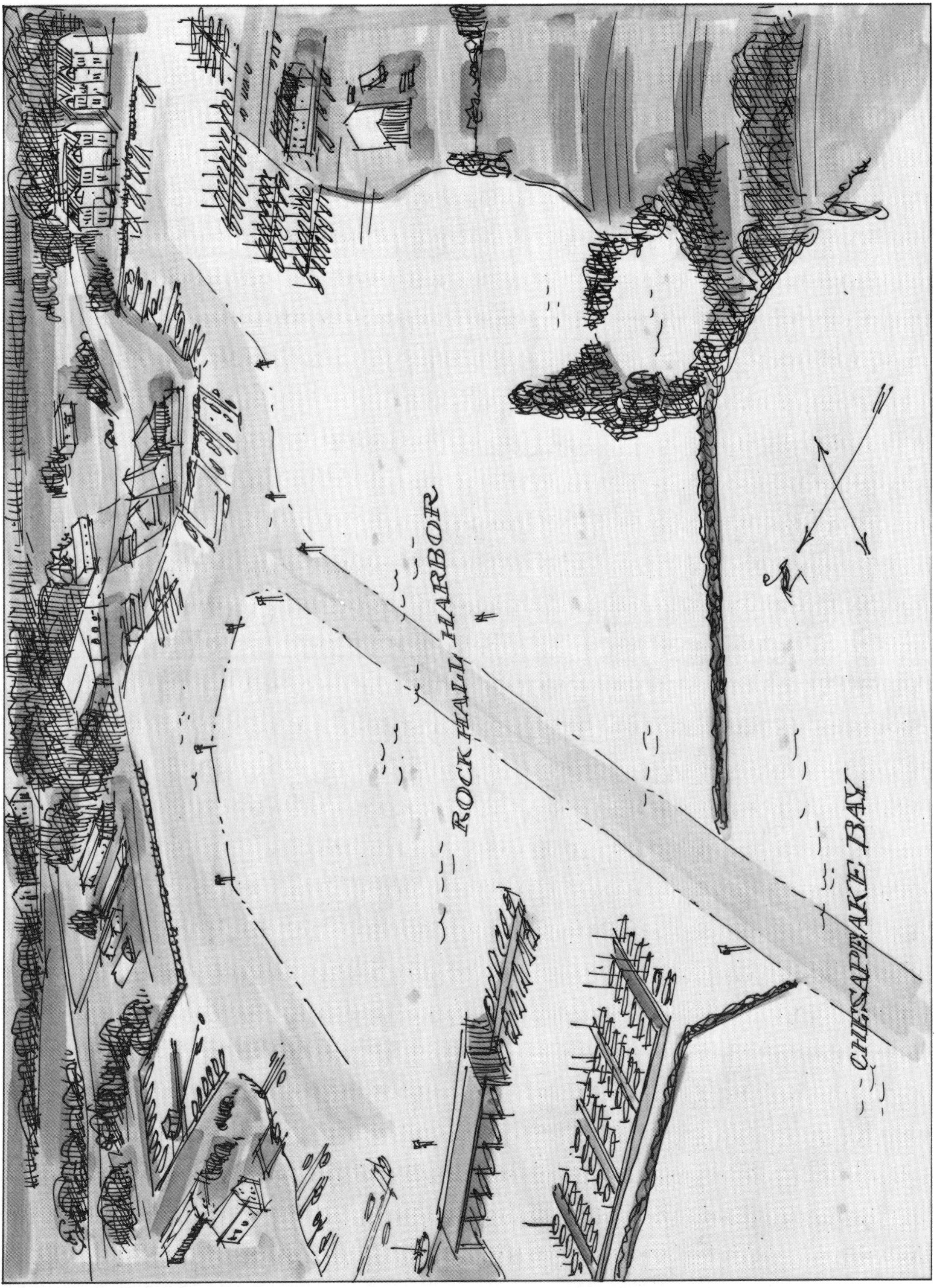
ROCK HALL HARBOR
CHESAPEAKE BAY

COMMON USEFUL KNOTS

SQUARE OR REEF KNOT
Properly tied (with the parallel lines coming out on the same side as shown) this knot will not slip or jam. It is most frequently used for tying two lines of the same size together or two ends together.

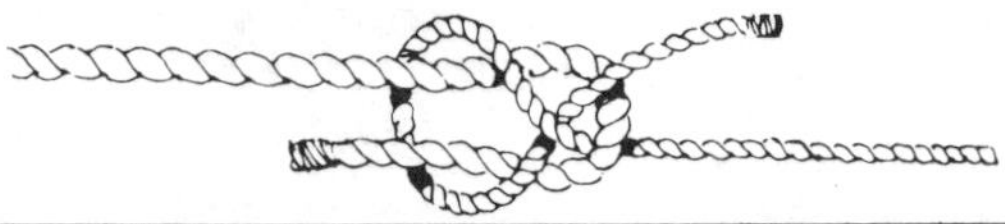

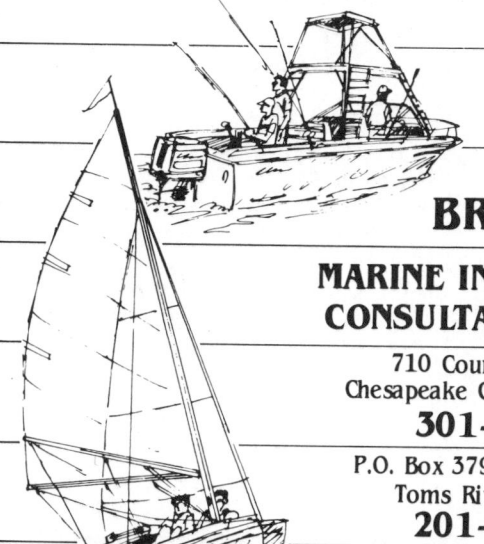

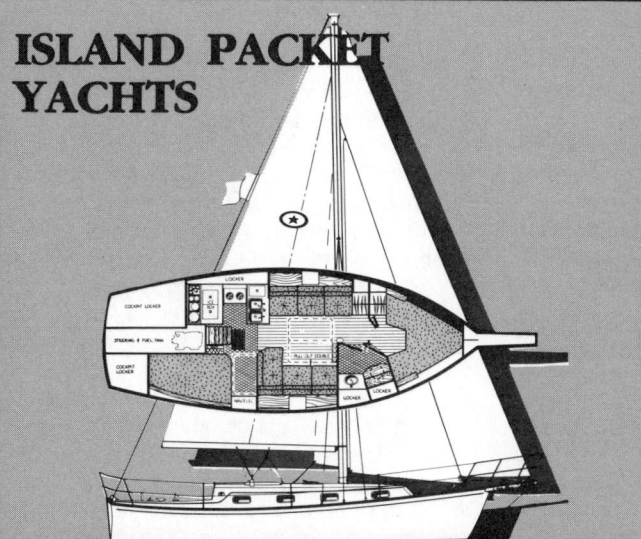

A Walking Tour of
ROCK HALL

by Andi Manchester

If people are shaped by what they eat, then towns are shaped by where they're located. Close to the mouth of the Chester River, Rock Hall is only a few-hours' sail away from popular Bay towns, near inland routes to major cities, and close to some of the best fishing in the area. Smitten with the Bay's bounties, a group of English settlers founded this fishing village in 1707. In colonial times it was a landing for the Annapolis-Rock Hall Packet used by prominent figures like George Washington and Tench Tilghman (he came through town in 1781 en route to Philadelphia with news of the British surrender at Yorktown). Later it was the terminus of an auto ferry between Rock Hall and Baltimore. Over the years Rock Hall has earned a reputation as The Seafood Capital of Kent County and in 1916 was a focal point of the area's oyster industry. In fact, it is claimed that during one period 1,000 skipjacks and bugeyes worked in the surrounding waters. But time takes its toll and modern fishing vessels have long since replaced those classic sailing ships. Lured by its convenient proximity to nearby towns and anchorages as well as to fine spots to cast a hook, recreational boaters and sport fishermen have discovered this port and have made their mark on the harbor's orientation.

Rock Hall's congenial harbor is entered rather dramatically through an opening between two rock jetties which protect the water and shoreline beyond. Once inside, a collage of waterside endeavors unfolds including marinas, restaurants, two condominium apartment buildings, commercial docks and lush wetlands. With all this vying for your attention you'd better keep track of the markers. The dredged channel may be friendly but the water depth elsewhere is apt not to be as kind to your boat bottom or your sense of humor. This is an active port with a relaxed parade of cruisers, sailboats, charter boats (for fishing and vacationing) and commercial fishermen constantly coming and going.

Several fine marinas ring the shore and offer a variety of amenities. Since Rock Hall's emphasis is on its harbor, most things are close at hand. If the walking distance from your marina into town is intimidating, tie up at the conveniently located public wharf and start your excursion from there or your marina may offer its guests complimentary use of a courtesy car. If you prefer pedal power to walking, the Mariners Motel advertises bicycle rentals as does The Sailing Emporium. Three miles east of town is Remington Farms, a wildlife research center open to the public, while six miles south is Eastern Neck Wildlife Refuge (a popular R&R spot for migrating birds) whose trails and roads are open to the public most of the year.

With fishing dominating the economy, it is no surprise that several restaurants featuring the local catch overlook the harbor. These include The Waterman's Crab House (part of Rock Hall Seafood which also offers carry-out service), Fur, Fin & Feather Inn, Hubbard's Pier and Seafood and Swan Point Inn (a bit more elegant than the others). Except for Swan Point Inn (which serves a Sunday brunch), these restaurants all serve breakfast. Since they cater to watermen as well as to tourists, they open EARLY in the morning to accommodate their customers' work schedules. Keenly aware that an inconvenienced boating diner is likely to opt for on-board eating, most restaurants offer free dockage to patrons arriving by water and free taxi service to and from marinas.

If you are like us, eating meals out is more the exception than the rule. Eating in, on the other hand, has us constantly running out of staples (like milk, bread and M&M's). Reprovisioning the galley is no problem, although carrying distance may limit your purchases. Farthest from the water is the Shore Stop Deli. Its left side is a well-stocked convenience store with a fresh deli counter; the right part is a do-it-yourself, eat-in-or-carry-out restaurant serving fried chicken, salads, subs, sandwiches and drinks. A service bar, complete with a microwave oven for food warming, offers accoutrements, and you can eat at one of the four snack tables in a cheerful dining nook. A little closer to shore is Bayfitters (formerly Clark's), a small supermarket whose deli department also makes sandwiches. Since Bayfitters is the home of Rock Hall's only fresh bakery, we decided to see if lack of competion resulted in inferior baked goods. Result: if you are in the mood for a fresh donut or pastry, it's worth the walk to get it. Nearer still to the harbor is George Myer's Grocery, reminiscent of an old-fashioned neighborhood shop with cartons of fresh fruit and vegetables on the sidewalk out front. If your menu calls for fresh seafood prepared on board by your favorite chef, try Cain's Wharf, Rock Hall Seafood or Hubbard's Pier and Seafood for your entree. Hubbard's retail store (in a separate building from their restaurant) advertises a full line of seafood though their specialty is clams. Each week they ship this delicacy to markets as far north as New England. In contrast to Hubbard's, Rock Hall Seafood's retail store is adjacent to their restaurant and offers a wide variety of seafood both raw and cooked. The real treat for us though was going behind their main building to see their soft shell operation. Over a dozen bins of peelers in various stages of the sloughing cycle are checked, re-sorted and culled hourly. It is fascinating to watch and the friendly staff patiently answered all of our questions and explained the process to us.

If you venture into town you'll discover the "downtown" is more an idea than a reality. There is a Main Street where a few businesses are clustered. Aside from Bayfitters and Myer's, there is a beauty salon, a video rental store, a restaurant and bar, a woman's apparel shop, a sloughing house and several other enterprizes. (The sloughing house is unique because it is located so far from shore. Instead of pumping Bay water through the bins, water stored in underground tanks is pumped through special filters and recirculated through the system.) There are other streets where you can find laundromats (there are two in town, Boulter's and Rainbow) and hardware (Dowling's in the downtown area is a full service retailer selling general hardware, lawn and garden supplies).

Need a specific marine hardware? Try the Rock Hall Marine Railway. With its dozens of cubbies and shelves full of all things imaginable, you're sure to find what you need. Looking

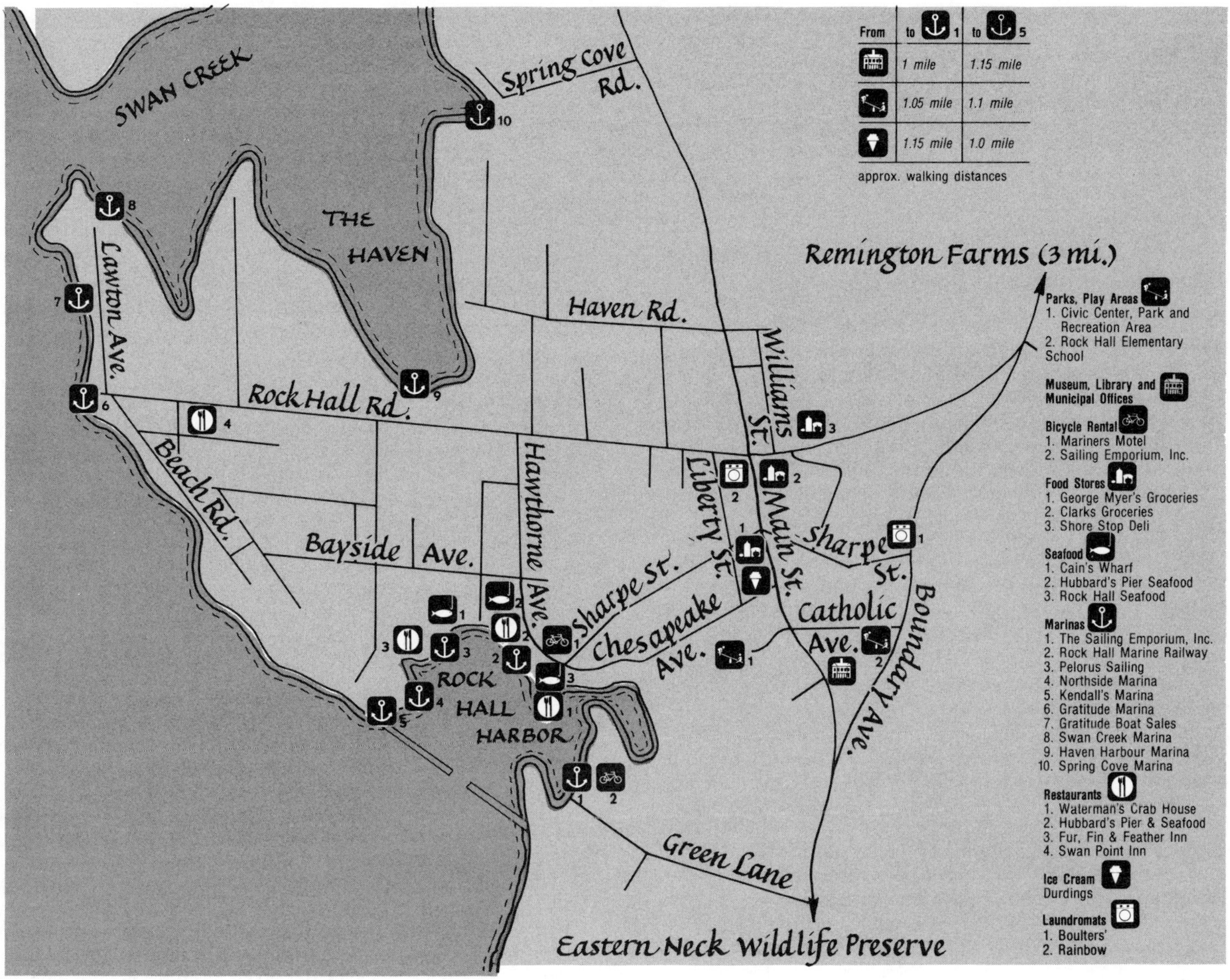

Rendering of author's map by Joan Machinchick

or a gift store? Try the Sailing Emporium. It is delightful inside and out. Inside is an interesting selection of items from canvas carry-alls to napkins and clothing. Outside we found a beautiful mural by the well known artist, Jack Schroeder. Designing the Maryland Duck Stamp and being an artist for the Smithsonian Institution are only two of his accomplishments. He has turned the side of the Sailing Emporium's main building into a huge chart of the Chesapeake Bay and its environs.

Rock Hall simplifies itself for the visitor by offering several guides catagorizing and locating local businesses and services. Listed under "Provisions and Sundries" is Durding's store, although if it were up to me I'd list it under "Ice Cream." In the name of research, we settled ourselves at the soda fountain for a milkshake, cones and ice cream soda. On a hot summer day, it was truly a pause that refreshed!

If exploring local artifacts sounds appealing, the Rock Hall Museum is for you. It is located in the red brick Municipal Building that once served as Rock Hall's elementary school. Although most of the classrooms have been converted into offices, two have been combined to house the museum. Items on display range from boat models to a sausage stuffer, paintings to oyster tongs, quilts to china.

A popular "happening" in the boating world is the "In-the-Water Boat Show" and in May, 1985, Rock Hall added its name to the roster of towns that host such events with its first annual show. Another heartily celebrated annual event is the Fourth of July. Festivities start on Independence Day with a parade, running race, and contests (like whistling with crackers in your mouth and pie eating contests) and are followed by an annual fish fry at the firehouse. July is also the month in which the Rock Hall Yacht Club holds its annual regatta. on the Chester River. Bands add their special flavor to this day of sail and log canoe racing. Remington Farms holds hunting and fishing demonstrations in September. As nature's finale to the boating season, geese and swan return to winter on the Eastern Shore in October, an awesome ritual to both see and hear.

Rock Hall's harbor may be familiar to boaters but the town probably isn't. If you want to reprovision, do laundry, sample the local culinary prowess, ruin your diet on ice cream, buff up on regional history, relax or explore, Rock Hall will hospitably welcome you. If you need more information, the Kent County Chamber of Commerce (301-778-0416) will happily be of help. ☐

BODKIN CREEK

on the Patapsco River

The Seven Foot Knoll Light serves as a useful marker for shipping in and out of the Patapsco River. And, for boaters approaching from up the Bay, it also provides a guidepost into Bodkin Creek. The Bodkin has been called one of the three best anchorages above Gibson Island on the western shore of the Chesapeake. (Sue Island and Rock Creek being the other two.)

Recently Dixie and I decided to visit the Bodkin, a natural stopover on a trip up the Bay. From the Bay Bridges we headed for Baltimore light off the mouth of the Magothy River. From there our course took us north, staying well west of the buoys of the Craighill ship channel.

The late August sun was broiling hot, and the wind was non-existent; so under awning, we motored by the four-plus miles of beautiful country shoreline which stretches from Gibson Island to the Bodkin. And as we motored, my mind went back several years to when I had travelled south along this lovely shoreline under very different conditions.

It was during the time when Dixie and I lived on the upper Magothy. Our next-door neighbor, Fred Mason, bought a used sailboat, a Contest 25, located on the Bohemia River. So, on a mild early spring day, Fred and I sailed it back to the Magothy River where it would be permanently moored.

As we passed the mouth of the Bodkin I noted that it was beginning to get dark. I wished we could put in there for the night. True, we were only three hours from home; but with dark coming on, I was frankly getting tired.

Well, Fred didn't suggest putting in, and so I didn't either, not wanting to appear over-cautious and all that balony. As it turned out, it would have been better to have laid over in the Bodkin.

We were about halfway down the coast when darkness closed in. And with it came a freshened breeze. The little boat was moving nicely now under the big genoa. Maybe we could get home a little before midnight.

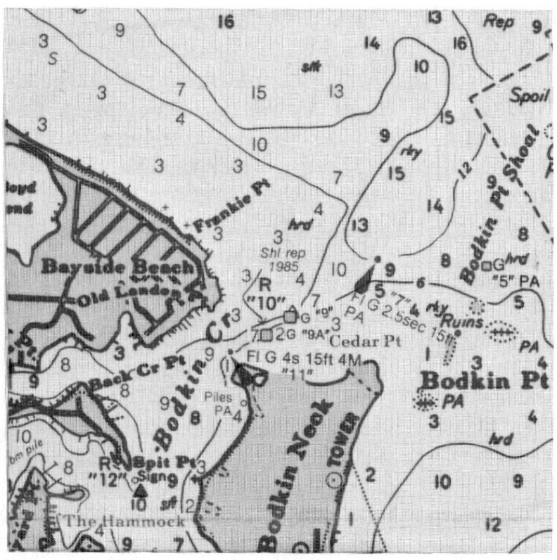

From NOAA Chart 12278—not to be used for navigation.

Gradually the intensity of the wind increased. Then lightning flashed across the black sky. The friendly lights along the shoreline were blotted out by sheets of driving rain. By this time we were bundled in heavy sweaters and foul weather gear. We hunched down in the cockpit and searched to pick up the flashing buoys. "This is insane," I thought to myself. "What am I doing out here?"

Then there was a particularly sharp gust, and a tearing sound from the genoa. Our spotlight showed a six-foot tear right down the middle of the sail!

Fortunately, the rain stopped just as abruptly as it had begun. But it was no simple feat for him to crab his way onto the wet foredeck and grapple—in the dark—with the wildly flapping genoa. If the wind grabbed it at the wrong time, it could easily carry Fred off the deck into the dark waters.

Once the big sail was doused and the smaller working jib hoisted, the boat calmed down. We sailed to the mouth of the Magothy and broad-reached up the river and home.

Returning to the present, I remembered several people warning of shoaling at the entrance to the Bodkin. Also, looking at the charts you will note that Bodkin Point shoals out a considerable distance toward the ship channel. We skirted the shoal and then followed the marks—"3", "5", and "7"—to the Bodkin's entrance. Most warnings we received were of shoaling around daymarks "9" and "11". We carefully motored around red daymark "10" and then "9" and found that with "9" is a "9A" before "11", which is located on a dolphin. We draw nearly five feet and came in on a moderate tide with no grounding.

Most cruising people recommend two anchorages on the Bodkin. One, on the east side of the main branch just across from Spit Point, is in the little cove above Old Bee Point. The second is farther upstream at Jubb Cove. Both are attractive and have good holding ground. On this trip we decided to explore Back Creek, the northern branch of the Bodkin.

As we motored toward Hickory Point (another favorite anchoring spot), we touched lightly on the shoal at its eastern side. We backed off easily and motored upstream; and although this is an attractive creek, I began to see why it was not a favorite of visiting cruising boats. The shoreline narrows considerably, and homes and piers crowd the water's edge. Depths, however, are good, ranging from eight to nine feet with no other serious shoals. We motored another half mile upstream of Hickory Point and anchored at the bend of the creek.

There are two main facilities on the Bodkin. One is the Hammock Island Marina, homeport to a congenial group of sailors. The other is Ventnor Marine, just past Graveyard Point. This almost entirely powerboat facility has gas and diesel fuel, water, ice, a ship's store, and repair service.

The best and most picturesque anchorages may be on the main body of the Bodkin and up in Jubb Cove; but as thoughts of previous storms flash through my mind, perhaps I would feel safer in the snug confines of Back Creek. Either way, the Bodkin is an attractive creek and deserves a visit—and a re-visit. □

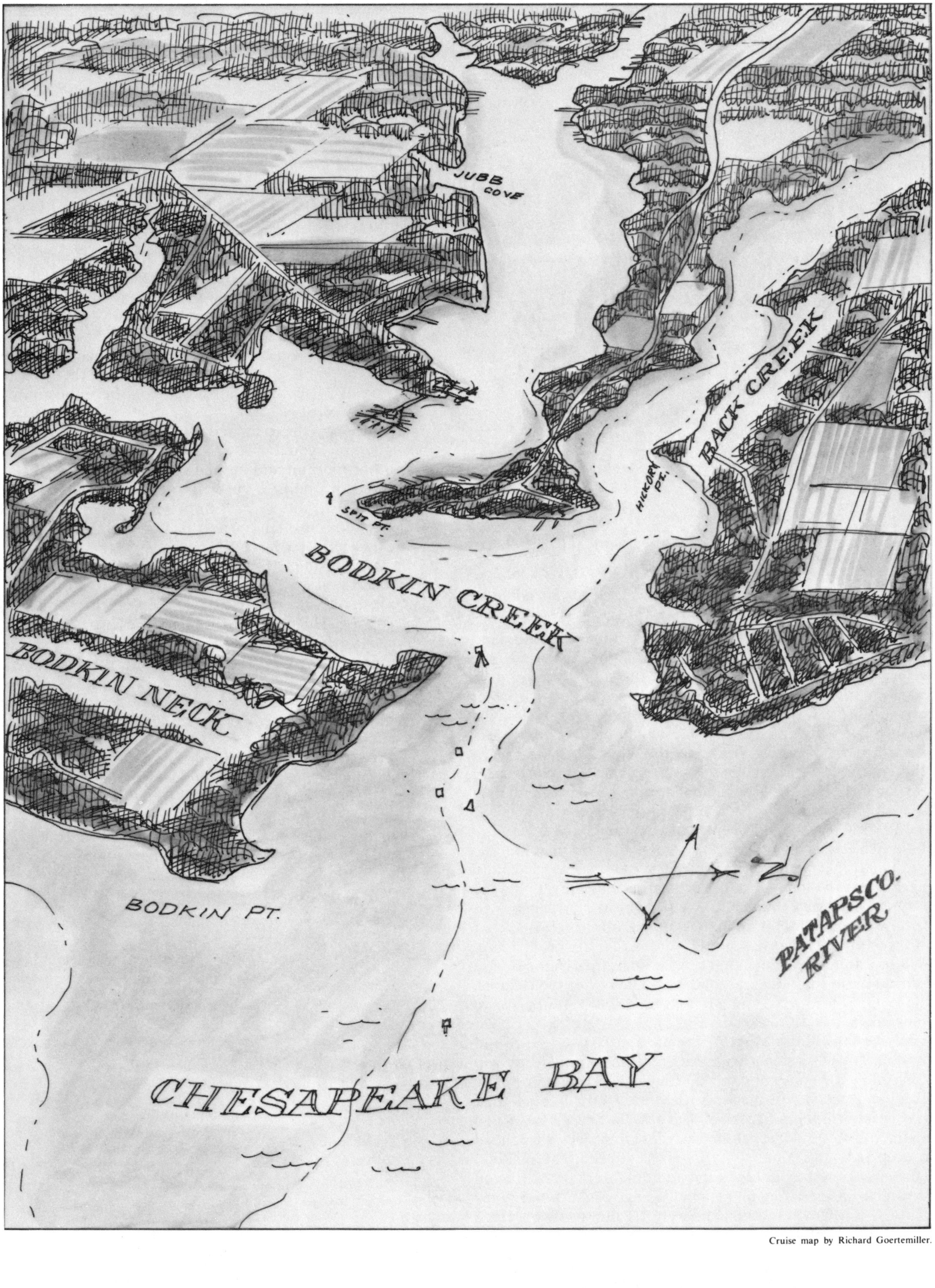

Cruise map by Richard Goertemiller.

ROCK CREEK

on the Patapsco River

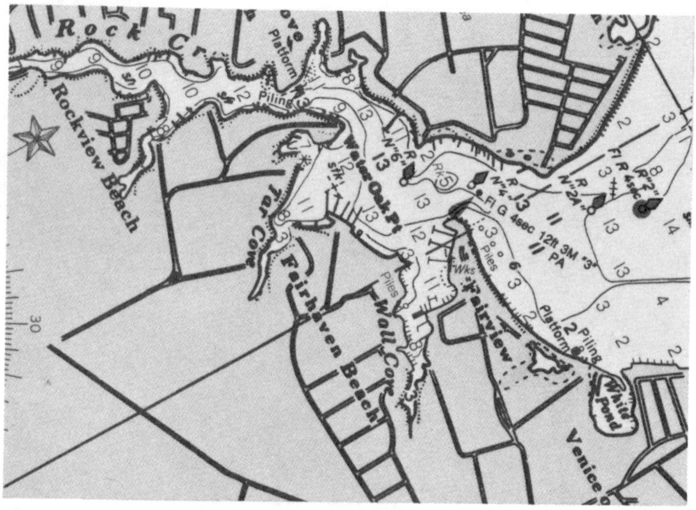

From NOAA Chart 12278—not to be used for navigation.

I seem to remember that the first lighthouse in Maryland was Bodkin Light, built about 1822. Before that time, the American Coast Pilot would direct the ship's captain with phrases such as "look for the high bank to port—a white house—large walnut tree—white rocks—etc." Times have changed, new lighthouses have been built, but the white rocks are still there. These, of course, are the White Rocks that mark the entrance to Rock Creek, across the Patapsco from Sparrows Point. The area is familiar to me because my family used to frequent nearby Alpine Beach when I was a child.

Rock Creek, largest center of yachting activities on the Patapsco River, offers three fairly good-sized marinas and the prestigious Maryland Yacht Club. The creek is easy to identify because of the formation of rocks at its entrance. From the Bay, an easy way to avoid any shoals on the Patapsco is to follow the major ships' channels upstream. You'll find that Brewerton Channel has paired buoys that are easy to see. While I don't recommend getting in the ship's channel, you can do as we did—stay a good half-mile out of the channel, close enough so that you can read the buoys' numbers with binoculars.

Entering the Patapsco from the south, you will round Bodkin Creek's outer marks, leaving them to port. Here you can follow the buoys of Craighill Channel curving in from the Bay, and which will merge with Brewerton Channel. Just northeast of Bodkin Creek you will pass the Seven-Foot Knoll Light, a large, circular lighthouse whose iron sides are painted a deep red. This squat structure is easy to spot and makes a convenient marker. Entering the Patapsco from the north you can pick up the Craighill Channel Range Light, a tall, four-sided tower which is approximately 2¼ miles east of North Point. From either direction you will have a prominent light structure for guidance.

The important thing to note when heading for Rock Cree is the North Point shoal, which extends from the eastern sid of the creek's entrance, northward toward the Brewerto Channel. Using extreme caution, we followed the chann marks till we reached flashing red "4-B," then took a course c 254°. This led us right to the white rocks at the creek's mout a little over two miles distant. From here the entrance is snap.

Once past the rocks and the small fleet of fishing boats tha surround it, you'll pick up the red nun, and just beyond tha another red nun and lighted spar off the point at Fairview Around this point is the well-known Maryland Yacht Club You may be able to pick up a spare mooring there, and th dining room is often open to visiting yachtsmen. Speak to th dockmaster, of course.

Once inside, the creek broadens considerably. To port between Fairview and Water Oak Point, you will see Whit Rocks Marina, which boasts a restaurant and slips wit electricity. There are fuel docks and some supplies, also.

As you round Water Oak Point you will see anothe marine facility, Oak Harbor Yacht Yard. This too is a larg marina with fuel (gas only) and a travel lift. Just beyond this to starboard, you will pass Pasadena Yacht Yard, a somewha smaller facility. They have a railway and lift for haul-outs an repairs.

We wanted a more secluded part of the creek to spend th night, and so far the shoreline was dotted with homes, larg and small. Just past Pasadena Yacht Yard we found a snu little cove on the port side that suited us fine. Although ther were homes all around us in the cove, the wooded banks lent a air of privacy as we settled down for dinner. □

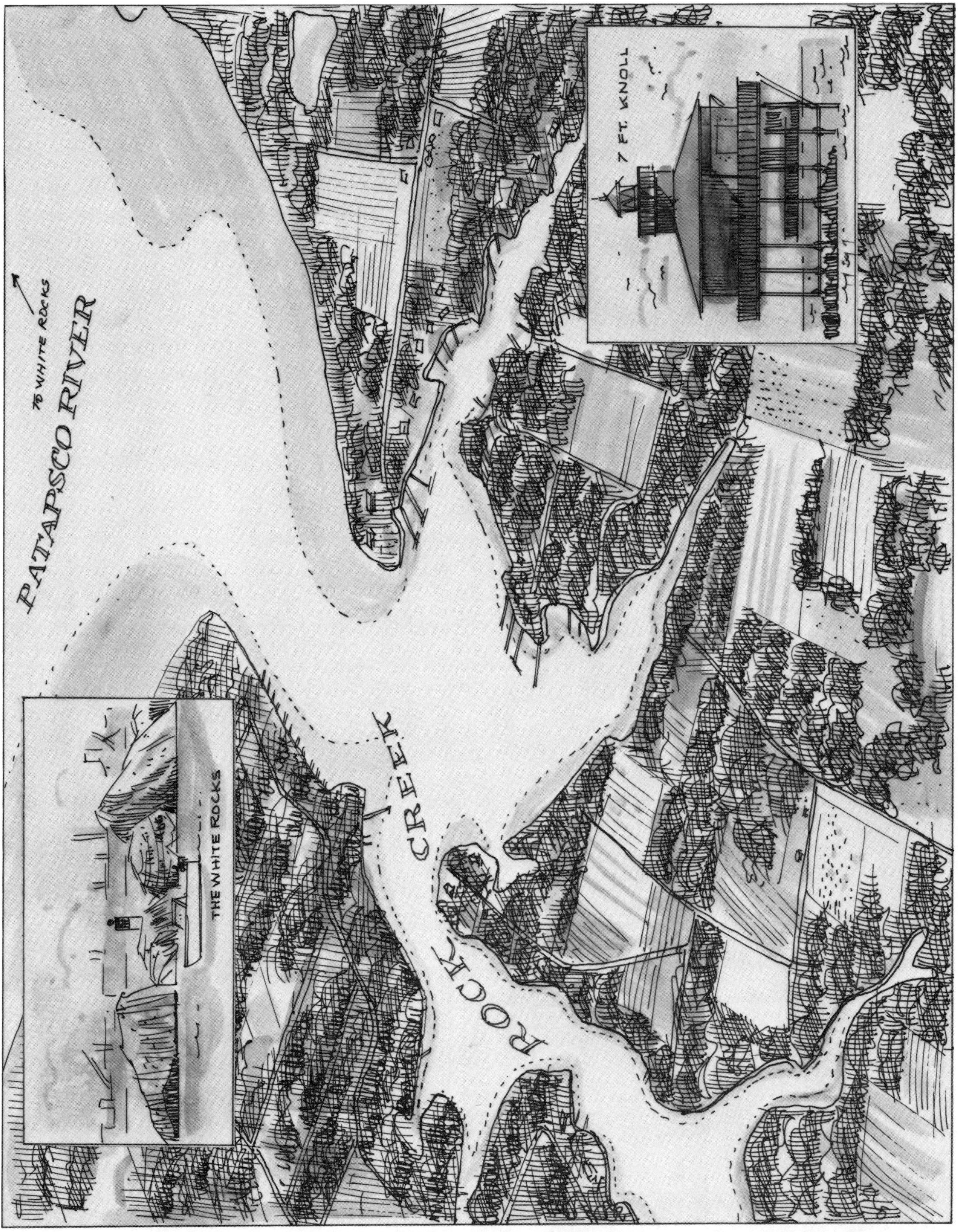
PATAPSCO RIVER
TO WHITE ROCKS
ROCK CREEK
7 FT. KNOLL
THE WHITE ROCKS

STONY CREEK

On the Patapsco River

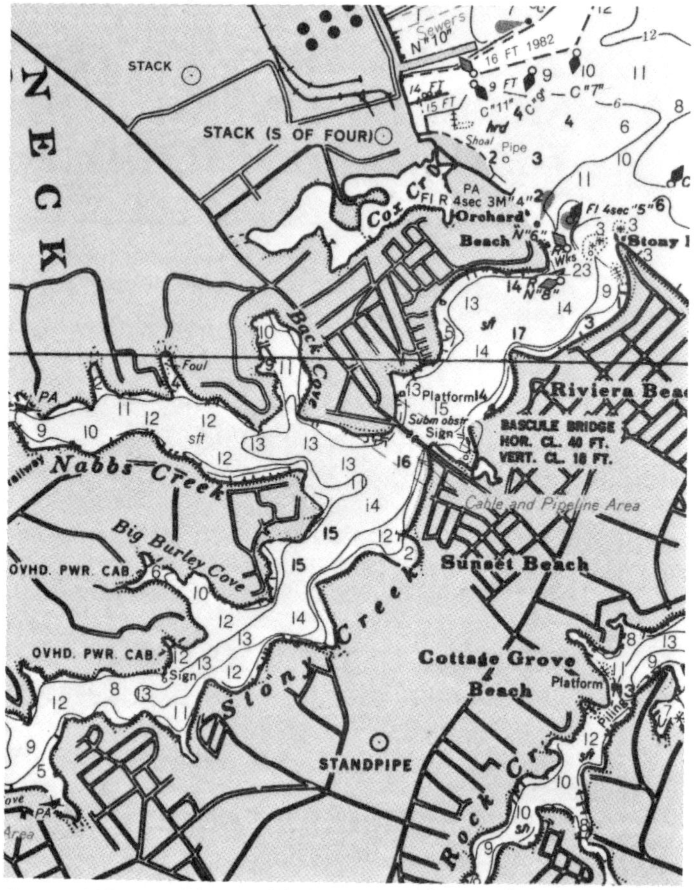

From NOAA Chart 12278—not to be used for navigation.

The line of buoys marking the shipping lanes into Baltimore is among the most recognizable navigation aids on the Bay. Boaters coming from north and south should have little difficulty picking up the entrance to the Patapsco River. Nevertheless, the river is not numbered among the favorite cruise sites of most boaters, and it is only the delightful reward of Baltimore's Inner Harbor that makes the trip worthwhile.

Surprisingly, there are several welcome reliefs from the commercialism of an international port, and Stony Creek is one of them. The creek is located on the southwest side of the Patapsco, 5 miles above Bodkin Point and it has depths of 12 feet or more almost to its head.

The easiest way to find Stony Creek is to follow the line of buoys up the Patapsco. Since there is ample water on either side of the shipping lanes, it is neither necessary nor prudent to stay within the lanes.

Proceed upriver until you reach R "4B" (FL R 4 sec). From this buoy, a course of 270° M will take you to N "2", 2.3 miles away off Stony Creek. From there, it is .7 of a mile to "4" (Fl R 4 sec) (3-mile visibility) and "5" which mark the creek's entrance. Pick up N "6" and N "8" and you'll be safely in the creek. The east side of the entrance is obstructed by rocks, their various stages of visibility determined by the tide. There has been some shoaling at the creek's entrance, however, there is still ample water.

The drawbridge, .8 of a mile above the creek's mouth, is 40 feet wide with an 18-foot clearance. It will open on call with the exception of one hour during the morning and one hour during the evening rush hours.

Nabbs Creek, a tributary which branches off to the right just above the bridge has depths of 11-14 feet for its one-mile length.

For the most part, the creek has fairly high banks lined with attractive homes and farther upstream some apartment complexes. However, if you should anchor in the lee of the shore in the creek proper and the wind should change direction, a change in location might be needed. We encountered a stiff southwest breeze and found the going quite choppy until we managed to get under the lee of the shore. For more protection you might want to take advantage of the several coves located on Stony Creek, or Back Cove, off Nabbs Creek, which has depths of 10-11 feet.

There are a few marine facilities which provide various repairs, marine supplies, groceries, water and ice. However, Greenland Beach Yacht Basin, to the right just past the bridge, is the only marina supplying fuel. The gas dock hours are 8 A.M.-6 P.M. on weekends and 3 P.M.-6 P.M. on weekdays. Boaters leaving Baltimore's Inner Harbor, where the gas docks close considerably earlier, sometimes take advantage of the facilities at Stony Creek, 7.3 miles from the Inner Harbor.

One of Stony Creek's most serious drawbacks is the lack of any 6 mph speed limits especially near marine facilities. I heard reports of damage and injury as a result of the large wakes on the creek.

All-in-all, Stony Creek provides a delightful respite from the hustle and bustle of the Patapsco. □

PHOTO BY BOB GRIESER

BALTIMORE'S INNER HARBOR

on the Patapsco River

About 6½ miles north from the Magothy River is Seven-Foot Knoll Light. This is a good point of reference since its large, round shape is easy to spot and will be your turning point to head into the Patapsco. Three and a half miles up the Patapsco from Seven-Foot Knoll are the white rocks that mark the entrance to Rock Creek. These rocks rise some 15 feet out of the water and used to serve as navigation aids for early Bay shipping long before lighthouses were constructed here. Now there is a light to warn mariners of their presence. Rock Creek would make a good stop for fuel, supplies, and emergency repairs.

To starboard, about 6 miles from Seven-Foot Knoll Light is Fort Carroll. The fort is a concrete and stone structure standing about one-quarter mile outside of the main channel. Further upstream, you will pass under the Francis Scott Key Bridge, and another three and a half miles upstream the Patapsco will divide—right at Ft. McHenry. The right-hand branch will take you into what the charts call "Northwest Harbor," which terminates in Baltimore's Inner Harbor.

Several marinas in the inner harbor have tie-up facilities. The one with the floating docks on the south shore is privately owned; the other on the west side is city-operated and has fixed piers. In addition, a designated anchorage marked b white buoys is available right in front of the World Trac Center. Holding ground is hard mud in 20-25′ of water. O weekends it is quite crowded, so setting two anchors on Bahamian moor might be a good idea. Leave your dinghy tie up at the city marina.

Good provisioning for food and beverage needs is availab in the 1000 block of Charles Street (west on Pratt Street t Charles, right on Charles)—about one mile from the wate front.

Baltimore's Inner Harbor complexes, together with th Charles Center Plaza in downtown, have been credited wit the rebirth of this major East Coast city. The Inner Harbor main attraction, Harborplace, opened in the summer of 198 and every year the anniversary of its opening is celebrated o July 4th weekend with an elaborate fireworks display. Harbo place consists of two glass-enclosed pavilions located on th corner of Pratt and Light Streets, along the north and we shores of the harbor basin. These buildings house more than 1 eating places, markets and specialty shops.

But there are many other attractions in the Inner Harbo

continued on page 9

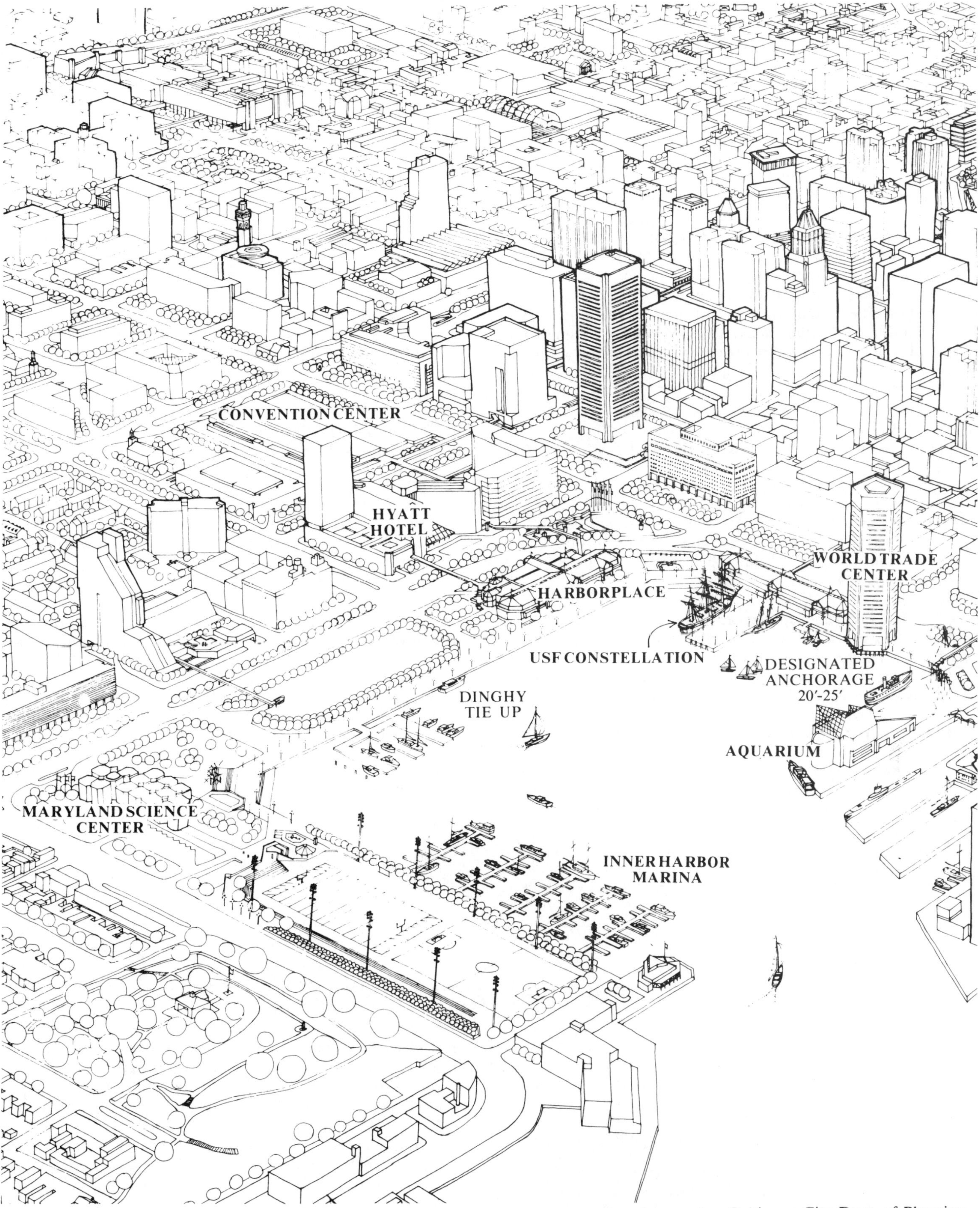

Drawing courtesy Baltimore City Dept. of Planning

The Maryland Science Center [(301) 685-5225] houses a museum and planetarium and is located adjacent to the Inner Harbor Marina [(301) 837-5339], which has 158 slips for visiting and locally-owned private pleasure boats. The Rusty Scupper Restaurant is located next to the Marina, and houses a marine supply store.

The World Trade Center [(301)837-4515] is a 32-story pentagonal office tower that rises 430 feet above the water. The entire 27th floor is devoted to the Top of the World Exhibit Center and public observation deck affording a panoramic view of the entire port and region beyond.

The National Aquarium in Baltimore [(301)576-3810], located on Pier 3 and Pratt Street, is an audio-visual experience of the world of water, featuring over 5,000 marine creatures, dolphins, sharks and seals, as well as a tropical rain forest.

The Pier 6 Pavilion water stage provides a floating bandstand for concerts and theatrical productions that are given during the summer months. Call (301)727-5580 for tickets and the performance schedule.

Inner Harbor summers are also highlighted by a series of international festivals with ethnic foods, entertainment and crafts. The annual Mayor's Inner Harbor Regatta also takes place here. It is reputed to be the largest regatta ever held within the confines of a major American city. The regatta is usually held the third weekend in May. The Baltimore City Fair, usually held the second weekend in September, is also a featured attraction found in the Inner Harbor. It is the largest urban event of its kind held in the country, and is a showcase for Baltimore's "neighborhoods"—Italian, German, Polish, etc.

Docked near the Harborplace pavilions are the U.S. Frigate *Constellation,* the Navy's first commissioned warship and the oldest American warship continuously afloat. Call (301)539-1797 for tour information. The submarine *Torsk*, which sank the last two Japanese warships in World War II, is docked at Pier 4 and Pratt St. Also docked here is the floating lightship *Chesapeake*. Both are open to the public as tourist attractions [(301)396-3854].

The *M.V. Port Welcome* [(301)727-3113] makes its home port at the Inner Harbor right across the street from the famous McCormick Spice Company (which is also open for tours [(301)547-6166]). The *Port Welcome* has a passenger capacity of 500 and cruises to Annapolis, St. Michaels, Havre de Grace, the C & D Canal, as well as around the Inner Harbor. The *Baltimore Patriot* [(301)685-4288] operates from the foot of Constellation Dock. This tour boat is designed especially to take visitors on 1½ hour sightseeing trips around the Port of Baltimore. The *Baltimore Defender* [(301)752-1515] departs from the western finger piers of the Inner Harbor and offers a brief cruise to Fort McHenry, birthplace of the "Star Spangled Banner." Fort McHenry is the scene of many military re-enactments during the summer months, and is accessible by land or water [(301)962-4290]. For a good anchorage in a quiet area, try the cove almost due south of flashing marker #13 in Ferry Bar Channel.

The Hyatt Regency Hotel, located directly across the street from the Light Street Pavilion of Harborplace, is a new and exciting hotel in Baltimore. It is a lavish and convenient way for the cruiser to pamper him/herself. Call (301)528-1234 for reservations.

Also within walking distance or a short cab ride is Little Italy, one of Baltimore's more famous "neighborhoods." It is the location of many fine Italian restaurants.

For those planning a cruise to the Inner Harbor, the above information is just a small portion of the many activities going on in Baltimore. For a very complete visitors package on all of Baltimore's highlights, call the Baltimore Office of Promotion and Tourism at (301)752-8632.

A visiting yachtsman can find the best of both worlds while visiting Baltimore: the convenience and excitement of the Inner Harbor, and the solitude of anchoring in a quiet cove in the Middle Branch of the Patapsco River. Located just around the corner from Ft. McHenry, you will find good water depths and, at present, very little activity. The redevelopment of the Middle Branch area provides many exciting opportunities for boating, aquatic study, and other leisure-time activities. With its less developed shoreline, the Middle Branch complements the more densely developed Inner Harbor, thus offering Chesapeake Bay cruisers a clear choice when visiting the Baltimore area. Long-range plans call for several marinas, shops and eating establishments in this area. The beauty about anchoring in the Middle Branch is that it is still relatively unknown and there is little commercial traffic.

So, if you are in Baltimore, and the nightlife and bright lights of the Inner Harbor are not your thing, consider the Middle Branch as a possible alternative. □

GALLEY TIPS

Keep a small box of baking soda open in refrigerator to absorb odors. If it gets damp or has been used more than a month, dissolve remnant in water to wash refrigerator interior or pour down drain to freshen it.

To add new appeal to your boating fare, swap ideas for good galley meals and snacks with your marina neighbors and cruising acquaintances once in a while. Here's a recipe I wheedled from a friend. Mix cream cheese, horseradish, dry mustard and orange marmalade to make a delicious dip or spread for crackers.

Learn to use a pressure cooker (preferably a 4-qt. size) if you are tired of cooking the same old things, but limited by your galley stove's capabilities. It can increase your repertoire by decreasing cooking time. Easy to use, and big enough to hold a complete dinner for most crews, the kettle (without the pressure gauge) can also be used to cook spaghetti, crabs, or lobsters.

Keep things dry (bread) or clean and dry (towels) in lightweight, inexpensive foam ice chests.

COMFORT TIPS

Make your own sun awning: Buy a king-size sheet (with as high a polyester content as you can find); sew pockets for battens; spray with Scotch-guard-type waterproofing. Use nylon cords or shock cords for tie-downs, and you have an awning that will resist mildew and rot.

Neutralize a jellyfish sting by sprinkling it with Adolph's (or some other brand) meat tenderizer. Try using vinegar to soothe the welts. welts.

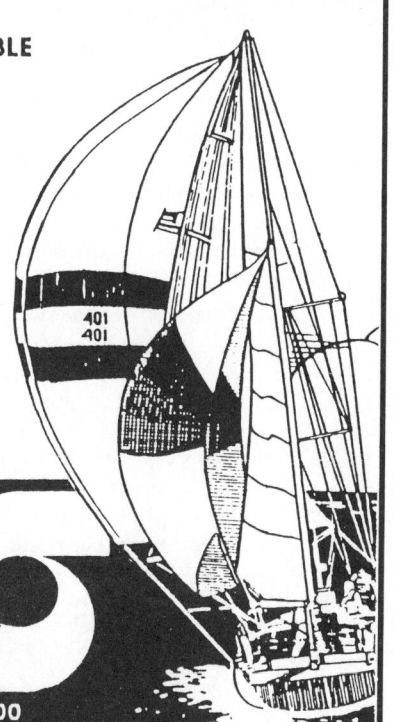

DOBBINS ISLAND

on the Magothy River

For many years the Magothy River was our home river, and we loved it! Unlike most of the tributaries within the Baltimore-Washington area, there is a slower pace here.

We have to admit that the Magothy River presents a problem at its entrance. The channel is only about 200 yards wide, and if several boats arrive at the same time, it is a little tight. But once you squeeze through, the Magothy broadens to allow ample room for any number of boats. There is seldom a racing fleet to conflict with, and the many creeks and coves here absorb the heavy traffic.

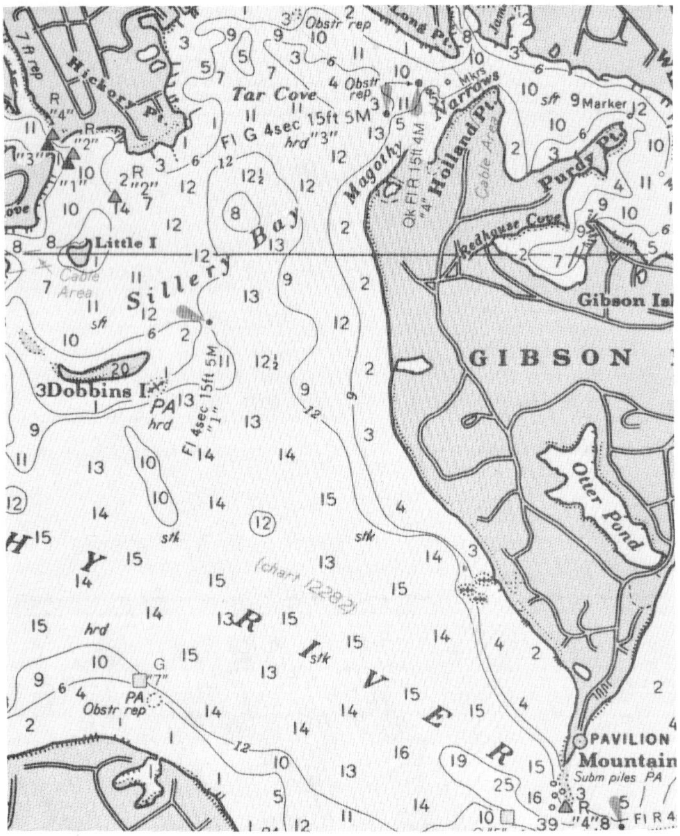

From NOAA Chart 12278—not to be used for navigation.

Although the Magothy shows the signs of nearby population centers, as you poke into its headwaters it is not unusual to find evidence of its early-day trade. Across from Beachwood Park near Riverdale, for instance, lie the rotting remains of the town wharf. The melon boats touched here, it is said, with loads of fruit from the Eastern Shore bound for Baltimore.

The Magothy River has much to recommend it, and here's how to get to one of the best anchorages in this area. The entrance to the river is almost due west of Baltimore Light and is guarded by a black beacon (a large wooden structure about eight feet across) with a flasher on top. There are two red beacons on the starboard side which mark the shoals off Mountain Bar. It is advisable to continue into the river to #5, and leaving it to port, take 339° to the black flasher on the eastern tip of Dobbins Island, about ¾ mile away. One of the most famous anchorages on the northern Bay, Dobbins Island is in Sillery Bay. Also known locally as "Dutch Ship Island," its protective arm encircles the anchorage and breaks any southerly winds.

On its southern side Dobbins shows high red clay banks with a tree topping, but the northern side is more hospitable. Water depths range from 10 to 12 feet, and the holding ground is good. This is the anchorage we recommend.

The island *cannot* be circumnavigated by most cruising boats because of the sandbar which connects its western tip to the mainland. So we remember with glee the looks on startled faces as we gracefully sailed past several folks wading halfway between the island and the mainland in less than knee-deep water! Apparently they had no idea that a 20′ sailboat carrying four adults and a child could quietly pull up the centerboard and, with a light breeze off the port quarter, drift over the bar in less than a foot of water. □

Dobbins Island

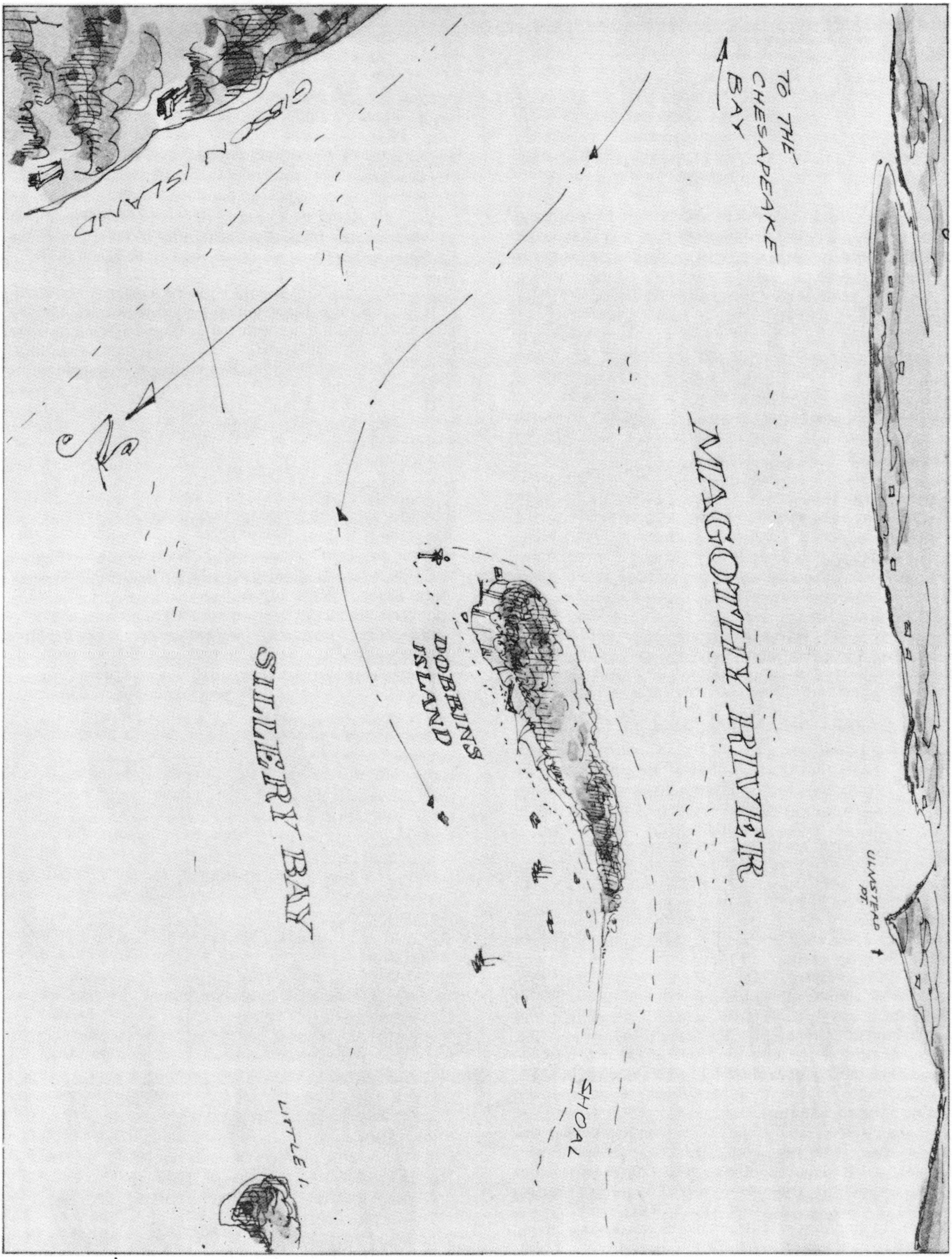
TO THE CHESAPEAKE BAY
GIBSON ISLAND
MAGOTHY RIVER
ULMSTEAD PT.
DOBBINS ISLAND
SILLERY BAY
SHOAL
LITTLE I.

BROAD CREEK

on the Magothy River

Once inside the entrance of the Magothy, which although narrow is well marked, the river offers many creeks and coves to explore. On the north shore the private community of Gibson Island rises high above the water. Many beautiful homes cling to its steep sides, presenting a somewhat Mediterranean atmosphere.

Immediately up river stands Dobbins Island. Perhaps one-half mile long, Dobbins (or Dutch Ship Island, as it is locally known) marks the opening of Sillery Bay. There is a good anchorage here, but go further up the Magothy; there's much good scenery to enjoy.

Almost at the headwaters is Riverdale Restaurant, a restaurant on the Magothy which is very popular with local inhabitants. The traveling yachtsman can tie up to its docks or anchor in its cove and row ashore for a meal. It is famous hereabouts for its seafood, and on weekends it really "jumps."

When you're ready to settle down for the night, go back down the Magothy and try Broad Creek.

Broad Creek is easily accessible and attractive with a couple of good anchorages. From the Magothy River's entrance mark ("The Old Man," as it is known), take course 310° (approx.) to the Broad Creek entrance mark, R "2," a distance of about two-and a-half miles. Broad Creek is better marked now than in our earlier boating days, with daymarks on the two shoals—port and starboard—that nearly close off the creek's entrance. These are both easy to see and getting past these shoals should present no real problems.

As you proceed upstream on Broad Creek there are a couple of shoals that deserve your attention though. To starboard, for instance, you will spot a break in the shoreline and a little cove with a couple of houses. On either side of this cove's entrance there are shoals projecting out toward the creek's main channel. Give them an ample berth.

The worst shoal is on the port side, further upstream. You can see it easily on your charts. If you go slowly and favor the east side of the creek, you should have no trouble.

Broad Creek makes an abrupt right turn just beyond that shoal and reveals a small island. The water around the island is pretty shallow, and on our first visit there we spotted a pole driven in midchannel to warn boaters of the "thin water." After a moment's indecision we chose (correctly) to take the starboard side and curved around into a small cove where we anchored to wait for the other boats in our party. The second boat chose the wrong side of the pole and ran aground. The third boat came to his rescue, threw him a line, and attempted to haul him off, backwards—in other words, the same way he came in.

For some reason the direction of pull on the tow line was such that the rescuer was swung into the shallows himself and was also driven aground. I was preparing to retrieve our anchor and attempt to help when the fourth boat in our party came around the bend and quickly sized up the situation. He threw a line to the would-be rescuer and, giving his engine the gun, jerked him out into deep water—which, in turn, pulled the number two boat off. The three of them, still all strung together, motored over to us and rafted up.

Here, on the south shore of Broad Creek, just opposite the little island, is a pretty little anchorage. The shoreline is unsettled; tall trees come just about to the water's edge. The island across the way is small with some beach (which invites a visit), and a sparse covering of stunted trees.

I have heard of several boats running aground attempting to get up into Broad Creek, and that puzzles me. The first reported grounding occurred at the outside entrance marks, a red and a black. The portside shoal may extend out from the black to some extent, which might have caused them to bump. But the word we have is that if you keep a little closer to the starboard mark, you should have no trouble.

Also, I understand that two boats were a little further upstream and one ran aground, apparently near the small cove just beyond the #2 daymark. (That's possible because we ran aground there as we were leaving, but were able to swing off without much trouble.) The second boat reports they were out where deep water was supposed to be and they, too, ran aground.

As I said, I don't see how that happened. The water should be good enough to carry ten and twelve feet nearly to the head of the creek. But you won't find me arguing with anyone about whether they ran aground or not. I, too, have the ability to go aground even when people say it's impossible to go aground. Still, the bottom here is soft enough to cause no great inconvenience. And with a creek as inviting as Broad Creek, I think it's worth the effort. □

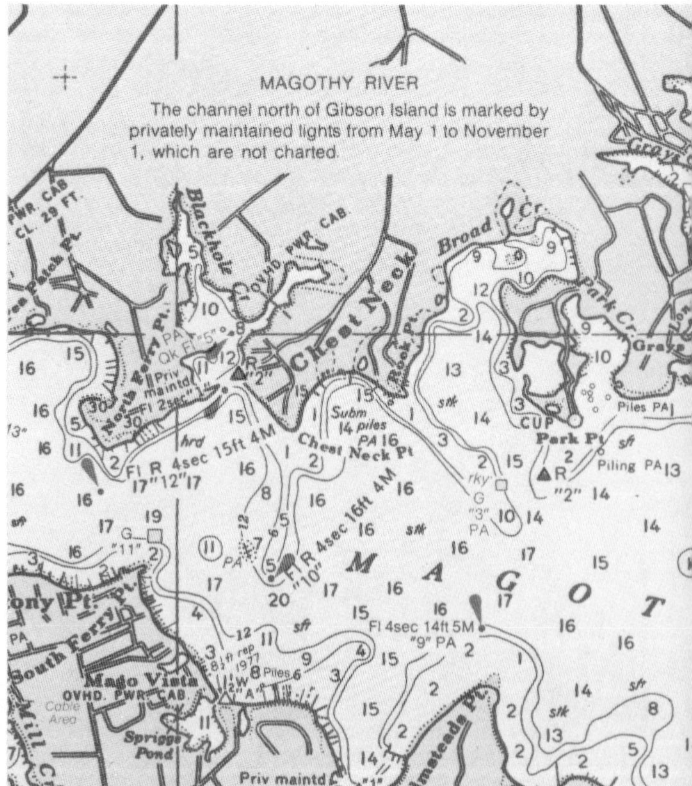

From NOAA Chart 12278—not to be used for navigation.

BROAD CREEK
WE WENT
AGROUND HERE X
PARK PT.
MAGOTHY RIVER
RKS.

THE CHESTER RIVER

Salthouse Cove
Reed Creek
Grays Inn Creek
Corsica River
Cacaway Island
Comegy's Bight
Chestertown
Kent Narrows

Many cruising families who travel the Bay place the Chester River high on their list of prime areas and perfect anchorages.

Upstream, the Chester River, which is the second longest river on the Eastern Shore, displays beautiful countryside and lovely estates to the visitor with time to explore. From old Hail Point where, in Colonial times, merchant ships were inspected, to Chestertown, 26 miles above Kent Island's Love Point Light, the land quietly reflects the personality of the people.

The Chester River above Eastern Neck Island fans out in four reaches, and it is said that only a chart or a local waterman can solve the riddle of where lies the main course. These four branches are Gray's Inn Creek, Langford Creek, the main extension of the Chester, and the Corsica River — each one as inviting as the next to the cruising yachtsman!

The Chester River is broad and beautiful, with an easy-to-follow path of buoys to lead the way upstream from Love Point to the Corsica.

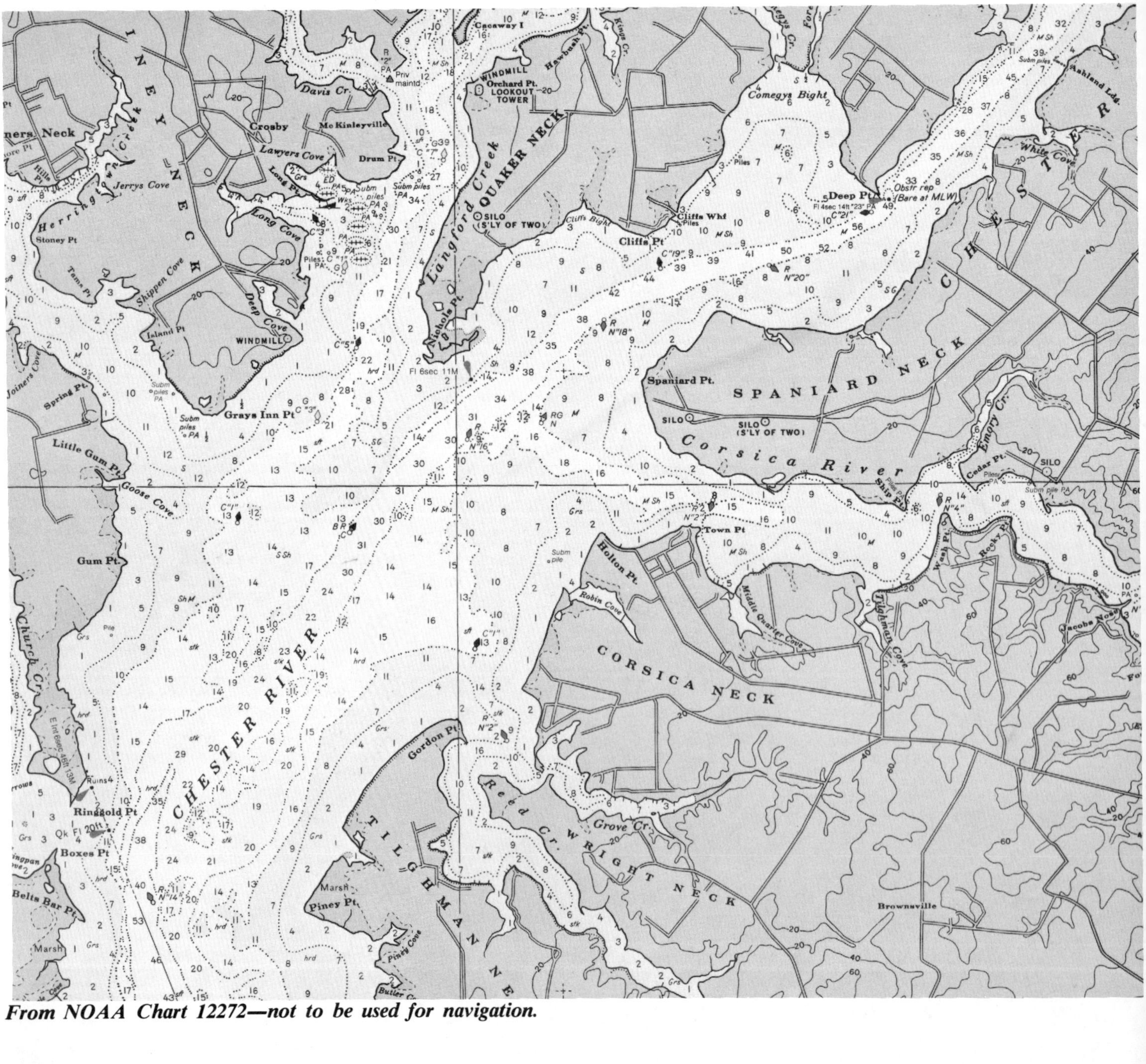

From NOAA Chart 12272—not to be used for navigation.

Love Point Light marks the main entrance to the Chester River between Love Point on the northern end of Kent Island and Eastern Neck Island.

Illustration by Richard Goertemiller

SALTHOUSE COVE

on Queenstown Creek

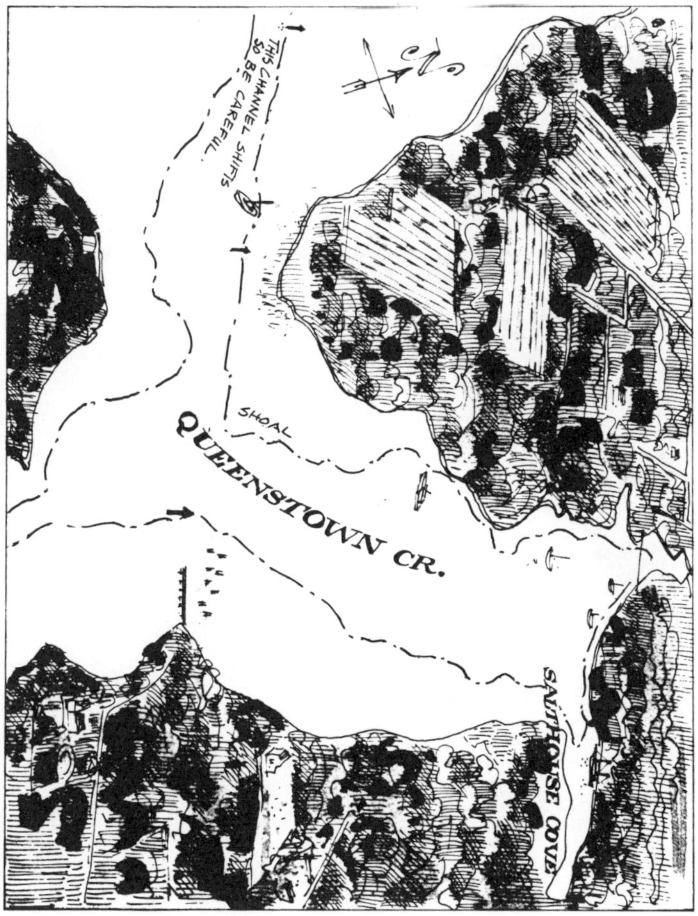

If ever there was a constantly changing channel, it is the one into Queenstown — one of the most popular places on the entire Bay. Hardly anyone who cruises has missed this charming tree-surrounded haven.

As often as our boat has tiptoed in, carefully searching for Queenstown's elusive channel, once inside we've never had any trouble putting down a firm anchor.

Queenstown is still one of the best cruising spots we know of, changing but little over the last ten years. Except the channel that is, which the charts claim has ten feet in spots. The trick is to find where the channel has shifted to. It seems that practically every month the sand bars shift, changing the entrance just enough to trap the unwary.

For a change, instead of anchoring near Queenstown, go all the way up to Salthouse Cove. Here you'll find a lovely body of water with trees overhanging its banks, giving a perfect picture of wilderness seclusion. Water depths in mid-channel range from six feet at the entrance to four feet further upstream. It was late afternoon when our anchor splashed down into the cool green waters. Carefully avoiding occasional jellyfish, we jumped in after it.

There were not more than a half-dozen boats in Queenstown Creek, and as dusk fell we dutifully hoisted our anchor light. This time of day is, to me, the best part of cruising. The wind usually dies to a faint whisper, gathering darkness blurs the countryside, the trees becoming black cutouts silhouetted against an indigo sky. Other boats sharing your anchorage become dim ghost ships, and in the distance a channel marker winks its message to any latecomer. □

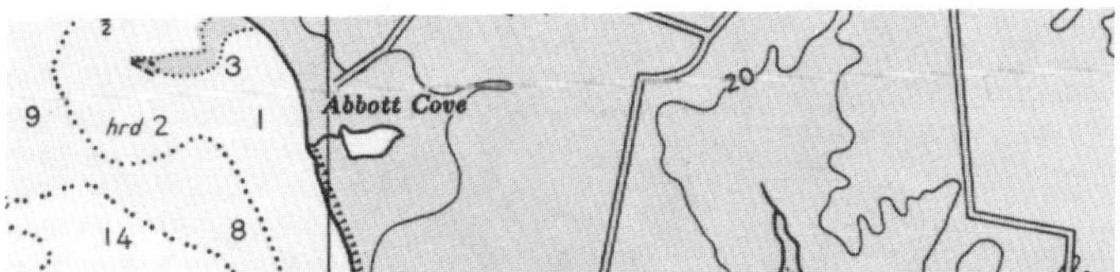

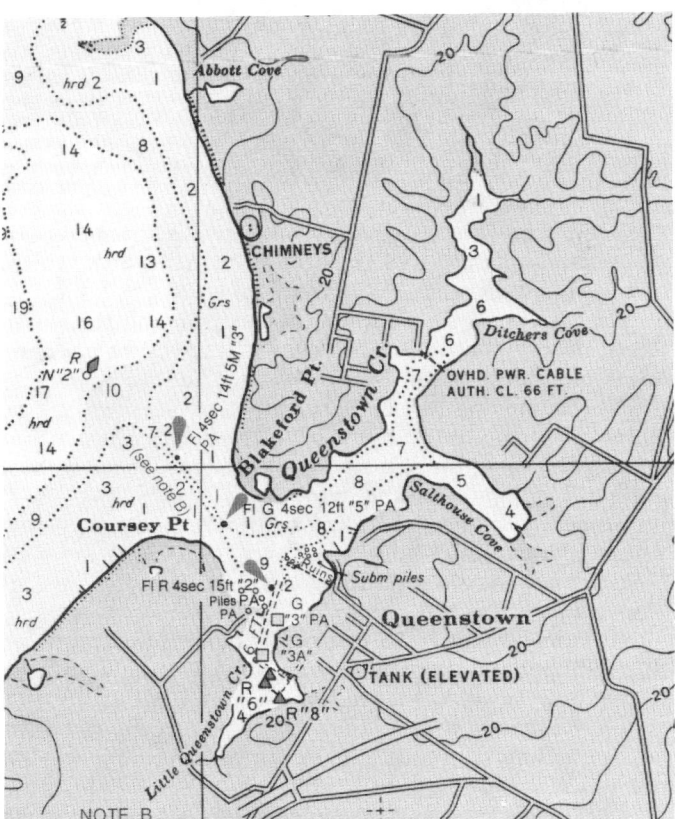

From NOAA Chart 12272 — not to be used for navigation.

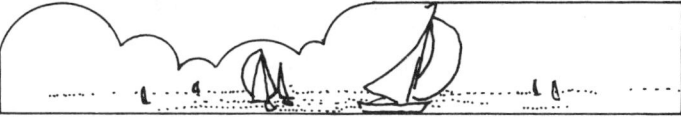

REED CREEK

on the Chester River

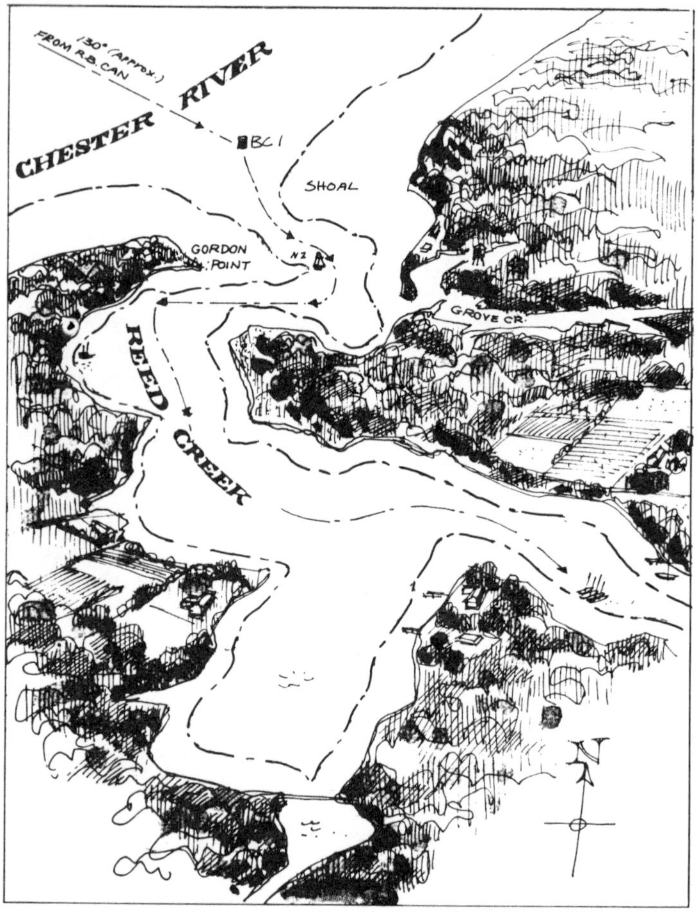

Reed Creek is a spot on the Chester which has not received much attention but which is worth more than a little praise as one of the finest anchorages you could find.

On the east shore between Queenstown and the Corsica River, the entrance to Reed Creek is marked by a black can #1 about one-third mile off shore and a red nun where the shoal marks the opening. We had difficulty locating the black can, which blended into the shoreline; so we used the water tower on shore as something to aim for as we approached from the red and black mid-channel buoy.

Some cruising guides warn against trying the entrance without "local knowledge"; however, the buoys are Coast Guard maintained, and there is no reason to miss the enjoyment of this fine creek.

As you leave the black can astern and line up a range with the red nun, be aware that the shoal on the port side bellies out into your path. We touched bottom with our four-foot keel and found that by bearing to the starboard side until halfway to the nun and then favoring the port side of the channel the rest of the way, we got in easily.

The opening to the creek and the first two bends are somewhat tricky, and our simple solution was to turn due west after we cleared the nun and to head for the bank—you can come in fairly close. Then turn and head due south until the river widens again. From here on to your anchorage just keep to the center.

The water depths at the entrance are mostly seven to ten feet; and once inside, seven-foot depths are carried for a mile or so up the river, with some deeper spots here and there. There is a small bay halfway in, whose shores are lined with three or four very large homes.

On past this bay about a quarter of a mile further up the creek the banks are lined with farm fields and trees. The anchorage here is quiet and serene, the perfect place to drop your hook.□

GRAYS INN CREEK

on the Chester River

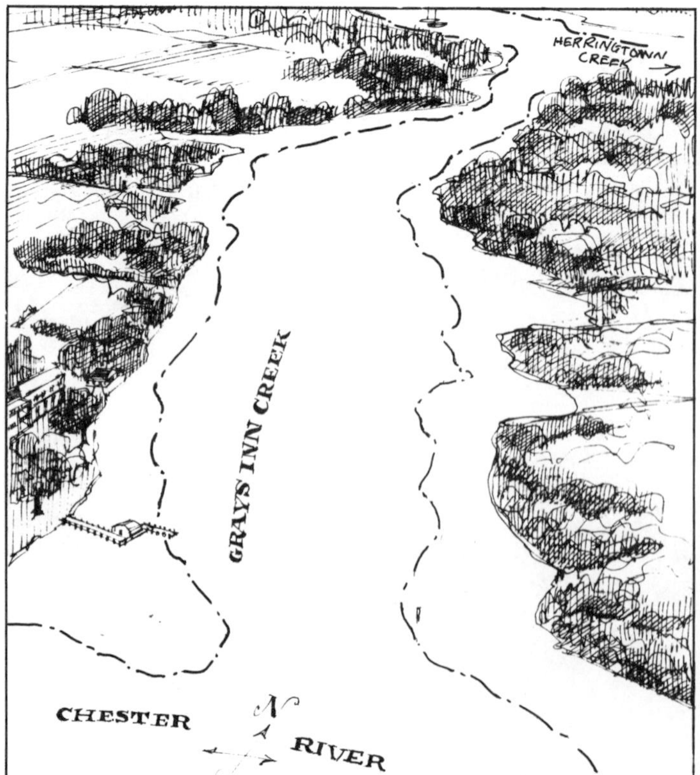

On the western shore of the Chester, almost 12 miles upstream from Love Point, is Grays Inn Creek, with wooded marshes and farms along its banks. The peninsula created by the creek, the Chester River, and the Bay is the location of one of the earliest areas of settlement on the Eastern Shore. Located along the banks of Grays Inn Creek was New Yarmouth, a 17th century settlement, and the site of the first Kent County courthouse. This town was of some importance until 1696, when the court was moved to Chestertown (then known as New Town). Once the county seat was relocated, New Yarmouth rapidly declined.

Although the mouth of Grays Inn Creek is broad, it is not easy to enter. According to the *Coast Pilot*, the best way to avoid the long shoals on both sides of the entrance is to leave black can #1 close to port and head for the end of the wharf at Spring Point on the west, or port, side of the creek.

Then keep 50 yards off the wharf and follow the creek on up, staying in mid-channel. On the north bank of Herringtown Creek is a marina with gas and supplies and a railway for boat repairs.

Although a few houses can be seen in this area of the creek, the wooded banks provide a screen and shelter to the yachtsman who prefers privacy. Our favorite anchorage would be just past the point of land opposite Herringtown Creek. The little cove formed here has tree-lined shores and a quiet atmosphere.

Grays Inn Creek is on that part of the Chester River where much yacht racing takes place. On one visit we were treated to a ringside seat to watch log canoe races and at the same time were able to see a great swarm of Windmills weaving in and out of a fleet of racing Hamptons. This was quite a show and indicates that many weekends can provide some fine entertainment for visitors to Grays Inn Creek.□

The wooded banks of Grays Inn Creek provide a screen and shelter to the yachtsman who prefers privacy.

CORSICA RIVER

off the Chester River

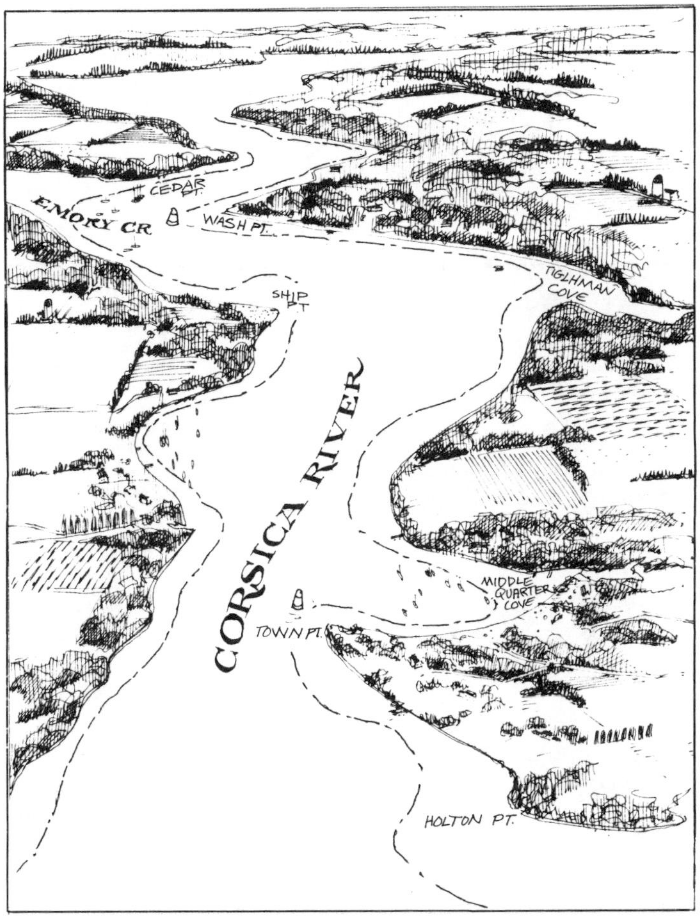

The Corsica River, located off the Chester River about nine miles north of Kent Narrows, is broad and meandering, with pasture and woodlands lining her banks. The country is really beautiful here, like a scene from an old Flemish painting.

At the mouth of the Corsica, the south bank is known as Corsica Neck. Two large, mansion-style homes, along with various other houses, occupy a large portion of the Neck. The most conspicuous landmark, Pioneer Point, is located between Holton and Town Points and was formerly the estate of John J. Raskob, who first placed the name of F.D.R. into nomination for president. The estate now serves as an "R and R" site for the Russian Embassy.

There are three principal anchorages on the river. First, in the cove off the Raskob estate just beyond Town Point. Be sure to honor the red nun #2 before heading in to avoid the sand bar. Second, north of red nun #4 at the mouth of Emory Creek. This is our favorite anchorage on the whole river. The middle of Emory Creek has fourteen feet of water and carries six feet almost up to its banks. The cove formed here by the creek is known locally as Red Wharf Cove and provides good protection from a northwesterly wind.

Emory Creek gets its name from the Emory family, who still occupy the brick home which can be seen on the left bank as you enter the creek. This is the oldest home continuously owned by one family east of the Misssissippi. Now known as Poplar Grove, the house was originally known as Brampton

Hall. The Emory family changed its name during the Revolutionary War when English-sounding names grew unpopular.

A third popular anchorage is at the Centreville Landing. There is at least seven feet of water at the wharf; just leave the private channel marks to port heading up.

The trip to the Landing is for the adventurous because the dredged channel is not easy to follow and the trip up the narrowing river becomes uninviting at times. □

CACAWAY ISLAND
on Langford Creek

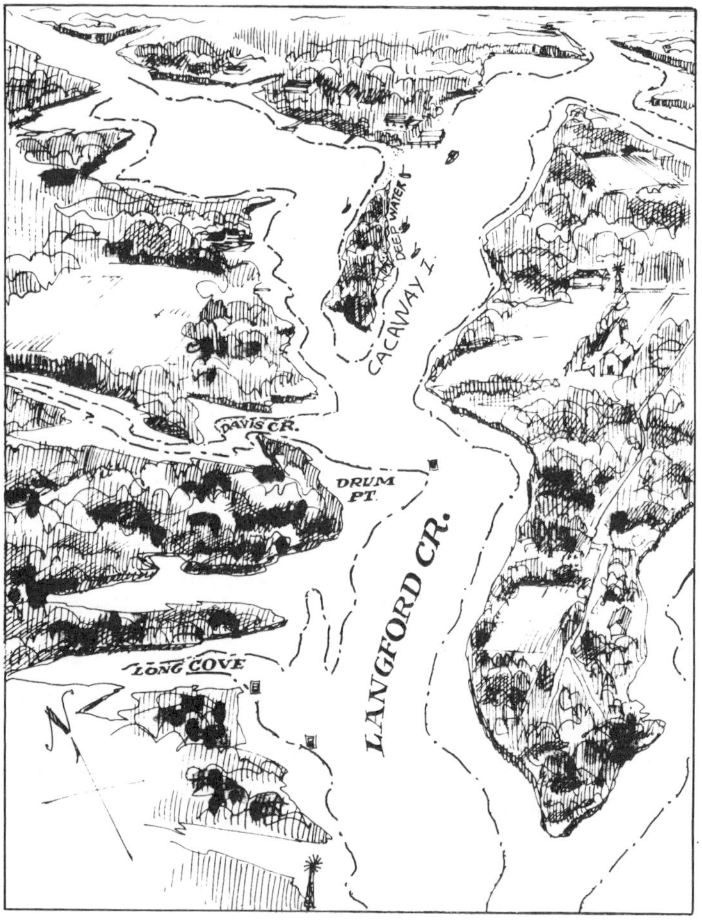

Part of the intrigue of cruising the Chesapeake Bay is its infinite variety. No matter how much of an expert you consider yourself, I guarantee there's always a surprise just around the next bend. Cacaway Island is a good example of what I mean.

We've been up and down the Chester River on many a cruise, and never considered this little gem. Langford Creek which surrounds the island is just not that impressive looking. Well, let me tell you, Cacaway Island can be the highlight of a summer's cruise.

The entrance to Langford Creek is easy to find as you leave Eastern Neck Island behind, because there's a string of black cans to port that lead right into the creek's entrance. To starboard just opposite Grays Inn Creek, there's a black an red can marking the shoal off Nichols Point. Further eas of this can are the range lights off the point. The black an red can, as well as the range lights, are left very much t starboard as you follow the black cans up into Langfor Creek.

As you pass the last can, #7, you will note, to por Davis Creek marked by a red daymark and duck blind. Ther are quite a few boats moored in the creek, and an exceller marina facility is located on the creek's south shore.

Cacaway Island on the chart looks something like a upside-down high-top boot. Its toe points northeast and i the curve formed between it and the instep is the most popula anchorage.

There's a long sandbar extending from the toe towar land, making it all but impossible to circumnavigate the island. W chose to anchor just east of this sandbar. The water dept measures nine feet where we are, about 50′ from the islan and I am curious to find out how close to shore we could hav anchored. So swimming in from the boat, I keep putting m feet down to feel for the bottom and find that within 12 pac from dry land there is a water depth of six feet!

A word of warning, though; this island is privatel owned! The visiting yachtsman is advised to ask permissio before trespassing. As so often happens, there are som visitors who cannot police themselves and who therefor make it impossible for the rest of us to enjoy such privatel owned places.

Either side of Cacaway Island or opposite the entrance c Philip Creek is a good anchorage if you want to catch southerly breeze. In rough weather you'll want to go farth upstream. On the west fork a snug spot is off Pastor Poin

At the head of Langford Creek is old St. Paul's Churc which stands amid oaks and sycamores that were probably century old when the church was built. Its silver chalice an plate bear the date 1699, having been used in the origin church, built of wood, on the same site. St. Paul's is believe to be the oldest Episcopal church in Maryland that has bee used continuously as a house of worship. Thirty-four pew were constructed in the church and rented out at so man pounds of tobacco per year. Or, one could buy an entire pe outright for 1,000 pounds of tobacco. The tomb of th internationally known actress, Tallulah Bankhead, is in th graveyard. □

COMEGY'S BIGHT

on the Chester River

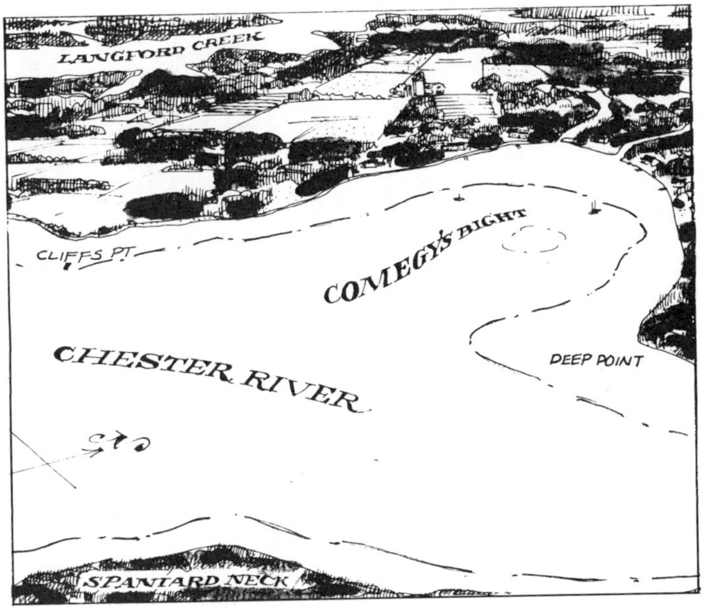

It was just north of the Corsica that we discovered one of those "serendipity" cruising spots in which the Bay abounds. On the west shore of the Chester just two miles north of Nichols Point on Quaker Neck lies Comegy's Bight. For the navigator, a course of 050° M from N "14" off Piney Point will bring you to the range lights off Nichols Point. From there continue north on the Chester, past N "18" to "20", and from there a course of 020° M will run you right into Comegy's Bight.

Now a bight is, by definition, "a curve, a bend, a loop . . . as a curve of shoreline that forms a small bay or cove." And that's an apt description of Comegy's Bight. At its mouth the bight measures a little over one-half mile wide and is slightly more than one-half mile long. The water here measures from seven to ten feet; but if you draw over six feet, beware of the six-foot shoal smack dab in the middle of the cove. Otherwise, there is plenty of water.

The open end of the bight faces south, and its encircling arms provide a cozy protection from nor'westers or northerlies. Sprouting off the top of this little bay, or bight, are two shallow streams, so shallow that only a flat-bottom skiff can navigate them. If you tow a dinghy, they are interesting but marshy (and buggy).

We entered this anchorage leaving the red nun #20 astern and motoring almost due north to the point where these two streams empty into the bight. The bottom is soft, sandy mud and will hold a Danforth or plough anchor very well.

As we sat at anchor and surveyed this cozy bay, a feeling of relaxing calm settled over us. The quiet shoreline was marked by few homes, and these, being older and more conservative, blend into the brief wooded patches that here and there come down to the water's edge. Behind us, the infrequent boat traffic passed too far away to be a bother. As dusk settled, the tree frogs on shore serenaded us to sleep.

The nearest supplies are south of here around the corner in Langford Creek. We've found the marinas to be friendly and hospitable, but that's no surprise. That's about how we found the whole Chester River. □

CHESTERTOWN

on the Chester River

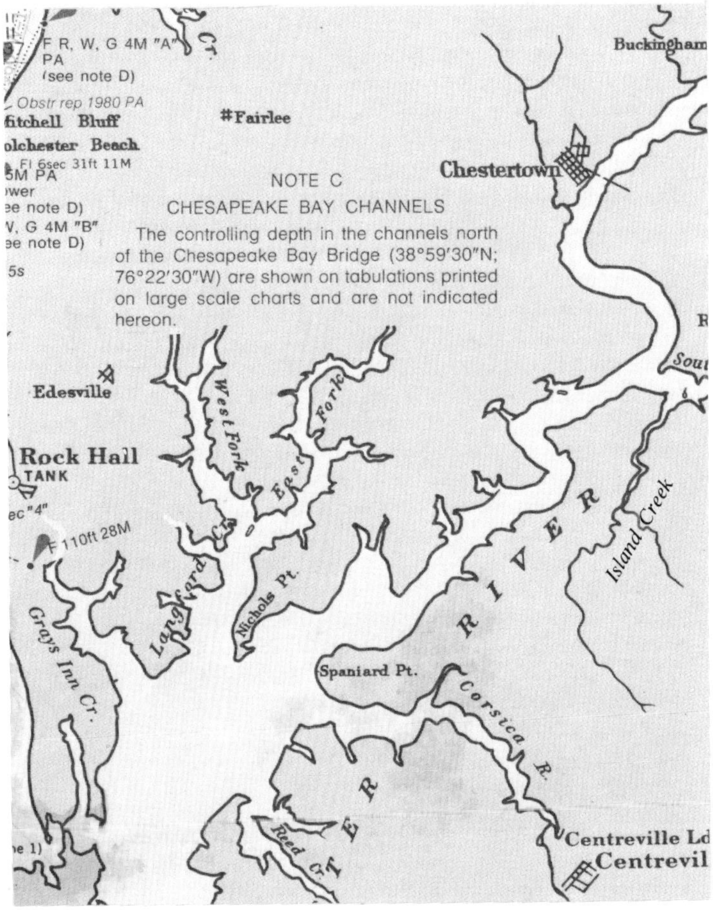

From NOAA Chart 12260—not to be used for navigation.

The 26 miles from Love Point Light (Fl 6 secs, 38 ft., 7 miles range) to Chestertown can provide the boater with enough attractions for an entire vacation, if not an entire summer. Nearly three miles across at its widest point, the Chester River gradually narrows to about ½ mile at Chestertown with good navigating depths in its well-buoyed channel.

To port, just off Can "3" a mile and a half upriver from Love Point Light is Eastern Neck Island. My first experience with this island was that it was the proverbial lee shore in a heavy northwesterly blow. At that time I was unaware of, and due to our dire circumstances, uninterested in the island's history. But in calmer times I was amazed and impressed by it. It seems the island was the site of the first lasting settlement on the Eastern Shore, New Yarmouth. In 1696 the Kent County seat was moved from New Yarmouth to Chestertown, a move which heralded New Yarmouth's demise, and today there is no sign that the town ever existed.

The tiny island was also the birthplace of Revolutionary War naval officer, Captain Lambert Wickes. Born in 1742, his credits included being the first naval officer named by Congress in 1776 to carry the American flag to Europe; the first in the Continental Navy to capture a British vessel in British waters; and the first to command an American warship in Europe after the war. It was aboard his ship *Reprisal* that Benjamin Franklin made his secret mission to gain the support of the French in the Revolutionary War.

Once you reach Chestertown you can anchor out and dinghy to the public landing at the foot of High Street, or tie up at one of the town's two marinas. However, if you plan an overnight stay, to my mind the river here is just a little too wide for comfort and I prefer the safety of a marina. Both marinas are within walking distance of Chestertown's business district.

In any event, you'll want to explore this fascinating town, second only to Annapolis in the number of beautiful eighteenth century dwellings which have survived. An added bonus is a whole street lined with these impressive structures.

Chestertown's ships kept her in touch with ports around the world. She was, however, a far cry from the rather sedate community of today. Gambling, dancing, horse racing and theatrical performances were commonplace. During the lavish period preceeding the Revolution, wines, liquors, cordials and rums were all cheap, plentiful and generously consumed.

In May , Chestertown will celebrate the annual commemoration of its May 3, 1774 "Tea Party." There will be a parade, the re-enactment of the tea dumping, entertainment, races, crafts, exhibits and numerous other events to delight both native and visitor alike.

An interesting aside on the actual tea party can be found in the wry account of the event in the pages of the *Kent County News*. The paper stated that they "threw overboard the tea, but didn't destroy the rum." I suppose the fun-loving natives of Chestertown had their priorities in order.

Although there are many fine dining facilities in the Chestertown area, if you are a boater you will probably wind up at the Old Wharf Inn. We can be in it, around it, on it all day and all night, yet when it comes to dining out, of course, we want to look over the water. Some people can never get enough of a good thing. ☐

Notes

KENT ISLAND NARROWS

Connecting Chester River and Eastern Bay

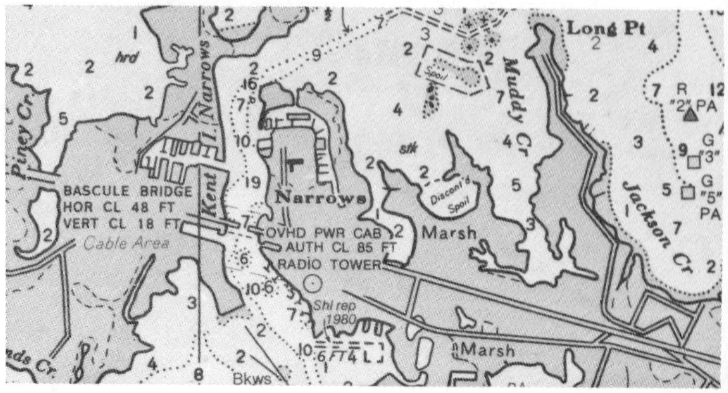

From NOAA Chart 12270—not to be used for navigation.

The quickest route between the Chester and Miles Rivers is through the Kent Island Narrows.

On entering the Narrows from the Chester River, Beacon "35" through the Narrows to Beacon "3," REMEMBER—KEEP BLACK TO STARBOARD! Coming from the Chester, you will be surprised at the strength of the current. We have measured currents of 2 knots while motoring to keep the boat stationary over the bottom. Although some cruising guides report the current through the narrows is always in a northerly direction, this is not the case. Local knowledge reports the current goes in the direction of the tide. The current goes north when the tide is coming in, south when the tide is going out. As in the C&D Channel, it is best to maintain a good engine speed.

Several years ago the Coast Guard changed the rules prescribing the opening signal to be used when approaching a drawbridge. A vessel approaching a drawbridge shall sound a signal of one long blast (4-6 sec.) followed by one short blast (1 sec.). Horns or whistles may be used, but bells are only to be used as fog signalling devices. If the bridge can be opened right away, the bridge tender is to respond with a similar signal. If the draw cannot be opened, or must be closed immediately, the bridge tender will sound 5 short blasts repeated until acknowledged by the vessel with a signal having the same meaning.

The bridge across the Narrows is on a restricted opening. All land traffic going to and from the ocean beaches via the Chesapeake Bay Bridge also crosses this bridge. To help alleviate a car traffic problem, the Coast Guard has adopted the following opening schedule:

May 1-October 31
Mon.-Thurs.: Hourly openings from 7 A.M. to 7 P.M.
Friday: Hourly openings from 6 A.M. to 3 P.M., and again at 8 P.M.
Saturday: Openings at 6 A.M., 9 A.M., Noon and 3 P.M. After 3 P.M., hourly openings until 8 P.M.
Sunday and Monday Holidays: Hourly openings from 6 A.M. to 1 P.M. and again at 8 P.M.

November 1-April 30
The bridge will open on signal 6 A.M. to 6 P.M.

There are several marine facilities in the Narrows providing repairs, fuel, restaurants, and transient slips. Once through the bridge, it is clear sailing to the Miles River. ☐

A Walking Tour of:
CHESTERTOWN

by Andi Manchester

One peanut-butter-and-jelly sandwich and two games of Concentration® above Kent Narrows, well above the Chester River's most popular drop-anchor creeks and gunkholes, is Chestertown. Although rich in history, at first glance it betrays no basis for its existence. Once a major Bay port, only the Customs House and grand merchants' homes are left as a tribute to that era.

Chestertownians are proud of their colonial heritage and have restored many 18th century buildings, but the town's orientation is far from being a "restored" landmark. Since 1782 it has been home to Washington College, but its character isn't shaped by that relationship. During hunting season it is a popular sportsmen's stop, but that influx doesn't dominate the town either. While several industries are located in the surrounding countryside, their presence shadows neither the skyline nor the town's aura. You can't stereotype Chestertown or put it in any one category, yet its charisma and charm make it a favorite port-of-call to both land and water travelers.

If your itinerary includes an overnight stay you can either anchor or dock. The river is calm and wide enough to make anchoring-out pleasurable and a public landing at the foot of High Street makes dinghying ashore no problem. If you prefer the creature comforts and facilities electric hook-ups and marinas provide or simply like the convenience of being tied up in town, you can stay at either Kibler's or Scott's Point marinas.

The marinas are at the waters' edge of an approximate three block area known as Scott's Point. They share that boundary with the new Wilmer Park named for Philip G. Wilmer who served 14 consecutive terms as mayor of Chestertown, from 1935-1963. It boasts well over 500 feet of bulkhead, a tree and bench-lined promenade/jogging trail, picnic benches, playground, open field, and a pavillion (funded by Washington College but available to the city for its use).

Starting at the marinas and continuing up the river elegant 18th and 19th century homes stand not only as a tribute to their builders but as a welcoming committee to arriving boaters. If architecture of this period interests you, then "A Walking Tour of Old Chester Town" was written with you in mind. Stop #1 on this tour is a stone's throw from the entrance to the marinas' parking lots, on the corner of Water and Cannon Streets. This is the Hynson-Ringgold House, built in 3 stages by 2 different families, and "home" to Washington College presidents since 1944 (the college owns the house). Our youngsters aren't into architecture, but this corner interested them, too, for the unusual terrain tree roots have given the cobblestone sidewalks. The walking tour (available from the Chamber of Commerce and several area merchants) continues from here down Water Street before meandering into downtown. In addition, three annual tours are offered during the year. The "Candlelight Walking Tour" and "Christmas in Historic Chestertown" are open houses featuring selected 18th, 19th, and 20th century residences (admission charged). Guided walking tours (tickets required) are part of the annual Tea Party Festival activities held each May. (I could ramble on for 12 pages on the Tea Party Festival. Let me just say that even the kids agree that this is a 4-star event!)

We opted for a do-it-yourself-tour starting with a stroll up Cannon Street. We found the back side of downtown shops on our right and a modest, primarily residential area on our left. One of the few commercial endeavors was Chestertown Seafood (about 2½ blocks from the water) advertising seafood, bait and fish for sale.

Next we decided to explore that portion of town that has made Chestertown so popular: the downtown district. In a project jointly funded by the city and area merchants, broken portions of cement sidewalks are being replaced with more colonial cobblestone. The result is quaint and warmly inviting, adding to the area's already friendly ambiance.

High Street is a major downtown thoroughfare whose western side of the street looks like a life-size model train village. Interesting little shops occupy the first floors of two- and three-story buildings that line a broad sidewalk. The opposite side of the street presents a different picture. Toward the river end is the Imperial Hotel which, after major renovation, is restored to its original 1902 self. Not just a place to find lodging, the hotel has three separate dining rooms serving full course breakfasts, lunches, and dinners. Up a block, in the heart of town, is an inviting park. It has bench-lined, crisscrossing paths and a fountain that was originally installed in 1899.

In our wanderings we found two libraries. At the river end of High Street's commercial area is the Chestertown Library, a private collection specializing in novels and local history. Started as a small literary club meeting in women's homes, it has grown to fill the first and second floor of a building the club bought over 40 years ago. In contrast, at the other end of High Street's business district is the Kent County Public Library, a full service library in a modern one-story brick building. It features a children's film series in the summer and reciprocity with other Maryland county libraries should you decide on the spur-of-the-moment to borrow a book.

An interesting addition to the commercial district is White Swan Tavern.

Joe Manchester's photos show a part of the High Street business district and a view of Chestertown from the water.

Originally built as a tannery in the 1790's, it is now a fully restored bed-and-breakfast inn. Although breakfast is served to its guests only, it is open to the public for tours daily at 2 P.M. and for afternoon tea Mon.-Thurs. from 3-5 P.M.

Along with food and clothing, downtown merchants sell everything from freshly ground coffee and hand-carved duck decoys to Brio toys in stores that range from specialty shops to all-things-craftsy-boutiques. There is even a place to rent bicycles (Bikeworks), two laundromats, an A&P, and a few places to buy food that someone else cooked. Ambrosia, a cross between a gourmet 7-11 and a carry-out, sells delicacies like hearts of palm and artichoke hearts, and hunger pleasers like hearty soups, sandwiches, quiche, and baked items. Mrs. Kelly's Tea House is open for light meals (breakfast and lunch only) and snacks (they sell fresh desserts and 7 different varieties of tea) served in a cozy atmosphere. Unruh's is a luncheonette catering to those who don't want fancy or quaint, just a regular meal served in unceremonious style.

If you are an ice cream devotee, as we are, then I'm sorry to tell you that the closest thing to an ice cream parlor is the carry-out soda fountain at Stams Drugs. There, at an old-fashioned counter, you can buy cones, sundaes or floats, but it is strictly an eat-as-you-walk affair. The other drug store in the downtown area, Chestertown Pharmacy, also sells ice cream but it is pre-packaged rather than hand-dipped. Be forwarned: both pharmacies close early on Saturday and are closed all day Sunday. In fact, many downtown merchants have limited weekend hours.

About 1/2-mile from the center of town is Washington College. More than just a place of academics, in the summer months it presents a dinner theater with several different productions to appeal to a variety of tastes. (For more information call (301) 778-1358.) About a block from here, advertising 24-hour emergency care, is the Kent and Queen Anne's Hospital. Just a mere 0.2 mile farther (about 0.9 mile from the center of town) is a busy intersection of highways and a small shopping center with such chain stores as Acme, Penn Jersey and Radio Shack. Fast food addicts can find both a Roy Rogers and a Pizza Hut. Two family restaurants are located in this hub of activity, Danny's and Buzz's Steak House. If you have gotten this far don't forget: there are no cabs or buses in Chestertown, it's feet all the way back!

One way back to the waterfront is down Washington Street and Maple Avenue (Rt. 213). On this route you'll find large Victorian houses complete with gingerbread and stained glass windows.

After all our explorations we decided to treat ourselves to a relaxed dinner close to our marina. There, overlooking the water at Kibler's Marina, only a few yards from our slip, we dined at the Old Wharf Inn to the delight of our children, our taste buds, and our feet!

If you are still looking for an excuse to visit, perhaps one of the two other annual events that I haven't yet mentioned will give it to you. In early May the Chestertown Garden Club will hold its annual Flower Mart, a house and garden pilgrimage (tickets are $10.00). Later in the month, on Memorial Day weekend, is the annual Tea Party Festival. Beside all the goings on it offers (parade, re-enactment of the tea dumping, entertainment, races, crafts exhibits, puppet theater, sound and light show at dusk), there is the annual Tea Party 10-Mile Classic, probably the largest and best known long distance run on the Eastern Shore.

For more information on all that Chestertown has to offer, you can contact the Kent County Chamber of Commerce at (301) 778-0416. □

Rendering of author's map by Joan Machinchick

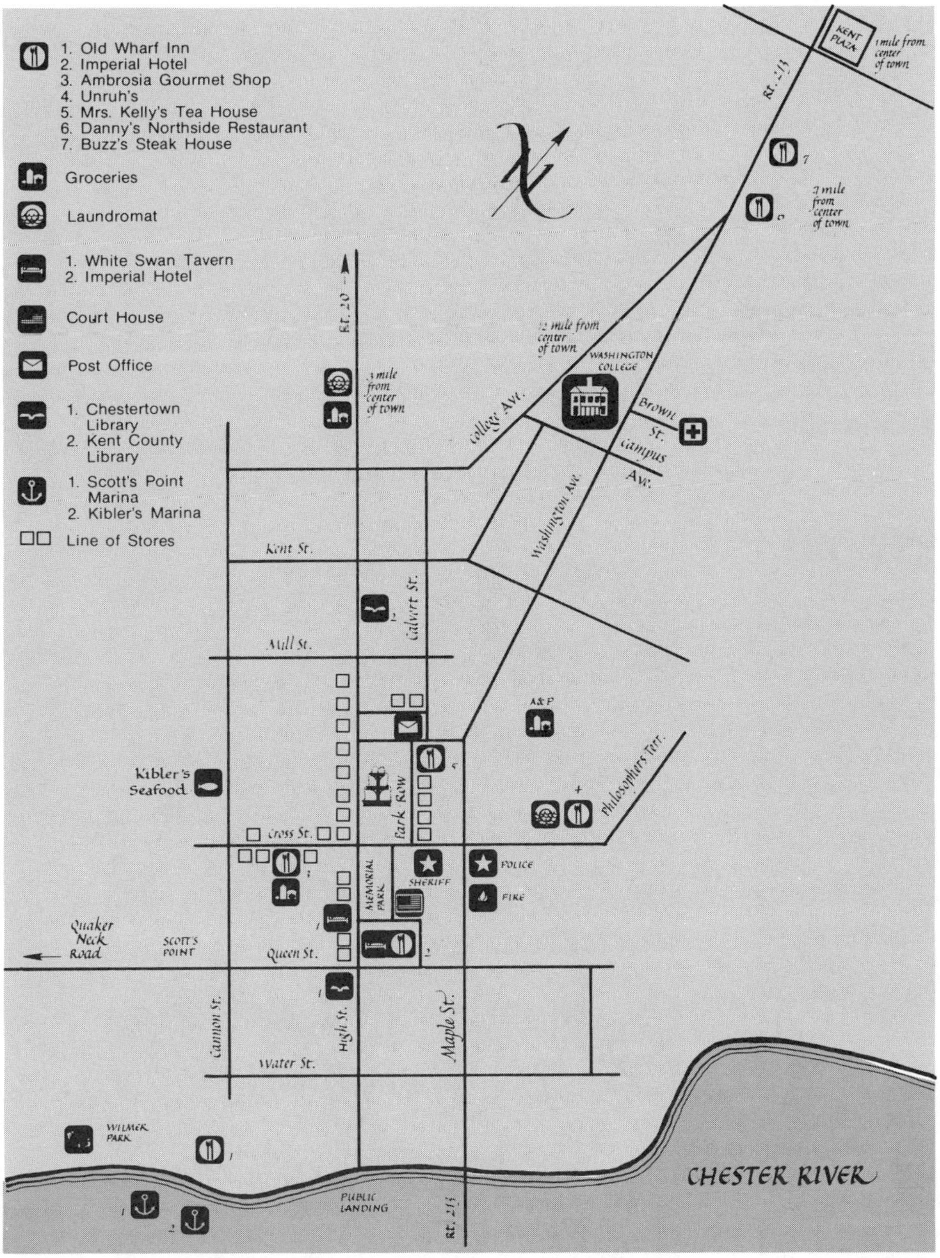

MIDDLE BAY:
CHESAPEAKE BAY BRIDGE TO POTOMAC RIVER

The beauty that remains in the Middle Bay has changed little since the time Captain John Smith first "cruised" that area in 1608. From the hustle and bustle of the port of Annapolis on the Severn River to Thomas Point Light, faithfully guarding the entrance to the South River with its many quiet coves, you can find just about anything here. The Rhode and West Rivers together provide peaceful anchorages and commercial amenities. Cruising spots on the Western Shore can provide the cruising yachtsman with an idyllic quality unmatched anywhere on the Bay.

On the Eastern Shore, as you round Bloody Point, Eastern Bay guides you toward the Wye River, whose every creek and cove has its own "story" of days gone by. The Miles River then leads you to the ever-popular cruising spot of St. Michaels, with its own special charm.

The Choptank is the longest river on Maryland's Eastern Shore and is almost five miles wide at one point. It averages 20- and 30-foot depths, although there are a couple of 60+ foot depths some six miles upstream where the Tred Avon joins it. On our many cruises to Oxford, we have been intrigued by the north shore of the Choptank and the beautiful rivers and woods there. The Choptank's 15+ miles provide the cruising yachtsman with unlimited anchorages and points of interest as it meanders from its mouth at Tilghman Island and beautiful Broad Creek to the entrance of the Tred Avon and historic Oxford and on to the city of Cambridge.

This section of the Bay also offers the yachtsman a variety of lifestyles, from the simple life on the Islands of Smith and Tangier to the modern, populated areas of the Patuxent and Potomac Rivers. The Potomac River is a huge body of water, having several large tributaries of its own. On this one body of water you can find a variety because it stretches through the quiet, rural areas of Virginia and Southern Maryland all the way up to the Nation's Capital.

This Middle Bay section is definitely unique. At night a quiet cove will give you a haven from the everyday world, but just around the bend civilization begins all over again.

Middle Bay Charts:

12220	12270
12230	12271
12233	12282
12260	12283
12261	12284
12263	12285
12264	12286
12265	12287
12266	12288
12267	12289
12268	

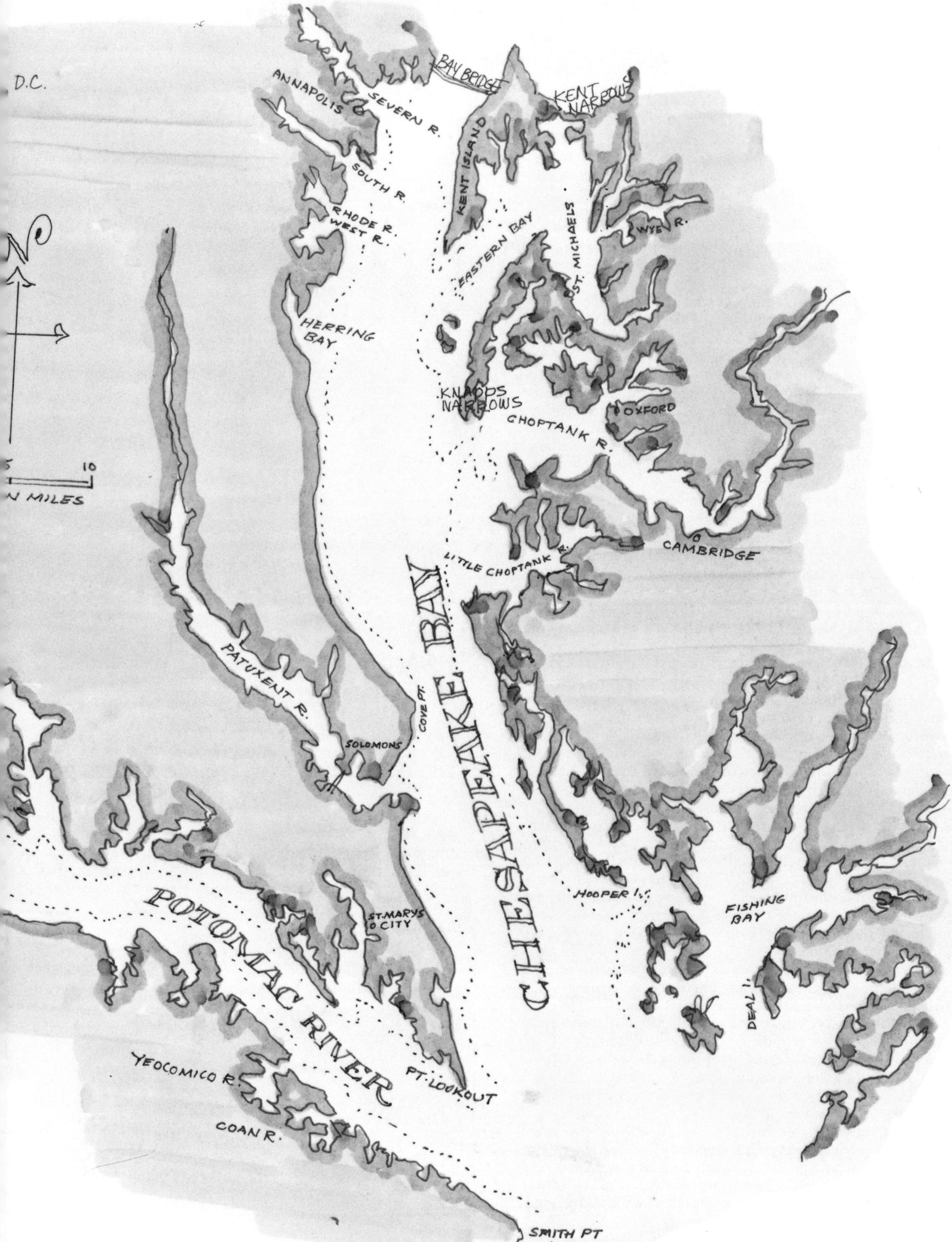
D.C.
ANNAPOLIS
SEVERN R.
BAY BRIDGE
KENT NARROWS
KENT ISLAND
SOUTH R.
RHODE R.
WEST R.
EASTERN BAY
ST. MICHAELS
WYE R.
HERRING BAY
KNAPPS NARROWS
OXFORD
CHOPTANK R.
10
N MILES
CAMBRIDGE
LITTLE CHOPTANK R.
CHESAPEAKE BAY
PATUXENT R.
COVE PT.
SOLOMONS
HOOPER I.
FISHING BAY
POTOMAC RIVER
ST. MARYS CITY
DEAL I.
YEOCOMICO R.
PT. LOOKOUT
COAN R.
SMITH PT

WHITEHALL BAY, WHITEHALL CREEK, RIDOUT CREEK

Mouth of the Severn River

Whitehall Bay is a convenient anchorage just south of the Bay Bridge and within easy cruising distance of most of the upper Bay. If you yachtsmen are discouraged by the crowded conditions of the Annapolis harbor and the heavy traffic in the vicinity of Spa and Back Creeks, Whitehall Bay may be just the spot for you. You can anchor here for the night and have an easy run into Annapolis the next day for supplies at the many facilities.

Whitehall Bay has general depths of 6 to 13 feet. The entrance channel is about 300 yards wide between Whitehall Flats on the west and North Shoal on the east, both with depths of 3 to 4 feet.

To enter Whitehall Bay, be sure to give Hackett Point a wide berth, as the shoals here extend a fair distance south before curving westward in a hook shape to the red flashing entrance marker "2". The usual trick for those who are not too sure of the area is to line up Can "1" out in the Chesapeake Bay with the northernmost radio tower on Greenbury Point and keep these in range on a heading of approximately 309° M. But there are 16 towers, and it may be hard to pick out the northernmost. An alternative is to range on the only tower that stands in the water. Take a heading of 312° M (approx.) from Can "1". In either case, keep going until "2" (Fl 4 sec 12 ft. 4 M) bears about 009° M, and take a course to pass it well to starboard, and slip into the creek. Be sure not to confuse "2" (Fl 4 sec 12 ft 4 M) with "2" (Fl R 2.5 sec) further to port and much closer to shore, marking the entrance to Mill Creek.

Most yachtsmen head for the easternmost part of Whitehall Bay to be clear of the boat traffic of those who live on the upper branches. Whitehall is not the private anchorage that is found on the Eastern Shore, but there is no commercial traffic, which can be rough on a raft of boats. The local boatman is a resident whom we have found courteous and friendly. As a result, the area is quiet and comfortable.

The cove is fairly small, and there are several snug spots in the upper branches. Whitehall Creek is navigable for about two miles past Sharp's Point, and the shallows are clearly marked. On our cruise to Whitehall Creek the red daymark #4 got us lined up for the green #5 which marks a sharp turn to port toward red daymark #6. The only concern I had at this point was that the beam seas might ease us to leeward out of the channel. Frequently checking with our flashlights and crabbing our way, we safely rounded #6 into somewhat calmer waters.

Whitehall Creek has several things in its favor as a cruising spot. First is its easy entrance. Second are the marine facilities available to the boater here.

Whitehall Creek also offers a number of attractive anchorages. As we wound our way past daymark #7, we found our way into Ridout (pronounced *ride-out)* Creek. Even in the dark the entrance is easy to negotiate. The tall trees on both banks were swaying and sighing in the wind, but down on the water all was calm.

I went onto the foredeck as Dixie throttled back; when headway stopped, I slipped the anchor over the side. Water depths range from eight to ten feet, so I let out seventy-five feet of rode. I watched as we swung gently to the end of our rode, then waited to be sure there was no chance of dragging.

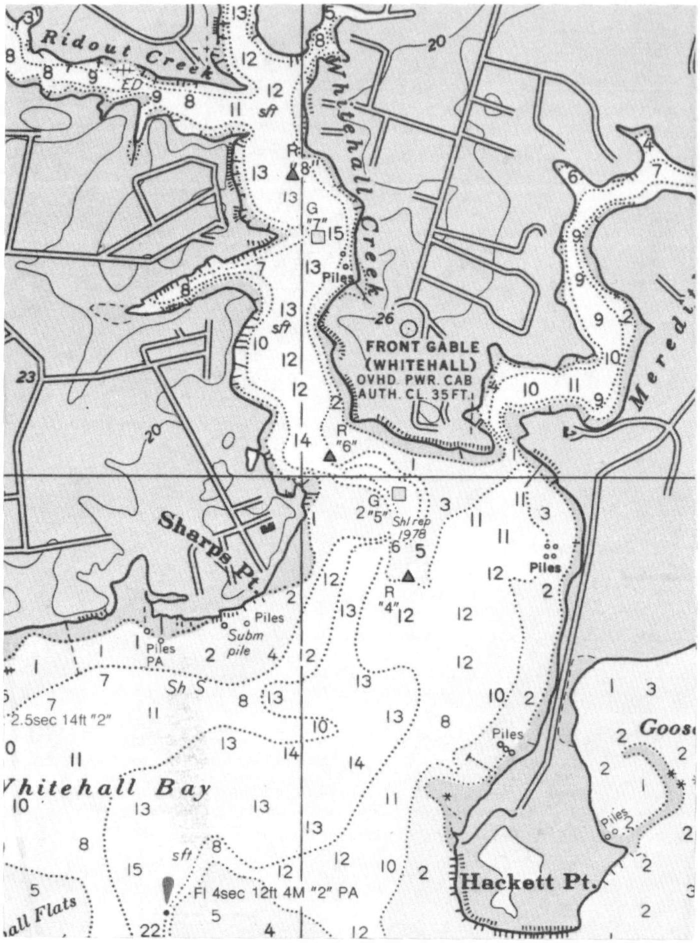

From NOAA Chart 12282—not to be used for navigation.

The next morning a warm sun filtered down through the trees and sparkled on the water. The wind had blown itself out, and a light breeze was riffling the water. Ridout Creek is one of those truly beautiful creeks of the Chesapeake Bay, a creek you'll want to come back to. I know we'll be back.□

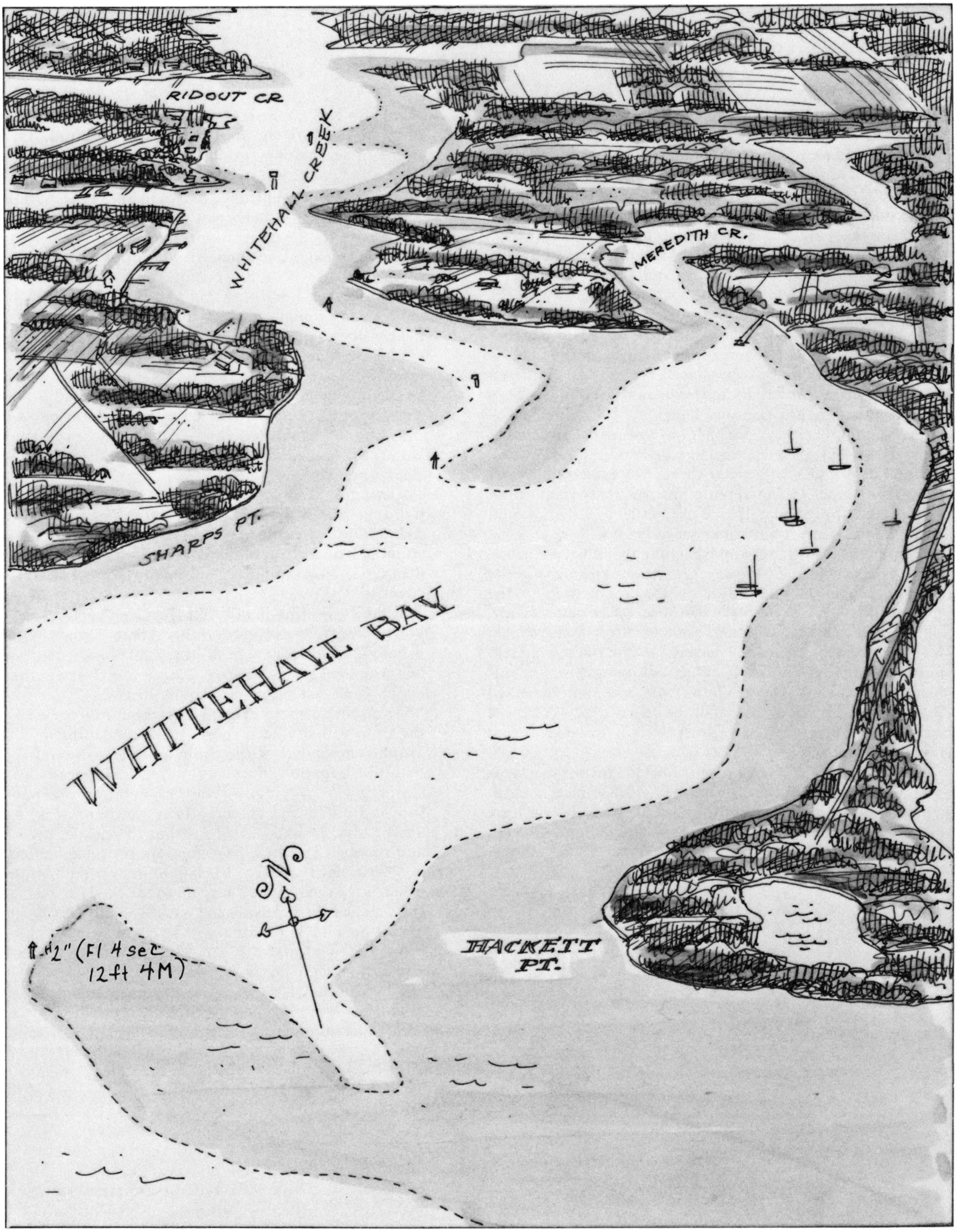
RIDOUT CR
WHITEHALL CREEK
MEREDITH CR.
SHARPS PT.
WHITEHALL BAY
HACKETT PT.
"2" (Fl 4 sec 12 ft 4M)
N

LAKE OGLETON

mouth of the Severn River

At four P.M. we passed under the center span of the Bay Bridge. The wind was really piping out of the south. Two-foot seas were topped by white foam, and as we ducked around several moored freighters, we began to think about the night's anchorage. Whitehall Bay was out as far as we were concerned. We had spent too many uncomfortable nights there being bumped around by a stiff southerly.

We didn't feel like Annapolis harbor either. Crowded anchorages are unnerving, and my mate and I were pretty bushed and didn't feel like motoring further down to the South or Rhode Rivers.

As I went through my charts, I pulled out a new one that shows the Annapolis harbor in great detail. Chart #12283 is 1:10,000 scale. We looked over Back Creek and remembered anchoring there many years ago before all the condos, docks and extensive dockworks were built.

We studied the chart. Further out toward the knuckle of Tolly Point our eyes fell on Lake Ogleton, and we found ourselves intrigued with what we saw. A moderate length dredged channel (5 feet reported at low tide) leads to an inland lake approximately one mile in length. This would give us good protection from southerlies.

An hour later we were approaching the outside mark, a black 4-second flasher. However, as we looked again at the charts, this mark was shown on the wrong side of the channel! Black and green marks should be left to port on entering—but the charts showed it as a starboard mark. Well, what do we do now? Every navigation book says to leave black & green to port on entering, doesn't it? With misgivings, we left this black to starboard. The wind was from port and I reasoned that it would give us a push off if the charts were wrong and we went aground. The charts must be right, because we had no trouble getting in.

From Chart 12270, one might conclude that #1 marker is on the wrong side of the channel, but #12283 makes it clear. The channel doesn't extend quite to #1, and if you look closely, you will see on #12283 that there's slightly deeper water on the norhtwest side of the entrance end of the channel than on the southeast side. So you'll hardly go wrong if you honor #1 and shape your course to honor #2. This course will not quite parallel the line of the channel.

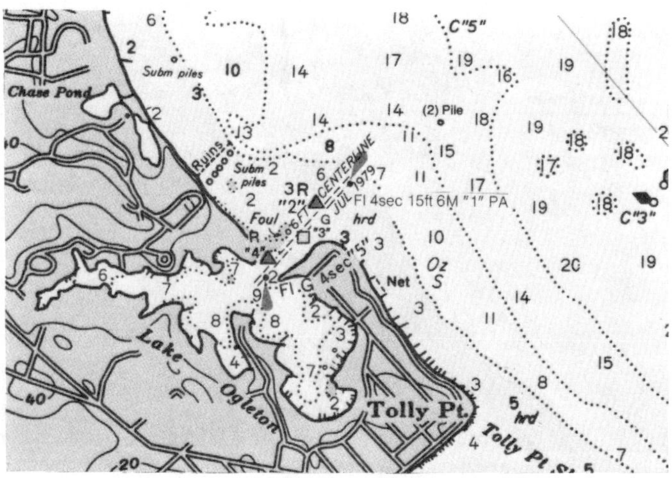

From NOAA Chart 12270—not to be used for navigation.

There are five entrance marks in all — alternating black and red, the last a black with a green four-second flasher. Once past that, you're home free. On the starboard side there is an extensive shoal around a masonry bulkheaded point of land with a black-topped gazebo.

Past the last mark, facing you from the south shore, is Oak Point, which seems to divide Lake Ogleton into two nearly equal parts. The port side appears crowded with extensive docks and many boats. To starboard there were fewer docks, and just west of Oak Point was an attractive wooded cove with fewer houses. We motored around the shoal spot just opposite the cove, headed south toward the tall, wooded bank there, and dropped anchor in ten feet of water. The banks with their tall trees cut the wind down to a gentle breeze.

Lying in our bunks we read until our heads were nodding. Suddenly, *Kerplunk, Flutter, Flutter.* Now what? I didn't know what the noise was, but it was on our deck and I stumbled out to investigate. There, strutting up our side decks, was a mallard hen, her bright, shiny eyes watching me suspiciously.

"I'm sorry, Mrs. Duck, but I just won't get any sleep with you making all this commotion out here. Shoo!" With that I ushered her over the side. Returning below, I undressed for bed when *Kerplunk, Flutter, Bump, Bump.* It was that duck again. Well, I'd show her a thing or two.

Not bothering to dress, I leaned out into the cockpit for the mop which I keep there. Flashlight in hand, I peered around the corner of the cabin and there she was. I poked with the mop. She danced out of reach, her beady little eyes staring at me. Trying to retain my modesty, I crouched as low as I could and came halfway out onto deck. I poked again. Mrs. Duck scuttled just out of reach, glared at me, and did an unmentionable thing on my clean decks!

With that I saw red! Flashlight in one hand, mop in the other, I charged. All the way up to the bow I chased her. As she reached the headstay she paused, and that's when I got her. It wasn't a hard slap, more like a wet push with a soggy mop; and she took off, squawking her anger at me.

That's when Dixie popped out of the forward hatch, spotlight in hand, saying, "What on earth is going on?"

Mop in hand, naked to all, I could only sputter something about chasing ducks and retreated to the cockpit. On the way my bare toes encountered something unpleasant. And as I mopped up Mrs. Duck's memento and washed my feet, I tried not to think of how silly I must have looked.

We did, however, enjoy our stay in Lake Ogleton. This is a perfect anchorage for folks who don't want to spend the night in Annapolis harbor and wish to avoid the long haul to Whitehall Bay. Just look out for a certain Mother Duck with a gleam in her eye for a clean boat deck. □

OAK POINT
LAKE OGLETON
TO ANNAPOLIS
NOTE: ON CHARTS THIS GREEN APPEARS TO BE ON STBD. SIDE. LOCAL BOATS LEAVE TO PORT UPON ENTERING
FL.4 sec. #1

Notes

ANNAPOLIS

on the Severn River

A thriving tobacco port in colonial times, present-day Annapolis is a major boating center, and a popular anchorage for cruising yachtsmen. Many fine stores and restaurants are within easy walking distance of City Dock.

Briefly the capital of the United States, and the capital of Maryland since 1695, Annapolis is without peer among colonial cities. The State House, completed in 1779 and the oldest in the nation in continuous legislative use; St. John's College (originally known as King William's School) founded in 1696; and the William Paca House, home of one of the signers of the Declaration of Independence, are but a sampling of the many historic homes and buildings open for inspection.

Annapolis has been the home of the United States Naval Academy since 1845 and the cultural life of Annapolis is sparked by a symphony orchestra, an opera company, two theatre groups, and a summer band concert series, conducted at the City Dock by the Naval Academy Band.

The In-The-Water Boat Shows, held at the City Dock in October, and Chesapeake Appreciation Days, a two-day festival held at Sandy Point State Park (just east of the city) either the last weekend in October or the first weekend in November, cap the fall tourist season.

The entrance to Annapolis is quite easy to negotiate, although very crowded. The big thing to note is a long shoal projecting from Horn Point on your port side (just north of

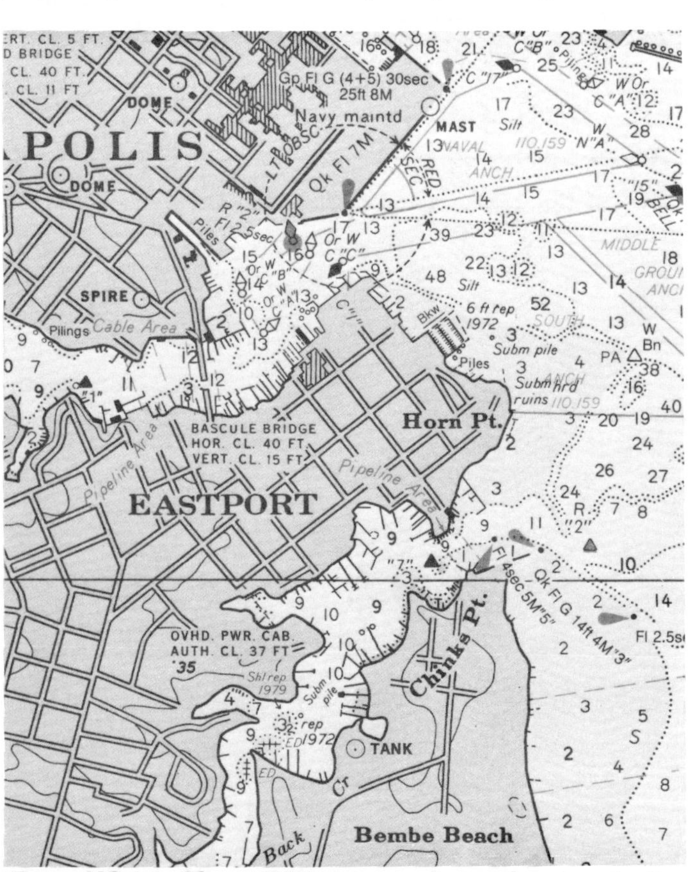

From NOAA Chart 12282—not to be used for navigation.

Back Creek). As you round Greenbury Point it is best honor the large "spider" platform light. (Incidentally, this w once a cottage-style lighthouse similar to the one at Thom Point.)

From the spider you can follow the fairway marked b cans, bells, and nuns for about ¾ mile. This will allow you clear the shoal mark, a daymark on a pole lit by a 6 secor white flashing light, and you can turn and head right into th harbor proper.

Anchoring is permitted in the harbor, where there is marked anchorage, but remember to use good sense in pickir your spot. There is a lot of traffic on a summer weekend, n to mention many sailboat races. Anchoring in the harbor on Wednesday evening can be quite breathtaking should you fir yourself in the middle of a "spinnaker finish" of the Annapol Yacht Club Wednesday evening races!

Slips, with showers, head and electricity are available a the City Dock for a fee on a first come, first serve basis. Th harbormasters office is the small, brick building in the harbo He will circulate the dock area to collect the fee.

The harbor itself, although close to the city dock an shopping, has a few disadvantages. The holding ground is fa to poor. It s location leaves it exposed to northeast winds, an no matter what the weather is doing, it's usually "bumpy" an always crowded. Rowing your dinghy ashore to the tie-up is fair distance, all the way to the end of the dredged basin on th square.

Spa Creek carries adequate depths for sailboats almost its head, but most yachtsmen prefer to anchor in parts of th creek that are shown on the chart. Less crowded anchorage available just off Truxton Park, which is a public park by th boat ramp, about ¼ mile above the bridge, portside. shopping center in Eastport should be able to satisfy all yo provisioning needs. It is about 1½ miles from the park doc where you can leave your dinghy. Truxton Park itself offe free tennis courts, a swimming pool, boat ramps, nature trai and picnic and barbecue facilities.

Over on Back Creek you can anchor just off the water ta opposite Bert Jabins Yacht Yard. It's about a mile's walk Edgewood Road, on the marina side, to a brand-ne shopping center and supermarket.

Guided tours of Annapolis are available through Histo Annapolis, Inc. (301)267-8149 and Three Centuries Tou Inc. (301)263-5357. There are also guided tours of the Nav Academy.

If you prefer to guide yourself, these publications a available in local bookstores to enable you to do just tha *Maryland—A New Guide to the Old Line State,* compiled ar edited by Edward C. Papenfuse and his Maryland Archivi staff, published by Johns Hopkins Press; *Baltimore, Annapol and Chesapeake Country,* by James F. Waesche, published b Bodine and Associates, Inc.; and *Annapolis: A Walk Throu History* by Elizabeth B. Anderson from Tidewater Publisher

This thriving boating center is the ideal place to end a da on the Bay. The many attractions may entice you to spen more than a single night. □

PHOTO BY BOB GRIESER

Spa Creek *Annapolis*

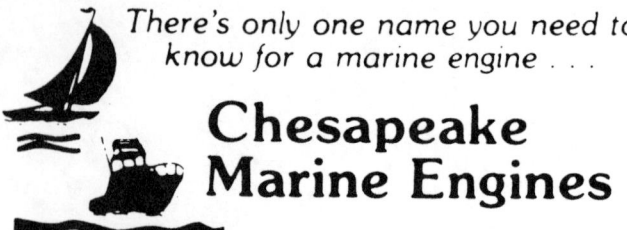

SALTWORKS CREEK

on the Severn River

On a recent cruise in the Severn River, we found the old railroad bridge has been partially torn down. Where we'd had to thread our way through the open arms of the bridge, we could now traverse the area in a wide expanse.

As we were exploring this beautiful river, we poked our way into Saltworks Creek. Talk about an Adirondack mountain lake setting. Saltworks has to be one of the prettiest miniature harbors on the Severn River! The creek is located on the south shore a little over a mile upstream from the high Severn River Bridge.

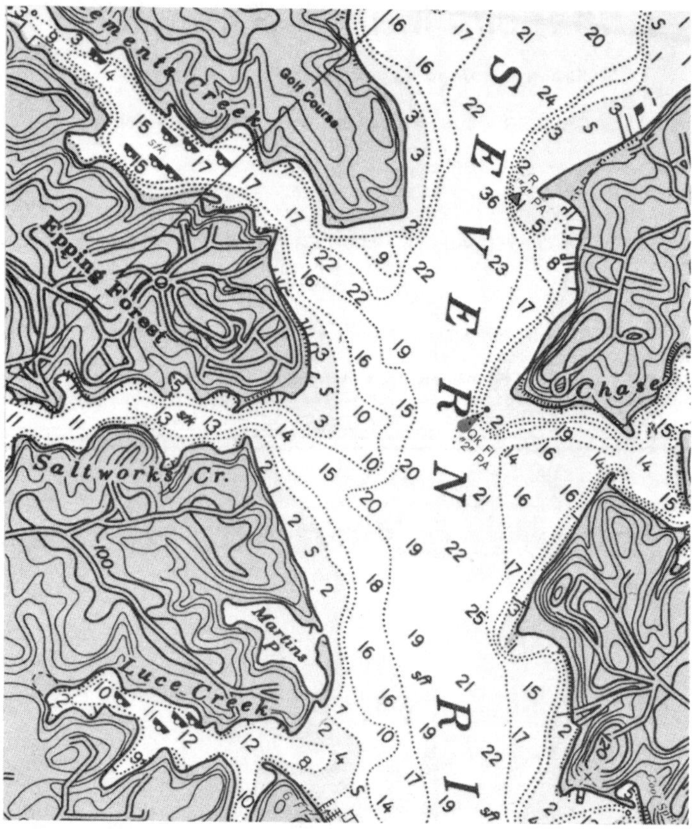

From NOAA Chart 12282—not to be used for navigation.

There is no real trick to getting into Saltworks Creek, particularly if you enter from the Bay side. The only shoal is the one extending from the upriver side of the creek's entrance. However, once you get past the 3′ mark there, it is safer to favor the starboard side of the entrance where there's an old red house on pilings at the river's edge. The red paint is fading, and the house, obviously unoccupied, is tilting backward as if the shoreside pilings were collapsing. Close by, inside the creek's entrance is a lovely new home with natural siding and steeply pitched roof. This will be easy to identify because there are three skylights on the roof, and a good-sized dock in front berthing several boats.

There are no tricky sandbars to block the entrance, so if you keep to the middle, you should have no problem getting in. The best anchorage is about 250 yards upstream in 13 feet of water where NOAA chart #12282 says "Stk." Of course you can go further upstream since the creek carries six feet of water or more for over one-half mile.

Saltworks Creek is reminiscent of a beautiful mountain lake, with high, wooded shores that allow only a glimpse of scattered houses perched high above the anchorage. There is an occasional pier along the water's edge, but as darkness falls, the setting can't be very different from the days when the early Puritans were first settling these shores over three hundred years ago. □

Notes

Notes

CHASE CREEK

on the Severn River

The upper reaches of the Severn River are guarded by three bridges. Well, *guarded* may not be a precise description. Two of the bridges seem to be obstacles sometimes, but the third—the bridge upstream—is tall enough to permit easy passage to the Severn's headwaters. It's the first two bridges that have sometimes been a problem.

In our early boating days, the downstream drawbridge had a reputation as a reluctant respondent to a boat's pleadings to open. Some boaters even insisted that the tender was not there at all—that a real bridge tender just didn't exist! Ah, well. Such is the frustration of waiting for *any* drawbridge to open.

There must be a new bridge tender nowadays. We heard a female voice on VHF last fall identify herself as the bridge tender. And when we came within hailing distance of the bridge and gave our toots, the draw lifted very nicely, thank you.

It was just as well it did, because the nor'easter we had battled all day from Solomons picked that exact moment to let loose. In my mind's eye I can still see the dark gray sky, the flat white shape of the bridge, and the slowly opening green iron jaws through the torrent of rain and wind. We hit the throttle and turned on our masthead light—just to make sure we would be seen—and slipped through with room to spare.

With a toot of thanks to the tender, we peered through the rain to find the opening for the second obstacle—an unused railroad bridge a little over a half-mile upstream. Until recently the entire bridge was still standing, with the opening section swung roughly perpendicular to the main bridge. This presented no problems unless there was an inordinate amount of boat traffic. Now, the north end of the bridge—including the swing span—has been removed. We skirted the remaining southern portion and made for the third bridge. We call this the Route 50 Bridge and it is eighty feet at its central span—enough to clear most any sailboat I know of. We motored resolutely under the bridge, with the rumbling of auto traffic falling on us like a blanket.

Our destination, St. Helena Island on Round Bay, was only three and a half miles farther upstream, but as the rain and wind picked up when we left the shelter of the bridge I began to have my doubts. Maybe we should look for an anchorage nearby. We had been into a couple of the creeks on the south shore—Saltworks and Clements—but that would put the wind on our stern. We could probably handle that all right, but a strong stern wind does take away some of your steerage and, in the failing light, I wanted perfect control of the boat.

To starboard was Cool Spring Creek. In the shelter of our dodger we studied our charts. It looked snug, but maybe too snug. What's this one further up, Chase Creek? A number of cruising friends had mentioned Chase Creek. "It looks good," we said to each other. "Let's try it."

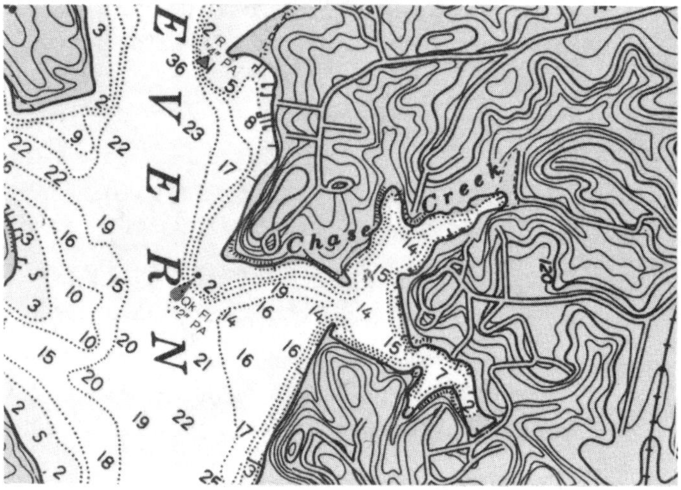

From NOAA Chart 12282—not to be used for navigation.

Chase Creek has a quick-flashing red buoy to mark a shoal off its upstream side. That should make it easy to find. The mouth of the creek is only about a mile from the high bridge.

The rain continued in torrents. Now there was lightning as well. Bright flashes lit up the shoreline in eerie blue detail that dropped back into the dark gray of approaching night. For a while we couldn't make out the creek's entrance. The shoreline on each side of the opening retreated into a gathering gloom that we just couldn't see through.

"The red buoy," I said. "We'll just head for its flashing red light, then when we're within a couple of hundred yards, we'll just turn and head in."

More pouring rain, an occasional flash of lightning, then, through the gloom we saw the buoy's flashes. By the time we made our turn to run into Chase Creek, we were thoroughly chilled. As we passed through the entrance visibility improved and we saw that there was ample room with no shoals to worry about. Chase Creek is actually Y-shaped. The port branch held quite a few anchored and moored boats, mostly sail. The starboard branch seemed much prettier with tree-lined slopes on one side while the north side was lined with pleasant-looking houses. This branch continues maybe three hundred yards then curls around a sandy point for another hundred yards or so.

I inched my way through the rain onto the foredeck, and as Dixie slowed us to a stop, let out our anchor. Chase Creek provided a snug, protected anchorage, and only an occasional puff of wind found *Moon Song* as she swung on her 12H anchor. Within a few minutes we had the stove lit and hot coffee brewing; as the warmth and aroma filled the cabin, I settled back to savor the day. I must have been exhausted because almost immediately I fell asleep. The last thing I remembered was the drawbridge and lightning flashes.□

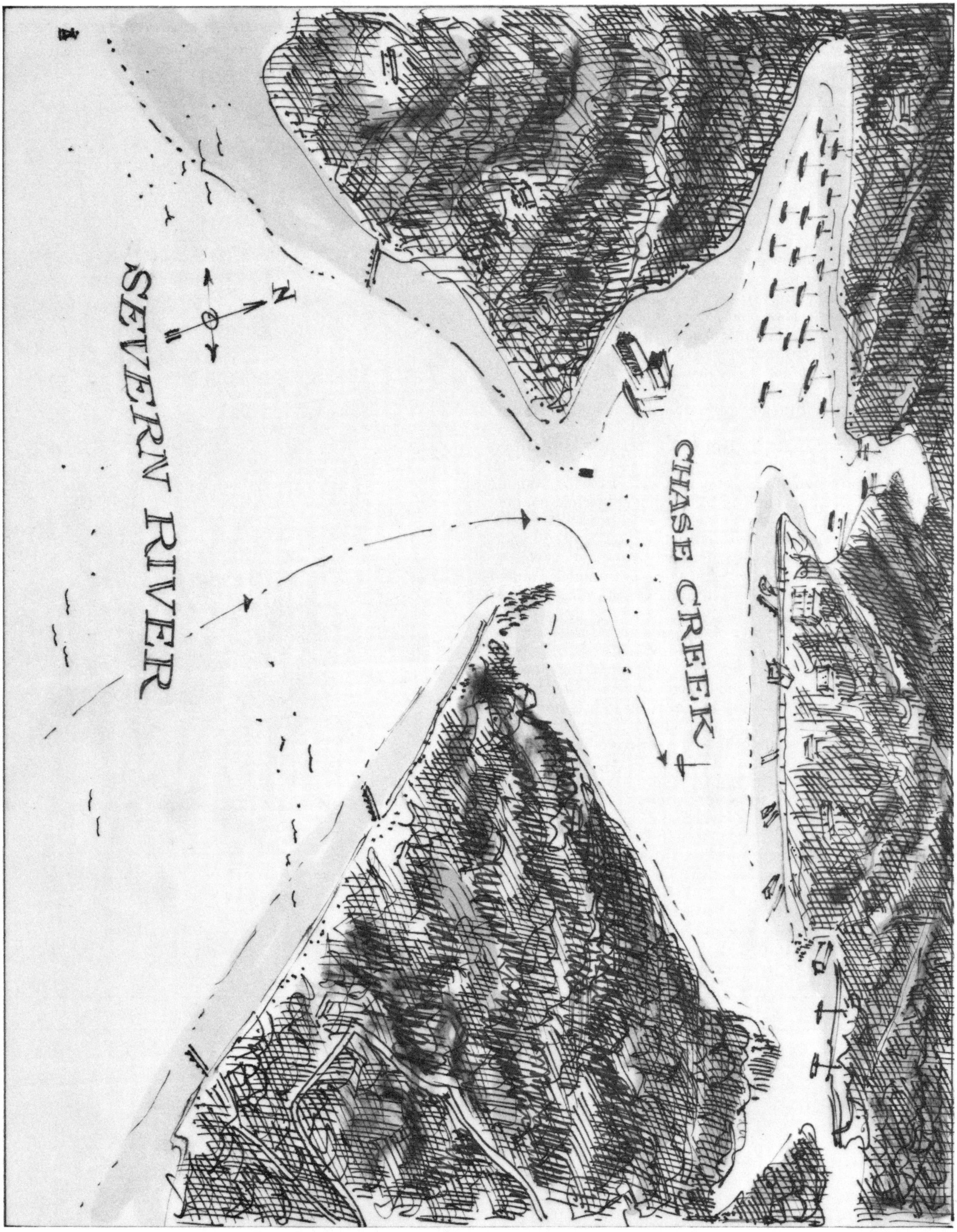
SEVERN RIVER
CHASE CREEK
N

LITTLE ROUND BAY

on the Severn River

Just about every creek on the Severn provides a comfortable anchorage in good deep water. Round Bay, five miles up the river, has several favorites, the best of which are Little Round Bay and St. Helena Island.

There's good protection all around St. Helena Island. Just don't anchor in the cable area directly west of the island. When the weather is really "sticky," perhaps you could slip around and drop your hook inside the protecting arm of Long Point. The shores here are fairly well settled, but you will be protected from any nor'wester that might hit the Bay in midsummer.

Other choice spots are Hopkins Creek and Maynadier Creek, SSW of St. Helena Island.

If you draw over three feet, give a wide berth to the shoal jutting out just opposite Mathiers Point. Stay mid-channel until you round the sandspit at the entrance to Hopkins Creek, then circle around to port, where you can drop your hook. The sand bar will keep any wave action at bay while it permits the breeze to find you, even on a hot summer's night. Water depths range to 11 feet, and the shoreline has few houses and little activity.

But if you want to find a really good anchorage on a hot summer night, turn west around Mathiers Point into Maynadier Creek. The channel leading around this point is an ample 14 feet or more, and the creek opens up inside with depths of eight to 10 feet. The bottom is soft mud and provides good holding ground. There are few homes or buildings along the shore of this bay-like creek, and a feeling of solitude is welcome after a long day's cruise. Extensive marshes along its south and west shores suggest a dense mosquito population, so be sure you have insect repellent and good screens on your companionway.

Round Bay itself is wide enough for good sailing and small enough to offer protection from heavy seas. It is a beautiful body of water, about two miles across at its widest point.

Normally this part of the Severn River is busy with small boat regattas, and many white sails dot the water. Weekends afford the heaviest traffic, so the yachtsman will enjoy the weekdays more if he is seeking solitude. □

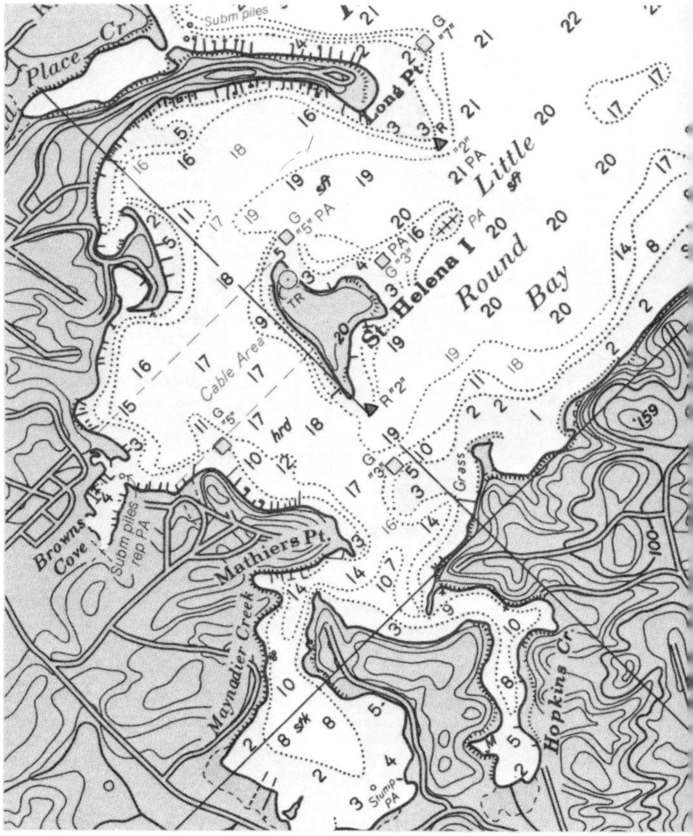

From NOAA Chart 12282—not to be used for navigation

Notes

SEVERN RIVER
LONG POINT
LITTLE ROUND BAY
"2"
CABLE AREA
"3"
"5"
ST. HELENA ISLAND
"2"
"3"
MATHIERS PT.
MAYNADIER CR.
HOPKINS CREEK
N

FISHING CREEK

off Thomas Point

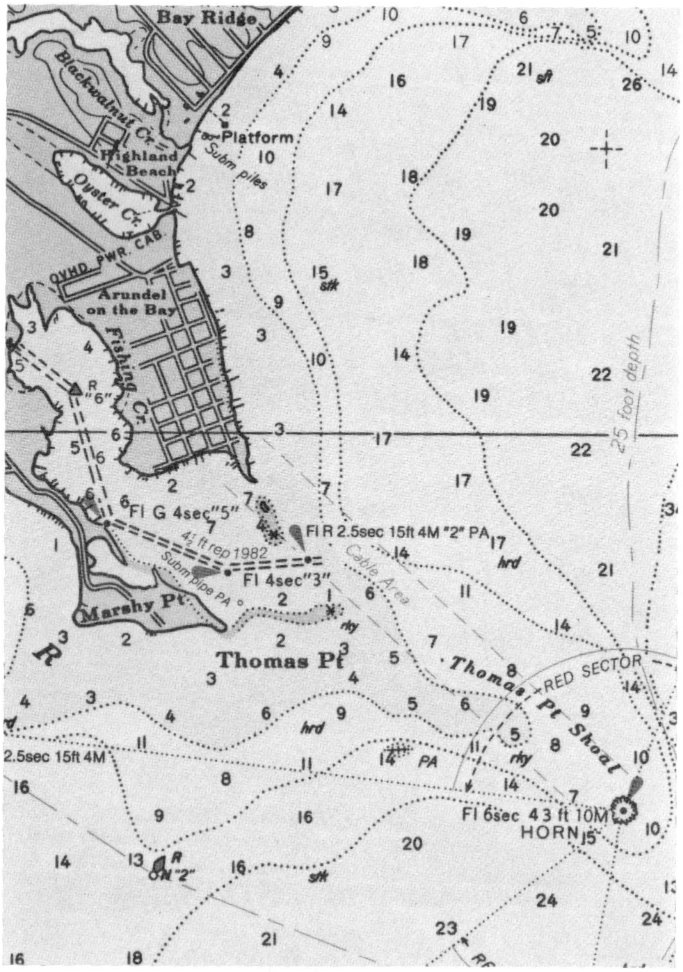

From NOAA Chart 12270—not to be used for navigation.

We were homeward bound from Solomons and a late departure had brought us to the mouth of the South River with only about an hour of daylight left. Whitehall Bay was still seven miles away, and home (up the Magothy) was almost twenty.

Then I remembered that several friends had mentioned Fishing Creek on Thomas Point. This little creek has been right under our noses and we had never had occasion to try it. Well, why not now?

Up ahead the bulk of the Thomas Point Light reflected the scarlet of the setting sun. This time we passed between the old lighthouse and the shoal and followed the shoreline north so that we could see more easily the entrance marker of Fishing Creek.

How often we have cruised up and down the Bay, using this lighthouse as a point of reference on our trips, and admiring its quaint cottage construction.

The first lighthouse on Thomas Point was erected in 1825, in an age when most lighthouses were masonry structures on land—beacons placed atop the keeper's quarters. For over fifty years navigators endured the inefficiencies of old Thomas Point Lighthouse, which was particularly dangerous since a shoal extended over a mile beyond the light into the bay. From its outer extremity to the shore, the shoal lay under only eight feet of water. In dense fog or heavy weather, navigators described the light as utterly useless.

The soft bottom of the Bay made it impossible to erect a lighthouse directly over a shoal until an Englishman, Alexander Mitchell, came up with a solution which had been in use in England as early as 1838. This was the screw-pile construction, which used a broad auger-like flange at the base of the pile to bore into the soft mud or sand, forming a foundation on which the lighthouse could be built.

The Thomas Point Light as we see it today is typical of such screw-pile construction. In recognition of its historical significance, the light was included in the National Register of Historic Places in 1975. Recent Coast Guard economy measures forced the removal of the light's three man crew favor of automation, but at least our favorite Chesapeake landmark is assured of preservation.

As we left the lighthouse to starboard, it seemed the best course would be about 345° M. This takes you roughly parallel to the shoreline; and if started somewhere near the lighthouse, will help you avoid the shoals.

As you spot the first red flasher 15 ft. "2" (Fl R 2.5 sec), start searching for the second lighted spar further inside the creek. This one is "3" (Fl 4 sec) with a white flashing light. When the two marks line up (form a range), you can turn and head in. There are shallows on both sides, so stay in mid-channel.

As you approach the second mark, start searching for the third—"5" (Fl G 4 sec). From there you turn on a course of 350° M (approximately) and head for R "6". We think that the best anchorage is halfway between "5" and "6". Simply turn off the fairway a short distance to keep out of the main channel traffic, leaving room to swing at anchor, and drop the hook.

A recent channel check reports some shoaling, so watch your depthfinder. You should be OK with a five-foot draft, or less.

Like Selby Bay, this is a real surprise anchorage for a peaceful night. And as you make the last anchor check before turning in, look back out to the Bay and be assured by the red winking light of the Thomas Point Lighthouse that all's well on the Bay tonight. □

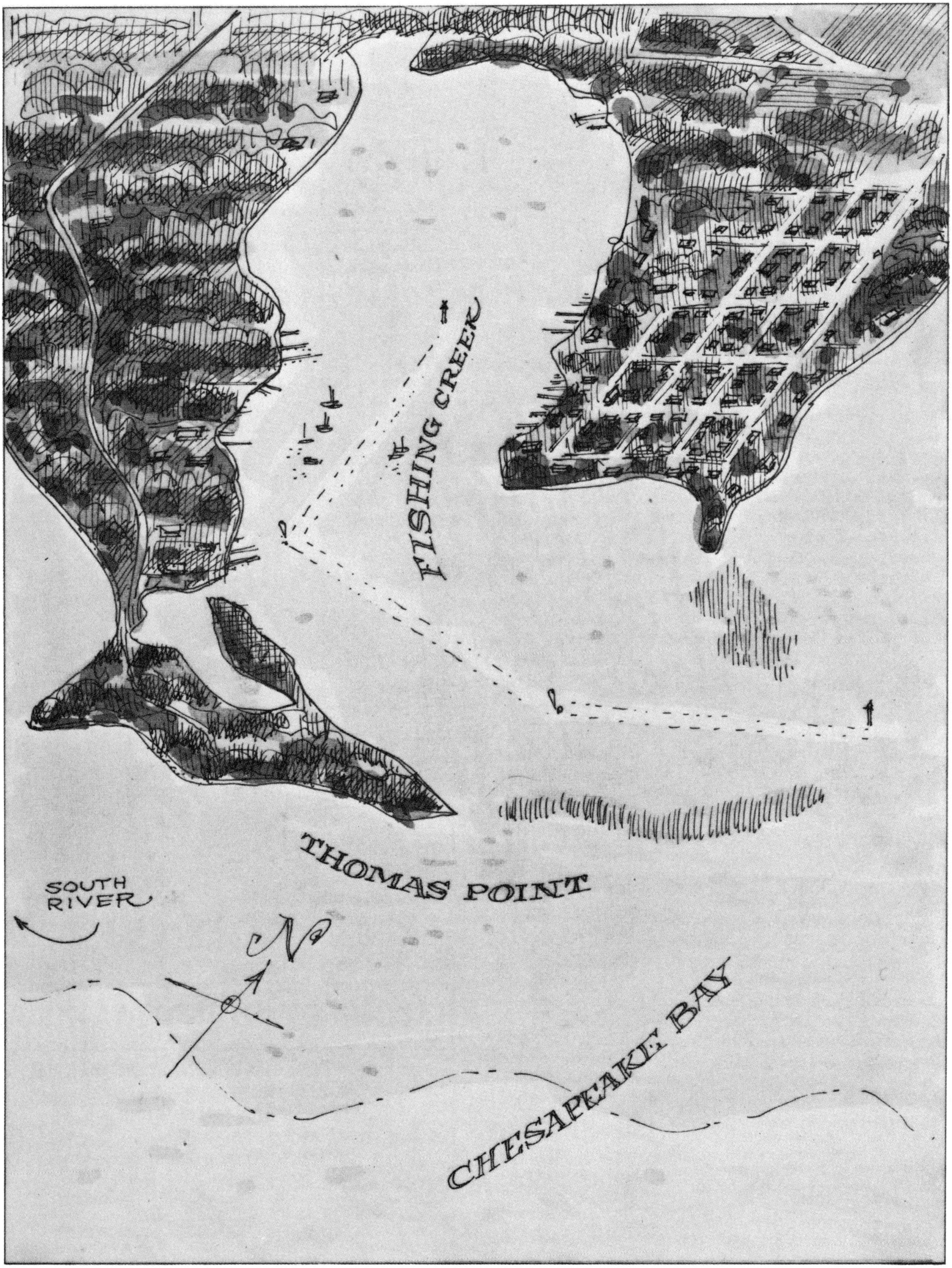
FISHING CREEK
THOMAS POINT
SOUTH RIVER
N
CHESAPEAKE BAY

SELBY BAY

on the South River

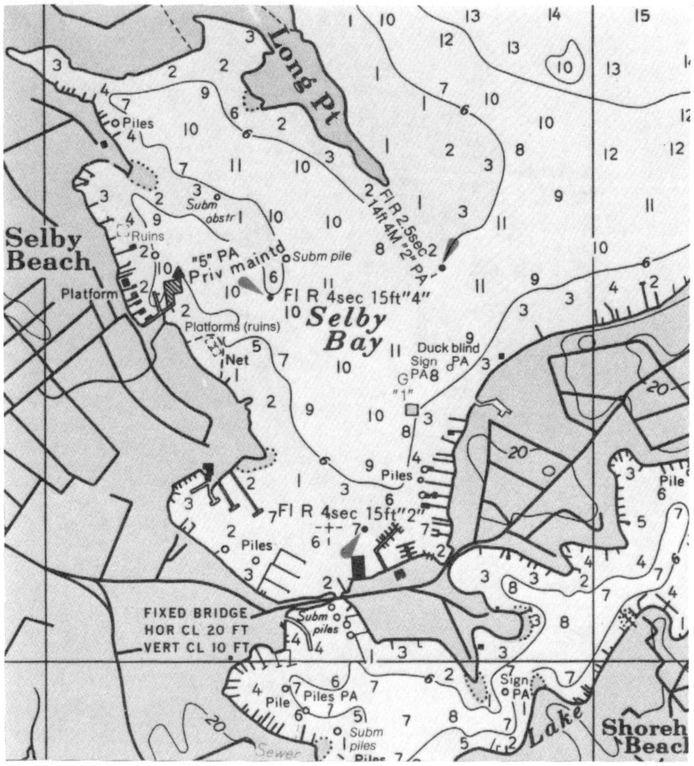

From NOAA Chart 12270—not to be used for navigation.

In an area which abounds with history, the South River has much to tell the visitor. On its hills can be found All Hallows Church, whose tombs and register read like a directory of this part of Tidewater Maryland in the 18th century.

Today the South River is a busy waterway but not as crowded as Severn or Middle Rivers. The creeks here are inviting, and more than once we've dropped our hook in their quiet green shadows.

Selby Bay looks inviting on the charts, but the several marinas there suggest a heavy traffic pattern which can make an anchorage uncomfortable. Indeed, several friends advised against ever anchoring in Selby Bay! However, we spent a very peaceful evening there in early June when the traffic should have been quite heavy.

It was late in the day, and we had intended to go further up the river to one of its fine creeks. Instead, as we passed Selby Bay we found ourselves intrigued with its possibilities; and as Turkey Point slid by, we rounded the red flasher and took a closer look at the busy shores there.

The place to anchor in Selby Bay is in the northwest corner where there is no commercial activity. As you round 14 ft. "2" (Fl R 2.5 sec), turn northwest and leave to port 15 ft. "4" (Fl R 4 sec) which marks a shallow tongue of sandbar that extends from the shore on a line parallel to your course; so don't stray too much to port! You might consider taking a course of 270° M from "2", and watching your depth; when it reaches about 10 feet, turn on your northwest course.

You can snuggle quite close to shore in the corner of the bay just opposite the little cove on the north bank. All around you is wooded land with wild birds and fish.

Selby Bay offers two distinct personalities. We were impressed with the contrast when we came topside after dark for the final anchor check before turning in. On one side the cool woods nearby throbbed with the calls of tree frogs, crickets, and other wild creatures, while across the bay in the distance the lights of the docks and marinas suggested much activity. The effect was pleasing and added to our pleasant evening in Selby Bay. □

Notes

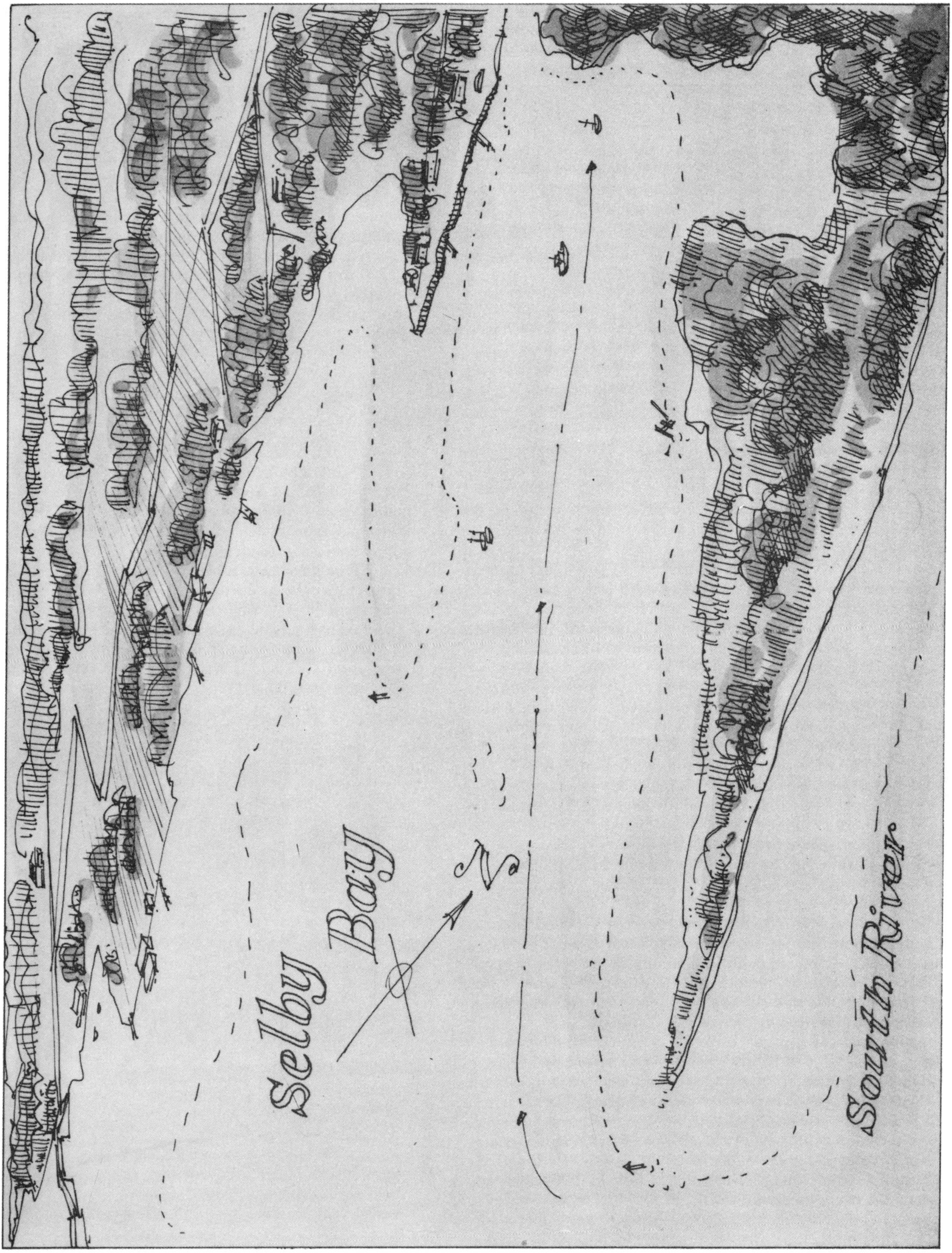
Selby Bay
South River
N

HARNESS CREEK
on the South River

From black bell #73 a course of approximately 338° will carry you right into the mouth of the South River, a distance of about three-and-a-half miles. From Thomas Point Light you'll take a course of about 286° M to clear "4" (Fl R 2½ sec 15 ft) off Marshy Point. Be sure you honor this mark because it stands a good half-mile off shore and might be hard to pick up, particularly if you're new to the area. There are quite a few crab pots in this part of the river, so keep a sharp lookout or you'll wrap a line around your prop. Also, there are a number of fish traps to avoid. These are not out in the fairway, however, and should present no problem.

Just past Turkey Point, to port, is Selby Bay, home of several large marinas, where you can get fuel, repairs, and supplies. Beyond Turkey Point you will find another pair of marks and about a mile beyond that, to starboard, is Harness Creek.

The entrance to Harness Creek lies 2½ miles from the South River entrance marker and just short of South River marker #10, on the north shore.

After you pass the four-foot shoal on the lower point, be sure to keep fairly close to the starboard shore to avoid the shoaling off Persimmon Point.

The creek's entrance is unmarked, so you'll just have to feel your way in. There's plenty of deep water, however, so you should have no problems. Just check your chart (I used #12271). Just inside the creek, on your starboard, is a favorite swimming area. Here the sandy beach drops off fairly sharply, so you are almost able to beach the bow of your boat.

This is the only spot we found where you can take your pet ashore conveniently. The rest of the east side of the creek, although in its natural, undeveloped state, has steep banks and "no trespassing" signs. The west shore is all privately owned and developed with one exception, where landing is all but impossible because of the steep bank. A couple of commercial fishing boats tie up at the head of the creek. You might go ashore there in an emergency. You are only about 1½ miles from Annapolis by road. In late May and early June strawberries fresh from the patch are sold along the road just above the fishermen's dock.

When you enter Harness Creek, the first little stretch is broad enough to hold a dozen boats or more. If you follow the eastern shoreline, there is a gap in the marsh which reveals a hidden cove, large enough for one or two boats—if they raft together. This is the famous Harness Creek "hurricane hole." The high banks and dense woods make this tiny anchorage safe in any blow.

On our cruise, the anchorage was jammed with boats of all descriptions: power, sail, single, and rafted up. Several dinghies paddled around, and here and there we could see the cheery glow of grills cooking evening meals.

We continued further upstream, wending our way through the crowd. The first point to port shows a thin strip of sandy beach with a field beyond where you might walk a pet. We carefully picked our way past a center-cockpit 40-footer and dropped anchor astern a small 23-foot powerboat. I paid out our anchor rode as Dixie backed down toward the marshy shoreline on the east side. We dragged. I retrieved the anchor, and we motored out to deep water and tried once more. Again we dragged. On the fourth try the anchor dug in solidly and we settled back to enjoy our surroundings.

Astern of us was an anchored houseboat which was soon joined by a sailboat. Within a half-hour I could see that they, too, were dragging anchor. With much shouting, flashing of lights, and roaring of motors, the pair moved away from the shallows and re-set their anchor.

When we had finished supper we relaxed in our cockpit, the warm darkness broken only by a few shorelights and the twinkle of anchor lights. Later, we had just snuggled down in our bunks and turned off our lights when I heard a loud shouting and horn blowing from across the water. I stumbled sleepily to the companionway and heard more shouts and horns, accompanied by bright, flashing lights.

The focus of all this attention was the 40-foot center cockpit sloop. Lights from several nearby boats were flashing on her as the breeze sent her backward, dragging anchor, till she was among several smaller boats and getting close to shore. The shouts continued for some time till several of her crew stumbled, half-asleep, on deck. In a few minutes they had motored her back into deep water and reset their anchor. It certainly appears that the holding ground is quite tricky on the upper part of the creek!

Harness Creek is a beautiful, snug little creek, close to the Bay and within easy reach of supplies. And, although our visit was made in late August on a Saturday night, I have a hunch there will always be a crowd there. My advice would be to get in early to assure yourself of room to anchor. Set your anchor very carefully—and check it frequently before you turn in. □

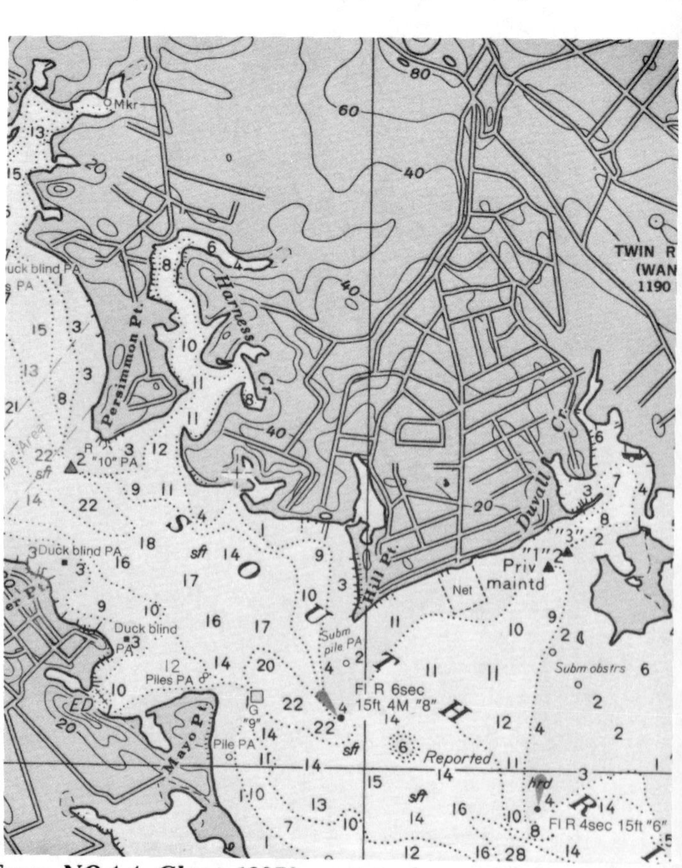

From NOAA Chart 12270—not to be used for navigation.

SOUTH RIVER
PERSIMMON POINT
N
HARNESS CREEK

GLEBE BAY

on the South River

Glebe Bay is on the south shore of the South River about 4½ miles upstream, below the South River Bridge at Edgewater. This bridge has a permanent limited boat clearance of 53 feet.

A green marker, "11" (Fl G 2.5 sec) pinpoints the shoal at the downstream side of Glebe Bay's entrance. This shoal is considerable, and as you approach from downstream don't mistake this aid as a mark intended for the north shore. This mark guards not only the extensive shoal off Cedar Point but also a few pilings as well (some visible, some underwater).

As you enter Glebe Bay, you'll want to favor the port side a bit. If you study the chart, you'll see why. There are more underwater pilings, right in the middle of the entrance to Glebe Bay. From the light we took a course that would keep us about 150 yards offshore as we rounded Cedar Point. Ahead you'll see a piling in the water just inside the entrance, about where the 2-foot mark and shoal are shown on Chart #12271. Although we were told later that this piling does not mark the shoal, we assumed it did and gave it a wide berth and found ourselves inside Glebe Bay with no problems. (Take it just to port and all will be well.)

One hazard immediately noticeable on your chart is an extensive shoal right in the middle of Glebe Bay, so don't try to cut right through the middle.

We looked around Glebe Bay; and although the shoreline is attractive, we decided that just about any place we would anchor would be too exposed. So we decided to head up into Glebe Creek. Keeping about 150 yards offshore, we skirted the southeast shore of Glebe all the way around to the low-lying point of land that guards the entrance to Glebe Creek. Beyond the point is a tiny bay with 11 to 15 feet of water, where we anchored for the night.

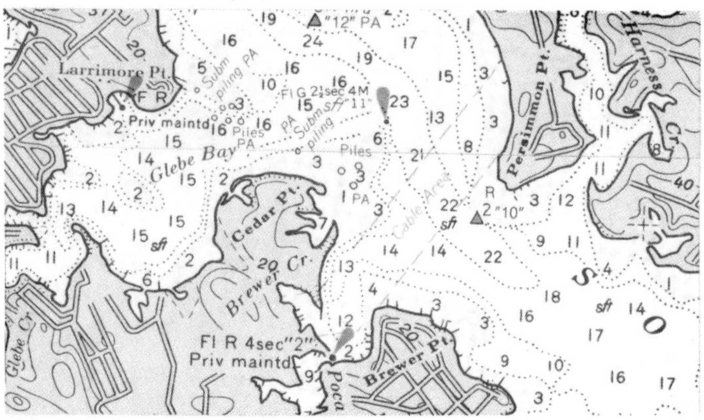

From NOAA Chart 12270—not to be used for navigation.

But anchoring did not come easily! Six (count them), six times we carefully lowered the anchor, swung delicately back on the rode, but when we'd put the engine in reverse, dragged the anchor across the lagoon. Each time we retrieved the dragging anchor we also brought up a quantity of mud and leaves. Obviously the leaves were preventing the flukes from really digging in.

We found our anchorage to be attractive and intimate. Most of the shore was lined with modest but attractive homes. There were many docks and piers, with the exception of the point of land on the northeast side. To hold the jellyfish at bay, several piers had enclosed swim areas in wire or net fences, where children splashed and shouted happily.

The only drawback was a runabout and waterskier that raced up and down the creek in defiance of a six-knot speed limit. Time and again they would zip into our little anchorage, circle our boat, and then roar off upstream. But after about a half hour, the waterskier withdrew as darkness closed in. The lights of the surrounding homes dotted the shoreline, and quiet descended as we fell asleep.

Morning was another thing, though. At dawn, as I climbed out into the cockpit with coffee and book in hand, I was greeted with a world of "shore sounds." First was the roar of a garbage truck, followed by the well-known rusty screech of brakes. A clatter of cans, a hoarse shout, and once again the roar of motor followed by screech of brakes. After making its rounds of the entire shoreline the garbage truck sounds faded into the background to be replaced by auto engines as people left for work. Next were several small airplanes flying over on their landing approach at a local airfield. Then, to top it off, we were treated to the tune-up runs of a fellow on a motorbike! I've never before been in an anchorage where we were so surrounded by sound.

After breakfast we motored out into Glebe Bay, around the shoal, and up to the Londontown Marina at Larrimore Point. There we gassed up and asked about the shoal, out in the middle. Indeed, there was a shoal we were advised, but a boat could skirt around on the western side. However, local knowledge was necessary since there were no marks there.

Glebe Bay was attractive and Glebe Creek well protected. We wouldn't mind going back again, but next time we'll take ear plugs. □

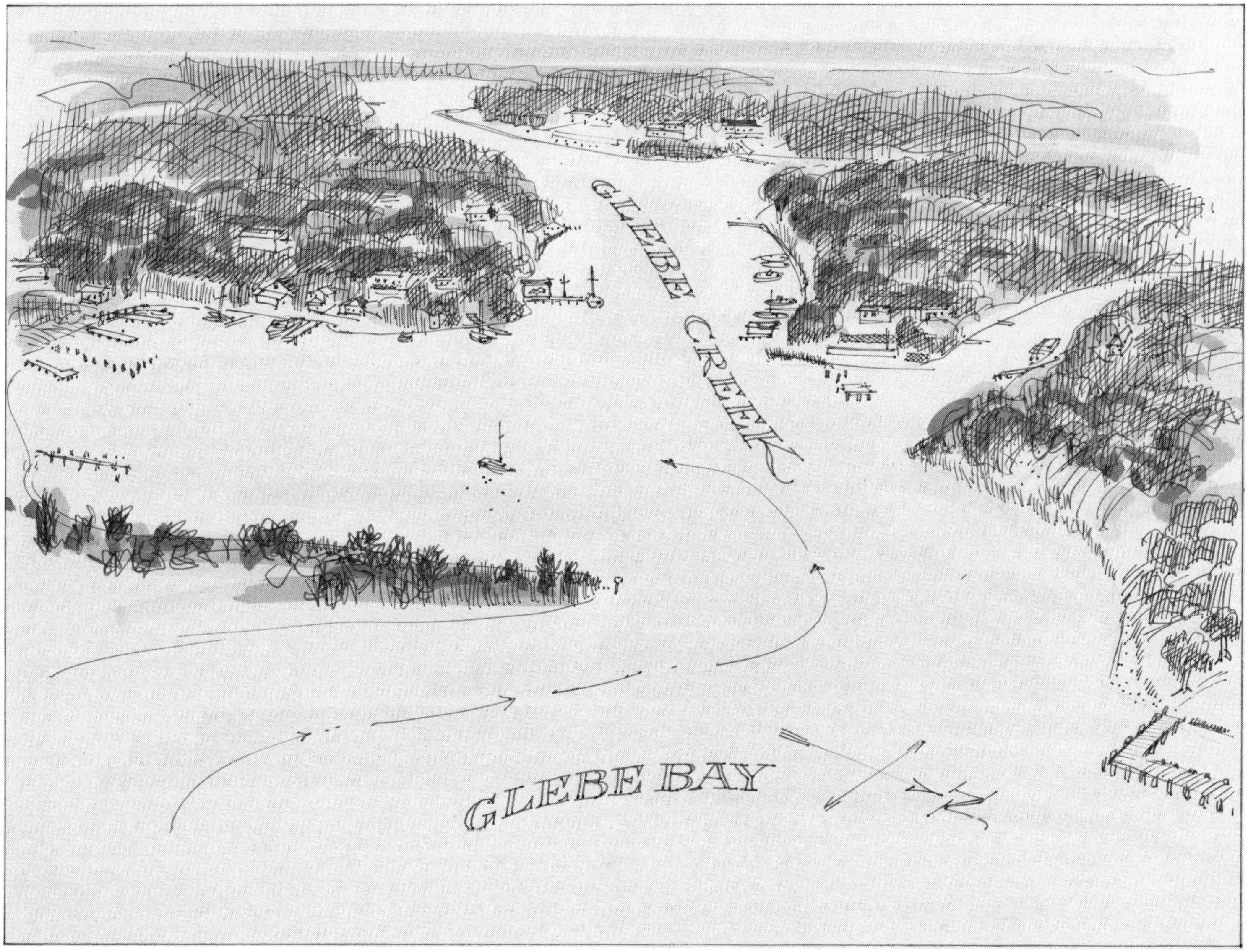

Notes

ABERDEEN CREEK

on the South River

One of the nice things about the South River is its many deep and navigable creeks. One of these perfect anchorages is Aberdeen Creek.

Starting from Thomas Point Light, take a course of 286° M

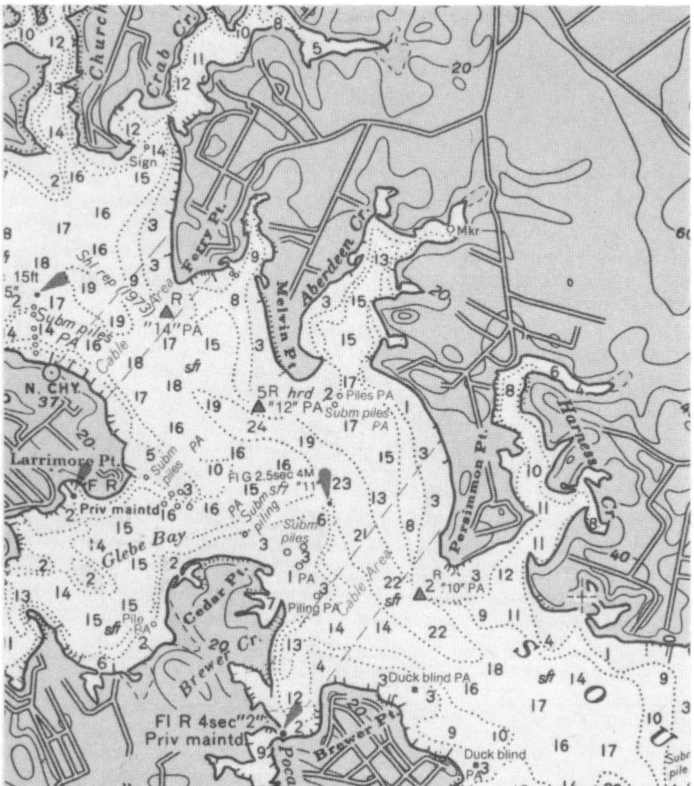

From NOAA Chart 12270—not to be used for navigation.

(approx.) to the red 2½ sec. flasher off Marshy Point, an then take about 320° M which should clear Turkey Point gre daymark just to port and the Hill Point Shoal marker "8" farth upstream just to starboard.

Across from Hill Point the black daymark "9" off May Point is easily visible, and about three-quarters of a mi upstream you should be able to spot the red daymark "10" th marks the shoal off Persimmon Point. Give this mark amp room as you round it and head into Aberdeen Creek. T creek itself is unmarked, although there are shoals projectin from each side at the entrance. Just favor the starboard sho a little. There's a duck blind to port, marking the shoal o Melvin Point.

We passed through the entrance to Aberdeen Cree without incident. To starboard, on slightly elevated groun we could see the grouping of buildings of a children's cam

The port side of Aberdeen's entrance is a wooded point land that curls protectively around the little bay where w would anchor. The end of this point dwindles off in a grass finger that ends in marsh.

Motoring in we took a heading of about 355° M for abou another 250 yards, aiming for the middle of three large house on the creek's western shore. The water here is a good 12 to 1 feet deep, and you can go fairly close to shore. We staye about 150 feet offshore, where we rounded up into a southerl breeze and dropped our hook.

The shoreline around Aberdeen Creek is wooded bu fairly low, which permits a breeze to circulate on hot summe nights. The setting sun cast a rosy glow on the opposite shor and the wake of an occasional passing boat traced a silver tra on the deep blue waters. Gradually a velvet-black nigh sprinkled with diamond stars replaced the summer sky, an we were lulled to sleep by the songs of tree frogs and a occasional loon. □

Notes

Notes

LONDON TOWN PUBLIK HOUSE

on Almshouse Creek, South River

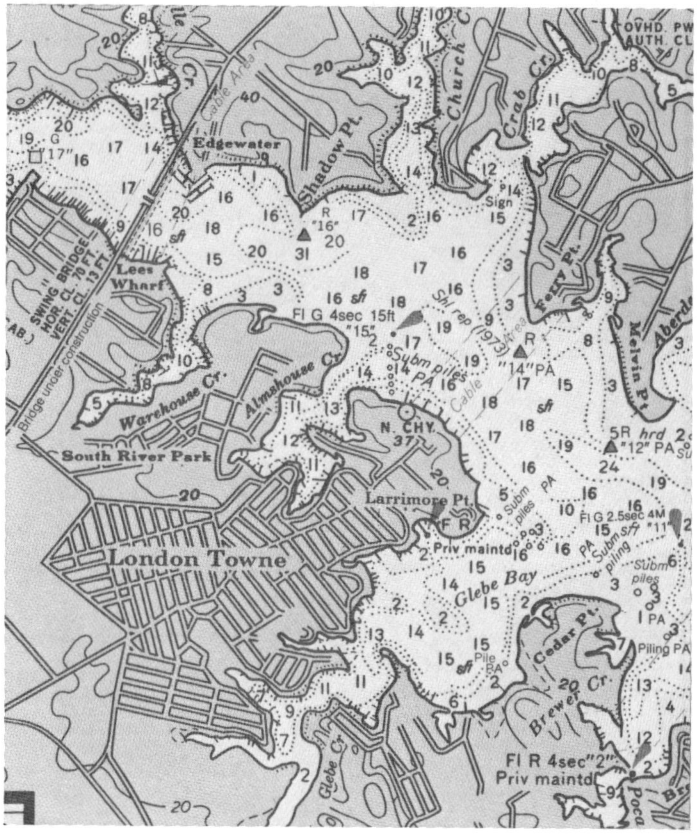

From NOAA Chart 12270—not to be used for navigation. Note: Chart does not reflect the completion of the new South River Bridge, now fixed structure vertical clearance 53 ft.

Your cruise of the South River should include a stop at the refurbished London Town Publik House, the only remaining structure of the once-thriving seaport town. The Publik House is located opposite Buoy 15, on the South River about six miles from the Bay. Deep-draft boats can be accommodated at the private pier. There is no dockage fee for boaters visiting the Publik House and Gardens.

London Towne was bounded by two creeks, Glebe Creek and Almshouse Creek, as well as by the South River. Thus the town provided easy access for sailing ships carrying the popular Maryland tobacco to foreign ports and bringing in their cargoes of European and East Indian goods for the surrounding plantations.

As the economy changed, and with the rise of Baltimore as the center of shipping and industry, shipping turned away from places like Annapolis, London Towne, and Port Tobacco for the more lucrative and accessible trading further up the Bay.

The Publik House, built somewhere between 1744 and 1750, served as an inn, and also provided ferry service for travelers using the main thoroughfare between Williamsburg and Philadelphia. Records indicate that George Washington, Thomas Jefferson, and Francis Scott Key, among others, made the crossing there.

The last private owner of the Inn sold the property to the Trustees for the Poor of Anne Arundel County in 1828, after the demise of the town. From that time until 1965 it was used as the county almshouse.

The Publik House is a solid structure built in the Georgian tradition, commanding an impressive view of the South River. Its style of brickwork is known as "all-headers," which means the bricks are laid side-to-side in walls two bricks thick. This pattern is similar to that seen in several Annapolis landmarks, such as the Paca House and Reynolds Tavern.

Today the Publik House is registered as a National Historic Landmark and represents a cooperative effort by Anne Arundel County and its citizens to preserve the remains of a small 18th century community.

Visiting yachtsmen may also wander through the London Town Gardens—eight acres adjoining the Publik House which are massed with native trees, shrubs and flowers.

Hours are 10 A.M. to 4 P.M. Tuesday-Saturday; noon to 4 P.M. Sunday; closed Mondays. The Publik House is also closed to the public during the months of January and February.

If you plan to overnight in the area, you might prefer an anchorage away from the heavy traffic areas. Perhaps you will want to slip away and drop your hook in one of the several quiet creeks nearby. Why not try Church Creek, or better yet, Crab Creek. Both creeks are just below the South River Bridge, fixed structure vertical clearance 53 ft. □

London Town Publik House

PHOTO BY HAROLD FLECKNOE

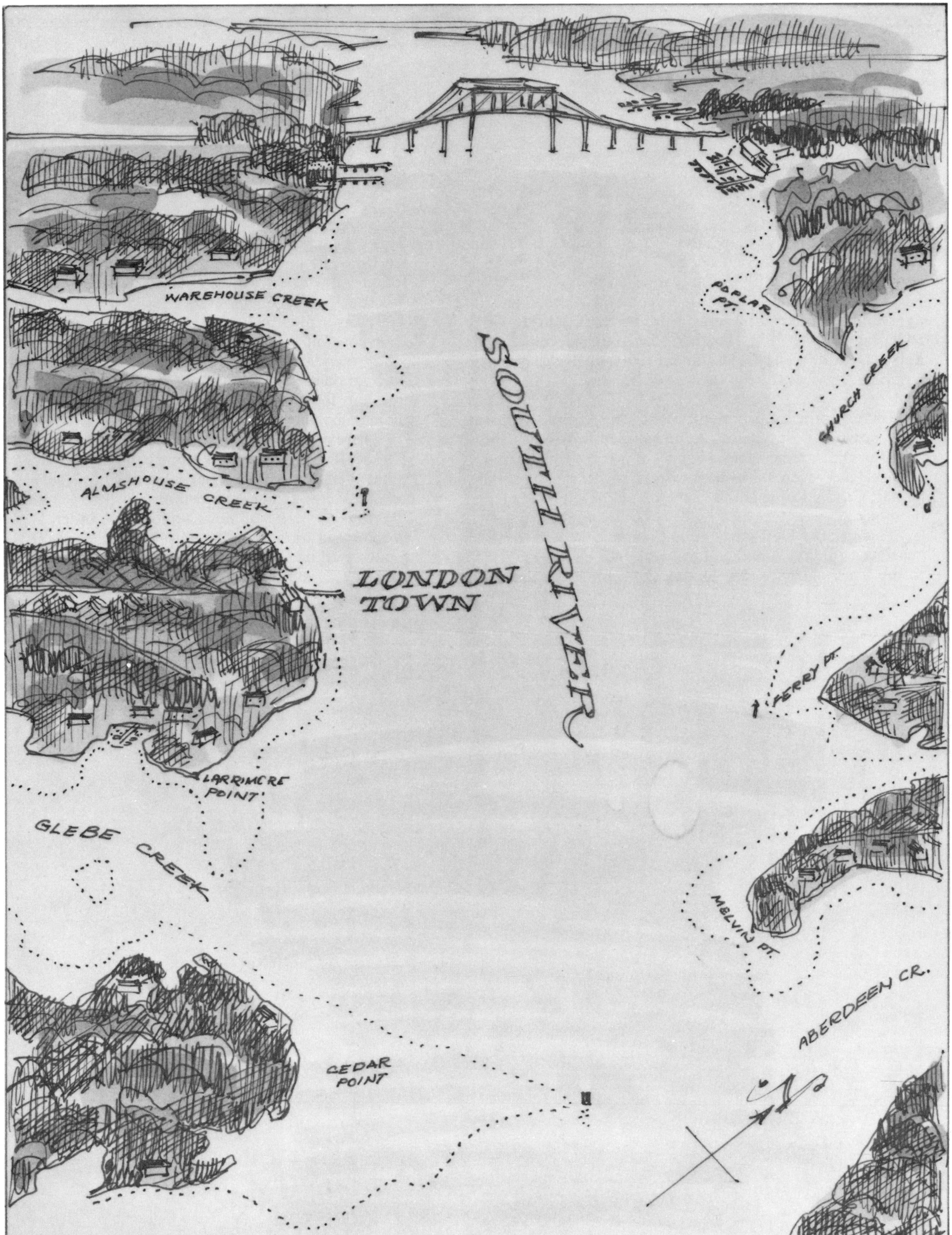
WAREHOUSE CREEK
POPLAR PT.
SOUTH RIVER
CHURCH CREEK
ALMSHOUSE CREEK
LONDON TOWN
FERRY PT.
LARRIMORE POINT
GLEBE CREEK
MELVIN PT.
ABERDEEN CR.
CEDAR POINT

RHODE AND WEST RIVERS

Located on the western shore of the Chesapeake Bay nine miles south of the Chesapeake Bay Bridge is one of the most complete and delightful cruising areas on the Bay. The West River and the Rhode River together provide peaceful anchorages and commercial amenities. The main Rhode River anchorage between Big, High and Flat Islands is scenic, secure and beautiful, while Galesville on the West River provides complete services for the boat as well as several fine restaurants.

To reach the mouth of the West River from the north, drop down the Bay below Annapolis until Thomas Point Light is abeam, then steer a course of 240° M to pick up the #1 black can which marks the northern corner of Curtis Point Shoal. Curtis Point is the eastern side of the West River mouth.

To enter the West River from the south proceed north up the Bay to Buoy #73; then turn west on a course of 293° M to the black entrance can. During the summer on very hazy days the marks may be hard to see against the low lying land to the west, but with reasonable care the entrance can be found with little trouble.

The Rhode River enters the West River just inside the West River mouth. From the water it is hard to decide which river runs into which, but looking at the chart it is clear that many years ago the Rhode emptied into the West River. The Navigational Aids Section of the Coast Guard has settled the question for us, however, as the West River is buoyed as the major channel.

There may be a little confusion on a trip into the West and Rhode Rivers with two #2 marks in a row. But when you remember that Rhode River is a branch of the West River it becomes clear. To help in identifying where you are, remember that the two marks do not resemble each other. West River #2 is mounted on a round steel pile and flashes red every 2.5 seconds. Rhode River #2 is on a tripod of wooden pilings and flashes red every 4 seconds.

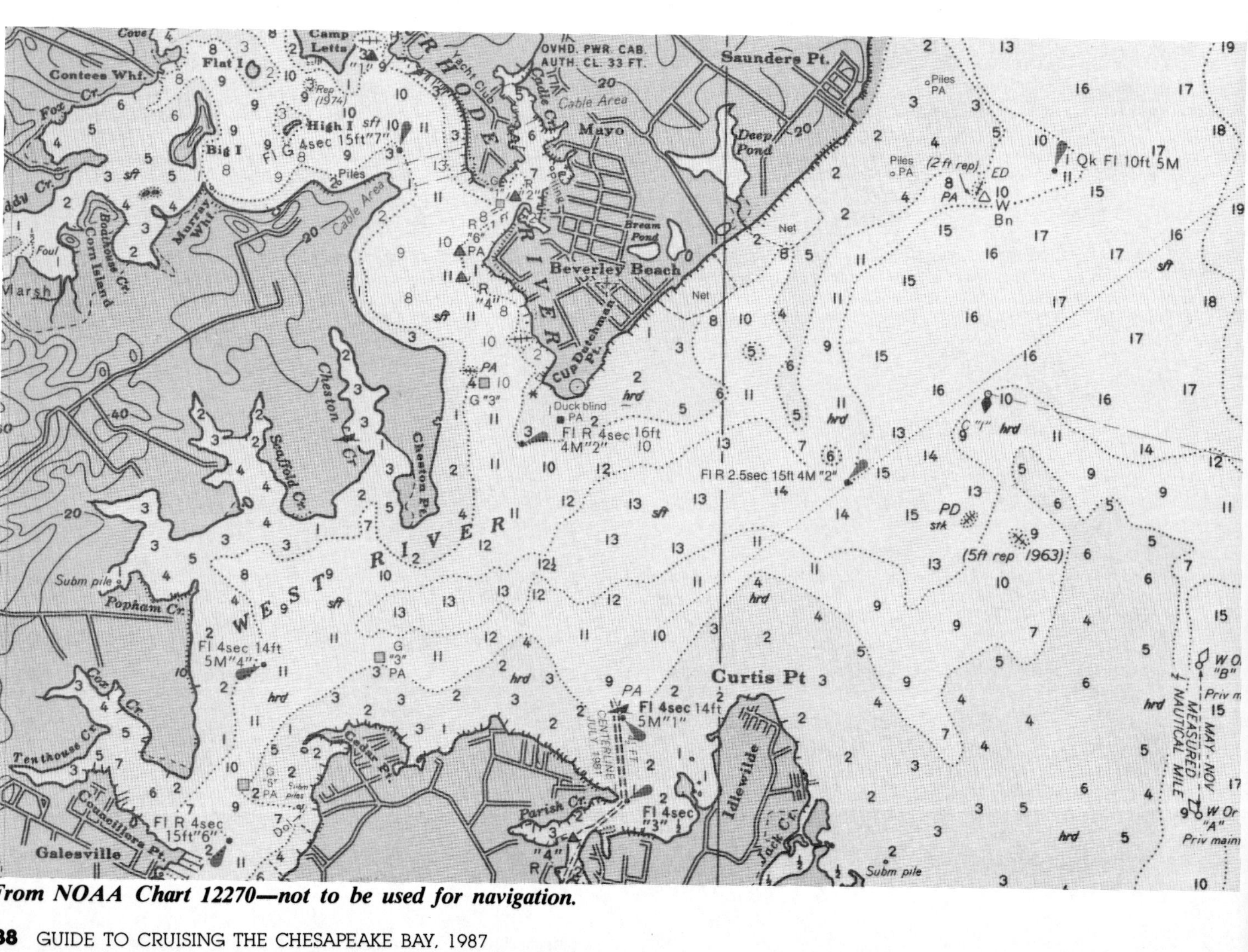

From NOAA Chart 12270—not to be used for navigation.

Directly opposite the mouth of the Rhode River and almost due south of it is Parrish Creek, more commonly known as Shady Side. The entrance to the creek is west of Curtis Point, and the channel is very narrow. There is not much to draw the cruiser to this location as the water is very shallow and with little room to swing, an overnight anchorage does not seem advisable.

If headed into Galesville, once past the entrance and can #1, steer a course of 260° M to pick up mark #4, then turn south on 199° M to enter the channel to Galesville. If you are sailing in on a southerly breeze, don't tack too soon after passing #5. The shallow water extends a little to the south of it. Although the channel is about 500 feet wide it takes the form of an "S" and, therefore, has to be run on a course with a continuously changing bearing. The boat traffic can be quite heavy at times in this area because of the constriction. On weekends sailboat races are often started at Galesville. It is therefore possible to encounter a small fleet leaving the West River under full sail. If the wind is out of the south, spinnaker starts are exciting to watch.

As you round mark #6, Galesville unfolds at the right. On the left South Creek forms a large bay. The shores are lined with the homes of permanent residents, many of whom maintain their own piers. The main commercial activity is located primarily on the western shore.

The Galesville Public Dock, the third installation along the shore, has a 20-foot ramp, a head and a small park.

For the adventurous and stout of foot, a walk of a mile to the west of the Public Dock reveals one of Maryland's finest five-part Georgian mansions, "Tulip Hill." This privately owned mansion dates from about !745, built by Samuel Galloway three years after his marriage to Anne Chew. The oddly-shaped chimneys, rare in colonial homes, have central arches cut out either for decoration or to relieve wind pressure. The wings on either side of the center section were added by Samuel's son, John, after the Revolutionary War. The Quaker Burial Ground is located about a half-mile from Tulip Hill.

Galesville is no busy metropolis, but it does have some amenities not found on the Rhode River. There are several very fine restaurants, each with a spectacular view of the river. A yacht brokerage, ship's store, and several full service marinas are here to meet your every boating need. Between Pirate's Cove and Steamboat Landing Restaurants there is a road where you can find stores selling groceries, liquor, etc.

After sampling the many wares of Galesville, an anchorage in South Creek across the West River from Galesville can be considered, but only when the wind is out of the south. If the forecast indicates that the wind may veer around to the north then the protection of the land will be lost and the anchorage will become exposed. If the wind is out of the northeast and strong then reflected waves could make a vessel lying to the wind roll unmercifully, a real detriment to sound sleep. If you have had an early dinner, and the light is still good, then it is but a short run up to the Rhode River and a well-protected anchorage.

The entrance to the Rhode River is guarded on the north by Dutchman Point. A large white two-storied building with a cupola is a good identifying feature if the #2 mark on the right hand side of the river mouth can not be seen in the haze. After entering the river a course of 348° M will serve for the first mile up the river.

Sailing instructions for the Rhode River depend upon wind direction. In the summer the wind is often out of the south or southeast and the banks of the river act as a wind funnel to the north, but when the wind is out of the west or north it seems to be channeled down the river. For a sailor on the Rhode, a reach is a rare occurrence.

A half-mile above the river mouth the channel opens up on the west side and forms a semicircular bay with good protection for anchored boats from the summer thunderstorms which generally travel from west to east in this area of the Bay. The western side of the river is undeveloped and many varieties of trees and the dense growth give the appearance of a forest. The eastern side of the river has been intensely developed.

Cadle Creek enters the Rhode River on the right three-quarters of a mile above the river mouth. On the chart a four-foot bar is shown across the mouth of the creek which will discourage deep-draft boats. The shores of the creek are heavily populated and its narrowness is not conducive to an overnight anchorage.

Continuing past Cadle Creek north up the Rhode River, be careful of the shoal which extends out from the western side of the river just in front of the lighted green #7 mark. The tendency is to use the mark as a range when approaching from the south, and if attention is not paid to the relative bearing of the light an accidental grounding could mar the delights that await around the bend. Ospreys guard the main anchorage of the Rhode River from their nest atop #7. Continue past the light, make a turn to the left and follow the shoreline in 10 feet of water. After the turn, High Island can be identified on the right bow.

On the chart High Island is shaped like a flat crescent. Extending out from each point of the crescent are shoals which should be given a wide berth when passing the island. At low tide only a few feet of water cover the shoals for a distance of 75 to 100 feet from shore. Once past High Island the river widens out and the three islands bracket the main anchorage.

Big Island on the west, Flat Island on the north and High Island to the east effectively surround the anchorage and give protection from wind and wave. High trees and bluffs surround this bit of deep water and while the wind may moan through the rigging or around the cabin in the middle of the night, the waves have little chance to form and the smallest cruiser can spend a night here in security.

By anchoring west of High Island most of the houses lining the east bank of the river can be screened and an unspoiled view surrounds the boat. During most weekdays the anchorage is deserted, so peace and quiet abound. On beautiful weekends, however, upwards of 100 boats have been counted at anchor within sight of the three islands attesting to the popularity of this anchorage.

Two other good anchorages are in the immediate area. One is tucked behind the west side of Big Island where seven feet of water affords further protection from easterly winds. The other is north of Flat Island in the mouth of Sellman Creek, a good spot in a west or north wind.

Big Island is mostly wooded ground and landing would be difficult. For those of an exploring mind, Flat Island and High Island have small beaches on which to land a dinghy with

West River

Galesville

PHOTO BY BOB GRIESER

ease. Flat Island's beach is on the eastern side of the island in a natural cove, and is large enough for a tent and the water is deep enough close-in for a small cruiser to ground its bow on the beach. Exploring the dense undergrowth could be an exciting adventure for small children.

The chart shows over six feet of water between Flat and High Islands. It is there somewhere, but while some skippers can find the clear spot with little trouble, there are an equal number who seem to run aground; it would be prudent to proceed slowly if passing between the two islands.

High Island, the smallest of the three, is just that. It juts high out of the water like a clay volcano. The island has a small beach across the northwest side under a bluff. On the southeast hillside, where a slope extends gently into the water, a larger beach exists with a lone tree on the edge of the water providing a cool spot of shade in the summer, as well as a handy place to moor a small boat. Two shoals extend like arms from the island out to the southeast forming a small bay. The shoals are hard sand and are enjoyed by swimmers from anchored yachts in the vicinity.

Camp Letts owned by the YMCA, is located on the neck of land between Sellman Creek and Bear Neck Creek on the northeast side of the anchorage. The camp features horseback riding and aquatic sports for young men and women. The camp is very active during the day as campers venture out into the river in canoes, sailboats, catamarans and water skis, and at night an occasional bonfire lights the early evening sky. At the early morning light, bugles awake the campers and can hurry an anchored crew awake, or merely notify them that they can catch 40 more winks. Most of the time the camp activities pass unnoticed.

Bear Neck Creek is worth exploring; it opens out onto the Rhode River northeast of High Island. Its entrance is well marked by a #1 daymark on the left and Carrs Wharf, a public facility extending out to deep water, on the right. Beware of cutting the point off Camp Letts too close as the shoal extends out farther than the chart shows. There are services available such as fuel, ice, water and some mechanical help on Bear Neck Creek.

As you continue up Bear Neck Creek past the second daymark, the creek becomes residential on the right, but remains wooded on the the Camp Letts-owned side.

A small shoal extends out from the left side of the creek just above a local marina, and should be given room to the right to prevent a grounding. Whitemarsh Creek opens up on the right a quarter of a mile above the mouth of the creek. At this point Bear Neck widens out, and on the left there is enough room for a snug anchorage for a shallow draft boat. Whitemarsh Creek is rarely used as an anchorage probably because it is too shallow for most cruising boats.

There are many beautiful spots in the world, some more accessible than others. For those fortunate few who are at anchor when the moon comes up out of the east like a silver ball, or see the dogwood in bloom on Big Island on a clear spring morning, or relish the russet leaves accenting the shoreline in the fall, the Rhode River is unquestionably beautiful; and like a fine wine its bouquet grows with each tasting. □

Energy Saving Boating Tips

Courtesy U.S. Power Squadron

REDUCE DISTANCE — Navigating a boat from A to B can represent many widely differing fuel expenditures, depending on the skipper. He can plot the shortest safe course, not just the easiest. He can steer it more carefully. Courses should be laid out using prevailing winds and tides to best advantage. He can find a weekend rendezvous closer to home. Two boat families can combine and by pooling save half the fuel ordinarily used.

REDUCE FRICTION — The tuned engine gets the most from every drop of petrol. Clean spark plugs, proper oil pressure, sharp timing, optimum engine heat — all make the boat go better and with less fuel.

HERRING BAY/ ROCKHOLD CREEK

on the Western Shore

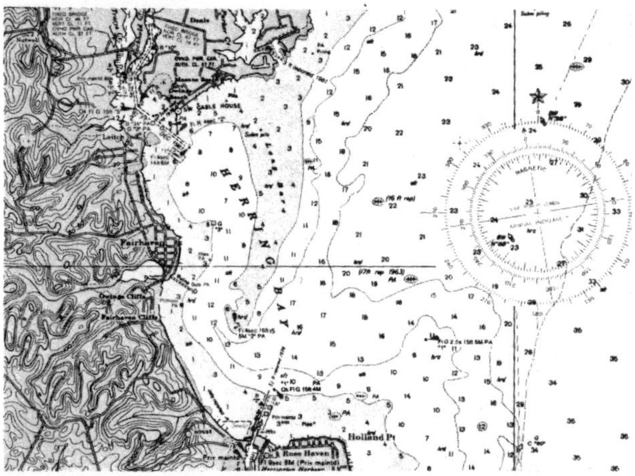

From NOAA Chart #12266—not to be used for navigation.

Herring Bay is about five miles from flashing green "71" (Fl G 4 sec), the big buoy in the large ship lane located between Poplar Islands and Herring Bay. From it steer a 267° M course to (Qk Fl G) "1" off Holland Pt. If you're approaching from the north, you may prefer to use a 223° M course from black and white N "32 B" east of Shady Side to flashing 2½ second "1" near Holland Pt.

For an approach from the south, use the three-mile run from black and white N "7B" off Chesapeake Beach past Holland Pt. to 15-foot "1," a 2½ second flasher, before turning into Herring Bay itself. In any event, advance chart study is recommended because markers close to shore are unlighted, and it's important to stay outside the one-fathom line.

Herring Bay itself is wide open and usually is not suitable for overnighting since it offers little protection from the weather. However, on the southern side of Herring Bay a well marked channel leads you into Herrington Harbour Marina, where you'll find a restaurant, swimming pool and tennis courts. A few transient slips are available, but should be reserved ahead of time. Although the charts do not indicate so, sources report the entrance channel has been dredged to 7 feet.

To lay your course into the marina, run 265° M from previously mentioned flashing "1" northeast of Holland Pt. to quick flashing green "1." These navigation aids illustrate the way the buoyage system is numbered, which sometimes confuses even experienced boatmen. The first "1" is for Herring Bay, the second "1" is for its tributary, Herrington Harbour.

Leaving quick flashing green "1" to port, turn to enter the marina via the 60-foot wide channel protected by long jetties. Run about 210° M between the sets of privately maintained daymarks, lining up the lighted beacons inside the marina basin. Look for the fuel pumps on the third pier to port where you'll be given directions to your previously reserved slip.

Powerboats and small sailboats might want to follow the markers at the western end of Herring Bay, where you will enter Rockhold Creek, which holds many marinas (some with transient slips). Workboats, fishing boats, and watermen abound here, giving the local restaurants good, fresh seafood and lots of local color. □

LONG BEACH,

Above Patuxent River

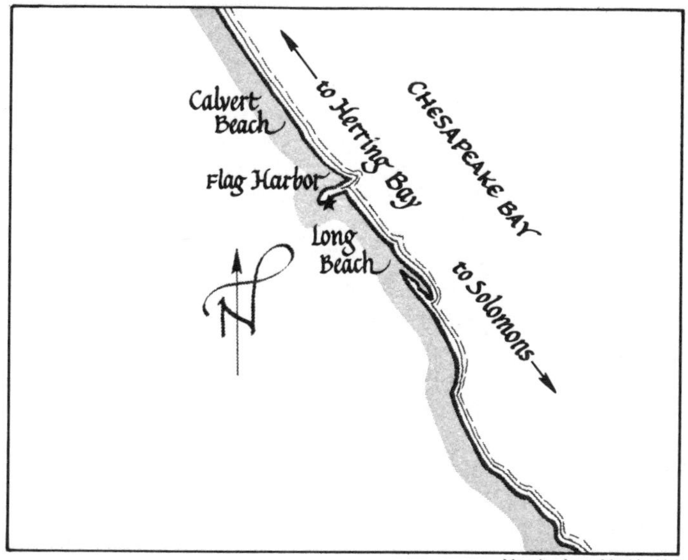

Map by Joan Machinchick

We have found a port of refuge along an inhospitable shore that is legendary for its lack of natural harbors—the 30-mile stretch from Herring Bay to the Patuxent River.

Flag Harbor Yacht Haven is about six nautical miles north of Cove Point Light, now dwarfed by the unused platform built to receive liquefied natural gas shipments. The marina, lying between Calvert Beach and Long Beach, shows clearly on charts, particularly NOAA 12264.

It is 2.1 nautical miles north of the Calvert Cliffs Nuclear Power Plant, conspicuous for its several large, round white towers. We were instructed to look for a row of white houses at beach level, then for a group higher up on the bank. Next we would see a black hole, then a white beach. When opposite the black hole, actually the marina entrance in shadow, we should head toward shore.

For boats cruising the large ship channel, look for the CP buoy about five miles north of Cove Point, or about four miles south of red N"2" off the mouth of the Little Choptank. Then turn west and go about four miles toward the power plant. If you're running nearer the western shore, look for the Calvert Cliffs plant, then the landmarks described above.

The best landmark is a 20-foot high white pylon erected on the beach just north of the entrance channel. Stone jetties extend seaward, the outer ends marked by small lighted red and green buoys. We noticed a brush stake in the channel, so left it to starboard in case it indicated a shallow spot. Entering on a rising tide, we had six feet under our keel; depths inside held about the same. However, entry could be difficult in adverse weather.

With about 175 slips, Flag Harbor Yacht Haven is predominantly a sailboat facility, but a fair number of cruisers ranging up to 40 feet are berthed there also. Although not a transient facility, Flag Harbor will accommodate overnighters in whatever slips are open.

Flag Harbor Yacht Haven is a fortunate addition to western shore capabilities for vessels with draft of over four feet. Perhaps in the foreseeable future the marina will have charted navigation aids to guide yachtsmen into its snug harbor. □

SHIPPING CREEK

off Eastern Bay

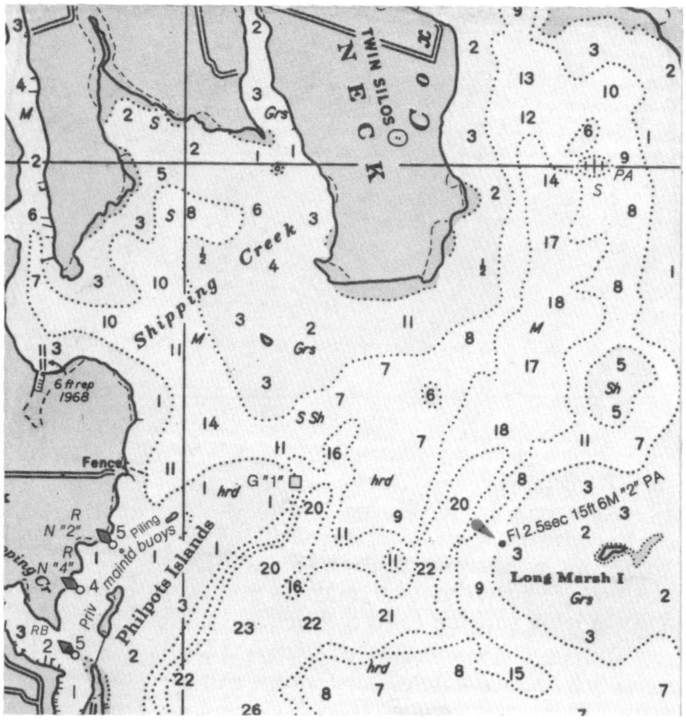

From NOAA chart #12270 not to be used for navigation.

In looking over our charts nowadays, we find that there are few creeks or coves that *Moon Song* hasn't explored. It's getting so that it's difficult to plan an extended cruise that includes a new anchorage each night. And it was only by chance that we found ourselves one bright and sunny day last summer heading up Eastern Bay.

The air was light and flukey as we motored out into the Bay, the water flat in a "slick ca'm." Sails up, we could make about two knots, no more. We cranked up the iron jib and dropped the main so we could rig the awning. Comfortable in its shade, we studied our charts. Of the three possible creeks we chose the closest—Shipping Creek, which is just across the island from Kentmorr Harbour.

From Bloody Point Light we continued toward Bell "1" (Fl 4 sec) approximately 1.4 miles southeast. From there we took the Maryland chart's advice of 072° M toward Bell R "2A" (Fl R 4 sec) off the harbor of Claiborne and held course for two miles before turning north, searching for the two buoys which mark the entrance of Cox Creek. There was such a thick haze that we couldn't pick them out right away. But eventually they materialized like ghosts—the red spar, which would flash red in the dark, and to starboard a black/green daymark. That's the one we were interested in, since it stands on the shoal at the outer limits of Shipping Creek.

We rounded G "1", giving it about a hundred feet since the shoal extends north beyond the mark. Still we bumped bottom. Immediately we turned north another hundred feet and found twelve feet of water. The shoal extended a little further north than I had imagined.

To starboard you will note a three-foot shoal on that side of the channel, so you can't just head straight for the opening of the creek. Instead, it's probably a good idea to do as we did—aim for the middle of the land between Shipping Creek and the larger house on shore.

On this course continue about halfway to shore, then turn north once more, holding that course till the creek's entrance opens for you. From there on in, it's simply a matter of keeping to the middle.

Shipping Creek is prettier than I had expected it to be. I don't know why, but I envisioned it as being somewhat barren. Instead, we found a lovely, quiet body of water—somewhat narrow for anchoring, but ample in a pinch. It is at the creek's entrance that you will find the best anchorage. There is ample room for several boats or a small raft-up. On the western shore is quiet farm land. Further upstream are several comfortable-looking homes with a sprinkling of workboats tied up out front—also a pair of large sailboats.

Picture yourself anchored here in Shipping Creek. The moon shines down on the cornfield edged with tall beach grass. You hear crickets and tree frogs singing, the splash of an occasional night-feeding fish, and the rasping squawk of a startled blue heron. What more could a cruising family ask for?

The next morning we headed out into Cox Creek to explore the possibilities there. Cox Creek has only one buoy—a flashing red about two miles north of the red flasher at the creek's mouth. But there are few probelms—only one, in fact, that we noticed. That is the shoal on the starboard side a mile and a half upstream. But this presented no problem, since at low tide marsh grass is visible.

As on the previous day, it was boiling hot as we motored out to the entrance of Cox Creek. When we got opposite the entrance of Shipping Creek, we gave up. We dropped anchor, put on swim suits, splashed overboard. This was one of the most cooling swims we've had in years! I remember drifting in the cool water and looking over at Shipping Creek thinking maybe we should go back in and anchor there for another night. □

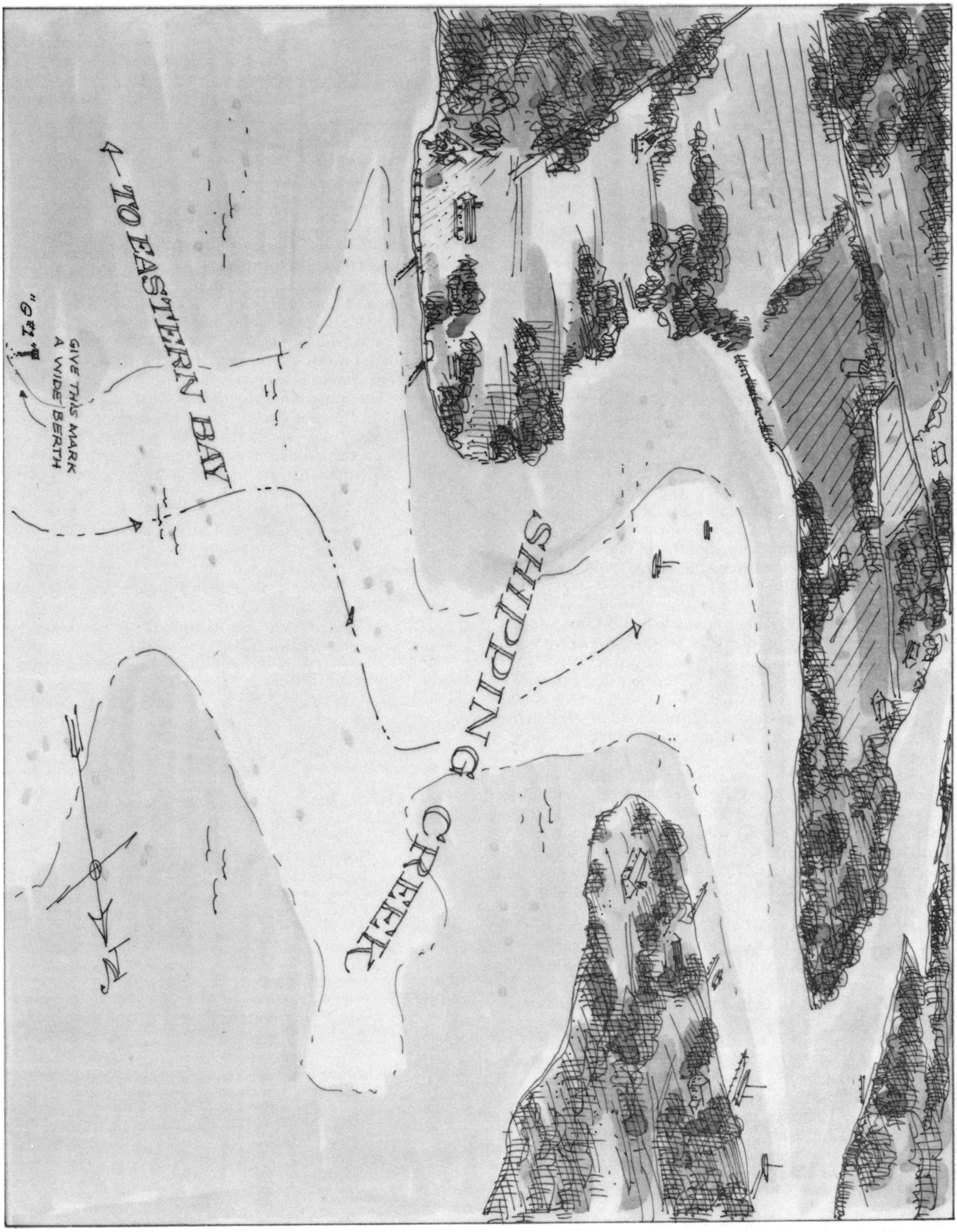
TO EASTERN BAY
SHIPPING CREEK
GIVE THIS MARK A WIDE BERTH
N

CRAB ALLEY CREEK

on Eastern Bay

"Look, look! Over there! It's a battleship!" Lynda's excited voice came over the radio.

"*Sea Gull,* this is *Moon Song.* What was that you said about a battleship?"

"*Moon Song,* this is *Sea Gull.* Yeah. Look over to port. At about 035°. I swear, it's a battleship—or a cruiser, or whatever you guys call those Navy ships with guns. Right up here on Eastern Bay?"

"*Sea Gull,* the heat must be getting to you! Wait a minute; let me check it out," I said. "*Moon Song* standing by on 68."

I popped back up on deck. We were heading northeast up Eastern Bay and, as so often happens in mid-July, the light breeze had all but died. A growing cloudbank was piling up in the west. But it was still early in the afternoon, and with any luck, we could get into the Wye River before it hit.

All around us the horizon was lost in a heavy golden haze. I focused binoculars on a light blue smudge which danced in shimmering heat waves. Yes, there it was! I could see a long, flat base and about a quarter of the way in from one end was what appeared to be the bridge. High above it was the antenna. In front of the bridge were its turret and gun.

I looked at the chart again. I was using NOAA chart #12270. The only thing on the chart bearing 035° from our position was Bodkin Island. I lifted the binoculars and, blinking to clear my vision, studied the "battleship" once more. Of course, it was the island. But if you squint your eyes a little, it does begin to look like some kind of warship. I wonder how many others have had the same impression, however fleeting?

The Bodkin illusion was interesting, but something else had caught my eye. To the north of the island, half cradled in the two arms of Cox Neck and Crab Alley Neck, lay Crab Alley Bay. And its western side led up into Crab Alley Creek. The chart showed depths of eleven, nine, and seven feet. Well, most boats would certainly have no problem with those depths. I'd have to keep Crab Alley Creek in mind for sometime in the future.

If you study NOAA chart #12270 you will see Crab Alley Bay is almost due north of Tilghman Point on Rich Neck. Bodkin Island stands as a sort of sentinel at the bay's entrance, almost six miles from Kent Point.

Another day found us motoring past Bloody Point Light toward black bell #1 about two miles to the southeast. From that point we set a course toward the black can #3 (approx. 067° M). As Bodkin Island came into view, we could see once again its distinctive battleship shape. This time there was the long arm of a steam shovel at work on the island, which added to the illusion. We resisted the temptation to head directly toward the island, since the long shoals which project from its south end are unmarked.

From can #3 we changed course to head for can #1 which marks the northeast end of the Bodkin Island shoal, course 030° M (approx.). This can is nearly three miles distant and, in the heat-haze, I couldn't pick it up even with binoculars. At black can #1 the course changes to 325° M (approx.), which will bring you to the next pair of marks, a black can #3 and red daymark #4 which are a little over a mile away.

As you pass these marks you will see two islands ahead to starboard. The nearest, Little Island, is no more than a mound of marshgrass. The other, Johnson Island, is much larger, with a few buildings. Between them, a marked channel leads up to a marina pier and a seafood house at Dominion. Crab Alley Creek lies west of Johnson Island, and a red and a black daymark guard two small shoals. There's a widening of the creek opposite Johnson Island, but we spotted a few crablines and decided to head further upstream. There is almost a mile more of the creek which shows six feet or more depths, so most cruising boats can find a comfortable anchorage in good protected water.

We anchored just north of the gap between Johnson Island and the mainland. All around us was quiet shoreline, with a few small, private docks. The homes were modest and were either watermen's residences or perhaps summer cottages—a guess, since we noticed a few were unoccupied. Upstream were a sprinkling of workboats at private piers and a few pleasure boats on moorings.

We'd gladly recommend Crab Alley Creek and its charm to all cruising groups. After all, it's easy to find. Just look for the "battleship" island. ☐

From NOAA Chart #12270—not to be used for navigation.

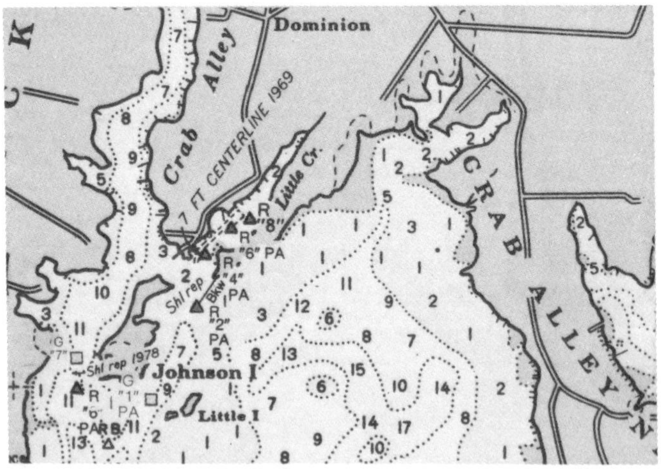

Notes

Bodkin Island – the Battleship
CRAB ALLEY CREEK
JOHNSON ISLAND
LITTLE I.
LITTLE CR.
N
CRAB ALLEY
BAY

THE WYE AND MILES RIVERS OFF EASTERN BAY

Shaw Bay
Lloyd Creek
Dividing Creek
Drum Point Cove
Tilghman Creek
Leeds Creek
Hunting Creek

When entering Eastern Bay from the north, give Bloody Point Light a good berth, and take a course of not less than 135° magnetic towards FL G "1." Leave this buoy on your port hand and you will avoid the extensive shoals that make out from Bloody Point.

Approaching from the south, take a course of 060° M from buoy "71" to "2" off the head of Poplar Island. There are shoals around the island too; the recommended course avoids them, but don't forget to allow for any southerly leeway or drift.

Proceed up Eastern Bay to R "4" off Tilghman Point, and shape your subsequent course from there.

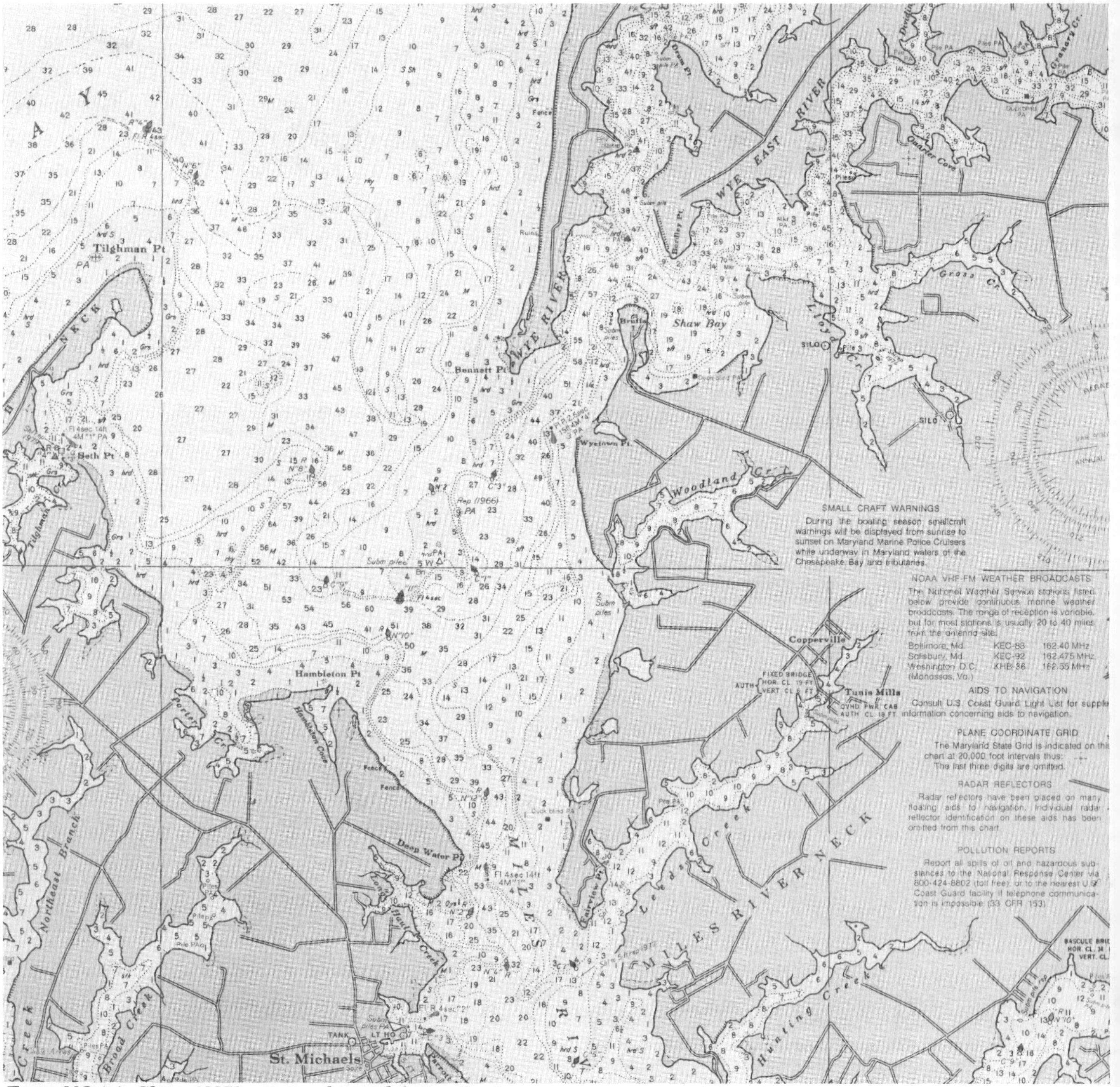

From NOAA Chart 12270—not to be used for navigation.

WYE RIVER

The Wye River is best described as a quietly winding stream whose waters meander through the peaceful countryside and whose grassy or wooded banks are only occasionally interrupted by stately and dignified mansions. All is serene with an air of suspended time. There is little to indicate the depth of its active past and history to the yachting families who love to frequent its many creeks and coves.

The river is actually divided, with its two arms encircling the 1800-acre Wye Island. The branches which are enjoyed by more knowing cruising men are known as Wye East River (or "Front Wye"), the Wye River, which runs in a northerly direction and is known as "Back Wye," and Wye Narrows, which connect the other two branches about four or five miles up. There is a bridge across Wye Narrows which unfortunately is fixed with a clearance of ten feet.

If you wish to cruise either branch of the Wye, our recommendation is Wye East River. This branch offers snug anchorages and beautiful scenery.

Getting into the Wye River is no great problem except at night, as there are no lighted marks to guide you in. The trick is to pick up the red nun #2 in the middle of the Miles River, then head almost due east for black can #3 which guards the shoal at Bennett Point (Note: #2 marks the northern end of a sunken island.) Just aim between those two marks, turn northeast until you pick up the red triangle on a pile #4, and follow midstream northward around Bruff's Island on your right. □

SHAW BAY

on the Wye River

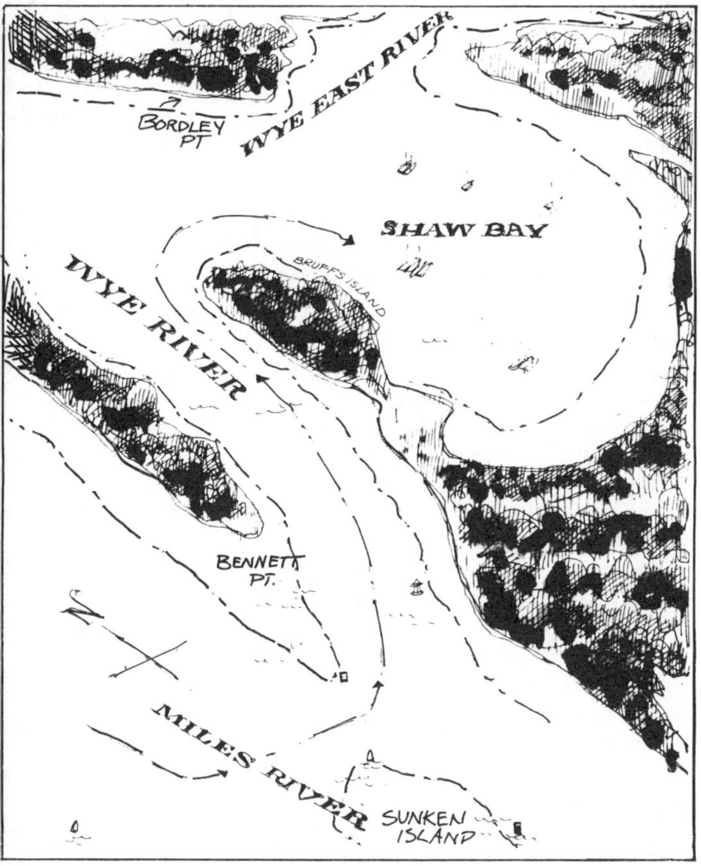

The submerged island marked by red nun #2 at the mouth of the Wye shouldn't discourage the novice cruiser, for once past this obstacle and Bruff's Island you'll find Shaw Bay, one of the most popular anchorages on the Eastern Shore. This bay is over a half-mile wide and deep enough to accommodate any size boat, or raft of boats, and still offer room for privacy. This anchorage is fairly large and open, which allows a nice breeze on a hot summer night.

The Wye River and Wye Island are rich with some three hundred years of history. Numerous settlements, manor houses, and estates are part of the area's historical heritage.

The shoreline is edged with lush meadows or cornfields with fringes of trees here and there that crowd close to the water. The creeks, thus wooded, have a close, comforting intimacy where cruising groups can ride out even the most severe storms in complete security. □

Shaw Bay is fairly large and open, which allows a nice breeze on a summer night.

PHOTO BY BILL CRONIN

LLOYD CREEK

on the Wye River

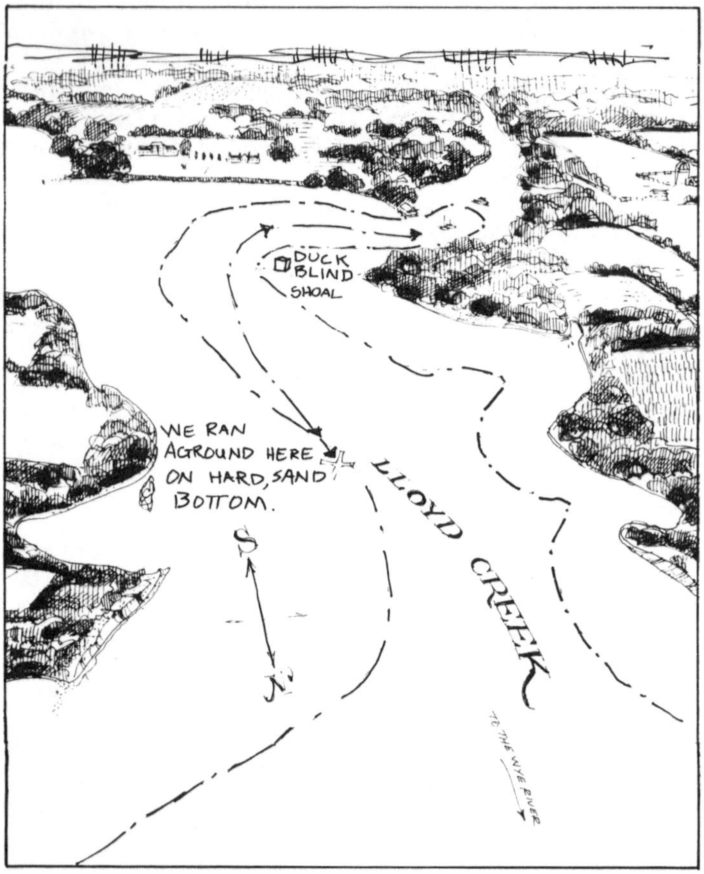

On the south shore of the Wye just past Shaw Bay is a long shoal aimed northwest toward Boardly Point. This mark has a tendency to blend into the shoreline, so watch out for it. On your NOAA chart #12270 such daymarks are shown as tiny, faint circles — hard to see even on the chart.

Rounding this mark, just follow the Wye East until you pass the next black daymark on the north shore. Then round gently into Lloyd Creek. "Keep to the middle" is oft-heard advice that certainly applies here.

Lloyd Creek has the Wye's typical beautiful shoreline of meadows and cornfields broken by wooded areas. Lloyd Creek is open to the northwest and consequently is quite exposed to summer storms from that direction. However, if a northerly is threatening, just go further upstream. On the west bank is a duck blind marking the shoal there. Give it a wide berth and head into the west branch where the seven-foot mark shows on your chart. The bank on the north side of this little anchorage is a bit higher here and will give you one of the snuggest anchorages you could hope for.

The Wye River has its share of history reflected by the famous names carried by its many mansions, such as Gross' Coate, Hope, and Lloyd. Situated on a tributary of the Wye East, Wye house has been the home of the Lloyd family for more than nine generations. A unique building in back of the house contains an orangerie, where orange and lemon trees were grown in tubs similar to those at Versailles. This 18th century greenhouse is still in use.□

DIVIDING CREEK

on the Wye River

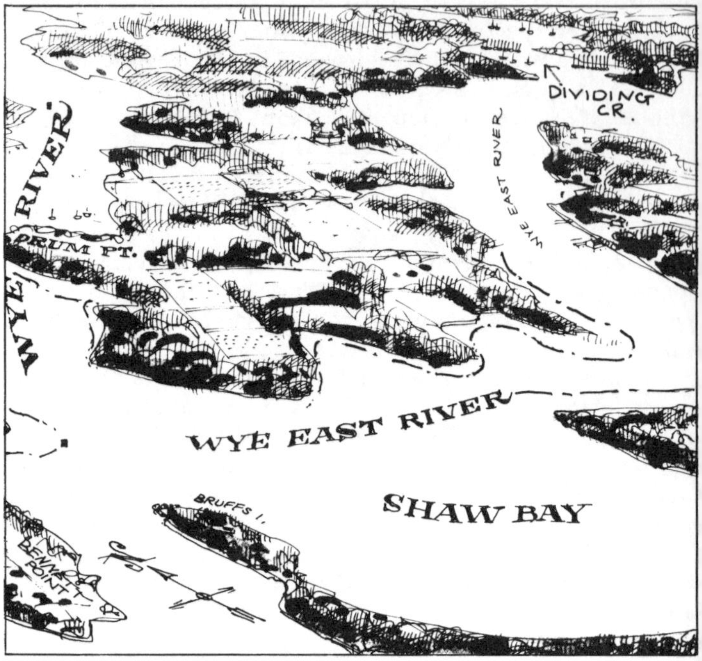

Past Bennett's Point, around Bruff's Island and Shaw Bay we wound our way eastward, with each bend of the river revealing the tranquil beauty of secluded coves and estates. Wye East River lies east and west, and the Wye River itself, north and south. Three miles north of Shaw Bay is Wye Narrows (or Back Wye as it was known several hundred years ago). The land which lies encircled by these three branches is known as Wye Island. Although the State of Maryland used to own the land with the intent of preserving it as one of the Bay's last undeveloped areas, it was sold in 1984 to a developer of residential estates.

We spent the night anchored in Dividing Creek, a mile and a half past Lloyd Creek on the Wye East River. Here we motored in past a 13-boat raft of Cal 25's and within a hundred yards found a 13-boat raft of Alberg 30's! At the same time there was a scattering of individual or paired boats, making it tough to find open water to anchor in. However, the creek has good deep water practically to the shore and we soon snuggled into our chosen spot. As evening shadows closed in, the tranquil waters were broken only by the fish feeding to the sound of tree frogs coming from the woods surrounding us.

The next day we explored further up the Wye East. The river turns and winds with small coves and creeks everywhere. There are steep banks and tilled fields edged with trees, vast wooded stretches that come down to the water's edge. Truly, the Wye River is one of the Bay's most beautiful and one we look forward to visiting again.

As the Wye East turns abruptly northward, we discovered Wye Landing. This is where the area workboats tie up and where many outboard boats are launched, so on weekends the area is quite busy. About two miles further up is Wye Narrows Bridge, which has only ten feet of vertical clearance.

On Skipton Creek was located the first county seat of Talbot known as York. Little remains today but a hole in the ground and some rubble.

Higher up is Wye Mills, which ground flour for the Continental Army in 1776 and whose wheels are still making flour. Nearby is the famous Wye Oak, grown from an acorn a full 100 years before the first white man came to America. □

DRUM POINT COVE

on the Wye River

From Bloody Point on Eastern Bay to Tilghman Point is only six miles, and from there to Bennett Point only another 2½ miles. Rounding the black #3 can off Bennett Point, Wye River turns almost due north. Around Bruffs Point is Shaw Bay, scene of some of the largest crowds of cruising boats you'll see anywhere on the Chesapeake. Sometimes I enjoy the companionship of others, but we usually seek out more secluded anchorages.

One such spot was up farther on the Wye River, just around Drum Point. We headed for it. A light breeze had followed us into the creek; and although our mainsail was furled, we had our big genoa ballooning out to catch the light air. We drifted lazily in the late afternoon's heat. The Wye River, which is as deep as 58 feet at its entrance, here measures only 40-feet deep.

We sailed slowly around Drum Point and saw the sprinkling of boats already there ahead of us. That was okay, though, since this cove is almost a half-mile wide and there's room enough for all of us. □

MILES RIVER

Buoyage in the Miles River may seem odd. The 1983 *Coast Pilot* says that the river flows into Eastern Bay "between Tilghman Point....and Bennett Point, 2.3 miles east-south eastward." The mouth of the river then, is on a line between the two points.

To enter the Miles, take R "4" north of Tilghman Point as your guide. The course then follows the increasing numbers on the markers, generally SSE, to Nun "12" about north of Deep Water Point, *just as if you were still following the Eastern Bay* numbers. Off Deep Water Point you will see "1", (Fl 4 sec) on a pile. Count the *river* buoyage upstream from there as if the mouth of the river were at the Point, and you won't go wrong.

The Miles River has widths of about one mile for a couple of miles south past Deep Water Point before it turns northeast, where one can find at least five more miles of navigable waters which offer many quiet coves and creeks. As you travel the Miles, there are numerous delightful harbors and anchorages along the way. If you should be irresistibly drawn to one, we won't blame you. First off, you'll pass the little harbor at Claiborne. When entering Claiborne don't keep too close aboard the entering markers. There's often shoaling near the edges of the channel. This is a beauty of a spot with tall trees that provide protection in a storm. Also located on the Miles is the town of St. Michaels, one of the favorite cruising rendezvous spots on the Bay. **See St. Michaels cruise and walking tour for more information.**

Although the Miles is often crowded with a continuous stream of pleasure boats, there are many secluded anchorages along its shores that make this truly one of the most pleasant rivers on the Chesapeake Bay. □

TILGHMAN CREEK

on the Miles River

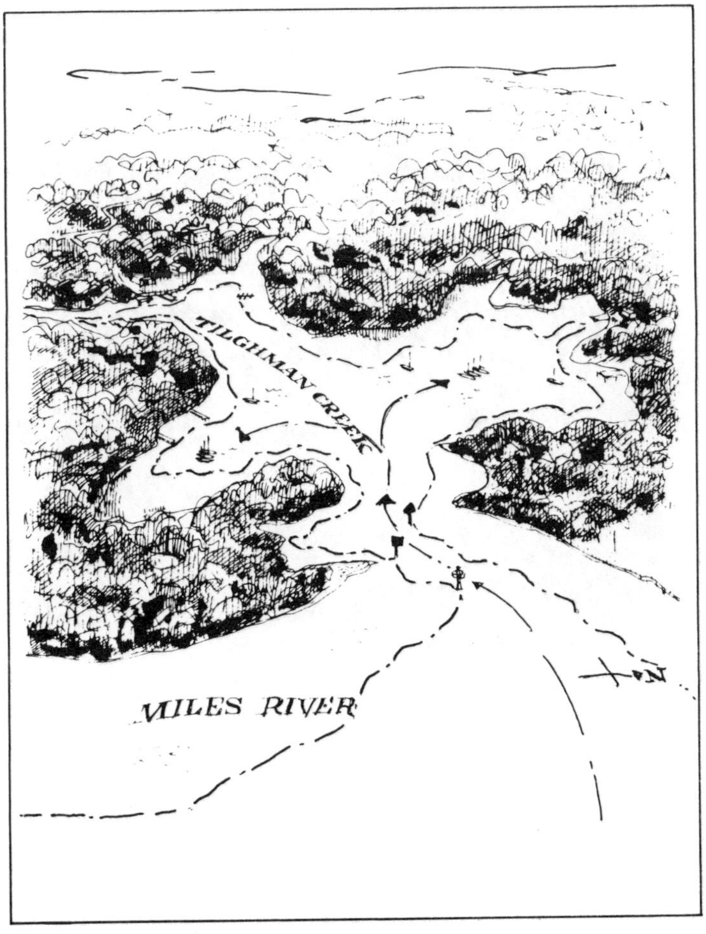

Tilghman Creek at Claiborne, Maryland, has long been a favorite stopover on the Miles River. The cruising yachtsman can find here a good midpoint for travel in many directions. Within easy reach are the Kent Narrows, St. Michaels, and Eastern Bay (a direct route to the Chesapeake). And if you have put in a long, hot day on the water, Tilghman Creek will provide one of the prettiest little wooded anchorages you could ask for.

Here, on the west bank, at the end of a quiet country road, is Rich Neck, the site of one of the original manors in Talbot

County, with a manor house dating back to the Revolutionary War. Directly across the peninsula from your anchorage and on the Eastern Bay side of Claiborne the slip of the old Claiborne-Annapolis ferry, established in 1919, still stands.

Tilghman Creek is about 6½ miles up Eastern Bay on the point of land at its junction with the Miles River. The visitor to St. Michaels often stops here overnight rather than anchoring in the busy town harbor.

The entrance to Tilghman Creek is well marked, and by swinging wide around the point of land on either side past the marks, there is no danger of going aground. The first cove to port behind Seth Point is fairly good and secluded but subject to the in-and-out traffic.

In the first cove to starboard is 11 feet of water and considerable room for an anchorage. Drop your hook out in the middle, as there are private docks on the west bank.

Further on up the creek to port, a third cove has 10 feet of water and is very wooded and secluded. On a calm evening the mosquitoes are busy here, coming from the southeast bank, and are quite fierce. This cove is particularly good in a northwest breeze, which will help blow the mosquitoes away.

All in all, Tilghman Creek offers another perfect anchorage for the boating family. □

Rich Neck Manor was once the home of Matthew Tilghman, called "Father of the Revolution in Maryland." — Grieser photo.

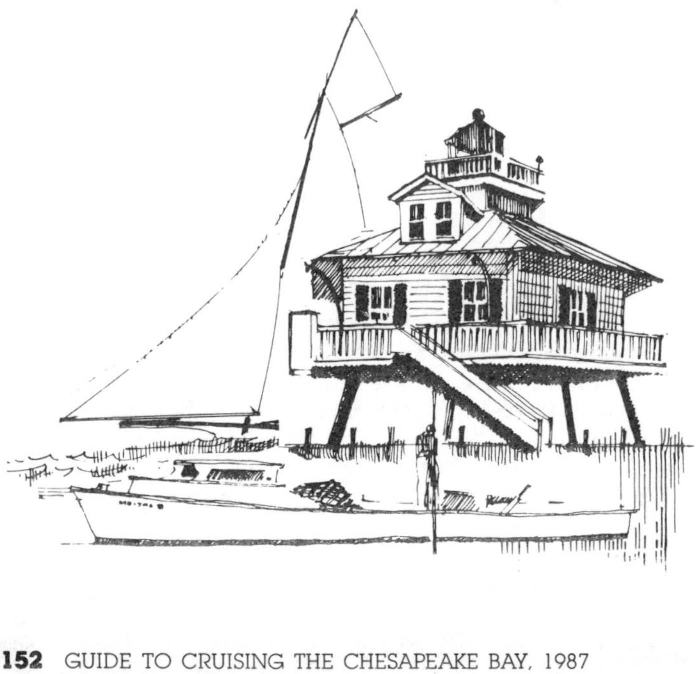

LEEDS CREEK

on the Miles River

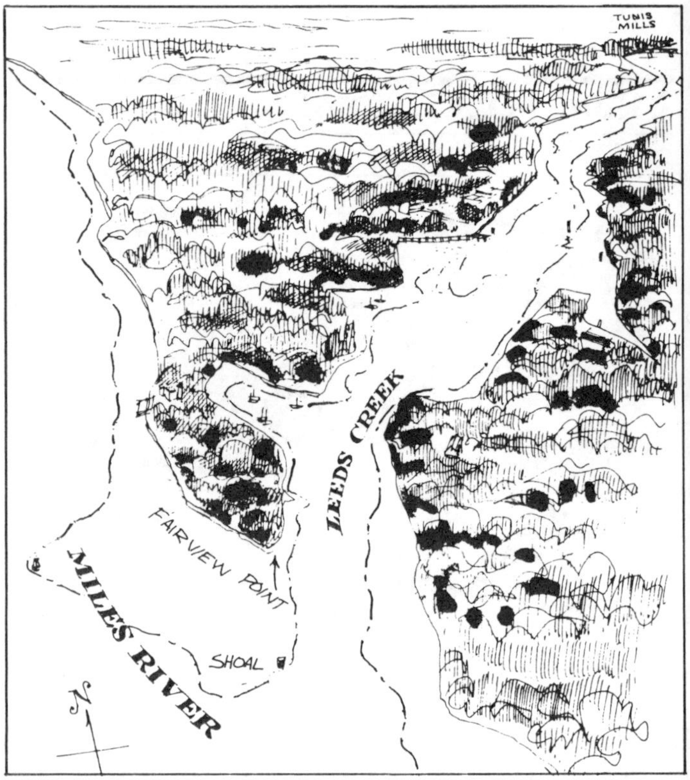

Leeds Creek on the Miles River is yet another beautiful cruising spot on our Chesapeake Bay. The great thing about this creek is its nearness to St. Michaels. How many times we've wished for a nice, quiet anchorage instead of the crowded St. Michaels' harbor, when all of its restaurants are really "jumping"!

At Deep Water Point just north of St. Michaels, make a jog right and then left at black flasher #1 to avoid the four-foot shoal that juts out almost a half mile from the east bank at heavily wooded Fairview Point. Continue south on 161° to black can #1, and Leeds Creek will be wide open to you. Although the channel is a little narrow at the entrance, it is straight and we had no difficulty getting in. Once inside Fairview Point we just followed the lefthand shore and around and into the little cove there where we dropped our hook. (If you find it too crowded, just continue upstream until you find a pleasing spot.)

There are wooded shores all around but with some marshy spots which made us suspect a heavy mosquito population during the hot summer months. Looking toward the narrow neck of land separating us from the Miles River, we could just make out the large castle-type structure which glowed red in the setting sun.

The next morning we motored farther up Leeds Creek to Tunis Mills, about 1¾ miles toward the headwaters. Over a century ago there was a sawmill here, when first timber was harvested on the Eastern Shore and large three-masted schooners were loaded for markets in Baltimore and Philadelphia. □

HUNTING CREEK

on the Miles River

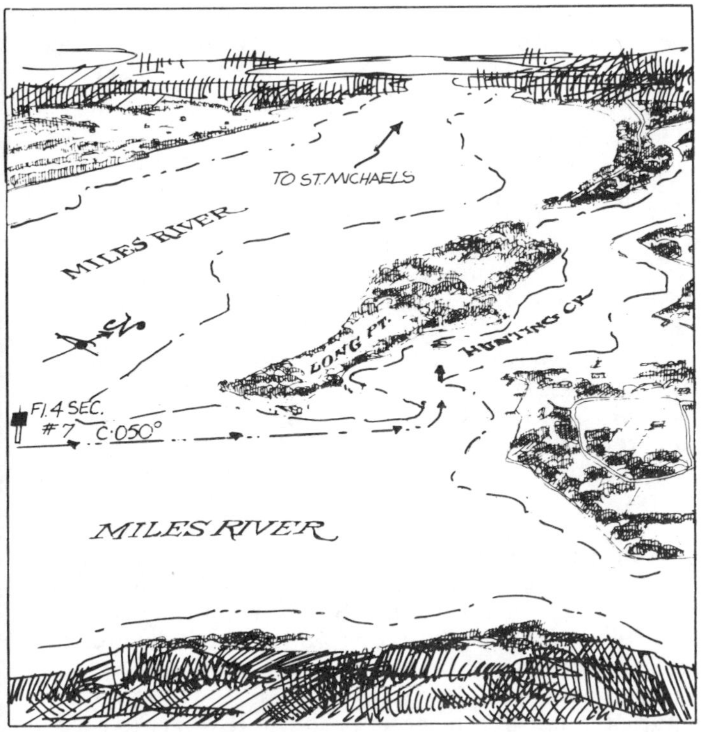

As boats congregate, you may opt to slip out of the St. Michaels harbor and find a quieter anchorage in the surrounding creeks. Favorites are Leeds Creek or Longhaul Creek, home of the Miles River Yacht Club. We have discovered another, perhaps more secluded, further south where the Miles River makes a sharp turn northeast — Hunting Creek.

After supper in St. Michaels as the sun began to set, we reluctantly hauled anchor and motored out into the Miles River, turning on course 115° to the black can #5. We could have headed right to the 4-second flasher off Long Point, but there's a shoal point that bulges out from Spencer Creek, and we thought it best to skirt around it before turning upstream.

About 2¼ miles from St. Michaels the Miles River makes an abrupt right-angle turn. It is here, in the crook of this elbow, that you will find the mouth of Hunting Creek. From the 4-second flasher which marks the river's turning point, we took a course of 050°, standing well off Long Point to avoid the submerged piles marked there on our chart. For a guide you will be able to use the small, white boathouse on the southeast tip of Long Point, and from there follow the chart into the creek.

At that time we picked our way carefully between these two shoals without any aids at all. Where there is a red daymark now was only a stick with a small sign tacked to it.

Hunting Creek meanders in a northerly direction for about a mile before turning northeast. We anchored in this bend, just out of sight of the creek's entrance. The trees in this section of the creek come right down to the water's edge, and heron and egret stalk the shores. □

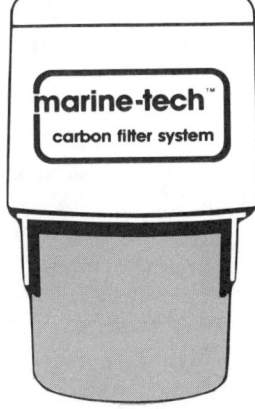

ST. MICHAELS

on the Miles River

St. Michaels is one of those truly unforgettable cruising spots of the Chesapeake Bay. Our first visit to this attractive little town took place almost twenty years ago, and I can clearly remember what an exciting event it was for us. Recently we took *Moon Song* into St. Michaels for a visit and found things pretty much as they had been, only better.

When entering St. Michaels take a course of about 233° from Nun "4" in the Miles River to St. Michaels Harbor Light "2" at the entrance. Pass it to your starboard, of course, and not too far off. The corresponding marker, black buoy "3" off Parrott Point at the other side of the entrance, is off a shoal that is both extensive and pretty shallow. Give it a wide berth, for it can be a trap for the unwary. Then look for the new buoys marking the fairway and anchorage as you enter the harbor.

As I maneuvered for space among the anchored boats, in the harbor, I found myself thinking about our smaller first boat. Things were a lot simpler then. That little centerboarder drew only 18 inches, and I could have gone anywhere in this harbor. Now, with our almost five-foot draft, I was concerned about St. Michaels' famous shoal spots.

We hear a lot of stories about people running aground in the harbor here—have even seen a few from time to time—so when we went ashore, we asked the local experts to point out where the "thin" spots were. They all agreed that there is only one spot to really worry about. The shoal lies mainly in the cove between Carpenter and Mulberry Streets.

Even knowing this, some people still manage to find themselves aground. What usually happens is this. The anchorage is often crowded, but there appears to be some open water west of the last boat. There is, but this is where the shallows begin. The late arrival may be able to squeeze in on a high tide; but when the tide falls or the wind shifts, they find themselves aground.

To those who would like to go ashore to stretch their legs, there are plenty of things to do and see in St. Michaels. Most interesting, of course, are the exhibits and displays at the Chesapeake Bay Maritime Museum. For visitors there is a dinghy dock located just west of the Crab Claw Restaurant. The museum has a gift shop, open to the general public, where you can find an interesting variety of Chesapeake Bay items.

The best known of all displays on the museum grounds is the Hooper Strait Lighthouse, one of the last Chesapeake Bay cottage-style lighthouses. The lighthouse was built in 1879 and remained in continuous service until 1954 when it was abandoned in favor of an automated light. In 1966 the lighthouse was moved to its present site on the museum grounds.

There are several floating exhibits at the museum, also, such as the skipjack *Rosie Parks,* berthed next to the lighthouse; the bugeye *Edna Lockwood;* and the *Mr. Jim,* an authentic "buy boat" of the Chesapeake. The museum has many interesting displays both indoors and out which document the history and industry of the Chespaeake Bay and is well worth a visit.

The walkway at waterside in front of the museum runs into Cherry Street, which leads the visitor across a footbridge and up to St. Michaels' main drag, Talbot Street. There's an ice cream store at the corner of Cherry and Talbot where you can pick up a cone (we consider such to be necessary equipment whenever we're browsing). To the right about a block, across from the High's store, is Lally's Bakery and Deli, which boasts, "Homemade at its best—we have the best sandwiches and soups to go."

The Two Swans Inn is a new bed and breakfast facility adjacent to Higgins Yacht Yard. Some cruising families enjoy a night ashore and the Two Swans fills the bill nicely. A new hotel, scheduled to be completed in July 1986, will also offer accomodations ashore. It will resemble a group of townhouses and it is associated with the St. Michaels Harbor Marina.

The St. Mary's Square Museum offers walking tours of the many historic spots and colonial buildings in town.

If you're interested in browsing, as we are, there are numerous little shops as you walk south that range from boutiques to fairly expensive. The specialty shops are quite interesting—such as Woodworks Etc., which is what the name says, or The Blue Swan, a Christmas/Easter shop.

Across the street is Valerie's Saltbox which offers crafts, antiques, and boutique—an interesting collection of items. Further south is the Village Shop, which specializes in imported cheese, produce, fine wines, liquors, as well as a butcher shop.

Back toward Hudson's Pharmacy is Town Hall Mall, a group of a half-dozen specialty shops. If you're in need of groceries, there's an Acme foodstore, Big Al's Seafood Market, as well as the Village Shop.

Dinner time can be a fun time in St. Michaels because there's such a variety. Talbot Street and the harbor offer a number of fine, intimate restaurants with varied menus and prices. Launch service is available from the new Harbor Ferry which charges $1 per person to take you anywhere in the harbor.

I've always thought that the perfect way to end the day is dining while watching our boat riding easily at anchor, reflecting the harbor lights as she awaits the dawn. □

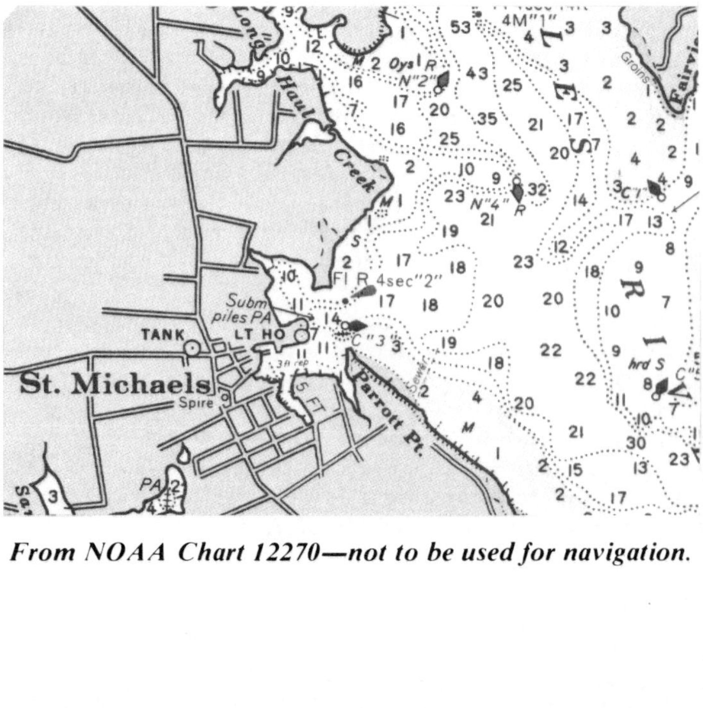

From NOAA Chart 12270—not to be used for navigation.

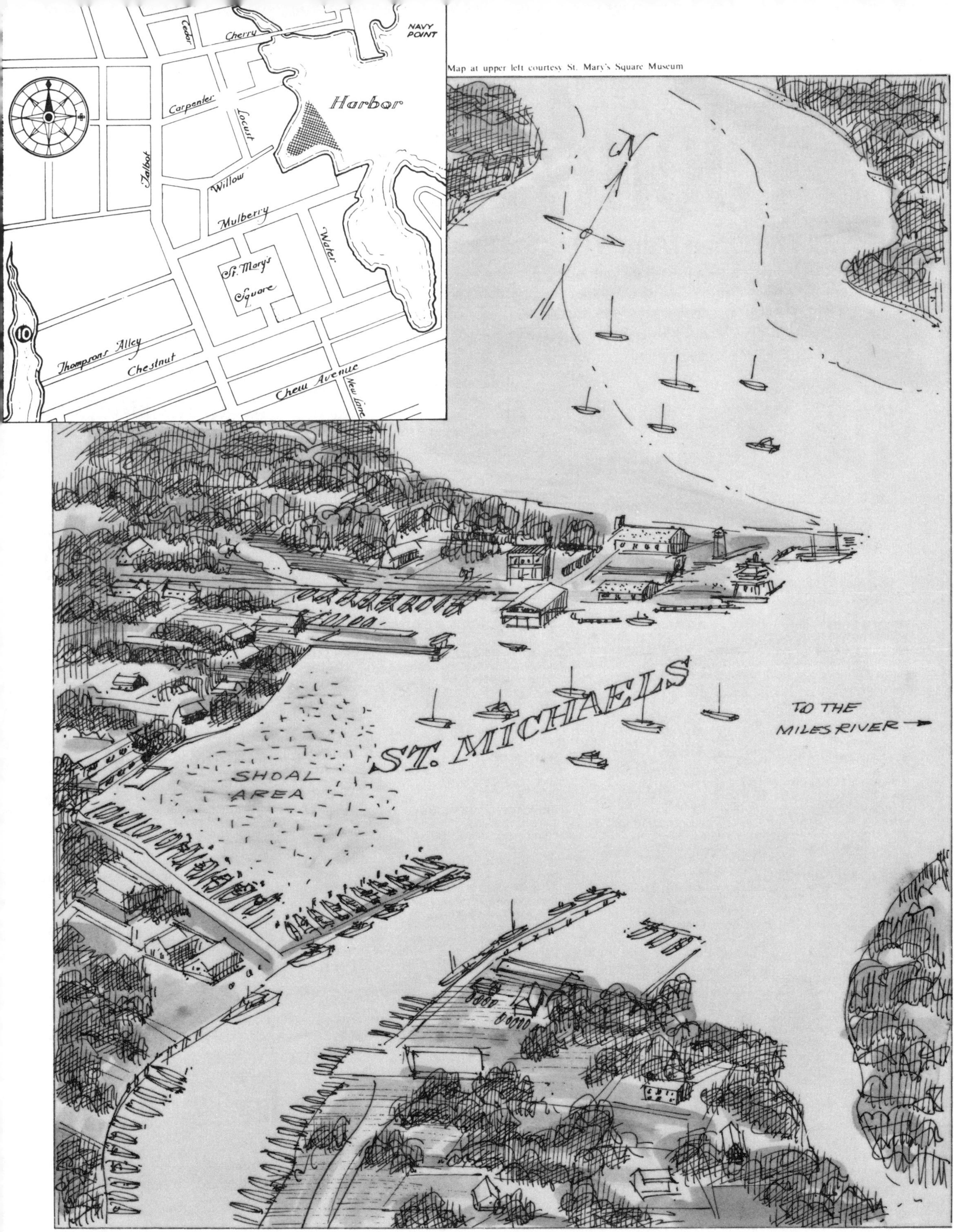

Map at upper left courtesy St. Mary's Square Museum

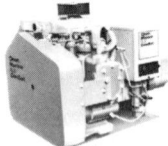

CRUISING TIP

Expand your cruising territory this year by checking the bus schedules. Sail to a new harbor over the weekend where you can leave your boat during the week. Then take a bus back to your car at your home port. Take the bus to your boat the next weekend and head for another new port. You'll see new sights both by land and sea. Another way to expand your cruising range is to sail your boat as far as you want in a week. Have friends meet you at your destination. You drive their car home and they bring the boat home.

A Walking Tour of:

ST. MICHAELS

If you could find a small picturesque harbor, add some vintage history, charisma and architecture, open fashionable shops and boutiques, build a wonderful maritime museum, and entice talented chefs to the pleasantest of restaurants, you'd create a multi-faceted, delightful town. Save yourself the energy, it's already been done. It's called St. Michaels.

On the Miles River, about sixteen miles from Bloody Point Light, is the friendly horseshoe-like harbor of St. Michaels. Several restaurants and marinas, a few houses, and the Chesapeake Bay Maritime Museum stand as an unofficial receiving line to greet you as you arrive. (In the future a hotel will be built where the St. Michaels Harbour Marina once stood).

The town of St. Michaels is over 250 years old. Although officially chartered in 1805, early accounts of trading here date to 1631 and in the late 1600's a parish church was built where the Christ Episcopal Church now stands. As St. Michaels grew it became a shipbuilding center especially noted for its "Baltimore Clippers," the fastest sailing vessels of their time. Today it is better known as a waterman's community and a popular yachting center. On pretty summer weekends the harbor bustles with activity as pleasure boaters make their way to anchorages and docks. To accommodate water-based visitors scattered throughout the harbor, the town has built a floating dinghy dock at Navy Point, just behind the Crab Claw Restaurant.

Pristine streets lined with well-maintained houses built over the last 300 years make up St. Michaels' residential neighborhoods. Though not open to the public, many of the homes have numbered plaques on them indicating that they are included in the "St. Michaels Walking Tour." (This complimentary tour, sponsored by the St. Mary's Square Museum, Inc. and the St. Michaels Business Association, is available at many businesses around town.) The tour takes you past 23 places of interest, a couple of which capture the imagination. During the War of 1812, St. Michaels' ship building industry attracted British attention. Accounts of the events of the Battle of St. Michaels show the ingenuity of the citizenry in repelling the foe. They craftily darkened ground lights and hung lanterns in trees which gave the town an illusion of being on higher ground. As a result, British firepower overshot the town, with an interesting exception. In the Cannonball House (stop #4 on the tour) a cannonball came through the roof, rolled across the attic floor and bounced down the stairs, much to the amazement of its horrified occupants. Several blocks from this landmark is the corner of Locust and Carpenter Streets, alias "Hell's Crossing." Although quiet and unassuming today, this

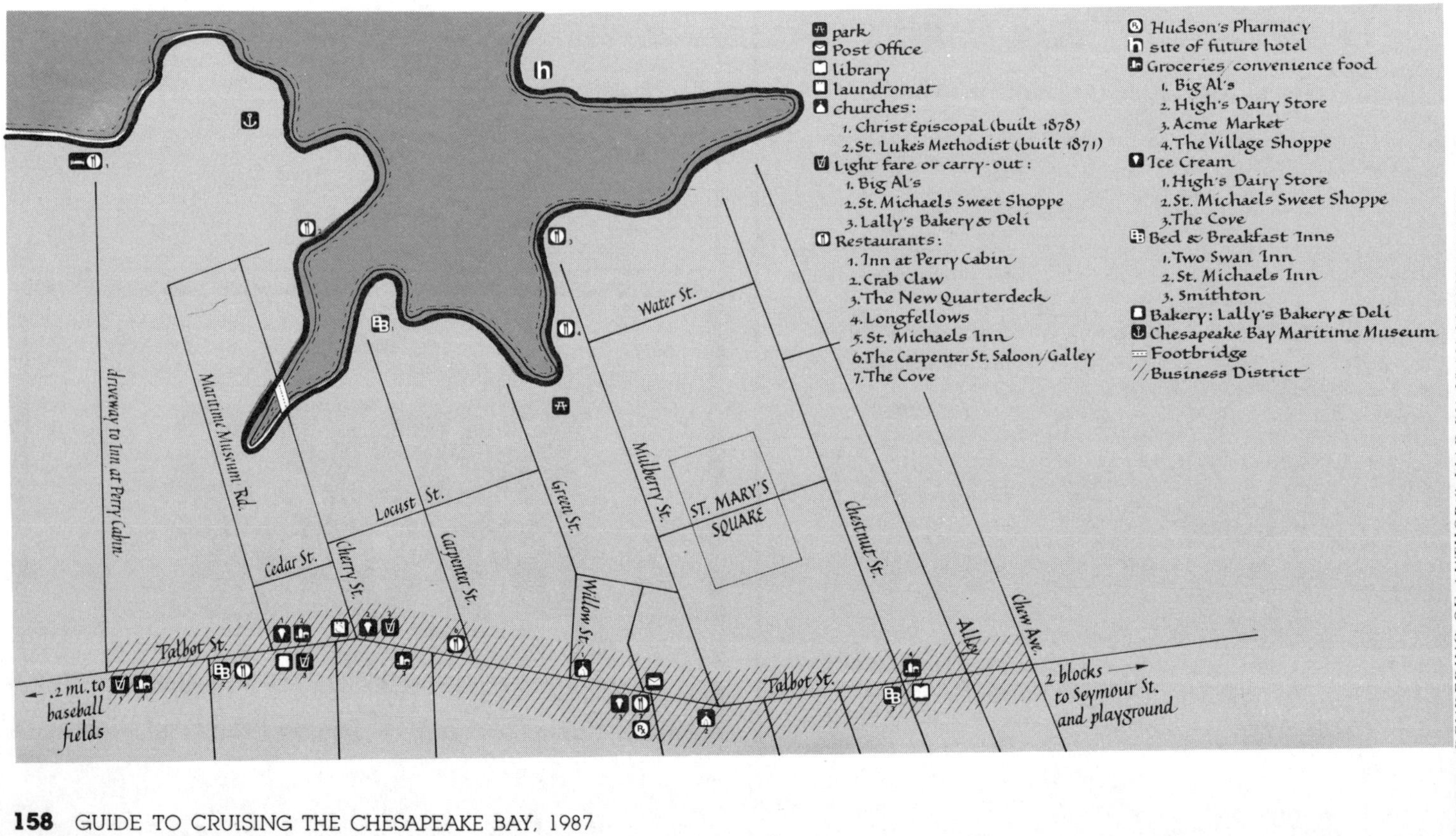

RENDERING OF AUTHOR'S MAP BY JOAN MACHINCHICK

intersection earned its nickname from the time when taverns and grog shops in this neighborhood were frequented by sailors from various ships anchored in the harbor. Fights between crew members of the different ships occured so often here that it was unofficially renamed. For more information on the town's past, history enthusiasts can see displays of local memorabilia in the St. Mary's Square Museum at St. Mary's Square (open weekends, May-October). The square itself was the focal point of one of the three wards that St. Michaels was originally organized into while the buildings on it have been transported from other parts of town.

The Walking Tour map not only highlights historic sites, it also features many local businesses. For the most part, stores with browse-and-buy appeal line Talbot Street (a busy two-lane thoroughfare that becomes Route 33 and links St. Michaels to Easton). Even window shopping is fascinating as these stores display a wide variety of wares from antique furnishings to brass hunting horns, fashionable sportswear to wicker baskets, Yule season nutcrackers (would you believe a cowboy?) to adorable handcrafted dolls and stuffed animals. Functional shoppers will not be disappointed either. There are a couple of well-stocked hardware stores, a laundromat, a pharmacy, a bakery, and we found four places to reprovision the galley. These are: Big Al's (which sells a little bit of everything, from fresh seafood to flowers), The Village Shoppe (in addition to pre-packaged items you can find a butcher shop, fresh produce, and imported cheese), High's Dairy Store and an Acme Market (the last two speak for themselves).

For us, a trip to St. Michaels wouldn't be complete without a visit to the Chesapeake Bay Maritime Museum. Founded in 1965, this museum has grown from one building to a 16-acre complex of restored and new buildings. At one end of the grounds is an aquarium, populated by a changing variety of local sea life (depending on what the staff catches). A chart picturing the different species of fish makes their identification easy (although our younger crew members prefer watching the turtles and crabs). At the other end of the complex is Hooper Strait Lighthouse, a "cottage" style lighthouse first lit in 1879. Inside you can get an appreciation of what being a lightkeeper was like. (I am always taken aback by the size of the coffee pot and skillet considering only two people lived there!) In between are buildings which display many aspects of the Cheapeake's history and traditions. You can trace the geological and social evolution of the area, see a waterfowl exhibit (including decoys and antique guns), view small craft, a skipjack and bugeye. In the boat shop you can watch as craftsmen restore and maintain the museum's growing fleet. Other facets of the museum are also expanding with work on a waterman's village, propulsion building and working crab dock being examples of recent projects. However, one thing stays constant: the untiring dedication of the staff and volunteers in preserving the Bay's heritage and passing it along to all who visit. That is why you see so many friendly people who are ready, willing, and able to answer your questions about the exhibits and the museum.

In some towns your choice of where to eat is mediocre, at best. Not so here. Many restaurants even offer courtesy transportation to their boating patrons. The St. Michaels Inn (a bed and breakfast that starts serving at 7:00 A.M.) will pick you up by car from your marina while waterfront restaurants sponsor water taxis that ferry patrons between their boats and dinner. (A toot of your horn or wave of your arm will signal them over.) Restaurants lining the harbor include The Inn at Perry Cabin (a restored plantation house offering lodging and elegant dining), The New Quarterdeck (at St. Michaels Town Dock Marina and serving three meals daily), Longfellows (featuring regional seafood), and the Crab Claw (informal dining where you can even have spread-the-paper-on-the-table-and-eat steamed crabs). In-town restaurants include The Carpenter Street Saloon/Galley (open for breakfast at 7:00 A.M.) and The Cove (located inside Hudson's Pharmacy, offers three meals daily at either table or counter service). For more impromptu meals you can get sandwiches at Big Al's (there's a carry-out window inside), a croissant breakfast or soups and sandwiches for lunch at Lally's Bakery and Deli (with a small eat-in area), and St. Michaels Sweet Shoppe where you can get hot dogs, snacks and ice cream (they have several tables inside and a walk-up window outside). We found three places to get hand-dipped ice cream, all with different atmospheres. For the most ice cream parlor decor, try the Sweet Shoppe. For more room but less atmosphere have your sundae at The Cove. Finally, there's walk-as-you-go-service at High's.

For more extensive exploring you can rent bicycles from the St. Michaels Bike Rentals at Town Dock Marina. Oxford is a pleasant ride away via the Oxford-Bellevue Ferry. This marina also rents pedal and sail boats. Those with a disdain for do-it-yourself tours can see the waterfront and river from *Patriot* (offering an 11-mile cruise on the Miles River) or board the "Train" at the Crab Claw (seasonal) for a land tour on a Disneyland-style tram.

Among St. Michaels' beautiful sights are its parks. We managed to find four recreational areas, although only two are convenient to the harbor. At the eastern end of Talbot Street is a large field which has been subdivided into two baseball diamonds. At the western end are the public schools complete with playing fields and a playground (at the corner of Talbot and Seymour Streets). In the center of town, behind the firehouse, is Church Cove Park. While it is a small park, it does have several picnic tables and some benches along the waterfront. The final grassy area (one our kids find ideal for frisbies and puddle jumpers) is on the museum grounds.

With all it has going for it, you'd expect St. Michaels to be "discovered," and it is. On a beautiful summer weekend the harbor is crowded with pleasure craft of every size and degree of luxury while the town bustles with visitors arriving by boat, car and bicycle. However, don't let its popularity deter you. We have never found St. Michaels so busy that we couldn't enjoy its charm and charisma. In fact, we find it rather habit forming. ☐

—Andi Manchester

Notes

KNAPPS NARROWS

at Tilghman Island

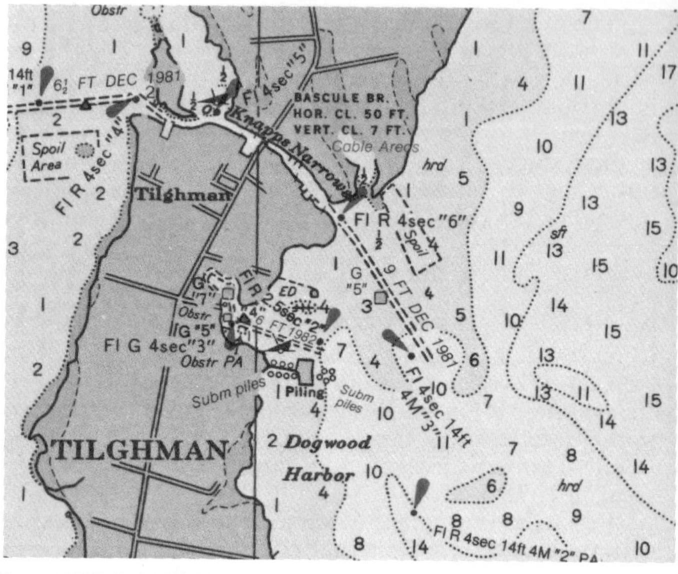

From NOAA Chart 12266—not to be used for navigation.

When traveling between the Miles and Choptank Rivers, or between St. Michaels and Oxford, the shortest route is Knapps Narrows.

By automobile, this would only take 15 to 20 minutes, plus the short ferry ride from Bellevue across the Tred Avon to Oxford. By boat you must retrace your steps up the Miles River, round Tilghman Point, and travel down Eastern Bay. This time you follow the south shore till you see Poplar Narrows. From there you squeeze through Poplar Island Narrows till you pick up the lighted beacons that mark the channel into Knapps Narrows. Or, you can avoid the Narrows by continuing south and rounding Blackwalnut Point, which would add six or seven miles to this leg of the cruise.

We usually take the shorter route through Knapps Narrows. Although subject to shoaling, the channel had plenty of water for our boat, which draws five feet. (Depth in 1981 was 6½ ft.)

To navigate the Narrows, you must toot for the drawbridge to open—no big deal, except that sometimes boat traffic is a little heavy and the water is narrow here. It can make your heart squeeze a little when you are part of a group of three or four boats milling about waiting for the bridge to open. However, the bridgetender is sympathetic to boat traffic, and you seldom have long to wait. The bridge tender also monitors Channel 13 so you can reach him by radio. Use low power.

Although no mention of current appears in the *Coast Pilot,* direct observation has shown that there may be a current of nearly 2 knots either way at the bridge. This current could affect your approach to tying up at a nearby bulkhead, or to "stooging around" while waiting for the bridge or boats in the vicinity.

Here at the Narrows you can view several working skipjacks and other workboats. There are a couple of marinas where you can fuel up, as well as two or three restaurants, where you can pull in for lunch and watch the water traffic pass by.

You'll notice the navigation aids seem to do a strange thing in the Narrows. Red markers are to starboard as you *enter from either end,* which means that there is apparently a reversal of the rule. This is not so, however, since entering the Narrows is considered to be "entering from seaward" whether from the Choptank or from the Bay.

If you remember this arrangement, you will have no trouble in the Narrows, but do use care in the approaches on the Choptank side. Keep a watch astern as well as ahead, to be certain that you remain in the rather narrow channel, or you may go very gently but firmly aground.

From "3" (Fl 4 sec 14 ft 4 M) a course of 124° M (approx.) will bring you to the Choptank River Light, a spider-like structure marking the entrance to the Tred Avon River.□

COMFORT TIPS

Another good item for bathing while cruising is the Solar Shower (available at most marine stores). It is simply a plastic bag about the size of pillow, clear on one side and opaque on the other side, which holds 2½ gallons of water. You simply lay the full bag on your deck and the sun will heat it to anywhere from 95° to 120°. The bag has a built-in heat sensor which signals when the contents are warmer than 95°.

Good foul weather gear is expensive, but well worth the investment. It's hard to enjoy a cruise when you are cold and wet.

Fight that sea-sick feeling. Tums or Rolaids serve in a pinch. Saltine crackers seem to work, too. Some of the newer non-prescription remedies can be chewed rather than taken with water and last all day. Be sure that you not only have a seasick remedy aboard, but that you have enough of it.

Bathe in comfort amid the jellyfish. Take along an easily inflated one-man rubber raft. Trail astern and fill with water. Since the jellyfish can't get in, you can soak in peace.

PHOTO BY BOB GRIESER

DUN COVE

in Harris Creek
above Tilghman Island

Depending on the weather and the time of day, you may wish to break your trip into the Choptank area for rest and shelter.

Up Harris Creek, just east and a little north of the eastern exit from Knapps Narrows lies Dun Cove, as pretty and protected an anchorage as one could wish to find.

On leaving the Narrows, go past daybeacon "3" about 100 yards. Then take course 042 magnetic for some 1½ miles. This will bring you to R"4" daymark in Harris Creek, while avoiding the shoal spots.

Then follow the markers in a general northerly direction, making sure to give "5" a wide berth. Continue on past "6," and set your course for "7." However, go only about halfway to it, and change to 279 magnetic. Take this course to the Cove's entrance. The holding ground is good and the anchored boats on the drawing will give you some idea of where you might like to stay. Just don't go too close to the eastern shore (the western side of Seath's Point). When you leave, don't go aground, as we did, on the shoaling out southerly from the point.

Dun Cove is generally quiet, a pretty spot, and basically unspoiled. Oddly, Dun Cove is the only place where we have ever heard the phrase " . . . bunch of city slickers" used seriously. It was used by a party of water-skiers who had just finished slaloming in and out around the anchored boats, rocking our hearts — and what is worse, our drinks — out unmercifully. Don't let this bother you. It has happened to us only once, and it didn't really spoil the tranquility of Dun Cove.

If you need boating help in this area, it's usually better to call the Marine Police rather than the Coast Guard because they maintain an operation at nearby Knapps Narrows. □

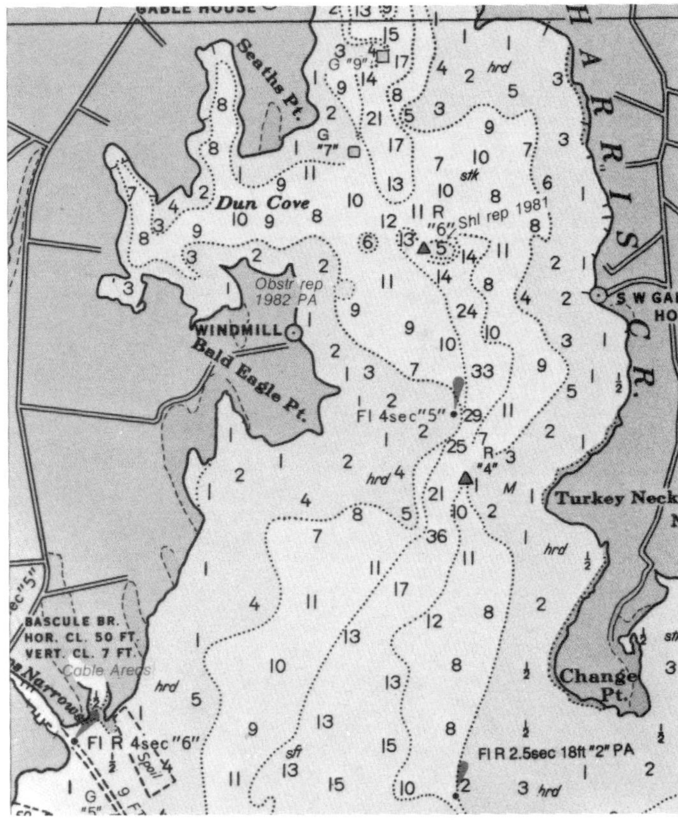

From NOAA Chart 12266 — not to be used for navigation.

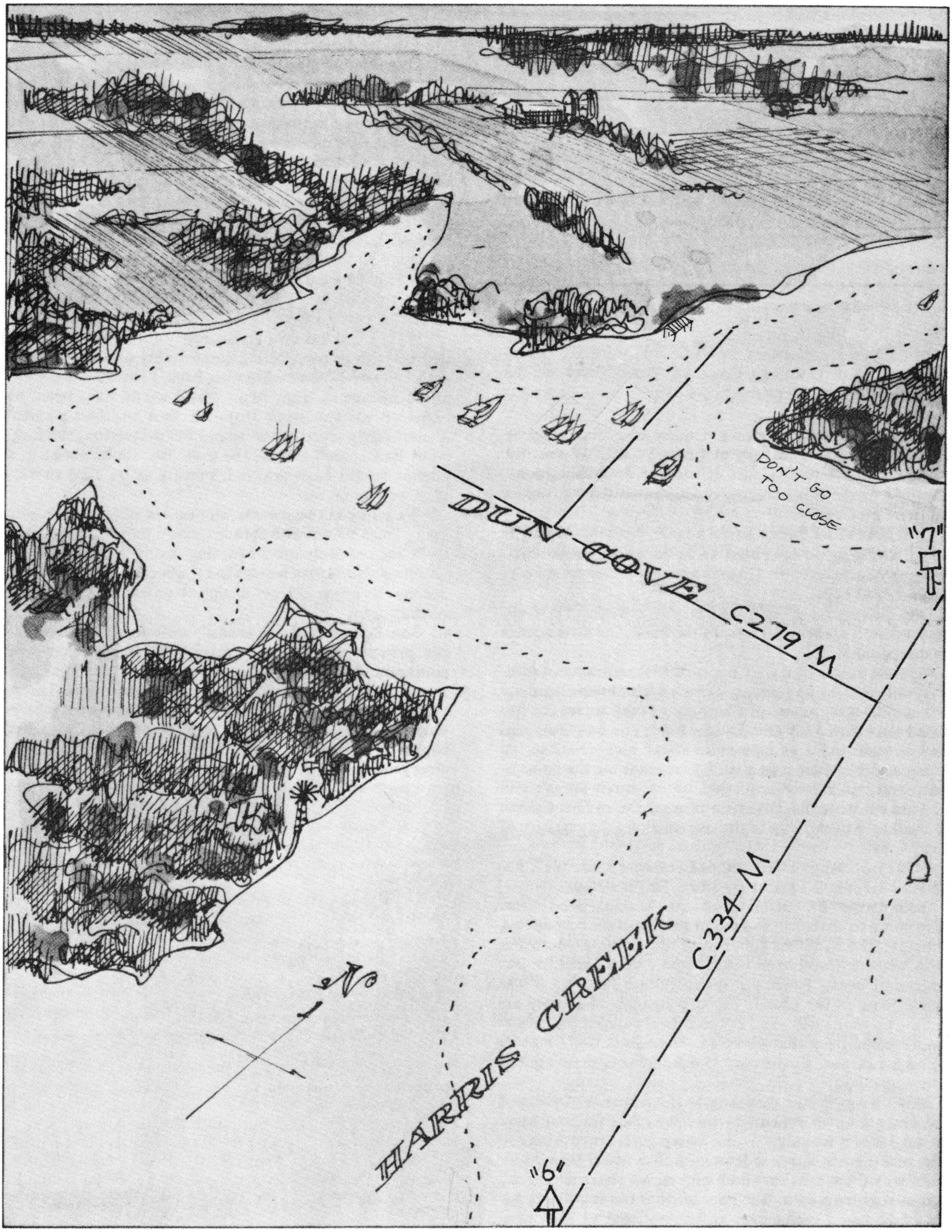
DON'T GO TOO CLOSE
"7"
DUN COVE
C279 M
HARRIS CREEK
C334 M
N
"6"

WATERHOLE COVE

on Harris Creek

From time to time incidents occur on a cruise that make that cruise truly memorable. Sometimes these are enjoyable, such as a perfect sunset, a congenial group, a perfect anchorage.

Sometimes these incidents are not at all pleasant. Everyone can remember a particularly hair-raising storm, an exasperating grounding, or a fouled prop.

But whether our experiences are pleasant or unpleasant often doesn't matter in retrospect. Taken as a whole, the good and the bad, our cruising memories become woven together like a tapestry, forming a vivid picture in our mind's eye.

This summer's cruise is a good example. Friends of ours in the Tartan 34 group, Arnett and Mibby Taylor aboard *Summer Wind*, invited us to join their group for dinner at Harrison's Restaurant on Tilghman Island. We gladly accepted. Dinner was planned for 6:30, so we hung around the lighted buoy #2 off Dogwood Harbor and waited for our Tartan host to show up.

As we waited, our VHF started picking up calls from the Tartan group as they approached. David Bourdon, Cruise Chairman-Commodore of the group, announced that because of the crowds at the restaurant's docks, the group could anchor up Harris Creek on Waterhole Cove and he would ferry people down to the restaurant. We accepted his offer, while the Taylors opted to take *Summer Wind* in toward the restaurant, hoping to anchor outside the channel.

The ferrying worked out fine, and in calm seas with little or no wind we motored back to Dogwood Harbor. Within an hour we were seated in the restaurant with the Bourdon's boat, *Celebration*, safely at the pier. The Taylors informed us that *Summer Wind* was indeed anchored nearby, just out of the entrance channel, and that we could hitch a ride with them back to Waterhole Cove.

We enjoyed a delightful meal, and as darkness closed in, the Taylors left with their other guests after planning for us to catch up with them. There's a long road built out over the water that leads to a large boat landing, and their dinghy would pick us up about half-way out along the road/causeway.

Leaving the restaurant, we were startled by sharp gusts of a brisk wind. In the darkness we stumbled across fields to the road and began our trek out the causeway. The wind was really blowing now, and on either side of the road angry whitecaps raced past us. Here and there potholes in the road splashed with water where the Bay took bites with each storm. We stumbled along till we could see the twinkle of a couple of anchor lights, and before long, Arnett rowed out of the darkness to take us out to *Summer Wind*.

His little dinghy bobbed and bounced its way back to the anchored boat, and we scrambled aboard, glad to be on a firmer deck. *Summer Wind* lay in shallow water with a falling tide. The 15-knot plus wind made her rock and bounce almost as badly as the little dinghy. Occasionally, in the dark, we could feel her keel come down with a jolt on the hard-packed river bottom. With the engine purring smoothly, I crabbed my way onto the foredeck to retrieve the anchor. Reluctantly it came up with a load of mud, and as I struggled, I could see out of the corner of my eye others of the Tartan group as they motored past us into deeper water.

From NOAA Chart #12266—not to be used for navigation.

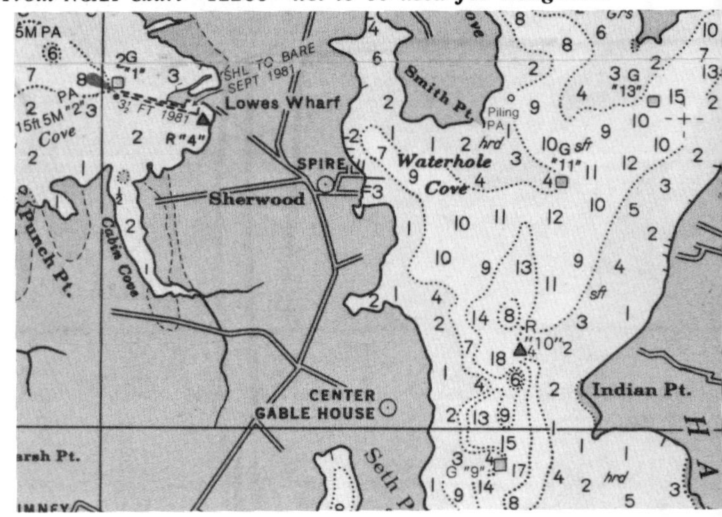

The writing of it doesn't really do justice to the situation. Images are stronger—of chill, black night with strong wind and splashing whitecaps, of ghostly shapes of boats, their running lights ablaze and engines roaring, leading the way out. We followed them, plunging and bucking past the flashing red buoy.

The rest of the trip back to Waterhole Cove was almost an anticlimax. I sat hunched on the foredeck, getting an occasional face full of cold wind and spray as I searched with a spotlight for the entrance marks to Harris Creek. The flasher off Change Point was easy to find; then came the white flasher off Bald Eagle Point; but its mate, a red daymark, remained elusively hidden.

I noticed that as we motored northward toward our anchorage, we were rolling heavily from beam seas and the strong easterly wind. At the same time, we were being blown west of our course line; frequent changes to our heading were necessary to keep from being run onto the shoal waters to port.

Finally the red daymark #4 reflected brightly in my spotlight. After that it was a simple matter to follow the buoys—"6," "7," "9" and "10"—and then run into Waterhole Cove, where we rafted *Summer Wind* with *Moon Song*.

Waterhole Cove is a delightful anchorage with wooded shoreline unspoiled by dense commercial development. The few homes visible from the water look comfortable and attractive, with several small piers and docks. There is one large dock which appears to be a public landing.

If Waterhole Cove has a shortcoming, it would be that its mouth is wide open to the east. Of course, that night the wind blew *strongly* from the east, making it a rough and bumpy night for us all. But on the average summer night, we would welcome the broad reach of this little cove, happy to be getting the faint breezes you can expect on those hot nights. By morning the breeze had let up somewhat, and we were treated to a beautiful rosy dawn.

So we have some pleasant memories of Waterhole Cove, but will also remember that dark night with whistling wind and plunging waves as we escaped the clutches of the falling tide. ☐

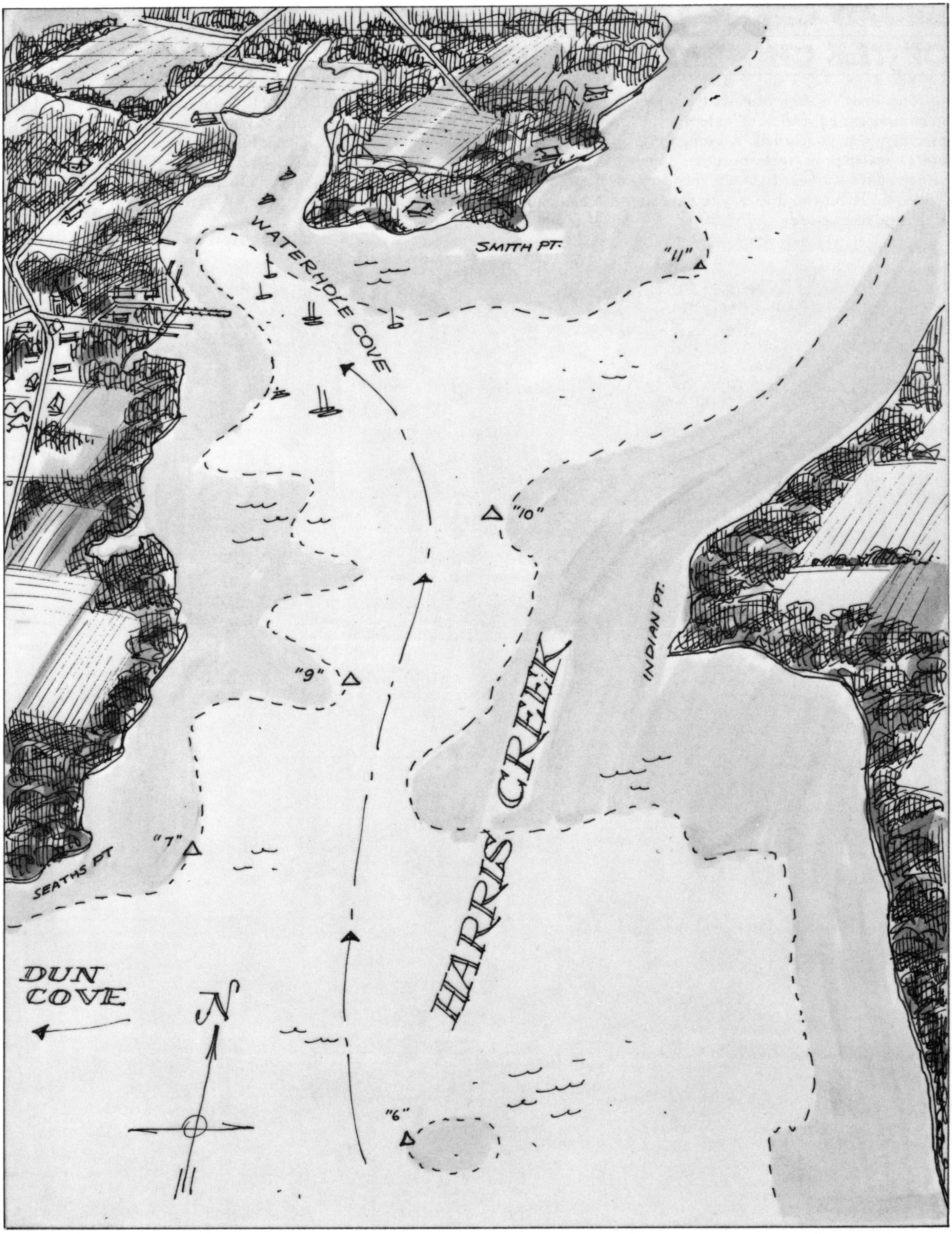
WATERHOLE COVE
SMITH PT.
"11"
"10"
INDIAN PT.
"9"
HARRIS CREEK
"7"
SEATHS PT
DUN COVE
N
"6"

BROAD CREEK AREA OF THE CHOPTANK RIVER

Balls Creek Grace Creek Leadenham Creek San Domingo Cr.

The Broad Creek area of the Choptank is perhaps the most underrated stretch of water on the Eastern Shore as far as cruising is concerned. Although cruising yachtsmen are quite vocal in praising the beauties of their favorite spots, very seldom have we heard anyone mention lovely Broad Creek. Wide and beautiful, it is easy to navigate with many miles of shoreline to explore.

Off Nelson Point at the mouth of the creek, the Choptank is almost five miles wide, and there's plenty of depth. Hence entering Broad Creek is easy. The hardest part is finding the entrance marker (Fl 4sec "1") SE off Nelson Point. It tends to blend into the shoreline behind it. Once you're inside and on a northerly course, there's no problem. □

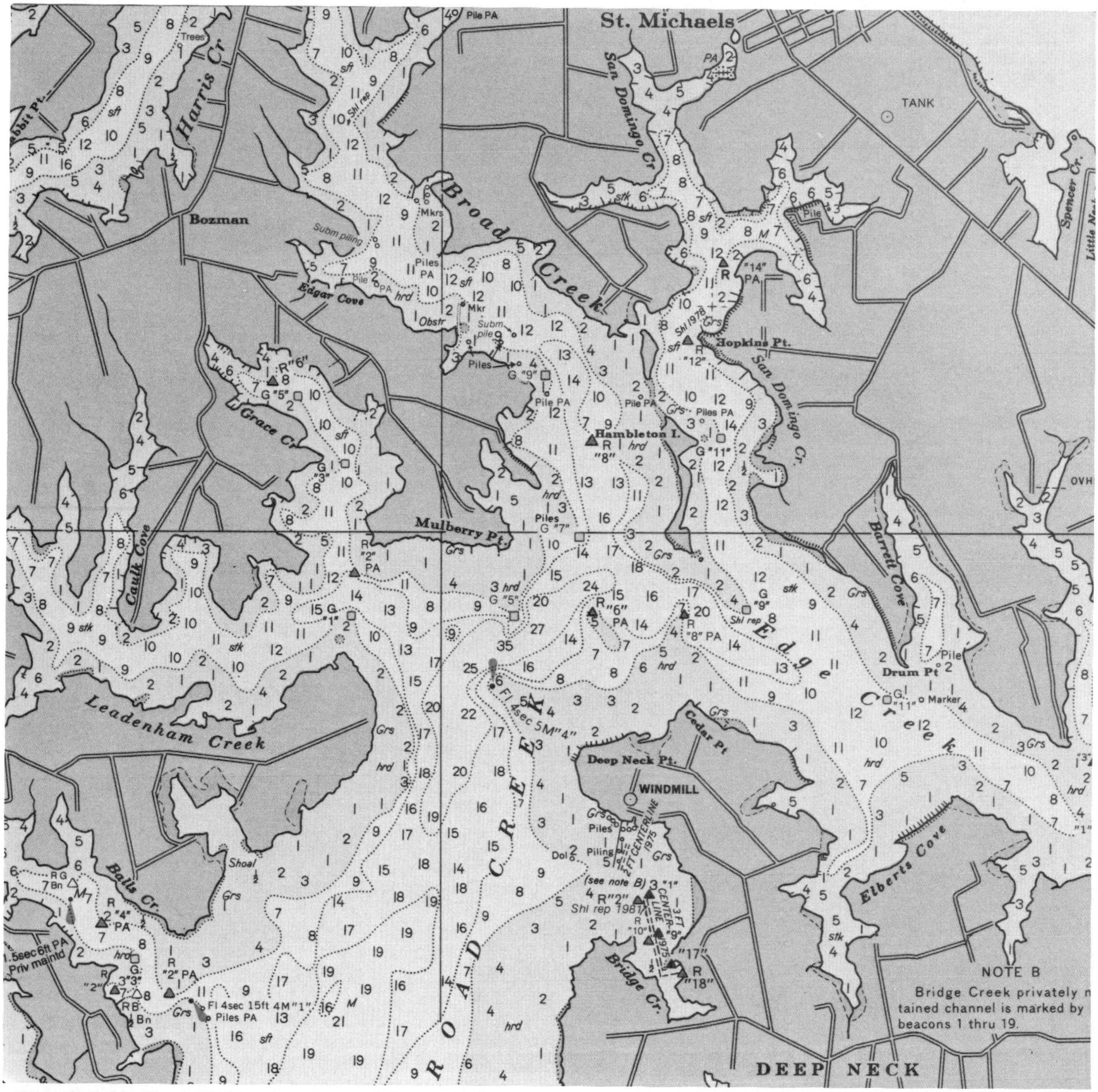

From NOAA Chart 12266 not to be used for navigation.

BALLS CREEK

off Broad Creek

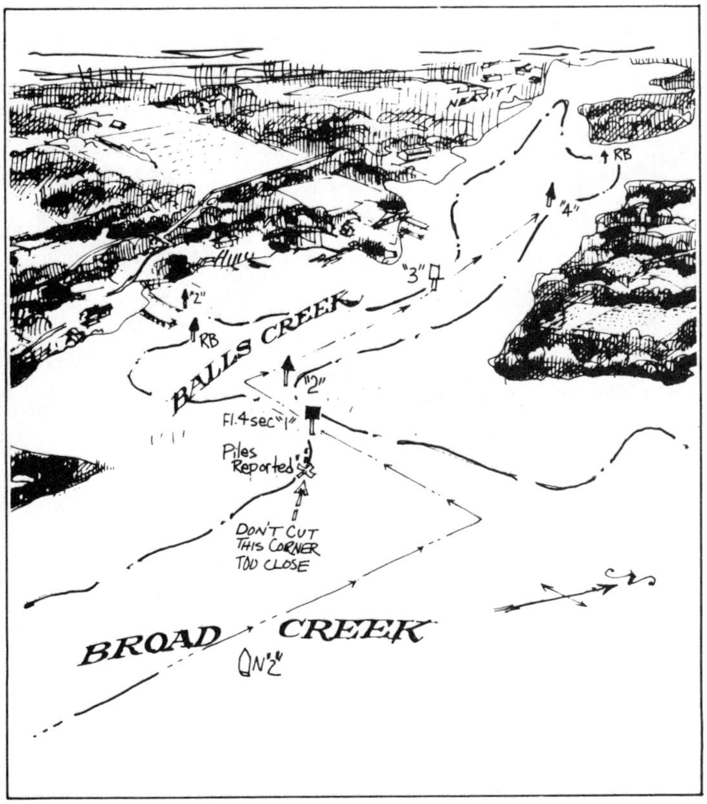

The Broad Creek entrance mark is difficult to spot since it has a tendency to blend in with the shoreline of Deep Neck to the east. If you draw less than four feet, you can pass on either side of Fl. G 4 sec. #1; however I always honor marks (simply because I'm too skeptical to trust the shallows completely). About a mile northwest on course 342° floats a red nun #2. From here you can almost head directly toward the entrance of Balls Creek. But, there is a slight bulge of shallows just south of the creek's entrance mark and I would advise you to just hold course 342° until the mark is abeam. Then turn and run right in on the first two marks. As you pass the second — a red daymark — turn northwest (again on about 342°) and you will pick up the next mark, a green daymark.

The best anchorage on Balls Creek is just past the red daymark #4. The water is deep enough to go all the way upstream to Neavitt, but there is too much activity there to suit us. We anchored in a depth of 8 to 9 feet of water over a mud bottom — good holding ground on a Danforth or plough anchor.

When we were on Balls Creek, the night was quite warm, and I noticed that several boats had stayed outside the creek and anchored just east of Nelson Point. Balls Creek is a tributary of Broad Creek, and the countryside is so beautiful hereabouts that just about any anchorage you select will be enjoyable. □

LEADENHAM CREEK

off Broad Creek

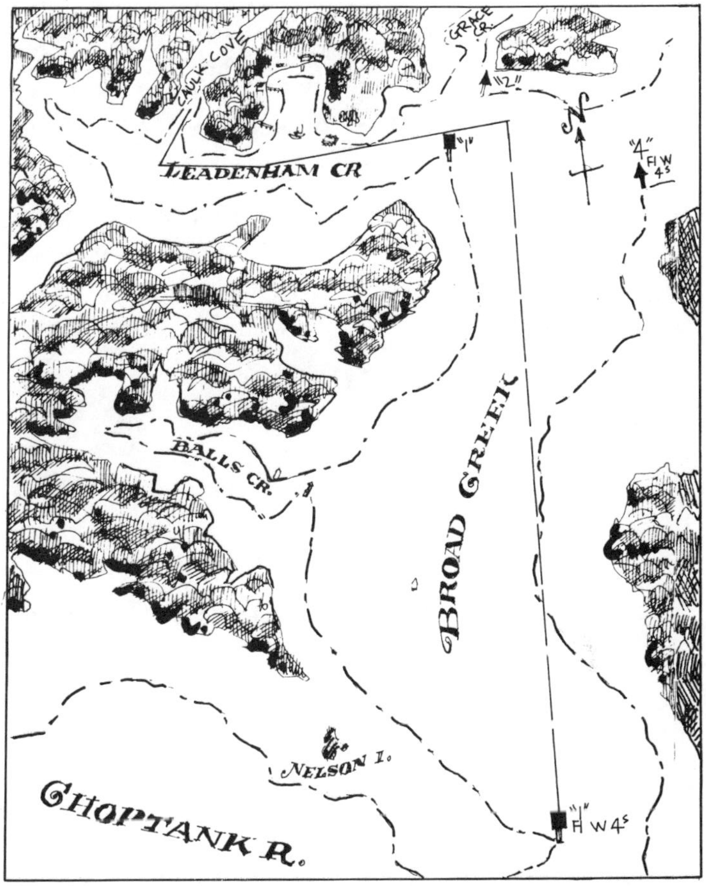

On our way to Leadenham Creek we peeked into Bridge Creek on the east shore. There were several buildings gleaming white in the afternoon sun, but lack of water depth discouraged exploration. We noted several homes and some long white barns similar to the many processing sheds found around the Bay. This little village looked out of place, because Broad Creek at this point shows only wooded banks lining the quiet, still waters with few homes or farms to be seen.

Broad Creek is evidently home to lots of boats. On any good sailing day they look like a flight of moths; and, if you are a stranger, they give you good guidance to deep water, and there's a great deal of it. Having been led to Fl 4sec "4," to enter Leadenham Creek take course about 313 magnetic which brings you to about mid-channel between daymarkers "1" on the south and "2" on the north. You are now at the entrance to Leadenham Creek and at the end of the line of markers. From this position take 245 M as your initial course, and then follow mid-channel to the first cove (unnamed) or the second (Caulk Cove) on the northern shore. Caulk Cove is very snug in heavy winds.

We like to anchor there. The holding ground is good and it's rarely crowded. Note that there are several houses along the shores of the cove, and some moorings and piers, too. Keep clear of them and "keep it clean." We all want to be welcome in this attractive cove another day. □

GRACE CREEK

off Broad Creek

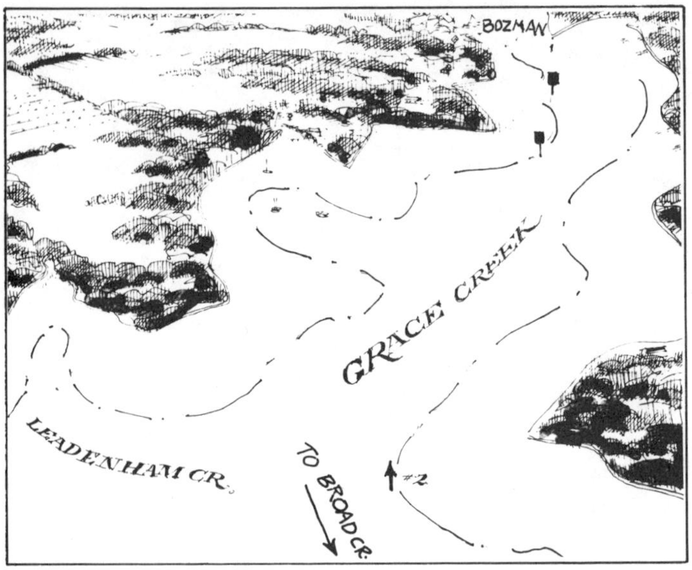

Our motor was humming along comfortably as we once again passed the Choptank Light, and by 5 p.m. we were at the entrance to Irish Creek. Old charts show a can and a nun marking the outward end of the Irish Creek channel. Now there is only a black can moored about a mile offshore of the creek's opening between Lucy Point and Deep Neck Point. Long shoals extend seaward (or Choptank-ward) from each point with a mile-long, curving channel between them. There is a nun #2 about halfway in that is supposed to mark the east side of the bend, but the crooked nature of this narrow channel warns that care must be taken to avoid going aground.

Irish Creek was tantalizingly close, but we were just bumping around as darkness started to close-in. Repeated castings of our lead line failed to reveal the 8-10 foot channel, so we just gave up.

As we headed out into the Choptank, we did a quick chart study and looked for an interesting anchorage for the night. Without hesitation we turned our boat up into Broad Creek, toward Leadenham Creek. Next to it was Grace Creek, which was new to both of us.

And the best part about Grace Creek is that it is easy to get into. No tricky channel. Leadenham and Grace Creeks share a common entrance with red and black daymarks like a gateway to show the entrance. As you pass the red mark, turn north for about four hundred yards, then turn west into the little cove on your port side. This is very snug and well out of the way of traffic with a holding ground of soft mud.

At the head of Grace Creek, at Bozman, are watermen's docks where a few supplies are available.

We anchored at dusk, able to see only dim outlines of the two houses on shore and few lights beaming us a welcome. It had been a wearing day, but the beauty of Grace Creek made it all worthwhile. □

SAN DOMINGO CREEK

off Broad Creek

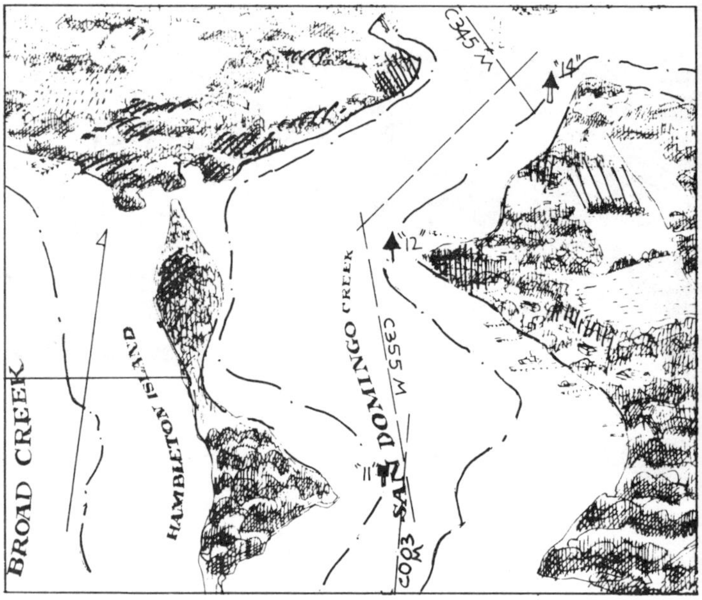

The head of San Domingo Creek is about as near as you can get to the Miles River and still be, as it were, in Choptank waters. If you wanted to shop in St. Michaels, for example, but were somewhere in the lower Choptank, you'd have to go right around via Poplar Narrows into Eastern Bay and the Miles River to get there, taking most of a day under sail or lots of fuel under power. However, for boats of lesser draft, it's quite practical to use the San Domingo "back door" to St. Michaels, anchoring and going ashore by dinghy. We have heard that the people whose properties back onto the upper parts of the creek are very accommodating, allowing one to go ashore and return over their land. (There's a ½ to ¾-mile walk into town.) Sounds to us like typical Eastern Shore hospitality, which, happily, we have experienced much more often than not. One might suggest that for an extended stay in St. Michaels which is most interesting in itself, it would really be better to go around to the "front door," i.e., St. Michaels harbor on the Miles River.

To reach San Domingo Creek, enter Broad Creek, remembering that marker "1" with Fl 4sec light must be left to port, unless you want to take a chance on the shoals that make out a long way SE from Nelson Point. For some reason, possibly because it blends with the dark shoreline, this marker is often difficult to pick out. From it, a course of 012 magnetic will bring you to Fl R. 4 sec. "4," about 4.8 miles up the Creek. From there follow the marked channel, first around to an easterly course, then to a southeasterly one, to "9." Again, follow the markers, now generally a little west of north, until you reach the head of the Creek, where the 7-foot depth is shown. After that, you're on your own, as to depth and distance from shore. Wherever you choose to anchor, shelter is excellent and the holding ground super, though sticky and hard to clean off the hook.

Like so many creeks along the Eastern Shore, San Domingo winds among farmlands and estates, some of them very old, but, as you might imagine, very pretty. Like so many, too, it has its champions who proclaim it "the prettiest spot on the Shore." Perhaps all of them are right! □

IRISH CREEK

on the Choptank River

A well known book on cruising the Chesapeake Bay describes the entrance to Irish Creek as one that will challenge your piloting skill. That's putting it mildly! It used to be a lot trickier than it is now, but our first attempts were frustrating—and fruitless. Being aware of the "shoaling reported 1976" noted on our chart, we still ran aground three times, and finally gave up.

It was some time later that I noticed in the "Notices to Mariners" that new marks had been placed in Irish Creek. I got out my chart, plotted the latitudes and longitudes, and confirmed my suspicions of our first trip. The "shoaling reported" area on my old chart was completely impassable. The channel had shifted a couple hundred yards to the east. Also, the Coast Guard had placed marks off Lucy Point, as well as Edwards Point. As you might guess, Irish Creek became a priority anchorage next time we were on the Choptank.

We made our next attempt around noon on a hot, sunny, windless day. Our run from "C-1" to "N2" was relatively simple. Then, instead of continuing this course (about 015°)straight on in, we headed about 042° and picked up #3 daymark. This stretch was pretty nerve-wracking since we expected to feel the bottom bumping our keel at any moment.

Rounding #3 we turned and headed for the new red daymark #4 off Lucy Point. This mark was easy to spot, and we had no trouble rounding it and picking up new #6 daymark off Edwards Point.

We were greatly relieved to be into the creek proper, with plenty of deep water all around us for maneuvering. Irish Creek is beautiful, but perhaps not as attractive as LaTrappe, or Island Creek, because it is rather low-lying. We found a good anchorage with protection from nor'westerlies straight up where the 8-foot depth shows on the chart. There is also a delightful spot at the entrance to Haskins Cove at the 9-foot mark.

A couple months later, I received several extremely angry letters from readers who had read my cruise of Irish Creek and decided to try it for themselves, with disastrous results. Once again Irish Creek became a priority cruise.

Before our next visit to Irish Creek, we decided to seek some local advice. We called Bob Daniel who lives on Irish Creek. A short conversation confirmed our thoughts about the creek's channel and brought an invitation to visit their dock when (if) we got there.

A couple hours later we found ourselves heading from the Irish Creek outer can #1 to the #2 red nun and nervously discussing the next couple of legs of the entrance. As we rounded the nun and took a bead on the #3, we discovered a workboat anchored right where we figured the main channel would be. Darn! We didn't want to pass too closely to him, but we were afraid of running onto the shoal.

With sweaty palms we steered past the crabbers and continued to the #3 daymark. Here we swung to port and aimed for the #4 daymark off Lucy Point. In looking over the chart (#12266) we had noticed a belly of shoal bulging out from the southwest shore at Lucy Point so that you cannot take a straight course from #3 to #4. By prior discussion Dixie and I had decided to give this shoal a wide berth. In other words, our course was not straight from #3 to #4, but rather a gentle curve out to port about two-thirds of the way up, and then curving gently back to #4. The tide was about half high on the flood, and our four feet seven inches made it in without a touch or bump.

It wasn't long before we were tied up to the Daniels' pier and they confirmed our thinking about the channel. There was no reason why a boat of five-foot draft couldn't get into Irish Creek—except perhaps during the extreme winter low tides. □

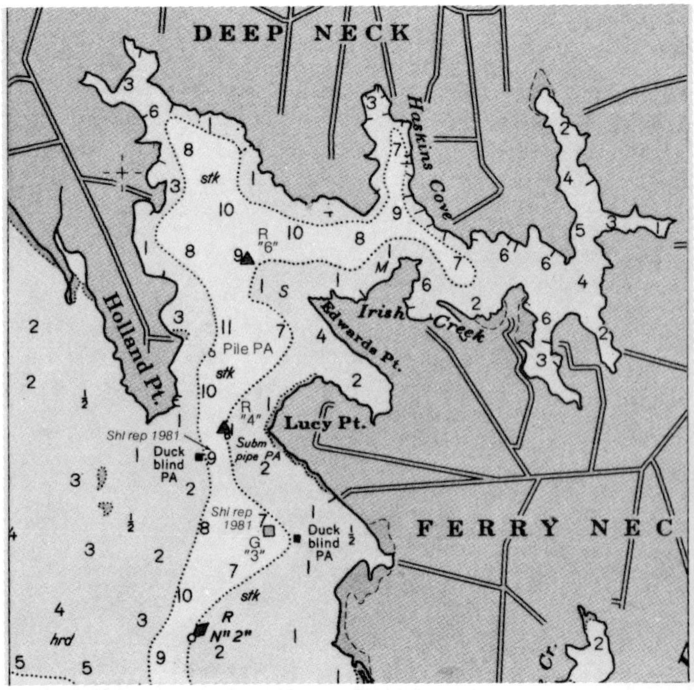

From NOAA Chart #12266—not to be used for navigation

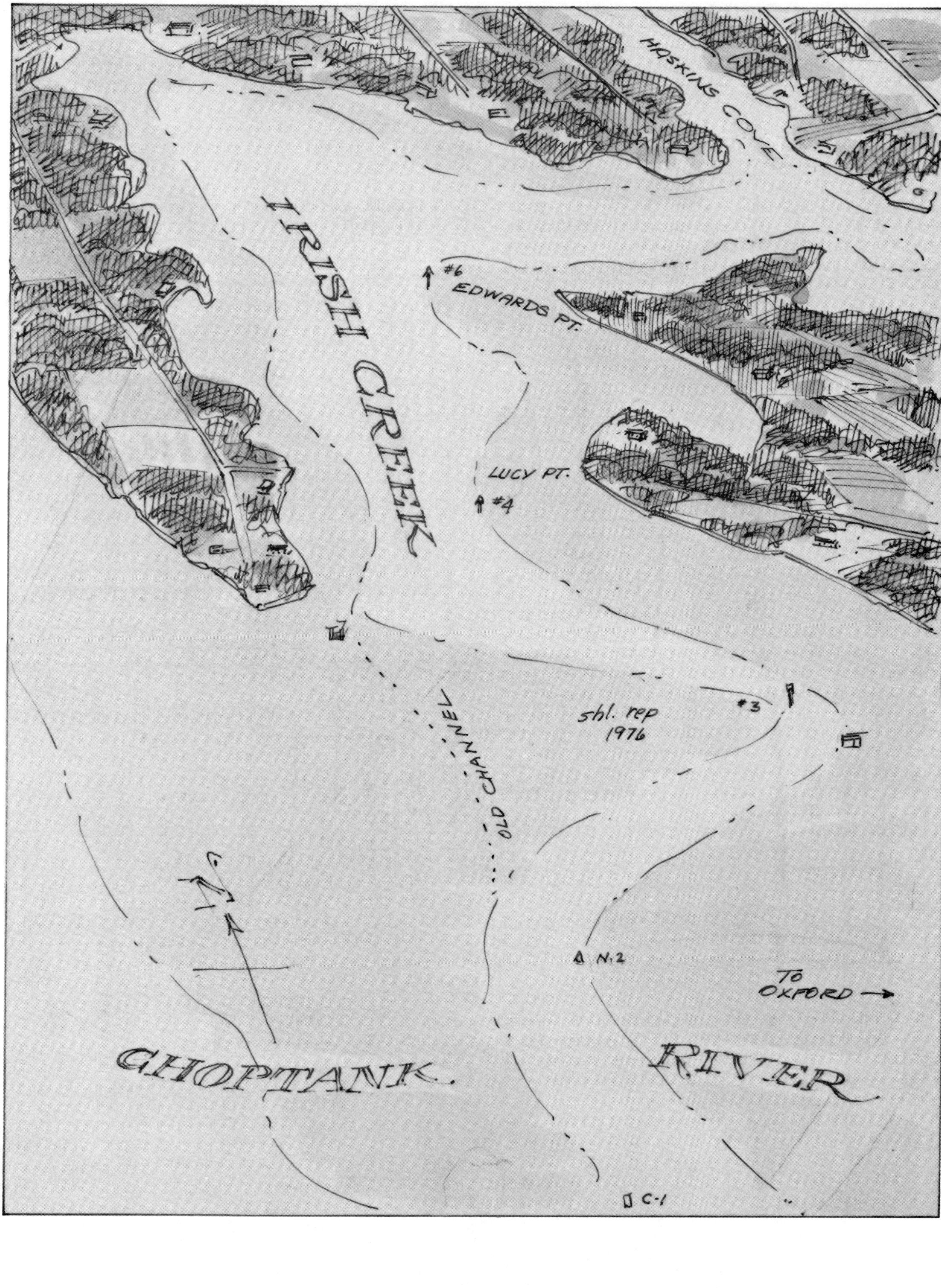
HASKINS COVE
IRISH CREEK
#6
EDWARDS PT.
LUCY PT.
#4
#3
shl. rep 1976
OLD CHANNEL
N.2
TO OXFORD
CHOPTANK
RIVER
C-1

OXFORD
on the Tred Avon River

A little over two miles up the Tred Avon from the Choptank River Light (014 magnetic) is the town of Oxford, cradled by Town Creek on the east and the Tred Avon to the west. There is limited mooring space or you can tie up at the public docks where the Oxford Ferry docks. There is now a limit to the time you may spend at the public dock. Or better yet, anchor in one of the lovely nearby creeks.

Once rivaling Annapolis as Maryland's largest port, it is today a charming, tree-lined village with about 800 residents. A commercial landing spot was recorded here as early as 1635. Named an official port of entry in 1683, it was then referred to as Thread Haven. Many folks believe that the town's heavy commerce in hemp, rope, and cordage led to this appropriate name. The name degenerated; first into Third Haven, and finally to Tred Avon. The village and river shared this name until the town was surveyed by a King's officer, rechristened Williamstadt in honor of King William, and later became known as Oxford. The town continued as a major port until the time of the Revolution. The outbreak of the war, coupled with the rise of Baltimore as a major port, contributed to its decline.

Today, Oxford maintains its importance in boatbuilding. The seafood industry is also very much in evidence, with a packing house and protected harbor for the watermen who harvest oysters, clams, crabs, and fish. Every August log canoes race in a three-day regatta hosted by the Tred Avon Yacht Club.

The oldest free-running ferry in the United States still operates here every day, connecting Oxford with Bellevue, across the river. Started in 1760, when fares were collected in tobacco, today's ferry is a modern diesel double-ender for passengers and vehicles.

Just up from the dock is the Robert Morris Inn, originally the home of the father of the "financier" of the Revolution. Part of the original house, built about 1710, is contained in the present structure. Today it houses one of the Shore's best-known restaurants.

Across Morris Street from the Inn stands the Grapevine House. In 1810, the story goes, a Captain William Willis, commander of the brig *Louisa*, brought over from the Isle of Jersey the grapevine which can still be seen growing in the front yard.

Other interesting old homes include the Bratt Mansion, built around 1848, as part of the Maryland Military School, and Barnaby House, which was erected in the 1700's. Byberry, at the end of Tilghman Street, is one of the area's oldest homes; records indicate it was standing in 1695.

The Oxford Cemetery is the burial place of Col. Tench Tilghman, aide-de-camp to George Washington. It was he who carried the news of Cornwallis' surrender at Yorktown to the Continental Congress in Philadelphia.

Oxford Neck itself boasts such plantations as Belleville and Plimhimmon, home of Tench Tilghman's widow, and Otwell, a Goldsborough home for over 200 years and a genuine reminder of rural England from whence came many of our early settlers.

But not all is old in Oxford. At the Fisheries Biological Research Laboratory on Boone Creek, the most scientific methods are being used to provide insight into the important commercial fisheries field. Research is presently being done on the various aspects of the commercial shellfish industry and the ecology underlying it. Near the end of the point at the western entrance to Town Creek is a modern house built essentially to the shape of the Hooper Strait Light now at the Chesapeake Bay Maritime Museum in St. Michaels.

All in all, historic Oxford is truly a cruising delight. □

See the Oxford walking tour for more information.

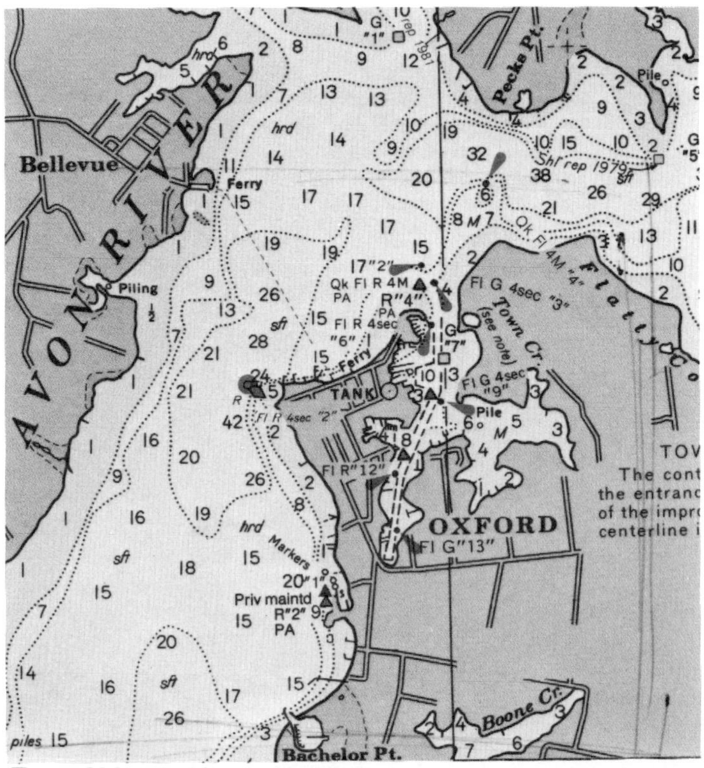

From NOAA Chart 12266—not to be used for navigation.

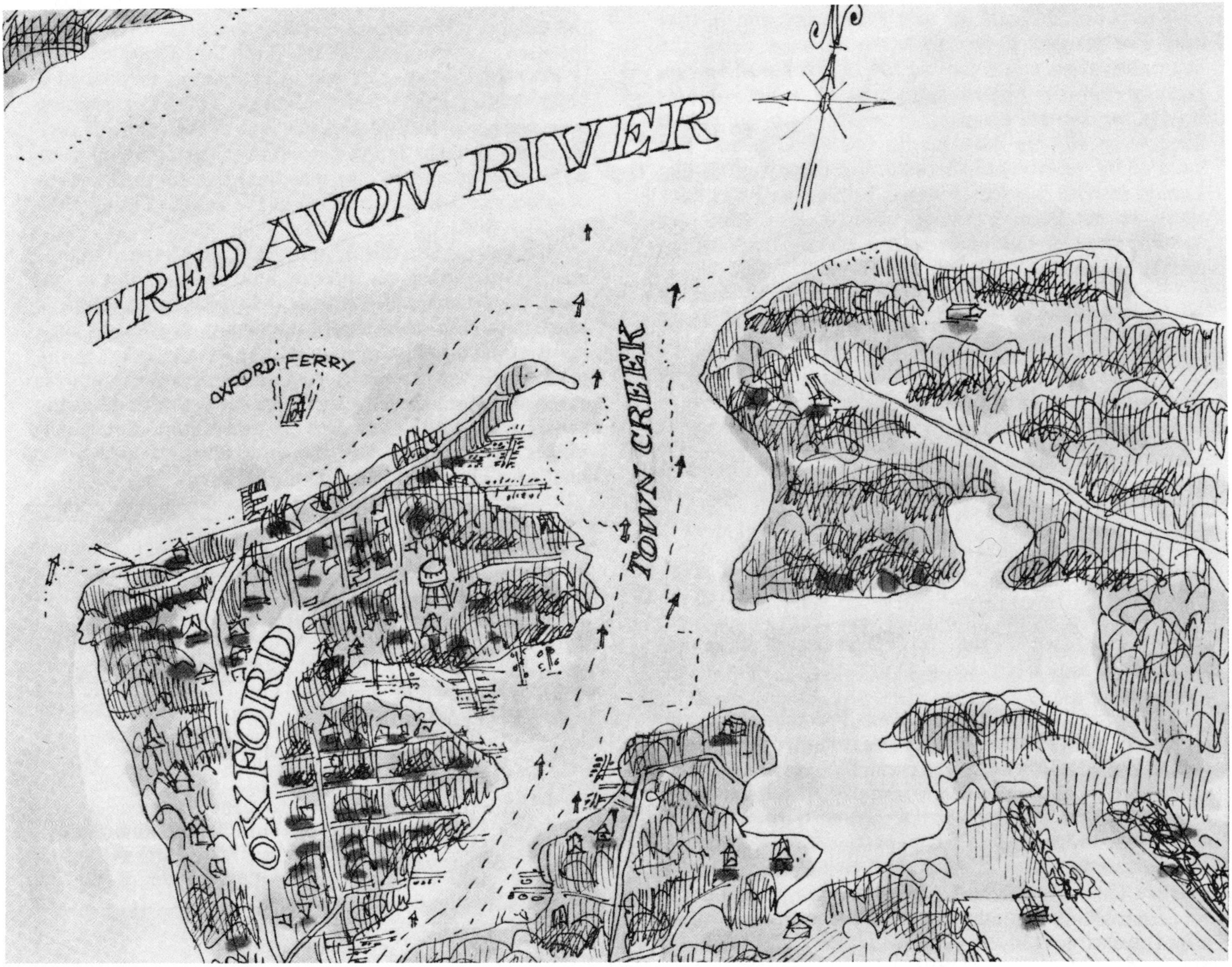
TRED AVON RIVER
OXFORD FERRY
TOWN CREEK
OXFORD

A Walking Tour of:
OXFORD

The story of Oxford reads like the plot of a Hollywood musical of the 40's, only without music. A small town is founded and begins to grow. It prospers and becomes prominent, even produces several famous historic figures. Then along comes a rival and our hero/town loses everything, becomes obscure. Time and pretty much everything else passes by until one day good fortune again shines down. Our town/hero recovers and though not nearly as prominent or prosperous, it successfully and contentedly carries on.

In 1683 Oxford was officially founded when the Maryland General Assembly had it laid out as a town (although it had already been in existence for about 20 years). In 1694 "Trade Haven" or "Tred Avon" or "Thread Haven" or "Third Haven" (Oxford was known by all these names) and Annapolis were proclaimed the only Ports of Entry into Maryland. The next year it was resurveyed and renamed Williamstadt (after King William), a name that lasted until Queen Anne ascended the throne (1702-1714) and its name was changed to Oxford. Regardless of what it was called, the town grew and prospered. Businesses in Liverpool and London set up branch offices here to trade goods for tobacco. Until the American Revolution, Oxford was an international shipping center nestled amidst wealthy tobacco plantations. However, Baltimore, with its accessibility to western areas was beginning to challenge Oxford's commercial status. By the early 1770's its economy was in a fatal decline.

After the Civil War, Oxford enjoyed a brief prosperity as the newly completed railroad was able to transport freshly canned and packed seafood to distant markets. This boom was not destined to last, and by 1910 Oxford had once again become not much more than another name on the map. However, the watermen remained, harvesting the Bay's bounties in the Tred Avon River and providing an economic foundation for the town. Shipbuilding grew to become another important mainstay of Oxford's economy. Recently, the town has been feeling the effects from the growth of two more industries: tourism and pleasure boating.

Despite these ups and downs, Oxford has given us several native sons who have earned themselves a distinguished place in history. They include Robert Morris, Sr., a wealthy and influential merchant and his son, Robert Morris, known as the "financier of the Revolution." Colonel Tench Tilghman, aide-de-camp to George Washington and carrier of the message of Cornwallis' surrender at Yorktown to the Continental Congress in Philadelphia, also hails from here. A monument honoring him has been erected at his grave in the Oxford Cemetery, just outside of town. The people of Oxford are proud of their unique history and have preserved some items from bygone days in a small museum on Market Street near Morris.

Oxford is a perfect port-of-call for those who are looking for a place where they can get away from it all. It is quiet, unhurried, and peaceful. Exploring can easily be done on foot; the size and terrain of this town should even appeal to armchair athletes. The streets are level, treed, and very pleasant. If you look at the shape of Oxford on a local map it seems to resemble an impressionistic triangle. One long leg lies along the Tred Avon River and for the most part is lined with private residences. Another long leg is bordered by Town Creek where the majority of boating facilities are located. Forming the third leg of the triangle is another branch of the Tred Avon River. Paralleling this shore is The Strand, a street whose houses face the water and have an unobstructed view of the lovely panorama. The town's architecture underscores its home-spun Eastern Shore charm.

Businesses and boutiques are not that numerous compared to those found in more "discovered" places. On the other hand, most other tourist haunts have larger permanent populations. (It's been estimated that Oxford has fewer than 800 residents.) The densest concentration of shops is on Morris Street, a main thoroughfare that runs the length of town and parallels the Tred Avon River. If you are into browsing, you'll love these shops with their diversified inventory. (It is here that we first saw the logo "There is no life west of the Chesapeake Bay" on bumper stickers and T-shirts.) Food needs are easily met whether you are eating on board or out. For the dine-at-home crowd there are two grocery stores. The first is Doc's Quik Shop Market which sells produce and meats as well as general groceries. Two doors away is Brigman's Tred Avon Confectionary which augments its groceries with other items from toys to lottery tickets. A smaller and more gourmet assortment of food can be bought at The Oxford Mews. They also carry a freezer full of convenience food from Stouffer's dinners to steaks sold by number instead of pound.

Restaurants are scattered around town, each having its own individuality. The Robert Morris Inn (on the corner of Morris St. and The Strand) has several dining areas. On our first visit we made the mistake of coming for dinner in sportswear expecting to be able to eat in the main dining room. We soon discovered that only properly attired patrons dine there (jacket and tie) as we were ushered into a more informal room. Eating here is a little like dining with history because part of Robert Morris's original house is now part of this colonial inn. Another option is The Masthead located in a small house on Mill Street. Town Creek Restaurant and Marina is at the foot of Tilghman St. and offers a small-eaters-menu (nice when you are in the mood for a smaller meal but you are neither a senior citizen nor under 12) and a carry-out. Pier Street Marina and Restaurant offers both indoor and outdoor dining as well as dockage if you come by boat. No discussion of eateries would be complete without mentioning ice cream. If you are in the mood for a hand-dipped cone, sundae, soda, or shake, try Brigman's Confectionery. There is a counter inside where you can get your favorite ice cream treat. You can also get sodas (we spoiled ourselves with cherry cokes) and sandwiches (a small variety of subs made daily).

Witnesses to Oxford's early days are scattered through town and highlighted in several different walking tours. "A Tourist's Guide," available from the Talbot County Chamber of Commerce, lists points of interest, biography and small sections of street maps of seven county towns including Oxford. "Oxford, Maryland," a street map that has been put together by local entrepreneurs, locates stores, restaurants, marinas, and nine points of interest. A third map, offered by the Oxford Mews, includes shops and sights but has no commentary.

One of Oxford's attractions could be a candidate for Ripley's Believe It or Not. It's called The Grapevine House (built in 1798) and its claim to fame is botanical. In 1810, Captain Wm. Willis brought a grapevine to Oxford from the Isle of Jersey (in England). To ensure its safe passage the plant's roots were buried in potatoes. Upon arrival the grapevine was planted here and has thrived and borne fruit ever since, although it is much smaller than it used to be.

Another attraction is the Oxford-Bellevue Ferry, not only a witness to the growth of this town but still very much a part of it. Although ferry service began on November 20, 1683, it wasn't until 1760 that Elizabeth Skinner established it as a regular line, with fees paid in tobacco (the accepted currency of the day). Until 1886 foot passengers crossed the river by sailboat while horses and wagons were transported via a small barge. In any case, there were never any cables used on this system. Today, it is considered to be the oldest free running ferry in the country.

In addition to getting acquainted with the town on foot and the obvious water oriented activities (like fishing and exploring by dinghy) visitors can enjoy the public parks or go biking. We found two park areas. The first would appeal to boaters who include athletic equipment as part of their travel gear. Located on the edge of town, where Morris Street turns into Route 333 and heads into the countryside, is a field, tennis courts, swings, and backstops. Those who prefer parks where you can conserve more energy than you exert will find the park across from Market Street on Morris Street ideal. This large, grassy area on the shore of the Tred Avon River has swings, picnic tables, benches, a beach, and tall shade trees—everything you need for a lazy summer day.

Biking is a popular activity among visitors. If you don't carry your own, a stop at the Oxford Mews Bike Boutique is a must. In this contemporary version of a general store, you can rent just the right size Schwinn bike by the hour, day or week. Along with a bike they supply a flag, basket, and maps of the town and countryside including two suggested routes to St. Michaels.

Oxford is an athletic town. Aside from a large number of local bicycling enthusiasts there are joggers, boaters, and people who are involved in fitness. One of the latter is Fletcher Hanks who sponsors an annual triathlon of swimming, biking, and running each June. Actually there are two versions of this contest. Both races have the same land course but one starts with a 5.6-mile swim while the other has a 2.4-mile swim. Don't sell the popularity or importance of this event short because it is held in a small town; it draws about 500 starters in all, including triathlon world champions. Contestants coming from about 38 states and several countries arrive early so they can test out the water in a practice swim a week before the race. There are also boat races in the Tred Avon River sponsored by the Tred Avon Yacht Club. In addition, an annual regatta sponsored jointly by the Tred Avon and Chesapeake Yacht Clubs is held each August.

Oxford has a lot to offer to people who want to slow down their pace a bit and relax. You really have to try hard to be hassled and uptight while you are here. Oxford means sitting back, putting your feet up, and ah-h-h. For more information call the Talbot County Chamber of Commerce (301-758-2300) or the Oxford Town Commissioners office (301-226-5122). □

—*Andi Manchester*

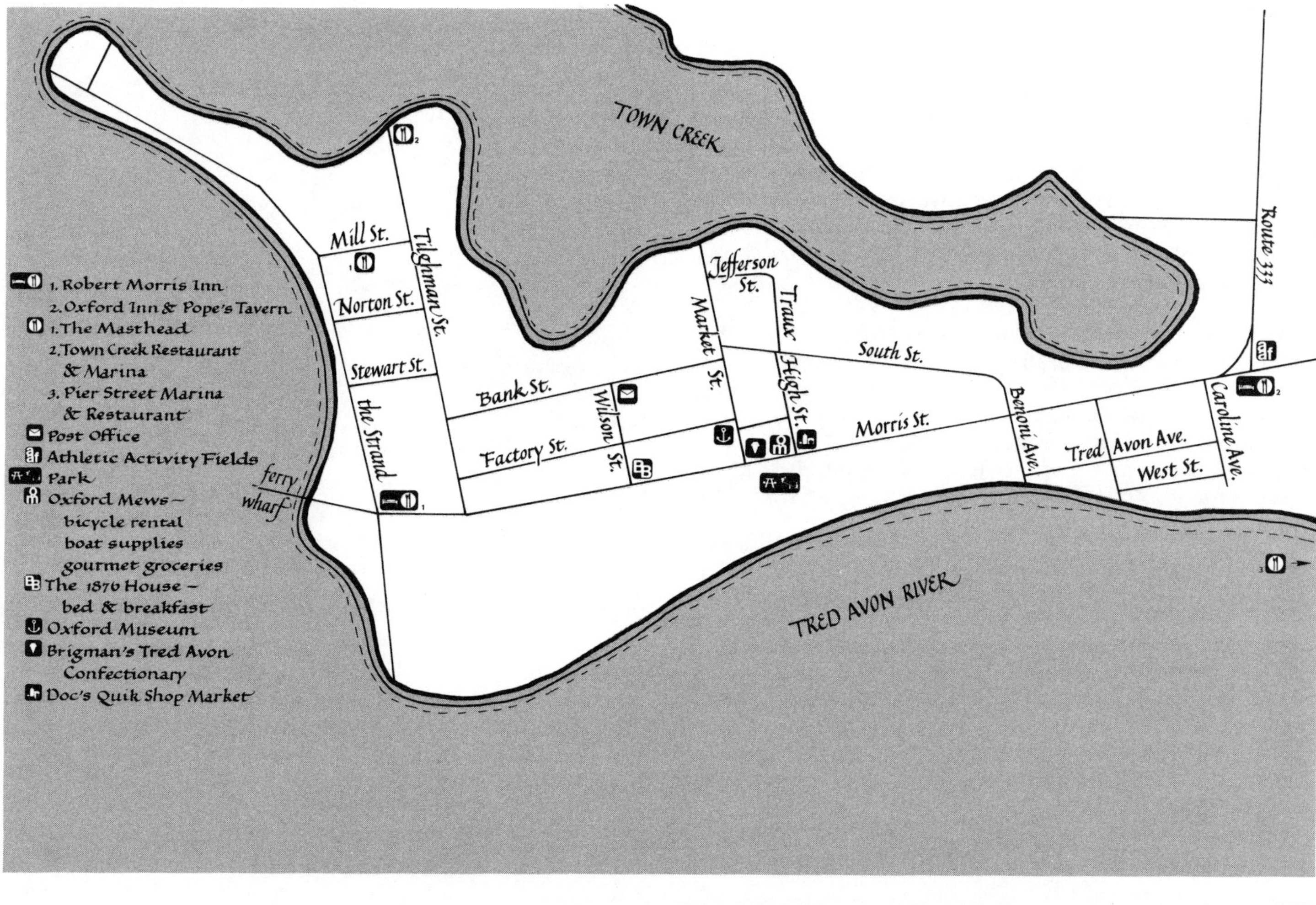

RENDERING OF AUTHOR'S MAP BY JOAN MACHINCHICK

PLAINDEALING CREEK
on the Tred Avon River

While in Oxford we decided to anchor for the night in Plaindealing Creek, instead of Oxford's Town Creek. On a previous visit we had experienced anchoring troubles in Town Creek. One time a real "zinger" of a summer storm passed through. Funny thing is, our two-boat raft stayed put throughout the storm, but it was afterward that a steady 15-knot wind caused us to drag. After resetting with a plough, we sat at anchor to watch into the late hours; and I remember thinking that this whole scene was pretty dumb. Here we were anchored just off the docks at Oxford Boat Yard that were crowded with expensive boats, and at any moment the mud holding our anchor might decide to give way, allowing us to go crashing into the boats at the docks. There must be a better place to anchor for the night, I thought to myself, than here in Town Creek (whose poor holding ground is well known).

On our next trip, we checked the charts and noticed Plaindealing Creek, just across the Tred Avon. I would recommend it to all; and a plus is that Plaindealing Creek is closer than the popular Trippe Creek.

Our three boats wanted to spend the night in Plaindealing Creek but have dinner in Oxford. So we left two boats with anchor lights lit and took the third into Town Creek.

We motored back to Plaindealing in the dark, and it was a little tricky. To begin with, the marks leading into Plaindealing Creek are unlighted, and, therefore difficult to pick up. Secondly, the face of the day marker — that is, the board with reflective border and number — faces the wrong way if you're coming from Oxford. There were a few sticks of an osprey nest to further disguise it in the darkness.

As we cautiously felt our way in, we noticed no lights on either shore to help us. On entering, just stay in the middle, and use the crab pot markers as a guide. Once inside, the river broadens and you can pull off to the port side where a forked branch leads off.

On a more recent cruise, we decided to look into the shoaling reports on Plaindealing. Nearing the daymark #1 we saw, just beyond, a waterman working a trotline. His boat was on the port side of the channel, though, and we wouldn't bother him. The charts show a shoal on the starboard side where the one-foot mark shows. This is the most likely place for new shoaling to develop, we reasoned, so we stayed to port.

When the waterman saw our course, he waved us forcefully away and signalled shallow water. We followed his advice and stayed in the middle. Slowly we motored our way upstream, with me amidships casting the leadline. The water depths measured eight and nine feet all the way, both going in and coming out. I know shoaling has been reported; we just didn't find it. That doesn't mean that a shallow spot isn't there, just that we didn't find it. So, as with any creek entrance, my recommendation is to follow the best advice available, watch your charts, and be extra cautious just to be safe.

If you have a depthfinder with an alarm, you ought to be able to steer a safe course by setting the alarm for a depth a couple feet greater than your draft, and correcting your heading according to the readings. Anyway, it would be good practice to do it a couple of times just for fun.□

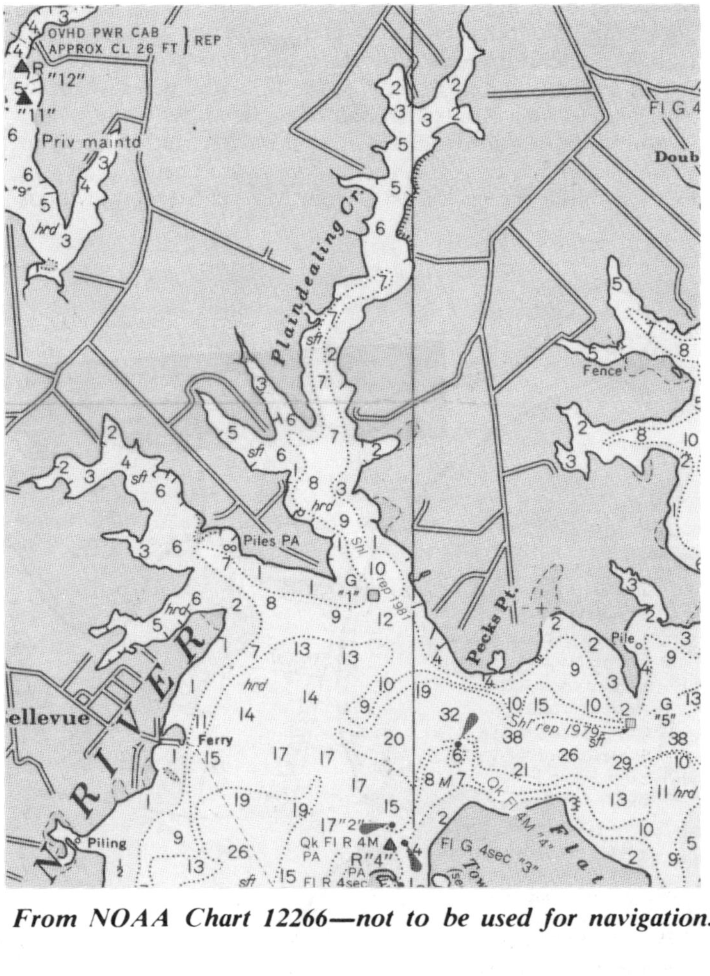

From NOAA Chart 12266—not to be used for navigation.

PLAINDEALING CR.
SHOALING REPORTED
PECKS POINT
TRED AVON RIVER

Notes

GOLDSBOROUGH CREEK

on the Tred Avon River

From NOAA Chart 12266—not to be used for navigation.

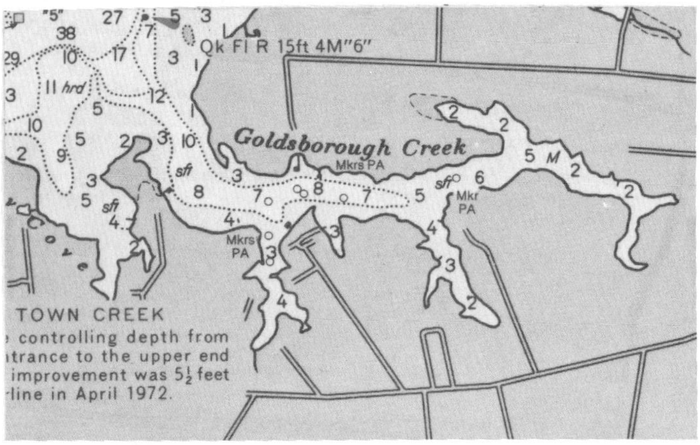

Great Day!

As I review our ship's log, that's the first thing I see about our cruise to Goldsborough Creek. "Great day!" And as I relive the details, I am reminded that it was indeed just that.

We had left the Miles River for Goldsborough Creek. The log shows that we had strong (15+ knots) headwinds down Eastern Bay; so in the interest of time, we were motoring. All we had to worry about were crab pots in Poplar Island Narrows. Recent NOAA charts show a channel that is supposed to be free of pots, but we noticed that a number of floats had apparently drifted into the "safe channel."

Our log, without further comment, shows that we cleared Knapps Narrows at 1605 hours. As I remember, there were no problems such as strong cross winds or bottom bumpings; but there were a fair amount of transiting boats—all jockeying for their half of the channel.

As we emerged from the Narrows channel, a ten- to twelve-knot southerly breeze greeted us. Up went our sails, and we boiled along the seven-and a-half miles to the mouth of the Tred Avon in smooth comfort. As we watched, sailboats that emerged behind us from the Narrows shook out their sails and chased after us.

Many sailors profess they have no interest in racing. But just let there be another sailboat nearby, heading in the same direction, and there occurs what I call the "sailor's reflex." We begin to take a keen interest in the set of our own sails. We glance repeatedly at the other boat. Often this is done surreptitiously because we seem unwilling to admit we are accepting a challenge. Perhaps there is an inner fear of being beaten. If we stay ahead and reach our anchorage first, we can strut and gloat. But if the other fellow passes us, we can pretend that we weren't really at "full throttle," though inwardly we feel rotten. It's as if we—or our boat—had failed some vitally important test. The whole thing is dumb perhaps, but we all seem to fall into this line of reasoning.

I also recall a November cruise when our destination was also Goldsborough Creek. And as we passed Broad Creek we could see huge "islands" (that's the only word I can think of to describe it) of Canada geese. At the time large formations of geese were taking to the air. We would see some of the same flocks later that evening in our anchorage.

This time we rounded the spar off Benoni Point and joined a dozen or so boats all sailing wing and wing up the Tred Avon. We used two charts—*The Guide to Cruising Maryland Waters,* published by the State of Maryland, and NOAA chart #12267—as we headed for Goldsborough Creek, about a mile upstream from Oxford's Town Creek. As we passed the green #5 we could see that there was a good-sized fleet of boats anchored in Flatty Cove, which stands between Town Creek and Goldsborough Creek.

The hour was growing late and because of the narrow look of the Goldsborough entrance channel, we gave a minute's thought to joining the group in Flatty Cove. But Goldsborough was our destination, and my memory of the creek was too good to pass up.

You can't head right into the creek from the #5 marker because the shoals pinch together in such a manner that you may run aground. So we continued northward another 300 yards till the small cove to port was abeam; then we turned and headed for the Goldsborough Creek entrance. We throttled way back and kept the cove dead astern, at the same time favoring Goldsborough's port side slightly. Our ten-foot lead line found no bottom as we slowly motored past the grassy shoreline.

Our destination was just inside the entrance where the deep water broadens just opposite a large boathouse. There are few homes or other buildings on this part of the creek, and the low banks are open for whatever faint summer breeze may be stirring. If the weather gets "blowy," you can head further upstream for a bit more protection. On the port side of the creek there's a good-sized sandbar, almost awash at high tide, which seems to be a gathering place for the local seagulls, which squawk and jostle each other for the occasional scrap of food they seem to find there. Keeping a discreet distance were a few dignified egrets and several heron.

Goldsborough's bottom is soft, sticky mud; anchoring is easy, with good holding ground. As the sun set and evening shadows turned the shoreline from rich greens to deep purple blues, we ate in the cockpit. Mosquitoes were taking the night off, and we enjoyed the tranquility of our surroundings.

Not much had changed since our first visit here several years ago. The highlight of that visit had been the Canada geese. It was early November, and the geese seemed to be everywhere. At that time as we sat in the lee of our dodger we could hear the heavy beating of their wings as they flew into Goldsborough and loud splashes as they landed. Their honking and calling was all around us. I remember thinking they were very clever not to fly into our rigging. There were great flocks in Flatty Cove as well, and their voices greeted each new flock of geese that was landing on both creeks. It was wonderful!

And so was this cruise. A flood of good memories came back to me as I re-read my spontaneous scrawl in our log—"A great day!" □

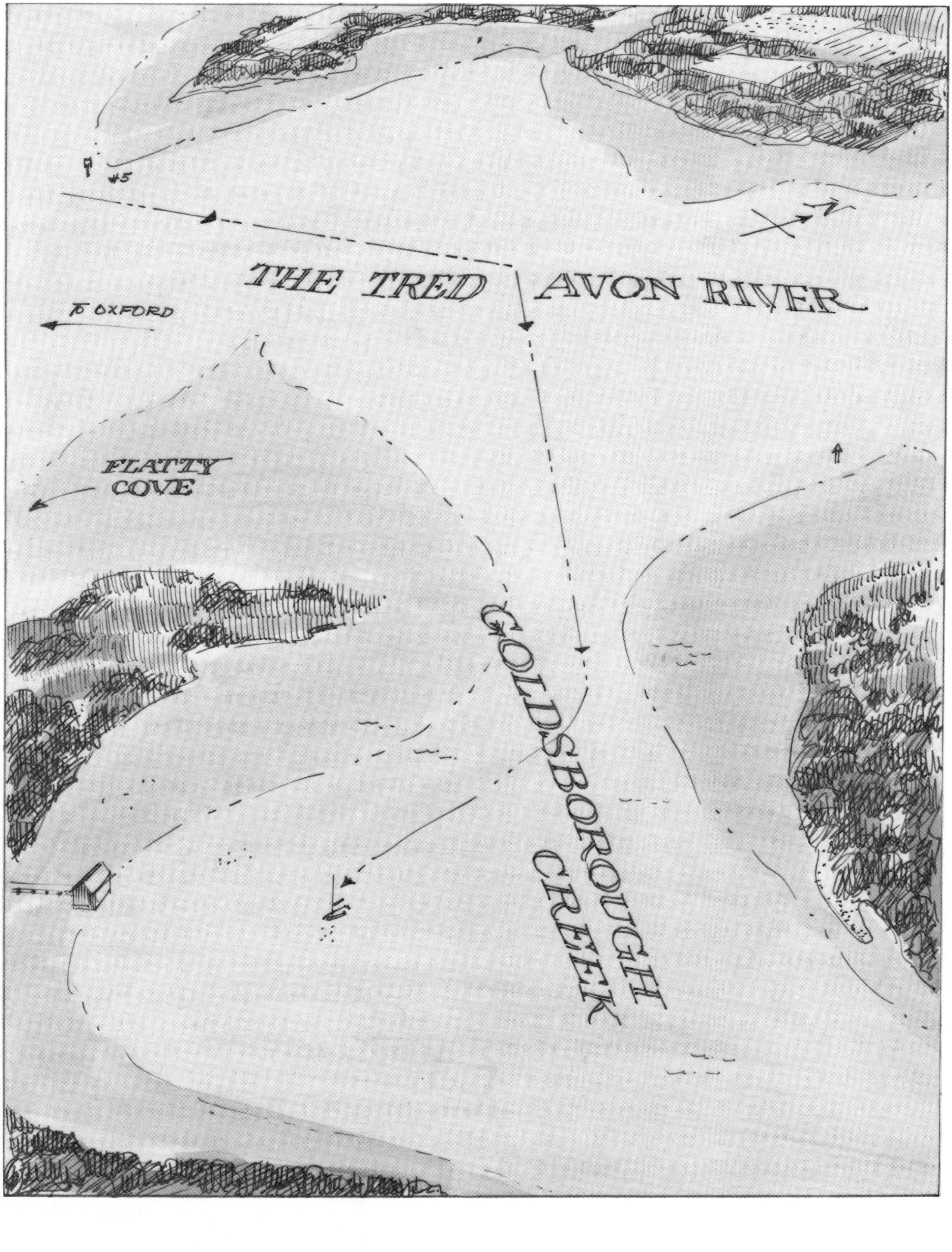
#5
THE TRED AVON RIVER
TO OXFORD
FLATTY COVE
GOLDSBOROUGH CREEK
N

TRIPPE CREEK/SNUG HARBOR

on the Tred Avon River

As we beat down the Bay toward Blackwalnut Point, the wind, blowing a steady 25 to 35 knots, was surprisingly cool. After rounding C "9" marking the shoal off Blackwalnut Point, we eased off to a beam reach inside the mouth of the Choptank River. We felt warmer and we enjoyed a comfortable sail to the Choptank River Light.

We continued north up the Tred Avon toward Trippe Creek, with our destination Snug Harbor. Just north of Oxford, it is one of the most beautiful spots on the Eastern Shore.

To reach Trippe Creek, ascend the Tred Avon to Oxford. Then, instead of turning in at Town Creek, as so many do, continue up the Tred Avon, carefully following the markers up the right-hand side of the river. There are shoals on the wrong side of the markers, which are daybeacons. Along this course are the lovely farms and woodlands of this most favored of rivers.

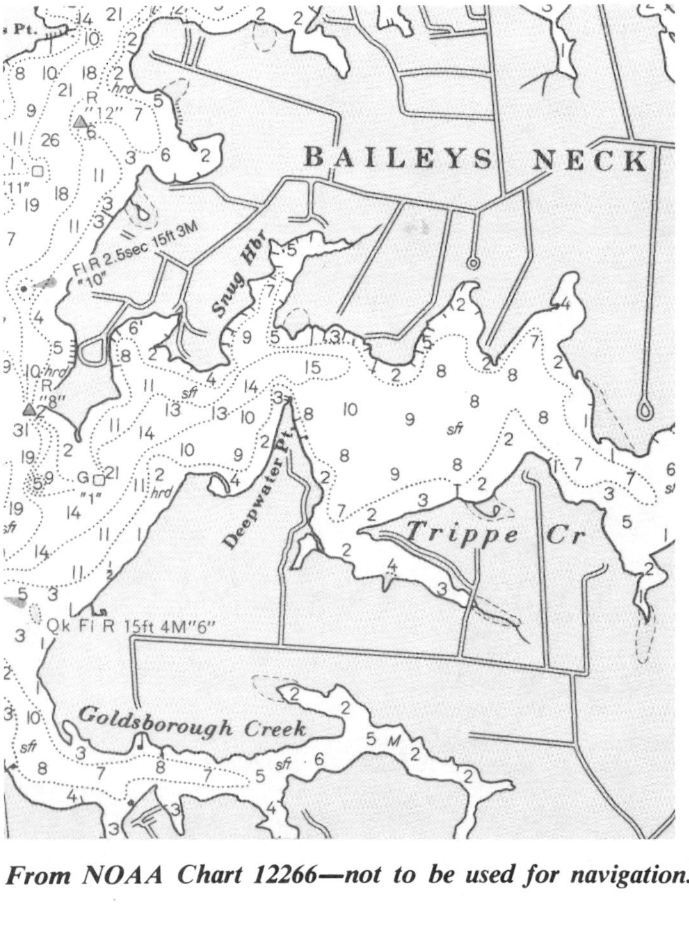

From NOAA Chart 12266—not to be used for navigation.

The entrance to Trippe Creek is about a mile and a half up the river from Town Creek and 4.5 miles from the Choptank River Light. The channel is deep and well marked with no surprises. You can navigate it at night, but the Trippe Creek daymark is hard to spot in the dark.

From daymark #1 a course of 065° M brought us to the mouth of our anchorage, Snug Harbor. Give Deepwater Point a wide berth. This charming and peaceful little cove is just the right size for a couple of boats to ride out a storm. Snug Harbor is wide open to the south, which is why we picked it. The brisk southerly wind had dropped to a gentle five knots, and we could look forward to a cool night's sleep.

Snug Harbor is fairly well settled, with a number of private docks. As we ate dinner in our cockpit, we watched the progress of an approaching storm. For an hour or more the clouds rumbled and thundered. By dark, lightning flashes had joined the thunder, and together they put on a fearsome display. The breeze had freshened and swung around to the west. I had let out a short rode when we anchored because of the limited swinging space; but as the wind picked up I let out another 30 feet. Total rode let out now was 110 feet. With our six feet of heavy chain, I figured it should hold us in any kind of blow. On the other hand, if the wind swung around out of the east, would we have enough room to reset the anchor if it should drag?

We first felt 15 or 20 minutes of heavy wind from the west; then it backed around and blew from the opposite direction. Next it shifted northerly. Torrents of rain fell, accompanied by immense flashes of lightning so bright the entire shoreline was illuminated in detail. I was on deck for over an hour to watch the set of an anchor line and the position of our boat.

Finally, about 10 P.M. the storm abated. We fell into our bunks exhausted. It had been a rough day—and night—but we felt we could rest easy in a place aptly named Snug Harbor. □

Notes

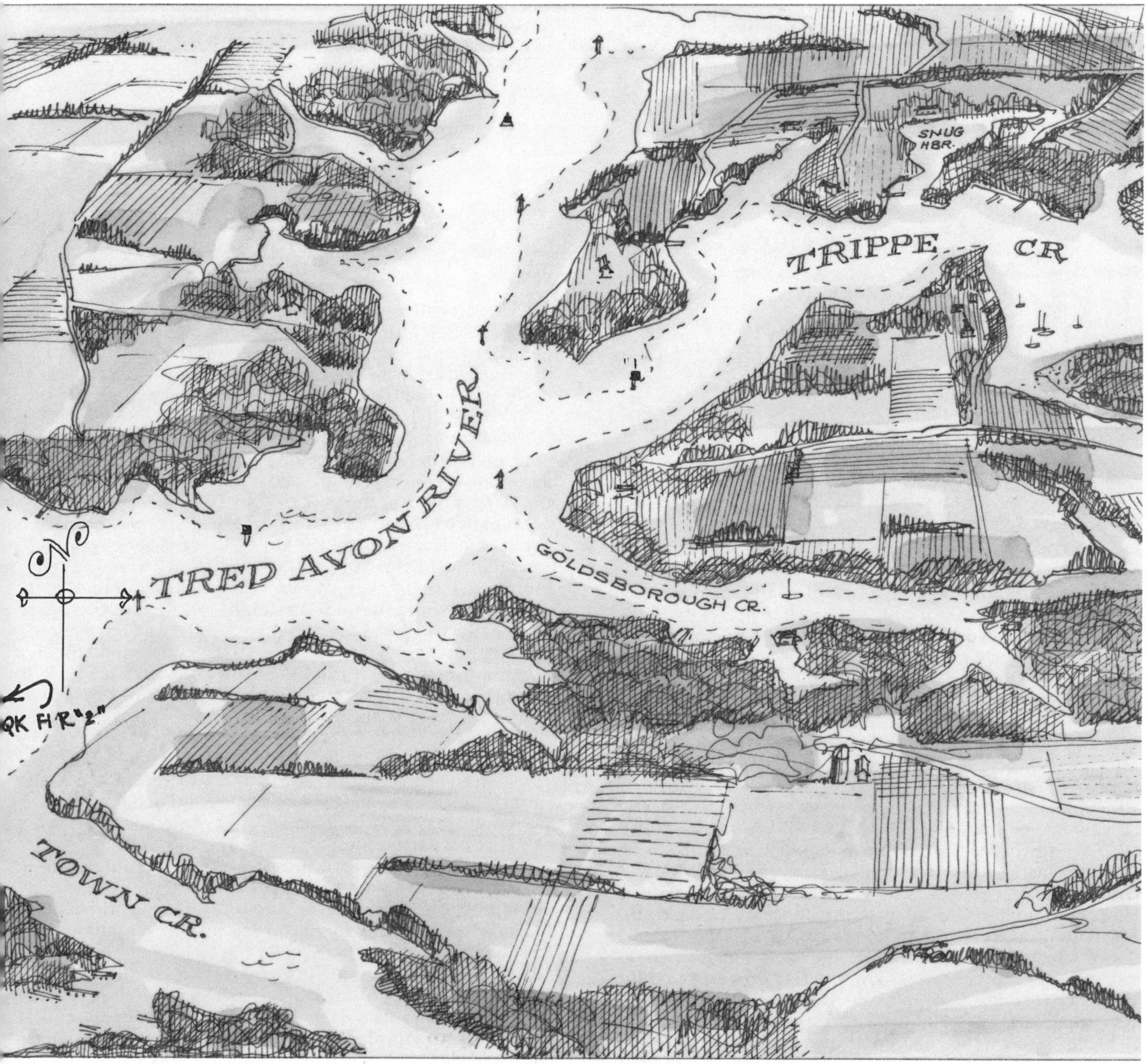

BOATKEEPING TIPS

For some of us, it's tough to read the charts without our glasses. To keep a pair handy by the chart table, buy an extra case and mount it on a nearby vertical surface. For quick reading of a small area of the chart, equip your navigation area with a small, handheld magnifier.

Make a list of those little things that annoy you about your boat. Identifying them is the first step toward fixing them. Deck slippery? Add non-skid material to your paint before you brush it on. Not enough water tankage? Add an inflatable tank for extended cruises. Hatch leak? Take it off and re-bed it.

A transient may spend the night in your slip when you are out overnight. And you may come home and find your dock lines gone. But you probably won't if you dye them a bright color so no one can mistake them for their own. It's easy to do with a couple of packages of commercial dye. To be really fancy, dye your boat's mop to match.

Try a car vacuum cleaner for boat use. It can be plugged into 12-volt current and is compact to store. Not recommended if your craft has bulkhead-to-bulkhead carpet!

PEACHBLOSSOM CREEK AND EASTON

on the Tred Avon River

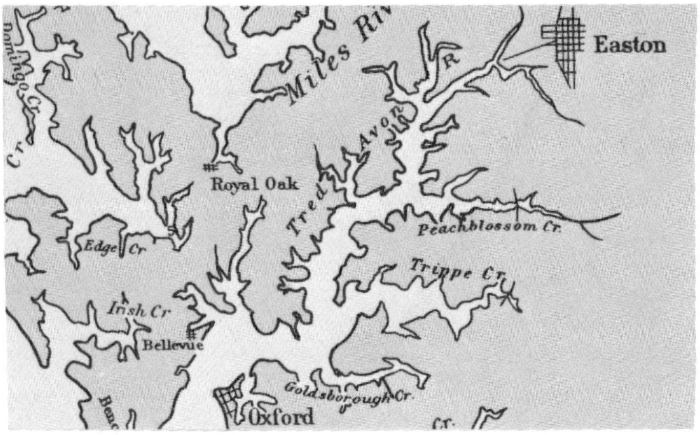

From NOAA Chart 12260—not to be used for navigation.

I was leafing through my stack of charts the other day and ran across one in particular that brought back memories of a recent cruise. The chart was not folded neatly as the others were, printed surface turned in for protection. This one was folded printed side out, as they are when we're using them in the cockpit.

The number in the corner read 12266. Turning it over, I saw the full length of the Tred Avon River. Ah, yes. I remember this cruise well. Looking back, it doesn't seem as harrowing now as it was then. Certainly, a cruise to Peachblossom Creek sounds about as exciting and hectic as vanilla pudding.

To begin with, we rounded the Choptank River "spider" fairly early in the afternoon, about 3 P.M. We could be in Peachblossom by 5 P.M., but the prospect of a short side trip into Oxford was irresistible. To tell the truth, I was looking forward to a meal ashore at the Oxford Town Creek Restaurant and, at the same time, we could gas up at nearby Mears Marina. After dinner we could cruise upstream to Peachblossom Creek, which is less than four miles away.

After refueling we tied up at the courtesy docks at the restaurant and took a short stroll around Oxford to stretch our sea legs. This was hot September, and back at the restaurant we had a welcomed shower first, and planned a hasty meal.

But the tasty food, good companions, and conversation delayed us, causing problems we hadn't anticipated. It was nearly 8 P.M. when we cast off dock lines and headed out toward Peachblossom Creek. The days in mid-September are shorter than those in July, and dusk was settling around us. We switched on running lights and headed north, up the Tred Avon. I remember glancing behind us once to see the rapidly sinking orange ball sun; and by the time we were off Goldsborough Creek, the sun was below the horizon.

By the time we got to the entrance of Trippe Creek, it was completely dark. We considered heading in, but no, darn it! We said we were going to Peachblossom Creek, and by golly, that's where we're going! What's a little dark anyway? Switching on compass lights we were greeted by their re-assuring red glow for a minute, and then they went dark again. A hasty check showed a blown fuse. No problem. Spare fuses were on board and easily replaced the old.

The new fuse blew immediately.

Well, it would have been nice to follow compass headings upstream so that we wouldn't miss the two daymarks just below Double Mills Point. But the next mark was lighted, and we should have no real problems.

It's only about a mile from "10" (Fl R 2½ sec) to "13" (Fl G 4 sec), but it seemed like ages. We worried about passing on the wrong side of a daymark and going hard aground. We were at fairly slow speed, but grounding in the dark would be no fun.

Finally "11" passed to port, and then "12" to starboard. We had a clear shot to "13" (Fl G 4 sec), where we would turn and head for "16" (Fl R 4 sec) which stands at the mouth of Peachblossom Creek. The distance on this leg is exactly one mile, but not a straight line. There's a slight dogleg caused by a shoal about half of the way up, marked by "15". It would have been nice to set a course and follow the compass; but with lights out, we couldn't see it well enough. We just had to cross our fingers and guess. The wrong side would put us aground, so we were pretty tense till we spotted "15" ghosting by in the dark.

Well, things should be clear sailing from here on in, just run a straight line to "16" (Fl R 4 sec), then turn and head into the opening of Peachblossom Creek. Even in the dark, we should have no problem.

That's what we thought!

As we made our turn into Peachblossom the tension drained out of us as we prepared for anchoring. I remember the beautiful feeling of relief that turned to alarm as we suddenly bumped bottom! The sensation on a keel boat is unique. There's a feeling like a giant hand that jolts you and seems to lift you briefly in the air. We staggered, I hit the throttle, and, after a brief struggle, we pushed our way into deeper water. What an experience!

Slowly we motored toward the south shore where some piers show on the chart. There, in the friendly glow of shore lights, we dropped anchor.

Peachblossom Creek is every bit as lovely as Trippe or Goldsborough Creeks. The homes (estates) are beautiful with well-tended lawns. There are two favorite anchorages—one where we were; but if weather get really rough, go farther upstream past Le Gates Cove to where the creek broadens out again. If you draw less than four feet, go yet farther upstream to the little bridge. Here Peachblossom Creek becomes more like a friendly country stream.

If continuing up the Tred Avon to Easton, at "18" (Fl R 4 sec) off Watermelon Point, watch the next two markers carefully to avoid being misled into Shipshead or Dixon Creeks. At green "21" the channel narrows to about 100 yards, but has depths of 10 feet or more. Less than a mile farther red "22" comes into view with the buildings of Easton Point Marina immediately beyond. Oil company structures stand nearby.

Taxi service is available for the 1.5-mile trip to Easton, or free shuttle service can sometimes be arranged at the marina. The city of Easton is still the county seat of Talbot county and with a population of 8,000 or more offers a wide range of shops and restaurants. It's one of the major centers of the Eastern Shore and grew up around a courthouse erected in the early 1700's. In Easton the first newspaper on the Eastern Shore was established in 1790, the first bank in 1805, and the first steamboat line to Baltimore began in 1817. Both Easton Point and Oxford were steamboat stops until the demise of water transportation about a half century ago. A modern change in Easton is the number of New York stock exchange offices that now occupy space downtown.

Each November the entire population turns out to host the Waterfowl Festival which attracts large crowds. But even without a festival the town is enjoyable with its courthouse green and Federal period houses. □

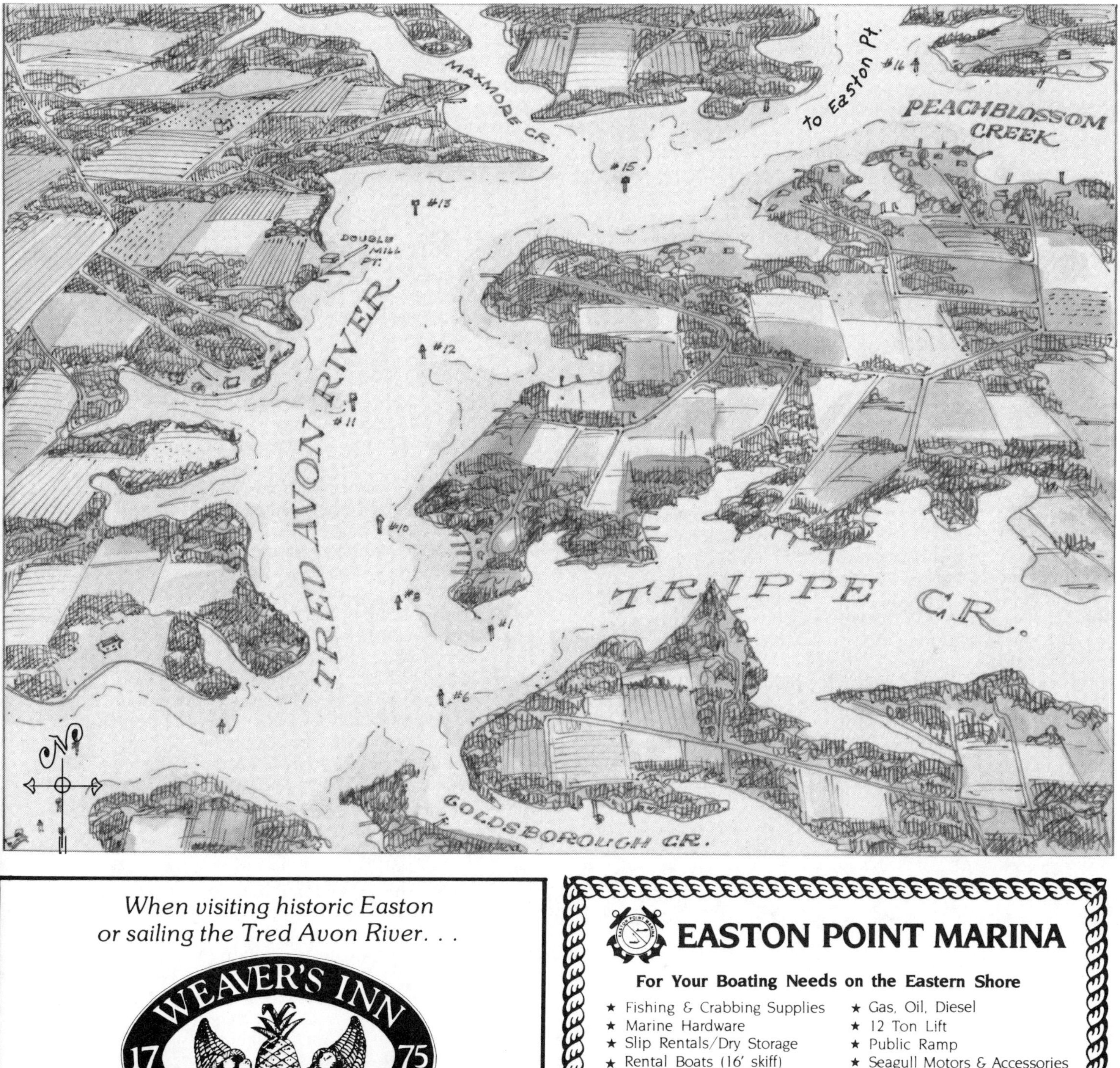

ISLAND CREEK

on the Choptank River

We've always enjoyed a visit to the Choptank River. There are other rivers and creeks on the Bay I can't say that about, but every time we've been on the Choptank has been a delight. We usually find a breeze, and the breeze is almost always fair.

On this particular visit we chose to use the Narrows for two reasons. First, to save time. Second, because we hadn't used this well-known short-cut for several years and just wanted to check out last year's dredging. *Moon Song* draws nearly five feet, and we had no trouble with the channel. There was the usual milling around, waiting for room at a gas dock; but the bridge tender is always quick to respond to a horn, and we were soon through the Narrows and out into the Choptank.

The day had started out cool and cloudy, and as we cleared the Narrows, a balmy warmth settled over us. We drew a course for the Choptank River Light and before we reached Nelson Island were caught in a heavy downpour of rain. There was no wind, just heavy, warm rain. The horizon disappeared and nearby boats on the same course became blurred. The water around us was beaten into a green-gray froth.

Just off the mouth of Irish Creek the rain quit, just as suddenly as it began. Ahead of us the Choptank River spider stood out wetly against the soft green horizon. We shed our rain gear and, as the afternoon got warmer, off came sweaters and shoes. To the west the black clouds were piled high and ominous, while ahead to the east gray clouds were beginning to part, showing a lining of soft turquoise blue. We motored on toward it and Island Creek.

Island Creek is just south of the mouth of the Tred Avon River, a little over a mile due east of the Choptank River Light. Its entrance is guarded by two marks—a 4-second green flasher #1 and a red daymark #2. We had read in "Notices to Mariners" that the #1 spar was leaning, but as we neared the creek's entrance, we could see both marks perfectly upright.

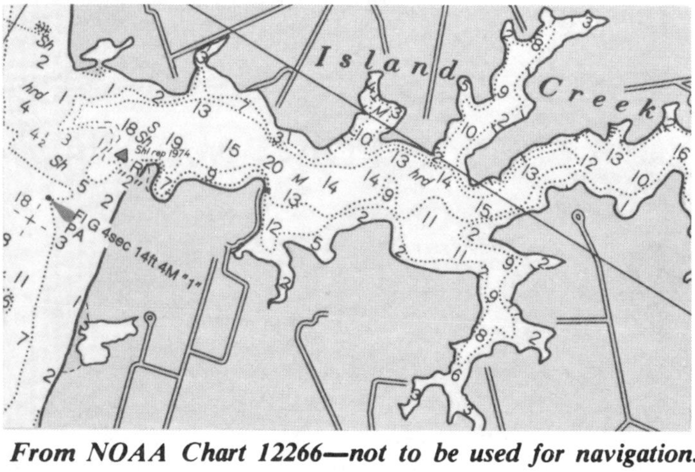

From NOAA Chart 12266—not to be used for navigation.

The entrance channel runs somewhat diagonally across the mouth of the creek with the first mark at the south or starboard bank. From there you take a course of about 035°. There's a short stretch where the water may be a little thin, but we've never had any trouble. As you enter, keep FL G "1" close aboard to port, because there's shoal water close to it to starboard. If you are a very confident navigator, you can leave this mark very close to starboard, and lay a course absolutely straight to "2" with less risk of grounding than if you follow the navigational rule implicitly. This is one of the very rare instances in which not honoring the mark could be the best policy.

The south bank at the entrance has a modern, well-worked bulkhead guarding a fairly new home. Your course takes you slightly upstream on the north bank. Shortly after leaving the red #2 mark you can turn and proceed upstream.

About a half-mile ahead on the point to starboard you can see what appears to be a crow's nest on a mast. There seem to be ratlines and flag as if just plucked from the foredeck of a pirate ship. It's tucked away in the trees, but you can't miss it.

Island Creek is fairly broad and, typical of most well settled areas on the Eastern Shore, has many large, attractive homes with well kept grounds. There's an air of contentment and charm here. About a half-mile upstream on the starboard side (just around the point from the crow's nest) is the first of two good-sized coves. This is a favorite anchorage and was already occupied by a raft of five elderly but elegant boats. It was late afternoon; grills were heating, and we could hear warm laughter and conversation. The social hour is one of the best parts about cruising.

Around the next point on the starboard shore is the second cove. We glided around the point and drifted up rather close to the south shore where we let out the anchor. The air was warm and overhead the clouds had broken up, leaving a bright blue canopy. We enjoyed a half hour or so of relaxation and then a good meal out in the cockpit where we could see our surroundings. To the west the setting sun turned orange-red on the horizon and sent a brilliant fiery wash over the few remaining clouds.

But, since the weather had been so changeable all day, we upped anchor and headed north across Island Creek to a small branch which offered more protection. We didn't go very far upstream, made a turn into the breeze, and put our anchor down for the night.

This unnamed (on the chart) branch of the creek has many homes, boathouses, and docks. Darkness was closing in as we flicked on our anchor light and sat back to enjoy the last brilliant blush of sunset. The shoreline blurred into black and purple shadows pierced here and there by an occasional light. A cricket chorus and the cry of a lone heron wove such a blanket of contentment that we were soon nodding off. We stumbled below to our bunks, secure in the knowledge of having a snug anchorage no matter how the weather changed. □

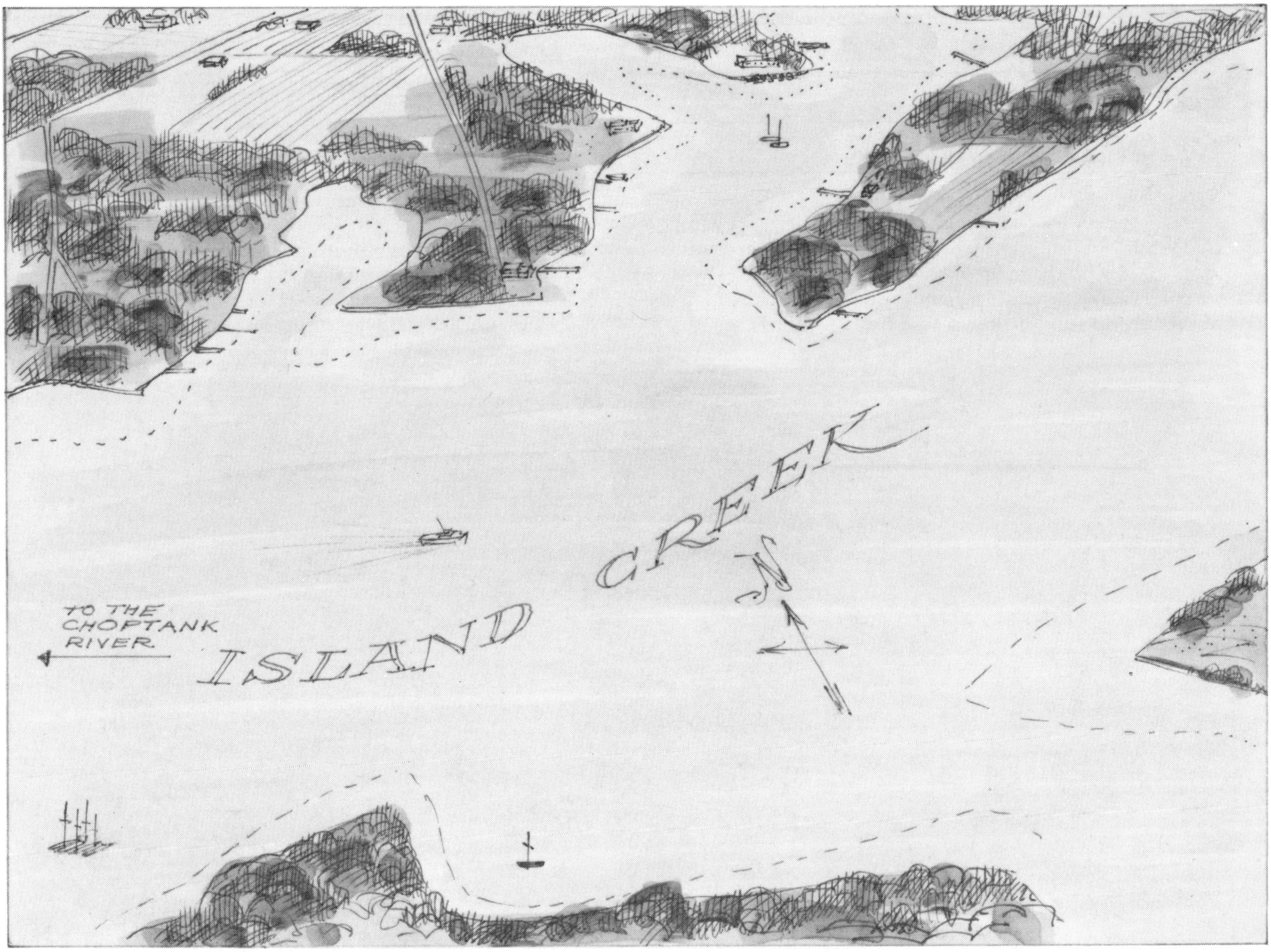

GALLEY TIPS

"Don't take the red mug, it's mine!" Ask anyone on our crew and they'll be able to tell you their "color of the day." Our boat mugs are all different colors. Remember which is yours the first time around and reuse it the rest of the day. Who wants to wash dishes more often than necessary?

Spices can put life in even the most ordinary canned or packaged foods that are so convenient to use on a boat, but so uninteresting to eat. And bless them, they are so small and easy to take along. Make a kit of a few you especially like, and vary them often. I recommend starting with some basics like cinnamon, basil and thyme and don't hesitate to experiment with them.

Make a firm base for dishes on table by using airline non-skid mats (thin, papery looking) placed under plates or placemats.

Keep pans or dishes from sliding around on the counter: lay a well-wrung-out wet towel on table or counter and place objects on it.

Make your own block ice. Search the plastic departments of your local stores till you find a heavy-duty container with a lid in the biggest size that will fit in both your home freezer and the boat's ice box. Your container must have a lid to support the sides of the container and keep it from distorting or cracking during the freezing process.

Utilize an inexpensive styrofoam ice box or large jug to transport foods from home to boat. Their cold-holding power is astonishing.

Utilize ice box space by putting foods in an assortment of plastic containers (labeled as to contents) that fit together in the ice box like a jigsaw puzzle. You'll get more food in and won't have leaky milk cartons or smashed eggs to pollute the bilges.

Fill a *good* vacuum bottle with boiling water the last thing at night, or after breakfast, to have a ready supply of hot water for soups or other hot pick-ups while under way. Mighty handy for early or late season cruising.

CAMBRIDGE AREA OF THE CHOPTANK RIVER

Lecompte Creek
La Trappe Creek
Sawmill Cove
Cambridge

While continuing to cruise the Choptank, one has to be impressed with the many natural harbors and coves available to the visiting yachting family. Indeed, there is hardly a direction one could take where there would be no creek to greet you nor cove waiting to welcome your anchor.

If you poke around and explore, you will experience sense of discovery and surprise waiting around every be between Castle Haven Point and Cambridge.

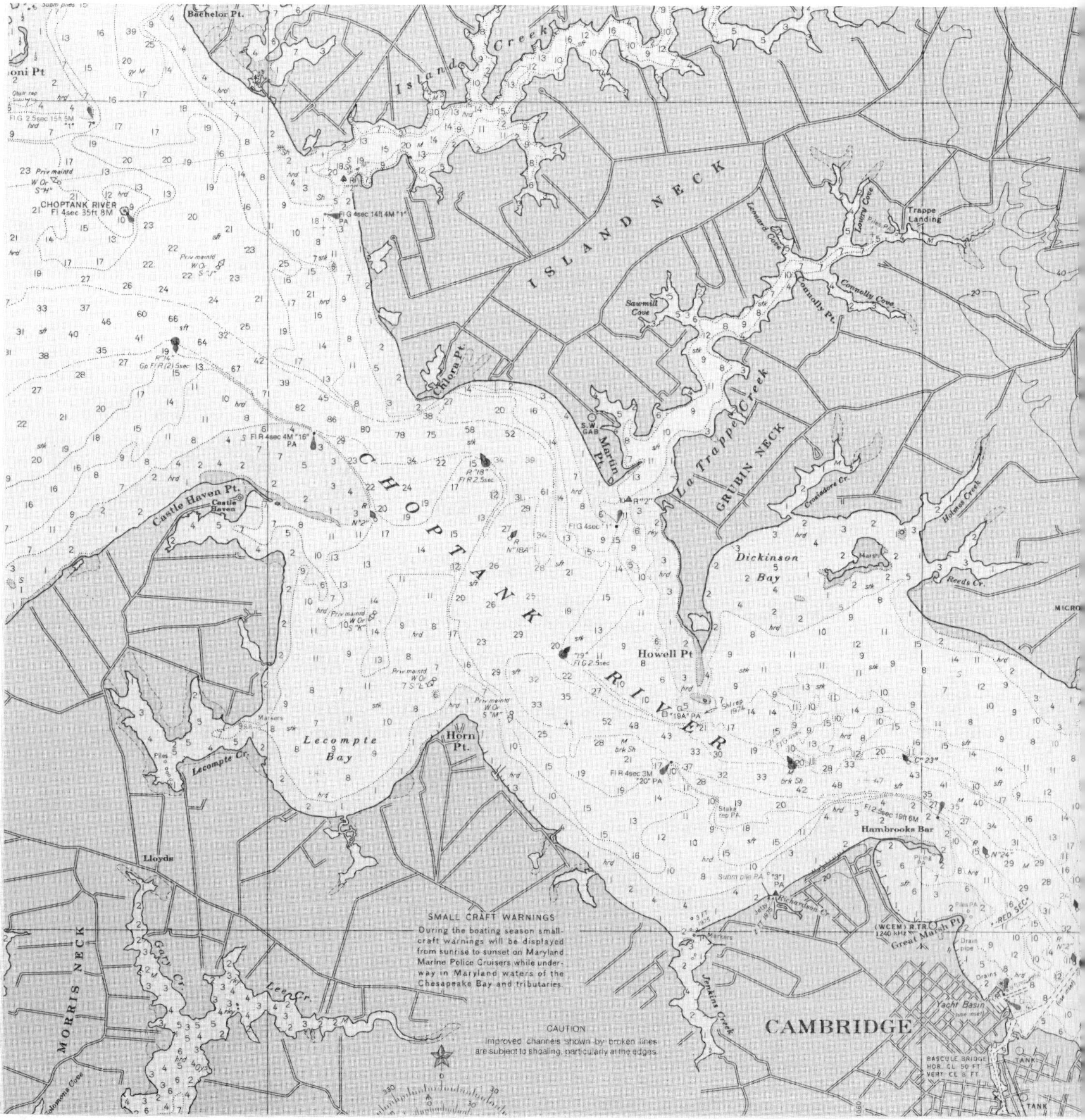

From NOAA Chart 12266—not to be used for navigation.

LECOMPTE CREEK

on the Choptank River

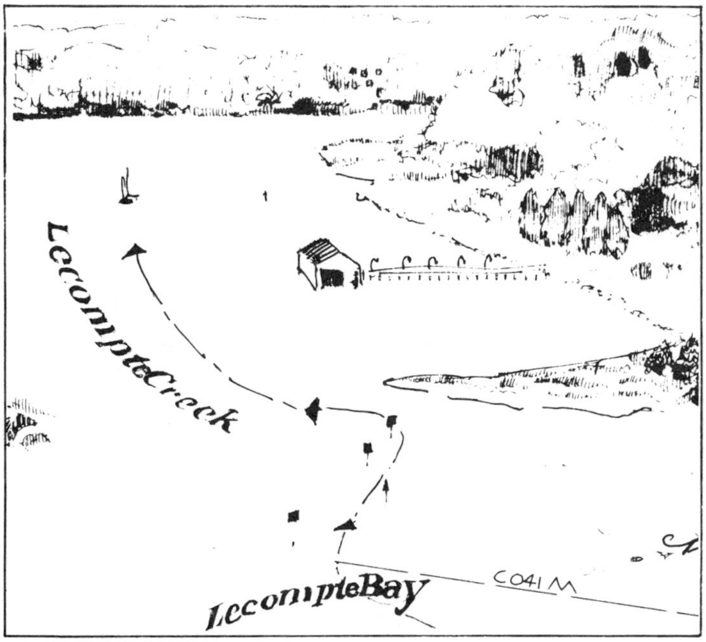

Although there are several fine spots to anchor in for the night within easy reach of Cambridge, we decided to venture into Lecompte Bay, which is on the south side of the Choptank just upstream of Castle Haven.

You will see by the chart there are two possible anchorages in the area—one at Castle Haven and another farther south in Lecompte Creek. Anchoring directly in Lecompte Bay, although it has plenty of water, is not advisable because you will have little or no protection from strong northerly or easterly winds.

Getting into Lecompte Creek is no problem since it is well marked by day beacons. The entrance is reminiscent of Fairlee Creek in that a series of marks guide you toward the beach on the north side of the entrance, then just as you feel that surely you are about to run aground, the final mark leads you parallel to the beach and into the Creek.

Lecompte Creek is snug and intimate and would provide a good anchorage in rough weather. The only major building there is at the entrance in the form of a handsome manor house with a boathouse and dock on the water. The semi-wilderness setting is very attractive.

If you are leaving Lecompte Creek and going toward Chlora Point, the *safe* course is 041° M, nothing less! This course leads toward Buoy "18" (Fl R 2.5 sec); this buoy will then lie just off to starboard. At the same time you will clear both the shoal of Castle Haven Point and N "2" that marks it. A long, shallow sandspit stretches out eastward and is marked by this nun at its tip. Across the middle of the sandspit you can see R "16" (Fl R 4 sec) which marks the starboard side of the Choptank River channel. But don't let a sight of "16" across the spit, bearing about 019° M from your spot in the creek, lure you into sailing right for it over the spit or hard aground you will be!

You might note, too, that there is a private white-and-orange spar "K" that you will pass on your starboard on the way out, some 1.5 miles from the mouth of the creek. □

LA TRAPPE CREEK

on the Choptank River

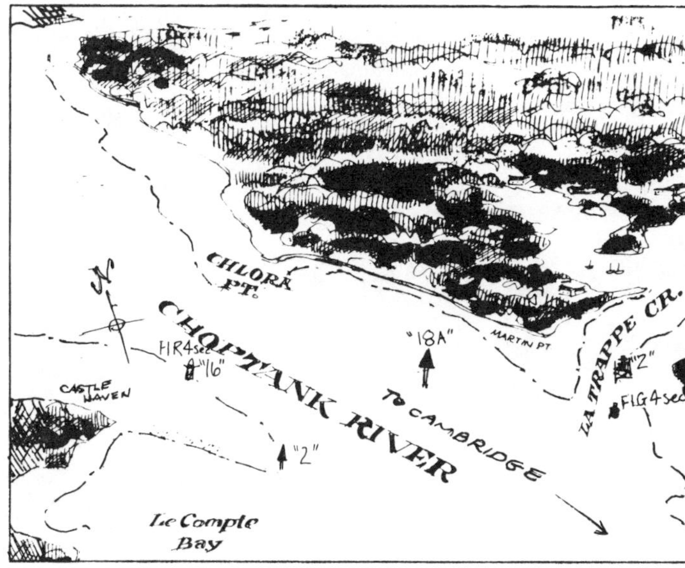

So, here we were approaching Howell Point as the evening turned indigo black. Buoy #21 passed and our red-lit compass pointed us to the lighted #20, and from there to the green flashing buoy#19. I scanned the La Trappe shoreline for our entrance flasher. Then I went below for a look at the chart.

Our course was 030°; as we swung a little to starboard, we brought the entrance four-second flasher on our bow. Although it was only a mile away, it looked extremely dim and weak. We motored on in the blackness, hoping we would find the second mark—a red #2—before we ran aground.

Then, at last, the first marker appeared out of the darkness. As we skirted this large concrete structure (looks sort of like a miniature lighthouse), we flashed our lights in front of us, searching for the red mark. Sure enough, the reflective red triangle lit up like a neon sign. From there on in it was a piece of cake.

To port was the cove we were looking for. A long sandbar extends northeast to give protection from southerlies. However, without a bright moon to light up the creek, it was impossible to spot the bar. We had come in on a high tide, and the bar was mostly awash. So we dropped anchor in midstream in ten feet of water just off the mouth of the cove.

If approaching from above Howell Point, after you clear "18A" carrying FL G 4 sec. "1" to port, immediately thereafter pass R "2" to starboard to enter the creek. Don't do it any other way in a sailboat. You will see a sort of little sandy hook to port, and an entrance channel beyond.

The next day, in bright sunshine, we explored the creek as it wound its way past a dozen or more of the most beautiful homes I've seen along a riverside. On our way back we motored into the cove which had hidden in darkness the evening before—and discovered a delightful anchorage I hadn't known existed.

The cove itself takes a northward turn, carrying eight feet of water into a second branch. This end is, perhaps, more beautiful than the other since there are no homes—other than the one to port—and the surrounding shoreline is covered by dense woods. It gives you the feeling of a secluded lake in a forest. There is also excellent protection from those frequent summer storms.□

SAWMILL COVE

off La Trappe Creek

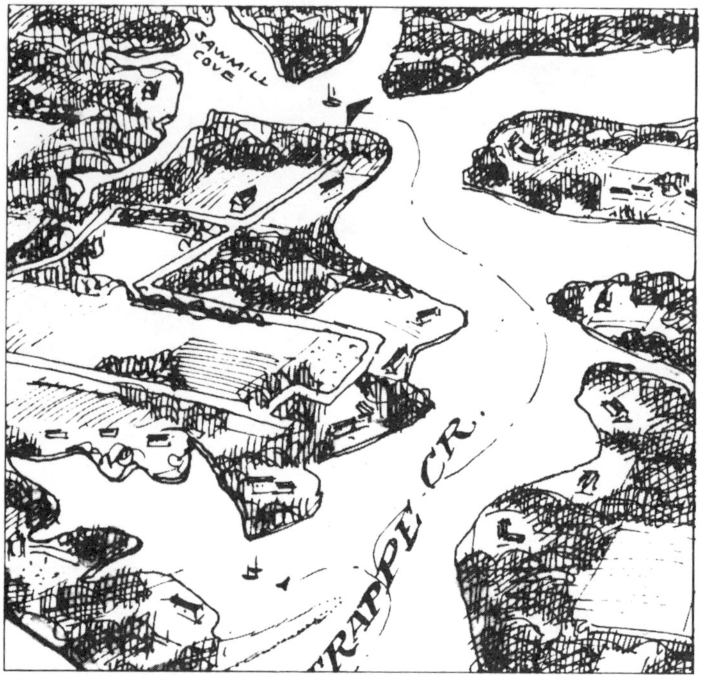

One thing that struck us as we left Cambridge was the water of the Choptank River. We hadn't noticed it on our way in, but as we rounded Howell Point and headed for our night's anchorage on La Trappe Creek, the water was crystal clear. We were astonished! Bay waters are usually murky, so clear water is always a great surprise anywhere on the Chesapeake. I guess we were on the 13-15 ft. shoal between green buoy #19 and the mouth of La Trappe Creek, because as we leaned overboard, we could see the bottom quite clearly.

At the entrance of La Trappe Creek the water became murky again about the time we got to the two outside markers. These markers are unusual because they both are concrete caisson structures — #1 with a green 4-second flasher, and about 350 yards further inshore, a red with no light. From green #19 the course into the creek is 030°. This should carry you right past the sand spit that projects northeast from Martin Point.

Many cruising families like to turn west around this sandy beach and into the cove to spend the night. This was our destination; but over the top of the sand spit, we could see this anchorage was already crowded. So we headed further upstream to see what we could find.

We found Sawmill Cove, but along the way the beauty of La Trappe Creek unfolded before us. Here and there, at well-spaced intervals, are large, private homes surrounded by well-manicured grounds. Behind them rises a dark forest of trees that gives an air of solemn Old-English countryside beauty. Total contentment and charm surrounded us.

The only shoal to beware of is the one to port about three-fourths of a mile upstream. Just around the next bend on the port side is Sawmill Cove. There are no obstructions at the cove's entrance — just keep to the middle. The trees crowd together at the water's edge, giving the cove a feeling of privacy and protection.

La Trappe is one of the most beautiful little creeks on the Chesapeake Bay. □

CAMBRIDGE

on the Choptank River

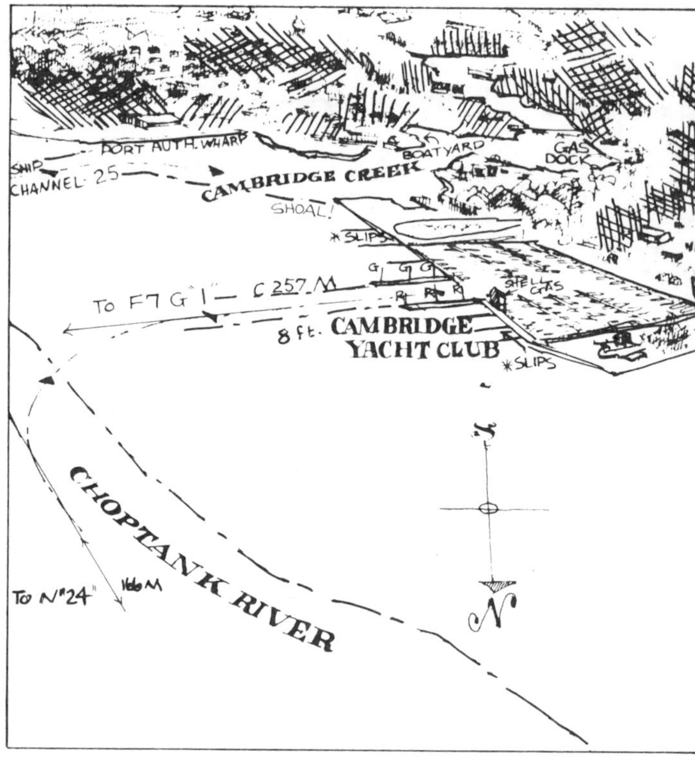

Cambridge, established in 1684, is one of three ports in Maryland that handle sea-going vessels. In fact, it is the second after Baltimore in size. While the volume of this traffic is insignificant from the yachtsman's standpoint, if you follow the buoyed channel shown on Charts 12266 and 12267, via Fl G "1," N "2," C "3," and N "4," all the way in, you will end up at the ships' wharf, where you won't want to be, and where the Port Authority won't want you to be, either.

Instead, when you arrive at N "24," come to Course 166 magnetic (towards N "4"); then, when Fl G "1" is abeam to port, take 257 magnetic to enter the yacht basin. The entrance has wooden jetties on both sides, marked with a F R light to starboard and a F G light to port. In this way you avoid shoal water around the entrance, yet don't go all around Robin Hood's barn to get in. Although the charts don't indicate so, our sources report the tank at Cambridge has been demolished.

The entrance (currently limited to about 7+ feet draft) serves both the Cambridge Yacht Club (to starboard) and the Municipal Yacht Basin (to port). The Yacht Club, well known for its hospitality, welcomes visitors from other clubs, serves excellent meals, has fine showers, electricity, water and fuel dockside, and has a dockmaster during the summer months.

The Club has a few slips available from time to time, which are fine for powerboats — especially twin screw vessels — but a little awkward for sailboats over 35 feet in length and drawing more than five feet.

The Municipal Basin also has a few slips ranging to 60′, and the facilities include a modern rest-room-shower-laundry building (which also houses the Dockmaster's office) and water and electricity. The Dockmaster is on duty most of the year, with extended hours during summer [(301) 228-4031.] Both dockmasters monitor Channel 16 during the summer months.

Vessels drawing over five feet may freely enter Cambridge

Creek. Depths run upwards of 10 feet, and anchoring is permitted. Avoid the very middle of the area, however, because there is boat traffic up and down the creek, and an occasional larger craft entering or leaving the Cambridge Shipyard (same premises as Yacht Maintenance, Inc.). Also, you'll see some slips just below the bridge to port. These are associated with the townhouses, and are private. Boats sometimes pass through the drawbridge to anchor in the upper creek for a perfect shelter from almost any wind that blows. On entering Cambridge Creek, to starboard there is a seafood packing house. You may see skipjacks tied up at the docks. You can buy fresh crabmeat here.

High Street serves the Basin, the small oyster boat wharf (Long Wharf, long the center of waterfront activity). Stroll along it and see 18th- and 19th-century homes, most of them in continuous use since they were built. The post office and a restaurant are on High Street. There is another rather elegant restaurant nearby. Both restaurants are an easy walk from either the basin or the creek. □

See A Walking Tour of Cambridge for more information.

PHOTO BY HYMAN RUDOFF

The Cambridge Municipal Yacht Basin

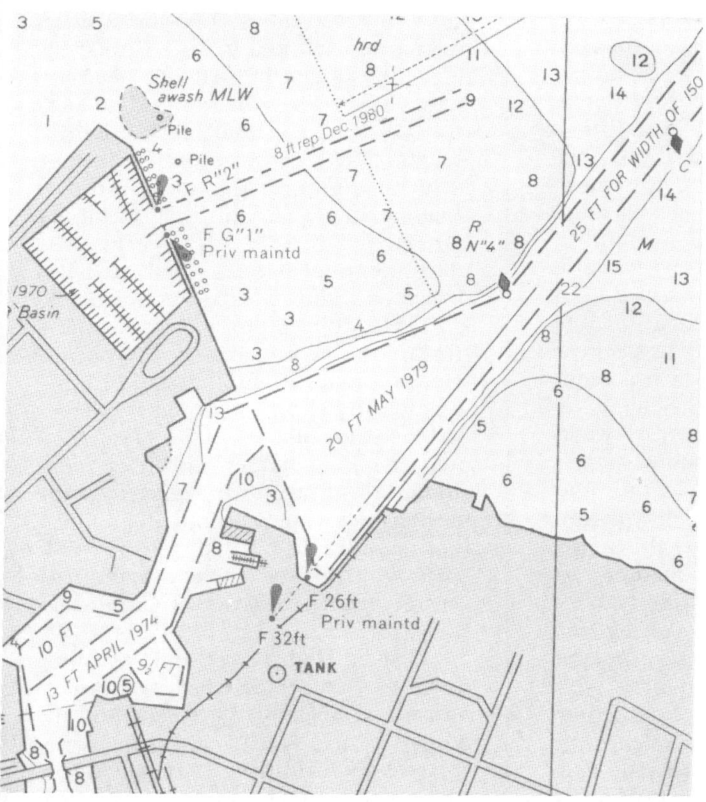

From NOAA Chart 12266—not to be used for navigation.

A Walking Tour of:
CAMBRIDGE

by Andi Manchester

The Dorchester County court house sits in its own little park. Photo by Hyman Rudoff.

Rendering of author's map of Cambridge by Joan Machinchick.

Looking for night life? quaint boutiques? epicurean fantasies? I can suggest a number of ideal places to cruise to but Cambridge is not one of them. Cambridge is more like a favorite easy chair: unpretentious, welcoming, relaxed. In a word—comfortable.

A pleasant cruise, about 16 miles up the Choptank River from the Bay, puts you at this quiet town's popular boat basin, a boxy harbor entered through a well-marked channel. Once inside you are surrounded by docks. Those on the right belong to the Cambridge Yacht Club while the rest comprise the Cambridge Municipal Boat Basin. A little to the right of straight ahead, at the far end of the basin, is a red brick building which houses the dockmaster's office, laundry equipment, a paperback book library (including a small selection of children's reading) and bright, clean, large rest rooms with showers. If you dock at the bulkhead, a well-manicured municipal park complete with tall shade trees, benches, and picnic tables lies a few yards from your slip.

To the left of the marinas is an area known as Long Wharf (aptly named because of a long wharf that used to stretch far into the Choptank River). A concrete walkway borders the river with benches that beckon the passerby to enjoy the view, and the fisherman or crabber to drop his line. Judging from the activity we saw this is a favorite spot for both. There is a fair amount of traffic here partly due to a circle where High Street (a main thoroughfare) doubles back on itself. In the middle of the circle is the Veterans' Memorial Fountain (seasonally lit at night). Behind the fountain, close to the water, is a monument to F.D.R. A plaque explains that after the late-president dedicated the Emerson Harrington Bridge here, the town had the elevator stack from the *U.S.S. Potomac* (a ship F.D.R. often traveled on) removed and mounted on this spot. Strolling up High Street, a wide brick thoroughfare, is like eavesdropping on another century; grand three-story houses built mainly in the 1700's and 1800's line its ample sidewalks. In one of them is the Dorchester Art Center. Volunteers hold it open so the public can visit rotating exhibits of the varied works of its members (open 10-5, M.-F.). Two blocks from the water, at High and Court Streets, the fine old homes give way to newer structures. On the left, set back from the street with a small picturesque park on its left, is the elegant Dorchester County Court House, built in 1852. The previous court house was destroyed by an arsonist's fire set in the office of the Register of Wills (sounds like a Perry Mason plot). Across the street, facing the court house, is another city landmark, Christ Episcopal Church, established in 1692. An inscription chiseled in its cornerstone indicates that this congregation has had less-than-excellent luck in buildings. The inscription reads: "Built in 1693, Rebuilt in 1794, and 1883." (A brochure chronicling the church's history, stained glass and courtyard is available.) Adjacent to the church is a cemetery that has been in use for over 300 years. The headstone of its oldest marked grave is dated November 24, 1678. People from all walks of life are buried here including five past Maryland governors and Civil War soldiers whose epitaphs proudly declare their political affiliations. If you are interested in the history of these homes (one was built in Annapolis and moved to Cambridge in 1750!) a walking tour of the entire historic district is available from the Chamber of Commerce.

An old, vacant, mostly boarded up hotel on the next corner launches the business district. It shares the real estate on this block with the post office and a variety of small enterprizes including the High Spot restaurant. The High Spot (open for lunch and dinner) isn't fancy nor do their hours accommodate late evening diners, but it is a local favorite. We sampled one of its claims to fame: home-made ice cream (available in both sit-down and carry out service). With only three flavors and five of us we could sample them all, and we enjoyed every lick and drip of them!

At the next intersection the business district jogs left and follows Poplar St. as it takes a gentle turn and becomes Race Street. These buildings date back only to the early 1900's (the previous structures fell victim to fire) and house an array of stores including a movie theater (first run) and several luncheonettes (Doris Mae's was the only place mentioned to us when we asked if there was somewhere to go for breakfast). We stopped at a pharmacy and a luncheonette and found the people friendly, helpful, and caring. Missing were trendy shops, national franchises and fast-foot eateries. (If you long for a quarter-pound burger with fries and a shake, about a 2-mile walk from the marina puts you at Route 50 and fast-food paradise.) Less than one-half mile from where Race Street started, the central business district of Cambridge ends.

East of High Street and extending down to Cambridge Creek is an interesting and diversified area. Behind the Court House is a forbidding stone, fortress-like building that had to be, and was, a jail. Despite its medieval appearance it was built in 1882. Not far away is another stone building that looks like it came from the same era of dragons and damsels. It is appropriately named "The Castle." But inside it is pure '80's fun; it's a roller-skating rink. (Open 7 P.M. - 12 P.M. Fri. and Sat. evenings.)

When your body clock strikes "Food," you'll find several dining-out options in this neighborhood. If you are in the mood for a meal served in an elegant atmosphere, where tables have tablecloths and the menu is not written entirely in English, try the Cator House. It is a tastefully remodeled turn-of-the-century home open daily for lunch and dinner. If you prefer a pizza parlor, you can find one across the street from Market Square, a new mini-mall. Or, if a snack is all you are after, try the mall where you can find a selection of hunger chasers from hot dogs to ice cream.

This section of Cambridge is changing very quickly. Several years ago the Rouse Company (whose creative genius brought us riverside centers like Harbor Place in Baltimore and Waterside in Norfolk) put together a re-development plan for Cambridge Creek. That plan is becoming a reality through the ambitious effort of independent developers. Already two townhouse complexes and the mini-mall have opened. A model layout of the proposed plan is housed in the Dorchester Public Library on Gay St., only two blocks from the mini-mall. (During July and August the library shows films for children on Wednesdays. Schedule available.) Beyond the creek, across the Market Street Bridge, is a predominantly residential area and the Dorchester General Hospital, a large red brick building which dominates the waterside skyline.

To the right of the boat basin is another residential area with churches, luncheonettes, and assorted other small businesses (including a small convenience market and a laundromat at Travers and Choptank Streets). Many homes here have interesting Victorian details and one even has a diamond pattern etched in its concrete walkway.

Paralleling the Choptank River is Water Street. If you set out in a northwesterly direction (heading out of town) you pass by some lovely and interesting waterfront properties. A big grassy field lies an inviting 0.3 of a mile away (approx.) at Oakley Street (named for THE Annie Oakley who lived in the Cambridge area for four years). However, this in *not* a public field. If you continue another 0.2 mile (approx.) to Glenburn Avenue a bigger field awaits you. This one *is* public and stretches to the end of the point.

If you choose your ports-of-call by local happenings, Cambridge offers several. In July, there is a Fourth of July fireworks celebration and both sail and powerboat regattas, followed by the annual Seafood Feast-a-val (admission charged) in August. September holds both the Dorchester County Historical Society Harvest Festival and the Dorchester Showcase (both free).

Perhaps you include bicycles as part of your traveling gear (there are no bike rentals in Cambridge). If so, Cambridge offers three biking tours designed to show you the town and its environs. The tours vary in length (5, 17, and 65 miles) and are available through the Chamber of Commerce.

The friendly and helpful people at the Chamber of Commerce can give you any additional information you may need for your visit to Cambridge. You can call them at 301-228-3575. □

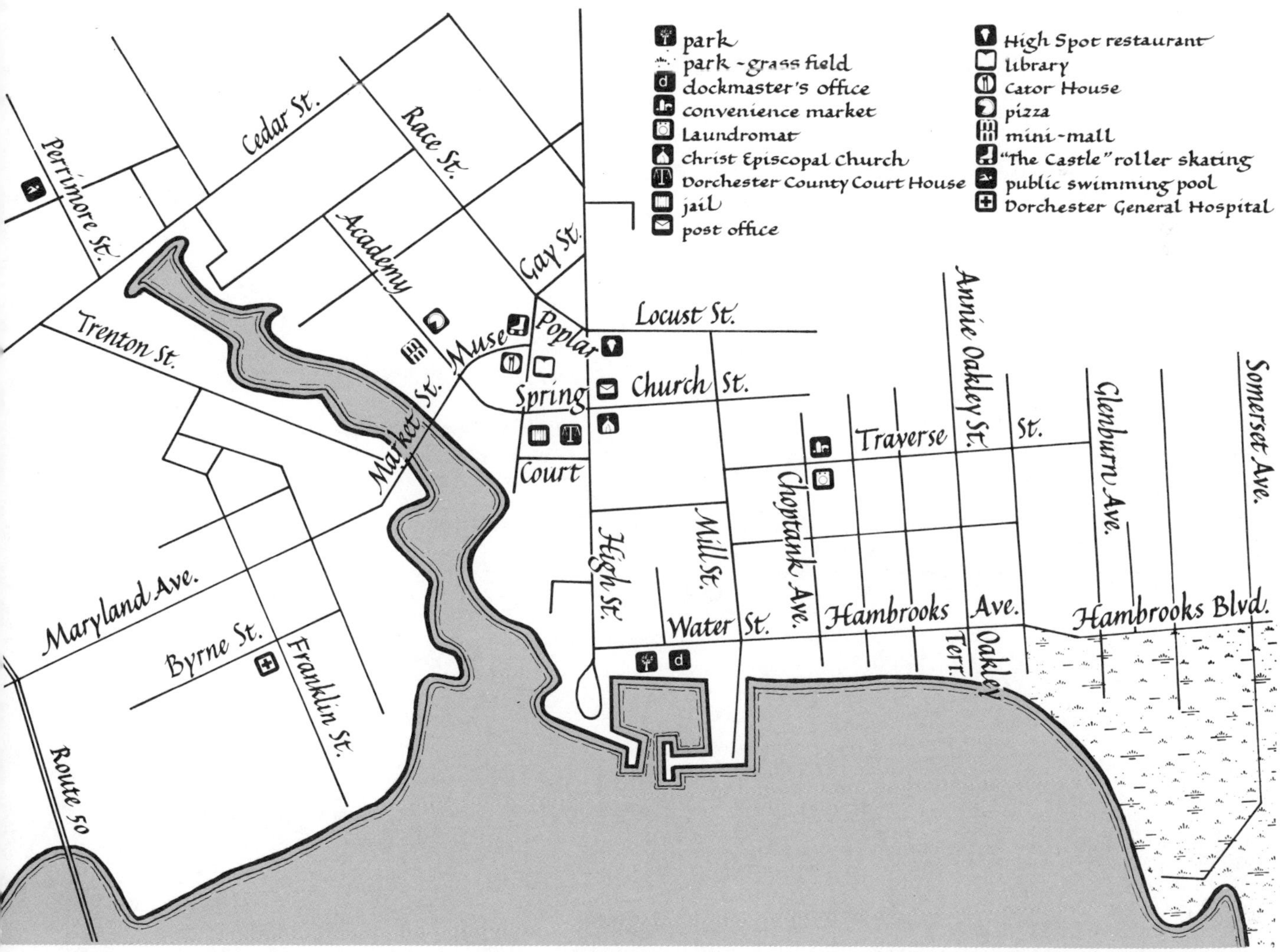

HUDSON CREEK

on the Little Choptank River

Not many boatmen are aware of the rich lore which surrounds the Little Choptank River. Settled in the 17th century, the river once boasted a thriving shipbuilding industry. The names of several mansions which dot the shores are those of families who settled in those early days.

The Little Choptank is thinly settled and has light boating traffic, and its many coves and creeks make it a pleasure to cruise. On the south shore as you enter is Taylor's Island, adjacent to Slaughter Creek. Also on the south shore of the Little Choptank is Fishing Creek, which holds many pleasant anchorages including Church Creek. Go all the way up in Church Creek, and you will be in the neighborhood of the old Trinity Episcopal Church. This tiny brick church, built in 1680, is a living reminder of its early heritage. The people here are said to be of pure English descent—even the folklore of Shakespeare crops up in the customs of the people.

On the upper reaches of the Little Choptank there runs through the forest a trail known as Tick's Path, named for a Dutchman, William Tick, who settled in this part of the Bay before 1670, and who, legend has it, hanged himself and whose headless ghost is often seen at night along the lonely path.

From BW "CR" (Mo A Bell) which is in the ship channel about west by north of Sharp's Island Light, a course of 138° M brings you to daymark "1" SW of Hill's Point, which is actually a low-lying island. Its distinguishing feature is a large colony of gulls.

Shoals around the island are extensive, and unless you want to anchor well off to the SE in 8-10 feet of water, and dinghy in to see the birds, avoid the place. Rather, take 150° M to "3" (Fl G 4 sec) and "5" (Fl G 2.5 sec) off the shoals at Ragged Point. Then follow the markers to "7", and turn northerly into Hudson Creek. The first mark in the creek proper is G "1", but don't go straight for it. Bear off slightly to starboard to avoid shallows that make out to the east of Casson Point. The place we chose to anchor was in the cove formed by Casson Point just west of red daymark "2".

Hudson Creek lies roughly 5½ miles from "1" (Fl G 2.5 sec) at Hill's Point and is a favorite of many cruising groups on the Chesapeake. The channel is well marked and shoals easy to avoid. The cove at Casson Point is larger than it appears on the charts with firm mud which will hold either a Danforth or plow very well. One hundred and fifty yards of the end of the point are grassy marsh which blend into the woods further up. □

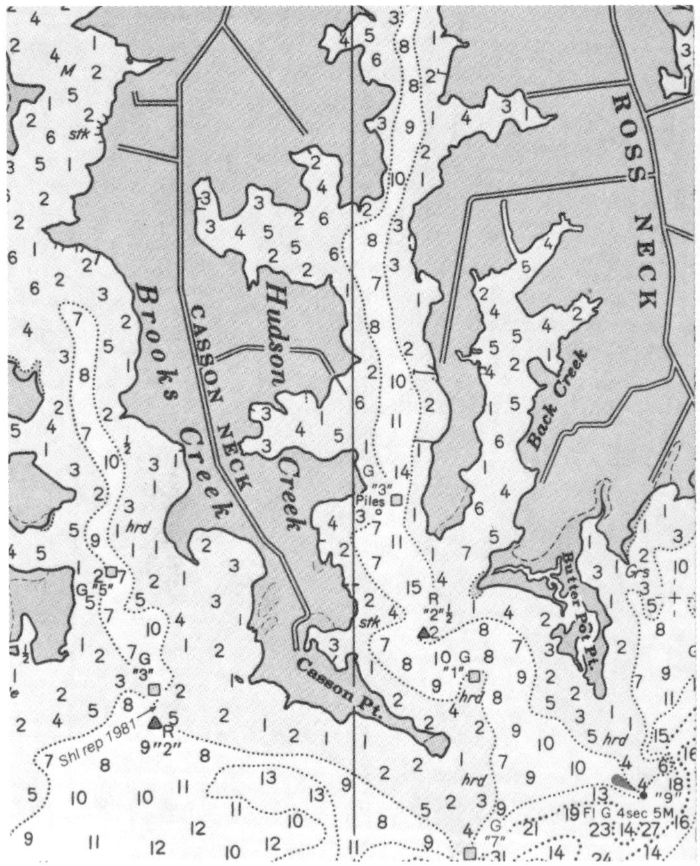

From NOAA Chart 12266—not to be used for navigation.

Notes

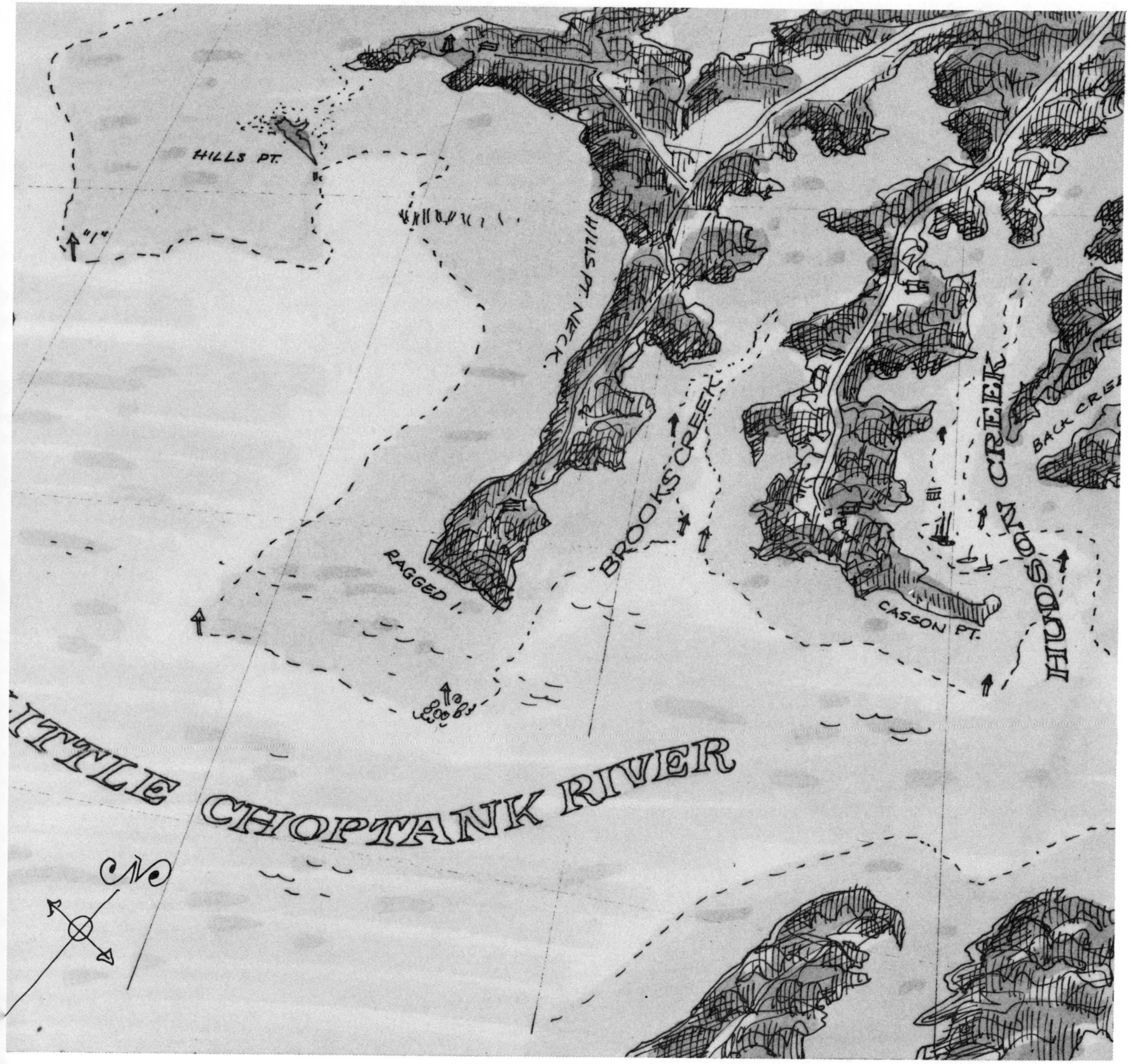

BOATKEEPING TIPS

Ask your handyman to install plastic kitchen sliding drawers in open locker (cupboard) space. They utilize those yawning depths, and create small areas for canned goods so storage in bilge can be minimized.

Secure laundry or towels for emergency drying while underway with old-fashioned spring snap clothespins.

Sweep deck or cabin sole with a child's play broom or whisk broom—often better than using a full-sized one. Use a small dustpan, too.

Stow favorite bric-a-brac objects while underway. Keep on board a collapsible cardboard box which may be opened when needed. Load it with knickknacks cushioned with towels and store where they are least likely to bounce around.

Use Lysol spray or liquid whenever you clean, or any product containing about 4.8 percent calcium hypochlorite (or mix your own, purchasing the ingredient at a lumber yard). It's the best way to guard against or remove mold or mildew.

PHILLIPS CREEK

on the Little Choptank River

The first time we visited the Little Choptank was in 1968, and the conditions were not at all ideal. We had been separated from our companion boat on the long leg up from Deal Island in weather that was dark and stormy with a strong northerly wind. Steep seas built up and broke over our bow as we motored into the teeth of the waves. Indeed, the next morning we found seaweed hanging from our boom! We rounded the northern tip of James Island (not to be confused with Janes Island at Crisfield) and literally flew down to round Ragged Point, where we turned north to motor up into Brooks Creek, our agreed destination.

As I recall, Brooks had only two marks in those days, making it easy to lose the channel and go aground, which we did — twice. I was forced to swim the anchor out into deep water (floating precariously on a life jacket) and then use our winch to pull ourselves off.

As darkness settled in, we were finally in deep water, putting out an anchor with plenty of scope. After hoisting a night light, we settled down, exhausted, for a troubled night's sleep. We were boating novices then, and groundings were quite traumatic.

Recently we have anchored in Hudson Creek, the next creek east of Brooks. The scenery here is charming. We usually spend the night in the cove formed by the curving arm of Casson Point with its sandy beach. Believe me, when the moon rises over the trees and illuminates the sandy beach and the waters all round your boat, there's nothing prettier on the Chesapeake.

There are times when both creeks are a little crowded with groups of visiting cruising clubs, and my advice is to go one step further east to Phillips Creek. Phillips Creek joins the Little Choptank at the latter's last lighted mark, a green 2½ second flasher #13 off Cedar Point. Our anchorage is in the broad cove north of Cedar Point and west of Cherry Island.

As you round Cedar Point you will find two homes here that have many martin nesting houses set on tall poles along the shoreline. From a distance, they look somewhat like the lights you see around a shopping center parking lot.

The only shoals to watch out for are the slight projection from Cedar Point to port and the long bar to the starboard side at the creek's entrance. The water is only two feet on this bar, and usually displays a crab float right where the water drops off. You will find that by lining up #13 on your stern and the tip of land to the north (where Phillips Creek swings away from Beckwith Creek) on your bow, you will usually be clear of this long shoal.

Once inside, there is ample water with depth of seven and eight feet. There is one house on the northwest bank of this harbor and relative privacy that makes this one of the better anchoring spots in the area.

On the east side of this little bay where Beckwith Creek branches off to the northwest stands Cherry Island, conspicuous by its square tower, reportedly built and later essentially abandoned by a branch of the DuPont family. It is visible for some distance. You can anchor to the south of the island in eight feet of water, but give the shoal on the island's western tip (near the tower) a wide berth. □

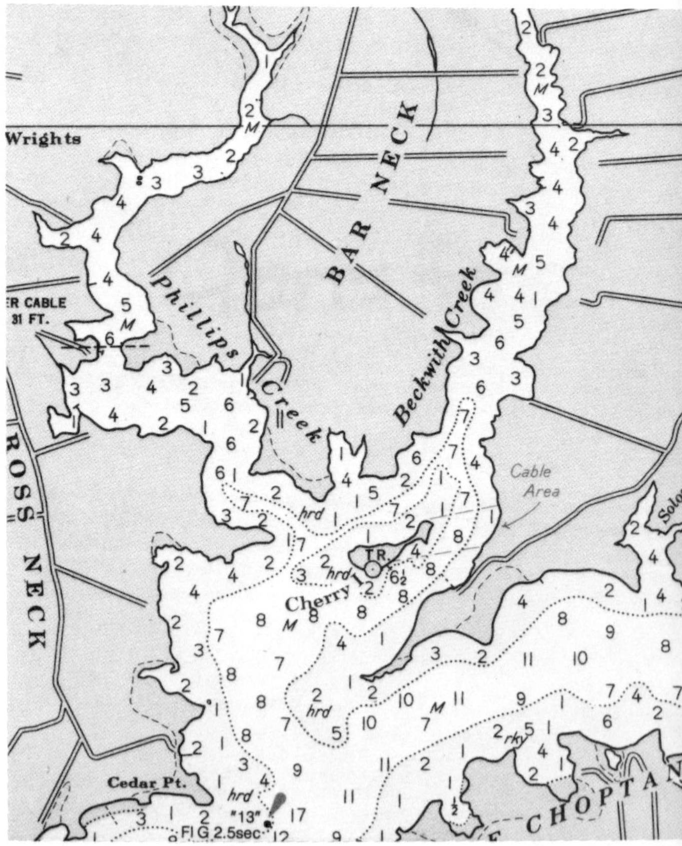

From NOAA Chart 12266—not to be used for navigation

BOATKEEPING TIPS

Make your boat a present of its own set of tools. If you try to share a set with car or house, the right screwdriver is always in the wrong place.

Restitch sail seams yourself—using the existing holes in the material. "Rip-Stop," a sticky-back fabric, is good for emergency patches.

Remove gas smell from your hands quickly by rubbing them with moistened kitcken salt.

Stick-on hooks are convenient in the head and galley areas. Ignore anyone who says they won't stick. Be sure to get the kind that points up and not out, to avoid injury.

Use empty cardboard egg cartons to make bumpers to keep refrigerator or shelf contents from shifting excessively in a seaway. A carton placed in front of shelf contents will absorb shock of jars and containers hitting door.

FISHING CREEK

on the Little Choptank River

Our cruise to Fishing Creek on the Little Choptank was "unplanned" because we had no idea of venturing into that river on this trip. We had pretty much already explored the Little Choptank, and thought we'd just about seen it all. But the threat of an afternoon thunder boomer brought us once again seeking shelter in the Little Choptank.

By the time we rounded Ragged Point, however, the darkened skies were brightening and a few puffy white clouds appeared to the southwest. The urgency to get an anchor down was lessened, so we pulled out our charts to see if there was some corner of the Little Choptank which we hadn't explored yet. Our eyes settled on Fishing Creek, and the choice was made.

Fishing Creek is farther upstream than Hudson Creek, on the south shore just beyond Madison Bay. There is a shoal north of McKeil Point which is marked by daymark "2," and a little farther upstream—about a half-mile—there is a green daymark, "3". We searched the chart for a protected anchorage and decided on Cherry Point. If the bad weather came out of the north, we would skirt around the point, putting it between ourselves and the weather. If the storm clouds appeared south or southwest, we would anchor north of Cherry Point. Although the threat of storm was abating, we still figured the direction would be from the southwest and anchored to the north of the curve of the point just west of the red daymark "4".

We dropped anchor at 5 P.M. and settled back to see what the weather would bring. We had 12 feet of water under us, and I had let out 150 feet of anchor rode. We should be safe in just about any blow.

By 6 P.M. the sky had brightened and there was no threat of storm at all, so we launched our rubber dinghy and took a ride along the shore. The scenery all around us was beautiful with a low shoreline covered by dense pine woods. Just opposite our anchorage was the wreckage of an old workboat, the sun-bleached ribs and keel sticking up like the bones of a stricken sea animal. In the water all around us were fallen branches blown from the surrounding trees. This is the only place where a rubber dinghy would have problems. We took our time rowing back to *Moon Song* and settled down for the night. Overhead a million stars shone brightly.

The next day we motored cautiously farther upstream. If you study chart 12266, you will see there's not much water just off the point, but there is plenty of depth just beyond. Indeed Fishing Creek has as much to offer as any other spot on the Little Choptank.

Just about the only place to pick up fuel and ice on the Little Choptank is Taylor's Island Marina on Slaughter Creek. The creek's entrance used to be tricky because of shoaling, but recent dredging to six feet and the addition of a green daymark between "2" (Gp Fl (2) 5 sec) and "4" (Fl R)

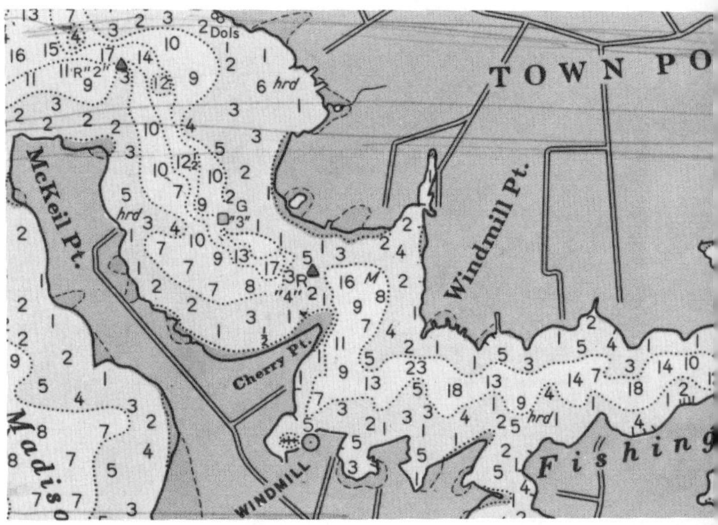

From NOAA Chart 12266—not to be used for navigation

make the channel easier to follow. The owners of the marina cautioned us that they have a very limited supply of groceries, but the fuel dock has five-to-six-foot depths and is accessible to most boats. We've found the folks there to be courteous and helpful to all—just another reason why you will find the Little Choptank a most pleasant area to include on your next cruise. □

Notes

CHERRY POINT
#4
FISHING CREEK
#3
#2
TOWN PT.
McKEIL POINT
MADISON BAY
LITTLE CHOPTANK RIVER
#11
SHOAL
N

SOLOMONS

on the Patuxent River

"Solomons has the potential to be one of the finest all around yachting centers on the Intracoastal Waterway," an experienced cruising man observed recently. More than a century ago its possibilities clearly influenced Isaac Solomon to locate his oyster processing plant on the Patuxent River after the Civil War when he chose Somervell Island for his business. Now as the pleasure boating era continues its momentum, new looks are appearing all around the harbor.

In pre-World War II days yacht building at the old M. M. Davis plant gave a special aura to the little fishing community at the mouth of the Patuxent River, but it took the war to catapult the area into the 20th century. Thousands of troops were trained for amphibious landings at the Naval Amphibious Training Base now known as Calvert Marina. The Davis boat builders turned to building utility craft as they built mine sweepers during World War I. When peace returned, the Solomons area took its first steps as a yachting center.

To reach Solomons you will need NOAA chart 12230, Smith Point to Cove Point, scaled 1:80,000. For more detail you may use chart 12264, Patuxent River and vicinity, scaled 1:40,000. If you're planning to do considerable cruising in the creeks close to Solomons, you may wish to indulge yourself by purchasing chart 12284, Solomons Island and vicinity, on a 1:10,000 scale. Only a half dozen harbors on Chesapeake Bay are accorded such detailed treatment and they're quite rewarding to chart buffs.

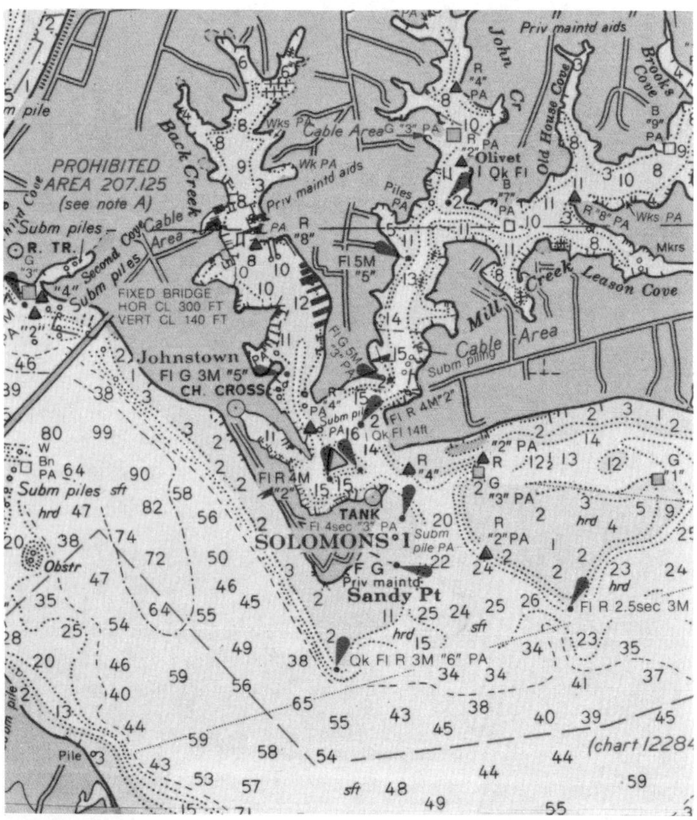

From NOAA Chart 12264—not to be used for navigation.

The navigation aids leading into Solomons harbor are easy to follow, but special study of the inner harbor configuration is strongly recommended. After you pass flashing "2" at Drum Point, there are two routes into the harbor; the mid-channel one is recommended. Leave flashing red "4" to starboard, turn north past red "2," but give the lighted pier and flashing green "3" in front of Chesapeake Biological Laboratory a good berth.

When you approach Solomons Island as marked on the chart, it's helpful to recognize that the island itself is a fish hook-shaped land mass connected to Johnstown on the mainland by a causeway. The inner harbor, entered between the island and Ship Point is divided into three main parts. The short northwest waterway called The Narrows leads to the causeway that brings the highway onto Solomons Island proper. Along The Narrows and the next segment, Back Creek, many marinas are located. You may leave the bulkhead island in mid-harbor to either starboard or port now that the latter channel has been deepened to over eight feet. The harbor's third part lies on Mill Creek, zoned residentially except for the El Paso terminal rebuilt on the site of the original M.M. Davis Boatyard mentioned earlier.

Although in the hot summer some boats will anchor in the Patuxent River between the flats and the shoreline, we don't advise it. The passing parade of fishing boats is not inclined to slow down for anchored boats and the evening and early morning hours will give you quite a jostling. The holding ground is good, but I would worry about a wind shift that might dislodge your anchor.

Most often anchorages are found on Mill Creek. About one-half mile up from the island, just past black lighted beacon #3, you will see boats snuggled up against the west shore, anchored in 10 to 15 feet of water. We've often spent the night here, and you can drop your hook fairly close to shore.

If this looks crowded, just go further upstream (noting that Mill Creek makes a sharp right turn at Olivet while St. John Creek continues straight ahead). We've spent some peaceful nights in the broad part of Mill Creek just past Old House Cove where the bottom is hard mud. And we couldn't keep our anchor from dragging in Leason Cove just opposite Old House Cove! Leason is a little tight for us; and if a sudden "duster" should spring up out of the west, as will often happen in midsummer, your anchor will have a tough time holding in the soft mud bottom.

In addition to marinas and boatyards, Solomons harbor is home to several restaurants, bars, charter fishing boats, gift and antique shops, lodgings and two grocery stores. One, Dockside Grocery and Marina, keeps a few slips for visitors. The other is Woodburns, located on the main drag in Solomons.

Allow time to visit the Calvert Marine Museum which has

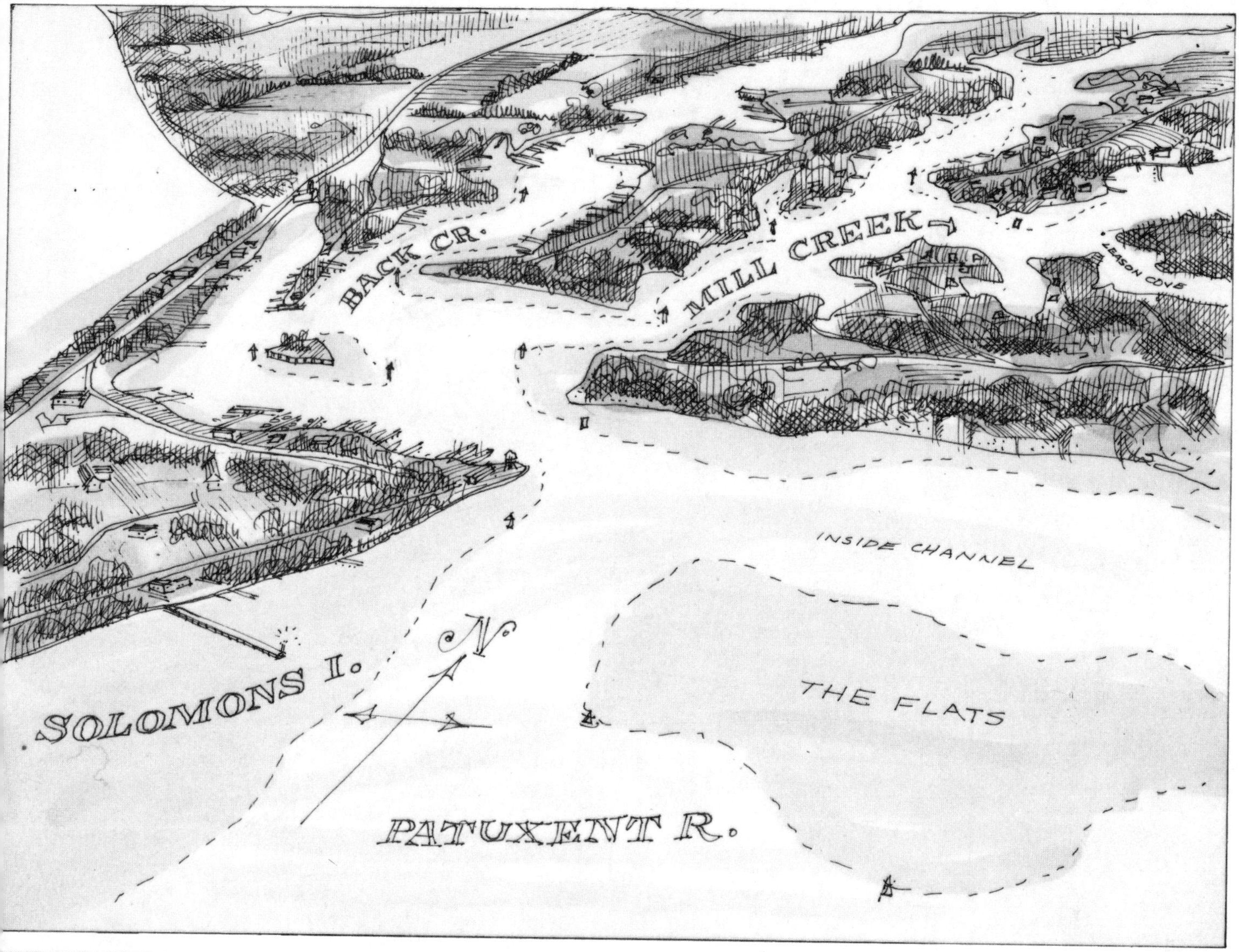

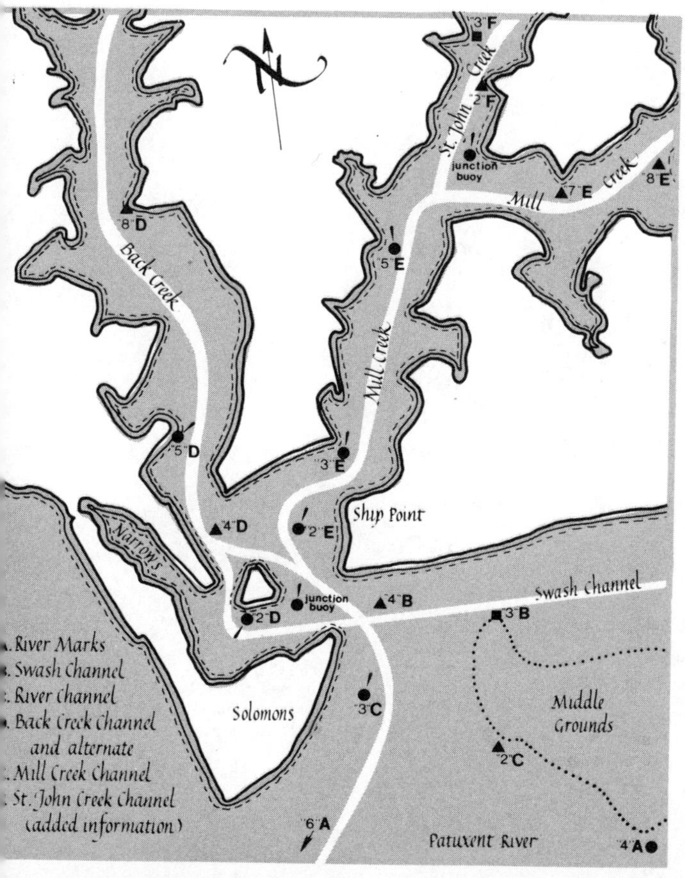

ANALYSIS OF HARBOR PATTERNS: LLOYD HAZLETON MAP BY JOAN MACHINCHICK

a courtesy pier near the transplanted Drum Point lighthouse on Back Creek. The lighthouse has been completely restored and furnished authentically. The remainder of the museum, housed in and around a brown building that was once the local school, has a surprising variety of engaging exhibits documenting the area's history. Fossils from world famous Calvert Cliffs date back to the Miocene Age. A new exhibit of underwater archaeological finds is also on display. Call the Museum [(301)326-3719] for hours. □

See A Walking Tour of Solomons for more information.

SWAN POINT

Where Luxury Comes to Life

Nestled in historic Charles County, Maryland, on the broad shores of the Potomac, Swan Point is being developed as one of America's premier recreational/residential communities.

Come build your dream home where there's incredible natural beauty and serenity as well as a host of luxurious amenities, including marina, tennis courts, swimming pool, and spectacular golf course.

Call now for choice lots. *Mon-Fri*: 202-543-0067. *Weekends*: from Wash. metro area, toll-free 870-2285; MD residents only, 301-259-4411; from outside MD, 1-800-242-SWAN. A U.S. Steel project. Sales by Weller-Davis, Inc., Box 15303, Wash., DC 20003. Shown by appt. only.

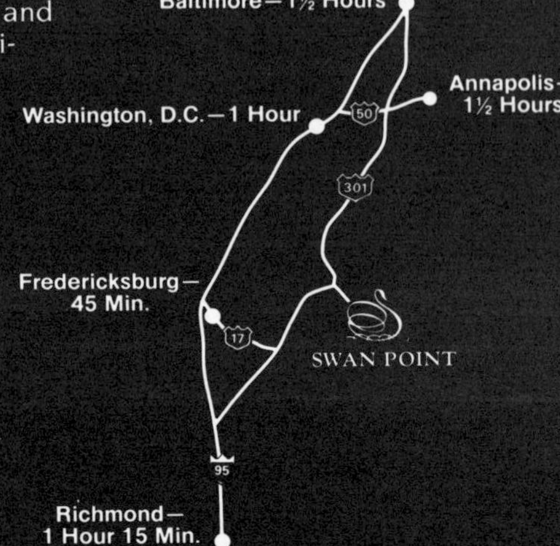

USS Realty Development
Division of United States Steel Corporation

EQUAL HOUSING OPPORTUNITY

WD

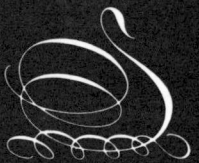

GALLEY TIPS

If it's hot, it's important for everyone onboard to drink lots of cool, refreshing liquids to avoid getting dehydrated. If it's cold, those hot drinks really warm a person up. For convenience and safety, try lashing a *pump* thermos, filled with the appropriate hot or cold drink, in a handy spot. You'll save spills and maybe even burns, and no one will go thirsty.

On a stormy day it's not a bad idea for the cook to wear some bib top pants from a suit of foul weather gear while at work. Keeps spills off skin.

We all seem to need a safe and dry spot to put valuables such as car keys, wallets and unexposed film when we are on a boat. They're in the way in the navigation table, and lockers sometimes develop leaks. If you have a swing stove, the empty pot that sits on it is a perfect place for these things—at least till it's time to cook dinner.

How many times have you needed a gimballed shelf? How many boats have one? When its rough and I'm pouring coffee, I put the coffee cups in the frying pan on the gimballed stove, instead of on the counter. They stay level while I pour. If a little spills, no harm is done.

A Walking Tour Of:
SOLOMONS

Solomons Island is for "Bay" people. It has always attracted those who stand on the shore and face the water rather than the land. In fact, because of the shape of this town, you are never very far from waters' view. The island takes its name from Isaac Solomon who established his successful oyster packing facilities here in the late 1860's. Because the surrounding waters remain ice-free year-round, fishing and oystering fleets were able to thrive and spawn a flourishing shipbuilding industry. Amidst such activity this modest fishing village evolved, its clapboard structures unpretentious and accommodating.

Today the shipyards are gone and watermen are no longer the town's main economic focus. The emphasis has shifted to pleasure boaters, the spare-time sailor who berths his boat here or makes Solomons an occasional port-of-call. Businesses geared to these visitors and temporary residents are creating a new industry, one which caters to boater's needs and interests.

One of those needs is a place to keep your boat. In Solomons, your choices abound. The marinas that dot the shoreline welcome transients and offer a variety of amenities including restaurants, pools, laundromats, groceries, bicycle rentals, ships stores, picnic areas and more. For visitors who prefer to anchor out, there is plenty of room in the snug harbor and creeks just beyond. Unfortunately, dinghy landings are not so plentiful, although you can use the Calvert Marine Museum's floating dinghy dock.

As we started to walk around, we soon discovered that you needn't be a long distance marathoner to explore Solomons, much to the joy and relief of our kids. Although once it was an island, a small bridge built on a bed of oyster shells in 1870 joined it to the mainland. Still, from stem to stern this narrow town is less than a mile-and-a-half long with only one two-lane road traveling the distance. The center, and mostly commercial area, is about one block wide while the more residential ends are a little wider. Level terrain made walking easy while the skimpy amount of paved sidewalk mixed with a generous amount of traffic occasionally made our leisurely stroll look more like a single-file hike (although when there are five of us we often look like a parade).

Another concern of boaters is where to dine if you are not eating on board. Should you decide to set your meal on a table that doesn't rock, there are a couple of picnic spots. The Calvert Marine Museum has a grassy area beside the main building where picnic tables await outdoor diners. Across the street, in a newly constructed park (summer '85) under the Thomas Johnson Bridge, is a boat ramp (Solomons' first public ramp on the river), parking lot, bathrooms, and picnic area.

Several marinas have restaurants on or adjacent to their property including Harbor Lights Restaurant (at Harbor Island Marina), The Dry Dock (at Zahniser's), and The Naughty Gull (at Spring Cove Marina). Two new and very appealing restaurants are the Solomon's Pier Restaurant (on a pier over the Patuxent River) and Lighthouse Inn (with abundant dockage if you come by boat). Pier 1 Restaurant and Tavern is a town veteran and one of the few places where you can order a simple "hamburger on a bun and French fries, please" or get breakfast (weekends only). The newly opened Fisherman's Inn is an informal addition to the eating scene. They serve breakfast (eat-in or packed to go) as well as sandwiches and ice cream. Not just hand-dipped cones, their menu includes sundaes, splits and other taste bud treats. If you want to eat your cone on the move, take advantage of their walk-up window. The only other place we could find to buy hand-dipped ice cream was at a High's convenience store located in a small shopping center at the northern edge of town. There is the Pizza Oven in the same plaza.

Since we constantly seem to run out of things (like milk and juice) we were glad to find a couple of places to buy groceries in addition to High's. Woodburn's Market, on the main street, sells fresh meats, produce and groceries. Dockside, at the Dockside Marina, is more like a well stocked convenience store that augments its foodstuffs with a variety of useful items.

Towns that cater to strolling visitors seem to specialize in shops that beckon browsers, like antique shops, ships stores, gift shops, craft shops, and sportswear boutiques. These small enterprises are not located in any one district in Solomons but are scattered throughout the town. A map of Solomons with a number of its shops and boutiques landmarked is available at many stores and marinas.

Walking and shopping are not the only activities Solomons offers. Children too long on a boat can stretch and move at a playground behind the Catholic church. Fishing is an obvious activity; there are several bait and tackle shops to get supplies. If you want to take a "busman's holiday" you can charter a boat for your fishing expedition. Biking enthusiasts can rent bicycles either at a stand in front of Dockside or from their marina (if available).

There are also festivals to enjoy. In spring is the annual Blessing of the Fleet complete with land festivities and a gala blessing of a decorated fleet with awards given to the fanciest boats. On the Fourth of July the Optimist Club sponsors a celebration which includes a carnival, sailboat and foot races, band concerts, and arts and crafts. An Arts and Crafts Festival is held in September with demonstrations, special exhibits, and a childrens' dog show. In October is the very special Patuxent River Appreciation Days (PRAD). Dedicated to celebrate and increase public awareness of the Patuxent's importance and heritage, PRAD features a parade, displays, arts and crafts exhibits, food, just a bit of everything. This festival is held on the grounds of the Calvert Marine Museum which also plays host to several outdoor concerts during the summer.

Perhaps what will be Solomons Island's greatest claim to fame is the contribution to knowledge and education being made by two of the town's distinguished residents, the Calvert Marine Museum and the Chesapeake Biological Laboratory.

The purpose of the Calvert Marine Museum is to explore this region through three themes: prehistory, estuary biology, and local maritime history. It does so by exhibit and example. Inside the main building (once a school) are many fascinating exhibits including one on fossils (incorporating findings from nearby Calvert Cliffs, whose exposed fossil deposits date back over 12 million years!), a working ship model and carving shop, a maritime history exhibit, and an exhibit on estuary biology including a hands-on, put-the-slide-under-the-microscope-and-take-a-look display. (This is not a large display but it was one of our favorites. Barnacles and jellyfish don't look very menacing at this stage.) Among other examples of the museum's three themes are Drum Point Lighthouse which can be toured, the *Wm. B. Tennison* (built in 1899, this bugeye is the oldest licensed passenger vessel on the Bay) which offers cruises May through October, and the J.C. Lore Oyster Processing House (a seafood packing plant from 1888-1978).

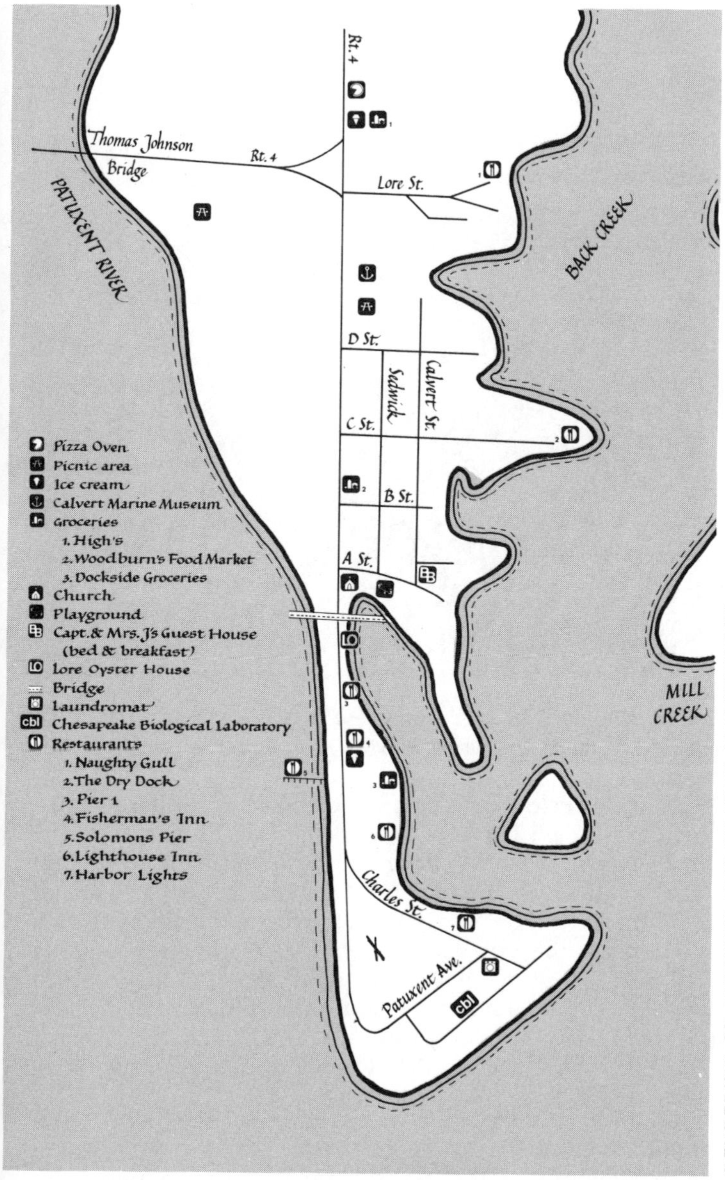

RENDERING OF AUTHOR'S MAP BY JOAN MACHINCHICK

At the other end of town, on the point, is the Chesapeake Biological Laboratory. From its humble beginnings as the one-man-show of Dr. R.V. Truitt, it has grown over the last 60 years in size, scope, staff and impact. Today it is part of the University of Maryland's Center for Environmental and Estuarine Studies and consists of five buildings, a staff of about 100 people, a research core of about 15 faculty members, about 38 graduate students, and offers both graduate level and undergraduate programs. Their scientific study revolves around three areas: ecosystem behavior, fisheries science and biology, and environmental chemistry, biochemistry and toxicology. Among other activities it has a speakers' bureau, consults with policy makers on environmental issues, and participates in PRAD.

With these two facilities in such close proximity to each other and sharing the mutual goal of public education and awareness of the Chesapeake environment, it is not surprising that they have recently joined forces. Together with The Maryland Historic Trust and The Philadelphia Academy of Natural Sciences' Division of Environmental Research at Benedict, Maryland, they have formed the Solomon's Environmental and Archaeological Research Consortium, better known as the SEARCH Consortium. By pooling resources they will be able to prevent needless and costly overlapping and be able to make better use of their time and energy. With an emphasis on public education, they will be building a new auditorium and library at the Calvert Marine Museum, as well as setting up additional exhibits there. Meanwhile, the museum has expansion plans of its own that will come in conjunction with the SEARCH endeavours.

All of these plans are exciting, even more so because they are moving from the drawing board to reality. The pragmatic people of Solomons have seen their economic base and educational facilities radically change and evolve. Like an adult in mid-life crisis, Solomons has studied its strengths and assets and chosen a direction of growth uniquely its own. Under the business-as-usual facade, this town seems to have an exuberance of purpose and an excitement of the new reality it is building. ☐

—*Andi Manchester*

BOATKEEPING TIPS

When you want light below, but want to keep cold air, rain or a following wind out, it's nice to have plexiglass replacements for your wooden hatch boards.

Use a partially inflated, large-size "Ziploc" bag as a passable substitute for the foam or feather pillows you have at home. The water-tight bags are also useful for storing left-overs, mixing batters, and keeping things dry. The bags come in two sizes—quart and gallon.

When it's hot on the Chesapeake, it is really hot. But you'll feel a lot cooler if you "air condition" your anchored boat with one of those brightly-colored air scoops rigged in the forward hatch. If you don't have one, inspect one in a maritime store or ask to see your neighbor's. You could make one yourself. But whether you buy a ready-made or save by stitching up your own, it will be worth its weight in gold (or cold) on a steaming, sultry, Chesapeake day.

MILL CREEK

on the Patuxent River

Our cruise coverage of Solomons Island includes the Mill Creek right nearby. On this cruise, we decided to spend the day anchored in another Mill Creek on the Patuxent. The duplicating of names is not unusual on the Chesapeake; there must be at least a hundred "Mill Creeks," as there are a thousand "River Roads." And this way of naming things is part of the charm of the Bay country. Names given in colonial days such as Point Patience, Old House Cove, God's Grace Point, Half Pone Point, and St. Leonard Creek, also add to the charm of this area.

As you cruise up the Patuxent, you will pass under the Governor Thomas Johnson Bridge linking lower Calvert and St. Mary's counties. The bridge has a 140-foot clearance. Further up the Patuxent, take notice in rounding Point Patience. Here in this narrow area, the river marks a water depth of 137 feet—one of the deepest points on the Chesapeake Bay!

Mill Creek, about five miles upstream from Drum Point, has one of the prettiest anchorages on the Bay. A black daymark off Half Pone Point leads to a red mark at the entrance with a nice, wide channel, which is easy to negotiate. Once inside the entrance, curve around to the left and drop anchor in the little bay which boasts 12 feet of water with a good holding bottom.

In stormy weather you can snuggle up to either the northeast or southeast shores, while on hot nights it is safe to anchor out in the more open part of this cove for a cooling breeze. Supplies and ice can be purchased up in Cuckold Creek.

Further up the Patuxent, around Half Pone Point, the river stretches away majestically in a straight line northwestward some 15 miles. The banks are higher than anywhere below, often higher than one hundred feet.

The Patuxent is a river of history whose manor houses played a special part in the social circles of early colonial days. Included were such estates as Robert Brookes' Delabrooke Manor, Rousby Hall, Resurrection Manor, and Preston, believed to be the oldest building in Tidewater Maryland, a distinction challenged only by Cross Manor on the Potomac. The buildings at Fenwick Manor have since disappeared from

PHOTO BY J.H. CROMWELL

Sotterley Mansion

the site, but not from history; for it was here that the Provincial Court sat, at least in 1659, as some historical records reveal.

And Sotterley, on a part of Resurrection Manor, looks down from high banks as one of the best known and kept manors in the area. It is located up the Patuxent from Half Pone Point, across the river from the entrance to St. Leonard Creek. In spite of its age, it is still a working plantation with a smoke house that still cures hams. Construction was begun in 1717, and one of its owners, George Plater V, is supposed to have lost the whole place—house and 5,000 acres—to his brother-in-law in a game of chance. The plantation is opened to visitors daily, June through September, and by appointment earlier and later in the season.

The dock is to the left as you go into Sotterley Creek. There is no dockage charge for visitors to the plantation. A telephone call from the end of the pier can arrange transportation and a tour of the house and grounds [(301)373-2280]. A modest admission is charged for adults and children 6 to 16. □

From NOAA Chart 12264—not to be used for navigation.

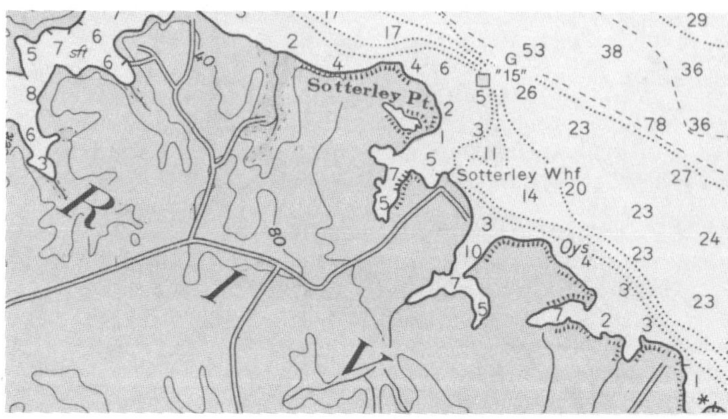

From NOAA Chart 12264—not to be used for navigation.

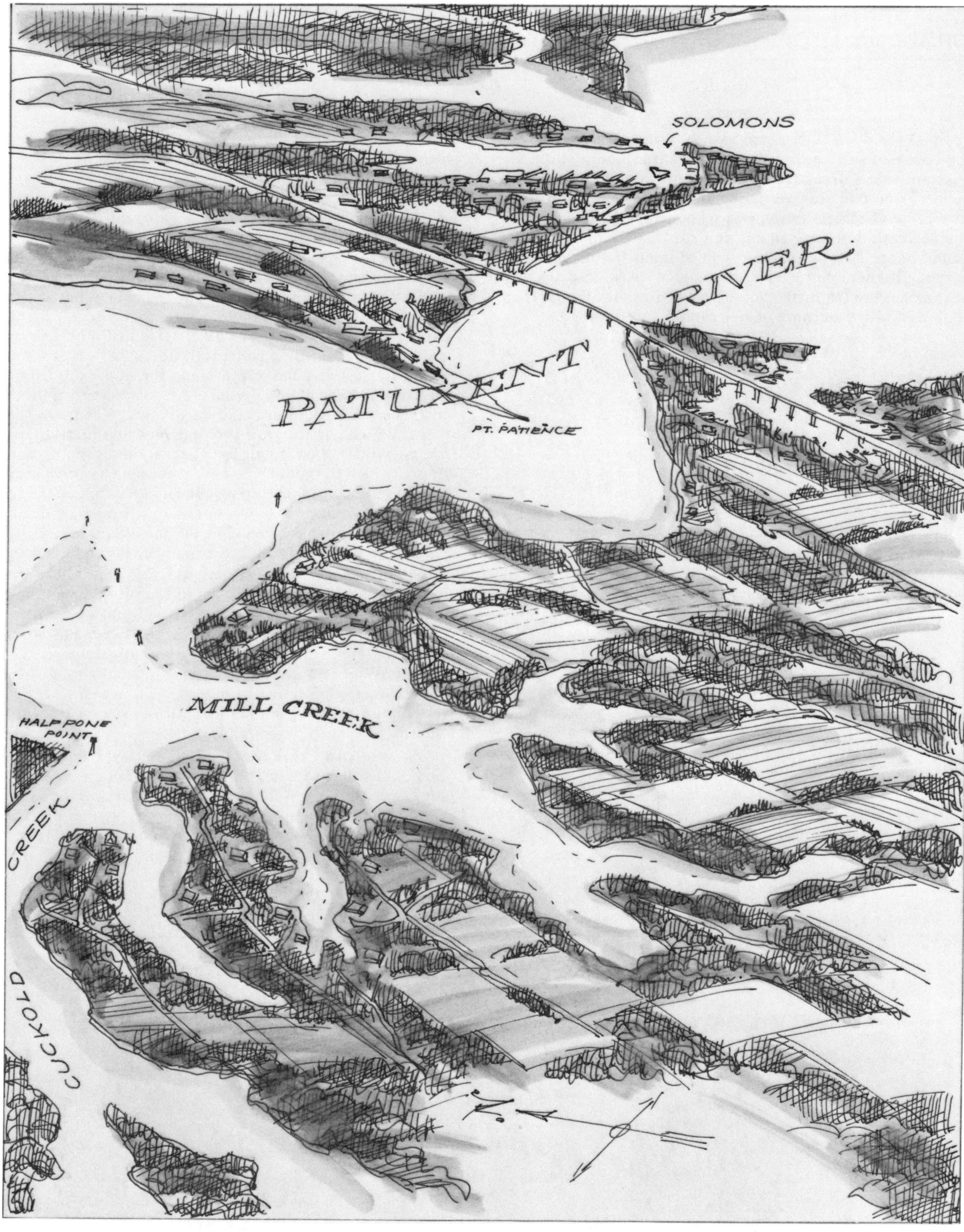
SOLOMONS
RIVER
PATUXENT
PT. PATIENCE
MILL CREEK
HALF PONE POINT
CREEK
CUCKOLD
N

ST. LEONARD CREEK

on the Patuxent River

St. Leonard Creek has been said to be the most beautiful of the Patuxent's tributaries. It was here at the mouth of the St. Leonard that a dramatic naval battle was fought during our country's second war with England. A blockading British fleet of two frigates, a brig, two schooners, and a number of smaller craft were driven off in a surprise dawn attack by Commodore Joshua Barney with a small flotilla of open barges. Barney, however, was unable to follow up his advantage; and the British force later contributed troops that took part in the burning of our capitol in Washington.

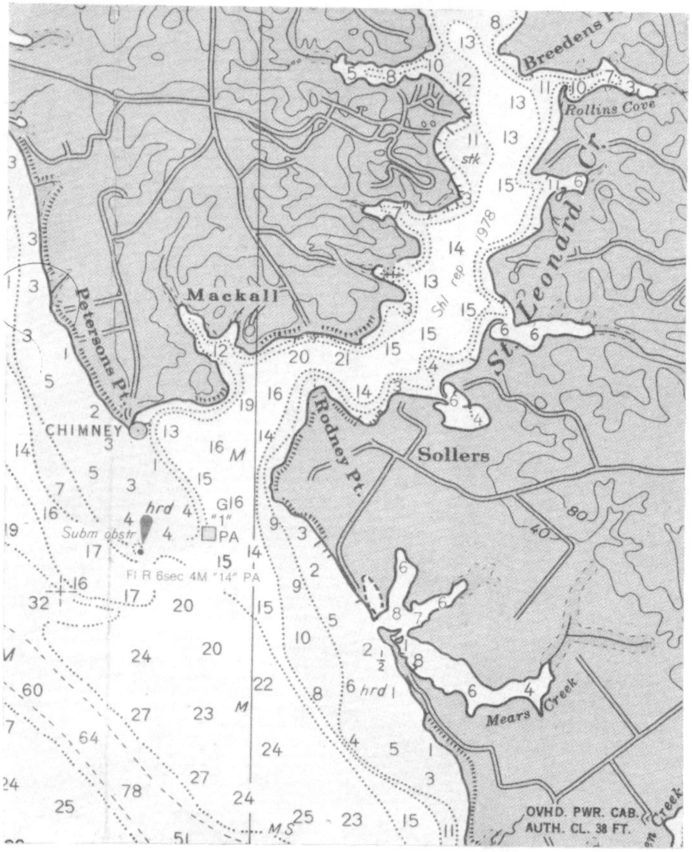

From NOAA Chart 12264—not to be used for navigation.

The buoys at the entrance of St. Leonard Creek can be a little confusing. When you enter the creek, take care that you don't honor the red mark #14 off Peterson's Point—that is, it should not be considered one of the St. Leonard entrance marks. This lighted red mark is a Patuxent River mark and *should be left to port* on entering St. Leonard. The entrance mark for the creek is a green daymark #1 about 400 yards to the east of the red #14 and should be left to port on entering.

If you are approaching from the west—that is, from upstream—here's the simplest way to enter St. Leonard Creek: head for the red #14 off Peterson's Point. Leave this mark to port and then come to heading 090°. According to Ken Brooks (who has often made the approach from this direction), ahead of you on the bluffs to the south of the creek entrance you'll see house and yard lights. Head straight for them. Watch carefully off the port bow and pretty soon the green daymark #1 will slide by. The mark faces south, so it will be pretty hard to spot till you have it abeam. Once past it, swing to port onto course 030° (magnetic) and head on up the creek.

After you have passed this mark, just remember to give all points a reasonable berth. For the most part, water is deep enough to permit access to the many coves and inlets. Most popular anchorages are at the creek's entrance, just around Rodney Point if the wind is out of the south, or on the port side, in the little cove behind Peterson's Point where the water is 8 to 12 feet deep. The shores are steep and wooded, providing excellent protection from a northerly.

The White Sands Yacht Club is located about 2½ miles upstream at the entrance to Johns Creek. Its marina offers fuel and supplies; its Polynesian restaurant promises escape to fabled "tropic isle" tranquility.

St. Leonard Creek was, by far, one of the most beautiful bodies of water we've explored on the Chesapeake Bay, with high, wooded shores and neat, well kept farms. Often you will see among the trees beautiful estates and homes perched on grassy fields that slope gracefully to the water's edge.

Indeed, as Captain John Smith observed on his explorations of the Chesapeake Bay, "...heaven and earth never agreed better to frame a place for man's habitation..."□

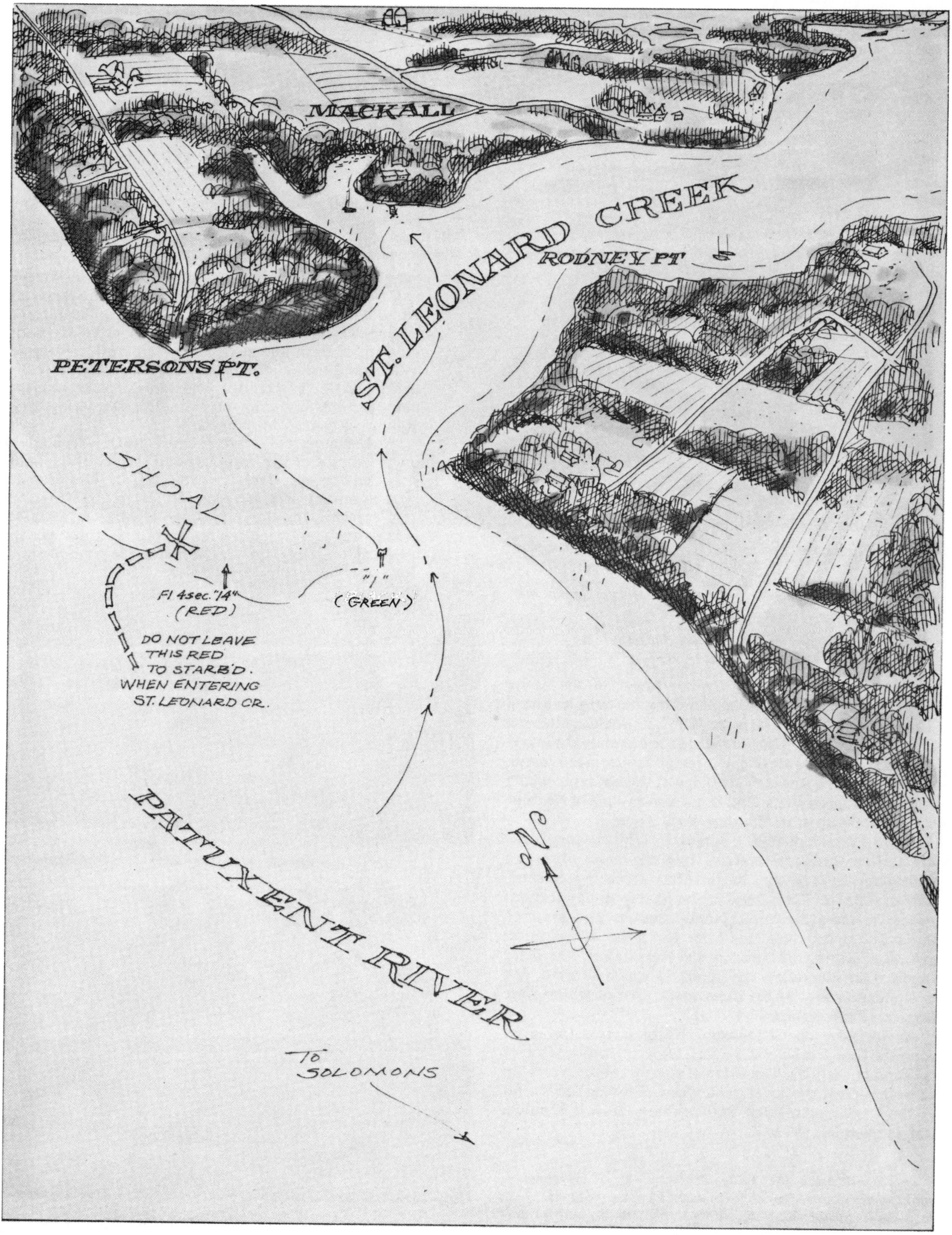
MACKALL
ST. LEONARD CREEK
RODNEY PT
PETERSONS PT.
SHOAL
Fl 4sec. "14"
(RED)
"1"
(GREEN)
DO NOT LEAVE
THIS RED
TO STARB'D.
WHEN ENTERING
ST. LEONARD CR.
PATUXENT RIVER
N
TO
SOLOMONS

THE POTOMAC RIVER: AN OVERVIEW

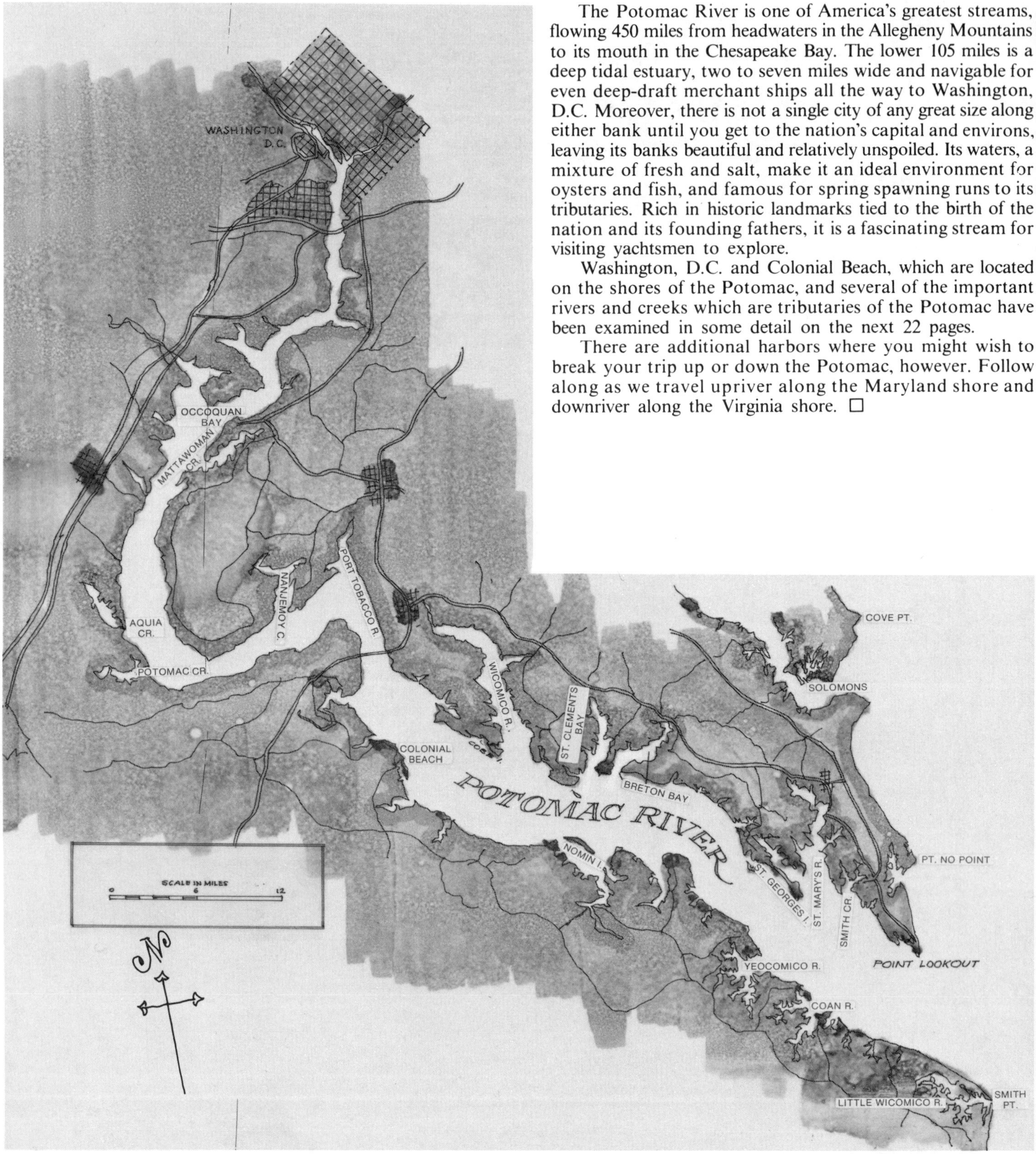

The Potomac River is one of America's greatest streams, flowing 450 miles from headwaters in the Allegheny Mountains to its mouth in the Chesapeake Bay. The lower 105 miles is a deep tidal estuary, two to seven miles wide and navigable for even deep-draft merchant ships all the way to Washington, D.C. Moreover, there is not a single city of any great size along either bank until you get to the nation's capital and environs, leaving its banks beautiful and relatively unspoiled. Its waters, a mixture of fresh and salt, make it an ideal environment for oysters and fish, and famous for spring spawning runs to its tributaries. Rich in historic landmarks tied to the birth of the nation and its founding fathers, it is a fascinating stream for visiting yachtsmen to explore.

Washington, D.C. and Colonial Beach, which are located on the shores of the Potomac, and several of the important rivers and creeks which are tributaries of the Potomac have been examined in some detail on the next 22 pages.

There are additional harbors where you might wish to break your trip up or down the Potomac, however. Follow along as we travel upriver along the Maryland shore and downriver along the Virginia shore. □

Maryland Shore

The Chesapeake Bay is at its widest point near Point Lookout. The soft, low headlands of Point Lookout are a beautiful sight, punctuated by the Point Lookout Light (Qk Fl 41 ft. 9M) standing offshore in 13 feet of water. Ashore is the old lighthouse built in 1830.

In nasty weather you can try the harbor of refuge at Lake Conoy, inside, about a mile and a half up from the point to starboard. There is a Maryland marine police facility there. Look for "2" (Fl R) and enter a dredged channel 100 feet wide. Be sure to split the jetties evenly (depth is 6 feet at the entrance, 4 to the sides). You may anchor out but not tie up or stay overnight except in dire emergency. There is an interesting old bar-restaurant on the Point and a park with some ruins of a Civil War prison camp.

Above St. George Island you come to the Potomac side entrance to Piney Point where Steuart Transportation Company operates a six million barrel tank farm. Huge tankers anchor out here to unload. Tugboats push barges loaded with gasoline and fuel oil up the Potomac to Anacostia where it is piped ashore. Piney Point was once the summer White House (destroyed by hurricane in 1933) of President James Monroe. In an emergency situation you can overnight at the dock here.

Just inside the entrance to Breton Bay to starboard is a lovely anchorage with 14 feet of water. Be sure going in that you give a wide berth to Huggins Point, clearing "2" (Fl R) and "4" going in. If in need of gas or supplies there is a marina to port at mark "5", or follow the winding upper reaches to Leonardtown (depths dwindling from 17 to 7 feet). This historic town, founded in 1708, is named for Leonard Calvert, Maryland's founder. It has an oyster shucking contest every October, a small business district, historical society and an ancient cannon. Breton Bay is named for an early settler, William Bretton, who deeded his lands to the Jesuits in 1668. St. Francis Xavier Church here is the oldest Roman Catholic Church still in use on the east coast of the United States.

Upstream above five miles is the Wicomico River (one of four on the Chesapeake bearing the name) and at its entrance Cobb Island.

Cobb Island is a popular summer resort dotted with cottages and served by a fine marina and clubhouse. Across a bridge are some more restaurants serving excellent seafood. There is a Maryland marine police facility here, too. When you enter the **Wicomico** you will note on the chart that there are four major shoals which carry far out from points to both port and starboard, so you must thread your way past them. There is deep water all the way up to Stoddard Point but there are numerous small and large shoals. Off to starboard at the entrance is a clubhouse on St. Catherine Island. Further upstream is a 300-year old mansion called "Ocean View" on a hilltop overlooking the river to port. Bushwood Wharf, about a mile above the entrance to starboard, was a steamboat port of call until 1932. Founded in 1683, it still has a dock with 6 feet of water, a store and restaurant.

Above Cobb Island the yachtsman comes to **Kettle Bottom Shoals**, designated on your chart as the "Middle Danger Area" established by the Navy to permit firing by the U.S. Naval Weapons Laboratory at Dahlgren on the Upper Machodoc Creek, Virginia side. You must watch for Navy range boats identified by a square red flag during daylight hours and a 32 point red light at the mast head at night. They may caution boatmen as far south as St. Clements Island. They will advise you to hug the Maryland shore past the danger area to the narrows below the Harry W. Nice Bridge which carries Route 301 from Mathias Point Neck to the Maryland side.

Approaching the **301 Bridge** you see at the base of the bridge some large, brightly painted smokestacks on the Maryland side. At the base of the bridge on the Maryland side is Aqualand Park, with a narrow well-marked channel to a gas dock and marina, not advisable with more than a four-foot draft. There is a marine police facility there.

Upstream about two miles to starboard is **Pope's Creek** (one of two on the river) where you will find some of the finest crab houses on the river, or anywhere for that matter. The pier is guarded by two shallow spots. You will find a small red nun "2" here marking the entrance. The pier is exposed and not suitable in heavy weather.

Towering on the Maryland shore, 7 miles from Craney Island, is the mighty Fort Washington near "80" (E Int R 6 sec 28 ft) built to protect the capital from the British. Although it is obsolete, it still makes a great tourist attraction with a nice park. Fort Washington Marina is on Piscataway Creek.

Virginia Shore

Alexandria welcomes touring sailors to its waterfront refurbished with parks and a historic clipper ship *Lindo* which is open to visitors. The city owns a 270-foot dock where you may tie up while touring the historic city. You are close to the foot of King Street with its charming boutiques, flower shops, restaurants, bars, antique shops and import stores. The Torpedo Factory has been turned into an air-conditioned center for arts and crafts. Ramsey House, at 221 King Street, dates from pre-Revolutionary War times and is a Visitor's Center. The city has a schedule of historic festivals—Scotch, Irish, Revolutionary War, Washington's Birthday, etc.

Mount Vernon, George Washington's restored home, is a major tourist attraction.

You may tie up at the boat dock, on the north or starboard side. Tour boats including a paddle wheeler, arrive from the Washington waterfront and tie up on the south or port side. A security guard will greet you and request you pay him the standard admission fee to visit the grounds. As you cruise by Mt. Vernon, ring your ship's bell in honor of our first president, as is the custom. At "67" (Fl G) you may wish to turn to starboard into **Dogue Creek** and the Mount Vernon Yacht Club. The yacht club is private, but welcomes visiting yachts from established clubs.

Downstream you round Mason's Neck, giving a comfortable margin to Craney Island, and come to Occoquan Bay. Turn at N "52" to course 351° M to reach "2" (Fl 4 sec). You can anchor out in Occoquan Bay (depths 5 to 6 feet). The channel is maintained to 10-foot-depths for barge traffic to above the U.S. Route One Bridge (vertical clearance 55 feet). Occoquan is a rapidly growing suburb with over 400 new slips for boats to 50 feet, many of them south of the bridges.

Enter Currioman Bay and Nomini Creek opposite St. Clements Island at "1" (Fl 2½ sec 16 ft). In Currioman Bay are cliffs at the base of which you can collect ancient fossils. **Nomini Bay** is broad and deep enough to anchor in, but Currioman Bay and Nomini Creek are shallow and unsuitable for deep draft vessels. In this case the best bet is to anchor off and dink in. The ancestral home of Robert E. Lee's family, Stratford Hall, in excellent repair, is near there. There is a recreation center visible from the water, and the mansion is open to the public during summer months, but has no dock. □

ST. MARY'S RIVER

off the Potomac River, Maryland Shore

One of our earliest and most pleasant recollections of anchoring out was our St. Mary's River experience. With a group of cruising friends we set out for Horseshoe Bend above St. Mary's City. The little flotilla was blessed with good weather, so all were enchanted by the river's pretty shores, the commanding site of the State House and the camaraderie of boating friends. Our children still talk about the water taxi when some of our party with dinghies ferried people to shore or to other boats.

We found no city on shore, but learned that the larger buildings were part of the St. Mary's College campus which has eclipsed the original capital in size. Visiting the Freedom of Conscience monument at the roadside near the water's edge gave us a better understanding of the basis on which the Maryland colony was established.

St. Mary's College of Maryland began in 1839 as a finishing school for young ladies and later became a high school according to an extensive account by historian Regina C. Hammett. In 1927 the school included a junior college, and by 1964, converted to a four-year, co-educational college. An extensive building campaign has given the school many attractive structures including waterfront facilities on the shores of Horseshoe Bend where sailing instruction is offered.

Courtesy dockage is available at the pier above Church Point where sailboats are tied. On a first come, first served basis yachtsmen may be granted transient privileges by applying to the college's admission office near the State House.

Gov. Leonard Calvert and his band of English colonists arrived at the St. Mary's site after having first landed on St. Clements Island. On March 25, 1634 they had celebrated mass and planted a cross on that Potomac island, then sought a permanent location. When they found friendly Indians in the present St. Mary's City area, they purchased the site from the Yaocomicos (also Yowaccococo, presently Yeocomico) who lived across the river.

To reach the St. Mary's River, our cruise group rounded Point Lookout, entering the Potomac on a course of about

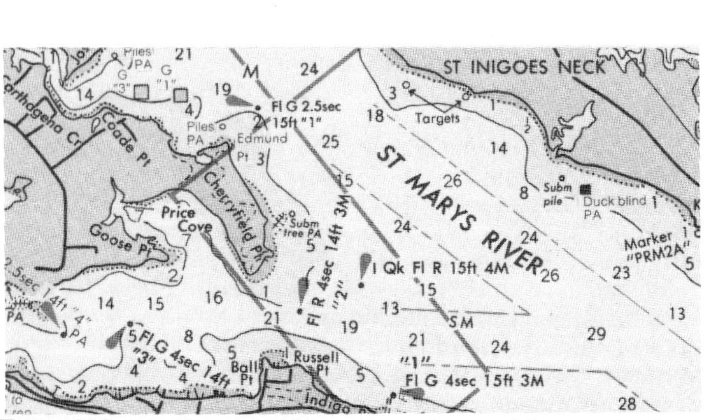

From NOAA Chart 12285—not to be used for navigation.

318° to the red and black junction buoy marking the entrance to the St. Mary's. The lower reaches of the eight-mile-long river are low and unremarkable on both sides. The St. Mary's ranges from 9 to 35 feet deep and is about two miles wide at its confluence with the Potomac.

The shores become higher as one progresses upstream; old homes may sometimes be glimpsed among the trees. To port in **Carthagena Creek** there's a modern, complete service marina tucked away behind Josh Point in an unspoiled setting carrying 11 foot depths. From Edmund Point follow the markers to Josh Point's red flasher "4," then head for green "5" and the marina piers. Supplies may be obtained here and snacks and cocktails are available in a setting dominated by a large fireplace.

To starboard on the river Webster Field, a Navy installation is situated along a level field on St. Inigoes (In-ee-goes) Neck. **St. Inigoes Creek** is easy to enter as the only shoal is on the south bank at Priests Point, clearly marked by lighted spar #2. Stay in the middle till you reach the two branches, one on each side. The river bends northerly and then east again. On your starboard side is a prominent sandy point with a wreck on the far side. Avoid this point and hug the docks to port till you reach the wide open bay where you can anchor in safety.

Overlooking St. Inigoes Creek, nestled behind a barrage of high box hedges, is Cross Manor, its original character obscured by quite modern porches. It is possibly the oldest brick house in Maryland. It stands on original manor land granted to Thomas Cornwallis. On the west side of St. Mary's are two venerable mansions of undefined age. They are Carthagena and Porto Bello, whose names recall the Spanish-English war early in the 18th century.

Protected anchorages beckon yachts to coves in **Milburn Creek** or **Church Cove** where waters range from 7 to 16 feet deep.

As one continues upriver the heights of **St. Mary's City** come into view. No metropolis greets the eye, nor did this first capital of Maryland ever become more than a cluster of buildings. Perhaps the idea of a "city" existed only in the imagination of the founding fathers. Certainly after the capital was moved to Annapolis in 1695 St. Marys' importance dwindled and so did the town itself.

Now above reconstructed Brome's (also Broome's) Wharf stands a replica of the 1676 State House, built in 1934 for Maryland's Tercentenary. In summer a square-rigged vessel usually lies at the wharf. This is the 57 foot *Dove,* a replica of the first pinnace which accompanied the *Ark* bringing the Maryland colonists to the New World. This new ship, built in 1977 at Richardson's Boatyard on the Eastern Shore, may be visited. A trained guide gives a complete tour for a small fee.

The State House and nearby Trinity Episcopal churchyard contain much of interest in addition to commanding an excellent view up and down river. In the church cemetery stands an obelisk marking the place where Gov. Leonard Calvert met the Indians under a mulberry tree to bargain for

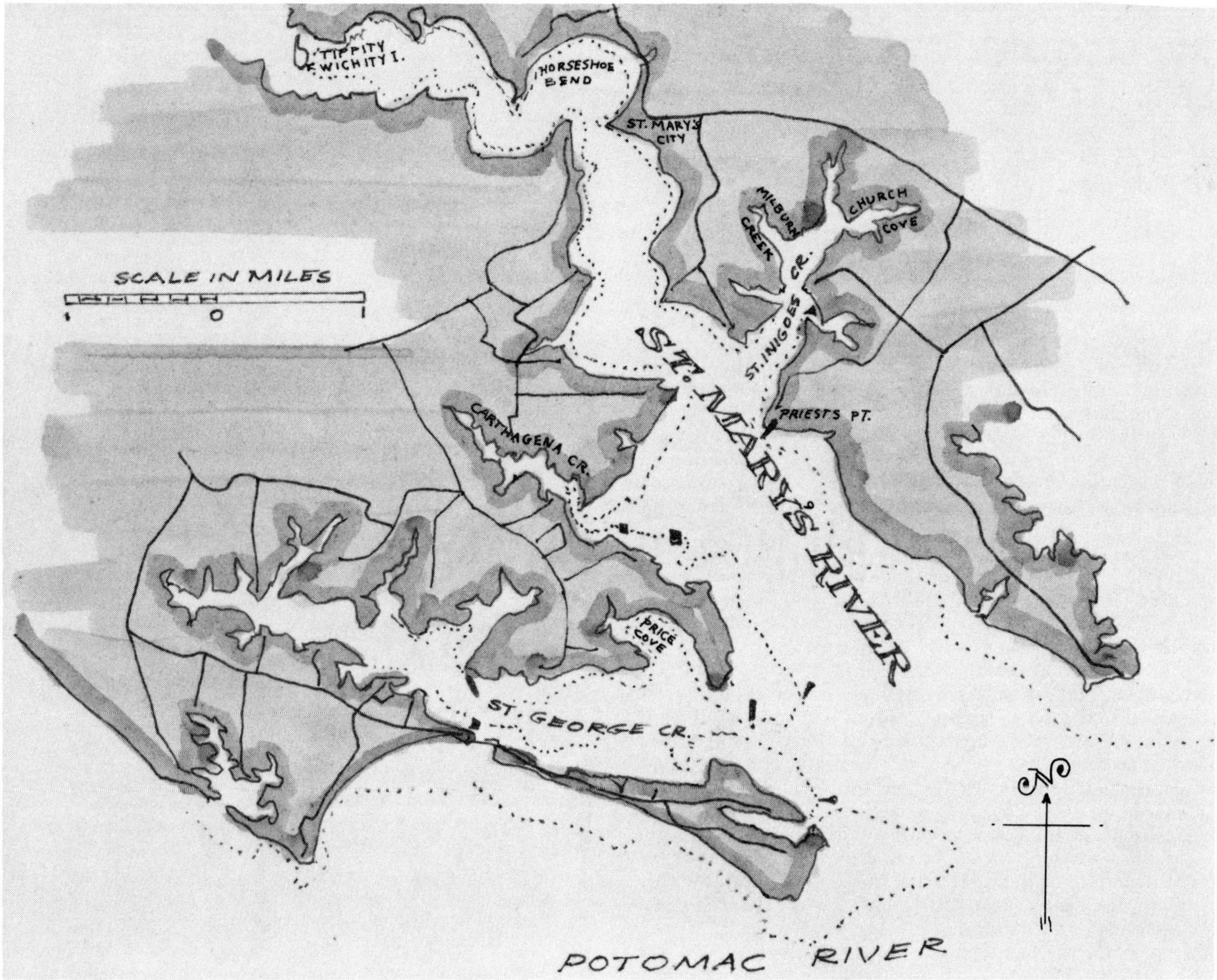

he land now known as St. Mary's County, the mother county f Maryland. A few years ago a new mulberry sapling was lanted at Founders' Day ceremonies which are held annually n March to commemorate the colonists' arrival.

Each year the St. Mary's City vicinity has more to offer isitors, and additional attractions were added for Maryland's 50th anniversary celebrated in 1984. Additions included a ew Visitor Center which is located in an area known as the Brentland Farm. The Visitor Center complex is a combination of restored and replica early 20th-century farm buildings which house a visitor information/ticket sales desk and orientation area, a museum gift shop, auditorium and an archaeological/historical exhibit. Archaeological sites may be visited now as excavation progresses to uncover original buildings' foundations. Also added was a reconstructed 17th-entury inn.

Charter Day is celebrated in June to mark the day in 1632 when the Calverts received their charter from the King of England permitting them to establish the Maryland colony.

Other events are included in the annual Summer Festival for those who may visit the old capital city during the boating season. A series of plays is presented in July and early August on a waterfront stage. Other events include a 17th century children's festival, Militia Day; and the finish of the Governor's Cup Regatta which is sailed from Annapolis to St. Mary's City in August.

There is a limited food service for visitors in the Brome-Howard House area on weekends. Reservations are available at the State House, phone (301)862-8522, for the plantation buffet dinner.

If sightseeing and shore expeditions are not your choice, try cruising upriver from Horseshoe Bend for about a mile. It's possible to anchor comfortably in 7 foot water near the island with the intriguing name, Tippity Wichity. □

ST. GEORGE CREEK

on the St. Mary's River, Maryland Shore

The lower reaches of the Potomac River contain many attractive creeks and rivers—enough to provide ample cruising and enjoyment for several weeks for the visiting boating family. Our first visit here was to Smith Creek, home of the Corinthian Yacht Club.

On the Virginia shore is the Coan River, whose several coves and branches we've found attractive. Further along on the same shore you'll find the Yeocomico. This river alone could be a cruising man's paradise; its three branches are beautiful and inviting.

Across the Potomac is St. Mary's River. This broad, beautiful river with shoreline that varies from wooded, flat land to tall banks, has an added dimension for the visitor. Here is where English explorers came to establish the first settlement in Maryland at St. Mary's City.

To port on entering is St. George Creek, and until recently we had not explored this interesting creek. However, the other day as I was checking *Moon Song's* log, a reference caught my eye: "Passing St. George's Creek. Half-dozen boats are coming out to join us. Check this creek for good anchorages." On the spot, I pulled out my charts and studied St. George Creek closely. It looked as if there were several coves and anchorages deserving a visit.

So recently we planned a cruise to St. George Creek. The creek's entrance is located 8½ miles northwest of Point Lookout. An easy marker to watch for is the red/black bell that stands about two miles off the entrance to St. Mary's River. From the bell a course of approximately 339° will take you to the red flashing spar at St. George Creek entrance, just south of Cherryfield Point. As you near the mark, to port is St. George Island; on its outer end is Island Creek, where a dredged channel leads into a restaurant whose food is quite good, I'm told.

The channel into St. George Creek is broad and well marked. The first, and perhaps most popular anchorage is in Price Cove, to starboard. Its entrance is broad with a prominent shoal on the west side at Goose Point which is barely awash at low tide. So keep to midchannel when entering.

Just past Price Cove a black/green lighted spar marks a portside shoal, and beyond that are a pair of reds spaced about a mile apart. As you approach the second red mark, you will note a red and green to port, marking the entrance to the channel which cuts between St. George Island and the mainland. There is a fixed bridge here with vertical clearance of 17 feet; if you intend to take this short cut out into the Potomac, be aware.

Continuing upstream just past the bridge you will find Swann's Pier, offering gas and diesel fuel (Texaco) as well as groceries, ice, bait, and tackle. Water alongside the pier is reported to be seven feet.

Beyond the bridge St. George Creek takes a right and then a left wiggle. Here is where you will find the bustling facility of the Harry Lundeberg School of Seamanship. I was amazed at the size of this operation. Two large six-story

From NOAA Chart #12285—not to be used for navigation.

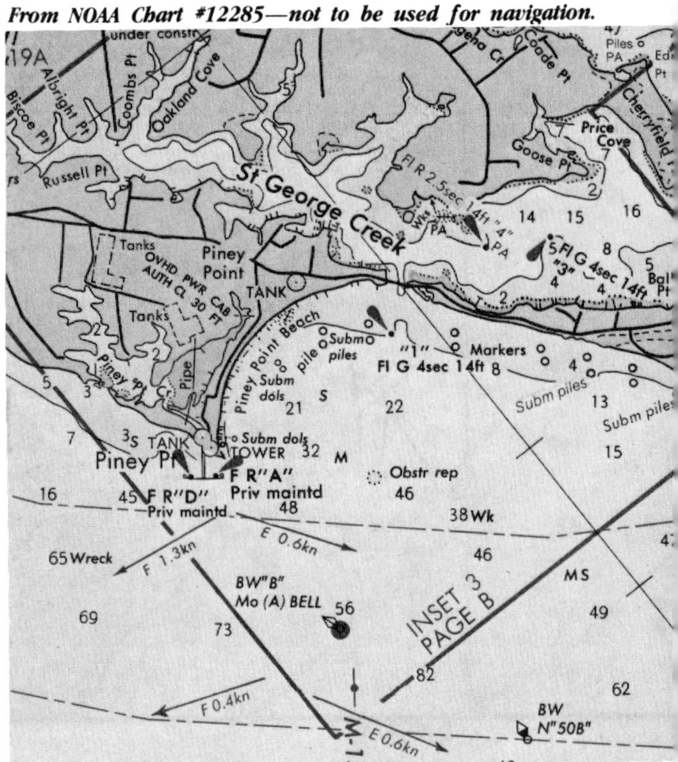

office/training buildings dominate the scene. A couple o small steamships, some tugs and barges, and a pair of cruise type ships, the *Earle "Bull" Shepard* and the *Charles S Zimmerman*, line the bulkheads. At the western end of th waterfront are the school's yachting piers, where *Manitou* the famous Kennedy yacht, is tied up.

St. George Creek is sparsely settled. Aside from th Lundeberg School and Swann's Pier, the shoreline is mostl wooded. Here and there a cornfield or a crop of soybean reaches down to the water's edge. The few homes along th creek are tucked neatly beneath the growth of trees. There i more boating activity in the area of the bridge as fishin boats come into St. George Creek for gas and supplies.

We rounded the bend, took a quick peek at Tarkill Cove then headed for our destination, Schoolhouse Branch. Th entrance of this little creek looks tight, but we found plent of room to get in and ample space to accomodate a good sized group.

Like many small creeks around the Chesapeake, Schoo house Branch has a combination of cultivated fields an wooded stretches lining its banks. The north shore, wher the creek bends toward the east is graced by well-manicure fields surrounding a couple of neat farm buildings.

The shores were deserted enough to encourage our usu on-deck showers, after dark, that is. As we settled in ou cockpit with a hot cup of coffee and dessert, the only thin missing was someone else with whom to share this anchorage. ☐

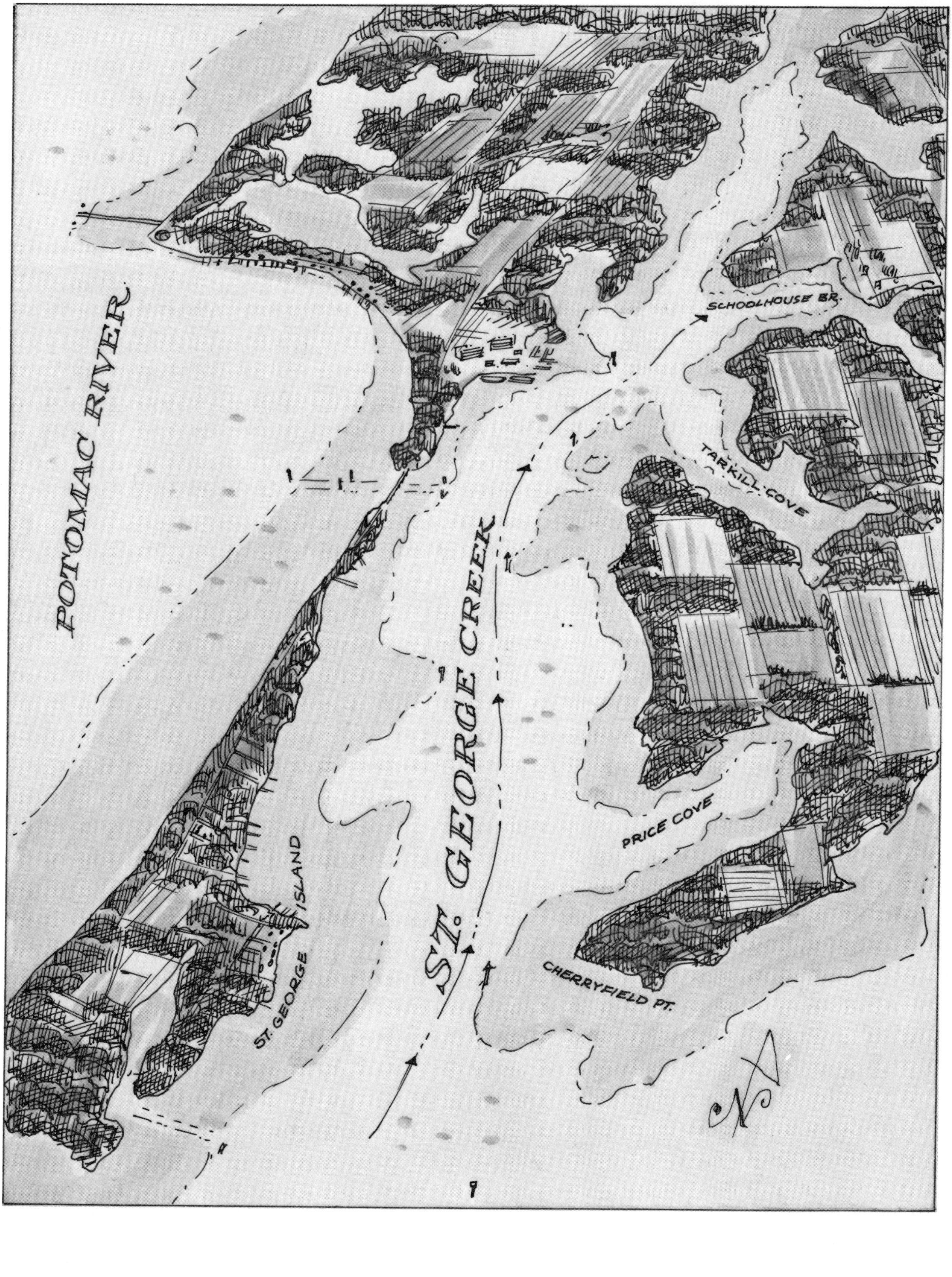
POTOMAC RIVER
ST. GEORGE CREEK
SCHOOLHOUSE BR.
TARKILL COVE
PRICE COVE
CHERRYFIELD PT.
ST. GEORGE ISLAND

ST. CLEMENTS ISLAND

on the Potomac River, Maryland Shore

At Ragged Point on the Potomac we circled the anchored fleet of fishing boats and searched the horizon for our destination, St. Clements Island. An August heat wave blanketed the river with a heavy yellow haze that hid the island from sight until we were within a couple of miles.

We tried to imagine what it must have looked like more than three hundred years ago as settlers led by Leonard Calvert arrived in early spring. The island at that time measured almost 400 acres and was a welcome sight to the colonists as their two tiny ships dropped anchor. They named the island for St. Clement, the martyred saint who was cast into the sea with an anchor fastened around his neck.

The island later became known as Blackiston's Island, and was owned by that family for some 200 years. In 1962 the name St. Clements Island was restored by the federal government.

In the course of time a farm with several buildings was established on the island along with a lighthouse and a small hotel. At Coltons Point across Dukeharts Channel a small summer cottage has been converted into the St. Clements Island—Potomac Museum. Visitors can see many historical mementoes as well as a turn-of-the-century photo collection of the hotel and farm buildings. Now the land area has shrunk to approximately 40 acres and time has erased all evidence of buildings. Today nothing stands except a huge 40-foot cross erected by the State of Maryland in 1934 to celebrate the tricentennial of the colonists' first landing. As you approach the island, the large stone cross stands dramatically against the skyline, presenting a moving reminder of colonial history.

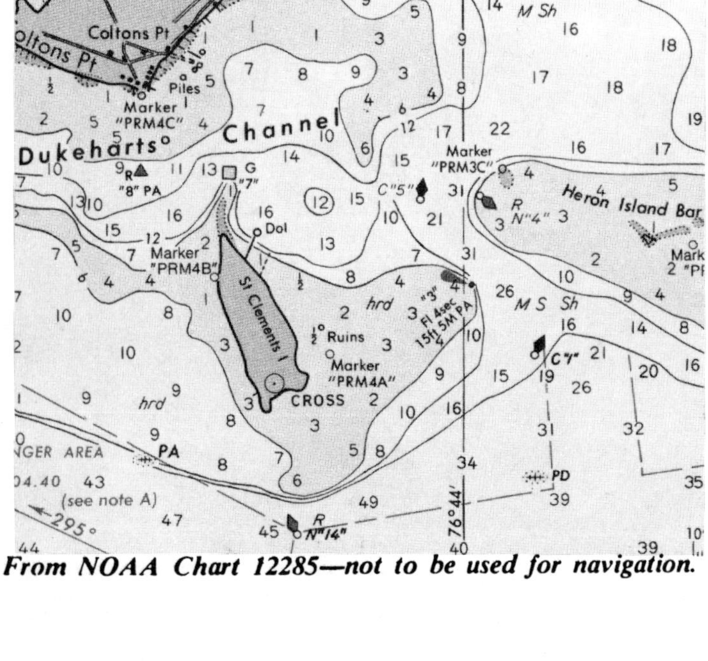

From NOAA Chart 12285—not to be used for navigation.

A long shoal projects northeastward from the island toward Heron Island Bar. (Heron Island Bar is visible only at low tide.) Those navigating these waters have a choice between circling north of Heron Island Bar and coming into St. Clements Island from the direction of Newtown Neck, or taking the more direct route by way of the channel between the two islands, a course which we chose.

This channel is quite wide and not the least risky, but from a distance we had a hard time spotting the two black cans and the red nun which mark the shoals on either side. As you approach the second can (#5), the new large dock will be easy to see. The dock, which must be close to 200 yards long, can accommodate quite a few boats, so just pick out an open spot and tie up.

St. Clements is an interesting place to go ashore, so don't miss the opportunity. To protect the island, which is presently a wildlife management area, the State of Maryland has placed a rip-rap around much of the shoreline as part of a much-needed erosion program. The island is the scene of an annual seafood festival and is noted for its nationally famous "Blessing of the Oyster Fleet," which takes place in late September.

The northwest end of the island thins out into a long sandspit that projects into Dukeharts Channel. On the southern end of the island the sandy beach slopes gradually up to higher ground with tall stands of grass.

By the time we settled in for the evening, quite a few other boats had joined us. All around, a congenial hubbub of activity settled along the dock as various boats became the centers of group dinners. Some families chose to leave the dock to anchor in the darkness where they would have more privacy, but we stayed where we were.

As we settled in our bunks for the night, I couldn't help but reflect on the vast changes that have occurred, not only on this tiny island but also throughout our entire country. It's been 350 years since that intrepid band of settlers—eager, brave, frightened, excited—set foot here to build a new world, and the echo of their voices is still preserved in places like this. □

ST. CLEMENTS ISLAND
DUKEHARTS
CHANNEL
VIEW FROM HERON ISLAND BAR
C"7"
C"5"
N"4"
HERON ISLAND BAR

Notes

CANOE NECK CREEK

on St. Clements Bay, off the Potomac River

The Fourth of July is a wonderful time to go cruising. Just about any where you go there's a good chance you'll be treated to a modest fireworks display which is all the more spectacular when viewed from the water. One Fourth of July found us on our way up the Potomac River to St. Clements Bay, where we planned to rendezvous with several other boats at St. Clements Island.

Our habit in traveling the Potomac is to follow the B/W nuns that serve as a fish trap line all the way upstream to Nomini Bay. One by one, the nuns measured the miles for us. From the B/W #45B to the #5 entrance bell off the Coan is about seven miles. The entrance to the Yeocomico is only 2½ miles further, and Ragged Point only nine miles beyond that. All in all, it took us about five and a half hours to travel from Smith Point to the spider off Ragged Point.

Power boat folks must think this an awful waste of time, but you learn to make use of these long passages on a sailboat. Best of all, it can be a time to do a little boat cleaning. One year I managed to clean all my teak trim, and polish the stainless, and troll for fish (snagging a huge blue that became our dinner that night).

Ragged Point was crowded with numerous fishing boats, and we swung wide to avoid their trolling lines. From Ragged Point we changed course slightly to 310° for six miles to the

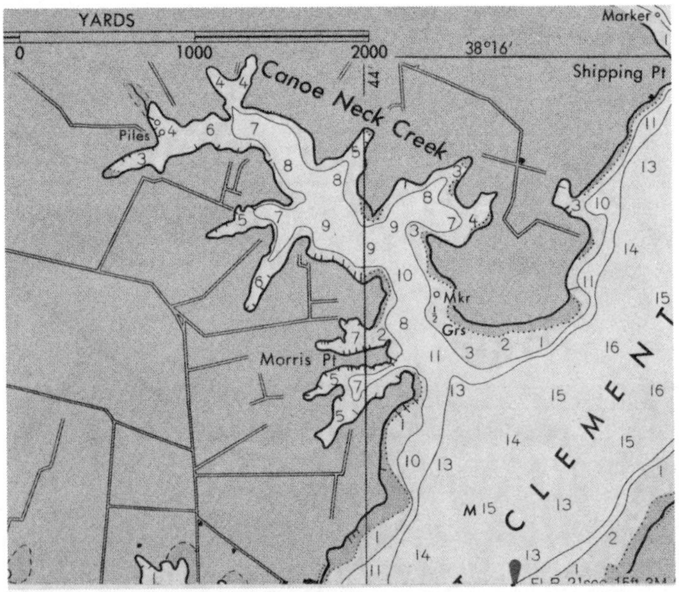

From NOAA Chart 12285—not to be used for navigation.

R/B nun that marks the eastern end of Heron Island Bar, a couple of sandy islands, measuring together about a half-mile, mostly underwater, and barely awash at low tide. Skirting the Bar (crowded with seagulls which chorused their displeasure at us), we headed on course 325° to clear the shoal off Newtown Neck, the east side of St. Clements Bay.

From here it is an easy matter to pick up the lighted red spar to starboard off Long Point; and about a half mile upstream to port is the entrance of Canoe Neck Creek.

We were intrigued with Canoe Neck Creek because, although some cruising guides haven't given it much of a recommendation, the charts show it to be fairly wide with an easy-to-negotiate entrance.

We passed the boathouses on the south side of the entrance and found the two creeks at Morris Point to be well populated with attractive homes and boat docks. We favored the port side of the channel until we were opposite the entrance to the first large cove on the north shore. There is an extensive shoal out from the starboard shore, so keep to port.

There were two other boats already at anchor — a sailboat snuggled up against the northeast shore, and a large cabin cruiser tucked away in the southeast fringes.

It was dusk as we dropped anchor and lit our anchor light. In the dim light, we bathed in the cockpit, large bath towels pinned to the lifelines providing privacy even though there were only two homes visible around the cove. Later, we dined under the stars on crab cakes, garden tomatoes, and squash, with pie and coffee to top it off.

As I said before, it was the Fourth of July; but we didn't expect to enjoy a fireworks display this far out in the country. However, on shore came the shout of several children's voices; and with a "whoosh" the sky was lit by an exploding rocket. More and more rockets took off; and as the children cheered, we on our boats cheered with them. For nearly an hour the shoreside display continued, and all the while the velvety warm night held not a single mosquito!

After the fireworks had subsided, we were, once again, alone in the darkness except for the twinkle of anchor lights from the two other boats in the cove. As we stretched out in the cockpit, our eyes heavy, heads nodding with sleep, we were startled by a loud screeching of heron from the east bank of our cove. This set off a cacophony of shrieking birds. The din was tremendous! Perhaps a fox was hunting along the shoreline. Whatever had startled them was nowhere in sight. Perhaps they were just adding their voices to the local celebrations of this most pleasant Fourth of July. □

dock no longer here
CANOE NECK CREEK
heron and egret point
ST. CLEMENTS BAY

Notes

PORT TOBACCO RIVER

off the Potomac River, Maryland Shore

If you are tired of fighting heavy boat traffic in the Bay, try some leisurely cruising in the Port Tobacco River. It is small and quaint compared to the larger and more regal Potomac. However, the scenery on these shores is stunning. I have spent many a delightful hour in these waters with the sails full and the

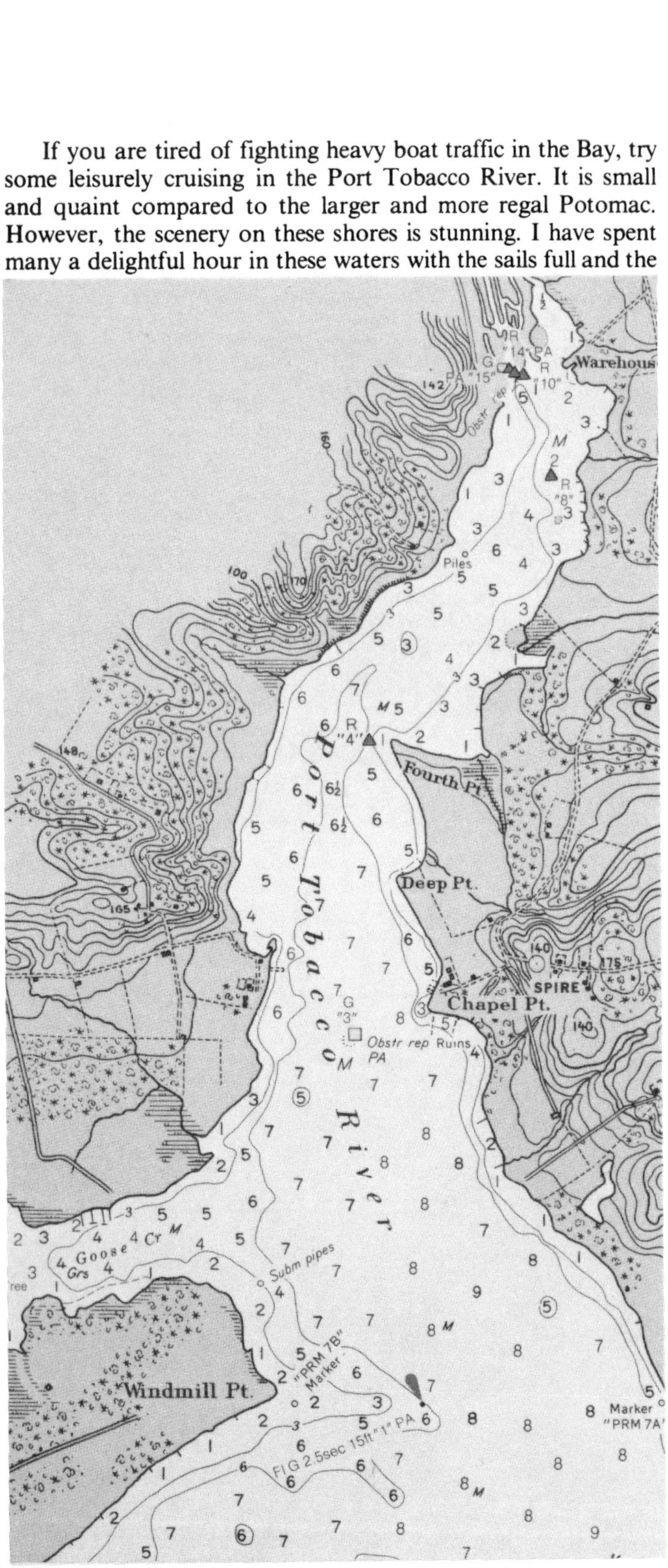

From NOAA Chart 12288—not to be used for navigation.

bow cutting through the blue water like a hot knife going through soft butter. I usually have one hand on the tiller and the other ready to work the sails. Normally the wind is not trouble-some, so I can concentrate on the treasures for the eyes. There are panoramas of green and tan river banks and small, sandy beaches.

Use NOAA Chart 12288 or Chart No. 16 in the *Guide to Cruising Maryland Waters,* published annually by the Maryland State Department of Natural Resources. This latter chart is excellent and gives important information needed to cruise these waters. If you trailer your boat, you can start your cruise of the Port Tobacco River at the town of Port Tobacco where there are launch ramps.

I will pick up my cruise northward from Cobb Island where there are several good marinas and restaurants. Along this route to Port Tobacco you will find some of the prettiest green scenery in the state of Maryland. This trip slices through a quiet, rural section of the state and lays out an outstanding view of farms, woodlands, and boating and fishing areas. Every once in a while, however, you see something that startles you and brings you back to the modern day. This happens as you pass under the Henry W. Nice Bridge; more commonly called the 301 Bridge. From the bridge to the mouth of the Port Tobacco River is a leisurely 6.5 miles.

A word of caution here: As you enter the Port Tobacco River and the companion cove of Goose Creek, the depths fall off rapidly. Care is necessary. Stay in the well marked, deep water channel particularly during low tide. The proprietors of two local marinas state that the approaches and their slips can accommodate up to five-foot drafts at Goose Bay Marina (in Goose Creek) and four-foot at Olde Port Marina on the Port Tobacco River. Off Windmill Point there is a particularly extensive shoal, marked by Fl G 2.5 sec "1" on pile (SG).

My boat is a light, centerboard San Juan 21 sloop with a draft of 8″ with the board up and 4′ with it down. The channel of the Port Tobacco River from its mouth upriver for about two miles is 10′ to 17′, after which it drops off to 5′ and finally 2′. Goose Creek, where I berth my boat, is charted at 2′ but I have sailed carefully with my centerboard 2/3 down (or a 3-foot draft). If you have a boat with a keel or draft larger than mine, I recommend you follow the compass headings and nautical distances drawn on Maryland's DNR Chart No. 16.

Goose Bay, marked on the chart as Goose Creek, is a sheltered cove near the junction of the two rivers. This is a good spot to go ashore for a picnic or a walk along the sandy beach.

Leaving Goose Bay behind and heading back into the Port Tobacco River, you will see St. Ignatius Roman Catholic Church (1798) with its inspiring pure white steeple visible high on a hill on the eastern shore.

The spot is appropriately named Chapel Point. Behind the church is St. Thomas Manor, built in 1741. The land deeds for the manor date back to 1662 when 4,000 acres were turned over

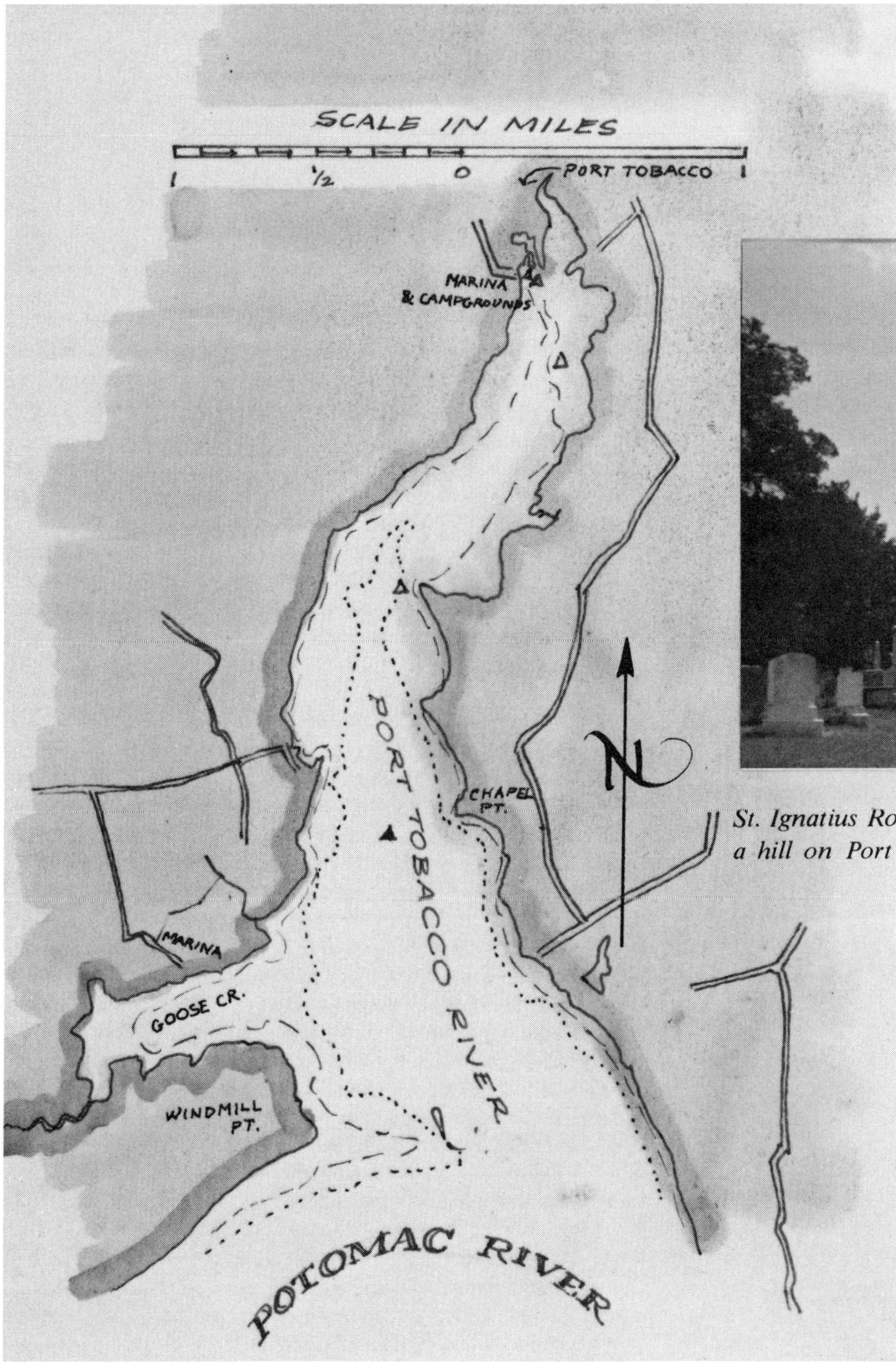

PHOTO BY SAUL PINCUS

St. Ignatius Roman Catholic Church (1798) is visible high on a hill on Port Tobacco's eastern shore.

to the Jesuit Order by Thomas Matthews. There is a fine anchorage or refuge from a Nor'easter under a high bluff at Chapel Pt.

Continuing up the Port Tobacco River, there are numerous historic buildings and sites situated inland. The Port Tobacco Court House, a marvelous example of Georgian architecture, has been restored and is used as a historic museum by the Society for the Restoration of Port Tobacco. There are quite a few old homes originally built by colonists and patriots that are fully restored and currently occupied as private dwellings.

The town of Port Tobacco played an important role in colonial times and in the Revolutionary War. The region supplied heroes, politicians and statesmen for the army of General George Washington, and for the budding republic. Although Port Tobacco seems aptly named because of its exporting of tobacco, it was not named for this reason. The original inhabitants, the Indians, named this area "Pertafacca" or "Potopaco" (sources differ on the exact Indian name) which means "in the hollow of the hills." The present name seems to be an anglicization of the Indian name.

All in all, the natural beauty of the Port Tobacco River matches anything I have seen on the entire Bay. The feeling of solitude and peace of mind I have felt while cruising these sparkling waters defies description by mere words. In addition, the fishing and crabbing are fine. Campsites, slips and picnic areas are readily available on this little river. ☐

MATTAWOMAN CREEK

off the Potomac River, Maryland Shore

Every cruising club has its favorite port of call in which it can raft up and have a party across the decks, complete with guitar, beverages, good food, songs, salty stories, etc. Our group favors Mattawoman Creek and has for many years.

There are many reasons for this but most important is its unspoiled natural beauty and the fact it is a comfortable day's sail out of Washington for everybody. It takes two days to reach Mattawoman Creek by sailboat from the Potomac's mouth at Point Lookout.

I'll never forget my first trip to Mattawoman Creek, one Memorial Day weekend roughly 12 years ago. I had never been below the Wilson Bridge further than Fort Washington, and my crew had no more experience than I did. Worse still, my crew had to work late so we couldn't get underway until late afternoon. The trip is about 26 miles and we had to do most of it at night—including the unknown part. We made it—with one hairy adventure. Coming around Craney Island off Mason Neck we encountered a huge freighter which dominated the narrow channel along the Maryland shore (depths 30 to 64 feet). She kept beaming a blinding

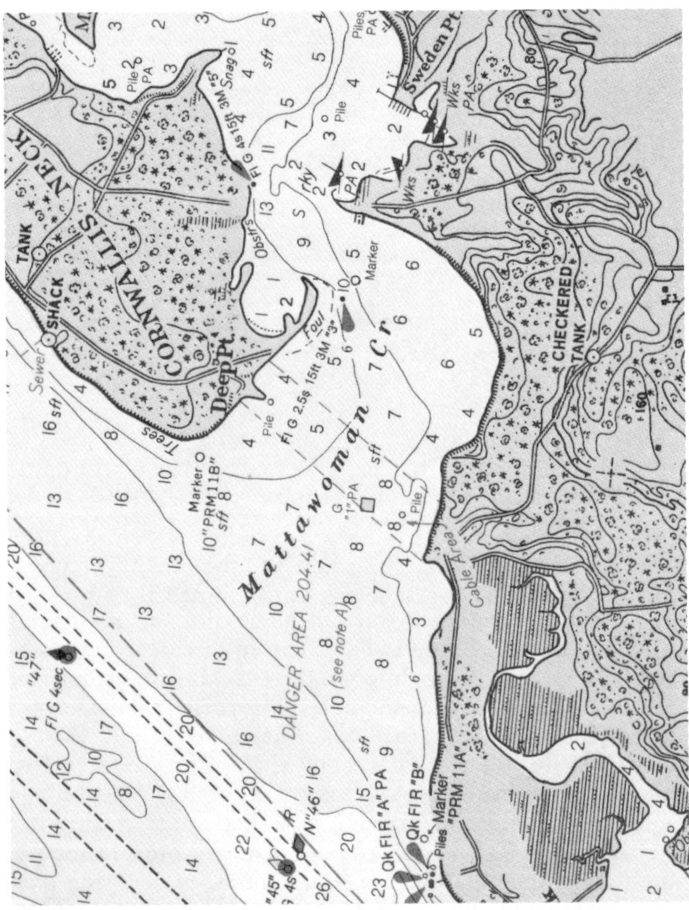

From NOAA Chart 12288—not to be used for navigation.

searchlight on us until I did the only safe thing—a 90-degre turn into shallow water out of her way. If I have to choos between colliding with a freighter or going aground, I'll hi bottom every time!

It was well after midnight when I picked up flashing greer Can "47" off Mattawoman. I decided to play it safe and go tc flashing green "45" before turning to a course of 90°, close tc the south shore to daymark "1" before carefully picking my way to Fl G 2.5 sec. "3" off Deep Pt., and then to Fl G 4 sec. "5" next to the north shore, staying clear of the shallows off Sweden Point. I picked up my club's raft of a dozen boats off Grinder's Wharf. This kept me in a channel from 25 to 13 feet deep. After happy shouts of greeting we were directed to one side of the raft tc tie up and join in the festivities.

In those days there was a restaurant and bar with a juk box ashore, an old wooden wharf, barbecue grills and ar outdoor open-sided shelter with a corrugated iron roof witl picnic tables. They made one of the best crab cake sandwiche I ever ate. Shallow draft boats tied up to the wharf.

But the restaurant closed, the wharf rotted away and so did the picnic facilities. The power boaters stopped coming but each year our club returned for a raftup.

Recently Sweden Point has been reborn. The State o Maryland has redeveloped this area and tied it into Smallwoo State Park, a memorial to William Smallwood, Revolutionar War general, plantation owner and Maryland governor.

On the creek front there is a newly built pier and sma marine shop where you can buy fishing gear and sandwiches There are no tie-up facilities or slips at the pier for cruis boats. There is a ramp for launching small motorboats. Yo can purchase ice and gasoline, but no diesel fuel.

The cove next to this facility is shallow and full of wate lilies. A graceful arched bridge crosses this cove to highe ground and Smallwood Park. There are charcoal grills an picnic tables scattered through the woods along a path up t the reconstructed Smallwood mansion. A park ranger wi show you about the interior, full of antiques. The general grave is marked by a large monument. There is a remarkabl oak tree here near the old slave quarters that is huge and ove 300 years old.

The banks of Mattawoman Creek are heavily wooded wit unspoiled natural scenery, dotted by houses mostly screene from view by the shrubbery. There is a lively traffic of sma power boats, and fishing is reported excellent.

My cruise mates and I recently enjoyed a great nev experience—a hurricane hole far up Mattawoman Creek. W cautiously picked our way with the depth finder up a narrov channel 23 to 10 feet deep through lily pads between beautifu wooded banks to a sandy beach about two miles upstream Deep water right up to the edge made it possible to put th bow up on the beach. Several other boats were there having barbeque picnic. Children were picking wild flowers. It was a attractive and unspoiled natural spot.□

PHOTO BY MICHAEL C. WOOTTON

WASHINGTON, D.C.

on the Potomac River

A visiting yachtsman cruising the intra-coastal waterway or the Chesapeake Bay might find it well worth it to take the 105 mile side trip up the Potomac River to Washington, D.C.—the nation's capital. A home afloat instead of a $100-a-day room ashore while exploring the delights of the capital city should prove attraction enough. There is a deep water ship channel all the way up to the Woodrow Wilson Bridge, marking the entrance to the capital. A clearly marked channel, 31 to 24 feet in depth, can take you up the Washington Channel inside Hains Point.

Just past historic Fort McNair, with its Armed Forces War College, on the starboard side is a waterfront lined with floating docks, restaurants, Capital Yacht Clubhouse, night clubs, open air fish market and marine repair facilities. Here also are the harbor police facilities and the commercial docks of excursion boats. The yachtsman has his choice of floating docks at the Gangplank Restaurant facility or riding on the hook at an anchorage on the port side of the channel off Potomac Park. The channel is deep, 18 to 24 feet, and can handle the largest cruising yachts. Washington Marina at the head of the channel has full marine repair facilities, gas and diesel fuel and can handle yachts of any size with fast service on replacement parts. The Metropolitan Police Marine Branch, with headquarters at a municipal pier next to the excursion pier, has authority over the anchorages in fair holding ground in protected water along the west side of the channel and at the Washington Sailing Marina Basin. Contact them on Channel 16 switching to 64 for conversation. The same goes for docking at the Gangplank.

Going ashore to register is no problem and the harbor police headquarters can grant you permission for a stay of one week at anchorage. The marina provides dinghy landing, shower and laundry facilities for boats at anchor.

The visiting yachtsman will find the area loaded with attractions for young and old alike. Waterfront restaurants and night clubs, banks, a supermarket nearby, and seafood plentiful on the wharfs are just a start. On the west side of the channel at Potomac Park are an 18 hole golf course, tennis courts and a swimming pool. There are bicycles to rent here that can be used to explore the historic spots, federal buildings and museums which are within a few blocks of the waterfront—remember this is a port city.

Taxis, Metro buses and a subway are easily accessible to take the visitor to any part of the city. At Pennsylvania Avenue and 14th Street is the newly reconstructed Federal Triangle. At 12th Street the old Post Office Building was turned into a galleria full of exclusive shops and tempting restaurants. Across the Triangle is the new Marriott Hotel with its own attractive shopping mall. Next door is the National Theater, recently refurbished and showing Broadway quality shows. Not far away is the famed Kennedy Center.

Even closer to the water is the mall stretching from the Capitol to the Lincoln Memorial including the Washington Monument, and nearby the reflecting pool with its Jefferson Monument and cherry blossoms. To the east are the White House, Treasury and other federal buildings. Lining the mall are Smithsonian museums.

But if all this culture is not the yachtsman's cup of tea he can find jazz and rock concerts at the George Washington University Marvin Center. Or he can pan for gold at the Long Branch Nature Center in Arlington, go to the changing of the old guard at the Tomb of the Unknown Soldier, visit the Vietnam War Memorial beside the Lincoln Memorial, or the Marine Corps Okinawa Memorial Statue nearby.

The Navy buff can come out of the channel, turn to port around Fort McNair and tie up at the McNair marina. Across the channel is the Anacostia Naval Station. It's a short walk to the old Naval Gun Factory with its Naval Museum.

Sailboats, unless they drop their tall masts, are prevented from going any farther upstream by low bridges. The Washington Channel ends in the Tidal Basin with no access back into the deep ship channel. You must go around Hains Point with National Airport on your port side to the 14th

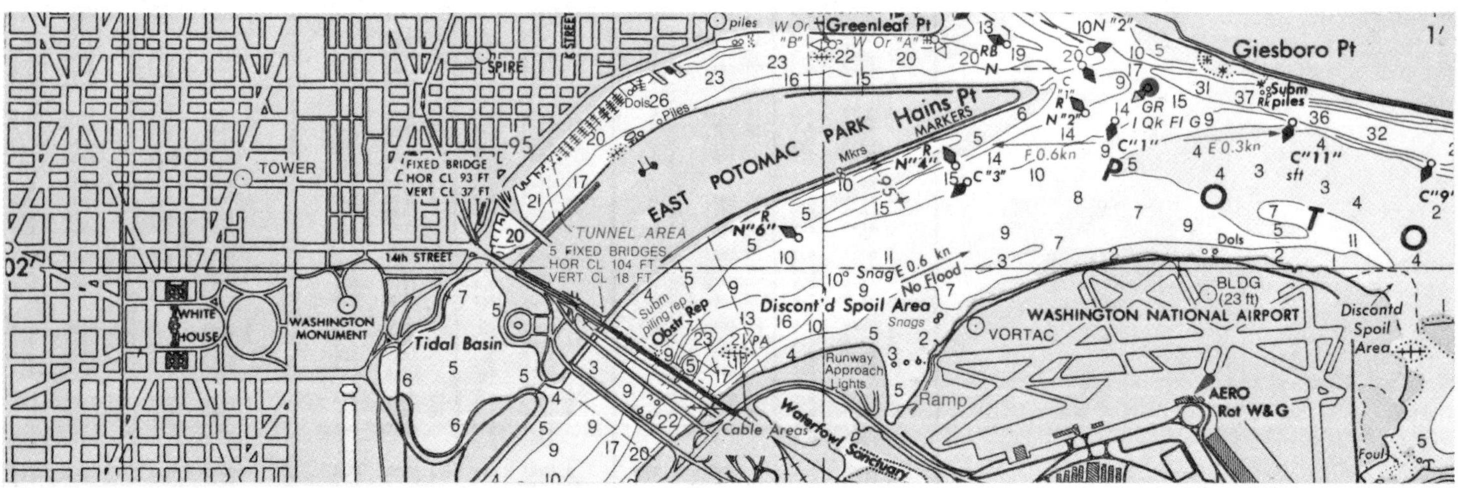

From NOAA Chart #12285—not to be used for navigation.

Seafood docks

"The Awakening" statue on Hains Pt.

Washington Monument

PHOTOS BY BILL MCMENAMIN

Headquarters of Harbor Police

Armed Forces War College

Street Bridges (vertical clearance 24 feet) depths 15 to 36 feet and past Thompson's boat house (canoes, sailboards, sculls) to the Georgetown waterfront now under reconstruction. The night spots, restaurants, an elegant new galleria, new shops and the old barge canal of Georgetown are well worth exploring, so anchor and dink ashore. Above here the channel deepens and the water becomes very swift, particularly in the spring. At the Key Bridge, Georgetown side, is the quaint old Washington Canoe Club. University and high school crew races are held in this area between Three Sisters Island and Thompson's Boat House. This has become a popular haven for sailboarders.

Above here is the end of the 105 mile navigable channel just as it was when John Smith explored it in the 1600's. Above Chain Bridge and the fall line is the rocky, dangerous channel that includes Great Falls and Little Falls—an area frequented only by expert kayakers and skilled local canoeists.

Coming back downstream out of the Washington Channel, the yachtsman might want to visit the Washington Sailing Marina on the west side below National Airport. To enter go south to the radar dome at the Navy Research Laboratory and make a 280° turn to the vicinity of the power station (large stacks), (Black Can #1) then turn north to follow the west shoreline past the partially submerged sunken barge (can "3" and nun "4" are off the barge.) Stay inside nuns "4" and "6" leaving them to starboard. There is a large spoil area off the end of the airport. Proceed into the Washington Sailing Marina basin and anchor out in 11 to 15 feet or, contact the dockmaster at the Potomac Inn for a temporary berth on one of the finger piers. Caution: beware the rocky ledge directly in front of the new clubhouse inside of Can "7." You may tie up temporarily at the dock in front of the crane but be careful not to drift down on the rocky ledge. Whatever you do, do NOT try to enter by the channel shown on the charts from flashing four sec. can "7" on the main channel. This channel was filled by Hurricane Agnes and never redredged.

In the event you desire a schedule of events that take place in Washington, contact the Greater Washington Board of Trade, 1129 20th St., N.W., Washington, D.C. (202)857-5900.□

COLONIAL BEACH

off the Potomac River, Virginia Shore

When cruising the lower Potomac River, be sure to include a stop at Colonial Beach, Virginia. If your stopover is to be brief and during daylight, you can tie up at the Town Pier which is on the Potomac at the public beach. From here you can walk to restaurants, a hardware store, a drugstore, churches, the laundromat, try the water slide, stroll the Boardwalk, or just lounge on the newly reconstructed main beach.

For a more sheltered anchorage and overnight docking facilities, you will find Monroe Creek to be a safe harbor. The Corps of Engineers dredged and widened the entrance channel a couple of years ago, but due to natural currents and some erosion control work upstream from the channel a shoal is again building to starboard. Be particularly careful after dark if you are not familiar with the entrance.

Once inside the entrance, marked with a QK FL R #4, Bay Yacht Center offers gas and diesel fuel, overnight facilities, travel lift, repair shop and an enlarged ships store. Another large reconstructed beach area is adjacent to the Yacht Center.

Approximately ¾ of a mile to starboard is Stanford

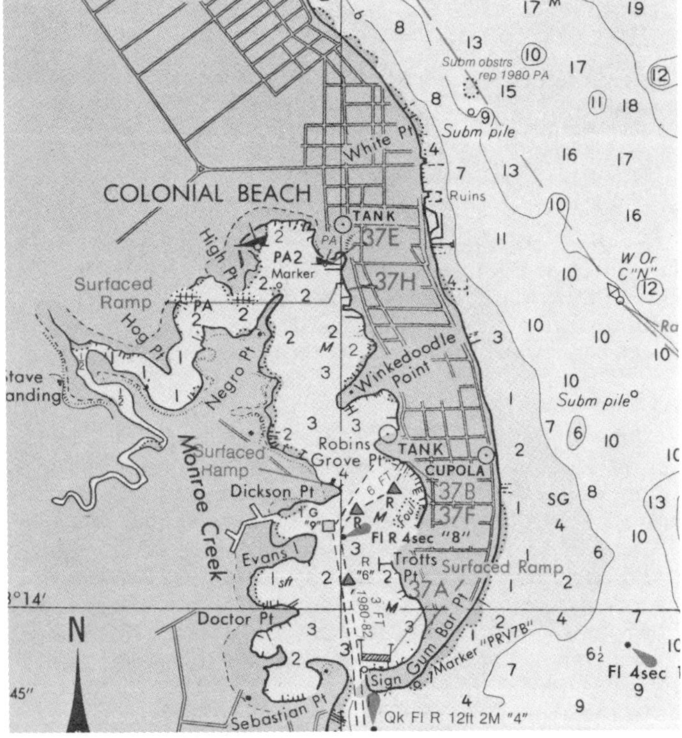

From NOAA Chart 12230—not to be used for navigation.

Marine which also provides gas and diesel fuel, travel lift, railway, shop facility and a well stocked ships store. Overnight slips are sometimes available.

Just before Monroe Creek takes a sharp turn to port, you will find Steve's Restaurant which is open year round and offers a varied menu as well as cocktails. Docking is available while you dine. Near Steve's there are two small marinas, Nightingale's and Atwell's, which may have vacancies for overnight. Parker's Crab Shore, near Stanford Marine, is open during the summer months and also has dockage while you dine.

Whether you tie up at one of the facilities or drop anchor in Monroe Creek, you will find 3′-4′ of water at low tide in most of the creek and about 7′ in the entrance channel.

Commencing with the annual Blessing of the Fleet at the Town Pier on the last Sunday afternoon in May, there is something of interest for the visitor to enjoy all season long. The Potomac River Festival takes place on the second weekend in June with a three-day celebration of parades, fireworks, beauty contest, drill contests and dances. The fireworks display from the Town Pier on July 4th is wel worth a visit and the Chicken Barbecue on the main beach i held annually on the third Saturday in July. The seconc weekend in August is always a favorite time as the annua Boardwalk Art Show, which typically brings over 200 artists and craftsmen to Colonial Beach, provides enjoyment fo residents as well as visitors. The Rod Run to the Beach is ar annual rally of restored antique cars held on the seconc Saturday in September and the Colonial Beach Classic, a 10-kilometer foot race, takes place annually on the first Saturday in October.

Colonial Beach is a good base from which to hire transpor tation to historic sites a few miles away. Down river from Monroe Creek (called Monroe Bay by local residents) is Wakefield, the reconstruction of George Washington's birth place. Adjacent to it lies Westmoreland State Park. Stratfor Hall Plantation, birthplace of Robert E. Lee, is nearby. Fo 250 years Stratford has been a working plantation, but it historic fame rests on the accomplished Lee Family, two o whom signed the Declaration of Independence.

There are two free, concrete boat launching ramps avail able for public use in Monroe Creek and water-skiing condi tions in this area are reported to be very good. ☐

NOTE: Shoaling reported in the entrance channel to Monroe Creek. Unless you have local knowledge, it is recommended that you make your approach in daylight, when the shallow area in mid-channel which must be avoided will be obvious.

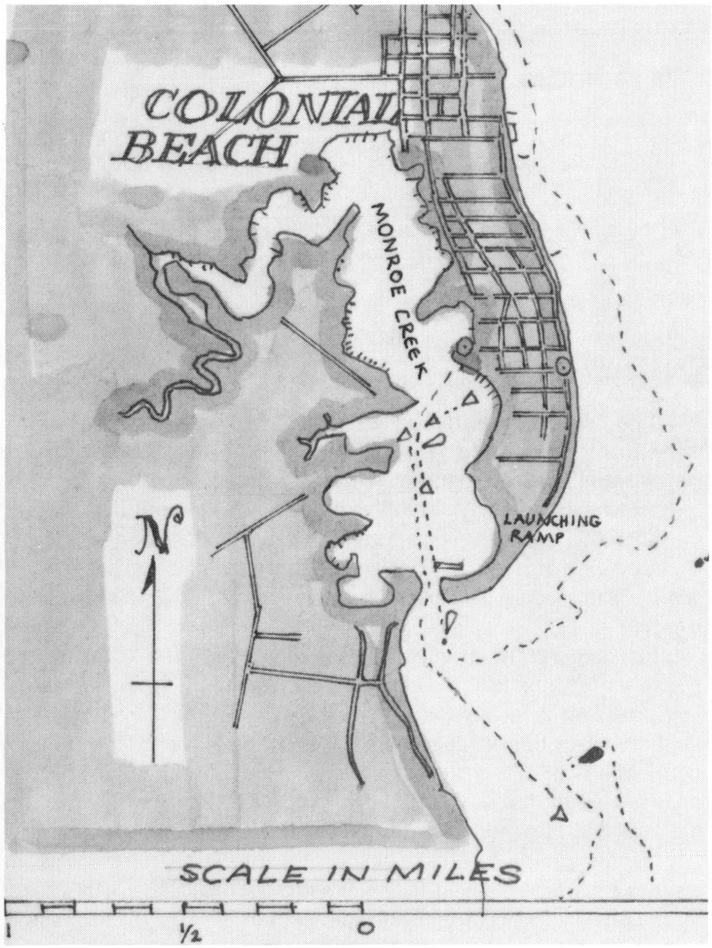

PHOTO BY MICHAEL C. WOOTTON

Notes

YEOCOMICO RIVER

off the Potomac River, Virginia Shore

The Yeocomico River has a legion of fans who admire its many good anchorages and marinas located along its tributaries. Conducive to its popularity are depths ranging from 7 to 18 feet even in many indentations. Like the fingers of an outstretched hand, the five-mile-long stream has several branches which in turn split into creeks and coves. With its wooded shores and many waterways, the river beckons to those who love the water. Its country beauty and serenity offer a strong contrast to the urban scene.

With these advantages, it might appear that this tributary of the lower Potomac would be teeming with boats. But somehow it never appears crowded. Amid an increasing number of pleasure boats watermen still ply their business as they have for generations.

The river lies nearly 12 miles up the Potomac as calculated on NOAA chart 12285. From Mile Zero on a line drawn ten miles across the Potomac's mouth from Point Lookout to Smith Point, it's easy to enter the Yeocomico. The magenta dashed line shown on the small craft chart indicates the boundary for fish nets and most crab pots. From flashing red "2" run about two miles to flashing green "3." The red aid is erected on a large black and white buoy, known affectionately as the birthday cake; the green one is sometimes hard to see against the dark shoreline. From here you may take the branch of your choice; ahead in the West Yeocomico to Kinsale, south to Lodge Creek, or north to Shannon Branch.

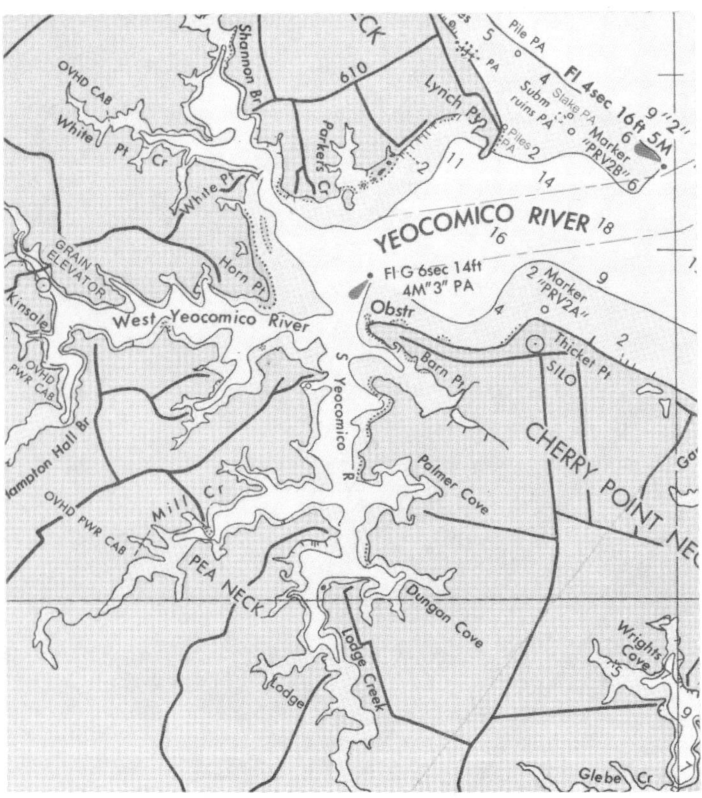

From NOAA Chart 12285—not to be used for navigation.

The course to Kinsale, less than three miles west, begins with a dog leg around Horn Point. If you honor red "2" off the point there'll be no trouble with the long shoal which extends to menace the unwary. Brush stakes abound here and elsewhere in the river, puzzling newcomers. Usually they denote oyster bottoms and are not aids to navigation. Just slow down, watch your depth sounder, stick to your charted course and proceed.

For a pleasant anchorage, look to port after clearing the Mundy Point shoal. Wilkins Creek with wooded shores and a few substantial homes is a favorite of cruising friends. This is an excellent anchorage, which is broad and deep (10 to 12 feet near its entrance with depths of 7 feet up at its head). There is only a hint of a shoal at its entrance, with the most prominent on the western side, clearly marked by a duck blind.

It's not far by boat to a restaurant at the marina situated in a cove by Allen Point on the West Yeocomico's north shore. The marina-campground combination has a variety of amenities including a swimming pool.

At the head of this branch lies the old town of Kinsale, now a ghost of its former self. Kinsale, named for the Irish town from which her early settlers came, dates back to the 18th century. Many of these early towns did not prosper as streams silted in or geographical location did not lead to further development. Kinsale was one of the more successful and even in 1926 it was larger than most villages along steamboat routes, as it had a hotel and more than one street. Even now grain hauling by boat continues from the storage tanks near a marina which stands near the country store. Kinsale Harbour Marina is being billed as a family sailing center, with sailing instruction and racing as primary activities, a Bed and Breakfast inn, and slips for 110 sailboats.

On a recent visit we saw the grain boat *Ward Brothers* tied near the storage tanks. Since these vessels are becoming increasingly rare, we searched for some information about the craft. It began its life as a sailing vessel but was later converted to power. Removing the mast and rigging and installing an engine lengthened the life of many sailing craft that were no longer economical in their original configuration.

Great House Point, shown near Kinsale on the chart, has an interesting story about its early history. For many years, according to an official report, the Bailey family's home, known as *"Great House,"* kept a light in its windows every night serving as a guide to mariners. Now a stone marker stands on the grounds of the home, a silent reminder of the War of 1812. In 1813 several British vessels entered the Yeocomico and in the ensuing battle a young American commander lost his life. He was buried on the grounds of the Bailey home and a monument erected to his memory.

The South Yeocomico offers good anchorages in Drum Cove, Mill Creek, Palmer Cove and Dungan Cove. When you

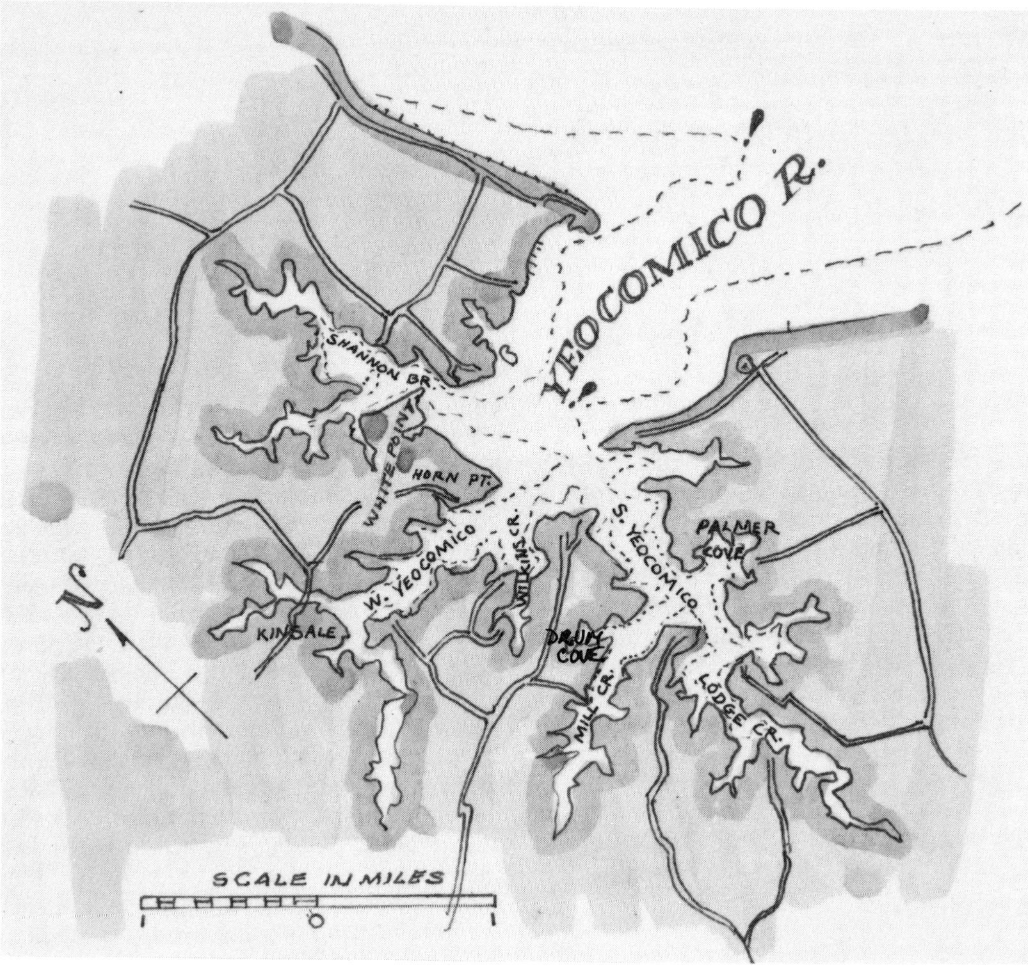

ter the South Yeocomico, just opposite the #2 daymark off arn Point, you can pass this point fairly close aboard, to be re to avoid the three-foot shoal off Tom Jones Point. As u pass the red daymark #4 at Walker Point, ahead on the rth shore you will see the opening for Drum Cove. The art (NOAA 12233) showed a shoal to starboard at the trance, and local knowledge confirms that visiting boats ve a tendency to follow the shoreline from red #4 and they nerally run aground here. Instead, locals have told us to give is shoal a wide berth (it's easy to spot because there are a attering of oyster stakes along its edge) and approach the trance from a right angle to the shoreline. There's plenty of ter inside the cove and the tall trees that cover its shoreline ovide a comfortable snugness. There are only two piers on e cove, and small cottages are tucked away among the trees.

Palmer Cove is on the port side of the South Yeocomico. ke course 102° (approx.) from the red #4 and you'll be in e of the prettiest anchorages on the Bay. The entrance to lmer Cove is about 400 yards wide, and there's plenty of om inside for a good-sized group of boats. The bottom is ft mud, so set your anchor well before you settle down for night.

Curiously named Harryhogan Point is said to have derived name from the Indian name Arehokin. In its well-known ipyard, established by Herman Krentz in 1932, was built e of the last skipjacks on the Bay. Nearby are a fishing ter and a small marina serving the boating public.

Farther south along Lodge Creek is an expanding marina tering to both power and sail. Lodge Creek, like other forks the Yeocomico, once had a steamboat landing, The first location of a Masonic lodge on this creek is said to have given the names to Lodge Creek and Lodge Landing.

The first branch, to starboard, is called Shannon Branch, where there is an attractive and roomy anchorage. As you enter this branch you will see, to port, an oyster and waterman's building. Along the starboard side of the shore is a sprinkling of modest homes, tucked in among the trees. Just around White Point, to port, is the White Point Marina. This is the largest marina on the Yeocomico with complete facilities for the boatman. You'll find a swimming pool, tennis courts, ice, fuel, engine and hull repairs, and transportation is available to a nearby restaurant and grocery store.

Shannon Branch, with houses along the starboard shore, also has a small marina and a seafood business on its banks. □

Notes

COAN RIVER

off the Potomac River Virginia Shore

Were we reading fact or fiction? Every cruising guide we consulted praised the Coan River. Such unanimity made us wonder if the authors were plagiarizing each other's material. There was only one thing to do: go and explore the river for ourselves.

What we found on recent visits to the Coan verifies our source material. This small river flowing into the lower Potomac is appealing as you approach its green shores where trees shade occasional buildings. Its well-marked main channel offers many pleasant vistas and a peaceful air that soothes the visitor. But remember you're in Virginia where brush stakes abound marking oysters beds! Good anchorages invite a stay, spots near red "18" and red"20" being especially popular with groups.

Although the Coan is long on scenery it is short on marinas and services. Nowadays there are two installations on the river catering to the boating public. One is a small marina at Lewisetta with 10-foot depths reported. It's on the tip of the point where the chart shows 6 feet; run north from red "8." There is fuel here, but limited space for transients. A store and post office serve the community where steamboats once stopped. The other marina in a cove at Stevens Point is mostly a repair facility, but the small store sells ice and soft drinks. Enter between red "12" and red "14" but keep alert for shoals.

Coan River, a Virginia tributary of the Potomac, is about seven miles from Point Lookout and 15 miles from Smith Point Light. We approached the Coan on a 285° course from the Point Lookout Light to Fl 4 sec bell "5," a river marker. Then headed for flashing green "5" off Travis Point and followed the navigation aids into the river. Alternatively you may cut across the magenta dashed lines and take your chances with crab pots and pound nets that abound within the magenta marked area. The channel runs sort of sou'west then does a short dog-leg south to a red lighted spar. This red lighted spar (#6) is a critical mark. Without it, you'd stand a good chance of going aground on the shoal east of Lewisetta.

Next comes a 90° turn west toward the two red daymarks off Honest Point, #8 and #10.

As you head toward #8 there is a prominent fish trap to starboard and all around you will be numerous bushstakes and poles marking oyster grounds. Local fishermen have assured us that there's nothing to fear about the stakes—frequently there's eight to ten feet of water around them. There sometimes seems to be no pattern to their dispersal, no fairways or paths between them; so your best bet is to follow the regular navigational aids.

The river's main waterway is buoyed, but its tributaries are unmarked, so we decided to follow the route most often described. Avoid the shoal off Walnut Point and pass close to red "12" when rounding the point. Encroaching shoals in the vicinity of daybeacon "12" off Walnut Point have restricted the existing channel to 30-40 ft. wide.

Walnut Point was once quite a thriving community with a summer resort hotel before the turn of the century. It also had a packing plant for seafood and vegetables until about 40 years ago, according to Frederick Tilp's book *This Was Potomac River.* Now amid lush green fields the aging remnants and sagging roofs of former structures are all that remain of more prosperous times.

One of the few commercial indications on the river is the group of new buildings on shore behind red "20." Shell piles on land and a few workboats tied at a wharf identify an oyster packing business. When we inquired about a store, we learned that the one at Lake (shown on the chart) no longer exists. In summer this facility is a tomato cannery, a continuation of seasonal business that kept many riverside communities active until a few decades ago.

At Bundick upstream from "21" we discovered a grain storage depot where trucks were delivering the harvest from nearby farms. A grain barge often awaits its load to take to market.

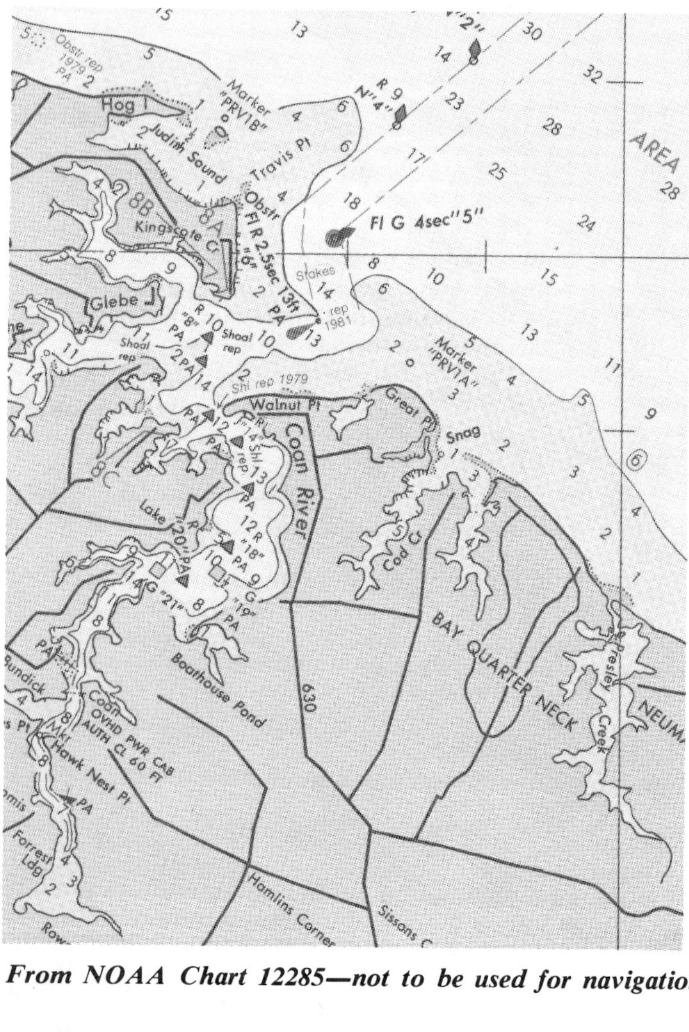

From NOAA Chart 12285—not to be used for navigation.

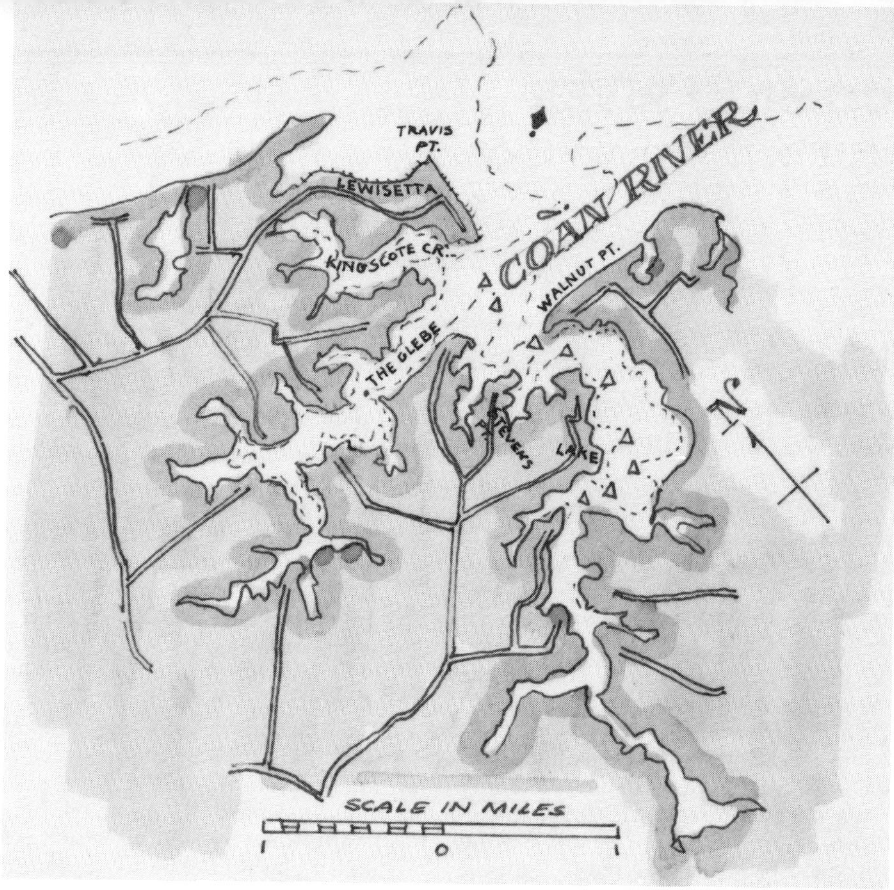

Bundick and Coan Wharf on the river's other shore were once connected by a cable ferry which ran until the mid 1930's. Now Coan Wharf's hotel and store are in ruins amid a tangle of brush. It seems incredible that this was one of the places decreed 300 years ago as a town site by the Virginia House of Burgesses. Obviously legislation did not insure success!

The tributaries of the Coan which may be seen from the Lewisetta vicinity are Kingscote Creek and The Glebe, so named because of the church lands along the shores. Neither waterway is buoyed, but Kingscote is somewhat more accessible than the meandering Glebe.

As you enter the Glebe, the area between Honest Point and Cowert is choked with oyster stakes. Once past the oyster stakes there was no real obstacle to our chosen anchorage, the first big cove to starboard about a half-mile upstream. At the mouth of the cove on the east side there is a bit of shoal that pushes its way out toward the Glebe's midchannel, but it was marked with brush stakes at the time of our visit and is easy to avoid.

This generous-sized cove, we were told by some local residents, is called Fisherman's Cove. It has a roomy mouth (where we anchored) just off the Glebe's main channel and a smaller anchorage area almost out of sight around the next corner. This would be the perfect snug place to ride out a storm or high wind. Depths range to 10 feet and more.

One of the numerous small boatbuilding yards which sprang up in earlier times formerly stood in this area. Until about 1960 the Headley brothers carried on at the yard established by their father about 1898. Sea Scouts led by Frederick Tilp sailed Potomac waters in their 30-foot skipjack *Silver Cloud* built by Giles and Sam Headley in 1945.

As we reflected on our visits to the Coan with its pastoral views and pleasant shores, it must now appear much as it did a half century ago. Far from metropolitan centers, this river offers refuge from the honk-and-hurry syndrome that sometimes threatens to overwhelm all of us. ☐

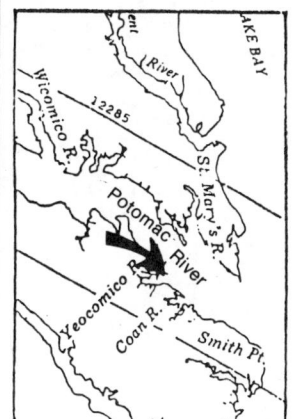

LITTLE WICOMICO RIVER

off the Potomac River, Virginia Shore

Approaching from the south, in good weather, you can start from a point halfway between Smith Point Light and BW N "C79" (this point is about a mile S of the light) and go between the light and Smith Point itself on a course of approximately 342° M, until C "1" is about 400 yards abeam to starboard. Then take 264° M directly to the jetties at the mouth of the creek. The southern jetty carries a light, "1" (Fl 2.5 sec).

The entrance to "Little River," the Little Wicomico, has been a problem which was corrected February 1985 by dredging to eight feet. Work and charter boats carrying five-foot drafts use the entrance routinely. Except on a NW wind and full and new moons, good power is required to fight the current which tears back and forth across the entrance twice daily, so check your current charts as well as your tide tables. In May 1985 a design study to rework the jetties began.

Don Chamblee, owner of Smith Point Marina (804)453-4077, said five feet can be carried from BW N "C79" south of Smith Point Light directly to "2" (Fl R 2.5 sec) off the jetties, and thence on in. Approaching from BW N "43B" you have to run halfway between "2" (Fl R 2.5 sec) and Smith Point Light until Smith Point Light is astern and then turn back hard to "2". You can go directly from C "1" to "2". You cannot go from C "1" to the mouth of the jetties or you will ground on the bar "2" marks. The bottom is not as it appears on the chart.

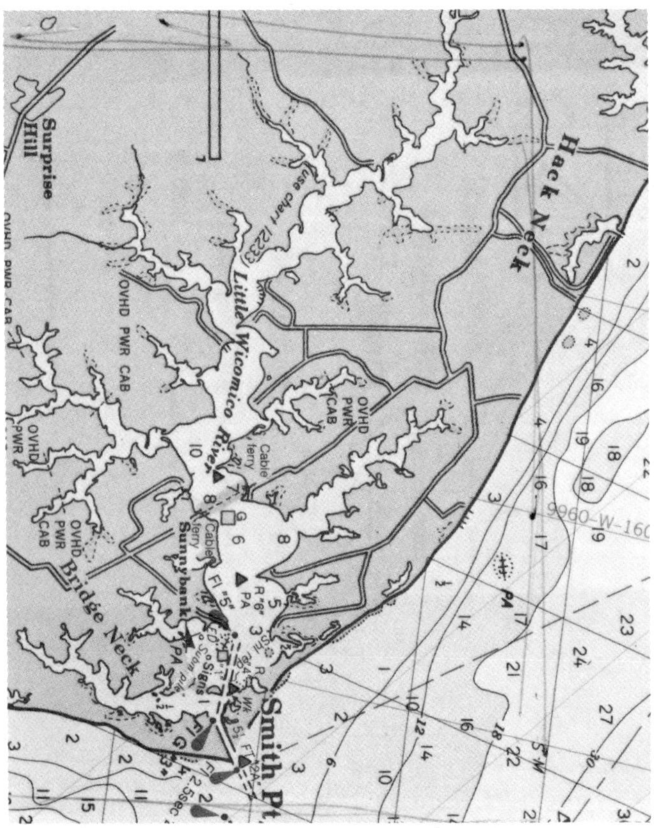

From NOAA Chart 12230—not to be used for navigation.

Once inside, look for each mark very carefully and honor them. Going into Sloop Creek (or Slough Creek, depending on your chart's spelling), you turn to port hard at its entrance "1" just past "4" daymark. There is a port shoal marked sometimes by a buoy which is between "4" and "5" in the main channel. Then you head for a "BP" gas sign on the shore. It is in Don's front yard; "2" is almost in line with the BP sign and at it you swing to starboard. Then the marks are "3"-"5"-"7"-"8".

Numbers "5" and "7" are on each side of a sandbar, and when you honor them you will almost be cutting a man's grass, but honor them. It looks tricky the first time in, but it is simple once you've done it. Strangers come to grief because they don't look hard enough for the marks, or don't believe it when they see them. In a narrow channel the marks are set on the shoal to leave the channel for the boats. Give marks a clearance.

You can also call Point Lookout Marine Operator and place a telephone call to Don Chamblee [(804)453-4077] to ask for existing local conditions. Don would probably be the one to have to come rescue you if you have a problem. Or call Smith Point General Rescue Ch 16 VHF and they will talk you in. Commercial boats work CB 21 and 9 is the emergency CB channel.

Of the marinas inside, Smith Point Marina caters more to transients with overnight slips available. Jett's Marina, across the river, is more of a convenience to the local boaters, having no transient slips (although Gene Jett allows as how he could probably tie up a boat in an emergency). Jett's gas dock is attended only in the early morning, at noon, and in the late afternoon; but Smith Point Marina is a full service marina. And arrangements can be made there for transportation to a nearby restaurant or for supplies.

Further up the Little Wicomico is Andy Cockrell's Marine Railway, offering hull and engine repairs, and nearby is J.D. Krentz & Son Marine Railway.

It is in the upper reaches that "Little River" is most beautiful, with many coves and creeks offering good protection in a natural, unspoiled setting where you can actually spot an occasional bald eagle wheeling in the sunlight above the river's placid waters. ☐

Note: In Little Wicomico River, a submerged object has been reported in the vicinity of the jetties at approx. 37-53-32N; 76-14-40W.

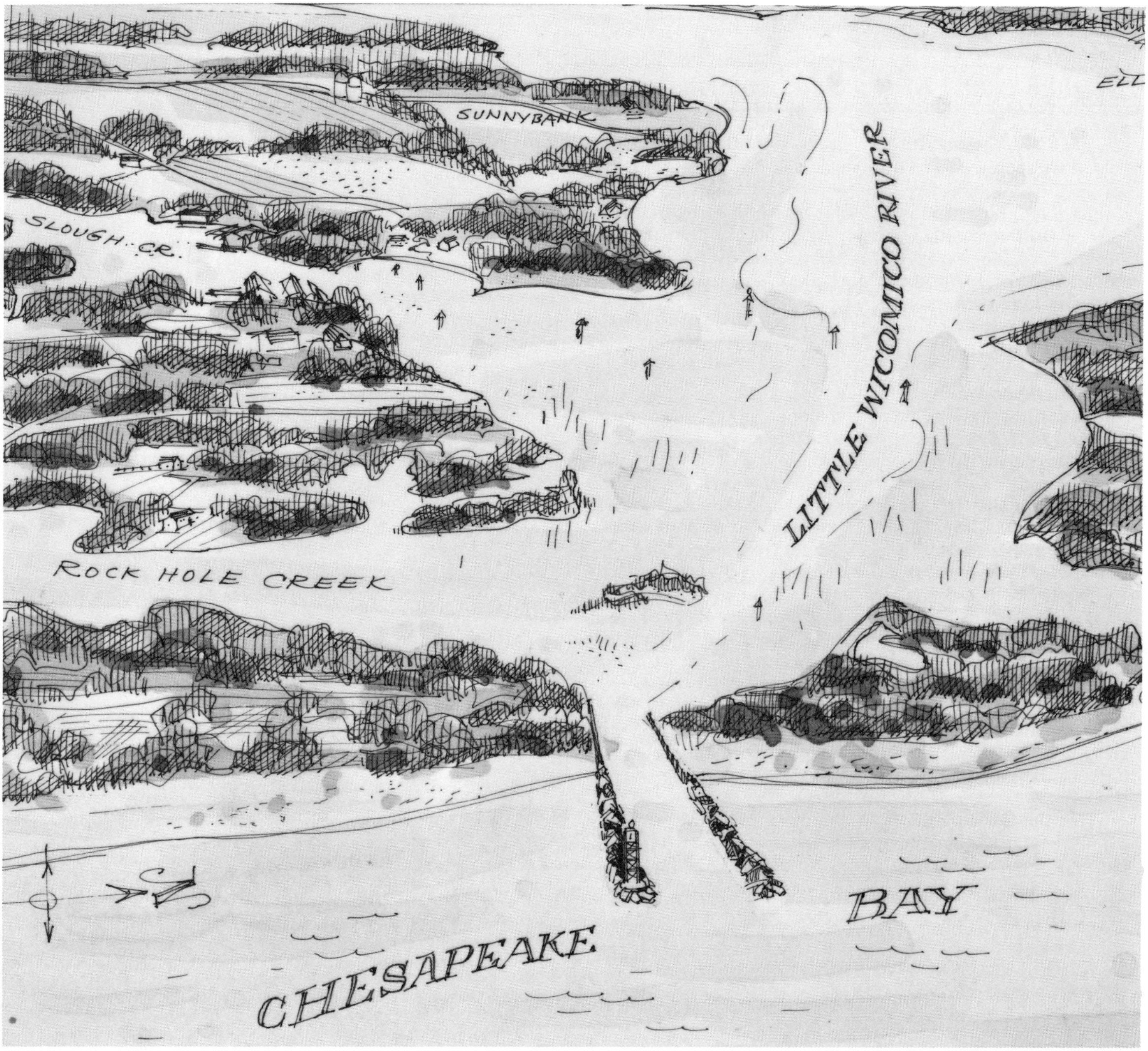
SUNNYBANK
SLOUGH CR.
LITTLE WICOMICO RIVER
ROCK HOLE CREEK
CHESAPEAKE
BAY

Notes

LOWER BAY:
SMITH AND TANGIER ISLANDS TO CAPE CHARLES

The lower Chesapeake Bay once was involved mainly in the seafood industry with little emphasis on tourism; therefore, not many yachtsmen were familiar with the beautiful cruising grounds here. But the modernization of Norfolk, right on the heels of Baltimore's Inner Harbor, is giving the lower Bay a tourist appeal all its own. Yet the deep, quiet rivers still make this section an ideal place to find peace and tranquility.

If you take the time to explore this area, most any of its creeks and rivers offer enough varied anchorages to suit the most avid cruiser.

Northern Virginia, where it touches the Chesapeake Bay just south of the Potomac, is a fairly untraveled area; and this is the reason more and more cruising people are becoming attracted to it. There are seven navigable creeks between the Potomac and the Rappahannock, all having deep water and bordered by small farms and woods. Whether you choose the Great Wicomico, the many creeks on the Northern Neck of Virginia or the Rappahannock, you will find pastoral quiet and charm that sets this area apart from any other on Chesapeake Bay.

This lower Bay section also provides an all-around beauty, cruisability and friendliness unmatched anywhere. Tree-covered banks and beautiful homes typify the landscape. Hundreds of inlets and creeks offer possibilities for exploration and a view of nature at her finest in any season of the year. The lower Bay abounds with fish and wildlife, with commercial fishing being a mainstay of the industry of the area. Boat-building on the Piankatank River combines with the distinct feeling of antebellum Virginia that you get while cruising the York and James Rivers.

Like the C&D Canal, Norfolk and Cape Charles are the beginning, providing the spot where mariners begin their journeys southward on the IntraCoastal Waterway.

Lower Bay Charts:

12205	12236
12210	12237
12220	12238
12221	12241
12222	12243
12223	12245
12224	12248
12225	12251
12226	12253
12228	12254
12231	12256
12235	

PHOTO BY BOB GRIESER

PHOTO BY BACKUS AERIAL PHOTOGRAPHY

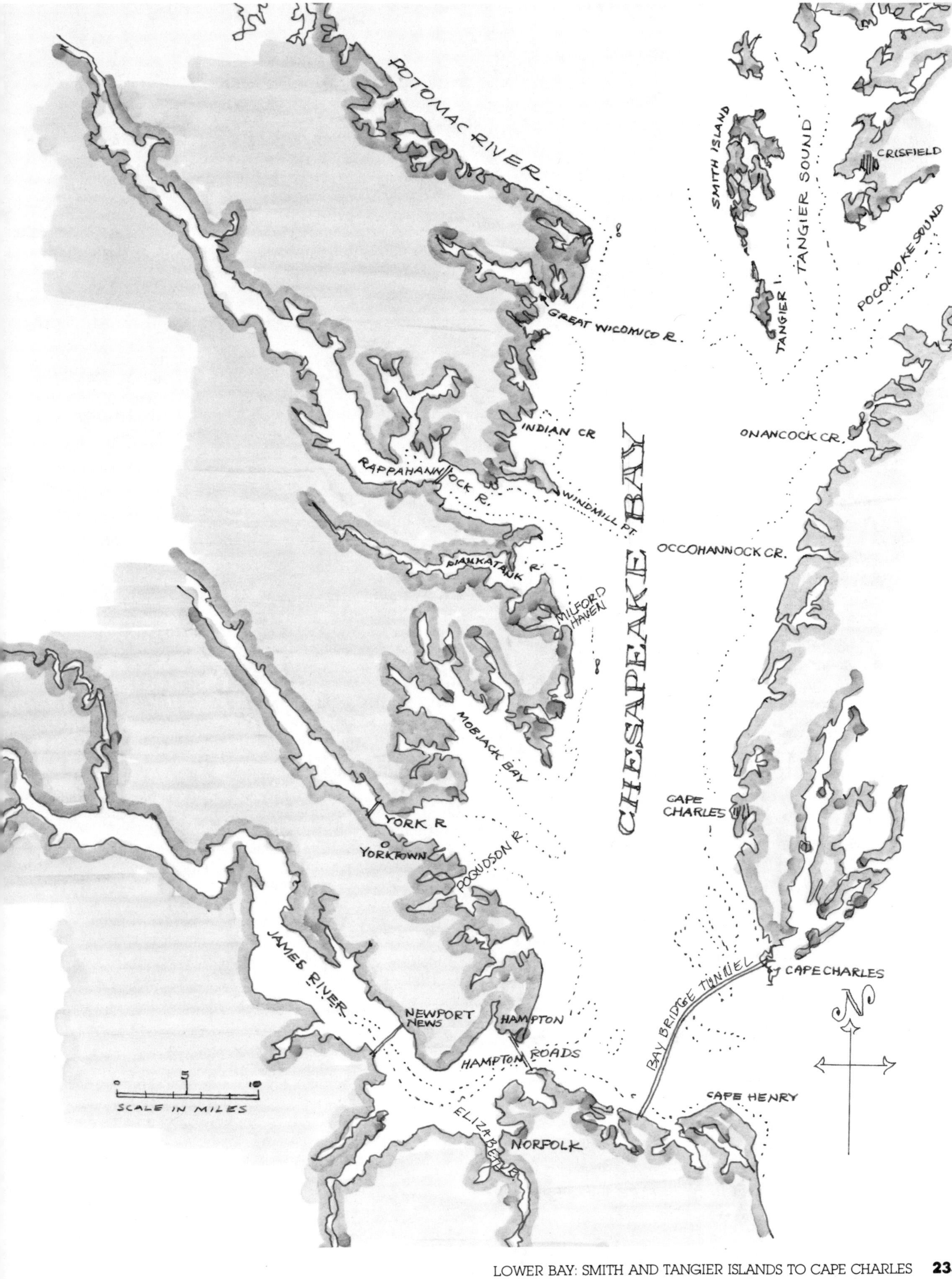
POTOMAC RIVER
SMITH ISLAND
TANGIER SOUND
CRISFIELD
POCOMOKE SOUND
TANGIER I.
GREAT WICOMICO R.
INDIAN CR
ONANCOCK CR.
RAPPAHANNOCK R.
WINDMILL PT.
CHESAPEAKE BAY
OCCOHANNOCK CR.
PIANKATANK R.
MILFORD HAVEN
MOBJACK BAY
CAPE CHARLES
YORK R
YORKTOWN
POQUOSON R.
JAMES RIVER
BAY BRIDGE TUNNEL
CAPE CHARLES
N
NEWPORT NEWS
HAMPTON
HAMPTON ROADS
0 5 10
SCALE IN MILES
CAPE HENRY
ELIZABETH R.
NORFOLK

CHANCE ON DEAL ISLAND

In Tangier Sound

It's been many years since we've travelled extensively on Tangier Sound. And although Crisfield is a more popular cruising spot for us nowadays, our first stopover in the Tangier Sound area was at Chance on Deal Island. From our dock on the upper Magothy we made our way there by stages, visiting along the way the old favorites of St. Michaels, Oxford, and Cambridge before taking the long leg to Solomons on the Patuxent River.

I mention Solomons here because that's the route we took to Chance a few months ago, which provided a couple of interesting sights along the way. For instance, on course 123° half-way from the old Cedar Point Lighthouse to the black bell #1 that marks the entrance to Hooper Strait you pass within a stone's throw of beautiful Hooper Island Light. To me this is one of the best examples of the iron caisson light structures on the Chesapeake Bay. Its lower portion is painted a bottom-paint red and the gently tapered upper cylinder, which housed the living quarters, is a sparkling white. The parapet is circled by a graceful iron railing, and on top of that is the light itself. The light was constructed in 1902 and stands about three miles offshore of Hooper Island.

On the same course 123° in another five and a half miles you'll pick up the black bell #1 that is the turning mark to head up into Hooper Strait.

If it were still there, you'd be able to see Hooper Strait Light. That lovely cottage-style structure had deteriorated to the point that it was about to be dismantled by the Coast Guard. Instead, in 1966 the Chesapeake Bay Maritime Museum acquired the light and moved it to their grounds in St. Michaels, Maryland, where it is on permanent display.

Now, only the iron platform remains, with its stubby little automated light. If you follow course 69° (approx.), you'll find nun #2 and shortly after that, on about the same course, the present-day Hooper Strait Light. Beyond the light is the low-lying peninsula ending at Bishops Head and a small cluster of white buildings that sparkle in the late afternoon sun.

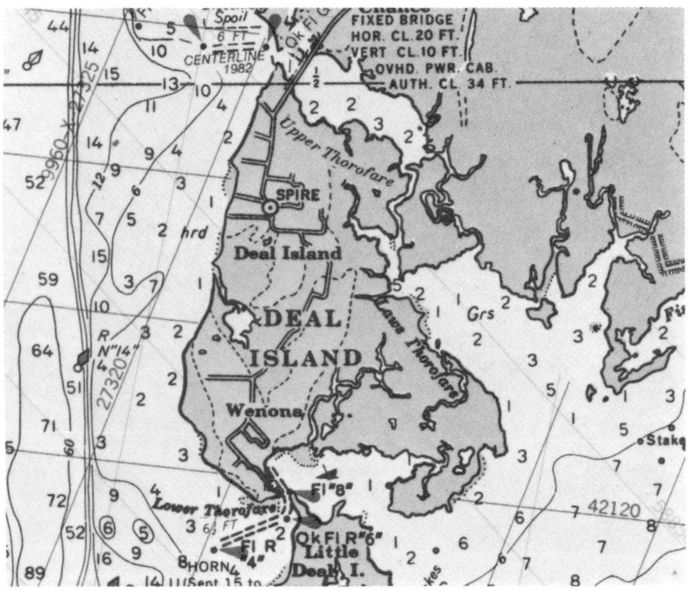

From NOAA Chart 12230—not to be used for navigation.

The light at Sharkfin Shoal was a disappointment, though. From such a descriptive name I was expecting a more imposing light structure, but found instead the same rusting iron platform with an automated light. This, too, was once a screw-pile cottage-style lighthouse, but was demolished in the mid-1960's. An automated light now marks Sharkfin Shoal.

The entrance to Chance is only two miles from Sharkfin Shoal Light, and here's where the crab floats become a hazard to the yachtsman. This is "crab country" and the floats seem to be everywhere, so be careful. If you approach Chance from the south, the same entrance markers are approximately thirteen miles north of the James Island Light off Crisfield.

The entrance to the harbor is easy to negotiate, but from offshore looks more complicated than it really is. The channel is straight for 600 yards or so, then makes a right-hand turn inside a sturdy stone jetty to starboard. To port, a sandy beach is usually busy with people fishing and picnicing.

The basin at Chance is snug and ample for most any size group, and there is six feet of water almost right up to shore. To port is a marina with restaurant and bar. However, when we pulled in for fuel, the facility was closed for the day. Since almost all business in Chance is centered around the waterman's schedule, we were told they would be open next day from 6 A.M. till 2 P.M.

On the south side of the harbor you can also get gas and water. Remember, though, this is a working waterman's harbor; you'll have to compete for dock or bulkhead space. There is a seafood packing business on the south shore where we were able to buy ice, but they open early and complete their transactions shortly after noontime. So come early when the office is open.

The east side of the harbor is fenced off by a highway bridge that separates the main harbor from a much-larger body of water called Upper Thorofare, which shows from 1½-foot to 3-foot depths. If you need less than a ten-foot vertical clearance, you could explore this end also.

Chance is home port for a half dozen working skipjacks, and it was interesting to stroll the docks and examine this vanishing breed of workboat closeup.

Our first visit here to Chance was quite an adventure, and one of those rare times that we tied up for the night at a marina. Just across from our slip was a large ferry boat, beached on the harbor's north shore. After dinner we walked across the marsh to investigate, but hordes of fierce mosquitoes forced a hasty retreat. That night sleep came easily—so easily that I slept through a wild and lightning-streaked storm that had Dixie and the ladies from the other boat scurrying around checking our dock lines. That must have been quite a sight—wind howling, nightgowns flapping, and angry voices trying to rouse me from my deep sleep! Needless to say, I was soundly scolded next morning.

The ferry boat is no longer there, and thus the main harbor is a good deal roomier. There was ample room for our three-boat raft. This time we were cruising in *Moon Song's* 32 feet of splendor, drifting lazily at anchor under a clear, diamond-studded sky. No storms, no hassle. I found myself wondering why we hadn't come back sooner. □

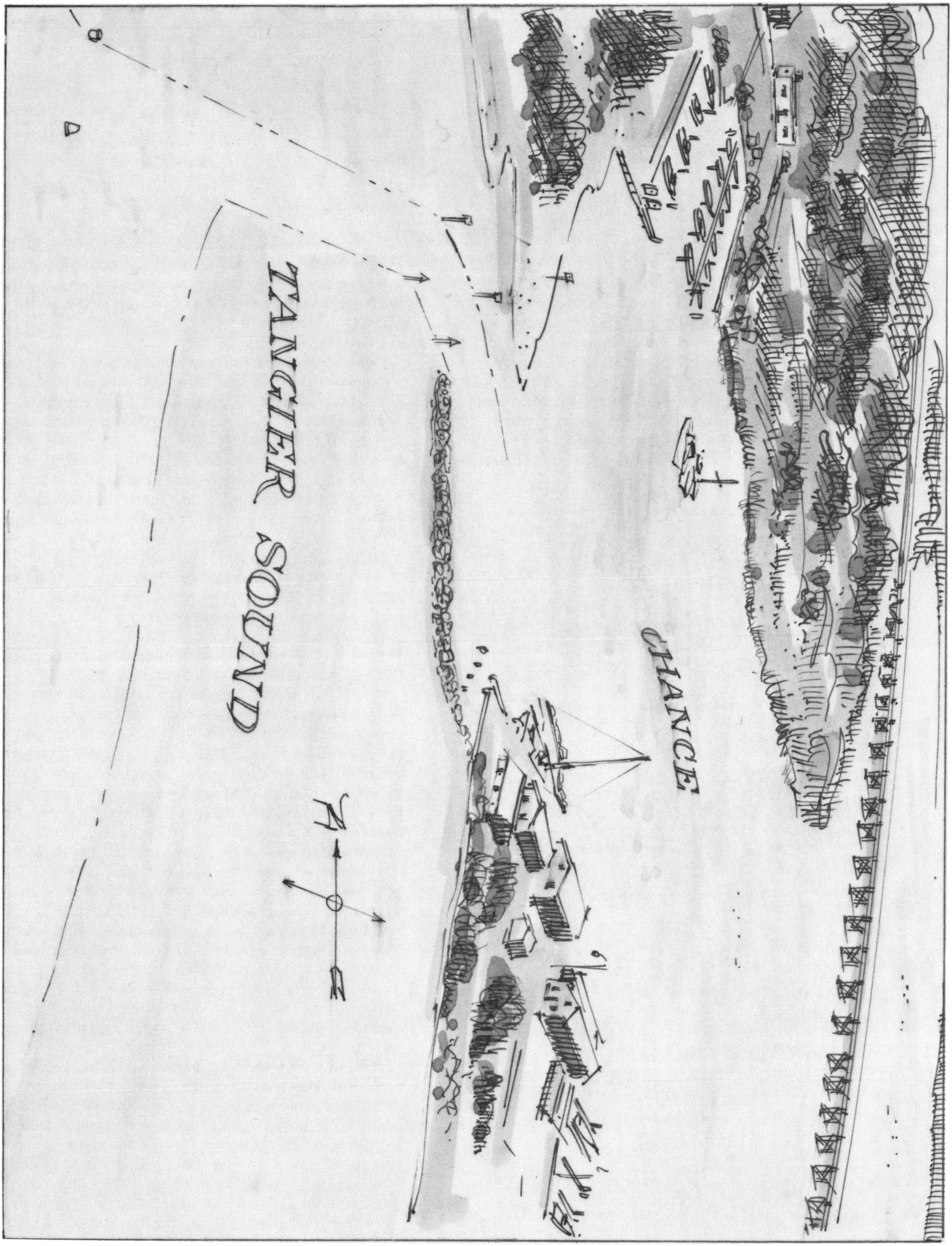
TANGIER SOUND
CHANCE
N

SMITH AND TANGIER ISLANDS

on the Chesapeake Bay

Whether you are new to boating on the Chesapeake or have been cruising the Bay for years, no other place holds the romantic lure of the two water-surrounded colonies of Tangier and Smith Islands. Located off the mouth of the Potomac River, these two islands and their inhabitants are completely cut off from land and are visited chiefly by boat (Tangier can be reached by airplane). And therein lies their charm.

Several years ago on our first visit to Smith Island we became involved in a conversation with an inhabitant and, after many questions about his island and its history, we mentioned our plans to visit his southern neighbor, Tangier Island, later that summer. To which he replied, "They're a little funny down there."

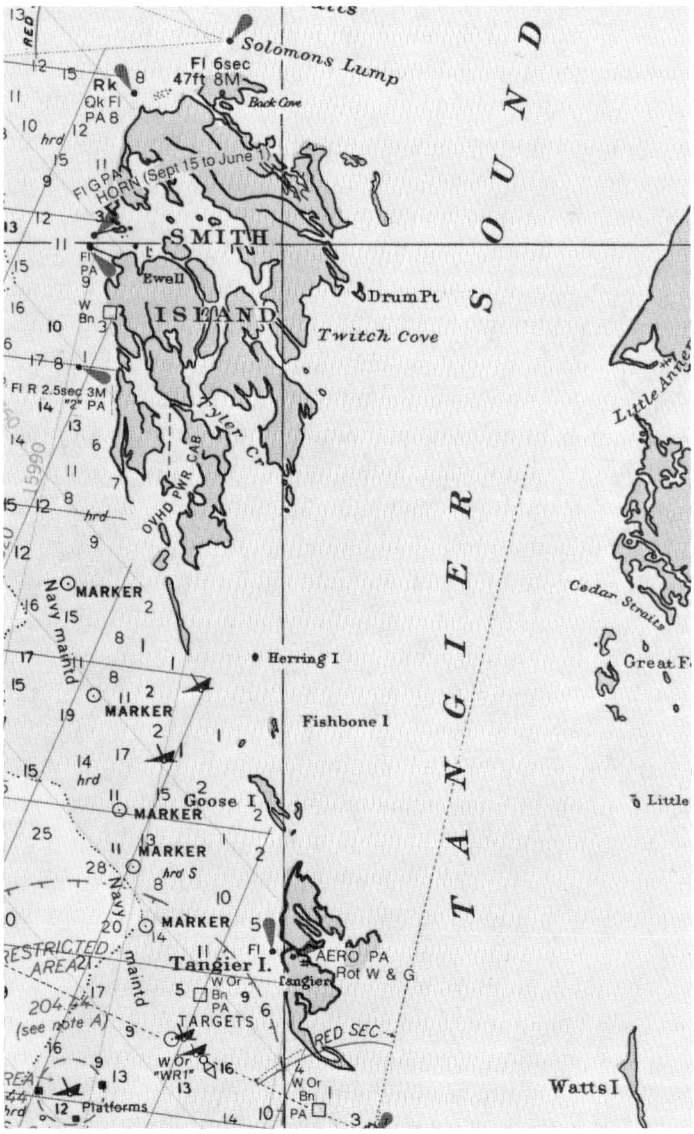

From NOAA Chart 12220—not to be used for navigation.

A couple of months passed before we were able to get t Tangier, and as we tied up at their "boat parking" dock, w were greeted by Frank Dize, who chatted with us briefly abou the island and its history. When we commented that earlier o we had visited Smith Island, he responded solemnly, "Yo know, they're a little funny up there."

This shy attitude is the natural outgrowth of a communit isolated from the world. And yet, little by little, the outsid world is making an impression on these proud, self-relian people. Electric power plants on the island now assure powe service to the islanders, whereas a few short years ago a electricity came from the mainland. Television antenna sprout from the roofs of many homes, and with the additio of boat tours, visitors to and from the mainland are mor frequent. And yet, with all this, the Tangiermen still spea with the same English brogue—faintly Elizabethan or Cornish– that their forefathers of 350 years ago spoke.

According to *Chesapeake Kaleidoscope* (by Anne Hay and Harriet Hazleton), there is some thought that the tw islands were at one time one big island. Today there is one va shoal and a sprinkling of marsh that all but connects the tw From the Bay you can see a string of telephone poles bridgin the gap between the two islands.

Both Smith and Tangier Islands have two entrances—or from the Bay and another from Tangier Sound. If yo approach the islands from the west (by far the easier entranc for either island), be aware of the U.S. Navy target ships ju offshore. The most famous of these is the *San Marcos* wreck about seven miles southwest of Tangier. The San Marcos the renamed battleship *Texas,* which the Navy towed to i present site, used for target practice, and sank in 191 (according to *This Was Chesapeake Bay* by Robert Burgess This underwater wreck is said to be responsible for the sinkin of seven boats, and even today it could pose a danger t watermen since it is suspected there are still live shells an bombs at the site. There is another target ship west of Kedge Strait to the north of Smith Island, about five miles offshor

There are three bombing targets west of Tangier at distance of one and one-half to three miles. These are easy t spot and are marked on your charts within a large restricte area. For full meanings of "restricted" and "prohibited" area refer to the *U.S. Coast Pilot.* In brief, they say: "No vessel permitted within the prohibited area without prior permissic of authorized agency. No vessel is permitted within a restricte area when firing is in progress. A warning that firing is, or wi soon be, in progress will be indicated by a red flag displaye from one of the six dolphin platforms on the perimeter of th prohibited area or by patrol vessels within the danger zone c by aircraft buzzing your boat." The target areas can b dangerous and should be avoided.

The best time to enter Smith Island is at high tid particularly if your boat draws over 4½ feet. The entrance protected by two stone jetties. Offshore about ¾ mi from the end of the jetties is a black and white can. From th

Photos by Bob Grieser

KEDGES STRAITS
SOLOMONS LUMP
FISHING PT.
BACK COVE
TERRAPIN SAND SPIT
BIG THOROFARE
EWELL
DRUM PT.
TWITCH COVE
BAY
SMITH ISLAND
RHODES POINT
TYLERTON
HOG NECK
HORSE HAMMOCK
HORSE HAMMOCK PT.
SHANKS CR.
SOUTH PT.
CHESAPEAKE
TANGIER SOUND
HERRING I.
GOOSE ISLAND
QUEEN RIDGE
TANGIER ISLAND
TANGIER
WHALE PT.
SAND SPIT
PROHIBITED AREA
SCALE IN MILES
1
0
1
2
3
N

can take course 095° to the lighted spars at the mouth of the jetties. Unless it's very foggy or "raining cats and dogs," you should have no trouble finding these marks. The advice we had was to not stick too close to the red marks, but rather favor the port side of the channel.

The entire channel is well marked and should give you no trouble; it runs generally easterly for about three-quarters of a mile before turning south. Water depths here are 7 to 14 feet. The next leg of the channel is the shallowest, with depths shown on the chart of 4½ feet. We entered at high tide and measured seven to nine feet except between marks #14 and #15. In fact, even at its shallowest (near spar #15) the channel was a little over six feet. But remember, this was a high tide; so if you enter at low tide, this spot could indeed be around 4½ feet. A current that can be as strong as two knots runs through the channel and can make tying up in the town a little tricky.

As you turn east after #15 you will see, on both sides of the channel, several shedding houses with watermen culling softshell crabs. (Both Smith and Tangier are homeports of impressive workboat fleets, and crabs are an important part of their economy.) Within a hundred yards of #15 to starboard is a small basin where much of the workboat fleet ties up here in the village of Ewell. If you ask, you can tie up to one of the pilings and dinghy ashore to the dock. We've done this in past years, but without a dinghy you'd have no way to get ashore except to swim. These pilings may be a little hard to spot at first, but they are located on the north side of the small tie up basin at Ewell. Other pilings are on the north side of the main channel just east of the basin.

Another place to tie up is at the private dock adjacent to the gas dock on the main channel. Just beyond the basin you will see a dock with "No Trespassing" signs. Further over is a private section of bulkhead next to the gas dock. This is where many transient boats tie up for the night, but ask permission first. Remember, the islanders earn their livelihood by the water, and being able to dock and unload their catch is important to them. If no tie up is available and it's getting late, a small anchorage is located east of marker #9 at the end of the first leg of the western approach to the island. This anchorage is exposed to wind and inconvenient for going ashore, but is known to local watermen as the only possible anchoring spot in the area.

There are two restaurants that are easily reached from the docks. On the road south past the Methodist Church you will find the small, white house where Mrs. Kitching serves meals. This is one of the most famous eating places on the Chesapeake Bay. Seafood is her specialty, as it is with other restaurants on the islands, and the meals are served family style. Across from Mrs. Kitching's is a general grocery store where you can pick up supplies and cube ice. When we inquired at the general store across from the church and graveyard in Ewell about the purchase of alcoholic beverages, specifically beer, we were told it is not sold on the island.

Further south on the same road there is another restaurant at the community of Rhodes Point. You might want to rent a bike to get there if you don't feel like walking a mile and a half, especially on a hot, sunny day!

There are several boarding houses that take guests from the mainland, either overnight or for longer periods. For all restaurant or overnight accommodations, it is recommended that you call ahead for reservations. Mrs. Frances Kitching can be reached at (301)425-3321; and Mrs. Bernice Guy at (301)425-2751; or contact the Maryland Office of Tourist Development toll-free (in Maryland) at (301)492-7126 an (outside Maryland)(800)638-5252.

Mosquitoes were no big problem on Smith Island when w were there, but biting flies were! However, long slacks kep them at bay. The only distraction while walking the island wa melted road tar. In the hot, summer sun there were places o the road that were really sticky. My advice would be to carr some sandals for shore walking and take them off when yo get back to your boat. I found that lamp oil will get most c the tar off shoes and boat. This is a slight inconvenience, mor than offset by the friendly people of Smith Island and th interesting village life.

A highlight of Smith Island in the summertime is the sigh of many flowering pomegranate bushes. They seem to b everywhere, and their glossy, dark green foliage and brillian red-orange blossoms add a cheerful note to the neat yard

The third community on Smith Island is Tylerton, dow on Tyler Ditch. This is a pretty village, but unfortunately can be reached only by boat. The ideal method of travel is b small dinghy with an outboard. The waterway around Tylerto is busy with crab shedding pens and houses, and workboat bustling about.

Ashore in Tylerton you will find the same neat homes an yards, as well as a grocery store and a recently complete primary school. The children attend high school in Crisfiel traveling daily on the mail boat, or commuting on weekend

From Ewell out the back-door channel, called the "Bi Thorofare," to Tangier Sound requires following a four-mil plus winding route that can be a little unnerving—particularl with a cross current or cross wind. It's easy to be blow sideways out of the channel without realizing it.

The Coast Guard Local Notice to Mariners reported tha the Big Thorofare Channel and Twitch Cove were dredged i early spring, 1982. We've been warned of a tendency to shoal i the vicinity of marker #33 near Tyler Ditch. And while we hav heard of many people going aground coming into or leavin Smith Island by way of this channel, we had no trouble, al though we prefer the western entrance. Either way, the visit t Smith Island is well worth it.

Tangier Island, like Smith, has two entrances. We entere by way of the eastern, or Tangier Sound, side, which has 8- feet. The Bay-side has been dredged to 9 feet.

Entering from Tangier Sound is quite easy. From blac bell #5 (about 1½ miles offshore) take course 245°. This wi take you right into the channel to the main public boat basi in Tangier. The channel is quite wide and very well marke To port just before the docks is a fairly large cove. The wate in the cove are extremely shallow, and the overhead powerli makes any side trip very dangerous. In 1979 a visitor in a sma sailboat was killed when his boat's mast struck the powerlin

The western entrance, that from the Chesapeake Bay, i easier to navigate, provided you can avoid the many restricte target ship areas. Offshore about 1¼ miles is a white an orange daymark, and the entrance channel is marked by lighted spar #1 about two hundred yards offshore. The channel i

Note: Shoaling has been reported in Big Thorofare Channel t 5 ft. between daybeacons "4" and "8"; to 5 ft. between "14" an "15"; to 5 ft between "29" and light "31"; and to 3½ ft. betwee "31" and Tyler Creek daybeacon "1."

at least 6 feet deep at low tide, reports the skipper of the tour boat *Captain Thomas*, despite the 3-foot depth indicated on chart 12228.

At the boat basin you may see one of several tour boats tied up so their passengers can go ashore to see the island and eat at Mrs. Crockett's restaurant. Just past these docks the channel turns to starboard and passes beneath an overhead power cable. Height at high tide is 50 feet, so if your mast is over 50 feet high, you should enter from the western side.

As you pass the next several large waterside buildings and docks you will see a number of workboats side by side in slips on the south side of the channel. Just east of the slips is a large boathouse with gas pumps where you can inquire about a slip. Not knowing better, we just moved into an empty slip, then walked ashore to find the marina owner, who ok'd our selection.

While we were setting our dock lines, five other pleasure boats came searching for slips; and a couple of young men began moving the moored workboats out of their slips, tying them all together at the bulkhead, and making room for the visitors.

There are two roadways on Tangier Island, running parallel in a southerly direction. Between them is a gut that cuts through the marshes, and a series of small bridges connect the two roads. Tangier Island is somewhat tighter than Smith Island, and the yards (all of which seem to be enclosed by chain-link fences) are small and neat. It is not uncommon to see frontyard graves, since the unsettled part of the island is largely marsh.

PHOTO BY BOB GRIESER

The islands were first explored in 1608 by John Smith, who, legend has it, first named them Russells Isles after Walter Russell, the physician accompanying him. Most famous of Tangier Island inhabitants is Joshua Thomas who came to be called the Parson of the Islands. Born in 1776, he married and established a home on Tangier Island, where he became attracted to the Methodist preachers who visited from time to time. Parson Thomas soon began to hold prayer meetings in the early 1800's, both on Tangier and Smith Islands. It wasn't long before he was spreading his ministry to the mainland in a small sailing skiff which he named *Methodist.*

During the War of 1812 British forces quartered 12,000 troops on Tangier Island and Joshua Thomas was, from time to time, required to hold services for them. In July when the British troops were about to leave for an attack on Baltimore, Joshua Thomas was asked to preach; and with great courage, he predicted the failure of their mission.

The most famous restaurant on Tangier Island is Hilda Crockett's located on the main road south of the boat docks. It's a short, pleasant walk and you will be surprised at the throngs of islanders on the roadway. Bikes and motor bikes are the favorite mode of transportation. South of the Methodist Church the road takes a jog past a small graveyard, and just beyond, on the left is Mrs. Crockett's Chesapeake House.

There is another restaurant, The Bayside Inn, on the next road west, just south of the tiny airport. It also has a few rooms for visitors who would like to stay over.

As we were eating at Mrs. Crockett's, we became involved in conversation with some folks across the table who had just flown down from New Jersey for the day and a meal at Mrs. Crockett's! Perhaps this will give you some idea of how popular and famous this place is.

As you leave Tangier, you might meet the *Captain Thomas* tour boat out of Reedville, her decks lined with people from the mainland eager to visit this isolated island where the people have changed little in almost 400 years. (See Cockrell Creek cruise for information on cruises and tours of Smith and Tangier.)

And this is what draws us all back to the islands, the people who have accepted little change over the years. It's as if they know, deep inside, that civilization has too many drawbacks. You can feel it all around you—that if the rest of the world fell apart there would always be a Tangier and Smith Island, with sandspits and marshes and the sea. After all, theirs is a heritage of almost four centuries of self-reliance. Judging from the numbers of people who visit the islands, they may be right. □

CRISFIELD

on Tangier Sound

Crisfield, which calls itself the "Seafood Capital of the Country," lies down in the southwest part of Somerset County on the Chesapeake Bay. Like Oxford, she sits on the shore with her feet in the water. From *Chesapeake Kaleidoscope* we learned that the last commercial sailing schooner on the Bay, the *Anna and Helen,* sank in Crisfield's harbor in 1958.

From Tangier Sound, the entrance is well marked by Janes Island Light, a skeleton tower on a cylindrical base, topped by a small house; it's almost 40 feet high. The channel is very easy to follow, being marked by C "1" and then daybeacons and lights. Once inside the Little Annemessex River the surrounding waters are not very deep; but the channel is quite wide enough and carries eight feet of water all the way into Somers Cove Marina.

On our visit we entered Somers Cove and found ample protection from the elements. Somers Cove Marina offers transient slips for visiting yachtsmen who may wish to go ashore and walk around the town. When we entered the cove, the wind was blowing 15-20 knots, and we had difficulty approaching the gas dock. So instead we motored across the cove into the lee of the Coast Guard station and dropped our anchor. We spent the night in the company of a 36-foot Dickerson ketch sailed by two ladies who also scorned the idea of a night at the docks.

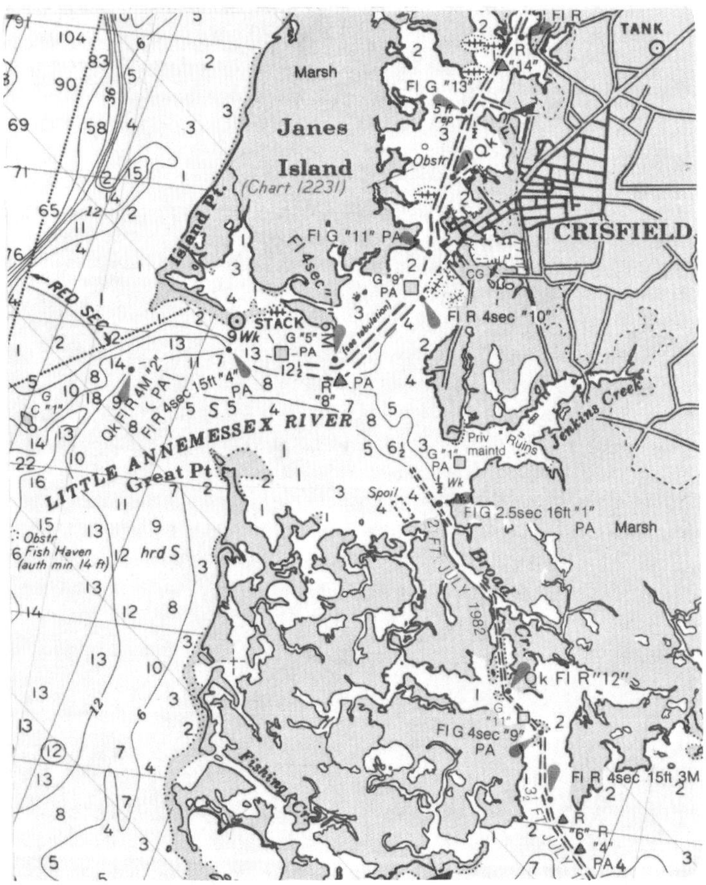

From NOAA Chart 12230—not to be used for navigation.

Several years ago the state of Maryland invested $6 million or more in an expansion of the Somers Cove Marina. The expansion includes a Tawes Boating/Visitors Center, which houses a library and museum collection related to the political career of former Governor J. Millard Tawes, a native son. It is touted as "the biggest small boat facility on the East Coast." Along with the marina expansion, two motels (Somers Cove Motel and The Pines) added a total of 40 rooms.

Should you wish to spend the night in the marina, and are unable to reach them on VHF channel 16 (they usually aren't listening, judging by the number of boats we heard call without a response), stand off the gas dock and hail the office. Someone will come out and assign you a slip and issue directions. If you anchor out, you can pull your dinghy up on shore at the marina. Information on cruises to and from Smith and Tangier can be obtained at the marina.

Crisfield is a fascinating little town. It is truly a seafood capital as the sights and smells will testify. The shells of millions of harvested oysters form the foundations of the shucking houses of today. The seafood houses are scattered around in reckless disregard for order, many of them on the island known as Jersey. The same sheds where hard crabs are picked in the summer serve for oyster shucking in the winter. The crab pickers here are known to pick a hundred pounds of meat in a single day! Crabbing as an industry began about 1873 when a shipment of soft crabs was sent from Crisfield to Philadelphia.

Very good shopping and provisioning are available within walking distance of the marina, including a supermarket, hardware and marine supplies, a liquor store and a drug store. Fuel prices are quite competitive here, with virtually every facility showing large price signs.

Crisfield has the distinction of being the only town on Chesapeake Bay with a hospital that has access from the water via its own dock and entrance channel (5-ft. draft), located off the river to the north of the town. Should a

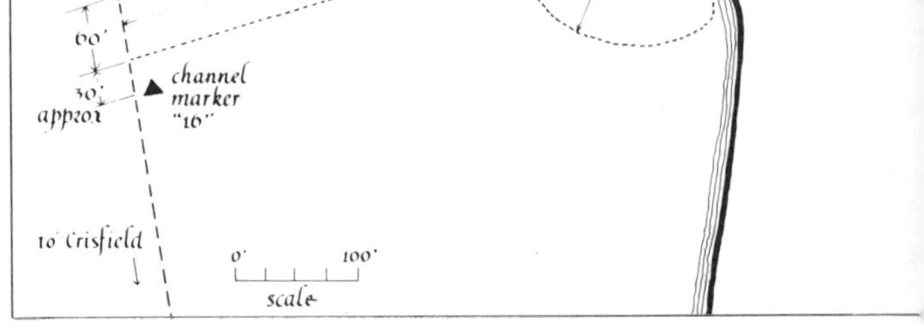

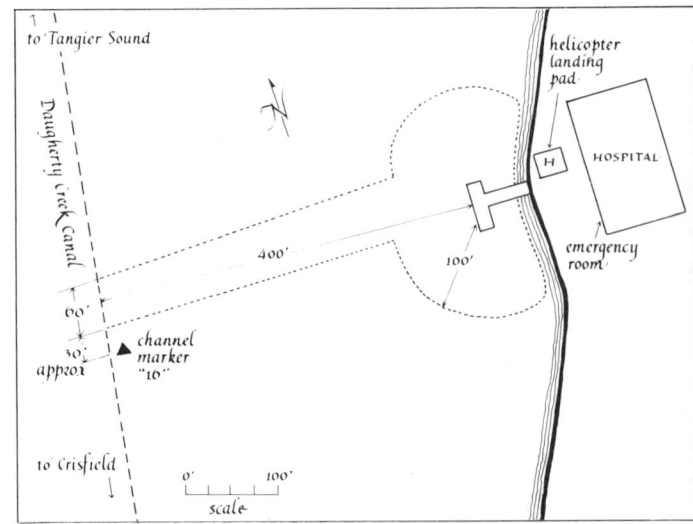

Dredged channel from Daugherty Creek Canal to McCready Hospital.

nedical emergency arise, you can tie up right at the dock and go directly to the emergency room. (See sketch.) The entrance channel is well marked with red buoys.

The original name of the town was Somers Cove. It was built on a 1663 land grant to John Roach and Benjamin Somers. Few of the town's original buildings remain due to the number of large fires which, within a few decades, destroyed the older structures.

For real family fun, the time to visit Crisfield is over the Labor Day weekend during the Annual Hard Crab Derby. Take the kids to watch the crab races or to nearby Deal Island where the skipjacks race on Tangier Sound.

Since Crisfield launched its plan to revitalize its economy, develop its harbor, and promote tourism, the boating family can find more and more of interest in Maryland's "Seafood Capital." □

POCOMOKE RIVER

The tributaries of the Chesapeake Bay have a real diversity of scenery. This is especially notable along the stunning Pocomoke River on Maryland's Eastern Shore. Said to be among the deepest rivers in the world for its width, it meanders a winding 30-mile course from Pocomoke Sound past Snow Hill, flowing through salt marshes and dense tropical-like forests until dwindling to a mere trickle just a few miles, as the crow flies, from the waters of Chincoteague Bay.

Here on the Pocomoke, you will find thick stands of rare and exotic cypress trees, nurtured by underground springs, mingling in profusion with oak, sweet gum, maple, dogwood, etc. There are few banks along the river to mar its beauty and, at high tide, the dense foliage rises directly from the sinister coffee-colored water.

Crisfield is a good spot from which to launch a cruise of the Pocomoke River. A re-check of supplies and a review of NOAA Chart #12230 (Smith to Cove Point) will prepare you for a safe and pleasant trip. There are no convenient gassing facilities between Crisfield and Shad Landing State Park Marina on the upper river, so go prepared. The Coast Guard

PHOTO BY MICHAEL C. WOOTTON

Snow Hill

maintains a station at Crisfield and a check with concerning the variable conditions at the mouth of the plus any available schedules of commercial traffic ar operation of the Pocomoke City bascule bridge w beneficial.

In planning your cruise, allow ample time for the 4 run from Crisfield to Shad Landing. Due to the e schedules of huge barges, anchoring out in the na waterway is discouraged and night travel is advisable or those who are well acquainted with the river.

Departing Crisfield, preferably on the rising tide, pr through Broad Creek into Pocomoke Sound. While trav the Sound, refrain from making short cuts and follow faithfully to avoid tangling with the numerous comm crabpots and fishnets in the area. As you approac entrance to the river, prepare for a 30-minute run throu "cut"—a dredged channel behind Williams Point that hu northern shore and allows a depth of at least four feet, e low tide. Heed all markers, be especially alert, and main maneuverable speed in order to heave-to in the eve narrow channel is occupied by a larger vessel or one infamous barges. The broad sweep of the Sound allows a view of the "cut" even from a distance. It is very importa to deviate from this suggested course; to run aground "cut" with a barge bearing down on you is an unse experience which can be easily avoided. Avoid the "n around the tip of Williams Point which is impassable for drawing more than a foot and a half. Marker #15, a entrance of the Pocomoke, is the only one on the river Shad Landing Marina. After passing it, stay center and the lookout for stumps and submerged objects; from th it should be smooth sailing with proper precautions.

The maneuvers involved in gaining access to the Poco River may tend to intimidate some would-be explorers river—perhaps that is why we have found traffic sparse, e the peak of the summer. However, when you roun interesting hair-pin curve at Shelltown you will probably that the preparations were worth the trouble. The uncro and peaceful ambiance of the Pocomoke makes this tr idyllic experience. Respect the placid solitude of the setti keeping your speed within the required limits.

Gracious homes repose along the shore and the hi colonial mansion, Beverly of Worcester (or Thrum Capp it was known long ago), is a landmark on the easterly near the state line. It is presently occupied and not open public, but its location (on a low bank quite near the w affords a close look at the mansion's interesting archite and curious filigree trim over the entrance.

As you leave Beverly of Worcester, the enticing aura stream beckons you on past the first clumps of fea cypress—as primitive in appearance as the cattle gr nearby, standing knee-deep in the shallows with white perched on their backs.

The winding curves of the river begin to narrow as th hamlet of Rehobeth appears on the portside. Ther

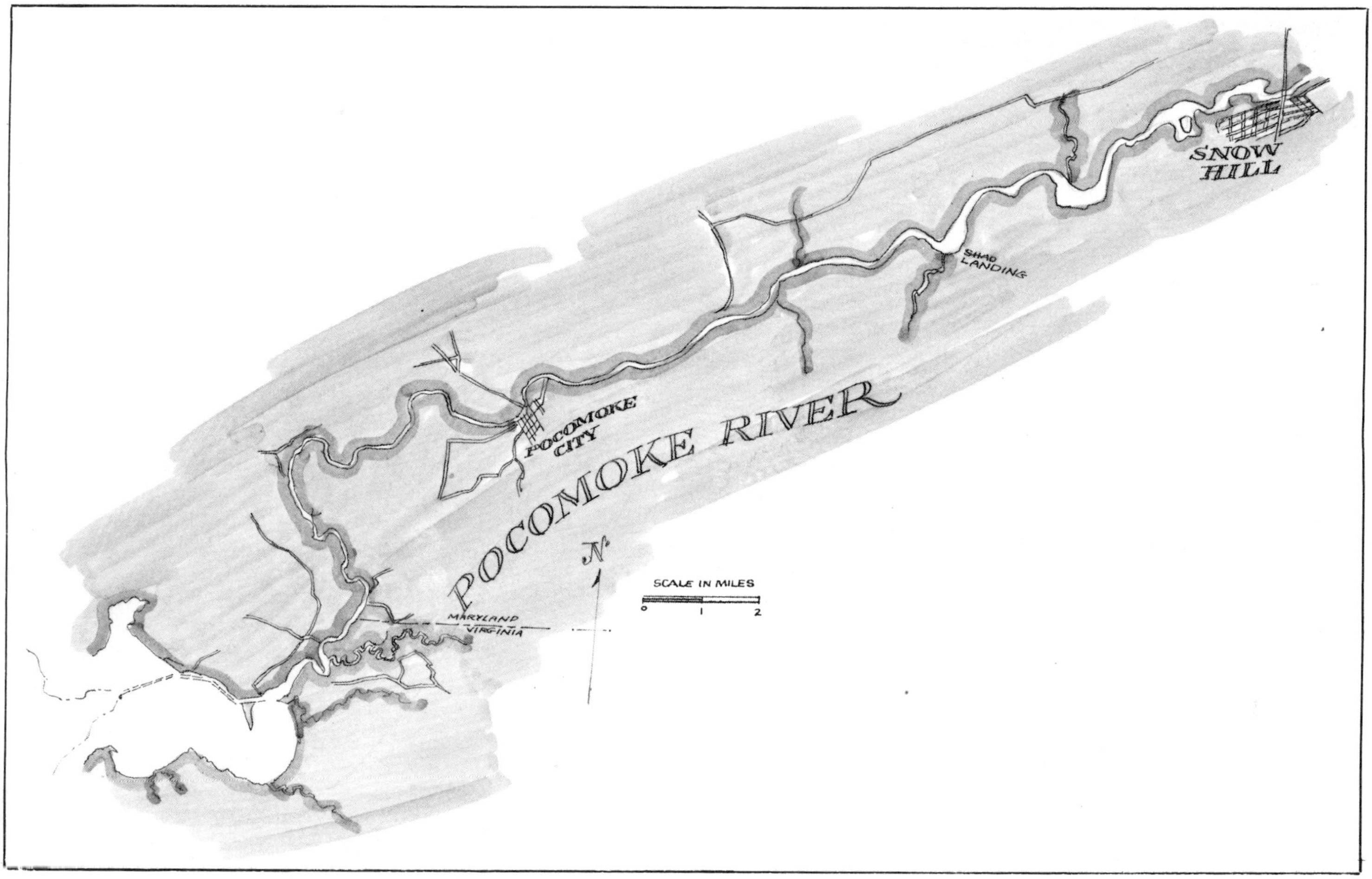

launching ramp and a small sturdy landing where one may tie up and stroll a short distance up the quaint street past a sprinkling of very old homes to the crumbling remains of the Old Coventry Episcopal Church, circa 1784. A trio of enormous sycamore trees, mantled in thick ivy, stand guard over the dank ruins of the church and ancient cemetery. Across the road, is the Presbyterian church founded and built by Francis Makemie in 1705. It is the oldest house of worship of that denomination in our country. The scene is exactly as Hulbert Footner described it in his book, *Rivers of the Eastern Shore*. I dare say much of the scenery along the river remains as it was when he recorded it four decades past.

Past Rehobeth and the marshlands of the lower Pocomoke, dark forests loom, punctuated by an occasional farm or an old manor house. Around a graceful bend in the river, Pocomoke City appears. At this spot the river is spanned now by three bridges: a railway bridge which is obviously no longer used and left permanently open; an interesting old bascule bridge with full-time tender; and a more modern soaring, fixed highway bridge with a clearance of 35 feet. A large and attractive new city dock, bordering a pleasant waterfront park, has recently been expanded to include both sides of the bascule bridge. Groceries and sundries are just a short walk up Market Street or across the bridge and an open-air market with fresh farm produce is adjacent to the city dock. Side streets of the city reveal some very attractive Victorian homes with well-kept dooryards blooming with old-fashioned flowers.

When you leave Pocomoke City, you will want to maintain a leisurely speed on the way up to Shad Landing in order to fully enjoy the natural beauty and wildlife of the river. A multitude of wildflowers bloom along the banks. The exquisite cardinal flower, with brilliant red spikes of blossoms, is an endangered species, but grows in great abundance in this area.

Bald eagles, great blue heron, kingfishers, and rare varieties of flycatchers are among the many wildfowl that thrive in the opulent wilderness of the Pocomoke River State Forest creating a bird-watchers paradise. It is said that no other Atlantic inland area supports a greater number of species.

There are two separate areas of Pocomoke River State Park: a few miles past Pocomoke City, you will see (on the north bank) Milburn Landing Area with no marina, but a small dock and launching ramp; and higher up the river on the opposite shore is the entrance to Shad Landing, which is clearly marked. There is easy access to the marina which is located on a wide canal. The slips can be reserved by calling (301)632-2566. Pets are not allowed anywhere within the boundaries of the park. There are many nature trails for hikers, and bicycles are available. One hundred and twenty campsites are rented on a space-available basis—an inducement to those with trailerable boats. The Atlantic beaches are only a short drive from Shad Landing. Marina facilities are open from Memorial Day through Labor Day, but openings and closing of all facilities may vary slightly according to weather conditions and demand.

Historic and picturesque Snow Hill is a distance of four lovely, wandering miles up the river from Shad Landing and the river is navigable for another two miles past the small highway bridge by boats with shallow draft. However, the part-time tender requires a five-hour advance notice to open the bridge. Snow Hill has some lovely churches and a small museum. A brochure from the office at Shad Landing will guide you on the tour and provide information. □

ONANCOCK CREEK

on the Eastern Shore

If you're coming down the Bay, look for the "ghostships" comprising the Naval firing range off Tangier Island's southwest shore. If you haven't seen them, heed this warning and don't venture too close, for they are old freighters used as target ships. All identifying names and numbers have been painted over. They are nameless hulks, and their empty portholes stare blankly across the water. Numerous shell holes have turned their superstructure to a lacework. The southernmost ship's back has been broken to such a degree that you can see all the way through it. Should you see one of them appear suddenly through a mist, the apparition is indeed ghostly.

Further to the east you will spot 41-foot Tangier Sound Light at the southern entrance to the sound. A magnetic course of 130° will take you seven miles to the beginning of the well marked channel up Onancock Creek.

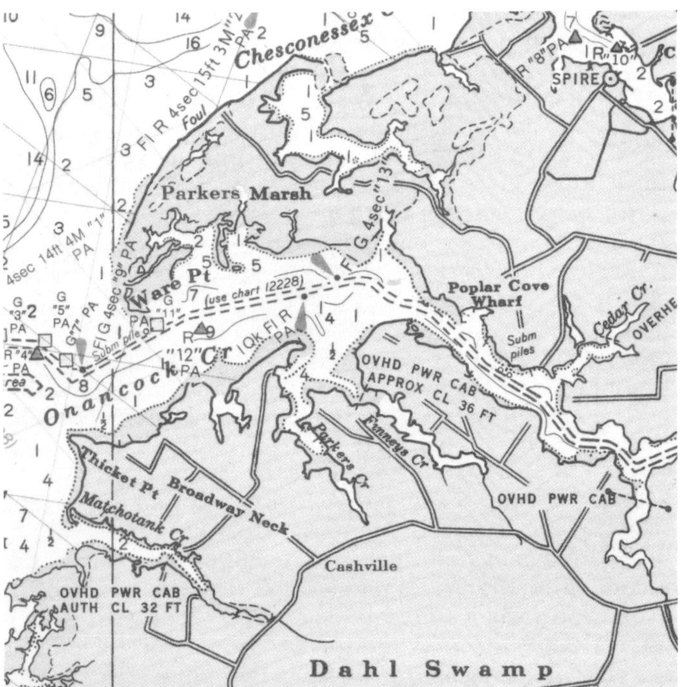

From NOAA Chart 12225—not to be used for navigation.

The entrance to Onancock Creek is quite easy to spot—especially if you are too far north (as we were). The three lighted marks and daymarks stand out against the low shoreline. As you pass Ware Point on the port side, you will enjoy the river better. The land is not the usual monotony of marshland, but lovely wooded countryside. Two favorite anchorages are off Cedar Creek next to daymark #26 and further up in a small bay just off the channel near #34.

You can also anchor near the town harbor in a pocket of water to the starboard side, just before the town dock. The town dock itself is available for tie-up when not occupied by the ferry from Tangier Island. When at the dock, the ferry takes up the entire pier, so be sure to check the schedule posted on shore to avoid any problems.

The ferry overnights on Tangier Island, leaving there to make its arrival at the Onancock town dock around 9:10 A.M., where she remains berthed until mid-afternoon before her sail back to Tangier. The schedule differs somewhat by season of the year, so be sure to check when making your tie-up.

Several transient slips are available at Hopkins and Bro. store. Ice, gas and diesel, electricity and water are available.

The village of Onancock is one of the three main towns on Virginia's eastern shore. Most of it is a short walk from the town dock where most transients tie up. There is water and electricity here, but you'll want to put out fenders since boat wakes can set you bounding against the dock. In town there are a couple of drugstores, a post office, and several small shops. The many handsome old buildings in the nearly 300-year-old town make it a pleasant place for a stroll after a long, hot cruise. Note the marker on West Market Street commemorating the site of the home of Francis Makemie, the founder of organized Presbyterianism in America. One of his first licensed preaching places was here in his home in 1699.

When you walk down the street, people say hello, and when riding a bike, people in passing cars wave. Shopping for hardware and consumer items is convenient, but the supermarket is a pretty fair hike from the dock (about a mile straight out the main street, past the bank and all the churches).

For the seafood lover, a simple restaurant on the main street, "Country Magic," has fresh seafood dishes and is located a short walk from the town dock.

We know of no better place on the entire Chesapeake. The combination of out-of-the-way location and a fine harbor make this one of the last unspoiled "original" towns in America, well worth the time and effort a visit might entail. □

CEDAR CR.
FINNEY'S CR.
PARKERS CR.
PARKER MARSH
ONANCOCK CR.

COCKRELL CREEK

on the Great Wicomico River

If you should be in this area at night, there is a trick you should know in order to enter the Great Wicomico. From the entrance you must keep the red nun #4 to starboard to avoid the fish traps off Fleet Point. Also be sure the red bell (old 4-second flasher #6) which has been changed to a Fl R 2.5 sec. is bearing 295° from the white flasher on its big 42-ft. structure about SE of Fleet Point—the Great Wicomico Light. This light often is obscured by an osprey nest, or else its luminosity is dim. Consequently, many visitors would pick out the red light (a 4-second flasher) off Cockrell Point farther upstream. If you time the 2.5-second flasher, you should have no problem distinguishing it from the 4-second #8. In the past, confusing these two aids could result in going aground off Fleet Point.

Many times we have made the decision to duck into the Great Wicomico to find shelter behind Sandy Point. The bight behind Sandy Point is well known and popular because of its beauty, its ready accessibility, its ease of entry, and its excellent protection. Carrying 16 to 22 feet of water in a roomy, easily read channel, one goes about two miles up the Wicomico and hooks hard to the left to daymarkers "2" and "4" marking the entrance to the bight. Then enter, taking protection in the 16 feet behind low Sandy Point. Deep water can be carried close

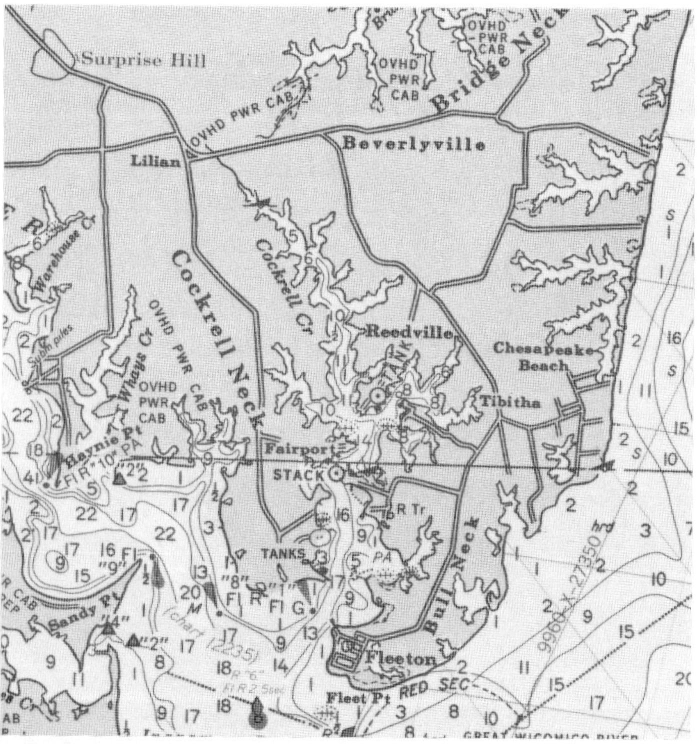

From NOAA Chart 12225—not to be used for navigation.

to the beach and holding is good. Protection is excellent from all directions except the northwest, but by staying close to the tip of the point, partial ease can be obtained from the chop funneling downriver on a northwesterly.

Be sure to check the set of your anchor carefully. Friends report anchoring in this bight a couple of times with poor results, trying both a plough and a Danforth.

There are some good anchorages up Cockrell Creek beyond the tall smokestack on the two main branches of the creek. In the afternoon when the fish dock isn't busy, you can tie up there for a short walk to the grocery store.

West of the tall smokestack is Laird's Marina, where fuel and supplies are available. Next door is Jennings Boatyard with travel lift, railways, and engine service.

Buzzard's Point Marina is further upstream. Just follow the large signs; after you pass the tall smokestack, follow the daymarks in the cove to port. Site of the Tangier Island Cruise boat, this marina has gas and diesel, ice, engine and hull service. Both marinas have courtesy cars to restaurants and grocery supplies.

Hungry for seafood? Then stop at Smith Seafood in the first cove to starboard after you round the tall smokestack. They offer all sorts of fresh and frozen seafood from steamed crabs, crabmeat, and soft crabs to shrimp, clams, lobster tails, scallops, and fresh fish. Stock up on items from their deli—freshly prepared daily—such as crab cakes, crab imperial, seafood salads, spiced shrimp; or select from their prepared-to-go menu of sandwiches and platters.

Reedville is one of the Chesapeake Bay's more interesting communities and is well worth visiting. As you view this busy harbor, you cannot help but be impressed by the fleet of menhaden fishing boats—all over 100 feet in length and rigged to fish the Chesapeake or the Atlantic Ocean.

CRUISE BOAT SCHEDULES

Smith Island Cruise leaves from KOA Campground at Smith Pt., Va. (804) 453-3430. Reservations required.

Leave 10 A.M., return 4:15 P.M. May-September, around $16 adults and $8 for children; includes tour of island.
Pack a picnic lunch or dine ashore. Charter moonlight cruises available. Group rates.

Tangier Island Cruise leaves from Reedville, Va. (804)333-4656. Leave 10 A.M., return 4:15 P.M. May-Sept. $16 adults, $8 children.

Pack a lunch or dine ashore. Charter moonlight cruises available.

REEDVILLE
COCKRELL
CREEK
N

HORN HARBOR

on the Great Wicomico River

There are two Horn Harbors on the Chesapeake Bay's lower western shore. One is called Horn Harbor on the Bay and the other Horn Harbor on the Wicomico. Both are lovely, snug spots of easy entrance in which one can idle away blissful days and serene nights.

The Horn Harbor on the Wicomico is just plain special. A little over three miles up the Wicomico from Sandy Point, and below the Horn Harbor Restaurant, is a tight gut in the North Bank with a switchback channel that leads into the snuggest hurricane hole in the Bay.

A tiny, perfect spot with high wooded banks, Horn Harbor gives seven to eight feet at MLW with five feet over the entrance bar. About a half hour up from Sandy Point on an atomic four, the entrance to Horn Harbor is guarded by fish stakes parallel to the shore. An eyeball evident dogleg entrance by day, Horn Harbor should not be tried at night by the uninitiate. The entrance is just past black "11" at the tip of Rogue Point. Swing in from starboard to a course of about 285° to cross the bar and then promptly north as the entrance is made. Four feet is carried well into the head of the creek.

From NOAA Chart 12235—not to be used for navigation.

You should plan to get supplies at the Fleeton, Fairport, and Reedville areas on Cockrell Creek either on the way upriver or coming out; or both. Leaving for a long run with topped tanks is usual, and it's always nice to snug down for a few extra sunny days in a very private secluded place with a full larder, a good reason for going nowhere, and with good friends. Within a mile upriver from Horn Harbor's entrance is the Great Wicomico River Campground, which is almost completely filled with yearly site rentals to recreational vehicle owners.

Just above the campground is Horn Harbor House Restaurant at Burgess, Virginia. (Burgess is shown on the charts.) The Beckers have been running this restaurant for over 10 years, serving steak and seafood meals that run between $5 and $10. The restaurant is only open April through October. Although reservations are not accepted, it isn't a bad idea to call ahead, (804) 453-3351, to make sure when meals are served.

Reedville and Fleeton are filled with people who go out of their way to be kind and helpful to visitors. An example is Sharon Jennings who owns the Jennings Boat Yard and whose telephone listing is 804-453-7181. On many past occasions, they have opened their yard gates after hours to help some poor out-of-gas transient. The Jennings Boat Yard is located on the left going up Cockrell Creek opposite the charted stack, and the Jennings have a big crane in plain view with the name painted on it.

In ports along the coast you will hear of this Horn Harbor and of the people such as Grady Lester who live close by: watermen, gentlemen, and friends to those who venture west of the Great Wicomico spider. You really should sit down now with your family or friends and charts and plan to join the ranks of people who like Horn Harbor on the Great Wicomico so well that they have sailed days just to be able to anchor there.□

Note: Horn Harbor on the Great Wicomico has silted some, depths inside run 4 to 7 feet. The entrance is still easy to eyeball in daytime. Approach the entrance from midriver on a course of about 030° as the eastern 1-foot shoal has made out farther than charted. Shoals are usually marked by saplings. Swinging room may be impeded by crab pots inside. Put them back if you have to move them.

Notes

PHOTO BY BACKUS AERIAL PHOTOGRAPHY

MILL CREEK

on the Great Wicomico River

Northern Virginia where it touches the Chesapeake Bay just south of the Potomac is a fairly untraveled area. Rarely will you find a housing development. Boat traffic is minimal, usually consisting of an occasional oyster boat or crabber. Although supplies are not too available, with careful planning one can linger in the area for quite a while enjoying the cool green wooded creeks and coves.

Duck into the Great Wicomico, round Fleeton Point, and head up Cockrell Creek to Reedville, where you can replenish supplies. There is also a fish-loading dock where

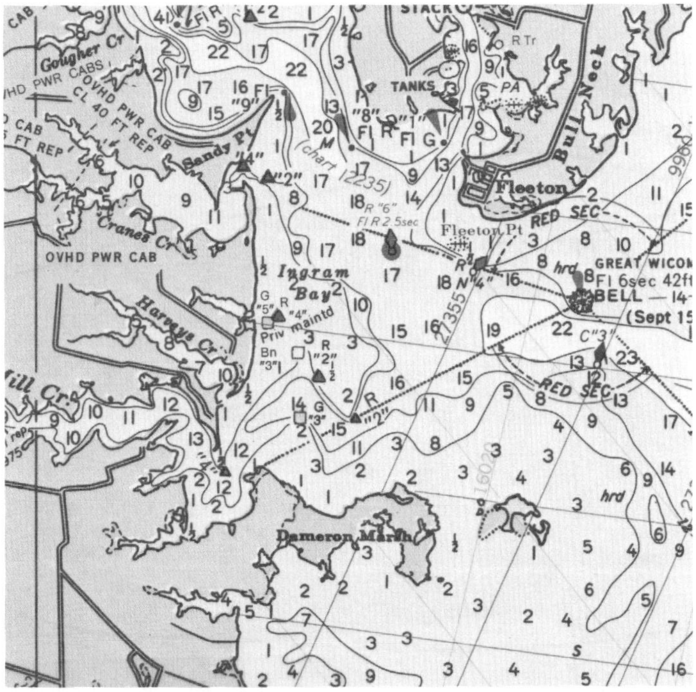

From NOAA Chart 12225—not to be used for navigation.

you can buy fresh fish — sea trout, blues or rock — and for couple of bucks, feed a crew of five or six.

This is also the home of several fish factories whose smok can discourage even the most avid cruiser. So, if they ar "cooking," we find ourselves motoring back to the Grea Wicomico for the night.

One good spot is Mill Creek on the south shore of th river. It is easy to sail directly from the Wicomico's 42-foo spider to the entrance channel. Take a course of about 251° t the red daymark "2" (about 1½ miles) and follow the marke in. As you enter Mill Creek proper, the last navigation aid is red daymark #4 perched on a sandbar that breaks roug waves from the Bay. Inside, keep away from points of lan which extend into shallows out from shore, and pick any co which looks inviting to you for your anchorage.

Less than a half-mile from the entrance of the creek is perfect cove with 12 feet of water. There are two tidal pools o this cove that are quite interesting. The entrance to the large one is only 10-12 feet wide, but is 4 feet deep in the middl

Before leaving Mill Creek next morning, we motore upstream to explore, and discovered what we then though was the source of this Creek's name. On the south bank abou one and a half miles upstream stands a faded, gray-painte grain mill whose rust-streaked loading arms still hover ove the water's edge. We later found that we hadn't reall stumbled upon Mill Creek's "mill," but a more recent, albe abandoned, facility.

In any event, the tall metal structure, built sometime in th 1950's, looked out of place here on this quiet, tree-line stream, and lent a charm that is typical of many creeks on th Northern Neck of Virginia. □

Notes

Notes

NORTHERN NECK OF VIRGINIA

Dividing Creek
Dymer Creek
Indian Creek
Antipoison Creek

Bounded by the Rappahannock River on the south and Potomac River on the north, the Northern Neck of Virginia has nine rivers or creeks which empty directly into the Chesapeake Bay. This area is a "cruising heaven" since most have navigable entrances, and once inside they nearly always offer a wide variety of deep coves for protected anchorages.

The area is also rich in history. Legend has it that once Captain John Smith, while fishing in the area, was severely stung by a stingray and nearly killed. A tribe of Indians just across the northern neck of land concocted a poultice that saved the Captain from certain death. The place where he was stung has been known ever since as Stingray Point and the creek where he found the cure now bears the name Antipoison Creek.

And, in the 1800s steamships made frequent stops along their shores. It is still easy to picture the steamer *Piankatank* chugging majestically into Dividing Creek to dock. Or, what a sight the *Lancaster* must have presented with her high, round paddlebox glinting in the sunlight as she cast off from the docks at Kilmarnock Wharf!

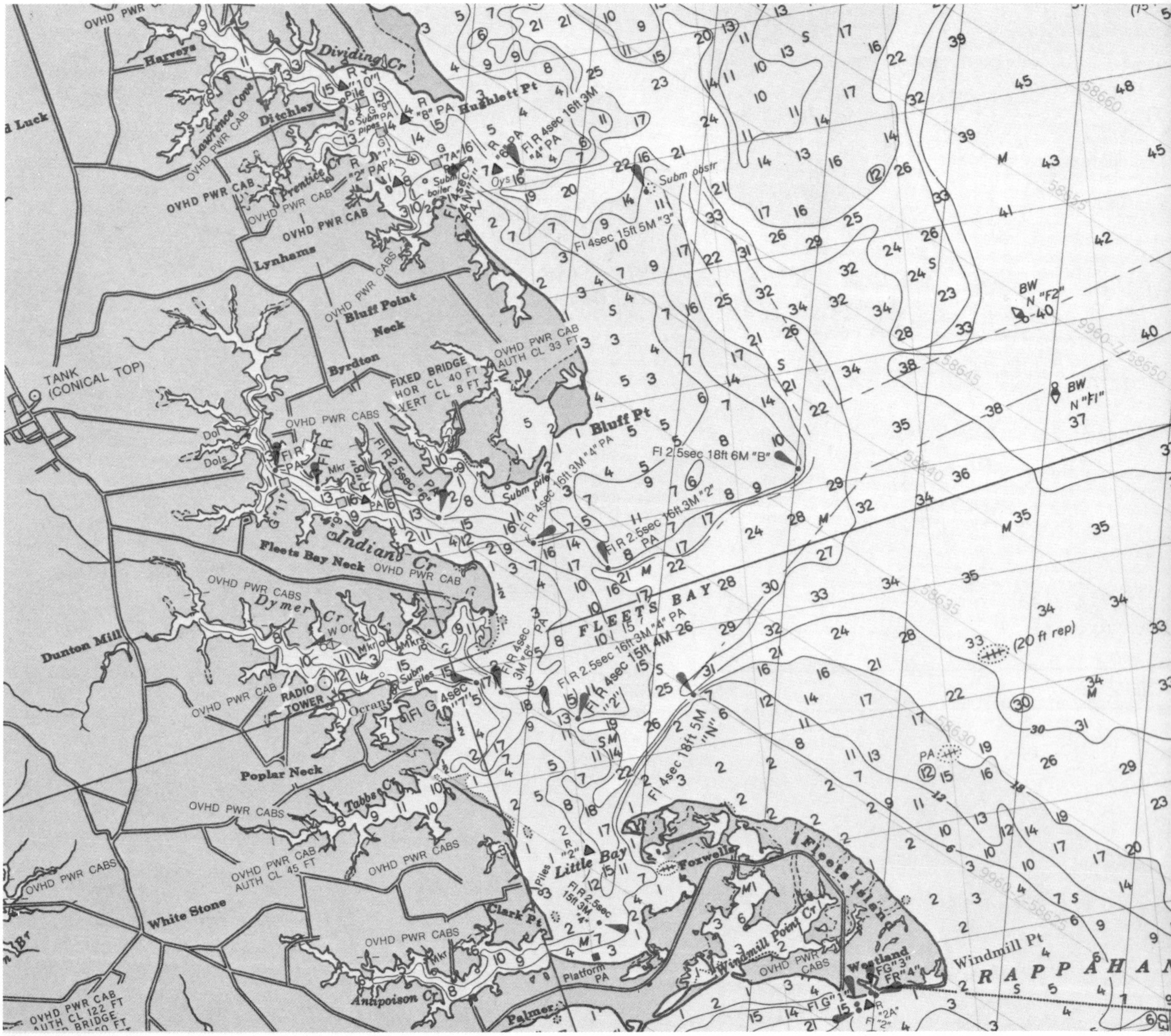

From NOAA Chart 12225 — not to be used for navigation.

PRENTICE CREEK

on Dividing Creek

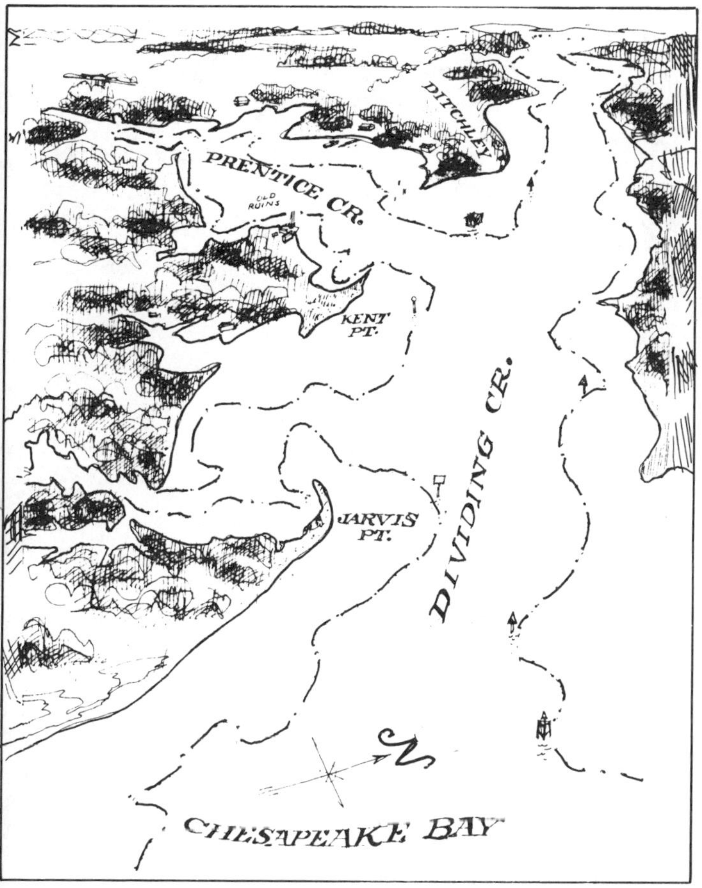

As we passed Wolf Trap and the Piankatank River, we studied our charts and examined those creeks within our reach before dark — our decision was Dividing Creek, which is about half way up to the Potomac River.

Dividing Creek is wide, with shoals projecting out from each bank. Darkness had fallen as we passed the two lighted marks at the creek's entrance (Fl. R 4 sec. almost exactly east of the words "Jarvis Point," and FL. 4 sec. "7" northeast of Jarvis Point), which made it difficult to judge the center of the creek. There are marks past the entrance, however, so daylight navigation is possible for some distance if care is taken rounding the points.

On the south shore at Kent Point, is a wide shoal with a local mark just opposite the red daymark. Jarvis Creek, also, is shoal. Just around the point is Prentice Creek, which we had picked as our night's anchorage.

On the starboard side of the Prentice Creek entrance is a duck blind which should be left at least 50 feet to starboard. We were in complete darkness when we tried to enter near the blind and went aground. On our second try we made it through a channel with 12 feet of water.

Although there is ample water further inside and the cove on the south side has ten feet of water and is recommended, we didn't go further than the point on the north shore marked "Ditchley" on our chart.

The area is very quiet with small farms and few houses. One thing we always notice in this area is the clear water. The effect is so refreshing we always promise ourselves that we'll return — and, of course, we will! □

LAWRENCE COVE

on Dividing Creek

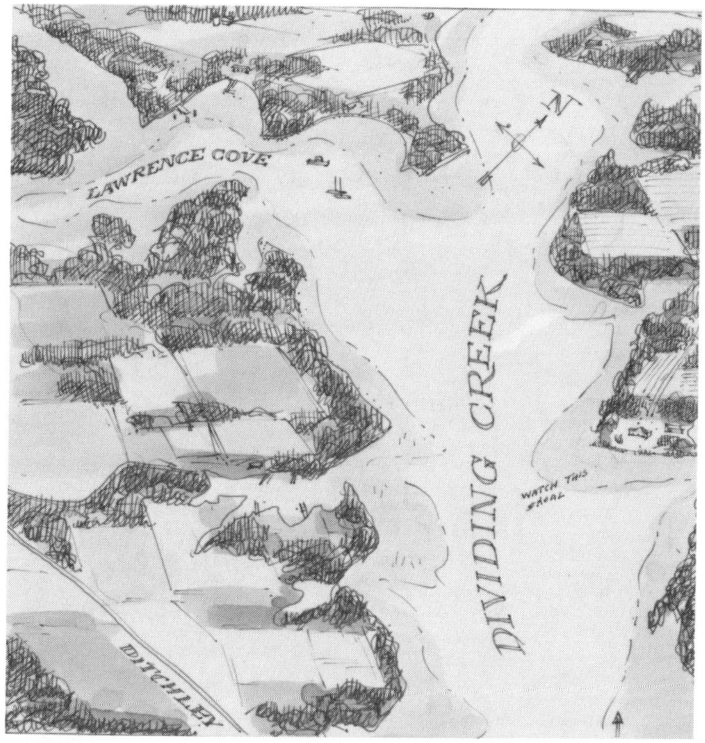

If you are approaching Dividing Creek from the north, say from Smith Point, locate black bell #1 which is about three miles off Dameron Marsh. From there a course of about 239° will put you at the entrance spar of Dividing Creek. The distance is about six miles. Note, though, that this course passes close to some four-foot depths, so if you draw more than this, a better plan would be to take 237° until Fl. R "4" is roughly 45° off your starboard bow, distant about .5 mile., and then turn for it. In this way you'll be in slightly deeper water all the way. If you draw six feet, continue until the light is abeam to starboard before heading for it.

Approaching from the south you would leave Windmill Point Light on course 347° (approx.) to the channel junction light off Bluff Point. This light is identifiable by its red and white checkered panel with the letter "B" in the corner. The Dividing Creek light is about two miles almost due north.

The channel into the creek is well marked with daymarks and lighted spars. As you enter, you will notice a large bay on the port side just past Jarvis Point. The water looks inviting, but this area is very exposed to the north and we passed it up.

Just about Ditchley a shoal projects from the port bank, and just ahead on the starboard side you will see a white frame one-story house with a small green roof. The house is quite prominent and the point trails off in a long three-foot shoal which should be avoided.

Our objective, Lawrence Cove, was just around the next corner to port. On entering you will see no marks, so keep to the middle going in. A really fine anchorage is in the first little bay at the cove's entrance where the nine-foot mark shows on NOAA Chart No. 12235. The starboard shoreline curves protectively around to give ample protection from the northwest, but the area could hold a good-sized raft. Further upstream are several other nice anchorages. □

BELLS CREEK

on Indian Creek

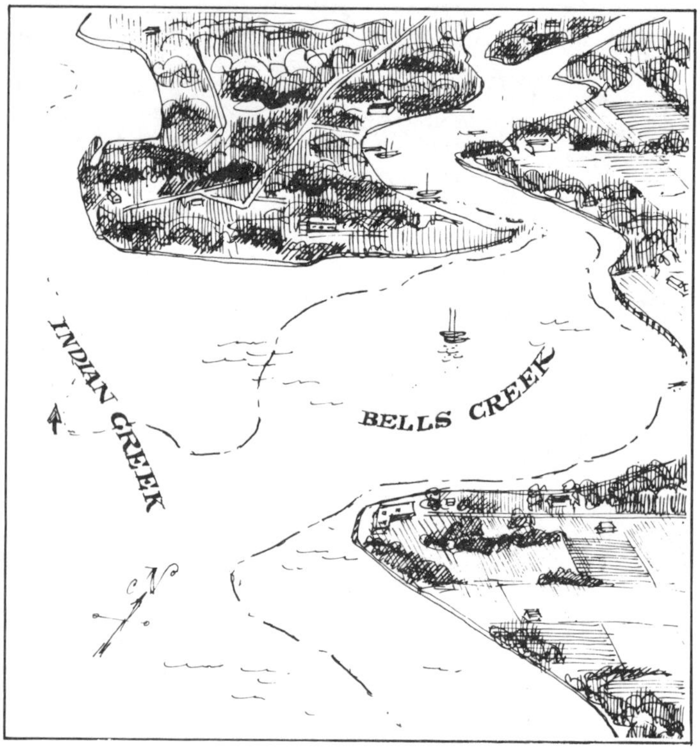

The entrance to Indian Creek is marked by two red flashers guarding the channel. As you come to the first red flasher, "2" (Fl R 2.5 sec), course 314° M will take you right into the head of the creek.

Indian Creek is considered to be one of the most attractive creeks in the area, well marked, with many appealing anchorages. The creek is also home of the Indian Creek Yacht and Country Club located just north of Bells Creek. About two miles upstream is the Chesapeake Boat Basin located at Kilmarnock Landing. This establishment has slips, showers, gas, ice, marine supplies and repair service, and can supply transportation to Kilmarnock, one of the finest towns in this part of the Chesapeake.

When rounding Fleets Island, perhaps the easiest mark to find is North Point Light "N" (Fl 4 sec) on a pile, marking the shoal off the northern tip of the island. From there a course of 353° M will bring you to the first entrance mark "2" (Fl R 2.5 sec), a light on a pile one mile south of Bluff Point. At this point it is easy to spot the next two marks, "4" (Fl R 4 sec) and "6" (Fl R 2.5 sec). Farther upstream you will be able to see the next pair of daymarks, which mark Bells Creek.

We chose Bells Creek for this night's anchorage and were not disappointed. On entering, I'd advise you go halfway up to the daymark on the northwest side of Bell's entrance, turn on course 025° M (approximately), and you should slip right in. As usual, our depth finder was not working; but the leadline showed 8-foot depths.

Rappahannock Oyster Company is located at daymark "8", where a full line of marine supplies and fresh seafood items can be found. We anchored in eight feet of water in the first cove; but if you've got a strong southerly blowing, proceed farther upstream around the point of land for a really snug harbor. □

HENRY'S CREEK

on Indian Creek

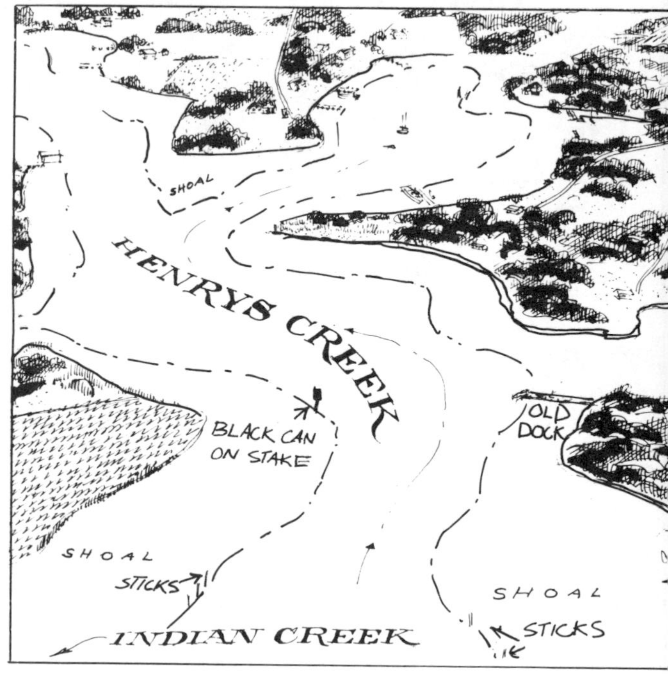

We've cruised back and forth past this area for severa years. But the only time we actually cruised into India Creek was during an extremely violent storm when w retreated to the sanctuary of Bells Creek.

Our destination this time was Henry's Creek. The creek' entrance lies about one-half mile northwest of marker "4" (F R 4 sec). There are long curving shoals on both port an starboard sides as you enter this pretty little creek, an without some help, I doubt we would have tried to go in However, a waterman's boat was just ahead of us, and w followed him in. Then I noticed some small sticks driven int the mud that showed precisely where the shallows were. wouldn't try it in the dark, but in daylight, the sticks are eas to follow.

We favored the eastern side where there is the ruin of a old dock, passed within a few hundred yards of the dock then turned and ran northwest to the sandy point farthe upstream on the starboard side. On the port side is one of th purely local marks we frequently see around the Bay— sturdy stick with a large can, painted black, nailed to the top

Just after the sandy point to starboard Henry's Cree divides. There is a nice anchorage on the western fork just a its mouth. We chose the eastern branch which seemed a bi more open once you pass the entrance. It is altogether pleasant spot to spend the night, and not too far off the Bay

At night, as we lay at anchor, a distant throbbing o engines drew our attention south toward Indian Creek. Jus visible over the sandy point we could see in the evening mis a largish boat with a long line of lights outlining the hull. I was a tour boat that takes parties out on evening cruises. Bu it didn't call for a great deal of imagination to see, instead the steamship *Lancaster,* her paddlewheel casting a showe of water that sparkles in the reflection of her lights as sh chugs majestically toward her next port of Ditchley o perhaps Reedville. □

PITMAN'S COVE

on Indian Creek

Pitman's Cove is a good place to know about for several reasons. We chose Pitman's Cove, by Grace Point in Indian Creek, because we were low on fuel and it was necessary to go to the marina farther upstream to replenish our supply. The attendant was friendly and very helpful with local information. He recommended we steam back downriver to Grace Point, opposite "12" (Fl R 6 sec), turn southwest, and anchor in ten feet of water.

The cove offers excellent protection, good holding ground, and scenic beauty, all the while still being a location that is close to the Bay and at the same time near a marina. We found it ideal as a stop-off point for both cruising sailors and yachts transiting the Bay northward or southward.

Indian Creek itself is quiet and relatively free of local traffic, compared to some other spots along the western shoreline. Well-placed fish stakes guard the upriver shoal spots once you have entered by way of the easy-to-follow channel from the Bay. The only trick we found, on a rather hazy afternoon, was in spotting the outside marker from the middle of the Chesapeake. Because of the other markers representing channels going into Antipoison, Dymer and Dividing Creeks, together with the maze of fishtraps between, it seems tricky. Nevertheless, our compass came to the rescue and brought us safely to where we wanted to be. □

HUNT'S COVE

on Dymer Creek

If you notice on your chart #12236, there are ample navigational aids leading into Dymer Creek from the Bay. The key marker is "N" (Fl 4 sec), north of Fleet's Island. From here, only about a mile offshore of the mouth of the creek, there are four marks—three reds and a green—in a line. There's plenty of deep water around all but the last one, and all are lighted so it should be no problem to enter Dymer, even at night.

It was only a little past noon as we rounded "7" (Fl G 4 sec) off Grog Island, and with a gentle following breeze and a whole sunny day ahead of us, we decided to explore further upstream before anchoring for the night. We sailed upstream for a couple of miles or so, enjoying the beauty of the shoreline. There was plenty of deep water and few troublesome shoals. A couple of inlets past Johnson Creek we circled around into the wind and reluctantly dropped sail. Motor humming, we wound our way back toward Hunt's Cove. We turned to run into our anchorage, as we were passing the point at Ocran.

Carefully, we searched the area ahead for the marker shown on our chart. Nothing! Closer we came. Still nothing. I guess we were spooked by the extensive shoal to port because, before I knew it, we were entering a thicket of oyster stakes off the starboard side. Watermen have assured us that stakes such as these usually indicate six to eight feet of water. I uneasily swung to port, just to be on the safe side. Before we cleared the stakes we had run aground. Rocking did little to free us from the sticky mud bottom.

Fortunately, a man and his wife came over in a skiff and offered to take our anchor out to deep water. In a few minutes we winched our way off and were free.

We turned once more into Hunt's Cove, this time keeping well clear of the stakes to starboard; motoring slowly we cleared the outer shoals. We anchored at the spot marked 10 ft. on the chart, although there is plenty of deep water upstream. The shoreline is wooded, broken by a few cornfields here and there and only a couple of houses. On the east shore, near the cove's entrance, a family had anchored so close to the sandy beach that they could almost step ashore! □

GEORGE'S COVE

on Dymer Creek

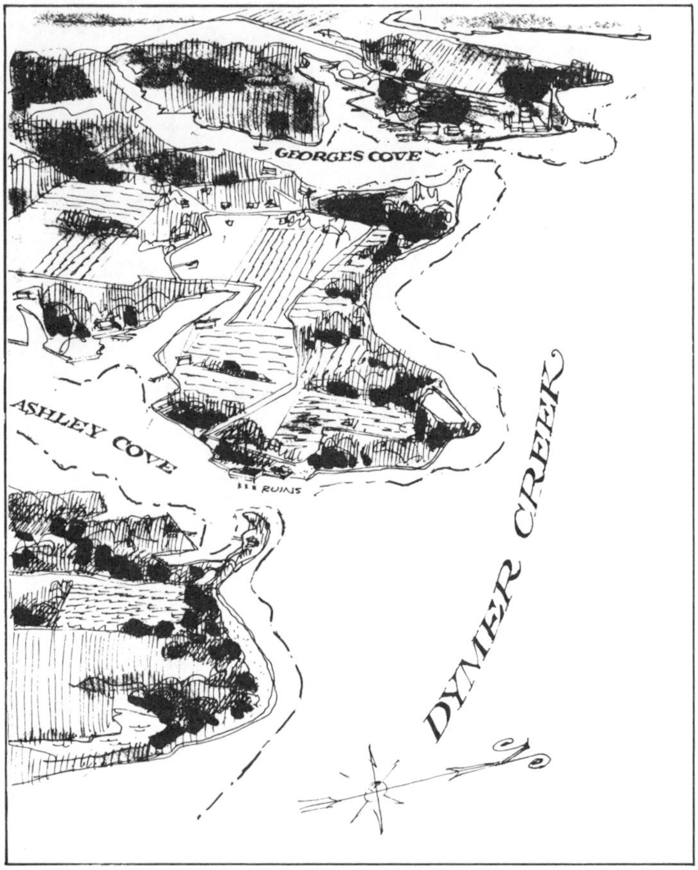

Our destination was Dymer Creek in northern Virginia, about ten miles south of the Great Wicomico River. We sailed into Fleets Bay, rounding the first of four lighted daymarks just as the breeze died. We drifted up into Dymer Creek, taking about a half-hour to put Grog Island abeam. There we reluctantly dropped sail and proceeded to motor toward our destination, George's Cove. On the south shore stretched a long white sand beach, uninhabited, and inviting a picnic. The beach terminates at Ashley Cove, which has deep water and a shoreline dotted with several beautiful homes. On the other side of the cove entrance are the ruins of an old fish factory. Years ago many such processing buildings with docks dotted the landscape in northern Virginia. Today most are reduced as this one is, to a jumble of bricks and the rotting ends of dock piles barely holding their heads above the persistent tide.

The next stretch of shoreline to port is thick with trees, as the land becomes a little higher. Behind the trees is farmland dotted with an occasional barn. As we reached George's Cove, we were intrigued by a solitary farm house, unoccupied, standing at the water's edge. She was quite ordinary in appearance, but a couple of huge oak trees beside her reached out their limbs, protecting her from the elements. The utter simplicity of the scene produced an air of quiet dignity and charm which invited inspection.

George's Cove has a narrow entrance, but it is easy to manage, with six feet of water in the channel. Inside just avoid the crab pot floats and you'll find plenty of water for anchoring. ☐

GROG ISLAND

on Dymer Creek

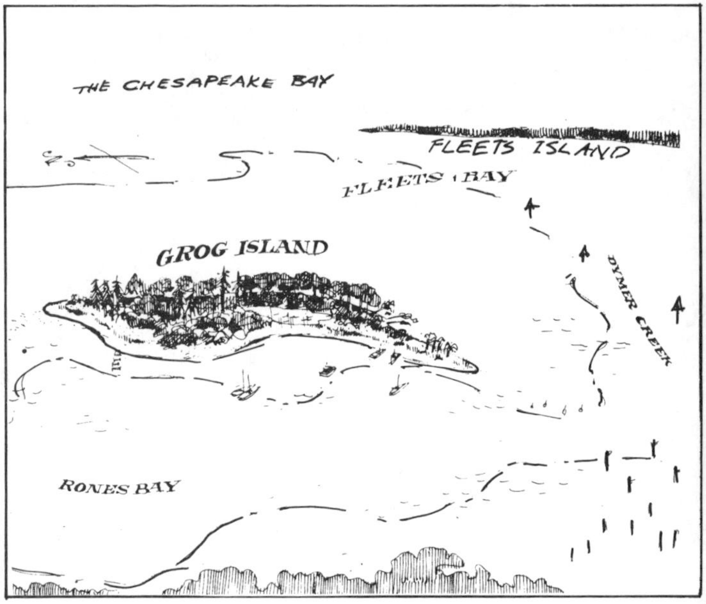

When you enter Dymer Creek from the Bay, Grog Island appears to be just part of the shoreline—or at most, a peninsula. Not very impressive or intriguing. However, as we motored out of Dymer next morning, we acquired a better perspective.

Grog Island stood completely separated from the north, its sandy beach shining gold in the morning sun, with a fringe of trees silhouetted against the sparkling waters of the Chesapeake. We realized that we had been missing one of the true gems of the Bay.

Perfectly situated to provide an ideal natural harbor, Grog Island offers good protection from all but sou'westerlies which are infrequent in the summer. The north shore of Dymer Creek, known as Fleets Bay Neck, is a low-lying prominence which projects out into the Chesapeake about two miles above Antipoison Creek. Just off the tip of this neck is Grog Island itself; a sand bar connecting the two is barely awash at low tide. It is shaped like the letter "L" in reverse. The bottom half points westward, giving protection from the south and providing a snug anchorage.

We learned the hard way how best to approach this little harbor. From Fleets Bay to the mouth of Dymer Creek there are three lighted dolphins to starboard, and then one to port. Continue for about 800 more yards before turning north and heading up into Rones Bay. The southwest tip of Grog Island is the most critical part of the entrance since there are shoals on both sides that try to close the channel.

As we approached this narrows, we spotted a maze of stakes, the kind that usually mark oyster beds. Four sticks had white rags tied to them and were in a perfect square pattern. Did they mark the port or starboard side of the entrance? Or was one pair for starboard and the other pair the port?

Cautiously we slowed to a near crawl and decided to run up the middle between the two pairs of marks. As we approached the stakes with an eye on the trusty (?) depth sounder, we watched its needle drop steadily: 12 feet, 10 feet, 8 feet, 5 feet. As it hit three feet, I was shifting into reverse. When we finally went aground, the engine was roaring, but to no avail; the sticky mud held us fast.

As we were rocking from side to side, a local waterman came by and offered to lead us in. Following him, we circled around and tried it again, this time leaving all four stakes to port. On our starboard side a sand bar stretched out from the tip of the island, its end marked by crab floats. Holding our breath, we slipped through into deep 12-foot water, where we circled several anchored boats and dropped our own hook.

The island has a nice sandy beach, perfect for picnicking and for your kids to run and explore. I went ashore with a friend and walked around the island, finding that several boats had pulled up on the beach to allow their families to lounge on the sand.

The anchorage at Grog Island is particularly charming because you can be so close to the Bay. As the light breeze ruffles the waters and moonlight reflects a golden pool, I can picture a pirate ship rounding Windmill Point and dropping anchor right on this very spot. On the 'morrow I might go ashore and search for buried treasure. □

Notes

ANTIPOISON CREEK

on Virginia's Northern Neck

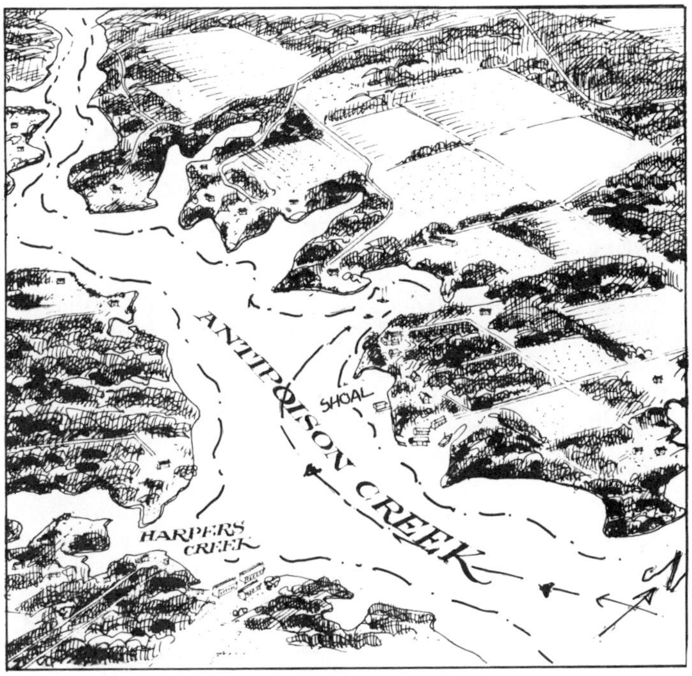

Situated on the Northern Neck of Virginia, Antipoison Creek is just north (around the corner) of Windmill Point. Indian Creek and Dymer Creek both empty into the Chesapeake Bay at Fleets Bay—a largish cove just north of Fleets Island. The entrance to Antipoison Creek is on Little Bay, a small body of water off the southern end of Fleets Bay.

Antipoison is well marked, and its entrance is easy to navigate. If you refer to NOAA Chart #12235, you will easily find Windmill Point on the easternmost tip of Fleets Island. Follow the north shore of the island all around the North Point where it touches Little Bay, and you will be just opposite the first daymark, "2", which is about a half mile north of "4" (Fl R 2.5 sec) at Antipoison's mouth. Give the flasher plenty of room as you make your turn and head right to the creek's entrance, some 700 yards away. It is best to favor the north shore somewhat since there is a shoal to port at the opening.

Just inside on the port side is Capt. Fitchett's dock where you can usually pick up some fresh fish. This is a favorite of ours when we're cruising the Bay.

At the first cove, just before Harper's Creek, on the port side you will find two herring packing plants. About 500 yards further upstream you will find a really prime anchorage with seven feet of water or more. As you approach this cove, the only thing to be aware of is a shoal which projects seaward from the eastern side of the cove's entrance. There's a stick with cloth tied on it to mark the shallow spot. Inside the cove you will find more sticks, which are not shallow markers, just oyster bed stakes, so don't worry. Its north shore is bordered by grassy fields with a scattering of trees. The east and west sides are more wooded, giving good protection from stormy blows.

You'll enjoy all of Antipoison for its quiet seclusion, its cozy wooded shores, and its lack of boat traffic. □

BROAD CREEK

on the Rappahannock River

The Rappahannock is a surprisingly large river. And, although storms can make her broad entrance quite rough, the intensity does not match the fury of the Potomac or York Rivers.

Entering the Rappahannock from the north is not difficult, but orienting yourself to the 36-foot beacon of Windmill Point Light which stands well offshore is important before turning westward. Take the light on your starboard hand. Then, with good visibility and smooth water, you may cut immediately west of the light and cross Rappahannock Spit in 7-foot depths. However, pound nets and crab pots are usually numerous within the magenta dashed lines denoting fish trap areas. Some skippers feel the short cut is not worth the nuisance. If you are planning to stop at Windmill Point Marine Resort, do not run a direct course from Windmill Point Light to the marina entrance markers. Instead, go about .5 mile south of the light, and then turn on a course of 300° M. Watching your depthfinder, you can steer a little more than 300° M, so long as your depth is not less than 10 or 12 feet. This course will bring you less than .5 mile off the markers. Windmill Point's resort facilities have made it a popular stopover with cruisers for over 20 years.

As you round Stingray Point from the south, keeping well east of Stingray Point Light, the Rappahannock's broad waters run on a generally northwest course (approx. 300°) to a fixed bridge (vertical clearance 110 ft.) about six and a half miles upstream.

Just west of Stingray Point is Broad Creek, the Rappahannock River entrance to Deltaville. The channel is marked with a lighted beacon at the outermost end and daymarks at convenient intervals to a lighted beacon at a turning area at the mouth of the creek. The 100′ wide channel carries 6′ or more into a broad, sheltered harbor. On the port side or east fork, there are numerous deep draft boats at Norton's sailboat dock which testify to the easy accessibility of Broad Creek.

Upstream at daymark "9" the creek makes a sharp turn to the west. In 1983 the local advice was to not cut too closely to "9" because the best water was at the point to starboard.

There are several large, well-run marinas on Broad Creek, most notable of which is Norton's Marine a short distance upstream. Here you can find a marine railway, travel lift, engine service and repairs, and ships store. A courtesy car is available from local restaurants. Deltaville Dockside Inn, which has motel rooms and efficiencies, has a courtesy car for transportation to stores, etc. □

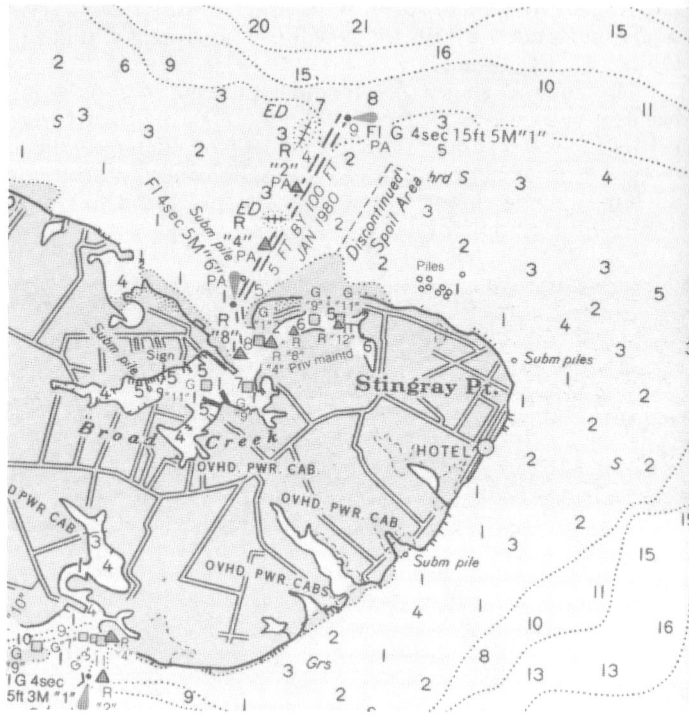

From NOAA Chart 12235—not to be used for navigation

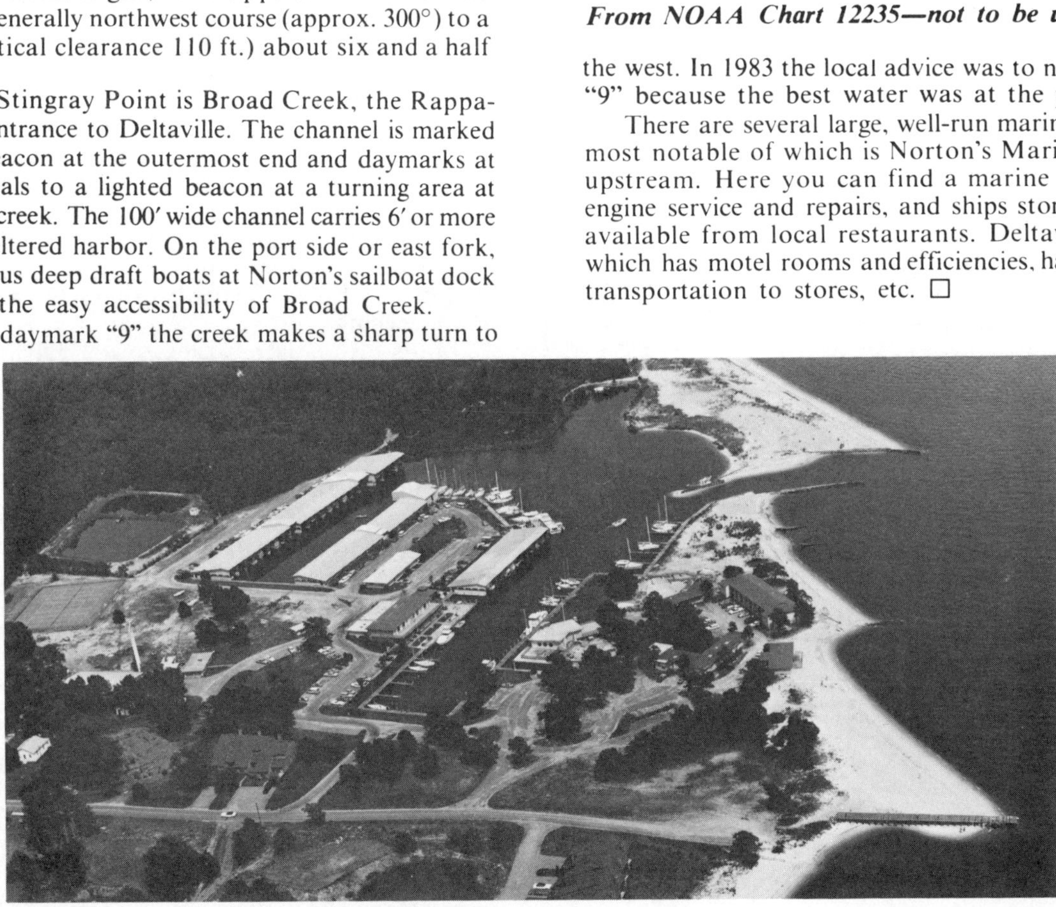

Windmill Point Marine Resort.

PHOTO BY BACKUS AERIAL PHOTOGRAPHY

BROAD CREEK
SHOAL REP.
STINGRAY POINT
RAPPAHANNOCK RIVER

CARTER CREEK

on the Rappahannock River

From Stingray Point Light you can take a course of 307° which will clear the shoal just west of Broad Creek. In about 3.2 miles you will spot a black daybeacon "7." Pass it to your port hand. The same course will take you right through the center span of the Rappahannock River Bridge—a distance of five miles. From the bridge, take course 335° right to the entrance marks of Carter Creek.

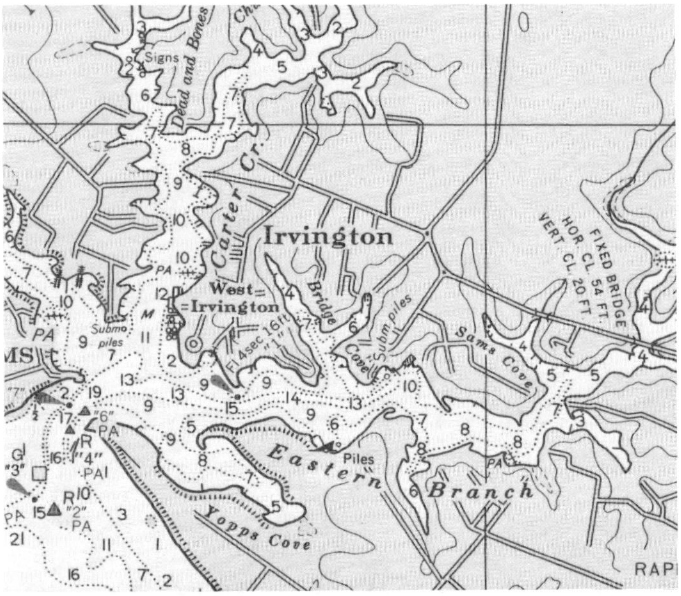

From NOAA Chart 12235—not to be used for navigation.

Conning in at night, look for the #1 lead mark, a 4-second flashing green. A swing to the north lines you up with the green 2½-second flasher, #7. Marks two through six must be logged, but fall easily in between. Once past #6, you can swing to the east for a nice run past the 16-foot 4-second flasher on the left at West Irvington. By staying in mid-river, eight feet should be easily carried up to the left turn at the head. Protection from all quadrants can be found at various spots along the creek, so feel your way along on soundings and keep an eye to any expected windshift due in before breakfast.

Conning in by daylight is obviously easier, more dramatic, and you probably will want to take more time to look at the area before you drop a hook.

Here you have several alternatives for anchoring: Weems on the west side in Carter Cove; straight on up Carter Creek past Tides Inn; or in the Eastern Branch at Irvington. The oblique left is the Western Branch, where most of the marine facilities are located.

Yopps Cove is the first inlet to starboard as you enter Carter Creek. This seems more than a cove, perhaps creek would describe it better. The entrance looks a little chancey at first, because charts show shoals projecting from both sides; but we found plenty of room to get in. And although there were half a dozen boats already anchored, there was plenty of room for us in seven feet of water.

PHOTO BY BACKUS AERIAL PHOTOGRAPHY

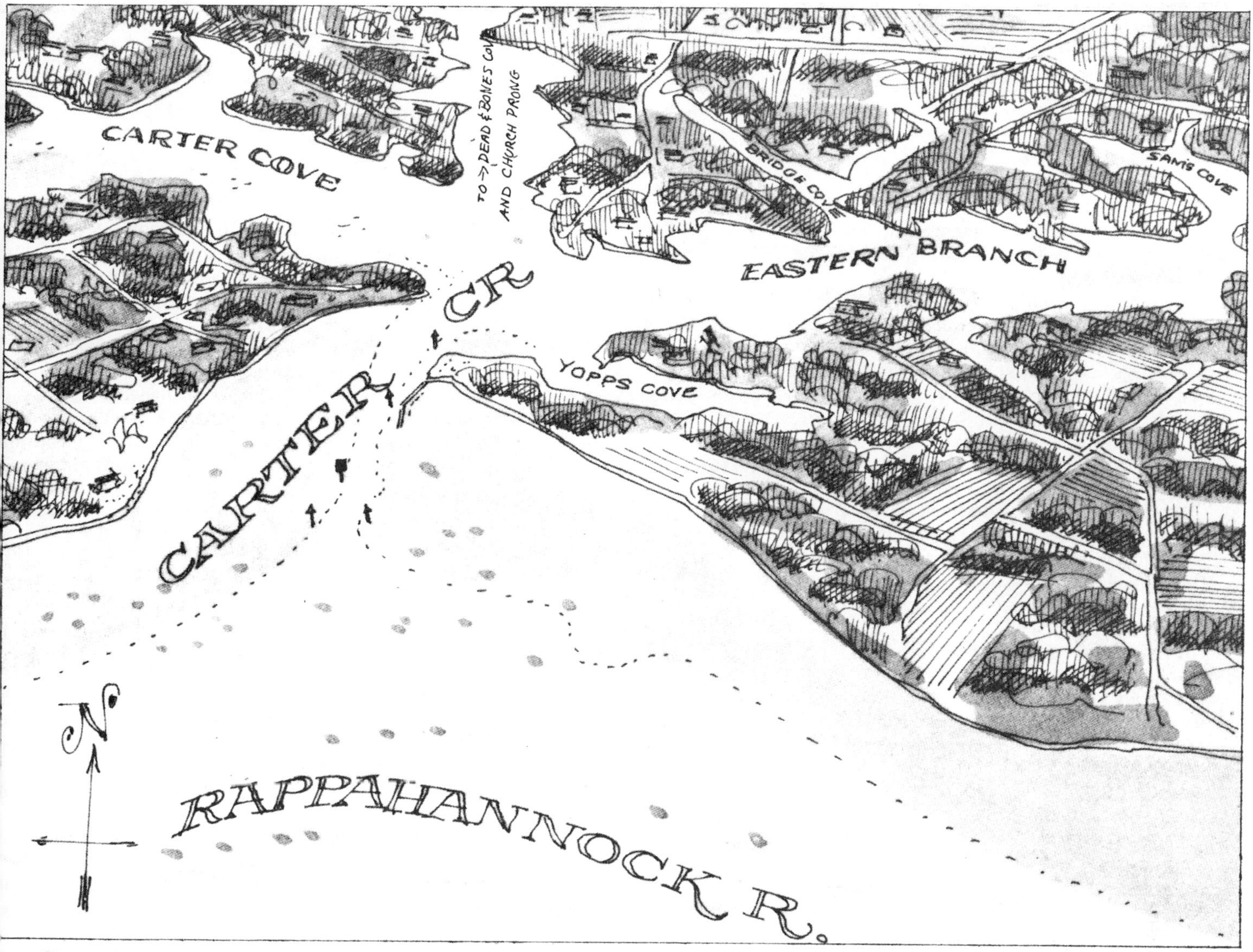

Carter Creek carries twenty to eight feet comfortably from its mouth to its arms but demands that its marks be honored, for the banks behind the beacons have only a foot or two over them at low water. Once inside the deep easy entrance, a sharp left shows you Carter Cove. This branch is largely commercial, but interesting. Humphries Shipyard is used by the big menhaden fishing boats and can handle even the largest yachts.

The Carter name in this area began with John Carter, who settled the place in 1649 as one of the fugitive Cavaliers from England. John Carter amassed great wealth in land and became prominent, both as commander in defense against the Indians and as a member of the Crown Council, where he is mentioned as early as 1657.

According to historians, John's son Robert born in 1663 of his third wife, became of such importance in the community that he was called "King" Carter. Robert "King" Carter died in 1732, enormously wealthy, leaving, it is said, 300,000 acres of land and 1,000 slaves. He married twice and had by his first wife, Judith Armistead of Hesse, four children; by his second wife, Betty Landon of Hereford, England, eight children. These children carried on his tradition, and the families into which they married represent the most famous names in Virginia. Among his descendents were three signers of the Declaration of Independence, four governors of Virginia, and two presidents of the United States, not to mention Robert E. Lee and a host of others.

The main branch, Carter Creek, holds most of the marine facilities of interest to the visiting yachtsman. First, on the point to starboard, is Carter Creek Yacht Service. As you head further upstream you will see the docks of Rappahannock Yacht Club, a congenial group whose family-oriented activities are well known in the area. Next, to starboard, is Rappahannock Yachts. Next door, is the Irvington Marina.

In addition to the many beautiful homes that line the shores of Carter Creek, you will find two of the finest yachting complexes on the Bay—the gracious Tides Inn to starboard and The Tides Lodge a bit further ahead.

If you wish to avail yourself of the many and varied facilities provided by the Inn and the Lodge, telephone them ahead at (804)438-5000 for the Inn and (804)438-6000 for the Lodge. In general, the Inn is formal and the Lodge casual in structure. To write ahead, the address of both is simply Irvington, Virginia, 22480. The Inn is open from mid-March to New Year's, and the Lodge from mid-March to late November. Contact them early, for people look forward to visiting the area and plan their trips far ahead.

Controlling depths of the channels in Carter Creek are about 15 feet in the entrance, 12 feet in the Eastern Branch to the wharves at Irvington, and 9 feet in Carter Cove, the western branch. The mean tidal range is 1.4 feet. ☐

URBANNA CREEK

on the Rappahannock River

Urbanna Creek is located on the south shore of the Rappahannock River, some 16 plus miles upstream from Windmill Point.

Urbanna is one of the four remaining towns of the 19 ordered built by the General Assembly of the House of Burgesses in 1680. Within the town limits stand some of the buildings from those early years: the Old Court House, renovated and used by the Middlesex Woman's Club; Landsdowne, where Dr. Arthur Lee, a forefather of Robert E. Lee, lived and is buried; the Tobacco Warehouse, authentically restored by the Association for the Preservation of Virginia Antiquities and now used as a public library; the Customs House, authorized in 1680 and now a private residence; and the Old Tavern, where Patrick Henry is said to have delivered one of his stirring speeches. Nearby is Rosegill, home of a colonial governor, and Hewick, where many colonial statesmen also gathered.

In the early 1900's Urbanna was a port of call for commercial vessels and steamships from Baltimore and Norfolk.

Today the town's commercial activity is centered around its seafood industry. Its local watermen provide a steady supply of the famous Rappahannock River oysters, crabs, and fish.

When heading up the Rappahannock, it's no problem finding the Rappahannock River Bridge. There's a simple way to set a course from the bridge to Urbanna Creek. Simply line up the center span of the bridge with the red bell #6 off Towles Point and the entrance jetties of the creek will be in direct line on course 286° (approx.). The bell is about four miles upstream, and beyond that, the entrance of Urbanna Creek is almost another three miles upstream.

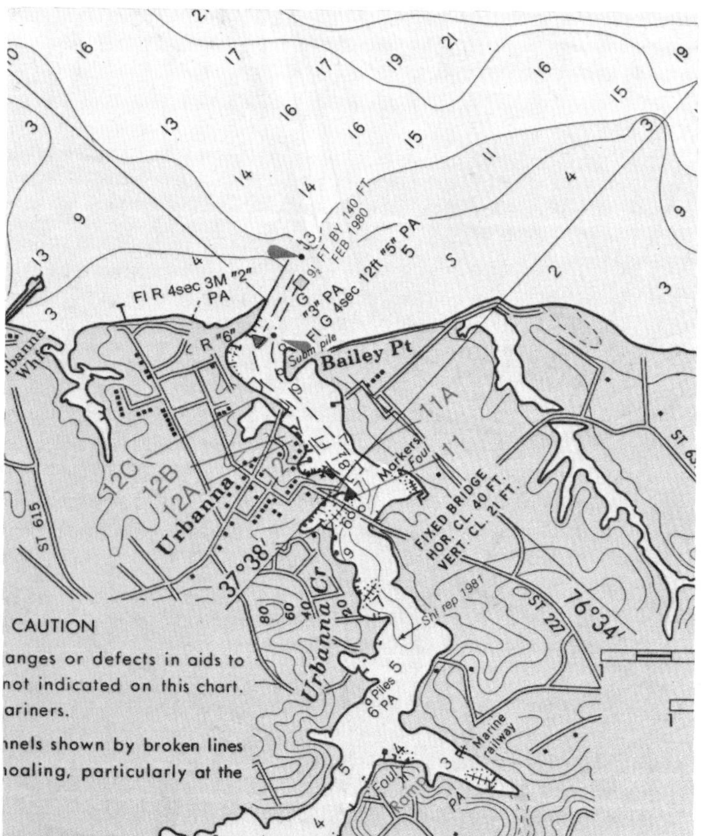

From NOAA Chart 12237—not to be used for navigation.

The entrance of Urbanna Creek is protected by a rip-rap jetty on the north side. Keep in the center of this entrance channel as there are shoal spots along the edges. Urbanna Creek channel daybeacons "1" and "4" have been renumbered to "3" and "6". Urbanna Creek Channel Light "3" has been renumbered Light "5". The channel is well marked with a black "3" and flashing "2" at the outer end, and off Bailey Point is a red #"6" and green flasher #"5".

The first public facility is Jamison Cove Marina, recognizable by the octagonal restaurant building next to the marina. Jamison Cove is primarily a transient facility operated by Urbanna Marine (see "Marina Hopping" in the December '85 issue). On our last visit there was a sign at the center dock that instructed visitors to take any empty slip. We did, and shortly an employee from Urbanna Marine drove down to leave us a shower key and answer our questions. All transient operations should be so easy.

The restaurant on the grounds is Chez Claude, serving fine French cuisine. A short walk up the hill is "town," where you can dine at the Urbanna Inn. The Inn is a bit less formal than Chez Claude, but also cheaper.

Past Jamison Cove are the dock and grain elevators of the Southern States Coop. During the harvest season, two small grain carriers call at the docks, hauling grain to Hampton Roads. The *John W* and the *Chief* are the last two small freighters plying the Bay, albeit part time.

Next up the creek is Southside Marine Service, a well equipped repair facility. Past Southside is Urbanna Marine. They are the largest facility in the creek, with several covered boat sheds, a ship's store and repair facilities. Both Southside and Urbanna Marine sell gasoline and diesel.

Between Urbanna Marine and the bridge is Urbanna Bridge Marina. It is a small marina and they do not usually have transient slips. Check with the owner, Mrs. Meyers, though, and she might find a place to put you for a night or two.

We have found the best anchorage to be opposite Urbanna Marina, almost to the bridge. There is plenty of room except during the Oyster Festival.

The highway bridge just around the corner has a vertical clearance of only 21 feet, which limits the upper reaches of the creek to mast-less vessels. However, this is a beautiful part of the creek with five and six-foot water depths. The shoreline here is sparsely settled with high, wooded banks that assure a beautiful and quiet anchorage.

The rest of the year Urbanna is a quiet little town where nothing happens. Almost every business in town is on the small hill overlooking the creek. Within a ten minute walk of the marinas, we found a drug store, laundromat, doctor, dentist, barber, beauty shop, grocery, liquor store, hardware store, gift shop, library, motel, restaurant and a dozen Labrador retrievers—my kind of town. □

Notes

TAYLOR CREEK

on the Corrotoman River

On the north shore of the Rappahannock, about ten miles upstream, is the entrance to the Corrotoman River, marked by a flasher on a pole. Once you are inside, the beautiful Corrotoman opens up with any number of anchorages available. Everywhere you look is a protected spot to drop your hook. On port side at both Ball Point and Bar Point are sandy beaches with swimmers and perhaps a beach umbrella or two.

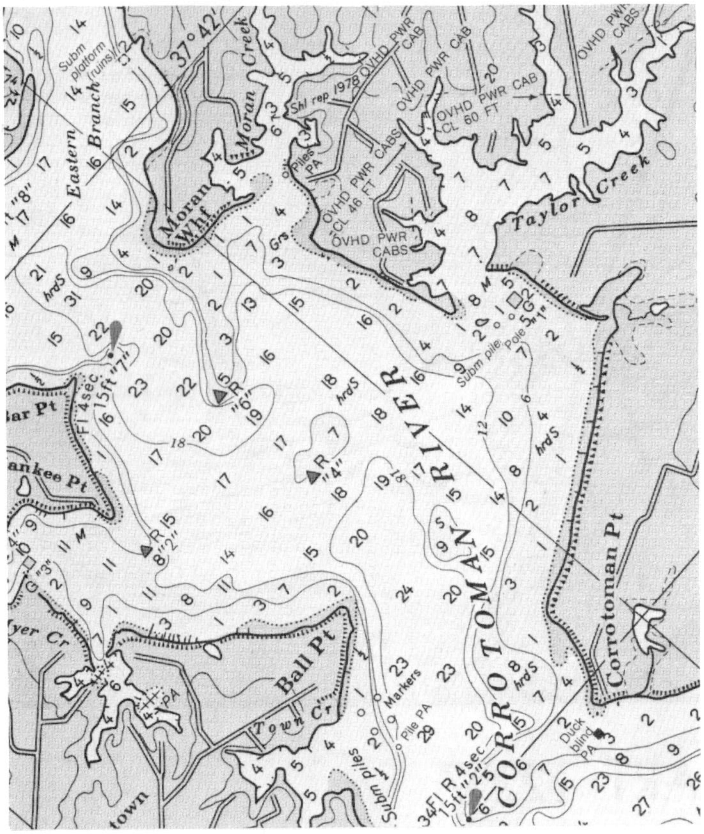

From NOAA Chart 12237—not to be used for navigation.

Take a few minutes to explore the two main branches, appropriately named the Eastern Branch and (what else?) the Western Branch, with their wooded shores and an occasional house nestled in the soft curves of the countryside.

On the Eastern Branch are some steeply banked shores where a boat can nestle right up to the water's edge. Up the Western Branch can be seen the wreck of an old oyster boat and barge, still tied up to a rotting pier. Beyond this a tiny ferry still plies its trade by Ottoman Wharf.

On our first visit to the Corrotoman we had a chance to visit Taylor Creek. This little tributary is quite beautiful, and its entrance, unusual. If you look at your charts, the water depths appear too shallow for comfort. However, we were guided by local knowledge and found no less than six feet all the way in. The entrance marker, Daybeacon "1," may be hard to see from the channel of the Corrotoman, because of its surroundings.

If you go up the Corrotoman toward "4," keeping it as nearly as possible dead ahead, you will find Taylor Creek almost due east when you are about 300 yards short of the marker. Turn eastwards, watching your depth, and you will soon see the solitary green daybeacon "1" with its entourage of stakes.

When entering Taylor Creek, local knowledge also advises that you stick closely to the oyster bed stakes to starboard. Ignore the telephone pole entirely. As you approach the creek entrance, you'll notice two stakes which are larger diameter than the oyster stakes. Pass between them, then swing around the black daymark leaving it to port, and you'll find approximately 6 feet of water all the way in. Do not try to cut between the pole and the small marshy island, as the water is quite shallow there. Once inside just pick a corner for yourself and enjoy a peaceful night. □

Notes

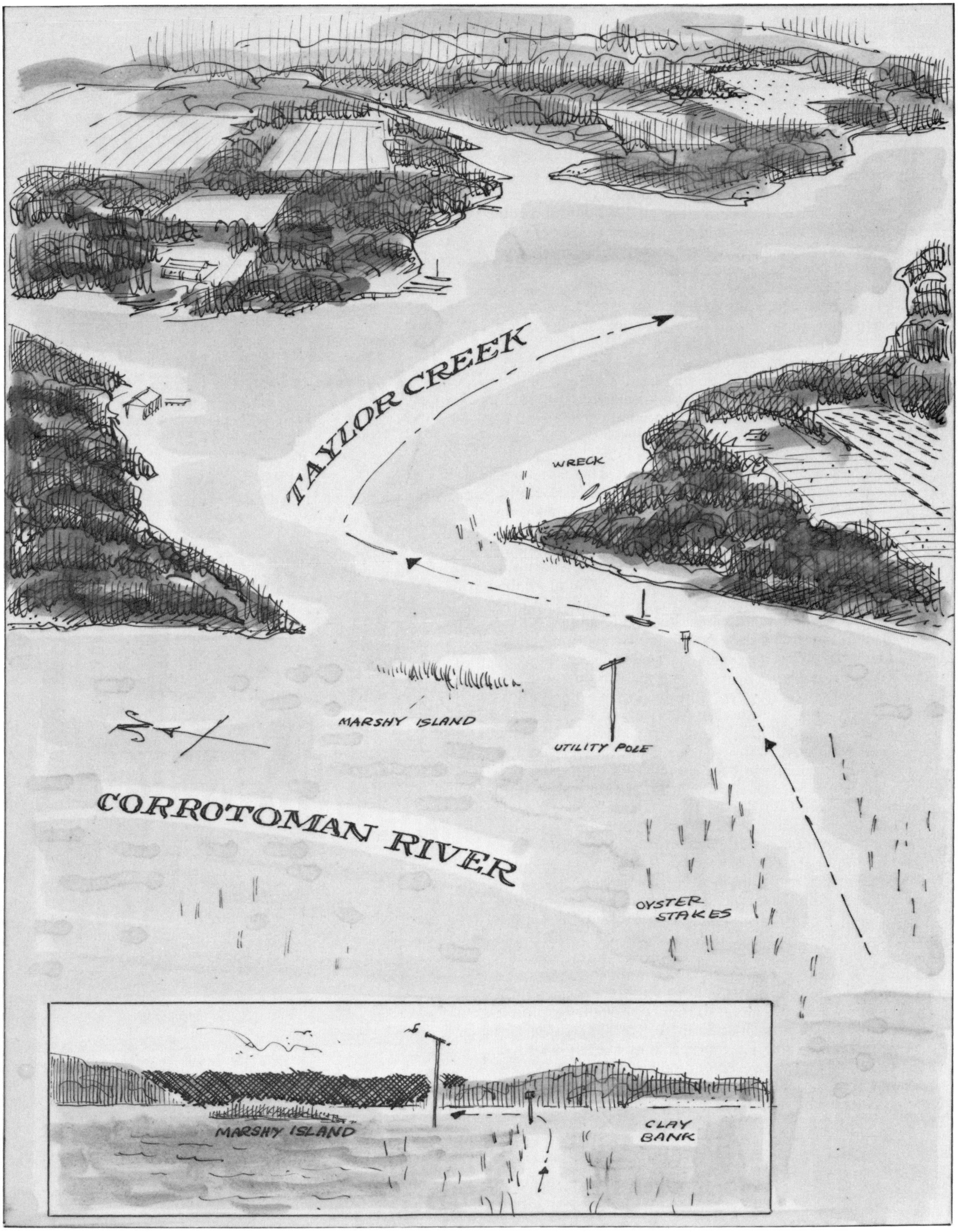
TAYLOR CREEK
WRECK
MARSHY ISLAND
UTILITY POLE
CORROTOMAN RIVER
OYSTER STAKES
MARSHY ISLAND
CLAY BANK

MYER CREEK

on the Corrotoman River

If you are searching for a peaceful body of water where you can while away a day or two, try the Corrotoman River, about three miles upstream of the Rappahannock River Bridge. The entrance of the Corrotoman is quite broad with only a single shoal to contend with—and that is clearly marked by a red beacon off Corrotoman Point across from Millenbeck. You won't be able to get supplies in Millenbeck; the harbor is shoal and the docks are filled with workboats.

Two miles upstream of the entrance beacon the Corrotoman divides. The right fork, called Eastern Branch, shows six feet or more of water some two and a half miles further. A favorite anchorage is in the little cove formed in Bells Creek. The water depths measure 12 to 14 feet, and the point of land to starboard just before the cove has a beautiful sand beach.

The Western Branch of the Corrotoman carries six-foot depths for some three and a half miles upstream. There are no navigational aids beyond West Point, but with a little caution the few shoals can easily be avoided. There is a fairly large curve of land between West Point and Merry Point, reminiscent of the small bay off St. Mary's City that provides an anchorage on those hot summer nights.

Just beyond this cove on the south shore is Ottoman Wharf, where a cable ferry still carries cars and passengers across to Merry Point. This is one of the few remaining cable ferries. Be sure to give it plenty of room ahead and astern, as passing too closely can cause serious accidents in running afoul of the cable. If you travel in this area by auto, take time to ride the little ferry. There is no charge for the crossing, and there is room for two vehicles on board. The operators are courteous and friendly, in the summer months ferrying as many as sixty cars daily across the river.

Another good anchorage is in 18 feet of water off John Creek. You will note that the entire length of the Corrotoman, including both branches, is deep enough for most boats, with such a wealth of creeks and anchorages that you should allow at least a full day to explore this area.

Myer Creek is about one mile upstream from the Corrotoman's entrance, on the western shore. The first mark on entering is a red daymark to starboard off Yankee Point. A snug anchorage in the event of southerlies is on the north shore of Ball Point near the sandy beach.

Upstream just beyond the next two marks is Yankee Point Sailboat Marina. The facility has expanded and carries marine and boating supplies, including fuel and ice. The second floor of the main building serves as a yacht club for members and contains a kitchen, bar, bathrooms, fireplace and general lounge area. The hospitable owners will arrange transportation to a nearby store.

One of this area's best anchorages is on the left branch of Myer Creek. There are seven and eight-foot water depths, with only an occasional home half hidden along the densely wooded banks. I haven't seen any anchorages more serene or inviting. □

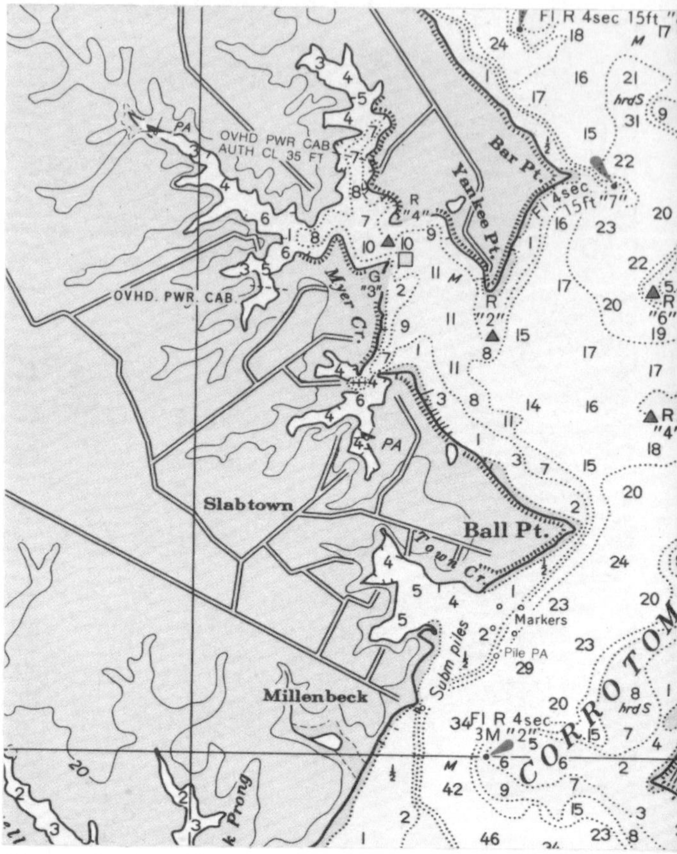

From NOAA Chart 12235—not to be used for navigation

Notes

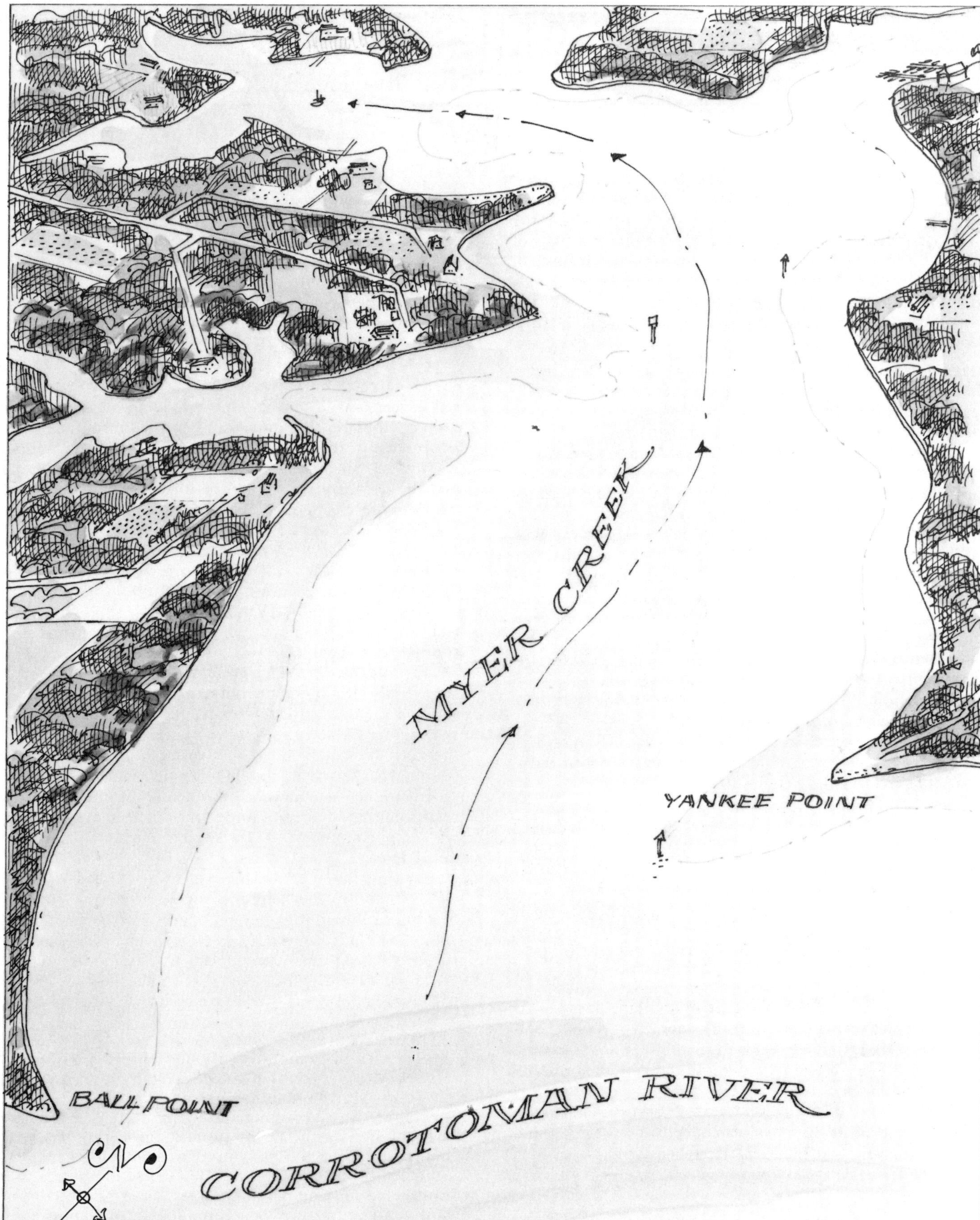
MYER CREEK
YANKEE POINT
BALL POINT
CORROTOMAN RIVER
N

JACKSON CREEK

on the Piankatank River

at Deltaville

Perhaps one of the best anchorages between the Hampton Roads area and the upper Chesapeake Bay lies between the Rappahannock and the York Rivers. It is the Piankatank River, which serves as a border for the Virginia counties of Mathews and Middlesex. Captain John Smith, in records of his travels in the Chesapeake, describes the Piankatank as a "little river." Although it is comparatively small, the Piankatank compensates by providing all-around beauty, cruisability, and friendliness.

It's not quite three miles across the mouth of the Rappahannock to the Stingray Light, and another mile brings you to the main entrance channel of the Piankatank river. A handy mark for the entrance to the channel is red buoy "2," Fl R 4 sec. A course of 255 will bring you to red lighted bell #6, you can turn onto course 322°. You will note that the whole area surrounding Stove Point Neck is crowded with the small fishing boats of weekend vacationers. The Piankatank-Deltaville area has earned a reputation as one of the loveliest spots on the Bay, and its many vacationing visitors agree.

The entrance to Jackson Creek is a little tricky here and should have your close attention. A lot of folks come to grief getting into the creek because the main channel does not run directly from the first channel mark straight into the creek. Instead, turn northeast (approximately 070°) toward the starboard bank where red #4 stands within a few feet of shore. From there you turn almost due west, keeping the next three green marks close to port till you come to red #10. At this point Jackson Creek divides into two branches. On the south branch, the county dock is located on the starboard bank. Across the creek is the Fishing Bay Yacht Club.

The north branch houses the main marina, Deltaville Marina, within eyesight of daymark #10. The marina's covered piers are crowded with local boats but can usually accommodate cruising yachtsmen. The Deltaville Marina offers gas and diesel fuel, engine repairs, and marine supplies, ice and beverages. Some recent additions include new open slips with 10′ of water, new bathhouse facilities and a laundromat. There is ample room for anchoring just beyond the marina. Nearby are several grocery stores.

The Deltaville area is alive with boat builders. Aside from the main boatyards, nearly every road and lane has its one-man backyard operation turning out workboats and sportfishermen. Deltaville seems to cover the entire peninsula formed on the south by the Piankatank and on the north by the Rappahannock.

Our choice for anchorages is the north branch. There are a number of workboats there, but water depth of six feet is found almost to the very end where there is less activity. Just watch out for the shoal on the starboard side at the nine-foot mark and you'll be okay.

NOTE: Shoaling to 2.5 ft. at MLW extends approx. 180° true, 35 ft. from light "10" off Stove Pt.

FISHING BAY

on the Piankatank River

You will have a good course for the Piankatank if, having been between the outer mark Fl G 4 sec. "1" and "3" in Hole-in-the Wall channel, you take a heading of about 330° toward Fl G. 4 sec. "3" in the mouth of the river. On this course you will be able to see Stingray Point itself after about 5 miles or so. Keep it a little to port; this precaution will keep you in a minimum depth not less than some 15 feet. Watch out for the ubiquitous crabpots that infest the Bay in depths below 15 ft. From "3" a course of 279° will bring you into the river.

Don't cut any markers beyond can "5," but proceed in a straight line southwest from "5" to "7," to "8" which is a 2.5-second red flasher on a 2- to 4-foot bar extending southeast from now very obvious Stove Point Neck. Often the southeast bar has people on it at low tide, possibly clamming, crabbing, or wading and swimming. The homes on Stove Point are lovely and the residents are among the fortunate few in this country who can watch moonrise and sunrise to the east, and sunset and moonset to the west as well. You give the bar marker and the marks at Stove Point a nice wide berth as you go to the northwest and then north to go up close to shore into the deepwater arms of Fishing Bay. You hold depth and good swinging room and put your hook down solidly in 16 feet in the northwest corner to get as much protection from the southwest as possible.

Fishing Bay provides good protection from the east and west. It also has other attributes. On a stifling mosquito-laden summer night in settled weather you can get a blissful night's sleep under the stars in the open cockpit by hooking over from the stern and catching the light wisp of a southwesterly that is nearly always present, and bug-free. The morning sun climbing quietly in the east will gently awaken you from a comfortable, restful night. Memories linger of the music drifting over the water from a party at the Fishing Bay Yacht Club as you were lulled asleep.

Fishing Bay Yacht Club is crowded, but its people are warm, friendly, and helpful in an emergency. There may not be room to tie up long but one can usually debark there. One should be a member of a yacht club having reciprocity with the Fishing Bay Club. A phone call to Taylor's Restaurant in Deltaville (804-776-9611), or Miss Lynne's Galley (776-6040) will usually get a car down to pick up your party for a meal out.

Ruark Marina, Deagle's Marina and Deagle and Sons Marine Railway are all to the left entering Fishing Bay. Ruark Marina and Deagle's Marina have transient slips. Deagle's Marina also has gas and diesel, a service yard (including travel lift) offering engine and other repairs and a small store with marine supplies, grocery items, ice and beverages. Both marinas will try to help you get to town for whatever they cannot provide. Everyone in the area is routinely kind and helpful. Cottages can be rented nearby, and you can tour the boatyards in the area and watch the construction of all types of Chesapeake craft.

Whether you use Fishing Bay and its facilities as a harbor of refuge, a vacation destination, a place for rest, or a place for a party, the area will not only "fill the bill" but will bring you back again and again the rest of your life. □

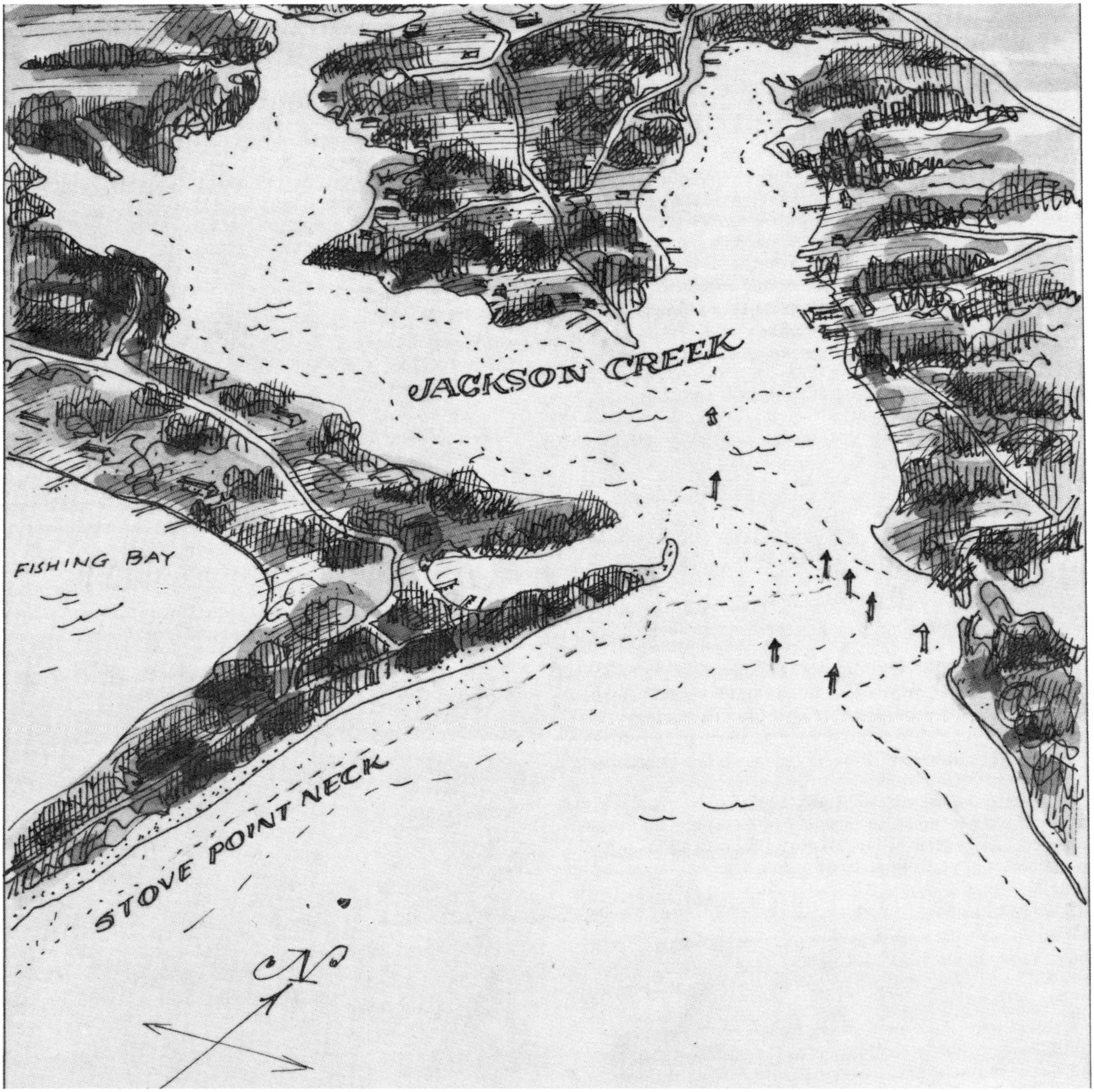
JACKSON CREEK
FISHING BAY
STOVE POINT NECK
N

HEALY CREEK
on the Piankatank River

Warm sunshine sparkled on the water and our white sails billowed out against a bright blue sky as we set a course for Windmill Point. And on a comfortable reach we were able to pick up Windmill Point Light smack dab on the nose.

In the distance we could see Stingray Point Light, and past that we picked up the channel markers at the entrance to the Piankatank River. With great care we sailed down around the lighted mark off Stove Point and, sheeting in our sails, beat our way upstream. The wind had shifted out of the north, and we passed Fishing Bay in a rush. There's a green flasher that marks a portside shoal just off Iron Point, so be sure you honor it. The marks to Healy Creek are less than a mile beyond, so we had time to ease our sheets and, as the breeze lightened, ghost our way up to the entrance at Horse Point, where we dropped sail and started up the engine.

If you study your charts, Healy Creek may not appear so inviting. The entrance is shown with a pair of privately maintained marks and questionable-looking channel, which almost turned us off. (I'm glad it didn't, however.) First a red then a black mark, and a red, bordered by a scattering of oyster stakes and crab floats, led us through a narrow opening in the shoreline and into the broad, quiet waters of Healy Creek.

There was plenty of water in the middle of the creek as we passed several impressive homes and large boathouses. Slowly we motored upstream enjoying the scenery. The banks rose on either side promising complete protection in a blow. Further upstream the creek splits and the water appears to get a little thin.

Our motor was throttled way back, and our quiet putt-putt did little to break the serenity of our surroundings. We reached a somewhat broader part of the creek and slowly did a wide circle, coasted to a stop, and I let the anchor slip quietly into the water. On both sides the wooded banks appeared uninhabited, and a flood of mountain laurel threatened to overwhelm the scene.

Upstream where the creek divides we could see what appeared to be several boathouses strung out together. A small launch came out of one and approached us, an older man at the wheel with his wife beside him just going out for a spin.

"Welcome!" he called over to us. We asked about the docks and boathouses, and he called, "That's all part of Chick Cove Farm. This used to be called Chick Cove, but they call it Healy Creek now. Come over and tie up to the docks if you need anything!"☐

Notes

COBB'S CREEK
on the Piankatank River

The entrance into Cobb's Creek reminds me of Fairlee Creek in the upper Bay. Two daymarks lead you parallel to shore until you are almost onto Ginney Point, a finger of land jutting out from the western side of Cobb's Creek entrance. Just when it seems you will go aground, the creek opens a narrow entrance to port and you can slip through in 8 to 10 feet of water. Inside, a small branch forks off to starboard where a boatyard and gas dock are situated. The main body of Cobb's Creek runs southeasterly. We anchored at the seven-foot mark on NOAA chart #12235.

There are several large old homes on the shores here with a fair amount of wooded cover to shield them from view and preserve the feeling of privacy. The bottom is thick mud, and the absence of traffic makes this a snug and safe anchorage. Further upstream about 500 yards the creek opens into another small bay, giving an anchored boat more room to swing, but offers only five-foot depths, which was a little on the shallow side for us.

West of Cobb's Creek, the river makes a 90° turn south and with another turn to the west flows under the Piankatank River Bridge with a 43′ clearance. The river continues winding its way for another ten miles until it disappears into marsh-lands. On the way upriver, there is shelter in the many elbows and inlets, particularly around uninhabited Berkle Island.☐

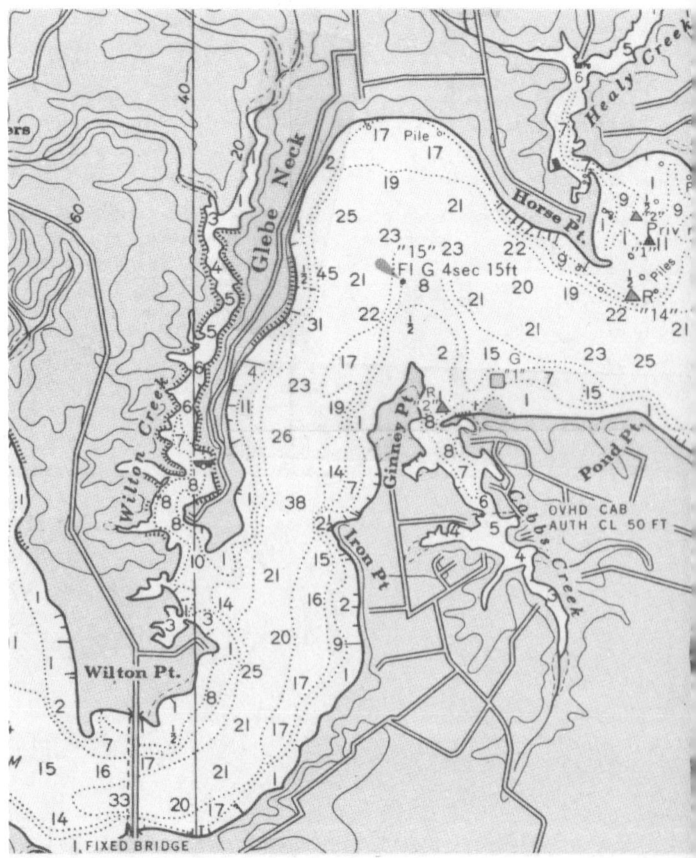

From NOAA Chart 12235—not to be used for navigation.

COBBS CREEK

HEALY CREEK
N

WILTON CREEK

on the Piankatank River

A gently winding river with sloping, wooded banks, the Piankatank creates a beautiful backdrop for the cruising family. From its mouth starting at Stingray Point to Freeport, one finds nearly 15 miles of river capable of carrying a vessel of six-foot draft. The only limitation is the fixed bridge ten miles from Stingray Point Light at Dixie, whose height at mean high water is 43 feet.

The best harbors are below the bridge anyway, and we picked out Wilton Creek for one night's layover. It gave us a chance to explore as much of the Piankatank as we could with our tall mast.

As we scurried straight up the Piankatank toward Wilton Creek, the blackening sky made us wonder if, perhaps, we should duck in somewhere nearby. But we continued upstream and noticed two shoals that might be difficult to spot the first time you visit the Piankatank. Both are on the south shore, the first at Roane Point and the second at Ginney Point just past Cobb's Creek. The reason they are hard to spot is that the shoals extend more than halfway across the river and thus the marks are well to starboard—where you would never look for them. But beware! Be sure to honor the mark off Ginney Point, as water depths of one-half foot extend far out from shore.

The best way to enter Wilton Creek (since it's unmarked) is to avoid cutting any corners. Don't attempt to turn in until you have the middle of its entrance dead abeam. Then turn and let the brush stakes show you where the shoals are.

From NOAA chart #12235—not to be used for navigation.

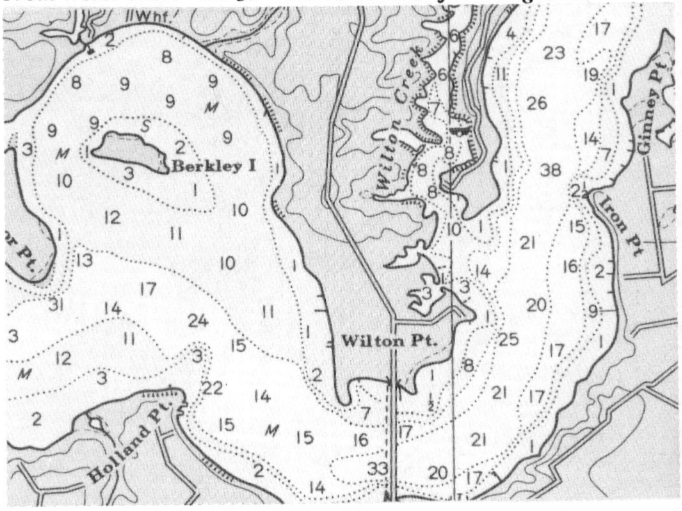

Wilton Creek is quite narrow, but carries five- and six-foot depths for almost a mile north. The shores are high and heavily wooded, reminding us of a mountain lake. Although the high banks cut down on the breeze and there was no air stirring when we anchored, the trees kept the creek pleasantly cool.

We dropped our hook just around the first big bend to the right in water depths of seven or eight feet. Around the next point was another lovely cove, already occupied by a visiting boat. Supplies can be obtained just across the Piankatank at Dixie, which is just at the bridge.☐

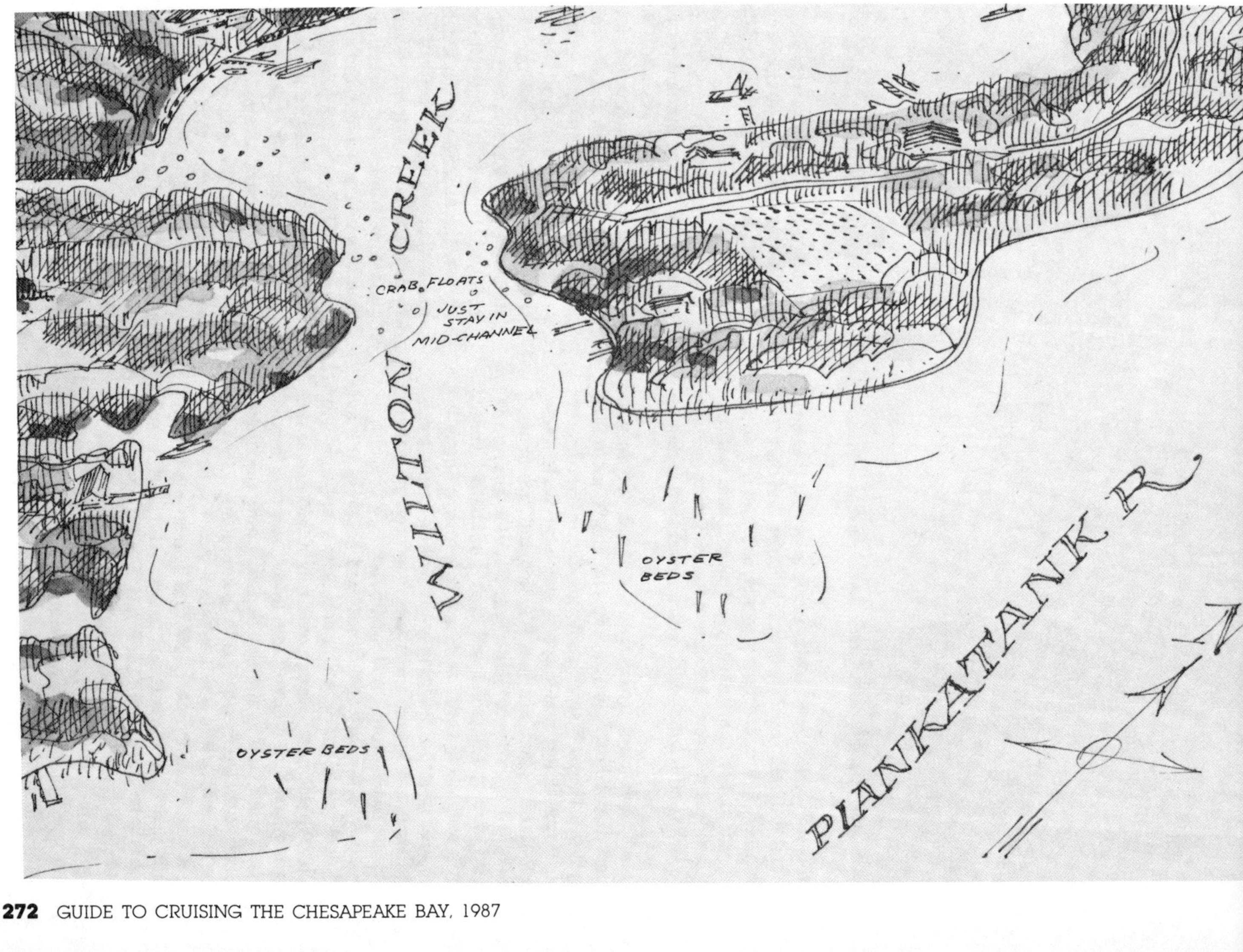

BERKLEY ISLAND

on the Piankatank River

Berkley Island lies way up the Piankatank River, approximately seven miles. The distance by itself isn't so bad. After all, you can spend a couple of days exploring the Piankatank and not get bored. The cruise up the Piankatank can be delightfully scenic, so take time to enjoy this beautiful river.

From the bridge take course 315° to avoid the end of Wilton Point and the somewhat trickier shoal to port off Holland. Berkley Island is about a mile northwest of the bridge. You'll probably want to swing around the east side of the island, but be careful. You'll note on your charts (we use #12235) that there is a prominent shoal extending eastward from the island. There are a couple of stakes in the water to guide you, so just give this end a wide berth and you'll be okay.

The favorite anchorage is just opposite Stampers Wharf in nine feet of water. The island is uninhabited most of the time, but there are two small piers if you should wish to go ashore. One dock is just opposite Stampers Wharf, and the other is at the island's western end. The island is beautiful and wild. Its elevated western end accommodates a cluster of trees, and from there the ground falls away to a grassy flat with another smaller clump of woods, which turns out to marsh at the island's eastern end.

Berkley Island is owned by the Virginia Baptist General Board and is utilized by them as part of their summer camp for boys. Through the years the Board has permitted individuals to visit the island. Visitors are encouraged to leave the island in the same beautiful state as they find it, making it possible for others to enjoy the beauty and solitude of Berkley Island.

Anchor to windward of the island so the evening mosquitoes will be blown away from you. The river bottom is soft mud, so a regular cruising Danforth-type anchor should set well enough. The high ground behind Stampers Wharf will give you ample protection from northerlies, and there are few homes in the area to disturb the peace of this anchorage.

The Piankatank carries deep water quite a way further upstream with several beautiful old—and new—homes scattered along its wooded shores. There is another good anchorage quite a way further upstream at Freeport on the south shore. In fact, you'll spot several others along the way. But for my money, you won't find any more attractive than in the quiet waters behind Berkley Island.☐

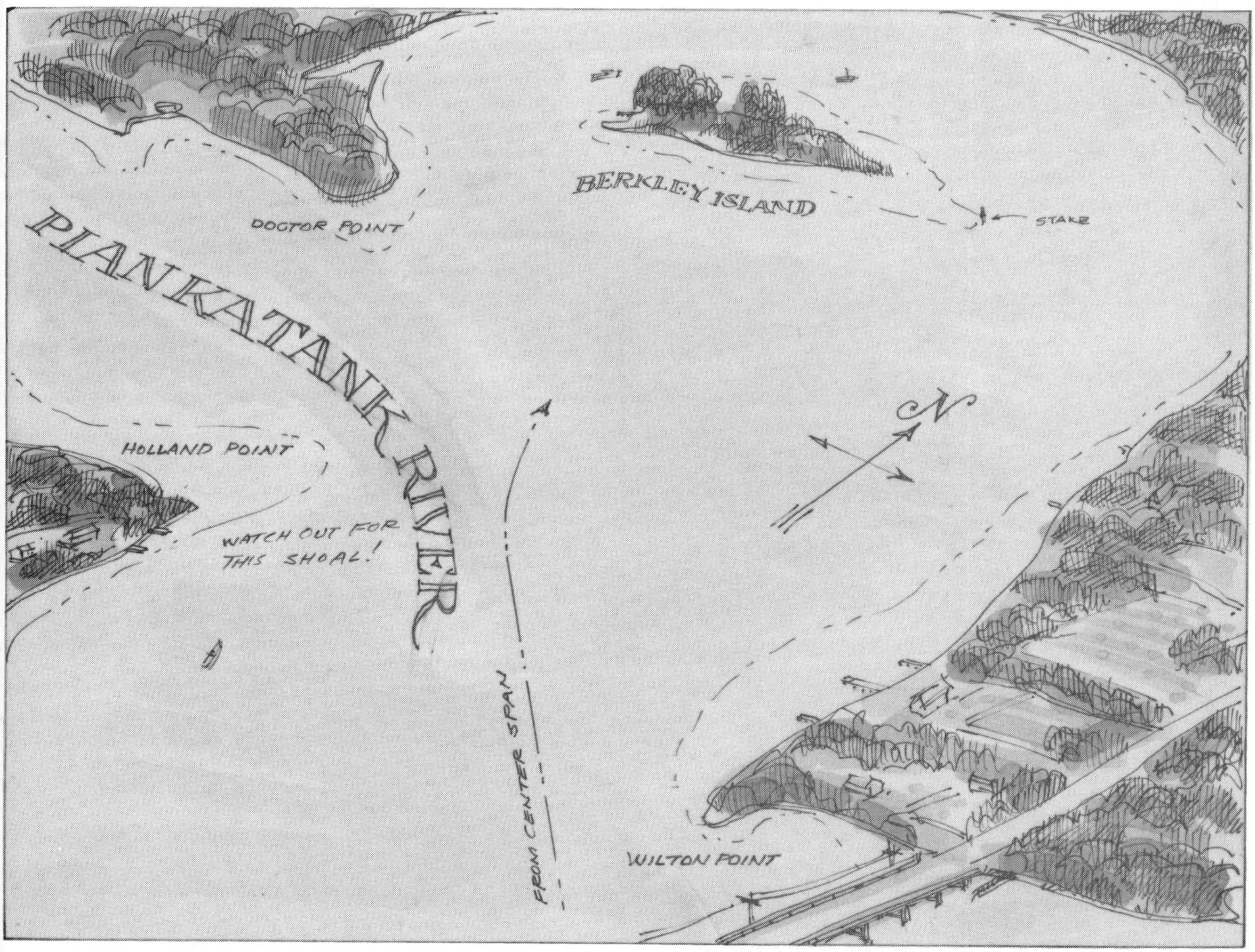

MILFORD HAVEN

at Gwynn Island

off the Piankatank River

As you travel around the Chesapeake Bay you will hear, as we did, occasional reference to the "Hole-in-the-Wall." And each time I heard that name, the urge became stronger to make its passage. I was being drawn to it irresistibly.

For those not familiar with Hole-in-the-Wall, perhaps a few notes about the area are in order. Gwynn Island, population somewhere between 700 and 800 people, is a small body of land located at the southern side of the mouth of the Piankatank River. The island is separated from mainland Virginia by a small bay known as Milford Haven. Access to Gywnn Island is by a small bridge that touches at its western tip.

It's fairly easy to enter Milford Haven through this northwest entrance, and we've done it a number of times. From the red marker that guards the southeast tip of the Stove Point Neck bar, a course of 197° will take you to the first entrance mark in Hills Bay, some 1¼ miles south. From that point a series of lighted spars will lead you through the swing bridge. Follow the channel northeast, past Callis Wharf and halfway to red daymark #8, then slip up into Edwards Creek. Many workboats moor here, but there's plenty of room to drop a hook with security.

The Hole-in-the-Wall entrance is something else. It brings you in on the southeast or Bay side, through the natural gap between Gwynn Island and its small neighbor to the south,

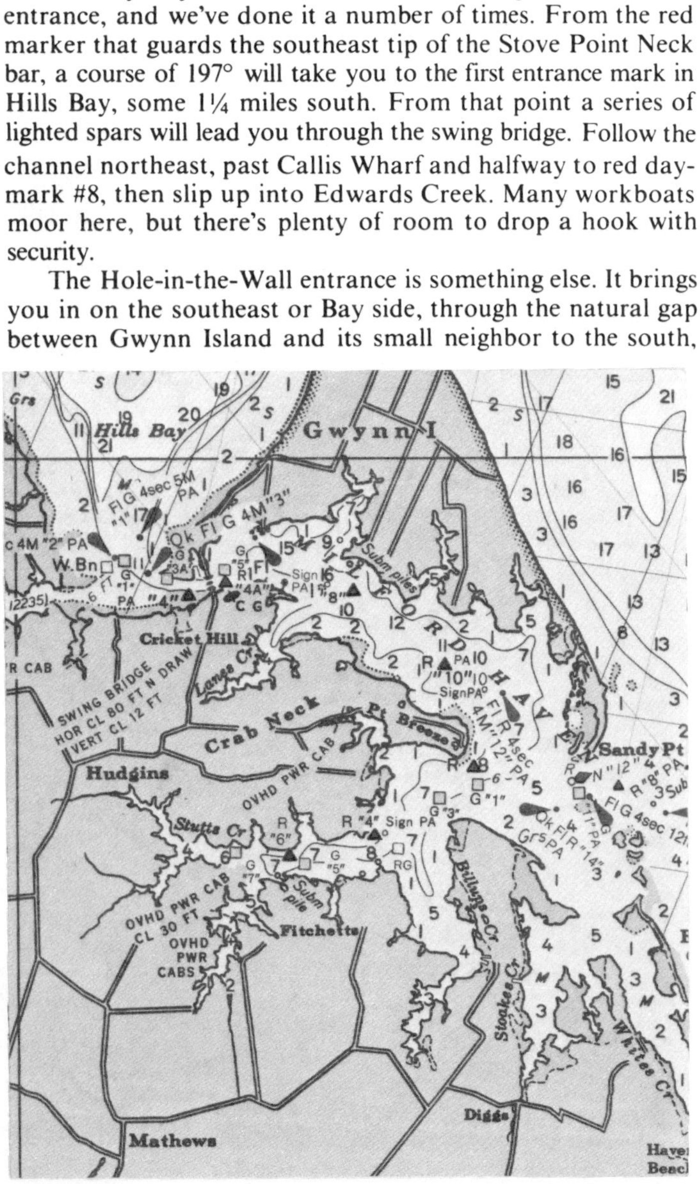

From NOAA Chart 12225—not to be used for navigation.

Rigby Island. The channel twists and turns its way in and out among several marshy shoals and sand bars but is about five miles shorter than going around the northern tip and down through Hills Bay and the swing bridge.

I remember, once, calling the Milford Haven Coast Guard Station Officer-of-the-Day for advice on entering from the Hole-in-the-Wall and he said, "We don't recommend it, but if you run it, try for high water and go slow at low water because a four foot draft touches. There's a bad spot at #6 and another at #12. And between #8 and #12 if you are a little wide, *forget it*. We ran it six times in 3 days and got 3 bumps." (He didn't say how to get your boat off the bar if you ground hard on high water.) The best time to take chances is on mid-tide with the water rising. Always carry a "push pole" a little longer than the distance from your keel to the top of your head while standing on your boat.

On a recent cruise we found ourselves just off the Hole-in-the-Wall entrance, midway between the two outermost spars #3 and #5. The entrance is easy to find and well marked by a bell # about four miles offshore and three lighted spars, each roughly a mile apart on heading 293° (approximately).

Hole-in-the-Wall gets a good bit of use, but it isn't the recommended entrance. Coming in from Hole-in-the-Wall the numbers go from "3" *up* to "14" and then *down* from "12" to "4A" and "5" at the bridge. Take red "14" on the right, then take reds on the left from "12" to "10" as then you are technically going out the other, better entrance.

If you try to head left from the hole entrance, depths drop to 5 feet past #3 right away. Most boats that anchor, do so between #5 and #6 outside the channel on the north side. The bridge still opens for one long and one short blast, and boats use the bay side of the swing span going both ways. Look at your chart. Be sure to have a new one, and for areas like Hole-in-the-Wall, get the 12235 NOAA chart.

At the lower end of Hills Bay lies Narrows Point. If you like leisurely dockside boating, you will enjoy the full service Narrows Marina (including a laundromat) and its adjacent resort facility the Islander.

Transient slips at the Islander are available at half-price to those who also rent one of their motel rooms. If you decide to stay at one of the Islander Marina's slips, there are two important things to keep in mind. The first is that a strong current flows perpendicular to the line of slips. The second thing to note is that daymarker #4, directly across the marina marks 1- to 2- foot depths. It is best to get the dockmaster to show you the limits of the navigable channel when you check in. A local store will come get you and carry you back to shop for groceries. Across the highway from the Islander is a public ramp and local restaurant. A nice campground on the island is Camper's Haven which leases or rents on a daily basis.□

NOTE: Shoaling to 2.5 ft. at MLW extends approx. 180° true, 35 ft. from light "10" off Stove Pt.

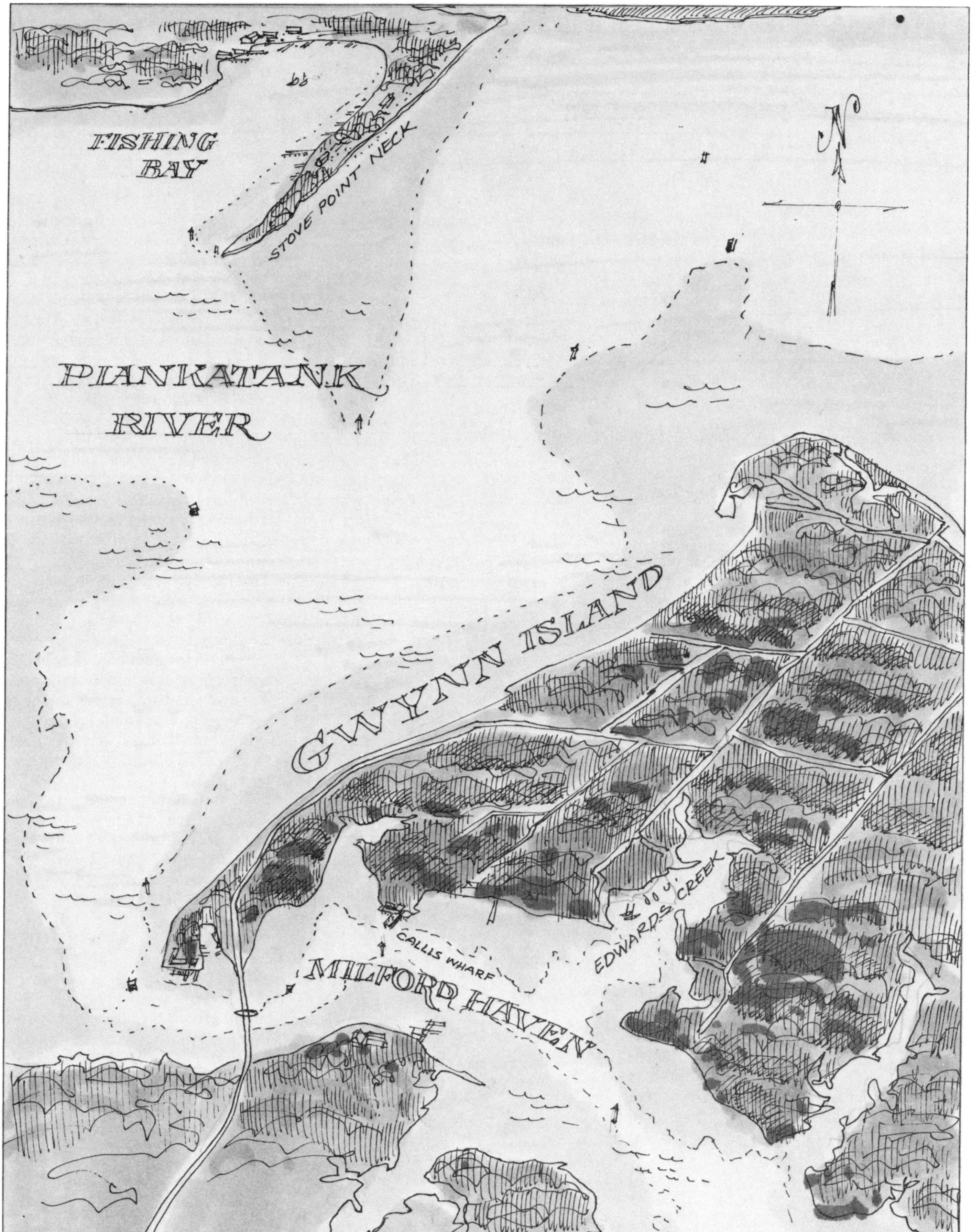
FISHING BAY
STOVE POINT NECK
PIANKATANK RIVER
GWYNN ISLAND
CALLIS WHARF
MILFORD HAVEN
EDWARDS CREEK
N

STUTTS CREEK

at Milford Haven

off the Piankatank River

We made two stops on our way to Stutts Creek. The first was at the gas docks at the Islander Motel-Marina to dump our trash. (Trash disposal is becoming increasingly difficult for boaters around the Bay, with a 50¢-$1.00 a bag charge not unusual. You have to sympathize with marinas, who in turn have to pay to have trash removed. This used to be part of their service, but increasing costs are being passed on to boaters.) It seems to make sense that if we want to insure clean waters, waterside communities will have to provide adequate trash disposal for boaters — preferably at no charge. Otherwise, the less conscientious will just decide to heave their trash over the side rather than haul it back home with them.

Our second stop was at Callis Wharf. The wharf is an interesting spot to visit while area watermen offload their catch. We visited the indoor peeler boxes here and picked up a "baker's dozen" soft crabs and then walked next door to the food market for supplies and ice.

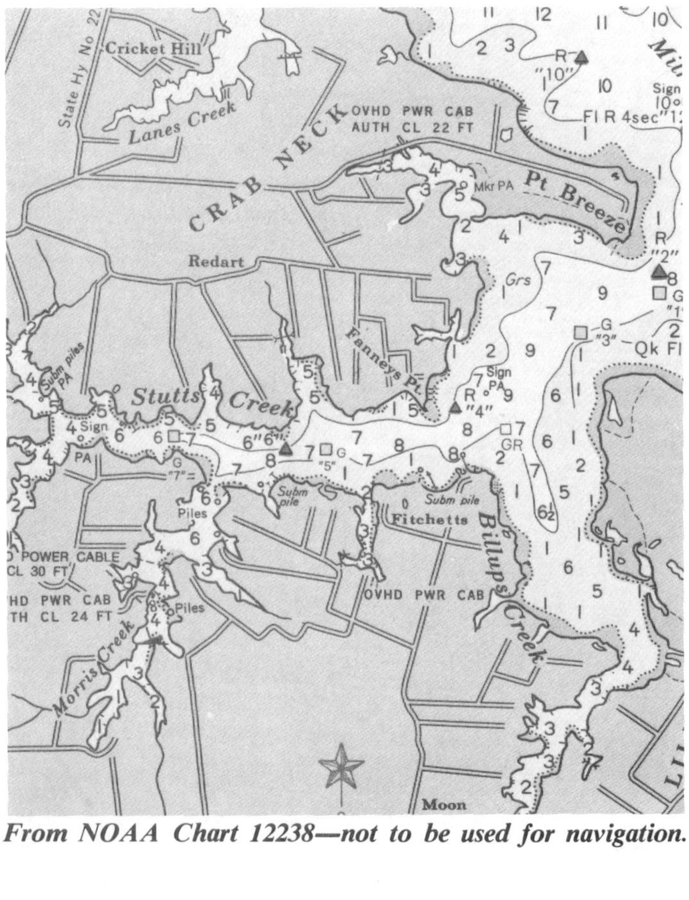

From NOAA Chart 12238—not to be used for navigation.

From Callis Wharf we followed the marked channel down to the entrance of Stutts Creek. **You will note that if you enter through the Hole-in-the-Wall the marks switch over beyond #14; that is, from that point on through the bridge you leave red marks to port as if you were leaving a harbor.**

The entrance to Stutts Creek is clearly marked by red and black daymarks appearing as a gateway to the creek inside. And what a beautiful creek it is. The first cove to starboard after Breeze Point looked inviting, with few signs of civilization, but many oyster stakes and crab pots would have kept us from getting very far out of Stutts' main channel.

To port we explored Billups Creek but decided against it for a summer night's anchorage. The channel is narrow going in, and many marshes along its banks promised hordes of hungry insects — the infamous "no-see'ums" and mosquitoes that abound in the summertime. So we headed further upstream and anchored in five feet of water in the cove just west of Fanneys Point.

On our stern deck we cleaned our soft crabs and discussed whether to try Hole-in-the-Wall the next day. We checked the tides and calculated that the channel would be at flood tide at 7 a.m. the next morning, and we would try it. As we settled back in our cockpit that evening, a full moon gleamed across the waters, illuminating the softly wooded shores and giving a ghostly beauty to the white-columned facade of old Fleetwood Manor.

The next morning we pulled up anchor at dawn and motored our way out of Stutts Creek and headed down to #14 which marks the start of the Hole-in-the-Wall channel. From a distance, there are four marks all in a bunch, plus two more out in the Bay, all looking very confusing. However, we found it was quite simple once we got right up to them.

We turned at #14 and headed up to #11 and #12. From there our charts were unclear about water depths and thus, the tension built up. From #9 we turned more easterly toward #8 where there were some four-foot marks shown on our charts. There was a nice strong northerly breeze blowing dancing, sparkling water across our bow, but the tension kept building as we rounded #8 and ran down on #6. Finally that mark was passed, and with immense relief we headed north up the Bay. □

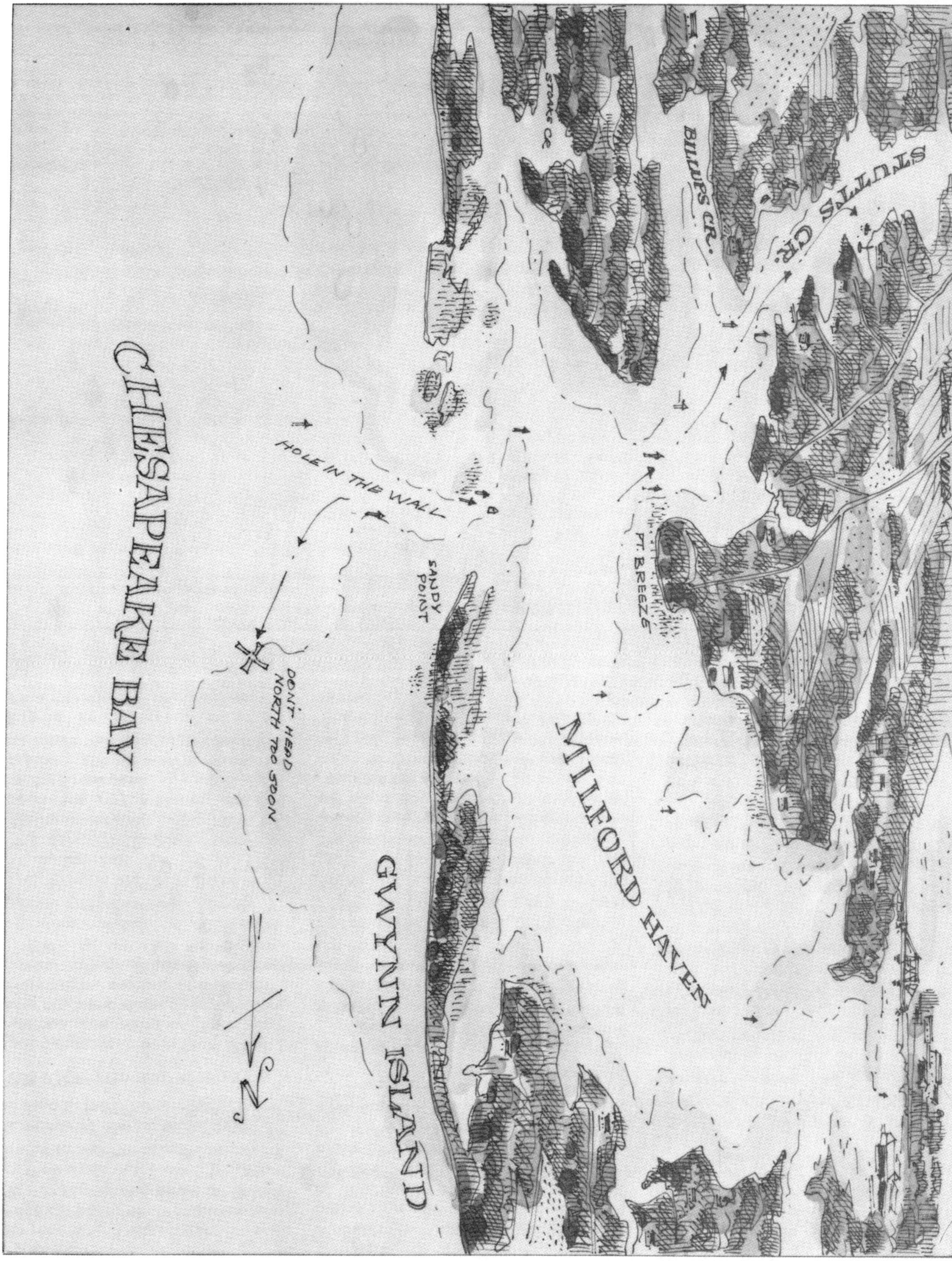
CHESAPEAKE BAY
HOLE IN THE WALL
SANDY POINT
DON'T HEAD NORTH TOO SOON
GWYNN ISLAND
MILFORD HAVEN
PT. BREEZE
BILLUPS CR.
STUTTS CR.
N

HORN HARBOR

north of Mobjack Bay

With a storm brewing, we decided to seek the sanctuary of Horn Harbor on the Bay's western shore above New Point Comfort. This Horn Harbor is not to be confused with the tiny, pretty hurricane hole Horn Harbor on the northern upper reach of the Great Wicomico. That one is small, has high wooded sides and a twisting daylight entrance. On last visit it had silted in to about six feet and was filled with crabpots, but would still offer excellent protection from long violent storms.

Horn Harbor on the Bay is easily accessible to craft with five or six feet draft. The entrance is generally about the same year to year, easily read on entering, and the marks are lit at night. If you are running the Rhumb Line between Annapolis and Norfolk, you begin to enter Horn Harbor at MO-A "H-H" below Wolftrap Light, just above New Point Comfort.

We picked up the entrance mark "HH" easily from the Bay. It stands tall and at night signals the Morse letter "A" (.-). The next two sets of daymarks are probably the most important since they mark the lower portion of the shallow bar which separates the Bay from Horn Harbor itself. As long as you remain within 100 feet of #2 and in the center of #'s 2A and 3 you will find water depths of 7 to 10 feet. A closer approach to these daymarks could cause the keel to touch bottom in the soft mud that lines the edge of the bar. Once clear follow the marks to red #10, where the channel takes a hard turn to port. From there you will be looking

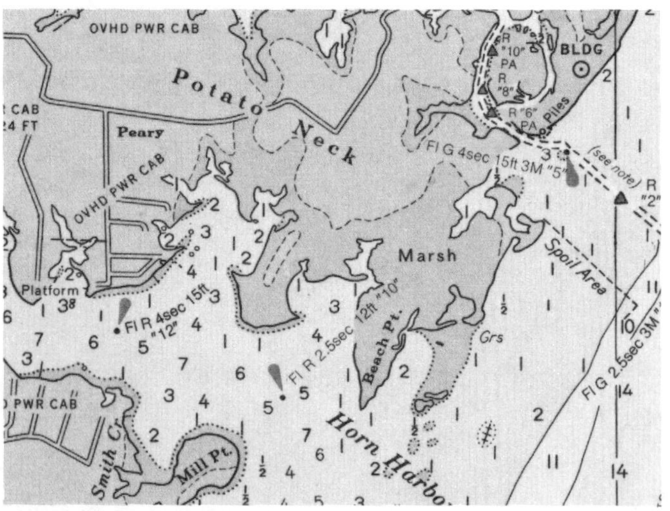

From NOAA chart #12238—not to be used for navigation.

NOTE: Shoaling to approx. 3 ft. MLW has been reported in the vicinity of entrance light "3."

upstream into the community of Port Hayward, Va. The distance between the next two daymarks appears to be long, but proved to be short, as we gazed about this placid community. Between marks 14 and 16 there is a row of stakes that are in perfect line with them and help identify the center of the channel in this area. They are not confusing and there is no danger here. The shallowest depth we found in the channel between these two marks was 5½ feet and then only for a very brief distance. From daymark #16 you will carry 6 to 8 feet all the way to the Horn Harbor Marina just beyond the last daymark, #19. If you draw less than four feet, you can find some really secluded anchorages beyond the marina in the upper reaches of the creek. We anchored our four-foot-draft Hunter 31 in seven feet of water on the south side of the channel between daymarks 18 and 19. Holding ground is excellent and is a composition of hard mud and sand.

We had not been anchored long enough to even start stowing loose gear when we were called on VHF 16 by the dockmaster of the Horn Harbor Marina, Mr. Wil Garringer, II, welcoming us and inviting us over. We took our dinghy to the dock where we quickly made friends and were treated to an excellent explanation of the history of the area.

A real treat was in store for us when he showed us the shop of the resident boatbuilder, Mr. Edward Diggs. In this tiny shed, nearly a century old, he has been creating masterpieces out of the finest raw oak timber. The art of boatbuilding was passed to Mr. Diggs by his father and his before him. At the time of our visit he was nearing completion of a 41 foot Chesapeake deadrise workboat for a local waterman. The craftsmanship exceeded anything handmade we had ever seen. It was in this same building that Mr. Diggs, under contract to a New Jersey firm, built the first six deep ocean lobster boats in the United States. An aged album and clippings from newspapers record the history making event. Everywhere we turned we saw the results of the skilled hands of Mr. Diggs, one of the few remaining master boatbuilders on the lower Bay. If you visit, be sure to ask to see the album.

Reluctantly, but in fading daylight, we bid Mr. Garringer a warm farewell and promised to return soon. As *Windless* slowly putted up the stream, we looked back and saw Mr. Garringer waving from the shore at the head of the pier. There was an urge to return but we wanted to explore the upper reaches of this lovely harbor. We found uncluttered homes, some over 100 years old. There are no loud, ugly noises here, just the quiet and peaceful sounds of nature. As we motored the dink back, we realized that we had almost become hypnotized by the beauty and serenity of our surroundings. □

Photo by Backus Aerial Photography

MOBJACK BAY

Severn River, East River, Ware River, Davis & Pepper Creeks, North River

NOAA Chart #12238 shows the Mobjack Bay to be shaped somewhat like a hand—the palm area being Mobjack Bay while the tributaries, like four fingers, spread out in separate directions. The four fingers are the Severn River, the Ware River, the North River, and the East River. Mobjack Bay is about seven miles long on the long axis (northwest to southeast) and about four miles across the mouth.

The approach from the Chesapeake is clearly marked with black and white buoys that mark trap areas. Note that the Corps of Engineers, who maintain the buoys, are changing their color to yellow.

The western side of the mouth is the Guinea Marshes, a very nondescript shoreline. The eastern side is marked by New Point Comfort Light and the adjacent abandoned lighthouse. Don't confuse the two—the light is on a 15 ft. platform about half a mile from the lighthouse. The lighthouse is visible from almost anywhere on Mobjack Bay.

Just in past New Point Comfort are Davis and Pepper Creeks. Davis Creek is a handy harbor of refuge off the Chesapeake but the two have little else to recommend them to the visitor. All four of the rivers off the Mobjack offer excellent cruising.

The Mobjack is almost too good to be true. An easy entrance, lots of protected anchorages, excellent marinas and repair facilities—whether a one night stop or a week long cruise the Mobjack is worth a visit.

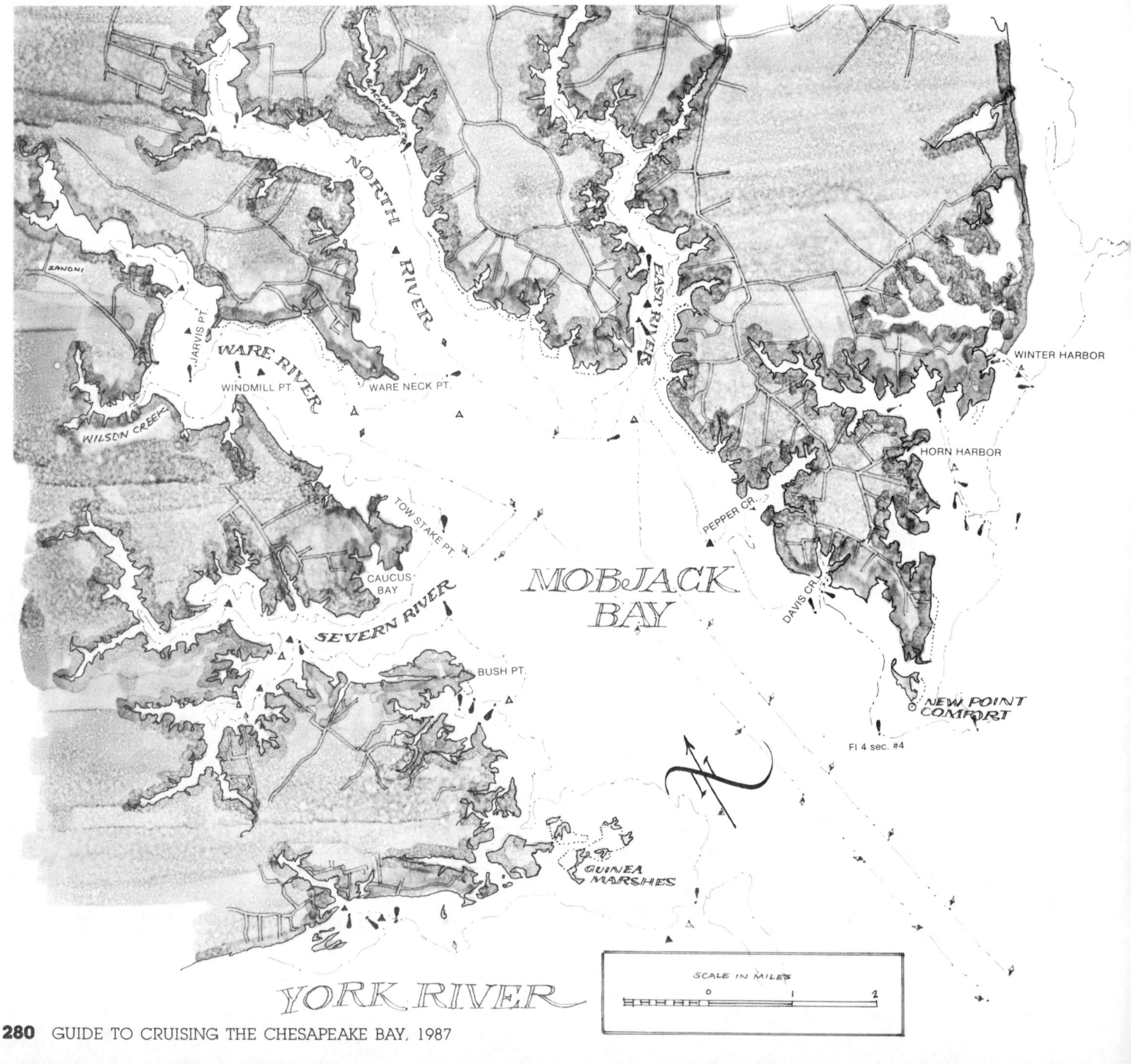

SEVERN RIVER
on Mobjack Bay

From New Point Comfort's flashing 4-second #4 (which looks like a square, flat table with red triangle reflectors suspended from its top and between its legs), we took course 295° to the 4-second flasher #1 at the mouth of the Severn River. You can check drift and tide by your position to B/W nun #14, which you should pass close aboard along the way on this course.

As you approach the Severn, the land mass to port will be Guinea Neck, which is quite low and flat. Much of what you see at water's edge is swampy marsh grass.

From a distance the entrance beacon to the Severn, #1, will blend pretty much into the land mass of Robins Neck. The Severn River stretches westerly for two miles, where it divides into Southwest Branch and Northwest Branch. At the fork of the river, Cedar Point on the south bank is easy to spot—a long, low grassy point of land with a couple of trees out near the end that are silhouetted against the horizon.

Off Cedar Point there are three marks visible to the right of a two-level duck blind. The first, a red daymark, belongs to the channel beyond leading into the Southwest Branch. To the right of that you will see #3, a lighted structure, and further right a short distance, a black daymark #1, which is the first port mark into Southwest Branch. Be sure to honor this mark as you turn into Southwest Branch.

To starboard between Stump Point and Bar Neck is a snug little cove where you can anchor out of the main channel. There are several oyster bed stakes to wind your way through, which can be harrowing since I always wonder if they might also mark shoal spots. The shore is fairly low and would allow a breeze on muggy, hot summer nights.

As you approach red daymark #4 the two marinas on this branch will become visible. Glass Marine to starboard (its name painted boldly on the roof of its large waterside building) is visible over the low grassy spit at #4. Glass Marine offers gas and diesel fuel, ice, marine supplies, and transportation, as well as engine service and boat repairs.

Opposite Glass Marine on the south shore on Rowes Creek is Holiday Marina. A well-marked channel leads to their docks, which provide both gas and diesel fuel, engine repairs, marine supplies, showers, etc. A favorite anchorage is in the stretch of water just beyond Glass Marine in 8 to 10 feet of water. Be sure to display an anchor light after dark.

Another nice anchorage on the Severn River is up on the Northwest Branch just beyond School Neck Point. As you round Stump Point, be sure to give the shoal on the north side of the point plenty of room. There are several bunches of watermen's stakes tied together with white plastic jugs attached that seem to mark the shoal's limits. School Neck Point, to starboard, is another of those long grassy points with sticks and plastic jugs as a shoal marker.

Run wide around this point and avoid the shoal on the west side by following the series of sticks stuck in the mud, and head toward Free School Creek as far as needed for protection from southeasterlies. The river continues for quite a way, carrying six feet of water well beyond Bray's Landing, but numerous oyster stakes have the effect of narrowing the channel in some spots. This branch is more wooded, with some comfortable-looking homes and well-tended grounds along the shore. □

WARE RIVER
on Mobjack Bay

As we motored out of the Severn River to explore the next river, the Ware, we began to notice a gray hazy build-up to the southwest. It took us about twenty minutes to reach the Severn's entrance flasher, and by that time the haze had turned into a dark cloud spread from horizon to almost overhead.

As you round Robins Neck, the next mark from Tow Stake Point is less than a mile away and easily visible on bearing 080°. If you are coming in from the New Point Comfort Light, this marker bears about 305°. There's considerably more shoal to the north of Ware River Point, so it would be safer to follow the B/W nuns which will lead you mid-channel right up to Windmill Point. Your general course will be about 315°.

By the time we rounded the mark off Tow Stake Point, the storm was making some nasty rumbling sounds. The telltale coppery glow let us know we were in for a real blow.

The storm hit with its usual cold draft of air, followed by a fierce blast out of the southwest. Then came heavy rain, blown

PHOTO BY BACKUS AERIAL PHOTOGRAPHY

Ware River

almost horizontally, that beat the water to a white froth. The point of this story is that the river's marks were close enough to be easily followed, even in poor visibility. Off Windmill Point there are two marks, (Fl G 2½ sec), "3" and beyond that, a green "5." You must leave this mark to port. Also, if you are proceding further upstream past Jarvis Point, be sure you find the red #6 that marks the next shoal. From green #5, bear about 280° to round this mark and clear the Jarvis Point shoal.

We anchored for the night in the little cove on the south shore between Windmill Point and the ruins at Roanes Wharf in seven to nine feet of water. There's quite a bit of room here and good protection from the south and southeasterlies. On the west bank of this cove is a long dock with a good-sized sailboat. We recommend that you not go further toward shore than the end of this dock.

Perhaps the prettiest anchorage on the Ware River is in Wilson Creek, just beyond Roanes Wharf. (There is no wharf today, but some pilings are still visible.) The channel into Wilson Creek has private aids, and if you follow a few simple guidelines, you will find ample water of six feet or more.

From Jarvis Point red #6 take course of 300° (approx.) to the long dock on the western shore with a small white house on the end. On your chart it's the dock that shows at the end of the road from Zanoni. From there turn and head for the creek's entrance, staying within 100′ of the next long dock. This dock has a small brown house with screened sides. To port you will see a private aid, draped with sticks of an osprey nest.

From here you're on your own. However, if you just keep to the middle, you should have no problems.

The shoreline on both sides of Wilson Creek has quite a few modest houses with a number of long docks. The scene is that of a comfortable little village—peaceful and intimate with well cared for lawns, cozy wooded areas, and majestic magnolias—with a mix of pleasure and work boats. Nicholson's Marina, also known as Old Shipyard, is located on the south shore, but has only a few slips and no other facilities.

If you wish to proceed further up the Ware River, be aware of the four-foot shoal spot west of Jarvis Point. There's a green daymark on its eastern side, so we suggest that route. The entire outline seems to be marked with fishermen's sticks many of which have white plastic jugs and ribbons of brightly colored plastic for better visibility.

As you approach the next mark, Fl G #9 just beyond Bailey's Point, be on the lookout for the three-foot shoal to starboard. There are the usual several sticks with plastic strips and a white jug that should be left to starboard, and beyond that the river has quite a few watermen's stakes most with fluttering colored ribbons.

To starboard just beyond #9 you will see the commercial fuel dock facilities of J.C. Brown and Company. Although the water is pretty shallow here, the long fuel dock has ten feet of water on its south side—a reminder of the days when gas barges were regular visitors to the pier. This dock has gas to offer to the visiting boatman, but no diesel, and welcomes all cruising families on weekdays, but is closed on weekends.

The Ware River carries six feet of water or more for another two miles, with no protected anchorages but with some beautiful homes scattered along a wooded shoreline somewhat higher than that of the Severn. □

NORTH RIVER

on Mobjack Bay

The third branch of Mobjack Bay is North River. From New Point Comfort the best route is along the fish trap channel of B/W nuns. A course of 325° will bring you to the North River's entrance. To starboard is B/W nun M-18, and to port a red and black beacon. Just north of this beacon is a lighted spar #1 off Ware Neck Point. Like most buoys on Mobjack Bay, the marks on North River are close enough to each other to be easily visible. The only significant shoal is off Horse Point marked by a green daymark #3. There are no notable protected anchorages until you get into Blackwater Creek.

The North River runs in a generally northerly direction for about 2½ miles, then takes a 90° turn west for another mile and a half before it swings north again. As you approach the first turn at Blackwater Creek, you will see, dead ahead of you, a scattering of small weekend cottages at Roys Point.

If you need fuel and supplies, better head up Blackwater Creek to The Yacht Yard at Mobjack Bay Marina. At this creek's entrance there's a red flasher #2 and beyond that you'll see a duck blind that marks the shoal off Roys Point. There's plenty of water here, so stay in mid-channel up to the red/green mid-channel marker at Greenmansion Cove.

The entrance to Greenmansion Cove is narrow but well marked by a red daymark. The creek has a tendency to shoal at the mark, so don't snuggle up to it. Once inside, you can circle to the left of the main dock to the green daymark, where you take a right to tie-up for ice and supplies. If you need fuel, go down the right side of the main dock. Stick as close to the docks and slips as you can, till you get to the covered boathouse at the end of the pier. Then swing to starboard to the fuel pumps.

Mobjack Bay Marina is one of the most popular marinas we've ever run into. Its patrons and those who keep their boats there have a warm feeling for the owners, Fleetwood and Bonnie Howell, as well as for each other; and you get the impression that it's all one big happy family. The Yacht Yard at the marina has fuel, ice, marine supplies, and a full service yard. Everyone will make you feel most welcome. A popular anchorage for the visitors is in Blackwater Creek around the seven-foot marks on your chart.

If you continue up the North River, you will see on the

BACKUS AERIAL PHOTOGRAPHY

North River

north shore about a mile before Cradle Point a beautiful and well kept estate—a large mansion with a small, neat pool house, newly painted white with gold roof. Back further in the cove you will see well kept farm buildings, a large, traditional barn painted black with white trim, several car garages, and other buildings. Everything looks brand new.

A popular anchorage on North River is at the next bend, just beyond Cradle Point. The river is quite wide here, and you can enjoy the view of one of the most beautiful estates on the Chesapeake Bay, Elmington, just by Elmington Creek. The main building bears a resemblance to Monticello and stands on the water's edge, where it has a view of this entire stretch of the river. In the background stands one of the largest magnolia trees I have ever seen. The North River has some of the most impressive estates we have seen anywhere, and Elmington tops them all. □

DAVIS & PEPPER CREEKS
on Mobjack Bay

NOTE: In Davis Creek, a depth of about 7 ft. is available through the channels and basin by favoring deeper portions of these areas.

There are two other creeks here on Mobjack Bay that have aroused our curiosity. These are Pepper Creek and Davis Creek and are located just a couple of miles north of New Point Comfort Light. From the 4-second flasher #4 at New Point Comfort, course 342° will take you to the entrance of Davis Creek. The channel into Davis Creek is well marked, and according to one local waterman, has ten feet of water all the way in to the public landing at the head of the creek. We were told to keep from 40 to 50 feet away from the marks, because there's a little shoaling at the east side of the channel.

As you pass the black spar that marks the outer end of the Davis Creek channel, take heading 005° to pick up the next mark. The marks are all close enough to each other that they'll be easily visible.

Davis Creek is cozy and narrow with absolutely no room to anchor once inside, so you'll have to take your chances at the public dock all the way at the end of the creek. There's a picturesque two-story red building with a white railed porch upstairs and a sign which reads, "The Crabbers and Fisherman's Wharf." You can get fuel and some supplies here. All around you there will be well cared for local workboats with hailing ports reading New Point, Peary, Gwynn, and Baron. Although Davis Creek does not offer the amount of room we usually like in an anchorage, its value is in its nearness to the Bay for an emergency stopover.

Pepper Creek, one mile north, has only two marks and both of those are at the creek's entrance. Neither is lighted, and they are almost ¾ of a mile apart. Because they are so far apart, the novice will find it difficult to stay in channel, particularly with a cross wind. Once inside, the channel is not marked, and local knowledge is required to keep from running aground. Pepper Creek is completely exposed from the southwest, and with inadequate marks is not the sort of place we would recommend as an anchorage.

But that doesn't matter, because Mobjack Bay and its tributaries, the Severn, the Ware, the North and the East Rivers, have enough good anchorages to provide a lifetime of cruising interest. The smell of giant magnolias mingles with the salt breezes of the nearby ocean. And the quiet charm of life—unspoiled by metropolitan glitter—makes this one of the best cruising areas on the Chesapeake Bay. □

EAST RIVER
on Mobjack Bay

The East River is about five miles north of New Point Comfort. At the river's entrance is a lighted spar #3 off Pond Point. To starboard you will see the deteriorating pilings of Diggs Wharf. Immediately to port is the wharf at Mobjack, with some large fuel storage tanks and dock. This is a commercial wharf, so don't try to tie up there. Upstream, just before Sharp Point, there are marks that lead back to a small marina, but our sources tell us that there's no facility there of any size.

Tabbs Creek, to starboard, has one of the snuggest anchorages you could hope for. Word is that a five-foot draft boat can squeeze through its narrow opening. You can't go far upstream, and if the usual moored boats are present, things will be very tight.

Zimmerman Marine is located at Marker 13 on the East River off Mobjack Bay, specializing in fine yacht care, repair and construction.

As you proceed up East River, the next prominent landmark is the cluster of buildings and storage tanks at Williams Wharf. To starboard, just around Williams Wharf Point, you will find Put In Creek. This creek has a beautiful little spot for anchoring, but you have to pick your way through the many crab pots. If the wind is blowing northeasterly, you might want to continue past Put In Creek to the entrance of Woods Creek, where you can have plenty of room to swing in 12 to 14 feet of water. The East River has long been a favorite of ours because of its easy-to-follow channel and scenic shoreline. □

PHOTO BY BACKUS AERIAL PHOTOGRAPHY

East River

PERRIN RIVER

off York River

The approach to the Perrin River is well marked and very easy to follow. Use chart 12238 to locate the entrance three-quarters of a mile northwest of red nun buoy #2. Respect this mark on the north edge of the York River ship channel. It stands sentinel to a large sand bar south of Jenkins Neck. A further note should be made of the fish traps which line the entire lower York River. From a distance they seem to form a rustic fence, but as you approach you will see that clearing them is no problem.

Once clear of red nun #2 you will quickly spot the first two red daymarks in the Perrin River to starboard. These aids are well placed and provide the visiting cruiser with the first glimpse of the natural beauty of this Tidewater estuary. On the day of our visit a fledgling osprey, standing watch over our approach on daymark #4, cocked its head and dove from its perch above us. It was as if mother nature herself had sent one of her growing new breed to welcome us with a display of soaring, as new wings stretched to glide through the sky above us. We were aware instantly that the once almost extinct bird could see us better than we him. With his approval we continued up river.

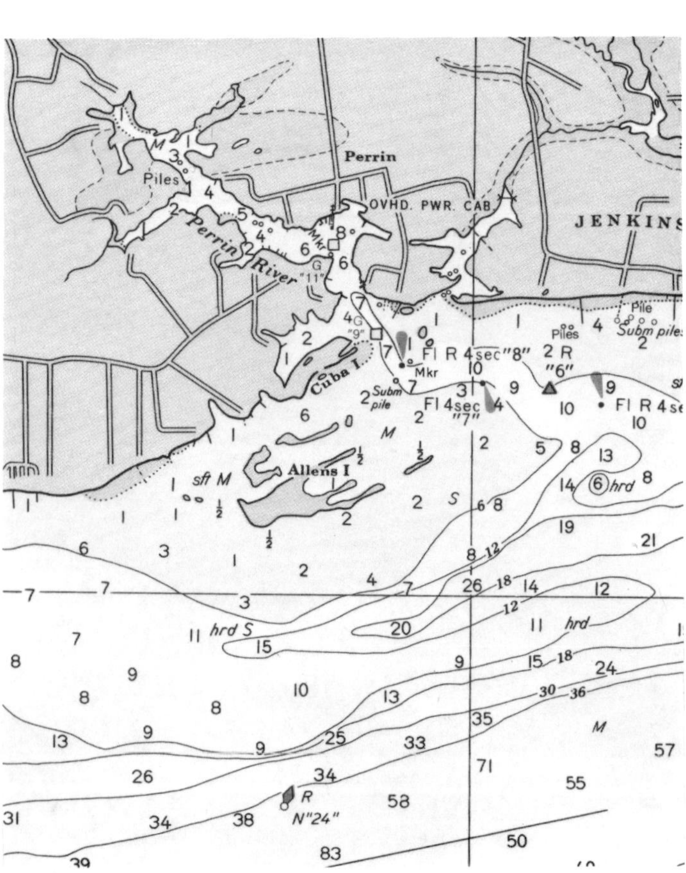

From NOAA Chart 12238 — not to be used for navigation.

Fl. 4 sec. #7 warns the mariner of a large sand bar to port. Don't be fooled by the passage of the powerboat crowd over the bar, there isn't enough water there for sailors. It isn't all bad though. If clamming is your thing, this bar is "first class." Many cruisers anchor just off the southern point of the bar and in no time fill a bucket with some of the southern Bay's most succulent clams.

The channel narrows at Fl. R. 4 sec. #8, but poses no serious problem if you remain between #8 and green #9 which is nearby. From here, stay in the middle of the channel past the crab docks to starboard. As you pass them you become aware of a widening of the river further up. Once clear of them you will see green daymark #11 as well as the expanse of yachts of all sizes at the marina about 200 yards above the crab docks.

Slowly emerging as a major yachting center on the lower Chesapeake is Cook's Landing Marina, on the Perrin River. It is the home of the Colonial Yacht Club and is a full service facility which is prepared to handle the need of any cruiser. It is 5 miles closer to the Chesapeake than the next full service marina.

No discussion of this area would be complete without a few words about the serenity of the shores and the people who live there. Peaceful and warm seem to be the best words to describe both. They reflect the real beauty one enjoys of this country setting. Unobscured by neon light and the city hustle-bustle the shores are uncrowded even though homes of the local watermen and farmers dot the banks. Friendly greetings and a truly warm welcome are offered to all who visit this river. The mutual respect of the cruising sailor and the local watermen is a hallmark of this storybook community. Everywhere is evidence of the famous Tidewater hospitality.

Transients are welcome, and directions to transient slips, fuel dock and marina office are posted prominently on the end of the first pier you encounter. All are well protected from weather and afford depths of up to seven feet. Electricity and water can be arranged. The fuel dock is further up past the piers and a full service boat yard is on a small branch of the river just to the right of the fuel dock. Boats of all descriptions and sizes form a neat line at their berths on both sides of this branch of the river. If you choose to anchor out, turn to port just beyond the green #11. You'll carry 5 feet about one-half mile up this branch if you stay to the middle. The channel here is not marked but has the advantage of being uncluttered by the fish stakes usually found in similar rivers. It is a short dinghy trip to the marina if you choose to ride the hook.

The two-story building contains the marina office, a ships store, heads, showers, ice and entrance to the marina's swimming pool. There is no snack bar or restaurant but vending machines are available. We made lunch on the boat and picnicked next to the pool under an umbrella. The piers are very near to the pool. Next to the pool is a playground for the young cruiser as well as ample parking for guests who arrive by car.

The marina keeps a watch on channel 16 VHF during normal working hours seven days a week, or can be reached by phone at either (804)877-3104 or (804)642-6177. It is open year-round. □

FAIRLY SHOAL
PERRIN RIVER
CUBA I.
N
SHOALING HERE
AT "NO WAKE" SIGN
YORK RIVER

Notes

WORMLEY CREEK

on the York River

From NOAA Chart #12238—not to be used for navigation.

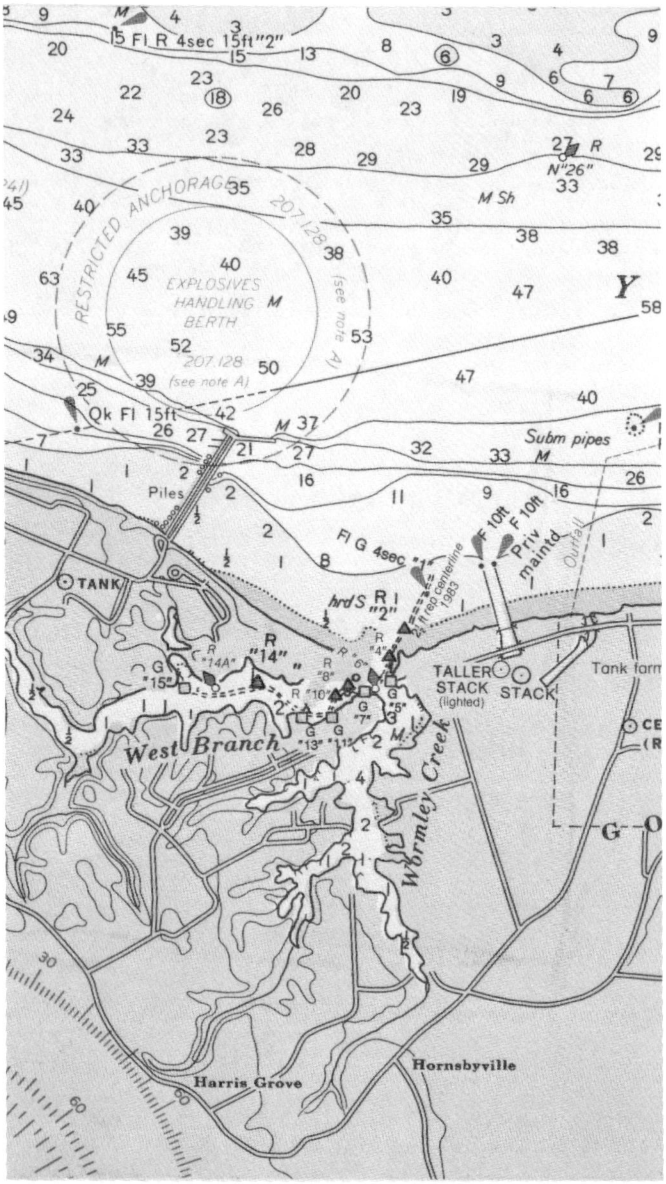

Wormley Creek is the forgotten harbor on the lower York River. It competes for visitors with Sarah Creek and the Perrin River, both with well-known marinas. Wormley Creek is also in the shadow (literally) of a major Virginia Power Company generating plant. To the first-time visitor it is all too easy to go across the York to the known harbors.

We like places off the beaten path though. Our curiosity about Wormley Creek was rewarded with the discovery of a new cruising destination. The skyline is dominatéd by the smokestacks of the generating station but the plant coexists with the boating community well—it is easy to forget they are there.

The smokestacks offer excellent guideposts to the creek's entrance. They are visible easily from anywhere between the Yorktown Bridge and the mouth of the York River. The entrance channel into Wormley Creek is simple to follow. The chart indicates a channel depth of five-feet and it is at least that deep.

Just inside the creek on the left is Wormley Creek Marina, which is the only marina on the creek. Owner Bill Reiser doesn't have a lot of visitors; when a transient boat stops by he takes the time to visit. The marina has six-foot depths at mean low water. Bill keeps a small ship's store and sells gasoline and diesel fuel. About half of the boats at the marina are work boats. Something is always in season—crabs, oysters, fish. Check with the watermen and you can ususally buy the makings of a truly fresh seafood dinner.

Wormley Creek Marina shares waterfront space with Raven Marine, a repair company. Raven has recently moved here from a location at Sunset Creek, where they built a reputation for quality work. Owner Scott Haley has a first-rate facility on Wormley Creek and is looking forward to expanding his business.

From the mouth of the creek, the dredged channel turns to the right, up the West Branch. The channel ends about a half-mile later at the piers of the Coast Guard Training Center on the north side of the creek. There is no room to anchor in the channel but it makes a pleasant side trip.

The Training Center has a number of boats used to teach the basics of seamanship to new Coast Guard personnel. Though it looks narrow in places, there is plenty of room in the channel for two boats to pass. Remember, though, that the other boat may be under the command of a student and give it plenty of room.

The main branch of the creek runs south from the marina and has depths of three to four feet. The scenery is beautiful, tree-lined shores with quiet residential neighborhoods. There is a boat ramp at the southwest corner of the creek. Along most of the creek the power plant, which I expected to dominate the view, is hidden behind the trees.

Most visitors, like ourselves, will find that their drafts will limit them to staying at the marina. There just isn't room to anchor out if your draft is more than three feet. Still, Wormley Creek is a welcome diversion off the beaten path. Stay with Bill Reiser and enjoy the peace and quiet. □

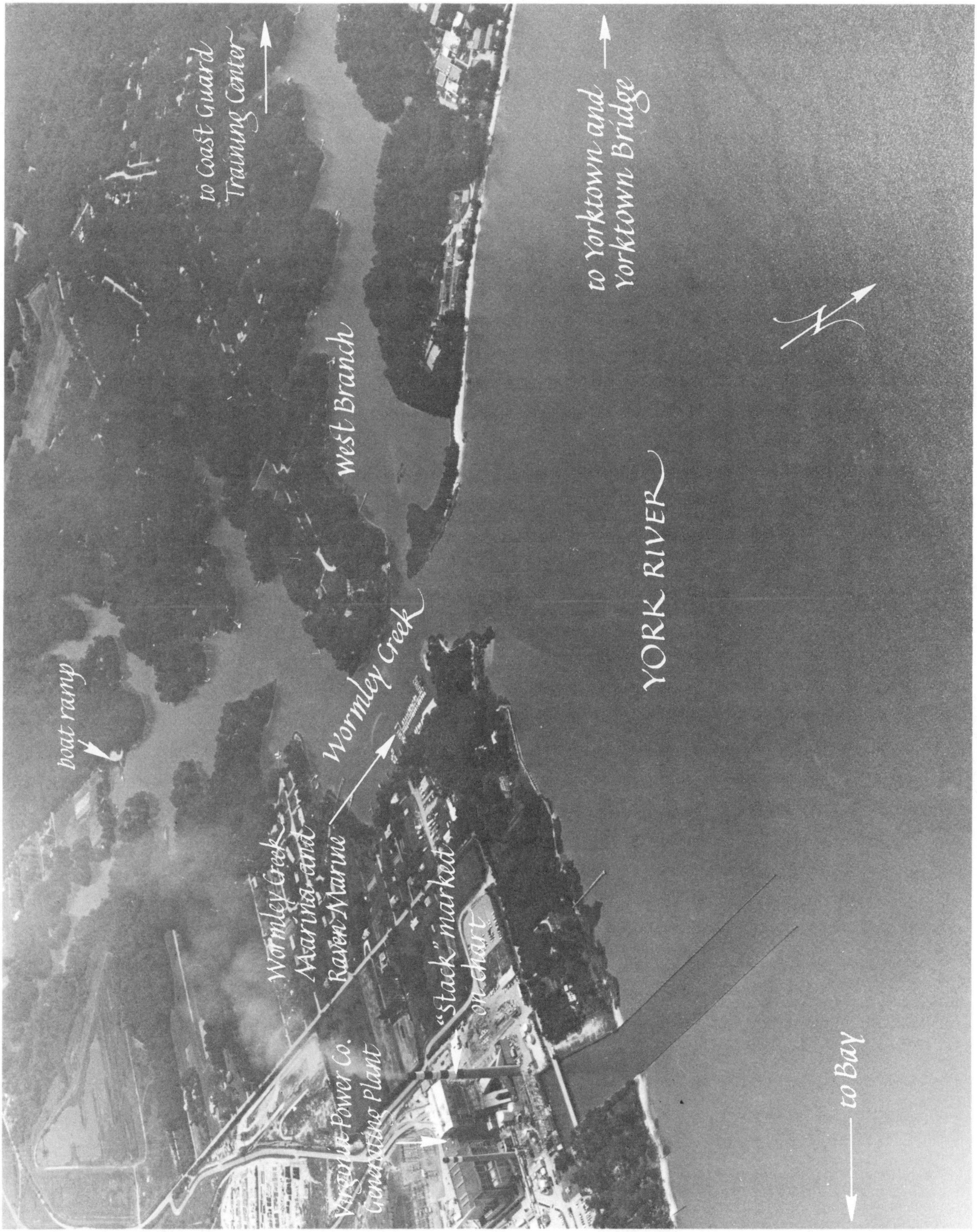

Photo by Backus Aerial Photography

SARAH CREEK

on the York River

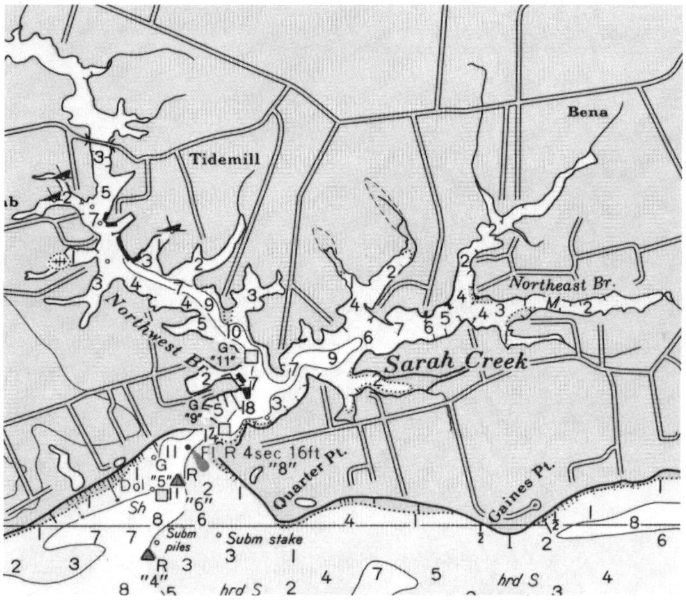

From NOAA Chart 12238—not to be used for navigation.

In late August we were exploring the Hampton Roads-Norfolk area, spending our last night in Hampton River. The contrast between the new and the old was evident as we sailed toward Old Point Comfort the next day. Nuclear submarines, gigantic aircraft carriers, and monstrous freighters steamed back and forth while the stalwart oystermen, unmindful of these giants of technology, scraped their living from the muddy bottom of Hampton Roads.

Our destination was Sarah Creek on the York River. From Old Point Comfort northward the homes along the shoreline rapidly thin out to be replaced by woods and marshes. A little over a mile offshore a double row of black and white nuns marks a small ship channel northward. Although there's plenty of deep water close inshore, we stuck to the channel, rounding the large opening of Back River, past Drum Island Flats, and then the even broader Poquoson River.

Gradually our course changed, and finally at Tue (pronounced TWO) Marshes Light we entered the York River. If you are approaching the York from the north, you may wish to take the shortcut across the York Spit. About a mile SSE of Guinea Marshes there is a natural channel that cuts across the three-foot-plus York Spit. The opening is marked by two daymarks and a lighted spar. This shortcut will save you a couple of miles.

Sarah Creek lies approximately five miles upstream of the mouth of the York River. While water depths of the York to the bridge above Sarah Creek average between 40 and 50 feet, there are also a couple of 70-foot spots; six- to eight-foot water carries almost to shore. There is one significant shoal to starboard off Gaines Point at red nun #26 and another on the downstream side of the entrance to Sarah Creek. Both are well marked and should present no problem.

As you pass the refinery and Navy pier on the south shore of the York, you are near a place of significance in American history. Here at Yorktown was fought the last major battle of the Revolutionary War. Buried in the mud of its shoreline are the rotting remains of the beleaguered British supply fleet, sunk during that battle. It hardly seems possible, as we motor past these peaceful shores, to envision the brutal and savage fighting that took place here. Today many of the original redoubts are still in place; a tall monument stands to commemorate the battle, and a Victory Center is nearby.

According to Chart #12238, the entrance into Sarah Creek is fairly straightforward. But as we turned at the outer marker, a lighted spar #2, it didn't look all that clear to me. The marks appeared to lead right up to the sandy shore, then stop. A large powerboat was making the entrance well ahead of us, and I watched with binoculars as he ran right up to the beach, then turned parallel to it, then disappeared behind some bushes. At least, that was the illusion he gave. Full of confidence now (if he can get in there, so can I), we followed the marks. When we turned at red #8 we could see the narrow entrance of the creek opening up to us.

Sarah Creek divides into two branches, the northwest branch and (what else?) the northeast branch. To port on entering is the York River Yacht Haven, a large marine facility. Here you can find not only fuel but also a laundromat, swimming pool, ships' store, and haulout services, as well as engine and hull repairs

Upstream on the northwest branch are Gloucester Point Marina and, beyond that, Jordan Marine Services, which also offers major marine repairs and service.

Sarah Creek lies in a triangle of historic landmarks, and York River Yacht Haven can arrange transportation to the nearby Yorktown Victory Center, Jamestown, Colonial Williamsburg, and Busch Gardens. They will also arrange transportation to nearby restaurants and grocery stores.

Just off the gas dock of York River Yacht Haven is a large and popular anchorage. Many cruising and racing groups from the Norfolk-Hampton Roads area find this the most convenient spot to drop the hook. Several boats followed us into Sarah Creek and while we were refueling, anchored here. We chose to proceed upstream on the northeast branch and anchored at the opening of the small creek to port about a half-mile from the marina's gas dock.

As darkness closed in we settled back in our cockpit with after-dinner coffee and enjoyed our surroundings. The shore was lined with pleasant, well-kept homes which hid discreetly behind trees and ornamental shrubs. In the darkness an occasional light winked through the foliage, and downstream the anchor lights twinkled like stars across the stilled waters. I dozed, and in the twilight of consciousness heard the distant, but distinctive clatter of an anchor chain being paid out. It didn't take too much imagination to persuade myself that this wasn't a late arrival. It had to be Captain John Smith's ship on the first leg of his historic exploration of the Chesapeake Bay. I wonder if he found Sarah Creek as charming as we did? □

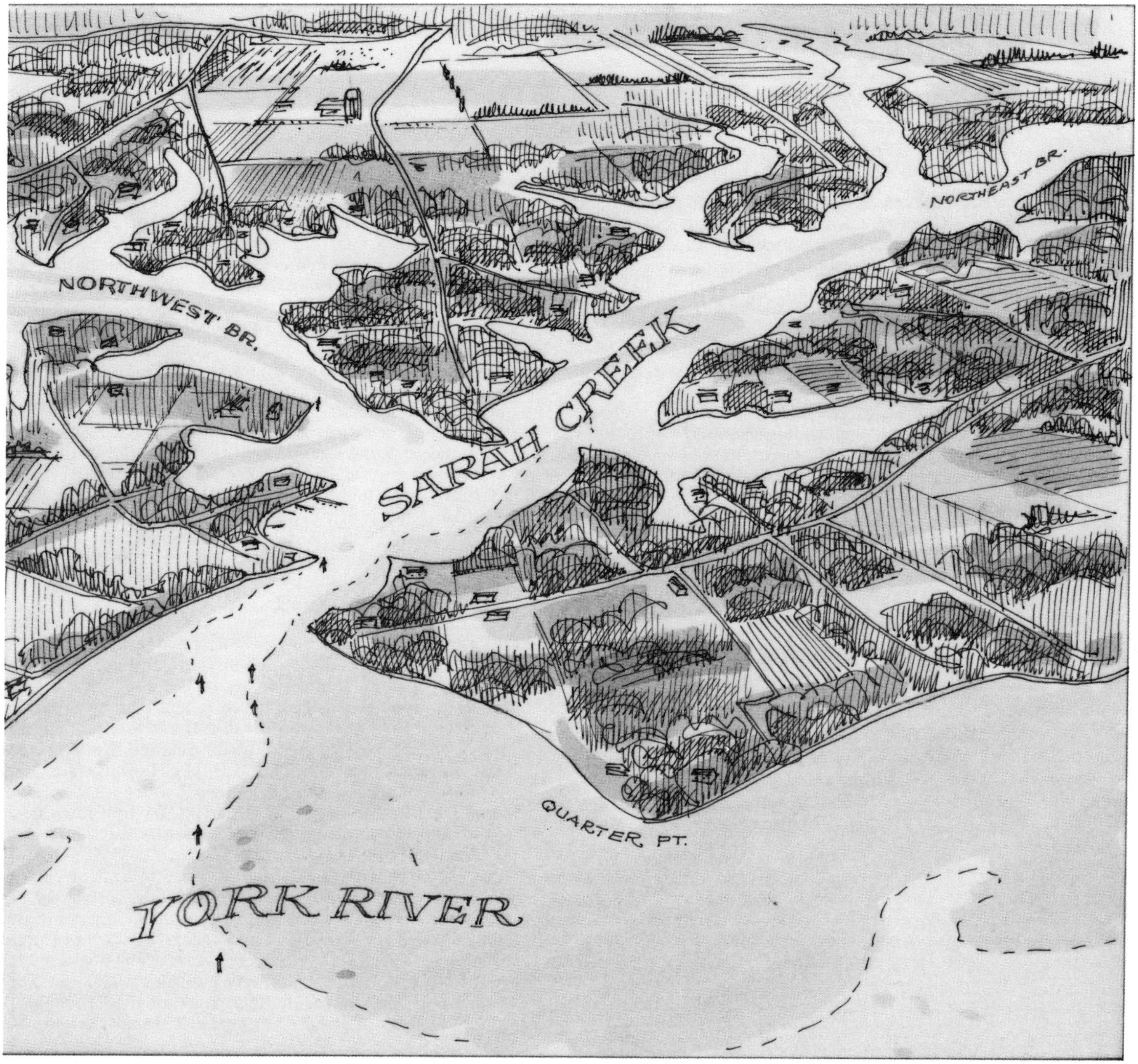
NORTHWEST BR.
NORTHEAST BR.
SARAH CREEK
QUARTER PT.
YORK RIVER

BACK CREEK

South of York River

Having cleared York Spit at the western end pair of York River Entrance Channel marks, we held about 250 (Mag.) just left of "3," cutting "2" to save time. Had the fathometer been on, it would have shown plenty of water as we passed by, but not over, a four-foot bar jutting down from the north about a third of a mile before "3." Curling a hook left and right around the next marks, we held roughly NW from "5" to "7," and then turned left from the Thoroughfare Channel into Back Creek to where we could see Mills' dock and Ewell's crab plant beckoning.

As you round green #7 entering from the east, and run for Back Creek green #1, you will become aware of an open expanse of water to port behind Green Pt. This is Claxton Creek. It affords good holding ground and is very close to the Bay if you want an early start the next day. Leave green #1 to port as you enter. While Green Pt. is a low marshy peninsula, it effectively reduces the chop from north or easterly winds. We waited out one of the Bay's famou summer afternoon storms with winds of 35 to 40 kts. i Claxton Creek and rode very comfortably. Depths of 6 to ft. are found in the center of the creek about half-way up 3 to 4 ft. depths carry up to within 50 yards of either shore The depths shown on chart 12238 are very conservative an do not tell the whole story of this good anchorage. There ar no houses or structures on the shores and there is no throug traffic. Nights are quiet and serene.

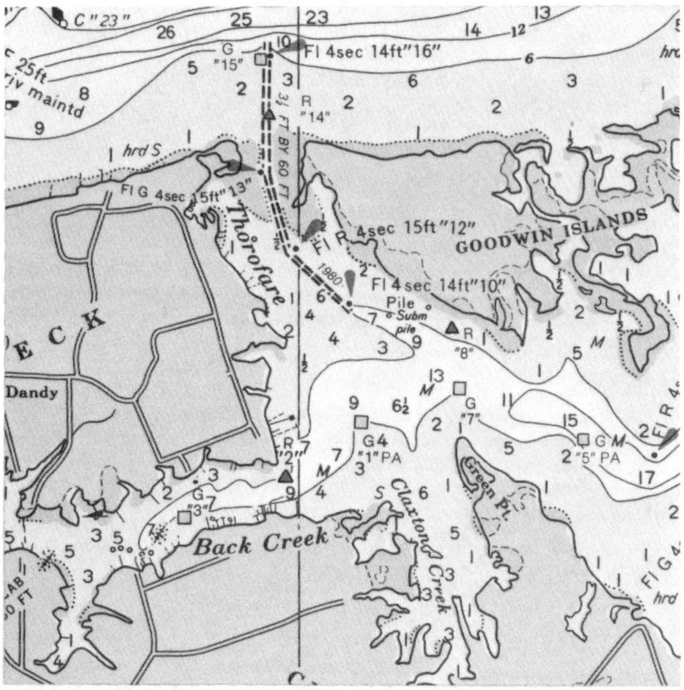

From NOAA Chart 12238—not to be used for navigation.

On the right further on up the creek, is Back Creek Park with floating docks, four ramps, toilets, a picnic and pla area, and six tennis courts. The park is a 26-acre are donated to York County by the Amoco Oil Refinery an developed by the Heritage Conservation and Recreatio Service of the Interior Department, Virginia Commission o Outdoor Recreations, and the Virginia Department o Highways and Transportation. You can't miss it. If you wan to check on their tennis program, call the York Count Department of Leisure Services, or the Park summe number 804-898-0096.

Just before the park there is a cove on the right where th Seaford Yacht Club has their new property and building They have an excellent growing club and are some of th finest people you will encounter on the Bay. There are goo spots to hook down off their cove, and there are some coz protected little bights on the left just before you enter th creek and before you get to the big Seafood Scallop plant b the old state dock. The "Sand Box" (Thoroughfare) to th York is quite shoal now. If you want to try it follow a loca and ask what he draws; or better yet, try it at low tide an you can get out and walk and look around. The worst i around the "10," "11," and "12" area.

The creek itself is as sweet as it used to be. You can carr 7 feet past the inner "3," and 5 feet past the fork in the mai channel. If you want to go into a branch, up high, or near th shore, do it on soundings and check the state of the tide Watch for crabpots everywhere. Most of the docks are buil out to the 5-foot line, and can be used as a guide. Remember when you come in the numbers start for the Thoroughfare and you go from green "7" to green "1" to turn left into Bac Creek.

It is the same fast, easy haven from the Bay in ba weather that it has always been, now with more nice homes docks, and people.□

PHOTO BY BACKUS AERIAL PHOTOGRAPHY

THE POQUOSON RIVER

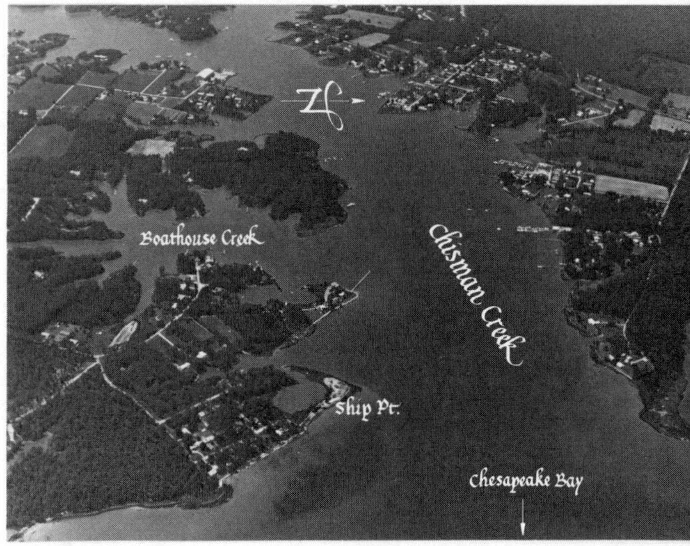

PHOTO BY BACKUS AERIAL PHOTOGRAPHY

The Poquoson River entrance lies 3.5 miles west of the York Spit lighted spider tower and is marked by R "2" (Fl 4 sec) and BW N "Y5". On a course of 226° M, follow a well marked channel down the wide mouth of the river. Good water extends for at least one-half mile to the east and more than a mile to the west of the marked channel. At N "8" the water narrows to about one-half mile.

There are few sights ashore on the wide expanse of the Poquoson River between R "2" (Fl 4 sec) and R "10" (Fl 2½ sec). If you turn to the east just past N "8" and move toward the southwestern tip of Cow Island (part of a wildlife refuge), you'll find a sandy beach superb for beachcombing and picnicing. Wildlife teems here, and it is not unusual to see turtles, raccoons and other small creatures. You can get within 200 yards of the beach and safely anchor in six to eight feet of water with a sandy bottom.

The southwestern branch of the Poquoson River is also well marked and easy to navigate. Respect "15" (Fl 4 sec) which marks a sandbar off Hunt's Point. After that there is good water all the way to "17". Anchorages are good here even though they are exposed to a chop from a northeast wind. The fetch down the river is unbroken to the north, but, in fair weather, the beauty of the homes which line the shore of this branch make the stopover worthwhile.

For better protected anchorages, choose either Chisman or Bennett Creeks.

Chisman Creek is to starboard after you pass R "10" (Fl 2½ sec) entering from the bay. It is navigable for three miles and is bordered, on both sides, by the attractive communities of Seaford to the north and Dare to the south. There are three marina facilities here. Anchorages abound on either side of the channel. If you draw four feet or less, you can find quiet anchorages in the smaller creeks farther up.

By turning to port at R "10" (Fl 2½ sec) you enter Bennett Creek. The channel appears narrow, but it is easy to navigate. The shallowest spot is at daymark "1", where there is six feet at MLW. A mile beyond, at daymark "10" (Fl R), you will see the large expanse of marsh behind Cow Island on the port hand. The area was named Poquoson by the Indians who lived there when the English settled in the area. The word means "Great Marsh" and the community has the distinction of being the oldest continuously named town in Virginia.

The "Great Marsh" is a wildlife refuge. Almost every day mark is home to fledgling ospreys during the spring. Watching adult birds gather food for the fledglings is an exciting pastime.

Proceeding beyond daymark "10" (Fl R) is not a problem even though the channel is not marked. Remain in the center as you leave "10" (Fl R) to starboard. Water depths of eight to nine feet are found all the way to Floyd's Bay. Anchorages are good on the southwestern side of the center, near a small uninhabited island, about 400 yards beyond "10" (Fl R). The area will accommodate six or eight boats and is out of the main flow of traffic which departs from three marina facilities in White House Cove.

White House Cove does not have suitable anchorages for gunkholers, but does not lack for marina facilities. Boats drawing six feet regularly transit these creeks and the 81-foot 1940 vintage motor yacht *Erica* is moored at the Poquoson Marina to port. Across the cove are Owens Marina and Chester's Boat Yard. Further up the creek there are four to five-foot depths in the center to another, smaller marina. Fuel, ice and supplies are available at all the marinas. Transient slips are few, but Dave Carpenter, owner of Poquoson Marina, will always find a berth for a visiting boat. The Ship's Galley restaurant at the marina serves locally caught seafood in a dining area shaped and decorated like a Chesapeake Bay work boat. □

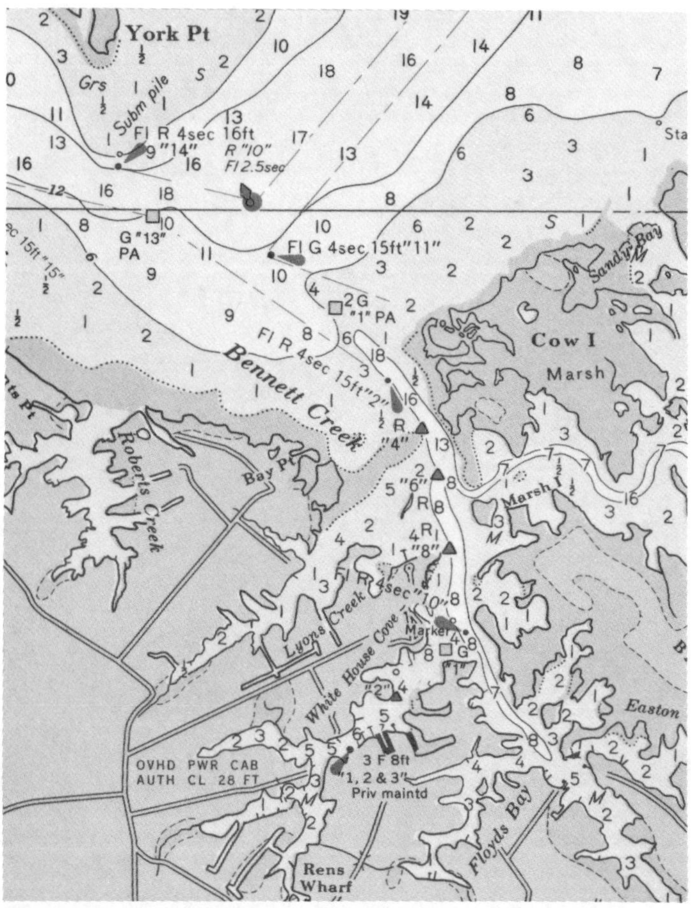

From NOAA Chart 12238—not to be used for navigation.

THE SALT PONDS

on the Lower Western Shore

We can thank the city of Hampton for dredging a channel into the "Salt Ponds," as it is referred to locally. It is located on the lower western shore of the Bay, just off Horseshoe Channel. As a result of the dredging, a new anchorage that is very convenient to the Norfolk area and much more secure and comfortable than others is now available to yachtsmen transitting the Chesapeake. Depths of six feet are found in the entrance channel and also in the Ponds. Eventually, Hampton intends to develop the area into a marine facility for pleasure boaters, but at present it is best used as an anchorage protected from rough Bay waters, while still open to a refreshing breeze.

Between the York River and Norfolk Harbor's entrance there is a secondary channel known as "Horseshoe Channel," about a mile off shore, and running about 023°-203°. It carries at least 10 feet of water at mean low tide. It is marked by a series of black and white buoys in pairs. North of markers "B4" and "B5," look for two red daymarks, both with green partners, that mark the way between the Horseshoe Channel and the lighted fixture at the end of the low rock breakwater that runs out from the north side of the entrance channel. Proceed inside (6′ controlling depth), making a 90° port turn once you are through the dredged cut. Head south about a half mile until the channel widens out, then drop the hook. You can row ashore to the barrier beach for a walk along the sand.

Located only about five nautical miles above the entrance to Norfolk Harbor, this is an ideal jumping-off spot for many destinations in the Lower Bay and the best secure anchorage in the area. □

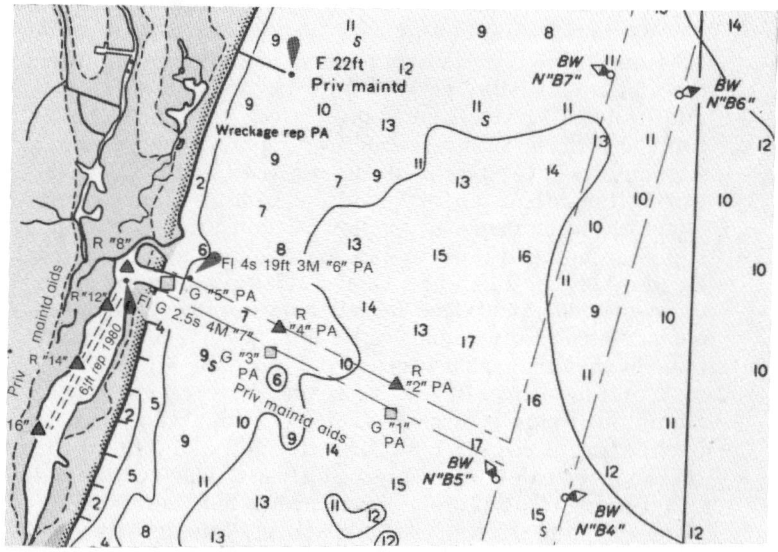

From NOAA Chart 12222—not to be used for navigation.

NOTE: Shoaling has developed on the N. side of the jetty entrance. Entering craft should angle toward the S. side of the jetty. Dredging planned for the spring of '87 should correct the problem.

BACKUS AERIAL PHOTOGRAPHY

HAMPTON RIVER

Hampton River is of easy access to craft arriving from the Chesapeake Bay and Atlantic Ocean, and it offers a multitude of services, good protection, and quiet charm coupled with the bustle of waterfront industry and pleasure. Coming down the Bay, you can hug the Engineer's Pier at Fort Monroe and go by Old Point Comfort fairly close. Often on an ebb current, the flow is "down the beach" and swings around Old Point to start an early flood into Hampton Roads. This can often be seen as a tide rip a hundred yards or so off Old Point. The current change can be as much as one-and-a-half to two hours earlier at points close to the shore than in mid-channel between Old Point and Fort Wool.

Coming in from the ocean against a strong ebb out of Hampton Roads, a surprising amount of time can be saved by holding a course from Thimble Shoal Light to the reasonably visible Fort Monroe Officers' Beach Club, and then turning to port, or left down the beach, in fairly shallow water and hold the course as told above. Please give the lines of pier fishermen enough berth not to upset them, and watch out for all the motorboats anchored and drifting in this popular fishing spot. Check your new charts. A straight shot to the northern tunnel island should provide no obstacles, but watch for the sign that warns you of the rotting underwater steamer dock pilings at the end of Old Point. The tunnel island rocks are comfortably steep to, but there isn't much point in cutting them close.

It is here that you hold close to "2" (Fl R 4 sec) on a tripod with no opposing mark, as the channel entrance is less than one hundred feet wide. You are then in a well-marked dogleg channel in behind very shoal Hampton Bar. Experienced local sailors have grounded so often on Hampton Bar that it has become a comfortable old friend, but it remains a very embarrassingly public place for a grounding. Give C "5" a wide berth for a shoal makes out from it in between dredgings; otherwise, follow your chart. Should you not have one, follow a local boat or go along the bridge holding 335° M from "2" to (Q R) "6", then turn to 298° M and go to "11" (Q G) and thence north into a routine channel. Marks "6" and "11" are both fixed and can be used to check instruments.

Entering Hampton Reach you will find Kecoughtan Veterans Hospital, Jones' Creek, and Hampton Institute on the right. Aptly named Sunset Creek is across from the tall Hampton University clock, and contains a variety of marine services. At the head of Sunset Creek is the Atlantic Ice Company, one of the few places where block ice is readily available. Immediately beyond Sunset Creek to the port side is the Hampton Yacht Club. Straight ahead is Hampton's commercial South King Street Dock and entrance to downtown. A city-operated transient pier is to the right of the commercial City Dock area. Deep draft can be found at the end slips only. Another marina is located upriver by a low bridge at the right. Limited anchorage is available east of the channel north of daymark "18". The low bridge at the end of the marked channel has been replaced with a new structure just north of the existing bridge. It too is relatively low.

Hampton houses one of the East's largest seafood industries. Some of the seafood plants operate small restaurants; ask around for directions and hours of operation, as most close early. In addition to the many restaurants, there is also the NASA Visitor's Center, Fort Monroe Casemate Museum, and Old St. John's Church, where the communion silver has been in continuous use since 1623.

When leaving Hampton, plan to spend a few hours at Fort Wool, located near the south end of Hampton Roads Tunnel. Fort Wool was originally built on a man-made island to defend Hampton Roads from the British during the War of 1812. Long abandoned, it furnishes the perfect spot for a quiet picnic. Access is by boat only; look for the pier on the south side of the fort.

Hampton is a harbor with bustling traffic of all sorts, at all times of the day and night. Due to this and the shoal sides, some people do not recommend you anchor out. However, other cruisers in this area report they anchor out here all the time with no problem. If you do decide to stay at a marina here, it is strongly recommended that you call ahead for a slip during the busy season.

Even with all the activity in Hampton, visiting yachtsmen will find more than ample sailing room around Hampton Roads and the lower Chesapeake Bay. □

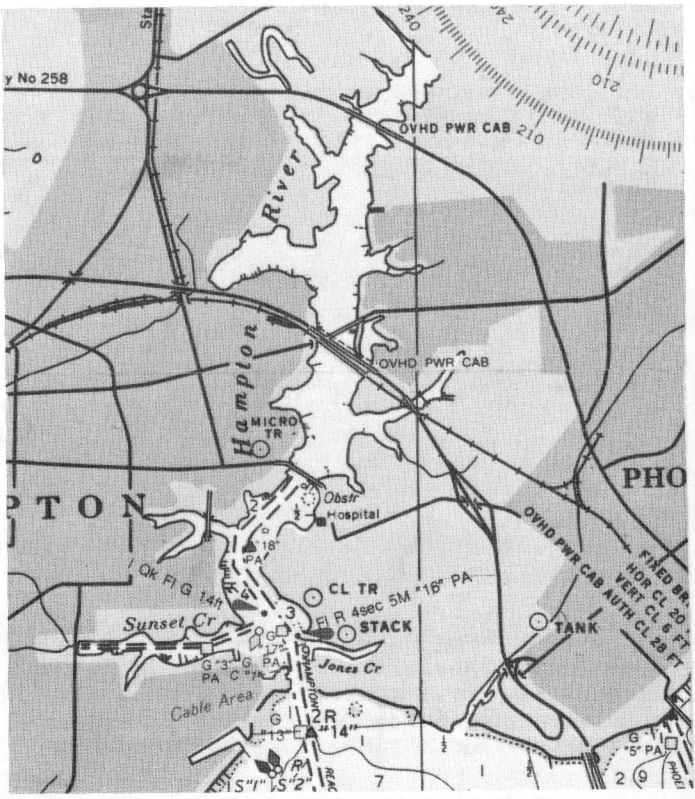

From NOAA Chart 12222—not to be used for navigatio

PHOTO BY BACKUS AERIAL PHOTOGRAPHY

ELIZABETH RIVER

For those not familiar with a commercial waterfront the Portsmouth Marine Terminal provides a convenient opportunity to observe the stevedore's art. The SS *United States*, once-proud flagship of US Lines, is in long-term storage at Norfolk International Terminal (chart 12245, just east of Elizabeth River channel "15"). Norfolk Navy Base (chart 12245, Sewell's Point) is home to a large assortment of naval vessels including submarines, destroyers, auxiliary ships, and aircraft carriers. The downtown waterfronts of Portsmouth and Norfolk are only a short distance along the Elizabeth River.

WESTERN BRANCH

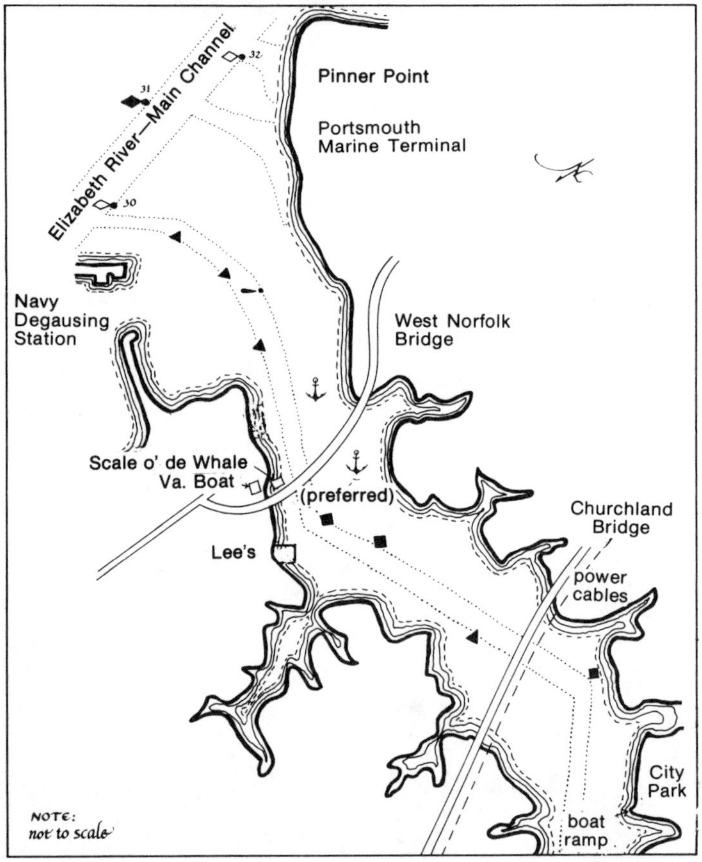

Western Branch channel turns southwest off the main Elizabeth River channel at R "30". The most prominent landmark is the Navy Degaussing Station just west of R "30." The cranes at Portsmouth Marine Terminal (located on the tip of Pinner Point) are also easy to spot. Daymarkers clearly delineate the Western Branch channel.

Two marinas on the north side of the channel have transient slips. Lee's Yacht Harbor is located in a facility west of the bridge; Virginia Boat and Yacht Service is just east of the bridge. The area between Churchland and West Norfolk Bridges provides a quiet anchorage with little to disturb peaceful sleep. East of the West Norfolk Bridge there is deeper water but unfortunately also more noise and traffic. All the bottom is soft mud and furnishes fair holding ground. The anchorage is quite protected except when a stiff breeze blows from due east.

Dine out at Scale O' De Whale, at the end of Virginia Boat's pier. They offer excellent seafood in a relaxed atmosphere. Prices are not cheap, but a night of elegant dining ashore is worth it.

Further up the Western Branch is Portsmouth City Park (just west of Baine's Creek). No pier is available for docking so access is limited to a dinghy or shallow-draft boat that can be beached. In addition to the usual picnic facilities the park features a minature railroad, tennis courts, nine hole golf course, and small boat ramp.

Charted soundings in the river are generally accurate, but deeper draft boats should proceed with caution outside the marked channel. The numerous small creeks off the Western Branch will tempt the curious gunkholer. However, all but the shallowest of vessels are advised to stay in the river and leave the creeks to canoes and Hobie Cats.

Carry an ample supply insect repellent during the warm months. When the wind dies the mosquitos and gnats swarm out of the surrounding low areas.

Do not plan on restocking the larder as groceries are not readily available. Western Branch is the place to relax and do nothing. Worry about shopping another day. ☐

Degaussing Station (foreground) with Portsmouth Marine Terminal in background. Note that the cranes are quite visible.

Virginia Boat and Yacht Service and the Scale O' De Whale Restaurant provide a stopover on the Western Branch.

HOLIDAY HARBOR

on the Elizabeth River

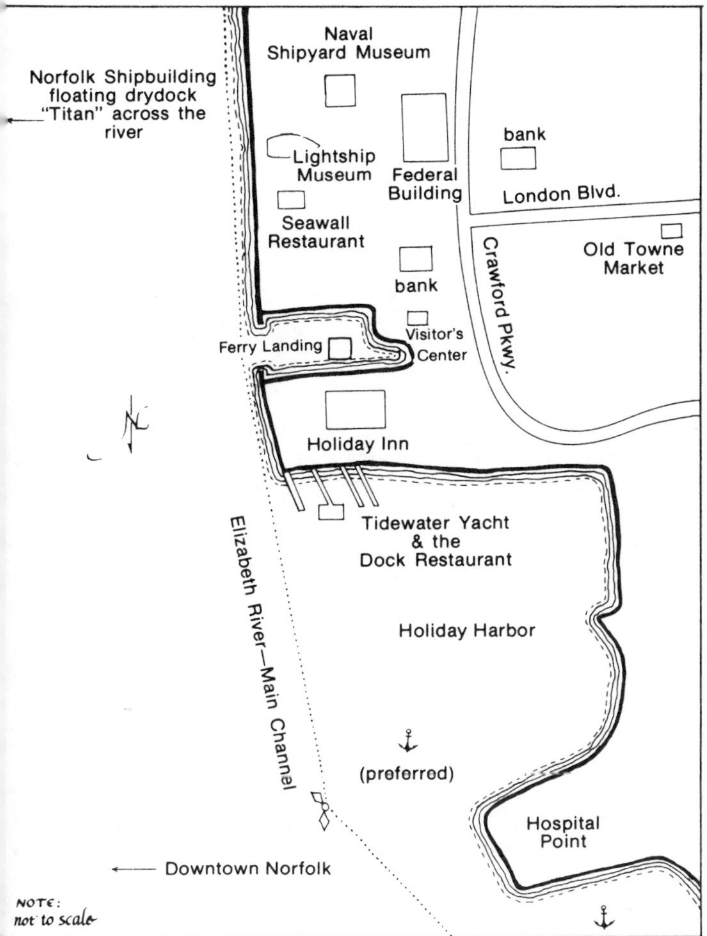

Holiday Harbor is one of the busiest yacht ports in Hampton Roads. The growing number of local boaters who call it home and the transient trade from the Intracoastal Waterway usually mean a bustling business every day of the summer. The reason for this popularity is apparent after the first visit. Not only is the marina well found and the anchorage quite protected, but the harbor is also convenient to the facilities and attractions of downtown Portsmouth.

Finding the harbor is simplicity itself. Follow the main channel of the Elizabeth River south just past R "36" (Q Fl R). The best anchorage is west of the channel south of Hospital Point. Additional anchorage is found north of Hospital Point, but is not as convenient to the marina and restaurant.

Tidewater Yacht Agency, on the south side of the anchorage, has transient slips. They also offer a complete range of marine repairs and supplies. The grocery store at the marina is modest, but will serve to replenish perishables such as bread and milk. Arrive early in the afternoon if you want the convenience of a slip and shore connections. Even with 100 transient slips they sometimes hang out the "no vacancy" sign. Tidewater Yacht will accept advance reservations for slips and offer a discount for cruising clubs visiting as a group.

Large merchant ships and tugs using the channel violate the "No Wake" signs regularly. Allow extra scope at anchor. A new breakwater offers good protection at the marina.

This is an excellent place to take a day ashore in the middle of an extended cruise. Downtown Portsmouth is close by; resupply at the newsstand, liquor store, or drug store as required. Four major banks have nearby offices. The Fifth Coast Guard District office is located in the Federal Building on Crawford Parkway. The closest grocery store, Olde Town Market, is about five blocks from the marina and offers free delivery. It is a small family-owned store that still does business the old-fashioned way.

The Portsmouth skyline is constantly changing as the city moves along in its downtown revitalization. A visitor's center has been built just south of the Holiday Inn; it is part of a large open air market. Visitors can take a ferry from there to downtown Norfolk to visit Waterside, the new waterfront festival center.

The Holiday Inn is next to Tidewater Yacht for those who need a night ashore or a break from the galley. The nearby Seawall Restaurant serves excellent seafood in a relaxed casual atmosphere. Both also offer a bit of night life. The Dock Restaurant is right at the marina; mooring is free if just stopping for one meal. More modest prices can be found at a number of cafes and cafeterias in downtown Portsmouth.

Two attractions along the Portsmouth waterfront are of special interest to the yachtsman, and both are free. The Portsmouth Lightship Museum is a restored lightship that is now drydocked in concrete. Next to it is the Portsmouth Naval Shipyard Museum, guaranteed to delight even those normally bored with history. Both are open 10-5 Tuesday through Saturday and 2-5 Sunday.

When you visit this section of the Elizabeth River be sure to cruise by Norfolk Shipbuilding and Drydock, just south of the anchorage on the east side of the river. Their two floating drydocks are two of the largest on the East Coast and can lift ships over a thousand feet long. Further south on the west side of the river is Norfolk Naval Shipyard, an historic complex that has overhauled naval vessels since the inception of the country's navy.

Holiday Harbor is a good choice for a day-long layover or just an overnight stop. Whether following the Intracoastal Waterway or cruising the lower Bay plan to stop by. Your neighbor could be from Maine or Florida just as easily as he could be from Annapolis. □

Holiday Harbor from Buoy 36, visible in the foreground.

LAFAYETTE RIVER

off the Elizabeth River

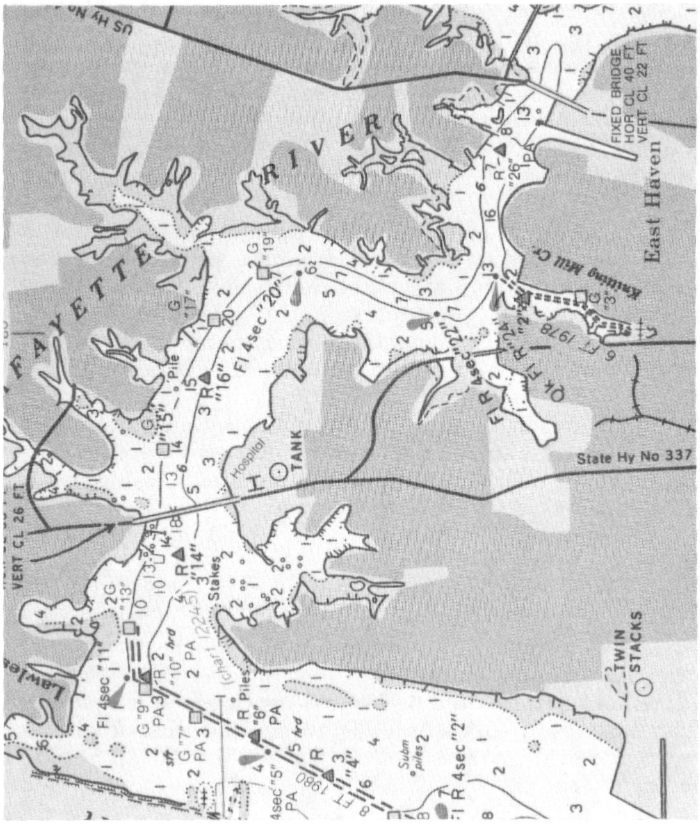

From NOAA Chart #12222—not to be used for navigation.

Normally the Lafayette River is a quiet, protected anchorage. Our trip there over a Labor Day weekend was anything but quiet though.

On Labor day weekend the three area yacht clubs sponsor a joint race. The first leg is sailed on Saturday from Hampton Yacht Club on Hampton Creek to the Norfolk Yacht Club on the Lafayette River. The second leg (Sunday) is up the James River to the Warwick Yacht Club on Deep Creek. On Labor Day the fleet races back to Hampton. We anchored Saturday night off the Norfolk Yacht Club expecting the usual peace and quiet. The party at the club seemed to last all night. The next morning, though, the fleet was off early. We tagged along, not really knowing what was happening, and were treated to a spectacular day of racing in Hampton Roads.

Most of our trips to the Lafayette are much quieter though. Only a few miles from our home slip, it is frequently our choice for a short, let's-spend-the-night-on-the-boat cruise.

The river is easy to enter and convenient to all the attractions of the Hampton Roads area. To the north is Hampton Roads, Norfolk Naval Base, and Norfolk International Terminal. Despite several years of well-publicized plans to return her to service, Norfolk International Terminal is still home to the S.S. *United States.* Even after years of inactivity, she is still a magnificent vessel and worth the detour to run alongside.

Farther south are the born again waterfronts of Portsmouth and Norfolk. Both cities have rebuilt their decaying downtown waterfronts with boating visitors in mind. The quiet waters of the Lafayette offer a sharp contrast to the hustle and bustle of Waterside at Norfolk and Portside in Portsmouth.

Access to the Lafayette is from the main channel of the Elizabeth River. The Elizabeth carries all sorts of commercial and military traffic, from trawlers to aircraft carriers. Be careful in traveling the channel, especially if you are not accustomed to sharing the water with large ships.

If entering the Lafayette from the north, resist the temptation to cut the corner around Tanner Point. Follow the long, marked entrance channel from the first marker and you cannot go wrong.

Just east of the first pair of markers is the Old Dominion University Sailing Center. The University's program started as a sailing club and has developed into a nationally ranked collegiate sailing team.

The Norfolk Yacht Club is next to the bridge on the left. Their facilities include a pool, several tennis courts, and large well kept docks. While they welcome visitors on a reciprocal membership basis, it is best to call ahead if you would like a visit.

There is plenty of room to anchor around marker "14." Several boats have permanent moorings south of the marker. Watch your soundings as you go south out of the channel, though, as it shoals quickly.

If you can pass under the Hampton Boulevard bridge (26 feet) by all means do so. The river is quieter there and the homes along the banks are truly magnificent. Like the anchorage outside the bridge, this area offers excellent protection in a blow regardless of the wind direction. My choice would be between markers "20" and "22."

Knitting Mill Creek is a pleasant side trip. There is not room to anchor and all the piers are private, but it is worth the time to take a look.

Except for the yacht club, there are no marinas on the river. There is an abandoned marina next to the Granby Street bridge where you can land a dinghy. Hagan's Seafood is next to the Granby Street bridge on the right—a small retail store with an excellent selection of fresh seafood. The row will make your dinner taste that much better. There is a grocery store at 38th and Granby (about three blocks from the bridge) and several restaurants within a short walk. The Lafayette Park and Zoo is less than a mile up Granby Street to the south.

For those seeking peace and quiet, off the usual trail, the Lafayette is a pleasant stopover. That is, any night except the Saturday before Labor Day. □

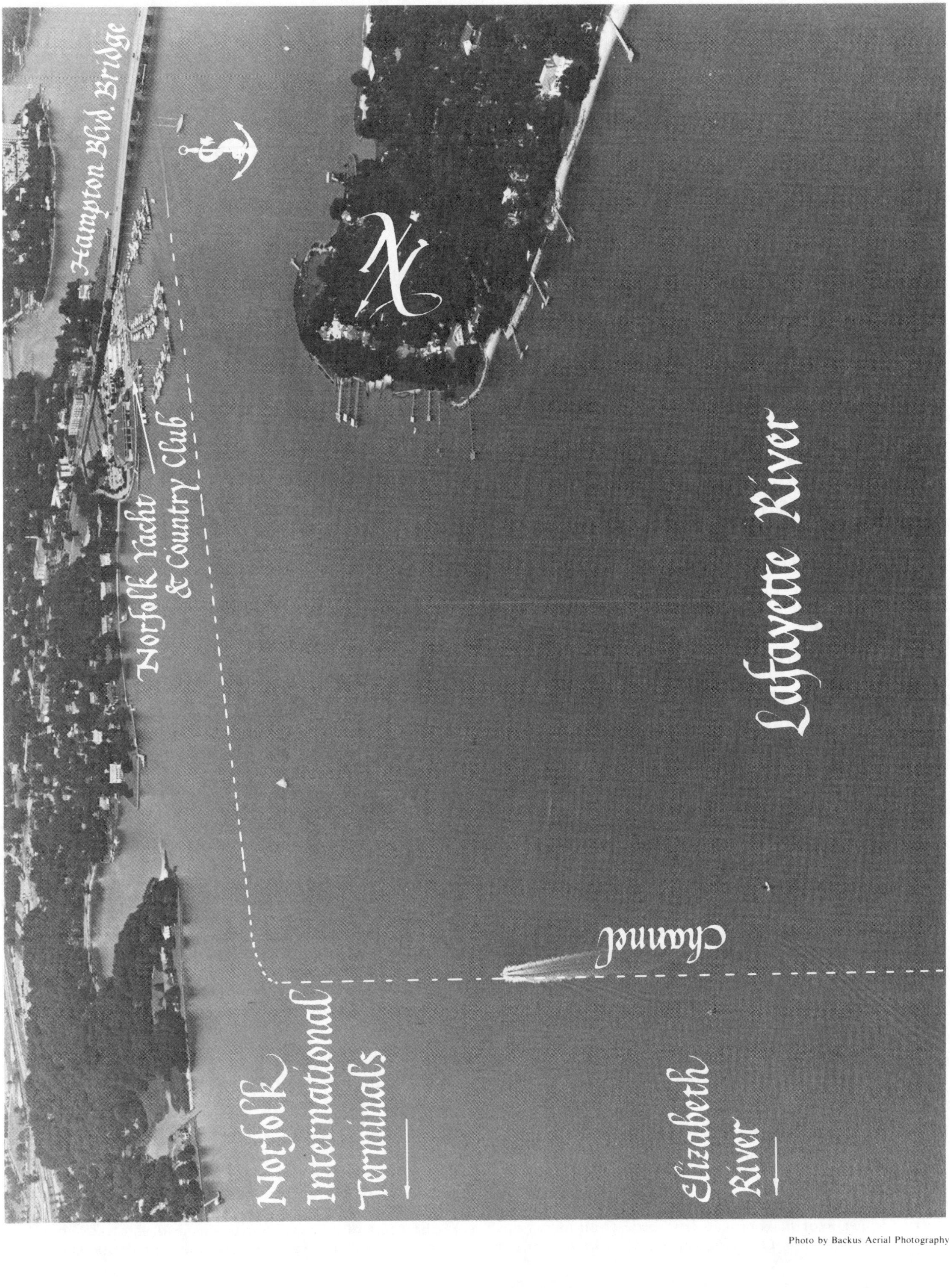

Photo by Backus Aerial Photography

A Walking Tour of:
PORTSMOUTH

First there were the Indians. A hardy people, they were able to withstand all nature's trials but one—the white man. On May 14, 1607, a group of about 104 of these fair-skinned creatures, in search of gold and silver and with plans to establish a trading post, landed on a little peninsula in what is now known as the tidewater area of Virginia. They named their settlement and the river it was on after their sovereign, King James I of England. The following year, their leader, Captain John Smith, explored a nearby waterway to be known as the Elizabeth River. The area had been "discovered". The beginning of a brave new world started for the European newcomer and the end of an era began for the Indian.

While the first recorded land grant on the Elizabeth River was in 1620, it wasn't until 1659 that the site of present day Portsmouth was included in an 890-acre tract granted to Captain William Carver. Unfortunately, Captain Carver's enjoyment of his estate was short lived, for only 17 years later he was hung and his lands confiscated for his involvement in Bacon's Rebellion. Carver's property became part of a 1,129-acre grant in 1716 to Lieutenant Colonel William Crawford, a successful merchant shipowner and member of Virginia's House of Burgesses. In 1752 the colonel dedicated about 65 acres of his estate for a small town he named for the English naval city of Portsmouth. The center of town was at the crossroads of two main thoroughfares and had a different public building on each corner—a church, a jail, a courthouse, and a market.

From its founding, Portsmouth's evolution has been tied to the sea. Today, ocean going container ships load and unload at the Portsmouth Marine Terminal, the Fifth Coast Guard District is based here, fishermen call it home port, ship building and repair are important businesses, and defense related industries add greatly to the city's growth and economy. The Naval Shipyard, begun in 1767, counts nuclear-powered submarines and super-carriers among the vessels it services. Its repair record includes the Confederate ironclad *Merrimac* which was drydocked in 1861.

Eager to get acquainted with this well-known town, we plotted our course, planned our provisions, and started on our way. As we neared Hampton Roads, traffic got busy. A passing submarine (be watchful, we felt its impressive wake well before we saw the ship), a Navy destroyer, tugboats and barges, pleasurecraft, and freighters at anchor (ever see freighters rafted up?) added to the activity we encountered. Once in the Elizabeth River we passed the Norfolk Naval Base where ships of the Atlantic and Mediterranean Fleets stand at-the-ready. A short cruise farther lay Portsmouth. Our exact destination: Tidewater Yacht Agency, Virginia's largest marina (about 300 slips). From there we could walk almost anyplace we wanted without fear of feet or children giving up. Facilities include a laundry, rental cars, gas dock, the Dock Seafood Restaurant, and a ships store which sells a little bit of everything (from milk to charts, jewelry to hardware).

After settling into our slip, we turned our attention landward. To the right is Hospital Point and the naval hospital complex. Ahead lies a quiet residential neighborhood and to the left is a Holiday Inn. Along the waterfront, just past the hotel, is Portside. Actually, it's not one place but a cluster of places. First, it's a ferry landing. Portsmouth's ferry service, North America's first pedestrian ferry, was established in 1636. Over the years technology brought improvements until 1955 when the downtown tunnel to Norfolk made the ferry obsolete. Revived three years ago, passengers can travel between Porstmouth and Norfolk on a charismatic replica of a Mississippi River paddle boat. Next to the ferry landing is the visitors' center which offers brochures highlighting local attractions, information from a friendly staff, the trolley tour ticket counter, and rest rooms. Across the street is the Olde Harbour Market, a collection of open-air stalls in a blue and white tent-like structure. Inside, an array of tasty treats await you including seafood, yogurt, oriental and Italian fare, and The Dipper ice cream stall (of course we indulged ourselves and enjoyed every nibble and lick). A plant store and pushcarts outside round out the commercial endeavors. A few steps further around the harbor is a stage used for family-oriented performances and weekly auctions. The co-ordinated entertainment (including movies and live concerts) scheduled for the season is called Portsevents (a calendar of events is available). Adding to Portside's festive ambiance are roving entertainers called the Portside Players. This talented group, including mimes, magicians, ventriloquists, jugglers, musicians, and minstrals, can pop up at any time to the delight of everyone. (Portside is open spring through early fall.)

Nearby is Riverfront Park, slated to be the only open space left in town. This patch of green has a lovely fountain, part of a jogging/exercise trail, and benches along a brick, flower-lined path. Overlooking the park is the Seaboard Coastline Building, built in 1894, expanded in 1914, and renovation/addition begun in 1986. Once it was a railroad building, later a City Hall, and it is now being transformed into a commercial property.

About a block inland is the historic Olde Towne district. Two of its best known homes are the Pass House and the Hill House. The former is so named because it was here during the Civil War that passes enabling travelers to go from federally occupied Portsmouth to neighboring Norfolk were issued. The latter is named for the family that owned it from the early 1800's until 1962 when they gave it to the Portsmouth Historical Association which uses it for its headquarters. (The Hill House is open to the public Tuesday-Sunday, 2-5 P.M.)

In Olde Towne's 200+ years of development, it incorporated many architectural types and details. For instance, there's the "English basement style" similar to houses found in Hull, England. Because of the land's close proximity to sea-level, basements were built above ground putting the first floor one story up. The "tax dodger" house was a clever 18th century money saver. Since taxes were assessed according to the number of full stories, the Dutch Colonial with its gambrel roof added another floor to a home while saving on taxes.

For a taste of the area's history and ambiance a guided tour is a must. The "Olde Town Lantern Tour" pamphlet outlines two walk-it-yourself excursions. The full tour takes less than an hour; its abbreviated version takes only 15 minutes. Both pass main points of interest while allowing you to adjust for time and stamina.

Although explore-on-your-own expeditions go through the heart of a town, tour guides lead you to its soul. If you have an extra 45 minutes and want a more personal look at

Portsmouth, treat yourself to the narrated trolley tour which highlights over 50 places of note. Knowledgable guides weave together architectural details with fascinating vignettes of past residents. One story involves the unassuming house at 401 Court Street. The California gold rush presented a serious problem for the western housing industry by combining a scarcity of wood with a rapidly growing population. Enter William Henry Niemyer, wealthy owner of a large local lumber company. He reasoned that you could cut sections of wood to exact specifications, load them on boats and ship them to the west coast to be assembled into houses. And so, an early pre-fabricated housing endeavor was born. When Niemyer's niece married, he gave one of his homes to the newlyweds as a wedding gift. Ironically, while many of Niemyer's houses can still be seen out west, this is the only one in Virginia.

Portsmouth's museums offer a pleasant change of pace. The Portsmouth Naval Shipyard Museum, at the foot of High Street, chronicles the area's naval history from the Civil War to today through models, artifacts, maps and memorabilia. (Free.) Nearby, the Portsmouth Lightship Museum uses exhibits and artifacts to explain the era of lightships. The restored 1846 Courthouse at town square houses two more museums. One is the Portsmouth Fine Arts Gallery which highlights the work of local artists and features touring exhibits from abroad. The other is the Children's Museum, a delightful blend of hands-on and dress-up experiences in three areas: optical illusions, water, and the city. (Admission.) Next to the courthouse, honoring outstanding athletes in many fields, is the Virginia Sports Hall of Fame. (Free.)

Wherever we go, running out of staples (like milk and M&Ms) seems part of our way of life and locating groceries is a priority. We found the Olde Harbor Market and the 7-11 great for odds and ends while Belo's appeals to the more serious shopper. (Belo's provides courtesy customer transportation back to your marina.)

As for shopping, Portsmouth is in the middle of a metamorphosis. Like a catapiller from its cocoon, within the next couple of years it should emerge as a lovely butterfly. Plans for the construction of high-rise buildings along the river call for shops and boutiques on ground level floors. These stores will replace the Olde Harbour Market which will then be dismantled. Meanwhile, work is progressing on High Street's face lift. In an effort to extend Olde Towne's charm to this existing downtown shopping district, brick sidewalks, landscaping, and new store-fronts are being added.

Rounding out Portsmouth's allure are a couple of annual events. Each June, the Seawall Festival is held in conjunction with Norfolk's Harborfest. Festivities combine entertainment and food with a host of activities including the Annual Seawall Art Show. The atmosphere is low-key, strictly family oriented, and sure to please. Around Thanksgiving, the Towne Lighting celebrates the coming of Christmas with an evening walk through Olde Towne. The Yuletide season is also welcomed with a special 3½-hour trolley tour. Not only can riders board and disembark to do their holiday shopping, but the trolley passes by beautifully decorated homes and makes a special trip to Coleman Nursery to see its fabulous animated holiday displays.

Charm and character permeate Portsmouth, blending all that has withstood the test of time with a surge of growth and progress. All this warmly welcomes you to explore and enjoy. For more information, contact the Department of Economic Development, 804-393-8804 in Virginia and 1-800-338-8822 out-of-state. □

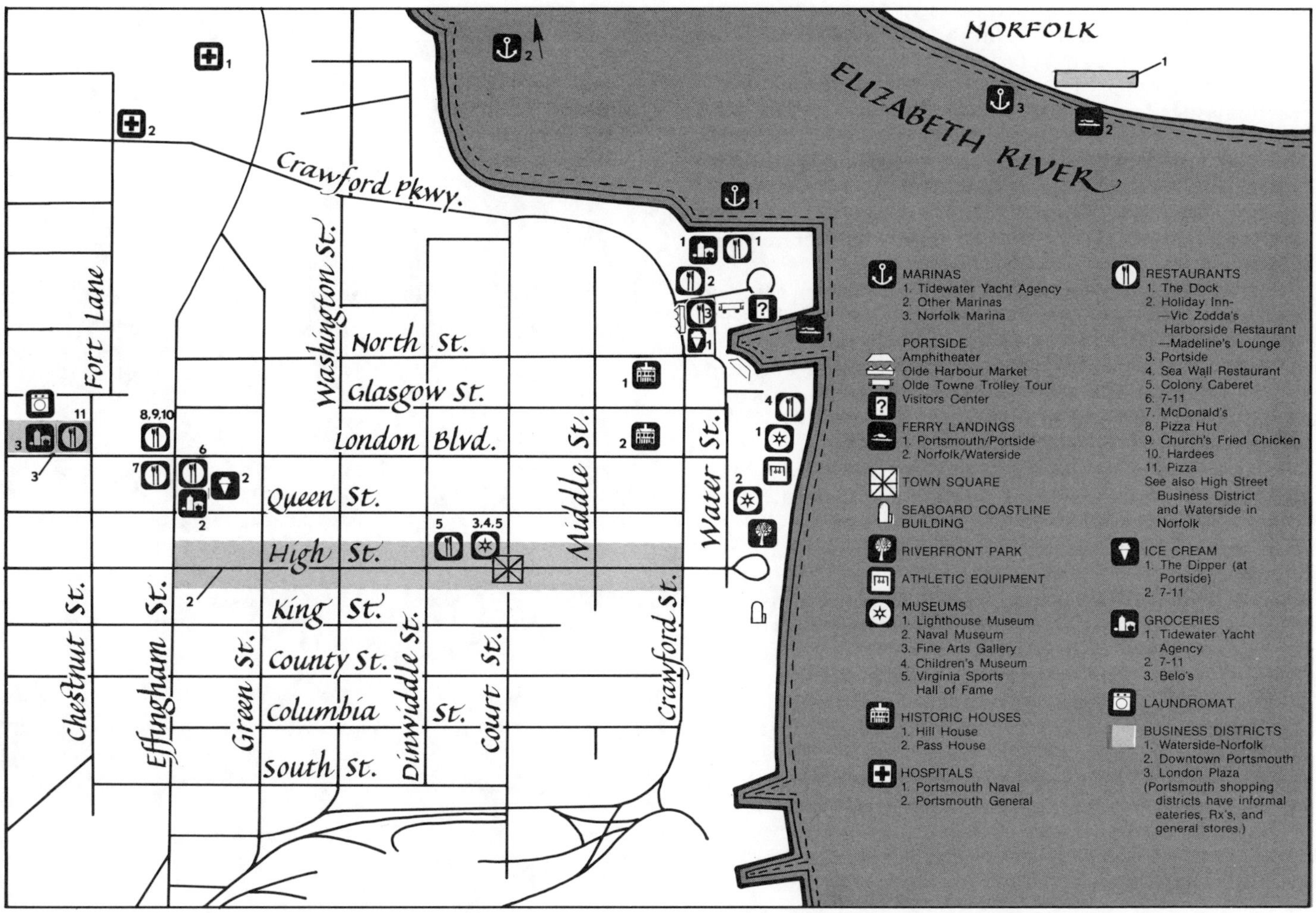

Rendering of author's map by Joan Machinchick

WILLOUGHBY BAY

on Hampton Roads

NOTE: Shoaling to 3 ft. MLW has been reported on the eastern edge of channel between daybeacons "1" and "3"; shoaling to 4 ft. MLW reported in vicinity of "3"; shoaling to 5 ft. reported across the entire channel between "3" and "5".

A nice spot to use as a destination, lay over, or jumping off point for the Intracoastal Waterway south from Norfolk to the Carolinas is Willoughby Bay. Good holding ground in 10-12 feet and a large, moderately well-protected anchorage lies under the north spit near the moored boats. The spit is rough on a southeaster, but protection can be gained by moving to the other side of the bay. The entrance is easy and deep, just a two-mile detour off your Intracoastal Waterway route along a nice straight well-marked channel. Marinas are available at the dockside complex, and Interstate 64 has an exit ramp adjacent to the long established Ocean View summer cottage area there. A rental car can allow you to see everything on the lower Bay from Williamsburg to Norfolk. Services are excellent and people nice at both Willoughby Bay Marina and Rebel Marine Service.

If you're traveling north, plan to leave the spit to arrive just below Wolftrap Light at the beginning flood and ride the flood all the way past the Potomac to below Solomons if your boat speed will allow. Check the Chesapeake Bay Current Diagram in the back of the NOAA Tidal Current Tables. If you try riding the flood north against a hard northerly blow it can be lumpy so you may want to use more gas, take longer, and ride more easily by leaving on an ebb and not going so far. Let your circumstances dictate your choice.

Willoughby Bay is a nice area for craft leaving the Bay for offshore trips, or for a short getaway for people from Hampton and Newport News who just want to weekend on their boats away from home creeks. Many an October trip up to Mobjack Bay from the city has seen a hard norther cause courses to be reversed and make boats run for a sheltered visit at Willoughby.

When entering Willoughby Bay one comes inside the southern Hampton Roads Bridge and runs south in a straight well-marked channel. Adhere well to marks, as the eastern bank of the channel is quite shoal. Stay on the red side and eight feet can be easily carried around to the very visible Willoughby Bay Marina Texaco dock, which is open all year and provides 110/220 volts dockside and berths up to 65 feet. A marine store is there with the ubiquitous ice and beer; tiled showers and toilets are provided; and there is an adjacent motel. Gas and diesel fuel and repair service are available; and groceries can be purchased about half a mile away.

Rebel Marine Service monitors channel 16 VHF and is also open all year. It offers hardware, head, showers, ice, beverages, a canvas shop and 24-hour salvage crews and divers. One of their best, unadvertised assets is a used paper book library to which visitors and locals add and take books at no cost. Someone built low shelves to facilitate central trading of reading material and one can spend an hour or so scratching around on hands and knees or sitting cross-legged shuffling through stacks of books.

Rebel Marine is also the birthplace and home of the famous Tugantine®, *Norfolk Rebel*, a 51-foot auxiliary sail-powered tug and fishing vessel that tows mostly inside the Bay but fishes off shore.

Willoughby Harbor Marina has opened just to the east of Rebel Marine. It has about 300 slips behind a breakwater.

A favorite overnight for local boats, a haven if not a hurricane hole, a convenient supply wayside stop if not an idyllic paradise, Willoughby Bay will vary your season's samplings of the lower Bay and beckon you back from year to year. □

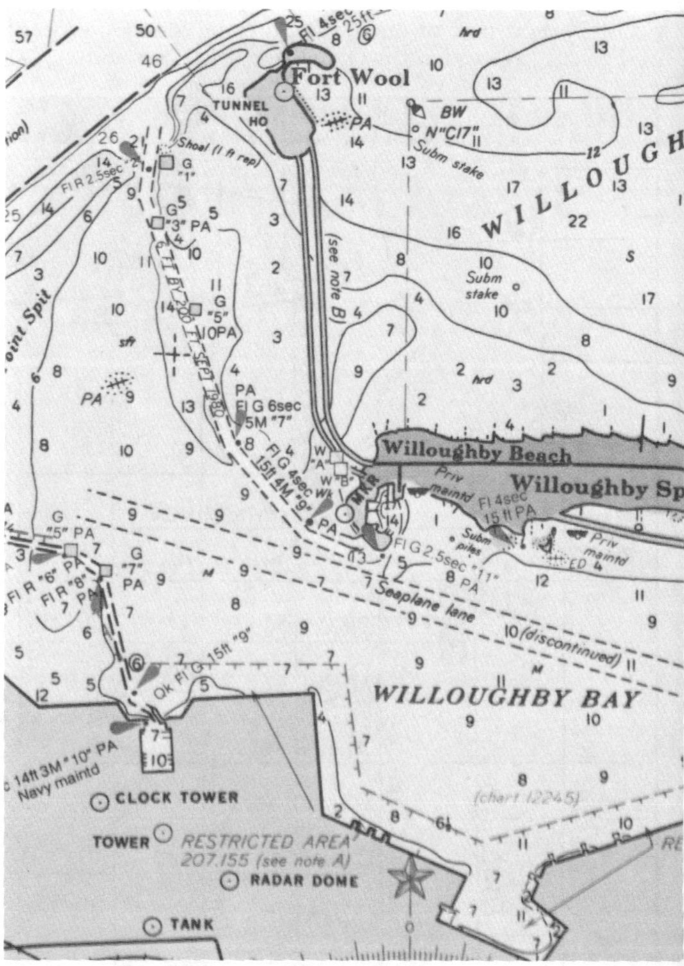

From NOAA Chart 12222—not to be used for navigation

BACKUS AERIAL PHOTOGRAPHY

NORFOLK

Norfolk is a vital port to commercial shipping, a mighty naval installation, a busy yachting harbor, and the beginning of the Intracoastal Waterway to Florida.

The entrance to the harbor, which includes access to Hampton Roads (the yachting area) on the north, Newport News (the commercial and shipbuilding center) to the northwest, and Norfolk to the south and east, is designed to make it easy for a 60,000-ton aircraft carrier, so it presents no unusual problems for yachtsmen. Entering, between Fort Monroe on the north and Fort Wool on the south, is straightforward, except when hampered by fog which seems to be fairly common. Currents can run as high as 2.6 knots, so if yours is a slow boat, use your current tables to advantage.

Anchorage is available immediately on entering the harbor, either to the south at Willoughby Bay, or to the north at Mill Creek, inside Old Point Comfort.

The Willoughby Bay anchorage is the more protected in all weather but is about two miles off the channel. The Mill Creek

From NOAA Chart 12253—not to be used for navigation.

anchorage offers the advantage of being much closer to the main channel, but has no facilities. Holding ground is good and you have a wake-up service from Fort Monroe in the morning when they blow reveille and mess call. Mill Creek is not suitable in southwest winds.

In entering Mill Creek leave "2" (Fl R 4 sec) to port from the main channel and follow the markers in. Anchor to the west of a line between markers "5" and "7" in nine feet of water.

As you proceed further up the main channel toward downtown Norfolk you will leave a big ship anchorage to starboard and pass a substantial portion of the U.S. Navy to port at Sewells Point. There is usually at least one aircraft carrier in port along with an assortment of destroyers, nuclear submarines and support ships. These vessels are ready to put to sea on short notice.

About a mile along on the port side, the passenger liner *S.S. United States* remains mothballed in a slip she has occupied since 1969. This vessel, which still holds the Atlantic Blue Ribband for speed, was built in 1952 in Newport News and was quite a technological marvel in her day—her hull design was classified top-secret by the U.S. Navy.

Continuing upstream in what is now called Craney Island Reach, the Portsmouth Naval Hospital is passed to starboard. Here you will see boats at anchor, just before a marina. The anchorage itself is secure, but bumpy. In this area, on the opposite side of the Elizabeth River, in what appears as downtown Norfolk, a new city tie-up facility has been developed.

For Norfolk, there are many indications of a rebirth emerging in this historic seaport city. Norfolk has a new look—modern high-rise office buildings share the skyline with an elegant cultural and convention center. An open mall, trees and park-like esplanades dot the downtown retail district. Millions of dollars are being poured into downtown office buildings, restaurants and hotels—all within walking distance of the waterfront. The Harborfest celebration (held annually, in the summer, usually in June) has attracted an estimated 750,000 people to Norfolk's waterfront. For more information on Harborfest and Norfolk's waterfront, call (804)441-5145.

Norfolk's waterfront profile has changed dramatically over the last few years. The Waterside, a festival marketplace developed by James W. Rouse, is situated next to the Omni International Hotel on the city's downtown waterfront. The multi-million dollar market, which opened June 1983, is being patterned after other successful Rouse marketplaces in Boston, Baltimore and Philadelphia, and is expected to attract up to 6 million visitors a year. It contains about 130 shops, restaurants, kiosks, fast-food booths and pushcarts. A marina has been built along the river in front of Waterside. It will be for visitors only.

Another attraction is the $22 million Virginia World Trade Center which is expected to draw more people to the downtown waterfront and to increase international trade in Norfolk. Another important element in the city's waterfront development is the proposed Cousteau Oceans Center. The Cousteau Society moved its world headquarters to Norfolk in 1980, and began planning for the center.

The Town Point Park is between The Waterside and the future Cousteau Oceans Center on the Elizabeth River. The park offers recreation and easy access to the waterfront. Another addition is a network of seven docks from Berkley Bridge to Freemason Harbor. These new docks enable cruisers on the Elizabeth River better access to the attractions at Norfolk.

The popularity of Norfolk's downtown waterfront is also evident in the sales of new and rehabilitated housing near the waterfront. Stately townhouses are being constructed near renovated turn-of-the-century homes in the city's Freemason Harbor district near the downtown western waterfront.

Norfolk is not an outstanding port for provisioning at present, but it looks as though this will change. Boats proceeding south are advised to tie up at Great Bridge, at Mile 12 of the Intracoastal Waterway, where excellent supermarkets, hardware and marine supplies are available, virtually at dockside.

Yachtsmen who are navy ship buffs can proceed further up the Intracoastal Waterway to view more fighting ships undergoing every stage of refit. Be watchful of the heavy commercial traffic on the river.

Back out on Chesapeake Bay (but also part of Norfolk and south of the harbor entrance at Ft. Wool) is Little Creek, home of a Coast Guard base, further units of the U.S. fleet, and many marine facilities. Entrance is easy, and there are no bridges for sailboats to worry about. Further south, Lynnhaven Inlet, the last before Cape Henry, is popular with sportfishermen, has plenty of marine facilities, but also has shallow water and a fixed bridge with a 35-foot clearance. This is the closest port for an outing to Virginia Beach with its many restaurants and summer fun.

See the sections on Hampton, Holiday Harbor and Elizabeth River (Western Branch) for more information on the Norfolk area. □

t left is a view of the Norfolk waterfront. Below is a 'oser view of Norfolk's Waterside, a festival market 'ace.

PHOTOS BY STEPHEN KNOX

A Walking Tour of
NORFOLK

by Andi Manchester

Cruising into Norfolk is an experience in itself. You leave the Chesapeake Bay at Hampton Roads, a VERY BUSY place. As you leave the Bay, the Hampton River is on your right, Willoughby Bay (a popular anchorage) and the Elizabeth River are to your left, and straight ahead is the James River. Following the Elizabeth River channel toward Norfolk brings you in front of the Norfolk Naval Base, the world's largest installation of its kind.

A short distance downriver is the heart of Norfolk and the city's only downtown marina. Be forewarned, only 1/3 of its 31 slips can be reserved and the rest fill up quickly. You register in the dockmaster's office, in the gazebo at the end of the marina's first dock, where you can also pick up a copy of *The Compass Rose* (a shopping and boating services guide). The marina's floating docks are wide, sturdy, and well-maintained and its staff is intelligent and friendly. Police and security personnel are very visible and take the safety and well-being of boaters seriously.

Our trip turned me into an incurable tugboat watcher. I've been captivated by their parade of shapes (one, two, and three decks high), styles (barge pushers, freighter tuggers), sizes (small, medium, and large), and colors (white, baby blue, dark blue, red, spring green, moss green), even combinations of colors. Tug traffic doesn't end with the daylight; all night long they glide quietly by, their running and deck lights reflected in shimmery patterns on the river.

Ship repair is a big business here. Freighters and naval vessels perched high in dry dock dwarf men and equipment around them. We dinghied up to one of these giants and were astounded by the sheer size of its rudder and props. Talk about feeling Lilliputian! A short distance from the marina (by foot or water) towards the naval base is the berth of a famous television "personality"—Jacques Cousteau's *Calypso*. We dinghied out to see it and Cousteau's experimental sailboat, *Alcyone*, with its revolutionary fixed rigid sail. Seeing *Calypso* on T.V. is one thing, dinghying along beside it is quite another. At a pier near *Calypso* are several NOAA deep sea research vessels, impressive though not as well known as their French counterpart.

Norfolk's land personality is as captivating and vibrant as its nautical side. A good place to start touring is at the Ask-Me kiosk at the street in front of the marina. Here you can get information about the area, buy tickets for tours, and board tour buses and trackless trolleys. Before setting out to explore on our own, we opted for a trolley tour to acquaint ourselves with the area.

The Norfolk trolley tour lasts about one hour and guides you through well-known neighborhoods, over cobblestone streets, and past major attractions. All the while you are treated to fascinating details you might miss by hoofing it on your own. (For example, St. Paul's Church, circa 1739, was the only structure to survive Lord Dunmore's bombardment of the city in 1776 and still has a souvenir cannonball embedded in its southeast wall.) You can get off the trolley at both the Chrysler Museum and the Douglas MacArthur Memorial to explore on your own and reboard another one an hour later.

A pamphlet at the information desk of the Chrysler Museum announces, "You Just Entered One of the Top 20 Museums in the Country. Don't leave Without Seeing A Dozen Reasons Why." These reasons, displayed in 40 galleries covering 50,000 square feet of exhibit space, include work by some of the world's greatest artists spanning 4,480 years and a variety of media. Founded in 1933 as the Norfolk Museum of Arts and Sciences, it was reborn as the Chrysler Museum after Mr. and Mrs. Walter Chrysler, Jr. donated their personal art collection to the city in 1971.

The MacArthur Memorial is a complex of four buildings: a theater, memorial, gift shop, and an exhibits/library/administration building. First we went to the theater where we watched a 22-minute film highlighting the general's life and career (the kids loved it) and then went to the memorial. MacArthur's tomb, in the rotunda of this converted 1850 Norfolk City Hall building, is surrounded by 11 exhibit areas chronologically tracing his life and career and displaying his gifts, medals, awards, and personal memorabilia. His 1950 Chrysler Crown Imperial limousine is in the gift shop building and the library boasts his 4,000 volume collection and over 2,000,000 other items research scholars find invaluable.

Most of Norfolk's attractions are within the one square-mile downtown area, hardly intimidating to seasoned walkers who want a more personal look at the city. For those whose intentions exceed their fitness, take heart—this is a town of considerate planners who have implemented a free downtown transportation system. (You can board, gratis, any downtown bus or the blue trackless trolley.)

Intrigued by the naval base as seen from the water, we wanted to tour it by land. A bus at the Ask-Me kiosk took us to the base where we boarded a different bus for the tour around this 4,800 acre complex. Established in 1917, the base has grown to include NAVCAMSLANT (Naval Communications Area Master Station Atlantic) which processes over 50 million messages annually, a heliport, the Naval Air Station whose 147 aircraft make about 116,000 flights a year, the Naval Supply Center which stocks over 900,000 different items (from milk to jet engines), and the Hampton Roads Naval Museum among its other operations. (Daily tours except during the Azalea Festival and Harborfest; admission.)

There are other ways to see Norfolk. Cycle enthusiasts can rent bikes at the information kiosk and treat themselves to an 8-mile self-guided excursion (1, 4, or 8-hour rentals, May 1 thru Sept. 30). Also, boat tours abound. The *New Spirit*, a 600 passenger vessel, offers entertainment (live bands and a "Salute to Broadway" revue) and dining (buffet luncheons and dinners, moonlight cocktails and snacks, Apr.-Dec., Wed.-Sun.). A replica of a 19th century Mississippi riverboat, the *Carrie B*, has a 1½-hr. daytime and a 3-hour sunset harbor tour. Several sailing vessels cruise on the Chesapeake Bay (the *American Rover*, the *Norfolk Rover*, and the *Bonnie Jean Rover*) and a paddle wheeler, the *Dixie Rover*, offers 3 different cruises. If you prefer to get around by taxi or rental car, three taxi companies and four rent-a-car agencies are ready to comply.

The downtown core is just the tip of Norfolk's attractions iceberg. Just across the Elizabeth River, only a few mintues away by passenger ferry, is the delightful town of Portsmouth. (But that's another article.) On a 12-acre site along the Lafayette River is the renowned Hermitage Foundation Museum. Housed in a Tudor-style mansion built in 1908, it boasts rare oriental and western art treasures. Another popular attraction is the Lafayette Zoological Park with a farmyard display, childrens' petting zoo, and 500 varieties of animals. A bit farther from the marina is the Norfolk Botanical Gardens. You can tour the 175 acres of flowering trees and shrubs by foot, trackless train, or canal boat. Virginia Beach is a mere 18 miles away, so close that buses run there regularly.

Anyone who has been to Norfolk in the past few years will inevitably mention Waterside, located next to the marina. Antiques, books, clothing, handmade crafts, toys, kitchenware—these and more test your self-indulgence. Food-wise, the specialty and old-fashioned markets and stalls stock just about everything a galley could use while all types of eating places challenge your dietary discipline. We conducted our own family-style taste test (which of course included ice cream!), and I can report that everything we had was well worth its calories. However, there's more to Waterside than shopping and eating. There's also an aquarium filled with marine life from the Chesapeake Bay, museum exhibits from the Mariners' Museum in Newport News and the Chrysler Museum, entertainment and an Ask-Me booth.

Shopping and eating outside Waterside is as varied as inside. A short block away is the Seldon Arcade, an impressive collection of boutiques and restaurants. Several blocks to the east is a plaza-type shopping center with a grocery store, drug store, liquor store, and even a McDonald's. A few blocks to the northwest is Granby Mall. Once a typical downtown street, it has been transformed into a brick-paved open mall in an effort to lure shoppers back from suburban shopping centers.

A discussion of Norfolk would be woefully remiss if it did not mention festivals. There are so-o-o many! The four day Azalea Festival, held at the Norfolk Botanical Gardens each April, honors NATO and marks Norfolk's role as its U.S. Atlantic headquarters. It features a parade, air show, dances, entertainment, exhibits, food, and the crowning of a queen. On Mothers' Day week-end each May, the Ghent Arts Festival combines food and entertainment with an outdoor art show. The biggest and most elaborate annual "happening" is Harborfest. Based at the waterfront and held the first week-end in June, this 3-day event draws over a million visitors. They can enjoy tall ships, military demonstrations, boat races, food, entertainment, and a fireworks display par excellence. Summerfest, which highlights artists, musicians, and food (or bring your own picnic lunch) is held annually at St. Paul's Episcopal Church. The 4th of July brings a variety of activities to the waterfront culminating with a spectacular fireworks display. Next to Waterside is the 6.5 acre Town Point Park. It is the site of over 220 free events annually, including ethnic festivals and food challenges, where local restaurants give out samples of a theme food and vie for tasters' votes. For a complete listing, consult the Festevents calendar of events.

Although I couldn't tell you about everything Norfolk has to offer, the Norfolk Convention Visitors Bureau would be happy to pick up where I left off. Call them at 804-441-5266 in Virginia or 1-800-368-3097 from out of state. Or, write them at Monticello Arcade, Norfolk, Virginia, 23510. □

Rendering of author's map by Joan Machinchick

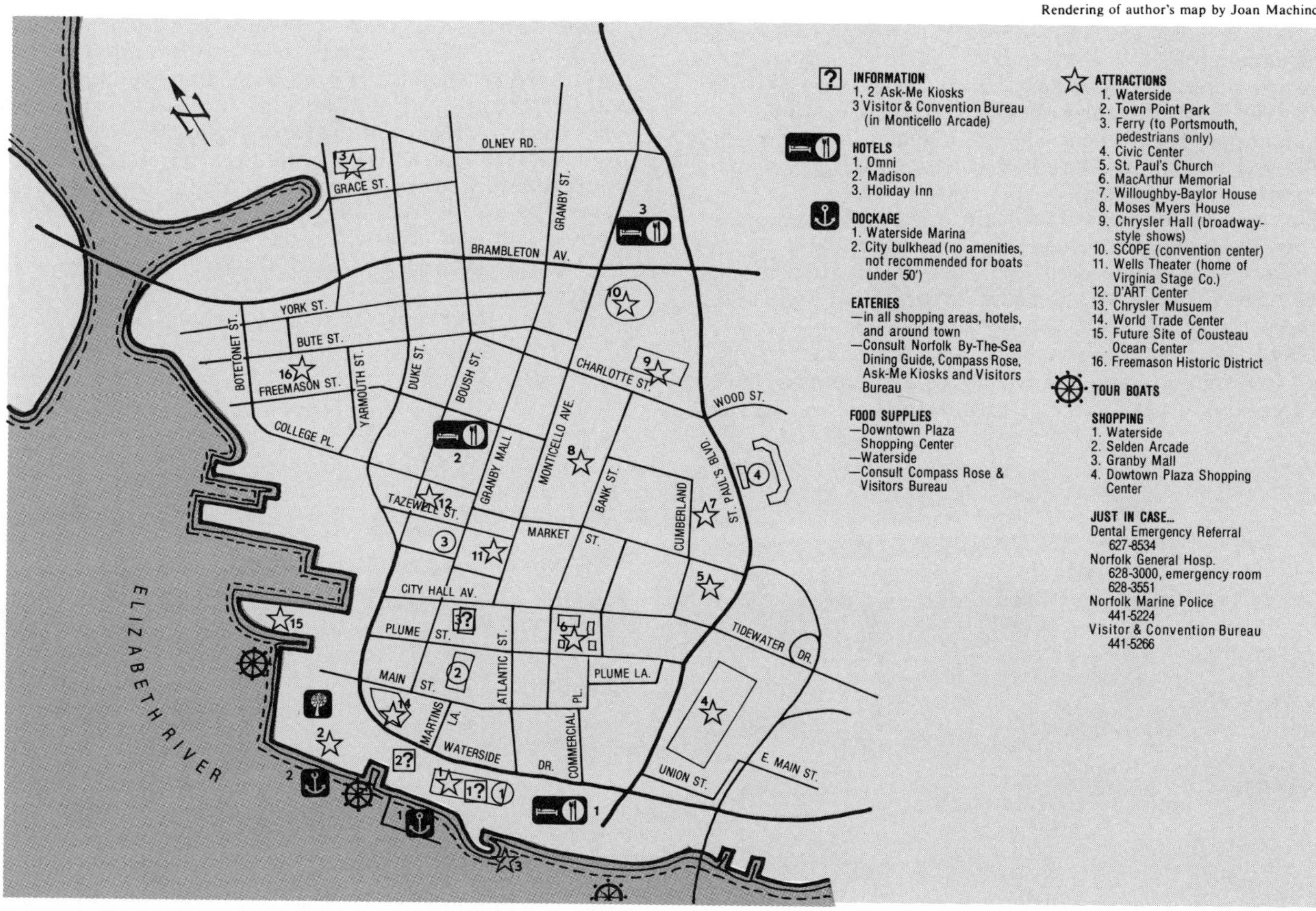

The James River is one of the largest tributaries of the Chesapeake and the first explored and settled by the English colonists. It is impossible to sail the James without thinking of those first settlers and wondering how the shoreline must have looked 400 years ago.

One change we can appreciate is the large number of markers set to guide you through the twisting channel. From Hampton Roads to Richmond the James is characterized by shoals and bends. Today it is easily navigated, but think how deceptively inviting the broad mouth must have appeared to early explorers. Charts 12248 and 12251 cover the James from Newport News to Richmond.

The mouth of the James is about five miles wide, with plenty of water on the north side (closest to Newport News).

Just at the mouth of the James are the Nansemond River and Chuckatuck Creek, both on the south side. The Nansemond is spanned by a new fixed bridge with a 65-foot clearance. The Nansemond is a quiet, undeveloped area with no marinas or other shore facilities and offers a certain unspoiled relaxation. The river is navigable all the way to Suffolk (about 15 miles), but there is little to see in the last five miles that you cannot see in the first five.

Likewise, Chuckatuck Creek offers little but solitude. The entrance to Chuckatuck Creek is long but well marked. **See page 310 for the Chuckatuck Creek cruise.**

On the opposite shore of the James is the city of Newport News, which offers quite a contrast to the peace and quiet of the southern shore. The Newport News side is dominated by Newport News Shipbuilding, which occupies about three miles of waterfront. The giant shipyard is the only one in the country that builds aircraft carriers and one of only two that builds submarines.

White Shoal lurks just north of the bridge. Even though it is clearly marked it snags many a sailor who tries to carry his tack just a little farther. A friend of mine has been caught so many times that his latest boat is named *Gotcha* with the hail port of White Shoal.

To the west of White shoal is the Pagan River. **See page 312 for the Pagan River cruise.** **The best excuse for a trip up the Pagan is a night tied to the dock at Tennis Seafood Restaurant. The restaurant is almost all the way to Smithfield, just past the bridge over Cypress Creek.**

One of our favorite overnight trips is to Deep Creek, about four miles past the bridge on the right. From our dock it is a good day's sail and a quiet, comfortable anchorage. **See the Deep Creek cruise.**

Next to Deep Creek is the Warwick River. It is difficult to navigate without the infamous local knowledge.

Past Deep Creek and the Warwick is the James River Reserve Fleet, a collection of naval and merchant vessels patiently passing the years, waiting for their recall to glory. The fleet is still impressive. Take the time to power through the fleet and turn up and down the rows. We do not recommend sailing as the rows of ships create wind swirls and eddies.

Past the Reserve Fleet on the right is Fort Eustis, an Army post. Though the chart does not show it to be a restricted area, there is nothing there of any interest.

Another of our favorite destinations is Kingsmill on the James. The marina is just north of buoy 38. Though small, the marina features visitor's slips at reasonable rates, clean showers, a sandy beach, and access to the Kingsmill complex. The dockmaster can arrange for reservations and transportation to Kingsmill Restaurant (coat and tie), tennis courts, golf course, and Busch Gardens. A wonderful spot to Spend a long weekend.

Across the river from Kingsmill is Hog Island and the Surry nuclear power plant. The chart shows the two domes at the plant; they are clearly visible on this part of the river.

Cobham Bay is a quiet anchorage, if somewhat exposed. In the hot summer months it is a good spot to catch whatever breeze is stirring. Be prepared, though, when the inevitable evening thunderstorm comes through from the southwest.

Jamestown was the first permanent English settlement in the New World. Jamestown Island was chosen by the group because its view down the river would give ample warning of any threat by water, and its being surrounded by water would protect them from possible Indian attack. The river was deep right up to the shore, so they could offload their ships easily. A replica of the Jamestown settlement has been built adjacent to the ferry landing at Glass House Point. Unfortunately, there is no easy access by boat. If you are determined to visit, anchor across the channel from the landing and row across.

The Scotland ferry crosses the river every 15 minutes between Scotland and Glass House Point. The landings are marked on the charts; be on the lookout for the ferries.

The Chickahominy River enters the James just above the ferry crossing. The entrance is well marked and easy to follow.

Deep Creek—looking just inside entrance.

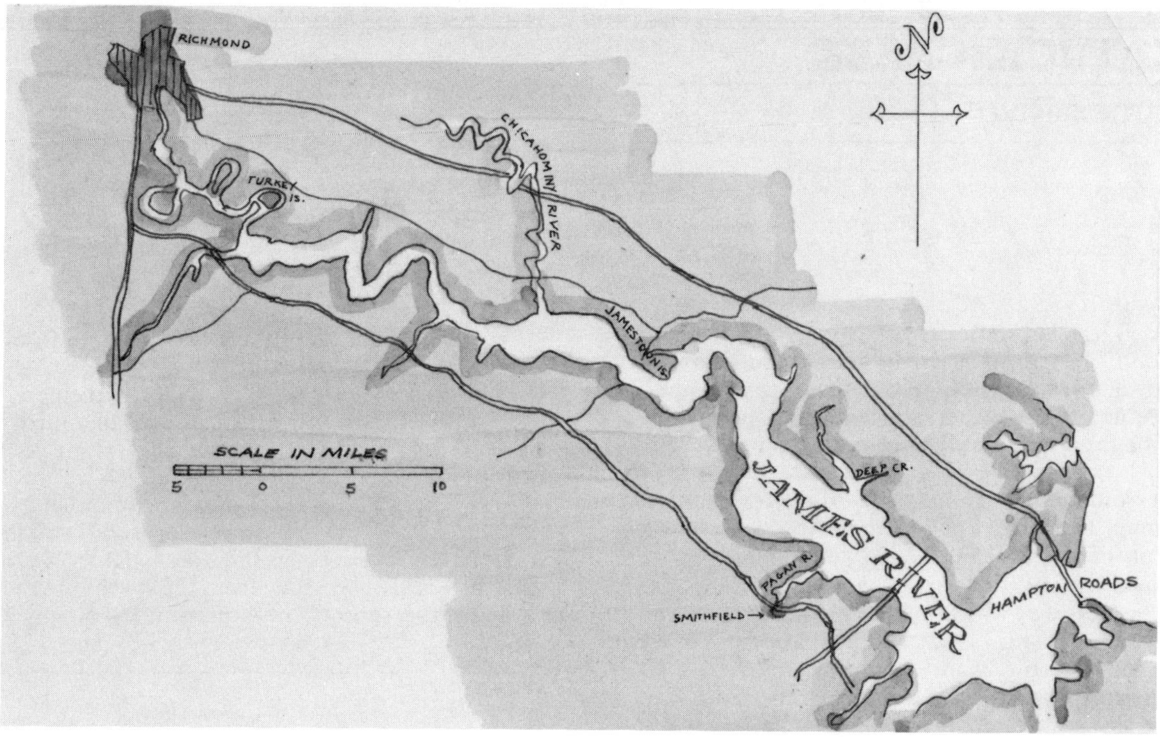

Like the smaller rivers and creeks at the mouth of the James, the biggest attraction of the Chickahominy is the peace and quiet. There is a swing bridge just inside the mouth, and just past the bridge is a fuel pier at the Riverside Resort Campground. The pier has seven feet of water at the end as well as a dinghy landing. The campground has a small grocery store that is open through the boating season.

About seven miles up the Chickahominy is Chickahominy Haven, which features a restaurant and fuel pumps.

With these two exceptions the rest of the Chickahominy is either undeveloped or lined with homes. We have never been to the head of the river, as our mast would be uncomfortably close to the power lines at about mile 8. I have always wanted to go to the lock at Walker Dam. The *Coast Pilot* says the "gates are hand operated; there is no tender. It is recommended that at least two strong persons be on board before attempting to use the lock."

Across from the mouth of the Chickahominy is the Eastover Manor. The four chimneys are shown on the chart; they are obvious. Like most of the plantation houses on the James, Eastover was built on a hill overlooking the river. The location offered a superb view and unobstructed breezes, the latter probably being more important to the original occupants.

As you continue up the James, there is a parade of plantation homes on both sides. Claremont, Brandon, Flowerdew Hundred and Westover are all marked on the chart. Though most offer public tours, none have public landings. If you want to visit one of the houses, row ashore and climb the bank. Your unorthodox approach may be rewarded with a special tour. The other option is to arrange transportation from one of the marinas in Hopewell.

The bridge at Jordan Point is known locally as the Benjamin Harrison Bridge. At the south end of the bridge, on the east side, is Jordan Point Yacht Haven. They welcome visitors and offer fuel, limited groceries, a pool and a restaurant.

There are two marinas in Hopewell, both on the Appomattox River just past the first bridge. Note that the bridge has a clearance of only 40 feet.

In fact there is little to lure the visitor as far as Hopewell. The James narrows quickly past the Chickahominy and though the scenery is beautiful it gets monotonous about here. For those who must do it all, the river is navigable all the way to Richmond, about 20 miles past Hopewell.

Our recommendation is to take the extra day or two and spend it on the lower James or around Hampton Roads.□

PHOTOS BY STEVE KNOX

Deep Creek—north end of harbor.

CHUCKATUCK CREEK

on the James River

The approach to Chuckatuck Creek is long and there are almost no facilities. Still, it is a good choice for a quiet, relaxing evening with no company. The nearby Ragged Island Wildlife Management Area is accessible by dinghy and will provide an afternoon's exploring for nature lovers.

The chart shows a shallow flat north of Pike Point—believe it. It is a long way around, but follow the marked entrance channel. Even so, proceed under the assumption that you will probably run aground on your first visit. We did the first time. The channel narrows considerably opposite Pike Point. The best way to follow the channel inside the harbor is to watch the stakes that support fish nets. They delineate both sides of the channel quite clearly.

The small island west of Pike Point is connected to the shore by a mud flat at low tide. If you approach at low water expect to see a clump of grass surrounded by mud.

The vertical clearance of the drawbridge is only 21 feet. As of this writing the bridge is unmanned and is opened only by prior arrangements. Check the *Coast Pilot* to find the current manning/schedule.

Anchor anywhere inside the harbor where the water is deep enough for your draft. Space is tight but the anchorage is well protected. Blyth Marine (on the south side) does not regularly offer transient slips but will accommodate a visitor if an empty slip is available. We recommend you anchor out and enjoy the peace and quiet.

Blyth does operate a small shipyard. They are equipped to haul and repair any size yacht.

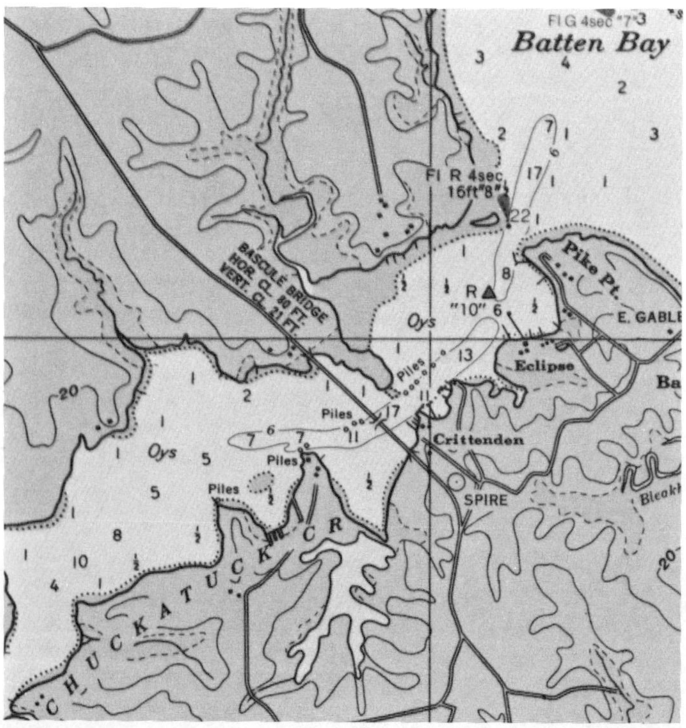

From NOAA Chart 12248—not to be used for navigation.

A small oyster and fishing fleet operates from Chuckatuck Creek.

The Ragged Island Wildlife Management Area is just north of Batten Bay. It covers an area of approximately 1500 acres of unspoiled river marsh. Several creeks allow access by dinghy. Deer, rabbits and squirrels abound around the several pine islands. The Virginia Commission of Game and Inland Fisheries has constructed several walking paths that start at Highway 17 by the James River Bridge. None of these are easily accessible from the south side though, so plan to enjoy the solitude of exploring by dinghy. □

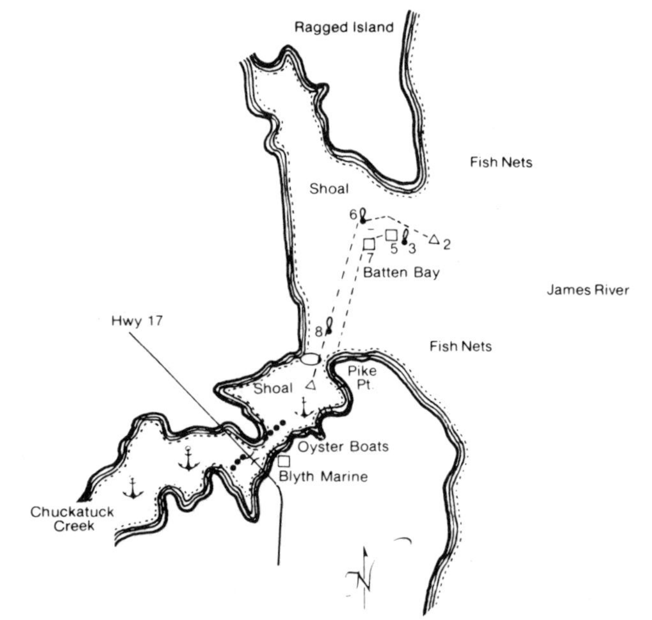

Chuckatuck Creek

DEEP CREEK

On the James River

Deep Creek is on the right about five miles up the James iver from the James River Bridge.

Coming in off the James the entrance is long, deep, and ell marked. (Despite charted depth, the creek has been redged and fathometer readings should run eight to ten feet or the main creek.) Shoal banks lay on either side of the hannel. Even though there is sufficient depth out of the hannel, it is unwise to cut any corners in this section of the ames for there are many broken-off stakes waiting just under he surface to hole one's hull.

The entrance to Deep Creek is between a low grassy spit n the right and the white city jail on a bluff to the left. Once nside you will notice the city dock beside the spit and a undred-foot trawler, with two forty-foot trawlers ahead of it aiting to load seed oysters. Ashore by the dock is Herman's Harbor House Restaurant. The south end of the harbor is illed with workboats. As the watermen go to work at aylight, we always anchor at the north end, between the after ange mark and Norman's (formerly Keffer's).

On our cruise everything was quiet except for the coming torm drumming rain against the cabinside and swelling the narshes with waves. Twenty or so oyster boats were securely ed at Menchville Marina across the creek; there were some ghts next door at Keffer's docks; and it looked like all the oats had returned to their nests at the Warwick Yacht and ountry Club at the creek's head. From here you can visit olonial Williamsburg, Busch Gardens, the Mariners' Museum in Newport News, or the NASA Visitors Center in Hampton by rental car from nearby Patrick Henry Airport. □

From NOAA Chart 12248—not to be used for navigation.

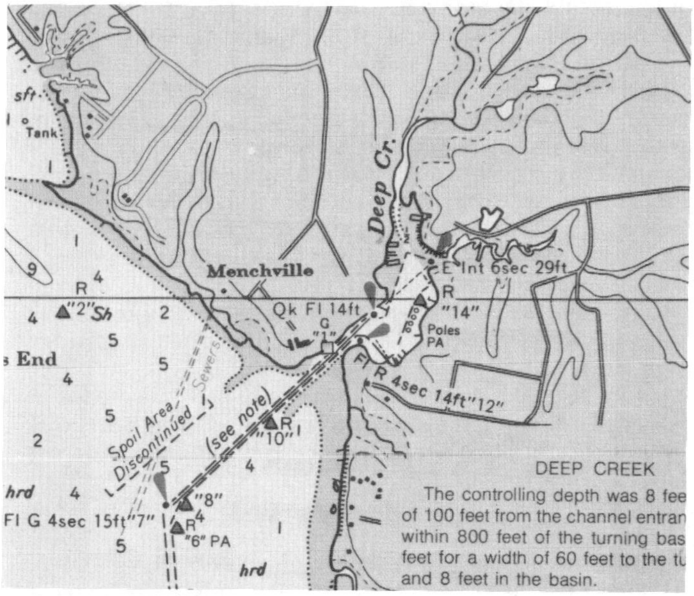

photo by Backus Aerial Photography

NOTE: Shoaling reported at entrance blocking southern half of channel. Navigate on the north side of the channel from the vicinity of day beacon "11" to 200 feet inside of the mouth.

PAGAN RIVER

off the James River

Heading up the James River, we passed close by Bell R "12" (Fl R 2½ sec) as we rounded Newport News coal piers to watch the fascinating process of loading coal from gigantic piles into waiting colliers. There were several fountains of water spraying over the coal piles to keep down the dust, and it gave the area an almost surrealistic feel.

Although there are fishing stakes along here on the southern side of the James River, the channel is plenty wide for sailboats and for the small merchant ships which steam up the river to Richmond. The northern bank of the river is occupied by the Newport News Shipbuilding Company, where there are several submarines and other ships, including an aircraft carrier, in various stages of construction.

The new James River Bridge is attractive, imposing and a little intimidating, although the vertical clearance is 50 feet. If that isn't sufficient for your boat, the bridge tender monitors VHF Channel 13 and will also open the bridge upon horn signal. Once through the bridge the shoreline suddenly changed, and it looked as if we had sailed back in history. To the north large, graceful homes and mansions abound, surrounded by lush green trees and magnificent deep green lawns right to the water's edge. The southern banks seem uninhabited, with thick, dark forests as far as the eye can see.

From the bridge we steered course 290° M for BW N "J1" or BW N "J3". We entered the Pagan River channel at "3" (Fl G 2.5 sec). It's well marked, although quite shallow on either side of the channel.

When we rounded Battery Park, at "14" (Fl R 4 sec) by the old oyster processing factory with its mounds of shells, the channel opened up as we passed through beautiful marshes, with 10-20 feet beneath our keel. The homes and farms lining both banks of the river are large and very pretty, and we sensed how it must have been years ago when graciousness was a way of life.

The only bad spot in the entire trip is Bob Shoal, which is marked on the chart as being only four feet deep! My fathometer generally reads about six feet at Bob Shoal, but I still am a little nervous when passing the shoal. The channel there is narrow, too, so I took "15" close to port, made for "16" (Fl R 6 sec) (marking the shoal proper), and then headed directly toward "17". Once there we were back in deeper water.

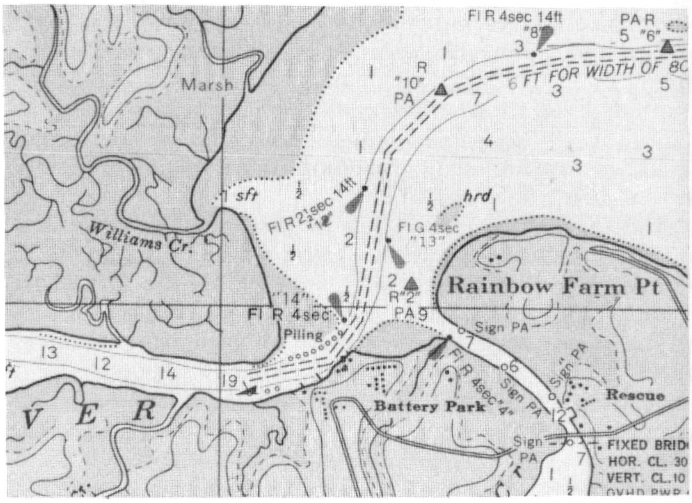

From NOAA Chart 12248—not to be used for navigation.

The scenery became even more gorgeous and lush as we rounded Chalmers Point, and the homes are larger and more impressive—a mixture of old and new. We continued through the marshes, with plenty of water, and past the fixed bridge. As we approached the new marina being constructed at the site of the old Tennis Seafood Restaurant, we gave the floating barge and crane plenty of room.

With marshes to starboard and old, elegant mansions on the high river banks to port, we arrived in Smithfield, home of famous hams, sausage and bacon. Although some people anchor to the side of the channel, we usually ask any of the friendly Smithfielders for permission to use their docks. This time we tied up to the docks by the new condominiums right on the river, with the owners' permission, of course.

A short walk up the hill and we entered the elegant and excellent Old Colonial Inn of Smithfield, for a delicious real Southern Virginia dinner, served family style.

For a relatively protected, uncrowded and beautiful cruise, next time try Smithfield, Virginia, on the Pagan River. It's only 21 miles from the entrance to Hampton Roads Harbor. □

Notes

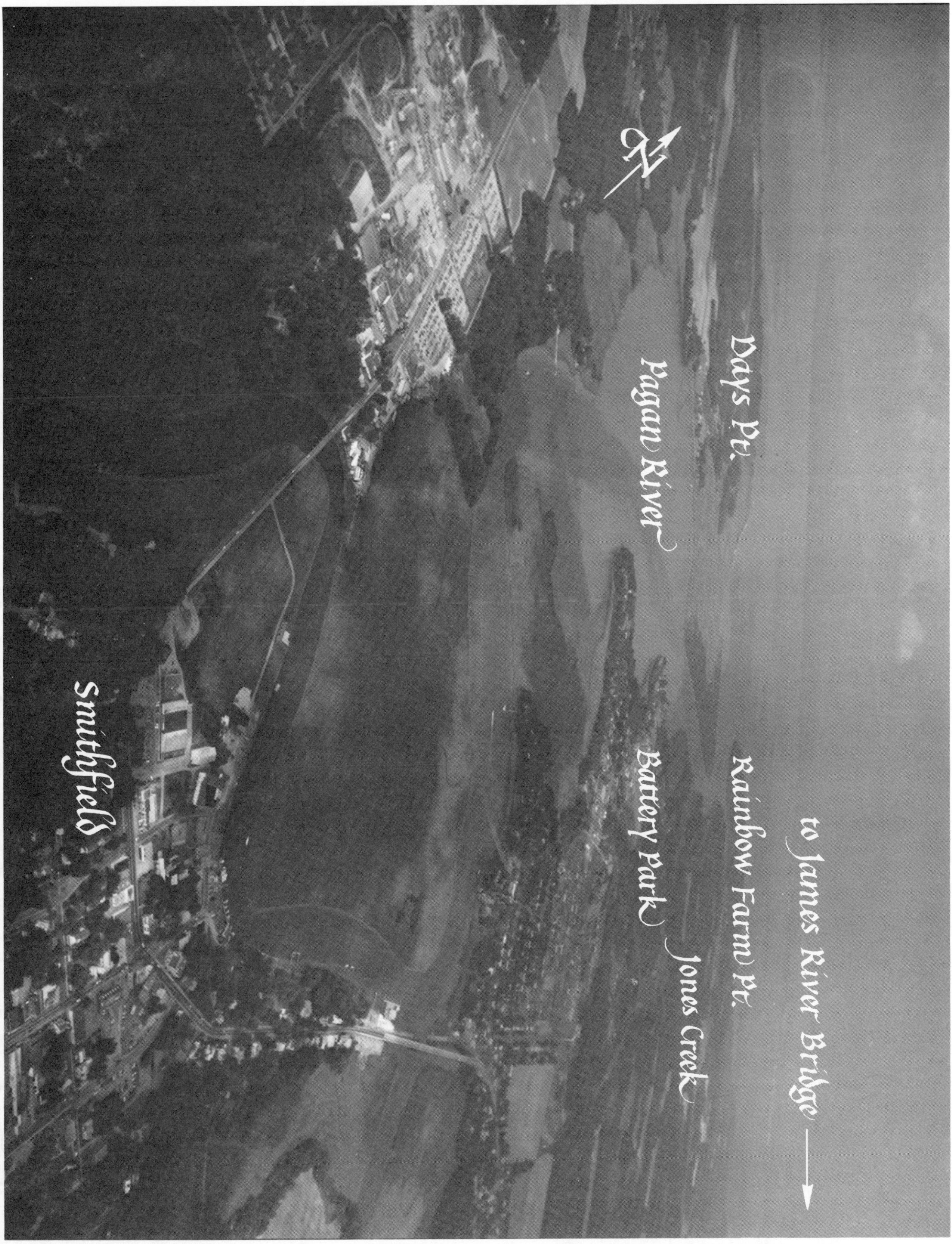

BACKUS AERIAL PHOTOGRAPHY

LYNNHAVEN INLET

Lynnhaven Inlet opens into several pleasant, protected bays and offers a variety of facilities and services. Broad Bay and Linkhorn Bay are both large but protected and easily navigated. Lynnhaven Bay is difficult to navigate without local knowledge and has little to offer the visitor. Several marinas with fuel and services are located just inside the Inlet.

A light and daybeacon mark the entrance from Lynnhaven Roads. The entrance area is prone to shoaling and only the marked channel is dredged. Do not stray outside the markers. Lessner Bridge (over the Inlet) has a vertical clearance of 35 feet.

Two channels turn east (left) just inside the bridge. As the chart shows, the two go around a small island and then rejoin. We recommend you use the first one because it is used by the commercial traffic and is dredged regularly. The south channel is prone to shoaling and the occasional visitor cann rely on the charted depth.

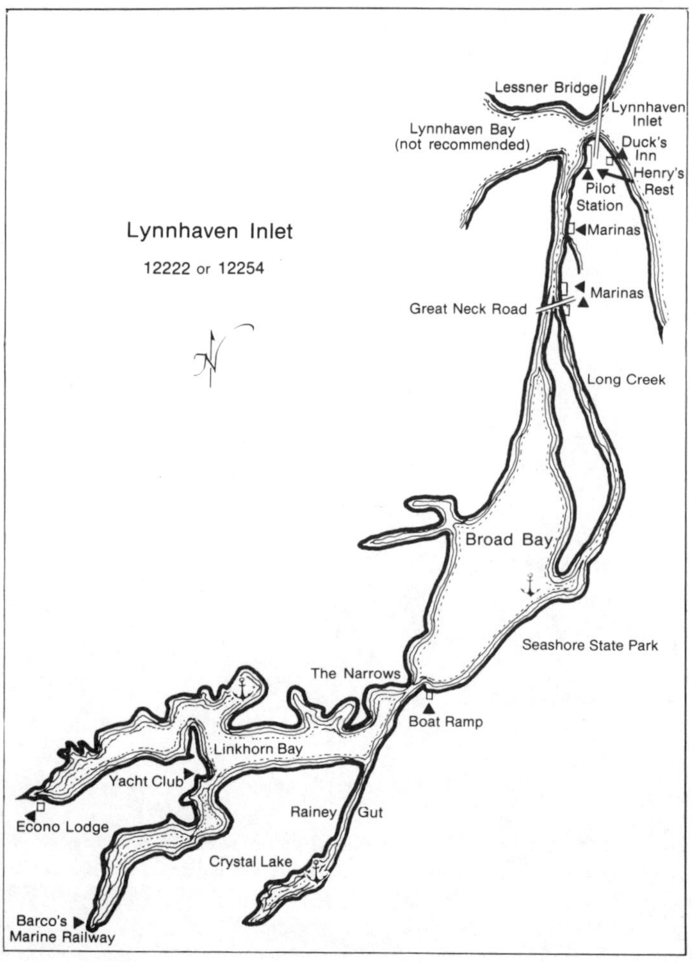

If you take the first channel to the left, you will immediatel pass the Harbor Pilot Station, Henry's Seafood Restauran and two marinas. Like the other marinas further in, thes seldom have transient slips. Henry's provides dock space fc their customers. The Duck Inn, a well known cafe and taver among locals, is just across the street.

About one mile from Lessner Bridge is a fork, with th main channel (on the right) continuing eastward to Broad Ba Long Creek (the left fork) runs north-eastward—a more scen (but longer) route to Broad Bay. The bridge just east of th fork has a vertical clearance of 35 feet over the main chann and 20 feet over Long Creek.

The area from the Inlet to Broad Bay is a no wake zone. is sometimes difficult to make headway against a maximu current without moving fast enough through the water t create a wake.

Most of the eight or so marinas near the mouth of the Inl have launching ramps. Most also have repair facilities.

At the eastern end of Broad Bay is The Narrows. A boa ramp on the north side provides public access from 64th Stre in Virginia Beach. The area around the ramp is shoa approach it with caution. The Narrows itself is well marke and presents no difficulty within the channel. Watch th current, though.

The Narrows opens into the northern end of Linkhor Bay. Rainey Gut continues eastward to Crystal Lake. You ca carry a four-foot draft through Rainey Gut. Crystal Lake is quiet, secluded anchorage surrounded by elegant residenti neighborhoods.

The Virginia Beach Yacht Club sits just east of Bird Nec Point.

Barco's Railway, the largest in Virginia Beach, is at the en of the southeast branch of Linkhorn Bay. A large supermarke is just around the corner from Barco's.

The best anchorage in Broad Bay is southeast of light "14. From there you can row ashore and explore Seashore Stat Park. Crystal Lake is usually less crowded than Broad Bay o Linkhorn Bay. Any of the coves off Linkhorn Bay would be good anchorage.

At the south end of Linkhorn Bay (almost to the lov bridge) is the Econolodge Inn (formerly the White Hero Motel) and Marina.

Several natural restrictions to the tidal flow occur insid the Inlet—the Inlet itself, the main channel just past the for at Long Creek, and the Narrows. During maximum flow thes areas will have a current up to two knots. Be careful. □

LITTLE CREEK

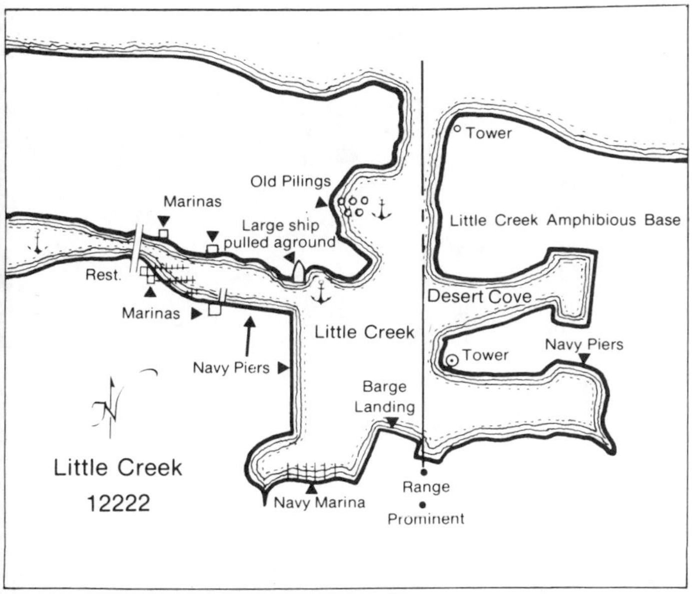

Little Creek is a popular harbor among Bay fishermen who find it convenient, about 4½ miles westward of Lynnhaven Inlet, to the productive areas around the Bay Bridge Tunnel. Because it is so close to open sailing waters, it is also a favorite with sailing enthusiasts. Locals are used to the large amphibious ships that come and go at the Little Creek Amphibious Base but visitors will find the "Gator Navy" quite different from the other ships seen up and down the Bay.

The approach to Little Creek is simple. The light on the east bank of the entrance is on a tall tower, quite visible by day or night. A lighted range guides you up the channel so it is really difficult to go astray.

Fisherman's Cove (the right hand turn just past "8") is the only area with civilian boating facilities. Most of the rest of the harbor belongs to the Navy. If you want to ride around and look at the ships, check your charts and *Coast Pilot* first to see what areas are restricted. Some of the Navy areas are closed to visitors.

There are marinas along both sides of Fisherman's Cove. All of them have launching ramps and most have at least some repair facilities. Most do not keep slips open for visitors but will accommodate you if they have space.

Little Creek is a small harbor with heavy traffic so we do not recommend you try to anchor for the night. If you just want to anchor for lunch, there is room on the west side of the channel just inside the entrance and on the north side of the channel just inside Fisherman's Cove (just east of the old ship that has been pulled up on the north beach). Note that Fisherman's Cove buoy "1" has been renumbered to "3," and buoy "4," a red nun, now sits in 5 ft.

The only restaurant in the harbor is on the south side almost to the low bridge. Chesapeake Bay Co. Seafood Kitchen is open from 8:00 A.M. until 9:00 P.M.

Since the bridge has a clearance of only 6 feet, few can venture past it. The area just past the bridge is deep and provides a secure anchorage for those who can reach it. There are, predictably, no facilities.

Though lacking room to anchor, Little Creek is a pleasant stop for the cruising visitor, and the port of choice for the visiting angler with a boat in tow. □

PHOTO BY BACKUS AERIAL PHOTOGRAPHY

CAPE CHARLES

on the Eastern Shore of Virginia

Cape Charles, on Chesapeake Bay's lower Eastern Shore, is a seldom visited harbor. Cruising sailors tend to bypass its out of the way location, thus missing some of its very real conveniences.

Cape Charles Harbor is nine miles north of the Cape itself, and almost 40 miles south of Onancock, the only other reliable, easy to enter haven on this shore. There are several creeks shown on the chart to the north of Cape Charles, but most are too shallow for our five-foot draft, or they require local knowledge.

Entrance to the harbor is simple and straightforward. Set your course for the Old Plantation Flats Light, which lies just south of Cape Charles Channel entrance. The light itself is a 35′ spider-type structure with the typical red and white diamond atop a white shed. From there, the channel is well laid out, combining markers and two converging ranges for the three remaining miles to Cape Charles Harbor.

The most frequent traffic seen on entering will be tugs pushing barges loaded with railroad cars and tows hauling sand or concrete products. This commercial traffic is active round-the-clock, but Cape Charles is not a busy or crowded harbor. The tugs and tows all terminate their activity in the outer harbor area where there is plenty of room for maneuvering.

The inner harbor is bisected by the Coast Guard Station. On the port side is the "Harbor of Refuge," and on the starboard, a seldom used turning basin. The Harbor of Refuge, a well-kept facility owned by the town, has dockage available for a flat fee of $10. There is also a fuel dock, but no showers. Water and electricity are included in the dock fee. To secure a slip, tie up at the fuel dock to starboard as you enter the inner harbor and go looking for the lady who runs the place. If you can't find her, ask one of the fishermen tied up nearby. He can probably direct you to an empty berth. Everything is very casual and low-key here.

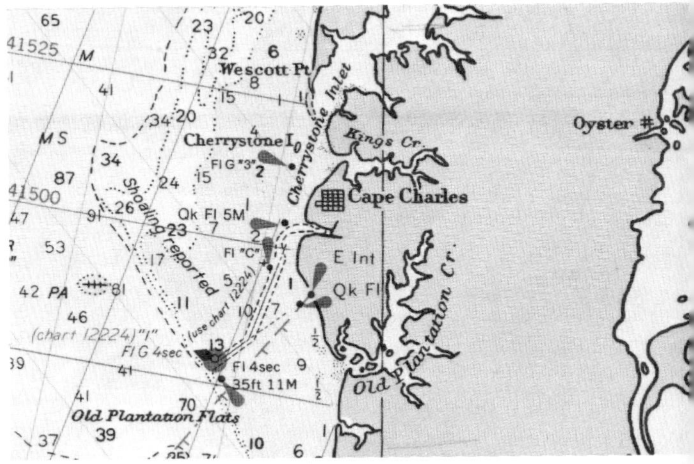

From NOAA Chart 12220—not to be used for navigation

For short tie ups, there is a dock right next to the boat ramps with about five feet at low water. Anchorage is available but frowned on by the Coast Guard. Be sure to fly an anchor light. We were one of three boats anchored out the night we were there and had no problems; holding ground was excellent.

Within sight a block north of the harbor is an excellent supermarket. The friendly manager of Be-lo will help get your groceries back to your boat if necessary. On the same

street is a laundromat, hardware store, bank, liquor store, drug store and restaurants. Only minor marine supplies are available. Cape Charles no longer has a motel but it has Etz's, a family-run restaurant. Seafood is the specialty, of course. Etz's meals are in the $5 to $6 range, and you will not leave hungry! The town has a taxi. Trailways has a morning bus to Norfolk at 8 A.M. and an evening bus north at 6:40 P.M.

Cape Charles abruptly sprang from farmland in 1884 when the New York, Philadelphia and Norfolk Railroad decided to extend its lines from Maryland to this spot. A small creek was dredged out so steamboats could meet the trains and transport passengers and mail across the Bay to make connections in Norfolk. Around the station a town was laid out six avenues deep and six streets wide. Stores, hotels and bars appeared. The railroad men and their families moved into newly built homes.

The Pennsylvania Railroad took over the line and made Cape Charles the headquarters of its Eastern Shore lines. The superintendent and his staff had their offices here as did the agents, dispatchers, trainmaster, clerks, draftsmen and all the men needed to run the steamships and train barges. A retired employee remembers that when the whistle blew for one of the three shift changes, it was like an army pouring out of the yard.

Cape Charles hardly felt the Great Depression because of the railroad economy. But in the 1950's, the economy of Cape Charles fell apart. The automobile ferry landing was moved to Kiptopeke, seven miles south. Trucks were now carrying the mail and produce; oil was coming by ship; vacationers were driving their own automobiles. In 1954 passenger and mail trains were discontinued. Only freight used this route. In 1958 the railroad closed its operation here. The population fell by more than half.

The town calls itself the drum fishing capital of the world and people come from 500 miles away from late April through June. Pick-up trucks are lined up for blocks to back their boats down one of the two free concrete ramps there. Fishing for other types of fish is good year round.

Retirees are discovering Cape Charles, purchasing for reasonable prices the solidly-built homes with their wrap-around porches left behind by the railroad people and enjoying the fishing, hunting in the fall and the nine-hole golf course. □

COMMON USEFUL KNOTS

SQUARE OR REEF KNOT
Properly tied (with the parallel lines coming out on the same side as shown) this knot will not slip or jam. It is most frequently used for tying two lines of the same size together or two ends together.

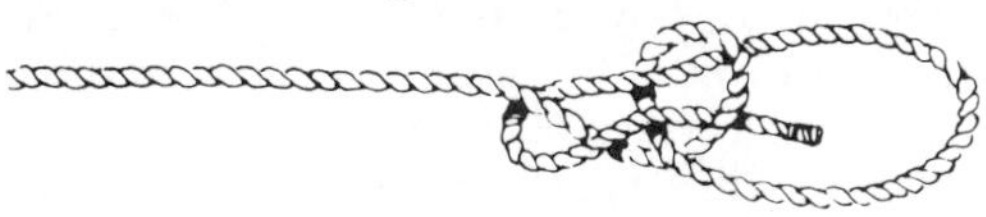

BOWLINE
(Pronounced Boh-lynn) – Sometimes called the king of knots. It makes a loop that will not jam and cannot slip.

FISHERMAN'S BEND
Used to secure a rope to a buoy or a line to any anchor. Also called Bucket Hitch because it is often used for tying a line to a bucket.

TWO HALF HITCHES
Easy to learn and easy to tie. A very useful knot for making a line fast to a piling, rail or post.

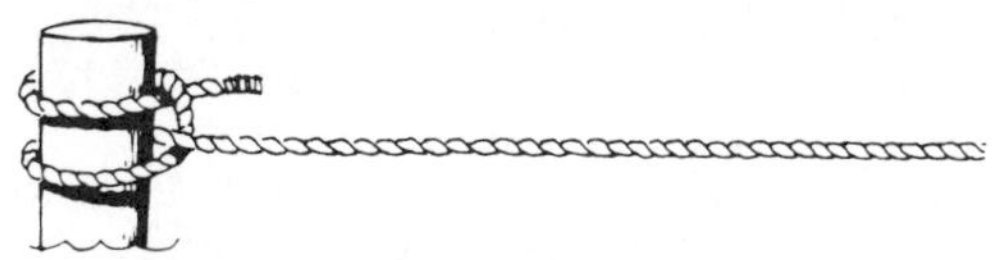

CLOVE HITCH
Also used for making a line fast to a piling, rail or post. Will not slip once it is taut, yet easy to untie.

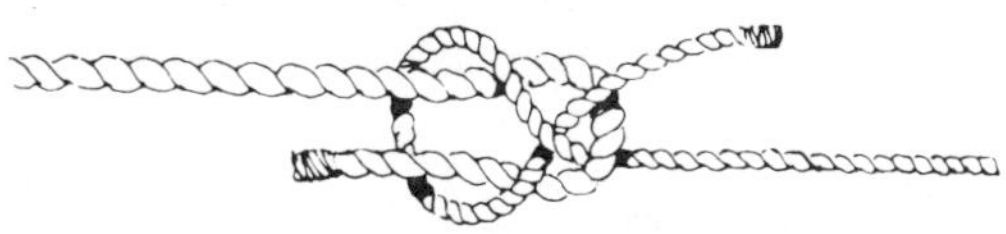

SHEET BEND
Most commonly used to tie two lines of different size together.

KINGS CREEK

on the Eastern Shore of Virginia

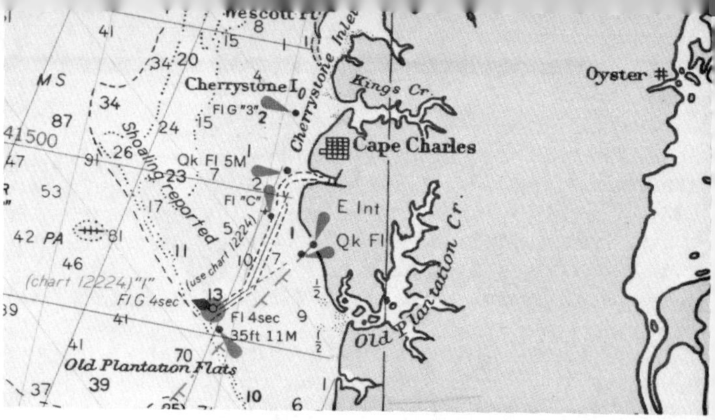

From NOAA Chart 12220—not to be used for navigation.

On one of the earliest trips we had ever taken at the beginning of any sailing season, our intrepid crew turned its attention to the seemingly remote body of water known as Kings Creek, on the Eastern Shore. We heard that the creek had character, and we were going to find out just what that meant! For all intents and purposes, the Eastern Shore has been the Bay's, "FAR EAST." We knew it held riches, but how to unlock them was the challenge.

Our course brought our family cruiser *Zephyr* in from the west. Even though there was a low haze on the water we were able to pick out the first of the navigation aids marking the entrance to the channels to Cape Charles City and Kings Creek. This aid, Old Plantation Light, is now marked by a single-legged day mark structure. The ruins of the foundation from a light house similar to the one at Thomas Point are about 50 yds. to seaward of the existing light.

Once Old Plantation Light (Fl 4 sec) and green buoy "1" (Fl G 4 sec) are sighted, look ahead and pick up the entrance range on a course of approximately 065° M, (excellent for checking magnetic compasses). Water on either side of the marked channel is adequate for most yachts. This is good to keep in mind if you should encounter one of the railroad barges that make daily round trips between Little Creek and Cape Charles City, Va.

As the next range appears on the port hand at approximately 030° M, turn to port and you should see the Cape Charles City breakwater ahead at just under 3 nautical miles. Once at the breakwater, leave the end to starboard and head straight for green "1" (Fl 4 sec) about 500 yards north. The water here is between 10 and 16 feet deep all the way to the daymark. From here on the channel narrows up to the next green daymark. The prudent mariner will not try to interpret the chart but believe it, and go all the way to green "3". Don't cut the corner; I'll tell you why later.

At green "3" turn to starboard and follow the well-marked and deep channel into Kings Creek. You will notice as you round "3" that there is a small island awash to the left of the marker. This is all that is left of Sandy Island. The rest, from here all the way north to where Savage Neck widens, is gone. Chart 12224 shows better than a mile of sand spit exposed. This was all devastated in last year's hurricane Gloria, and finished off by winter storms.

As you approach the land there are some notable things to see, among them several homes along the Cape Charles City shoreline. From near the first set of day marks after "3" you will have a more comfortable opportunity to observe these fine old homes. To port is Cherrystone Campground. It is one of the largest on the east coast, accomodating in excess of 7,500 campers and affiliated with KOA. It is set among a grove of trees with beaches and boat landings. Fishing and crabbing, as well as many other activities and amenities can be enjoyed by campers.

You will now find yourself approaching "10" and entering restricted waters. Don't fear because you'll find 12 ft. of water here at mean low water. To starboard you will see the masts and deck houses of the pleasure boats at Kings Creek Marina. It is safely tucked inside a sandy spit to your right and well protected from the elements. Rounding the sandy point you will see the rest of the creek, the marina and one house. That is it! The rest of the creek is not developed. The shallower your draft the better you will be able to enjoy the quiet and solitude of the creek. If you have a centerboard sailboat or a power boat you can get farther up the creek to a really secluded anchorage. Those with deeper draft can call the marina by landline (804)331-2058 or raise them on channel 72 VHF to inquire about a slip.

The marina is owned by Mr. and Mrs. Don Stiles. The Stiles live in a house over the water attached to the same pier complex as the pleasure boat pier and bait and tackle shop/marina office. Mr. Stiles has been working the water since he was eight years old and was originally from this area. Two years ago he and his wife Diana moved back after several years of fishing the waters off Chincoteague, Va. and bought the marina.

This year, the marina will provide a truly full line of yachting services. On the premises is a marine railway capable of hauling vessels up to 50 feet. During the black drum season Don says that this will be home to a fleet of approximately 20 charter boats.

On arrival you'll notice two piers. One is for the working fleet with its many work boats alongside. There, in all her historic splendor, is the beautifully kept skipjack *Eagle*. She has been converted to a pleasure yacht and has been seen at such notable gatherings as Harborfest. We chatted with two watermen who had arrived, that day, from Hooper's Island, Md., to work the warmer water near the mouth of the Chesapeake. We chatted a long time, until the day grew late and the sunset beckoned us to observe nightfall.

We found our stay here curtailed by the fact that "land things" had to be done at home and we retraced our steps out the channel on high water. The farewell with Mr. Stiles was only a goodbye, since I knew we would return to explore Cherrystone Inlet.

Now, if you remember, I said that I would tell you something important about the channel around "3" (Fl G 4 sec). On your way out of the creek simply follow the channel. I got anxious and turned 50 yards before daymark "3" and grounded on the sand bar that extends some distance out from the shore. We did get off without assistance, but there is no trick here, just follow the channel all the way to green "3". There is sufficient depth at low water for 4 feet and maybe 5 if you are cautious. If you come in at high water a boat with a 6-foot draft can make it easily.

So what about character? It is all over the place. From the skipjack *Eagle*, to the brogue of the watermen in their lounge." The Crabber's Shack" to the untouched shores and the osprey nests. It is the gentile way that the residents treat their guests and the pleasant, peaceful evenings surrounded by life in, on, above and around the natural beauty of Kings Creek, Va. The riches that are here rival those found by early explorers to the Far East. Our own "Far East" on the Bay, only miles away, waits for us all. ☐

PHOTO BY BACKUS AERIAL PHOTOGRAPHY

RESTAURANTS & MARINAS

C&D Canal

DOCKSIDE YACHT CLUB
C&D Canal
(301)885-5016
Open seasonally serving lunch and dinner. Dinner price range: $9.50-$19.95. Reservations not accepted. Dockage available for diners nearby. 4′-5′. House specialties; excellent fresh seafood and certified Angus Beef®. Accepts MasterCard and VISA.

BAYARD HOUSE
C&D Canal
(301)885-5040
Open year-round, 7 days a week serving lunch and dinner. Dinner price range: $10.25-$15.75. Reservations not accepted in summer except for large parties. House specialties include regional seafood, chicken and veal specials. Special salads daily for lunch. Entertainment on the weekends. Accepts MC, VISA and American Express.

SCHAEFER'S CANAL HOUSE
C&D Canal/Chesapeake City
(301)885-2200
Open year-round for breakfast, (Sundays only) lunch and dinner. Prices range from $12.00 to $20.00. Reservations not necessary (except weekends). Dockage for diners and overnight, 12′. Marina facilities on premises. House specialties: crab cakes, crab imperial. American Express, MasterCard and VISA.

SASSAFRAS RIVER

KITTY KNIGHT HOUSE RESTAURANT & INN
Sassafras River/Georgetown
(301)648-5305
Open year-round serving dinner. Price range: $7.95-$19. Reservations not necessary. Marina nearby. The Inn has 12 rooms. Features fresh seafood. Accepts major credit cards.

SUSQUEHANNA RIVER

BAYOU RESTAURANT
Susquehanna River/Havre de Grace
(301)939-3565
Open year-round serving lunch and dinner. Dinner price range: $3.50-$12.00. Reservations suggested. Marina and motel nearby. House specialties: seafood and veal, homemade breads and pies. Accepts American Express, MasterCard and VISA.

BAY STEAMER
Havre de Grace
(301)939-3626
Open year-round serving lunch and dinner. Dinner price range: $3.95-$13.95. Reservations suggested. Dockage for diners, 8′. Marina and motel nearby. House specialties include fresh seafood specials daily. Accepts MasterCard, VISA and American Express.

VIGNA'S
Susquehanna River/Havre de Grace
(301)939-3242
Open year-round serving breakfast, lunch and dinner. Dinner prices range up to $9.00. Reservations not necessary. Marina facilities and motel nearby. House specialties: Italian dishes, subs, pizzas, American dishes and daily specials. No credit cards.

NORTHEAST RIVER

WELLWOOD YACHT CLUB
Head of Northeast River
(301)287-6666
Open year-round serving lunch (summer only) and dinner. Prices range from $5.50 up. Reservations suggested. Marina facilities nearby. House specialties: prime rib, and seafood. No credit cards.

MIDDLE RIVER

DRIFTWOOD INN
Middle River/Hopkins Creek
(301)391-3493
Open year-round serving lunch and dinner. Dinners priced from $6.00-$18.00. Reservations not necessary. Dockage for diners, 10′. Marina and motel nearby. House specialties: seafood, steaks, raw bar, steamed crabs. Accepts MasterCard, VISA and American Express.

RIVER WATCH RESTAURANT & MARINA
Middle River/Hopkins Creek
(301)687-1422
Open year-round for lunch & dinner. Dinners $8.95 and up. Reservations accepted. Dockage for diners or overnight at marina on premises. Featuring steak & seafood. Dining on outdoor deck. Tiki Bar. Accepts major credit cards.

WORTON AND FAIRLEE CREEK

HARBOR HOUSE
Worton Creek
(301)778-0669
Open seasonally serving dinner only. Price range: $9-$14. Reservations suggested. Dockage for diners and overnight 6′. Marina on premises and motel nearby. House specialties: seafood and unusual foreign dishes. Accepts MasterCard and VISA.

GREAT OAK LANDING RESTAURANT
Fairlee Creek
(301)778-2100
Open seasonally serving breakfast, lunch and dinner. Dinner prices to $20. Reservations suggested. Dockage for diners and overnight, 6′. Marina facilities and motel on premises. House specialties: seafood and steaks. American Express, MasterCard and VISA.

SWAN CREEK AND ROCK HALL

FIN, FUR & FEATHER
Rock Hall
(301)639-7454
Open year-round serving breakfast, lunch and dinner. Dinner prices range from $3.95 to $20.95. Reservations not accepted. Dockage for diners, 7′. Marina facilities and motel nearby. House specialties: fresh seafood, Fisherman's Chowder, crab chowder, crab cakes. No credit cards.

HUBBARD'S PIER
Rock Hall
(301)778-4700
Open year-round serving breakfast, lunch and dinner. Prices range from $5.95-$8.95 Reservations not necessary. Dockage for diners and overnight, 10′. No electricity or water. Marina and motel nearby. House specialty: seafood. Restaurant opens at 4 A.M. No credit cards.

ROCK HALL INN
Rock Hall
(301)639-7141
Open year-round serving lunch and dinner. Dinners priced around $6.95. Reservations not necessary. Marina and motel nearby. House specialties: homemade soups and crab cakes, steaks, fresh seafood. Live music on weekends. Free transportation from local marinas. Accepts M/C and VISA.

SWAN POINT INN
Rock Hall
(301)639-2500
Open year-round for dinner. Price range is $4.75 to $14.75. Reservations strongly suggested on the weekends. Located one block in from Rock Hall Harbor. Marina and motel facilities nearby. Will pick up from local marinas. Features Eastern Shore specialties and continental cuisine and daily specials. Accepts MasterCard, VISA and Choice.

/ATERMAN'S CRABHOUSE
:ock Hall
301)778-1803
)pen year-round serving lunch and dinner. 'rices range from $3.95 to $18.95. eservations not accepted. Dockage for iners and overnight, 6'. Marina and motel earby. Specializing in steamed crabs and all eafoods and charbroiled steaks.

?ATAPSCO RIVER

:HART HOUSE RESTAURANT
altimore Inner Harbor
301)539-6616
)pen year-round for lunch and dinner. Prices ange from $9.95-$21.95. Reservations not ccepted. Dockage for diners, 20-30'. Marina acilities nearby. Motel nearby. House pecialties: seafood, steaks, prime rib. merican Express, MasterCard and VISA.

:ITY LIGHTS RESTAURANT
altimore Inner Harbor/Harborplace
301)244-8811
)pen year-round serving lunch and dinner. inners priced from $8.95 to $16.95. eservations suggested. Marina and motel acilities nearby. House specialties: :hesapeake seafood. Excellent view of arbor. Accepts American Express, VISA, MC, :arte Blanche and Choice.

HE GALLEY RESTAURANT
atapsco/Rock Creek
301)255-4424
pen year-round for breakfast, lunch and inner. Dinner prices range from $9.95 to 15.95. Reservations suggested. Dockage for diners and overnight. Marina facilities on premises. Motel nearby. House specialty: seafood. Live entertainment Fri., Sat. and Sun. nights. Accepts most major credit cards.

PHILLIPS HARBORPLACE
Baltimore Inner Harbor/Harborplace
(301)685-6600
Open year-round serving lunch and dinner. Dinner price range $5.95 to $18.95. Reservations not accepted. Marina and motel facilities nearby. House specialties: seafood, with daily featured selections on menu. Accepts VISA, MC, Choice, Diners Club, American Express.

RUSTY SCUPPER
Baltimore Inner Harbor
(301)727-3678
Open year-round serving daily lunch and dinner. Dinner prices range from $9.95 to $16.95. Reservations suggested. Marina facilities on premises; motel nearby. House specialties: fresh seafood, prime rib, steaks, daily specials, outdoor cocktail bar and raw bar on viewing deck. American Express, MasterCard, VISA, Diners Club and Carte Blanche.

SWENSON'S FAMILY RESTAURANT
Baltimore Inner Harbor/Harborplace
Open year-round serving breakfast, lunch and dinner. Dinner price range $4.00 to $7.50. Reservations not accepted. Marina and motel facilities nearby. Specialties are breakfast, burgers, salads, sandwiches and ice cream. Accepts MC and VISA.

MAGOTHY RIVER

CAPTAIN CLYDE'S RESTAURANT
Magothy River/Deep Creek
(301)757-4045
Open year-round serving lunch and dinner. Dinner price range: $3.00 to $12.00. Reservations not necessary but suggested. Dockage available for diners and overnight, 6'. Marina facilities on premises and motel nearby. House specialties: crab cakes, soft crabs, cream of crab soup. Accepts MasterCard and VISA.

RIVERDALE RESTAURANT
Magothy River
(301)647-9830
Open year-round serving lunch and dinner. Dinner prices range from $6.00 to $20.00. Reservations not necessary. Dockage for diners, 10-12'. House speciality: crab imperial, stuffed lobster. MasterCard and VISA.

CHESTER RIVER & KENT NARROWS

OLD WHARF INN
Chester River
(301)778-3566
Open year-round serving lunch and dinner. Dinner prices range from $8.95 to $17.95. Reservations not accepted. Marina on premises and motel nearby. House specialty: creamy crab bisque, fresh seafood. Accepts MasterCard and VISA.

YACHTSMAN'S RESTAURANT
Chester River
(301)643-6550
Open year-round serving Sunday Brunch and daily dinner. Dinner prices range from $8 to $18. Reservations suggested. Dockage for diners and overnight, 5'. Marina facilities on premises; motel nearby. House specialties; seafood, veal, steaks and poultry. MasterCard and VISA and Choice.

CAPTAIN ALEX'S SEAFOOD RESTAURANT
Kent Narrows
(301)827-6340
Open year-round serving breakfast, lunch and dinner. Dinner prices range from $5.95 to $18.95. Reservations suggested. Dockage for diners and overnight, 8'. Motel nearby. Features crab and oyster feast in season and nightly specials. Accepts MasterCard, VISA, Choice, Diners Club.

EBB TIDE CRABHOUSE
Kent Island
(301)643-6053
Open year-round serving lunch and dinner. Prices range from $1.95 to $15.50. Reservations are not necessary. Marina facilities and motel are nearby. House specialties: steamed crabs and fresh seafood. Accepts Choice, VISA, American Express.

FISHERMAN'S INN
Kent Narrows/Prospect Bay
(301)827-8807
Open year-round serving lunch and dinner. Dinner price range: $6.95 to $12.95. Reservations not accepted. Dockage for diners, 6'. Marina and motel nearby. House specialties: seafood. Accepts American Express, VISA, Choice and MasterCard.

Kent Narrows, continued

THE NARROWS
Kent Narrows
(301)827-8113
Open year-round serving lunch and dinner. Dinner prices range from $4.00 to $15.00. Reservations suggested. Dockage for diners and overnight, 15'. Marina facilities and motel nearby. House specialties: fresh oysters, fish, crab, deck dining. MasterCard, VISA, Carte Blanche, Diners Club.

POSEIDON INN/MEARS POINT MARINA
ChesterRiver/Kent Narrows
(301)827-7605
Open year-round serving lunch and dinner. Dinner price range: $5 to $25. Reservations not accepted. Dockage available for diners and overnight, 8'. Marina on premises and motel nearby. House specialties: seafood and steaks. Accepts American Express, VISA, MasterCard and Choice.

CHESAPEAKE BAY BRIDGE AREA

BAY SIDE CAFE AT QUEEN ANNE MARINA
Chesapeake Bay/Price Creek
(301)643-5065
Open year-round serving breakfast and lunch only. Open 7 A.M. to 4 P.M. Reservations not necessary. Dockage available for overnight 4'. House specialties: softshell crabs, fresh local seafood. Accepts MasterCard and VISA.

HEMINGWAYS RESTAURANT
Chesapeake Bay/Pier One Marina
(301)643-2772
Open year-round serving lunch and dinner and Sunday brunch. Dinner price range: $8.95-$15.95. Reservations not accepted. Dockage for diners and overnight, 6'. Marina on premises and motel nearby. Features crab dishes and baked stuffed flounder. Accepts major credit cards.

KENTMORR HARBOUR
Kent Island/Pier One Marina/S. of the Bay Bridge
(301)643-4700
Open seasonally serving dinner only. Price range: $5.95-$10.95. Reservations suggested House specialty: old Maryland style crabhouse. Accepts American Express, MasterCard and VISA.

SEVERN RIVER

ARMADILLO'S
City Dock/Annapolis
(301)268-6680
Open year-round serving lunch and dinner. Dinner price range: $6.00-$14.00 Reservations not accepted except parties of six or more. Dockage at City Dock, 6'-8'. Marina and motel nearby. House specialty: Mexican food. Accepts MasterCard, VISA, American Express.

HARRY BROWNE'S
Annapolis/Maryland Avenue
(301)263-4332
Open year-round serving lunch and dinner. Dinner prices range from $10.95 to $13.95. Reservations suggested. Marina facilities and motel nearby. House specialties: seafood, steaks, veal and pasta. MasterCard, VISA, American Express, Diners Club and Choice.

CARROL'S CREEK CAFE/ ANNAPOLIS CITY MARINA
Spa Creek/Annapolis
(301)263-8102
Open year-round,serving lunch and dinner, and Sunday brunch. Dinner price range: $12 to $20. Reservations suggested. Dockage for diners and overnight, 8'-10'. Marina on premises and motel nearby. House specialties: Buffalo tenderloin and veal. Accepts MasterCard, VISA and American Express.

CHART HOUSE RESTAURANT
Spa Creek/Annapolis
(301)268-7166
Open year-round for dinner and Sunday brunch only. Dinner prices range from $9.95 to $20.95. (Sunday Brunch, $5.95-$8.95). Reservations not accepted. Dockage for diners at dinghy dock. Marina facilities nearby. Motel nearby. House specialties: seafood, steks, prime rib, 60-item salad bar. Accepts American Express, MasterCard and VISA.

CHESAPEAKE HARBOUR MARINA
On the Bay, near Annapolis
(301)269-6799
At press time this new restaurant was still under construction. Latest information states the restaurant will be open year-round. Dockage available for diners and overnight. Marina on the premises.

FRAN O'BRIEN'S RESTAURANT
Main Street/Annapolis
(301)268-6288
Open year-round serving lunch and dinner. Dinner prices range from $9.50 to $21.95. Reservations suggested. Marina facilities and motel nearby. House specialties: prime rib and fresh seafood. American Express, MasterCard, and VISA.

HARBOR HOUSE RESTAURANT
Spa Creek/Annapolis
(301)268-0771
Open year-round serving lunch and dinner. Dinner prices range from $10.50 to $18.95. Reservations not accepted. Dockage for diners and overnight at Annapolis City Dock, 8'. Marina facilities and motel nearby. House specialties: crab cakes, crab imperial, crab Norfolk, bouillabaisse and prime rib. Accepts American Express, MasterCard and VISA.

LITTLE CAMPUS INN
Maryland Avenue/Annapolis
(301)263-9250
Open year-round serving lunch and dinner. Price range from $3.00 to $12.00. Reservations not necessary. Dockage at Annapolis City Dock. House specialties: varied nightly. American Express, MasterCard, VISA and Diners Club.

MARMADUKE'S PUB
Annapolis/Eastport
(301)269-5420
Open year-round serving lunch and dinner daily. Dinner price range: $5.95-$15.95. Reservations not accepted. Marina and motel nearby. Videotapes of sailboat races shown regularly. Pub type atmosphere. Features fresh fish daily, charbroiled steaks, homemade desserts, etc. Accepts MasterCard, VISA, American Express and Choice.

MARINER'S WHARF RESTAURANT
Severn River/at Old Draw Bridge
(301)757-2424
Open year-round serving lunch and dinne Dinner prices range from $8.50 to $13.9 Reservations suggested. Dockage for diner and overnight, 11'. Marina facilities nearby Motel nearby. House specialty: seafood. Liv music and dancing four nights. Deck open fc steamed crabs during summer. Accept MasterCard, VISA and American Express.

MCGARVEY'S SALOON AND OYSTER BA
Annapolis/Market Area
(301)263-5700
Open year-round serving lunch and dinne and brunch on Saturday and Sunday. Pric range: $3.75 to $16.00. Reservations nc accepted. Marina facilities nearby. Mote nearby. House specialties: seafood dishe steaks, hamburgers, raw bar, fresh fis Accepts MasterCard, VISA, American Expre Choice.

O'LEARY'S SEAFOOD RESTAURANT
Spa Creek/Annapolis
(301)263-0884
Open year-round for dinner only. Prices rang from $9.95 to $16.95. Reservations suggeste Dockage for diners, 6'-8'. Marina facilities an motels nearby. House specialties: fresh fish, man varieties, mesquite grill. Accepts all majc credit cards.

PENTHOUSE RESTAURANT/HILTON INN
Annapolis
(301)268-7553
Open year-round serving breakfast, lunc and dinner. Prices range from $3.95 to $20.0 Reservations suggested. Dockage for diner and overnight, 8'. Marinas nearby. Motel o premises. House specialties: seafood, tw outdoor harbor-side bars (in season), enter tainment, Accepts major credit cards.

REYNOLDS TAVERN
Annapolis/Church Circle
(301)263-6599
Open year-round for lunch and dinner. Dinne prices range from $4.95 to $12.95. Reservation suggested. Marina facilities nearby. Motel o the premises. House specialties: America cuisine, colonial style; seafood, crab an shellfish in season. Accepts American Express VISA and MasterCard.

RIORDAN'S SALOON
Annapolis/Market area
(301)263-5449
Open year-round serving daily lunch an dinner. Dinner prices range from $4.00 t $12.95. Reservations not necessary. Dockag at Annapolis City Dock, 6'. Motel nearby House specialty: daily seafood specials, prim rib, veal and homemade soups. Accept American Express, VISA, Choice and Diner Club.

RIVERSIDE INN
Whitehall Bay/Mill Creek
(301)757-9888
Open year-round for lunch and dinner. Price range from $3.00 to $10.00. Dockage for diners 14'. Marina facilities on premises. Hous specialty: Chesapeake Bay seafood, water side dining on Mill Creek. No credit cards.

TREATY OF PARIS/MARYLAND INN
Annapolis/Church Circle
(301)263-2641
Open year-round serving breakfast, lunc and dinner and Sunday Brunch. Dinner price range from $12.50 to $17.50. Reservation suggested. Marina facilities nearby; hotel o premises. House specialties: fresh seafooc Beef Wellington, Veal Oskar. American Express MasterCard, VISA, Choice and Diners Club

SOUTH RIVER

MIKE'S RESTAURANT & CRABHOUSE
South River
(301)956-2784
Open year-round serving lunch and dinner. Dinner price range: $7.95-$15.95. Reservations not necessary. Dockage for diners and overnight, 20'. Marina on the premises and motel nearby. House specialty: seafood and steaks. Live music Friday and Saturday nights from 9 P.M. to 2 A.M.. Accepts MasterCard, VISA, American Express.

PAUL'S
South River
(301)956-3410
Open year-round, serving lunch and dinner. Dinner prices range from $10.95 to $19.95. Reservations suggested. Dockage for diners and overnight, 12'. Marina facilities and motel nearby. House specialty: fresh seafood. Accepts all major credit cards.

PIER 7
South River
(301)956-2288
Open year-round for lunch and dinner. Prices range from $3.00 to $21.95. Reservations suggested. Dockage for diners and overnight, '. Marina facilities on premises; motel nearby. Boat rentals. House specialty: seafood steamed crabs. American Express, MasterCard, and VISA.

WEST RIVER

PIRATES COVE
West River
(301)867-2300
Open year-round serving lunch and dinner. Price range: $4.95 to $18. Reservations suggested. Dockage for diners and overnight, 12'. Marina nearby. Motel on premises. House specialty: seafood. Launch service. Entertainment. Accepts MasterCard, VISA and American Express.

HERRING BAY

HERRINGTON HARBOUR RESTAURANT
Herring Bay
(301)741-5101
Open year-round serving lunch and dinner. Lunch prices range from $2.75 to $5.50. Dinner prices range from $9.95 to $23.50. Reservations suggested. Dockage for diners and overnight, with reservations, 7'. Marina facilities, pool and motel on premises. House specialties: seafood and steaks. Dancing Friday and Saturday evenings. MasterCard, VISA and Choice.

THE SKIPJACK
Herring Bay/Tracy's Creek
(301)261-5514 or (301)867-1810
Open year-round, Tuesday-Sunday, serving lunch and dinner. Dinner price range: $6.95 to $12.95, buffet $5.95 to $13.95. Reservations not necessary. Marina nearby. House specialty: fresh seafood buffet. Accepts MasterCard, VISA and American Express.

SKIPPER'S PIER RESTAURANT
Deale/End of Drumpoint Rd.
(301)867-7110
Open seasonally for lunch and dinner. Prices range from $8.99 to $12.99. Reservations not necessary. Dockage for diners, 6'. Marina and motel facilities nearby. House specialties: freshly steamed crabs and clams, homemade crab cakes, BBQ, "beer batter" flounder, beef. Accepts VISA and MasterCard.

CHESAPEAKE BEACH

ROD N' REEL
Chesapeake Bay/Chesapeake Beach
(301)257-2735
Open year-round serving lunch and dinner. Price range: $5.95 to $23.95. Reservations not necessary. Dockage for diners and overnight, 7'. Marina on premises and motel nearby. House specialties: crab cakes. Accepts MasterCard and VISA.

MILES RIVER/ST. MICHAELS

CRAB CLAW RESTAURANT
Miles River/St. Michaels
(301)745-2900
Open seasonally serving lunch and dinner. Dinner price range: $3.95 to $14.95. Reservations not necessary. Dockage for diners, 10'. Marina and motel nearby. House specialty: Maryland blue crabs served all ways and other fresh Chesapeake Bay seafood. No credit cards.

THE INN AT PERRY CABIN
St. Michaels
(301)745-5178
Open year-round serving Sunday Brunch, lunch and dinner. Price ranges: $3.95 to $21.95. Reservations suggested. Dockage based on availability, 7'. Marina nearby. Inn with six rooms on premises. Features continental style dining with fresh seafood, beef, veal and lamb dishes. Accepts MasterCard, VISA and American Express.

LONGFELLOWS RESTAURANT
Miles River/St. Michaels
(301)745-2624
Open year-round serving daily lunch and dinner. Dinner prices range from $6.95 to $13.95. Reservations suggested. Dockage for diners, 3'. Marina facilities nearby (courtesy vehicle on call); motel nearby. House specialty: seafood. Accepts all bank cards.

MARTINGHAM HARBORTOWNE INN
Miles River/St. Michaels
(301)745-9066
Open year-round. Serves breakfast, lunch and dinner. Dinner price range: $10.95 to $20. Reservations suggested. Dockage for diners, 3'. Marina nearby. Motel on premises. House specialty: seafood. Eighteen hole golf course, swimming pool and tennis courts on premises. Accepts MasterCard, VISA and American Express.

TOWN DOCK RESTAURANT
Miles River/St. Michaels
(301)745-5577
Open year-round serving breakfast, lunch and dinner. Dinners priced to $12. Reservations not necessary but suggested. Dockage available overnight, 7'. Marina on premises and motel nearby. House specialty: Eastern Shore cooking, non-seafood entrees available. Accepts MasterCard and VISA.

KNAPPS NARROWS

BAY HUNDRED RESTAURANT/ KNAPPS NARROWS MARINA
Knapps Narrows
(301)886-2622
Open year-round serving breakfast, lunch and dinner. Dinners priced to $14. Reservations not necessary but suggested during the summer. Dockage available for diners and overnight, 6'. Marina on premises. Motel nearby. House specialty: local seafood. Accepts MasterCard, VISA and Exxon.

THE BRIDGE RESTAURANT
Knapps Narrows
(301)886-2500
Open year-round serving lunch and dinner. Dinner price range: $6.95-$14.95. Reservations not necessary but suggested. Dockage for diners and overnight, 8'. Marina and motel nearby. House specialties: Friday night seafood buffet $9.95 and Sunday buffet $7.95. No credit cards but accepts personal checks.

HARRISON COUNTRY INN
Knapps Narrows
(301)886-2123
Open seasonally serving breakfast, lunch and dinner. Price range: $4.00 to $16.95. Reservations not necessary. Dockage for diners and overnight. Marina nearby. Motel on premises. House specialties: vary daily. Accepts MasterCard, Choice and VISA.

TILGHMAN INN AND LODGING
Knapps Narrows
(301)886-2141
Inn open year-round (restuarant closed during winter.) Serving breakfast, lunch and dinner. Dinner prices range from $8 to $18. Reservations suggested. Dockage for diners and overnight, swimming pool, tennis courts and bicycle rental. Marina facilities and motel on premises. House specialty: fresh seafood. American Expréss, MasterCard and VISA.

TRED AVON RIVER

ROBERT MORRIS INN
Tred Avon River/Oxford
(301)326-5111
Open seasonally, mid-March through December. Serving breakfast, lunch and dinner. Dinner prices range from $11.95 to $28.95. Reservations not accepted. Dockage available for diners, 6'. Marina facilities nearby. Country inn on premises. House specialties: crab cakes and crab imperial, other seafood and beef. American Express, MasterCard and VISA.

MASTHEAD RESTAURANT
Oxford (301)226-5303
Open year-round serving lunch and dinner and brunch on Saturday and Sunday. Dinner price range: $7.95 to $20.95. Reservations strongly suggested. Motel is nearby, as are marinas. House specialties include fresh fish, veal, rack of lamb and filet mignon. Accepts MasterCard and VISA.

PIER STREET RESTAURANT
Tred Avon River/Oxford
(301)226-5171
Open seasonally serving lunch and dinner. Dinner prices range from $7.95 to $22.00. Reservations suggested for large parties only. Dockage for diners and overnight, 6'-9'. Marina facilities and motel nearby. House specialties: soft crabs, hard crabs, full seafood menu. MasterCard and VISA.

Continued

TOWN CREEK RESTAURANT
Tred Avon River/Town Creek
(301)226-5131
Open year-round serving lunch and dinner. Price range: $7.00 to $12. Reservations not necessary. Dockage for diners and overnight, 8'. Marina on premises. Motel nearby. House specialty: seafood and beef. Accepts MasterCard and VISA.

CHOPTANK RIVER

HIGH SPOT RESTAURANT
Choptank/Cambridge
(301)228-3410
Open year-round serving lunch and dinner. Prices range from $3.00 to $9.50. Reservations not necessary. Marina facilities nearby. House specialties: filet mignon, crab cakes, fried shrimp. No credit cards.

CATOR HOUSE
Cambridge
(301)221-0300
Open year-round. Serves lunch and dinner. Dinner price range: $9.50 to $14.95. Reservations suggested. Marina and motel facilities nearby. House specialties include a full line of seafood and char-broiled steaks. Accepts MasterCard and VISA.

CLAYTON'S ON THE CREEK
Cambridge
(301)228-1661
Open 11:30 A.M. to 11 P.M. seven days a week. Primarily a seafood restaurant specializing in crab dishes. Dockage available on the premises. Marina and motel nearby. Reservations suggested. Accepts MC, VISA and American Express.

LITTLE CHOPTANK RIVER

MADISON BAY MARINA
Little Choptank
(301)228-4111
Open year-round serving lunch and dinner. Prices range from $5.75 to $8. Reservations not necessary. Dockage for diners and overnight, 10'-11'. Marina facilities on premises. Motel nearby. House specialty: seafood. No credit cards.

PATUXENT RIVER

CALVERT MARINA
Patuxent River/Solomons
(301)326-4251, Wash. 855-1633
Open seasonally. Serves breakfast and lunch. Reservations not necessary. Dockage for Motel nearby. House specialties: crab cakes and other seafood. Accepts MasterCard and VISA.

THE DRY DOCK AT ZAHNISER'S MARINA
Patuxent River/Solomons
(301)326-4817
Open year-round serving dinner and Sunday Brunch. Price range: $9.95 to $17.95. Reservations suggested. Dockage available for diners and overnight, 20'. Marina facilities on premises and motel nearby. House specialties: prime rib and seafood. Live entertainment Friday nights. Accepts MasterCard, VISA, and personal checks.

DOCKS OF BENEDICT
Patuxent River/Mill Creek
(301)274-4429
Open seasonally serving lunch and dinner. Dinner price range: $6.99 to $9.99. Reservations not necessary. Dockage for diners, 3'-5'. Marina on premises. House specialties: fresh soft shell crabs and crab cakes.

GATSBY'S DOCKSIDE GALLEY
Island Creek/Broomes Island
(301)586-2437
Open year-round serving breakfast, lunch and dinner. Closed Mondays. Dinner prices range from $4 to $10.00. Reservations not necessary. Dockage for diners, 4'. Marina facilities on premises; motel nearby. House specialties: Weekend boater brunch, New England delicacies. No credit cards accepted.

HARBOR LIGHTS
Patuxent River/Solomons
(301)326-3202
Open year-round, serving lunch and dinner. Prices range from $2.50 to $19.95. Reservations not necessary. Dockage for diners and overnight, 14'. Marina facilities on premises. Motel nearby. House specialty: seafood. MasterCard, VISA and Diners Club.

SHORTER'S PLACE
Patuxent River/Benedict
(301)274-3284
Open year-round serving breakfast, lunch and dinner. Dinners priced to $15. Reservations not necessary. Dockage for diners and overnight, 8'. Marina and motel nearby. House specialty: seafood, carrot cake, pina coladas. Accepts MasterCard and VISA.

VERA'S WHITE SANDS RESTAURANT
Patuxent/St. Leonard Creek
(301)586-1182
Open seasonally for dinner only. Prices range from $8.95 to $14.95. Reservations suggested Dockage for diners and overnight, 12'. Marina facilities on premises, motel nearby. House specialties: Continental, Polynesian and seafood dishes. Credit cards for fuel only.

POTOMAC RIVER/MD SHORE

CAPTAIN JOHNS CRABHOUSE
Potomac River/Cobb Island
(301)259-2315
Open year-round serving breakfast, lunch and dinner. Dinner price range: $5.95 to $11.95. Reservations not necessary. Dockage for diners and overnight, 8'. Marina on premises. House specialties: steamed crabs and seafood in season. Accepts MasterCard, VISA, Texaco.

THE COB'S NEST
Neal Sound/Cobb Island
(301)259-2032
Open year-round serving breakfast, lunch and dinner. Dinner price range: $6-$18. Reservations suggested for weekends. Dockage for diners and overnight, 10'. Marina on premises. House specialties: seafood, prime rib. Accepts MasterCard, VISA, American Express and Gulf.

COLUMBIA ISLAND MARINA
Potomac River/Pentagon Lagoon
(202)347-0173
Open year-round for breakfast, lunch and dinner. Reservations not necessary. Dockage for diners and overnight, powerboats only. Marina facilities and motel nearby. House specialties: grill items, sandwich specials, catered barbeques and picnics. No credit cards except for gas.

DENNIS POINT MARINA
St. Mary's River/Carthagena Creek
(301)994-2288
Prices range from $2.50 to $6.00. Reservations not necessary. Dockage for diners and overnight, 11'. Marina on premises and motel nearby. House specialties: sandwiches and pizza. Campground and pool. Accepts Gulf, Chevron, MasterCard and VISA.

DOCK O THE BAY
Potomac River/Breton Bay
(301)475-3129
Open year-round serving lunch and dinner. Dinner prices range from $3.25 to $18.95. Reservations not necessary. Dockage for diners and overnight. Marina facilities on premises and motel nearby. House specialty: seafood and some steaks.

EVANS SEAFOOD
Potomac River/St. George Island
(301)994-2299
Open year-round serving lunch and dinner. Dinner price range: $4.99-$17.95. Reservations not necessary. Dockage for diners, 5'. Marina nearby. House specialty: crab cakes, crab imperial, all fresh fish broiled or fried. No credit cards. Take personal checks. Motel nearby.

FORT WASHINGTON YACHT CLUB RESTAURANT
Potomac River/Piscataway Creek
(301)292-6203
Open year-round serving lunch and dinner. Prices range from $5.95 to $12.95. Reservations suggested. Dockage for diners and overnight, 4'6" MLW. Marina facilities on premises, motel nearby. House specialties: seafood and steaks. Launch service. MasterCard, VISA, and Choice.

GALLEY TIPS

Seal some spare matches in a small plastic bag to insure having dry ones in an emergency. "Burp-to-top" plastic containers or band-aid boxes can also be used for this purpose.

Make a "sun tea"—without the bother of boiling and cooling. Fill a jug or jar with cold water, add tea bags (5 or 6 easily make a gallon). Cap and place in the sun for 2-4 hours. Presto! Beautiful, tasty tea that will never turn cloudy or bitter.

Avoid messes and soggy snack-food by pre-packaging individual portions of such items as chips, popcorn, crackers, cookies, small chunks of cheese, dried or raw fruits, etc. One of the "seal-a-meal" type appliances makes such packaging a quick, easy job. (Other galley "slaves" swear by zip-lock plastic bags.) Frozen seal-a-meals may not only serve as extra ice, but also may be heated in sea water, thus conserving stores of fresh water.

E RIVAGE
ashington Channel
02)488-8111
pen year-round, serving lunch and dinner. nner prices range from $9.75 to $14.75. eservations suggested. Dockage available at apital Yacht Club up to 100 feet. Motel earby. Call in advance. House specialty: esh seafood. Outdoor terrace. American xpress, MasterCard, VISA, Diners Club, arte Blanche.

UADE'S STORE
icomico River
01)769-3903
pen year-round serving breakfast and lunch. eservations not necessary. Dockage for ners, 4'-6'. Marina nearby. House specialty: omemade crab cakes. Accepts Gulf credit rds.

ELUCTANT NAVIGATOR
otomac/Herring Creek
01)994-1508
pen seasonally for breakfast, lunch and nner. Prices range $4.50 to $15. Reservations e not necessary. Dockage is available for ners and overnight, 6'-8'. Marina and motel the premises. House specialty: Sunday orning breakfast and all dinners. Accepts ulf, Chevron, MasterCard and VISA.

OBERTSON'S CRABHOUSE
otomac/Popes Creek
01)934-9236
pen seasonally (closed Nov.-March) serving nch and dinner. Dinner prices range from .95 to $16.95. Reservations not necessary. ockage for diners and overnight, 4'. Marina cilities and motel nearby. House specialties: eamed crabs, fried and broiled seafood nners. No credit cards.

CHEIBLE'S RESTAURANT
otomac River/Smith Creek
01)872-5185
pen seasonally serving breakfast, lunch and nner. Prices range from $3.25 to $13.95. eservations suggested. Dockage for diners. arina nearby; motel on premises. House ecialty: all you can eat-crabbettes. No edit cards.

OTOMAC RIVER/VA SHORE

NSALE HARBOR MARINA AND YACHT LUB
otomac River/W. Yeocomico River
04)472-2514
pen seasonally for Sunday buffet ($12.95), nch and dinner. Prices range from $5.95 to 1.95. Reservations suggested. Dockage for ners and overnight, 10'. Marina and motel cilities on premises. House specialties: afood, prime rib, box lunches for boaters, ecial parties arranged. Accepts MasterCard d VISA.

HE MOORING RESTAURANT
eocomico River
04)472-2971
pen year-round serving breakfast, lunch d dinner. Dinner prices range from $2.50 to 4.95. Reservations not accepted. Dockage r diners, and overnight, 7'. Marina facilities d motel on premises. House specialty: oiled fresh seafoods, fresh vegetables in mmer, steaks. MasterCard and VISA.

PILOT HOUSE RESTAURANT
Potomac River/Neabsco Creek
(703)221-1010
Open year-round for dinner only. Reservations not accepted. Dockage for diners. Marina on premises, 4'. House specialty: seafood. American Express, MasterCard and VISA.

STEVE'S SEAFOOD RESTAURANT
Potomac River/Colonial Beach
(804)224-7360
Open year-round. Serves lunch and dinner. Prices range from $4.50 to $11.00. Reservations not necessary. Dockage for diners. Marina and motel facilities nearby. House specialties: daily fish fry, seafood buffet on weekends. Accepts VISA and MasterCard.

WILKERSON SEAFOOD RESTAURANT
Potomac River/South 301 Bridge
(804)224-7117
Open seasonally serving lunch and dinner. Dinner price range: $6-$17. Reservations not necessary. Dockage available for diners, 6'. Marina and motel nearby. House specialty: crab dishes. Accepts VISA and MasterCard.

YEOCOMICO MARINA RESTAURANT
Potomac River/Yeocomico River
(804)472-2971
Open year-round, serving breakfast, lunch and dinner. Prices range from $2.50 to $15.00. Reservations not accepted. Dockage for diners and overnight, 7'. Marina and motel on the premises. House specialties: fresh local seafood and chargrilled steaks. Accepts MasterCard and VISA.

SMITH, TANGIER AND CRISFIELD

HARBOR SIDE RESTAURANT
Smith Island
(301)425-2201
Open seasonally serving lunch and dinner. Dinner price range: $8.50 to $12.95. Reservations suggested. Dockage for overnight, 6'. Marina nearby. House specialty: seafood. No credit cards.

HILDA CROCKETT'S CHESAPEAKE HOUSE
Tangier Sound, Tangier Island
(301)891-2331
Open seasonally serving breakfast, lunch and dinner. Dinner is $9.50. Reservations required for overnight stay. Dockage 8'. Marina facilities nearby, motel on premises. House specialty: family style seafood dinner. No credit cards.

FRANCES KITCHING
Tangier Sound/Smith Island
(301)425-3321
Open seasonally, April 15-Oct. 15, serving dinner and light breakfast. Dinner price is $10 plus tax and tip for family style meal. Reservations required. Motel nearby. Dockage available at the public dock. House specialties: everything is homemade. No credit cards are accepted; travelers checks O.K.

AUNT EM'S RESTAURANT
Little Annemessex/Crisfield
(301)968-0353
Open year-round for breakfast, lunch and dinner. Dinner prices range from $4.95 to $10.95. Reservations not necessary. Marina facilities nearby. Motel nearby. House specialties: prime rib, crab cakes, fried chicken. No credit cards.

CAPTAIN'S GALLEY
Little Annemessex River/Crisfield
(301)968-1636
Open year-round serving breakfast, lunch and dinner. Dinners priced to $15.00. Reservations suggested. Dockage for diners, 10'. Marina on the premises and motel nearby. House specialty: crab dishes. Accepts MasterCard and VISA.

HARBOR VIEW RESTAURANT
Little Annemessex/Crisfield
(301)968-3367
Open year-round serving lunch and dinner. Prices range from $5.95 to $10.95. Reservations not necessary. Marina facilities and motel nearby. House specialties: crab cakes, steamed crabs and shrimp. No credit cards.

GREAT WICOMICO RIVER

HORN HARBOR HOUSE
Great Wicomico
(804)453-3351
Open seasonally serving dinner only. Price range $7.00 to $12.00. Reservations not accepted. Dockage for diners and overnight, 10'. Marina on premises. House specialty: seafood. NO credit cards.

RAPPAHANNOCK RIVER

ANNABELL LEE
Rappahannock River/North end of bridge
(804)435-1450
Open year-round serving lunch and dinner. Prices range from $6.50 to $16.50. Reservations suggested. Dockage for diners, 8'. Marina facilities on premises; motel nearby. House specialties: fish and steaks. MasterCard and VISA.

BINNACLE II AT TIDES LODGE
Rappahannock River/Carter Creek
(804)438-6000
Open mid-March to December serving lunch and dinner. Price range: $7.25-$16.95. Reservations not accepted. Dockage for diners and overnight, 6'. Marina and motel on premises. House specialties: sauteed seafood, mesquite broiled ribs and chicken. Accepts MasterCard and VISA.

CHEZ CLAUDE
Rappahannock/Urbanna Creek
(804)758-2397
Open year-round serving lunch and dinner. Dinner price range: $10.95 to $14.95. Reservations suggested. Dockage for diners and overnight, 3'. Marina facilities and motel nearby. House specialties: local seafood. MasterCard and VISA.

DOCKSIDE HEARTH AT WINDMILL POINT MARINE RESORT
Mouth of Rappahannock River
(804)435-1166
Open seasonally serving breakfast, lunch and dinner. Reservations suggested. Dockage for diners and overnight, 7'. Marina and motel on premises. House specialties: seafood selections. American Express, MasterCard, VISA, Diners Club, Carte Blanche and Choice.

Continued

LOWERY'S RESTAURANT
Rappahannock/Tappahannock
(804)443-4314
Open year-round serving breakfast, lunch and dinner. Dinners range $5.95-$13.,95. Reservations not accepted except for large groups. Marina facilities and motel nearby. House specialty: seafood. American Express, MasterCard, VISA and Choice.

ROYAL STEWART DINING ROOM AT TIDES LODGE
Rappahannock River/Carter Creek
(804)438-6000
Open Mid-March to December. Serves breakfast, lunch and dinner. Price range: $22 to $26. Reservations required. Dockage for diners and overnight, 6'. Marina and motel on premises. Accepts VISA and MasterCard.

PIANKATANK RIVER

THE GOLDEN ANCHOR
Piankatank/Gwynns Island
(804)472-2151
Open year-round serving breakfast, lunch and dinner. Dinner prices range from $6.95 to $17.95. Reservations not necessary but suggested. Dockage for diners and overnight, 8'. Marina facilities and motel on premises. House specialties: seafood and steak. MasterCard and VISA.

BUCKROE BEACH

WATERVIEW MOTEL/BLUE MARLIN RESTAURANT
Buckroe Beach
(804)851-7811
Open year-round serving breakfast, lunch and dinner. Reservations suggested. Marina facilities nearby. Motel on premises. Waterfront rooms, close to fishing pier, game room. Accepts MasterCard and VISA.

HAMPTON & ELIZABETH RIVERS

FISHERMAN'S WHARF RESTAURANT
Hampton Roads/Hampton Creek
(804)723-3113
Open year-round serving dinner only. Dinner price range: $8.95 to $19.95. Reservations suggested on weekends. Dockage available nearby. Marina and motel nearby. House specialty: world famous seafood buffet and A La Carte menu, candlelight dining overlooking the harbour. Accepts MasterCard, VISA and American Express.

STRAWBERRY BANKS RESTAURANT
Hampton Roads
(804)723-6061/(800)446-4088
Open year-round serving breakfast, lunch and dinner. Prices range from $2.95 to $16.95. Reservations suggested. Dockage for diners, 3'-4'. Marina facilities, motel on premises. House specialties: seafood, tableside flambe', prime beef and daily luncheon buffet. American Express, MasterCard, VISA, Diners Club, Choice and Carte Blanche.

FISHERMAN'S WHARF RESTAURANT
Norfolk, Va.

Open year-round serving breakfast, lunch and dinner. Dinner price range: $8.95 to $19.95. Reservations suggested. Dockage available nearby. Motel nearby. House specialty: seafood buffet and a la carte menu. Located off I 64, next to Willoughby Marina. Accepts VISA, MasterCard and American Express.

NORFOLK'S WATERSIDE
Norfolk Harbor
Open year-round, seven days a week, serving breakfast, lunch and dinner. Price range varies. Many restaurants featuring all kinds of foods. This is very similar to Baltimore's Harborplace.

SCALE OF DE WHALE
Elizabeth River
(804)438-2772
Open year-round serving lunch (Mon.-Fri.) and dinner. Prices range $10.99 to $24.95. Reservations are suggested. Dockage is available for diners, 8'. There is a marina on the premises. House specialty is seafood. Accepts VISA, MasterCard, American Express, Choice and Diners.

SEAWALL RESTAURANT
Elizabeth River
(804)397-7006
Open year-round serving lunch and dinner. Dinner price range: $4-$14. Reservations suggested but not necessary. Marina and motel nearby. House specialty: seafood, pasta, steak and veal. Accepts MasterCard, VISA, American Express, Diners Club and Carte Blanche and Choice.

JAMES RIVER

KINGSMILL RESTAURANT
James River
(804)253-3900
Open year-round serving breakfast, lunch and dinner. Prices range from $15-$25. Reservations are suggested for dinner. There is dockage for diners and overnight, 6'. There is a marina and a motel on the premises. Hosue specialties include: veal and seafood dishes, shrimp and homemade desserts. Accepts VISA, American Express and Master Card.

SMITHFIELD STATION
James River/Pagan River
(804)357-3347
Open year-round serving breakfast, lunch and dinner. Dinner prices range from $3.95 to $19.95. Reservations suggested. Dockage for diners and overnight, 7'. Marina facilities and motel on premises. House specialty: seafood and Smithfield ham. MasterCard, American Express, VISA and Choice.

LYNNHAVEN, RUDEE INLET AND VIRGINIA BEACH

LYNNHAVEN FISH HOUSE
Lynnhaven Pier on Chesapeake Bay
(804)481-0003
Open year-round serving lunch and dinner. Dinner price range: $10.95 to $16.95. Reservations not accepted. Accepts American Express, MasterCard and VISA.

THE LIGHTHOUSE
Ocean at Rudee Inlet
(804)428-7974
Open year-round serving dinner. Dinner prices range from $13.95 to $27.95. Lunch only on weekends. Reservations suggested. Marina facilities and motel nearby. House specialties: western prime beef, shecrab soup, shrimp and home baked breads and desserts. American Express, MasterCard, Diners Club, Choice and Discover.

BLUE PETE'S RESTAURANT
Back Bay/Muddy Creek/Virginia Beach
(804)426-2005
Open year-round serving dinner only. Prices range from $7 to $20. Reservations not accepted. House specialties: fresh seafood and sweet potato biscuits. Pick-up and return to Captain George's (Pungo Ferry) and West Neck Marina or to Atlantic Yacht Basin (Great Bridge). MasterCard, American Express, Diners Club and Choice.

CAPE CHARLES

ETZ'S RESTAURANT
Cape Charles

Open year-round serving breakfast, lunch and dinner. Dinner price range: $5-$7.95. Reservations not necessary. Marina facilities and motel nearby. House specialties: seafood platter, crabmeat butter, and crab salad. No credit cards.

Safe Boating Tip

Courtesy U.S. Power Squadron

Check the current weather reports before you set sail for a day on the water and watch the sky for the appearance of sudden storms so you can get back to port safely.

● ON PREMISES
▶ NEARBY

	WATER DEPTH MLW	OVERNIGHT SLIPS	GAS	DIESEL	PROPANE	ELECTRIC	SHOWERS	LAUNDROMAT	RESTAURANT	MOTEL	POOL	HOLDING TANK PUMPOUT	ICE	BEER	GROCERIES	MARINE SUPPLIES	BAIT	ENGINE REPAIRS	HULL REPAIRS	HAUL-OUT SERVICES	LAUNCH RAMP	*CREDIT CARDS	*OTHER
&D Canal																							
OCKSIDE YACHT CLUB :&D Canal 301)885-5016	4′	●	●	●					●													AMEX VISA M/C	
CHAEFER'S MARKET & MARINA :&D Canal 301)885-2204	12′	30	●	●		●			●				●	●	●	●		●				●	
Elk & Bohemia Rivers																							
IARBOUR NORTH MARINA .lk River 301)885-5656	4′	●	●			●	●						●			●	●	●		●	●	Mobil M/C VISA	
OHEMIA ANCHORAGE ohemia River at Bridge 301)275-8148	5′ 10′	●	●			●	●		●				●	●	●	●		●	●	●		●	
OCUST POINT MARINA lk River 301)392-4994	4′	●	●			●	●						●			●		▶	▶	▶	●	VISA M/C	
OHEMIA RIVER MARINA ohemia River 301)885-5429	6′	●	●	●		●	●	●	▶		●		●			●		●	●	●	▶	VISA, M/C	Beach
OHEMIA VISTA YACHT BASIN ohemia River 301)885-5402	5′		●	●		●	●						●			●		●	●	●	●	VISA M/C	
ONG POINT MARINA ohemia River 301)275-8185	5′	●	●			●	●	●				●	●	▶	▶	●		●	●	●		Mobil	Soda & Snacks
OSTEN MARINA ohemia River 301)275-8168	5′	3	●	▶		●	●		▶	▶		▶	●	▶	▶	●	▶	●	●	●	●	●	Concrete 4 Lanes
WO RIVERS YACHT BASIN ohemia River 301)885-2257	5′	●	●	●		●	●				●	●	●			●		●	●	●		Gulf VISA M/C	
assafras River																							
UFFY CREEK MARINA assafras River 301)275-2141	6′	10	●	●		●	●		▶				●		●	●		●	●	●	●	Gulf Chev M/C VISA	
EORGETOWN YACHT BASIN, INC. assafras River 01)648-5112	20′	●	●	●	●	●	●	●	▶		●	●	●	●	●	●		●	●	●	▶	VISA M/C AMEX	Rental Cars Poolside Cocktails
RANARY MARINA assafras River 01)648-5112	18′	●	▶	▶	▶	●	●	●	●			▶	●	▶	▶	▶		▶	▶	▶	▶	●	
REGG NECK BOAT YARD assafras River 301)648-5360	10′	●	●	●	●	●	●		▶	▶			●	▶	▶	●		●	●	●	●		

● ON PREMIS
▶ NEAR

	WATER DEPTH MLW	OVERNIGHT SLIPS	GAS	DIESEL	PROPANE	ELECTRIC	SHOWERS	LAUNDROMAT	RESTAURANT	MOTEL	POOL	HOLDING TANK PUMPOUT	ICE	BEER	GROCERIES	MARINE SUPPLIES	BAIT	ENGINE REPAIRS	HULL REPAIRS	HAUL-OUT SERVICES	LAUNCH RAMP	*CREDIT CARDS	*OTHER
SAILING ASSOCIATES Sassafras River (301)275-8171	12′	15	▶	▶	●	●	●	▶	▶	▶	●	●	●	▶	▶	●	▶	●	●	●	▶	VISA M/C	Brokerage Yacht Sales & Charters
SASSAFRAS BOAT CO. Sassafras River (301)275-8111	12′	●	●	●	▶	●	●	●	▶	▶	▶	▶	●	▶	▶	●	▶	●	●	●	▶	M/C AMEX VISA	70 Ton Travel Lift
SKIPJACK COVE MARINA Sassafras River (301)275-2122	16′	●	●	●	●	●	●	●	▶	▶	●	●	●	▶	●	●	▶	●	●	●	▶	AMEX VISA M/C Shell	Launch & Rental Car
Susquehanna River																							
HAVRE DE GRACE CITY YACHT BASIN Havre de Grace (301)939-9448	6′	●	●			●	●		●			●	●				●				●		
HAVRE DE GRACE MARINA Susquehanna River (301)939-2161	6′	●	●	●	▶	●	●	▶	▶	▶			●	●	▶	●	●	●	●	●		M/C VISA	
PENN'S BEACH MARINA, INC. Havre de Grace (301)939-2060	6′	●	●			●	●		●	●			●	●	●	●	●	●		●	●	●	
TIDEWATER MARINA Susquehanna River (301)939-0950	7′	●	●	●		●	●		▶	▶		●	●		▶	●		●	●	●	●	P-66 VISA M/C	
Northeast River																							
ANCHOR MARINA Northeast River (301)287-6000	18′	12	●			●	●		●				●	●		●		●	●	●	●		
AVALON YACHT BASIN Northeast River (301)287-6722	4½′		●			●	●	▶	▶	▶			●	▶	▶	●		●	●	●	●		
BAY BOAT WORKS Northeast River (301)287-8113	4½′	●	●	●	▶	●	●	▶	▶	▶		▶	●	▶	▶	●	▶	●	●	●	●		
CHARLESTOWN MARINA Northeast River (301)287-8125	6′	●	●	●	▶	●	●	▶	▶	▶	▶	▶	●	▶	▶	●	▶	●	●	●	●	Mobil VISA M/C	Yacht Brokerage
JACKSON MARINE SALES Northeast River/Hance Pt. (301)287-9400	4-6′	●	●	●		●	●	●								●		●	●	●		●	
LEE'S MARINA Head of Northeast River (301)287-5100	3′	●	▶	▶	▶	●	●		▶			▶	●	▶	▶	●	●	●	●	●	●		
MCDANIEL YACHT BASIN Northeast River (301)287-8121	6′	4	●	●	●	●	●	●	▶	▶	●	●	●	▶	▶	●	▶	●	●	●	▶	Texaco Bank Am VISA	
NORTH EAST YACHT SALES Northeast River (301)287-6660		●				●	●		▶	▶			●			●		●	●	●		●	

SAFETY TIPS

The fire-engine red look is out. And it's easy to keep from getting sunburned, even during a long day on the water, if you use one of the new sun screens. They are graded by number from minimum to maximum protection and you should buy the one that suits your complexion and tanning plans the best.

Put on life jackets occasionally when going swimming. It's a practical way of becoming accustomed to the feel of a life preserver and could make the difference between panic and peace in a real emergency. Applicable to both adults and children!

Equip your boat, however low the freeboard, with a stable swim ladder. Very few people can scramble back on board even though they think its easy to do. Never use a transom board when engines are running. Danger from propellers is near and real.

Toot your whistle in an emergency. Specifically, put a whistle in the bilge, so the captain can attract your attention if necessary while working below deck.

MARINAS

● ON PREMISES
▶ NEARBY

Marina	Water Depth MLW	Overnight Slips	Gas	Diesel	Propane	Electric	Showers	Laundromat	Restaurant	Motel	Pool	Holding Tank Pumpout	Ice	Beer	Groceries	Marine Supplies	Bait	Engine Repairs	Hull Repairs	Haul-Out Services	Launch Ramp	*Credit Cards	*Other
SHELTER COVE MARINA Northeast River (301)287-9400	3′	●	●	●	▶	●	●	●	▶	▶	▶	▶	●	▶	▶	●	▶	●	●	●	▶	Phillips VISA M/C	New & Used Sales
Bush and Gunpowder Rivers																							
BUSH RIVER BOAT WORKS Bush River (301)272-1882	3′	3	●		●	●	●					●	●	●		●	●	●	●	●	●	Phillips 66	
TROJAN HARBOR MARINA Bush River (301)679-9813	4′	●	●			●	●						●	●	●	●	●	●	●	●	●	VISA M/C	
GUNPOWDER COVE MARINA Gunpowder River/Taylor's Creek (301)679-5454	4′	●	●			●	●					●	●			●		●	●	●	●	M/C VISA Choice Texaco	
Middle River																							
ANCHOR BAY YACHT SALES Middle River/Hopkins Creek (301)574-0777	9′	●	▶	▶	●	60 Amp.	●	●	▶			●	●	●	●	●		●	▶	60 Ton	●	VISA M/C AMEX	Yacht Brokerage
BEACON LIGHT MARINA Middle River/Seneca Creek (301)335-6489		●	●			●	●						●			●		●		●	●	●	
BOAT HAVEN MARINA Middle River/Norman Creek (301)687-7290	4′	●	●			●	●	▶	▶				▶	▶	▶	●	▶	●	●	●		M/C VISA	
BOATING CENTER OF BALT. Middle R./Sue Creek (301)687-2000	5′		●			●	●		▶				●	▶		●	▶	●		●	●	VISA M/C Choice	Soda/Cig. Candy Machines
BUEDELS'S MARINA AND BOATYARD Middle River (301)687-3577	5′	●	●			●	●	▶	▶	▶			▶	▶	▶	●		●	●	●		VISA M/C Choice	Propeller Recond.
CUTTER MARINE YACHT BASIN Middle River (301)391-7245	7′	●	▶	▶		●	●	▶	▶				●	▶	▶	●		●	●	●	●	VISA M/C Choice	
DECKELMAN'S BOAT YARD Middle River/Hopkins Creek (301)391-6482	20′	●	▶	▶	▶	●	▶	▶	▶	▶	▶	▶	▶	▶	▶	●	▶	●	●	●	▶		
DRIFTWOOD INN Middle River/Hopkins Creek (301)391-3493	10′	●	●	●	▶	●	▶	▶	●	▶		▶	●	●	▶	▶	▶	▶	▶	▶	●	VISA M/C AMEX	Rest. Lounge Live Music T.F.S.S.
ESSEX MARINA BOAT YARD Middle River/Hopkins Cr. (301)687-6149			●	●		●	●									●		●	●	●			
GALLOWAY CREEK MARINA Middle River/Galloway Creek (301)335-3575	5′	▶	▶	▶	▶	●	●	▶	▶			▶	▶	▶	▶	▶	▶	●	●	●	●		Marine Towing Marine Const. Pile Driving
GOOSE HARBOR BOAT YARD Middle R./Seneca Creek (301)335-7474	4′	●				●	●						●	●		●	●	●	●	●	●		

● ON PREMISES
▶ NEARBY

Marina	Water Depth MLW	Overnight Slips	Gas	Diesel	Propane	Electric	Showers	Laundromat	Restaurant	Motel	Pool	Holding Tank Pumpout	Ice	Beer	Groceries	Marine Supplies	Bait	Engine Repairs	Hull Repairs	Haul-Out Services	Launch Ramp	*Credit Cards	*Other
LONG BEACH MARINA Middle R./Frog Mortar Creek (301)335-8602	8′	●	●			●	●		▶		●					●		●	●	●	●		Paint
MARKLEY'S MARINA Middle River (301)687-5575	8′					●	●	▶	▶			●	▶	▶	▶	●		●	●	●	▶		
MARYLAND MARINA Middle River/Frog Mortar (301)335-8736	8′	●	●	●	▶	●	●	●	▶				●	▶	▶	●		●	●	●	●	M/C VISA Choice	Charter & School
MIDDLE RIVER BOATLAND Middle R./Sue Creek (301) 574-8281	5½′	●	●	▶		●	▶		▶		▶		●	▶	▶	●		●	▶	●	●	Choice VISA M/C	Hi&dri forklift New & used boat sales & service
NEW TRADEWINDS MARINA Middle R./Armstrong Creek (301)335-7000	6′	●	●	●		●	●	●					●	●		●		●	●	●	●	M/C VISA	
NORMAN CREEK MARINA Middle River/Barren Point (301)686-9343	10′	●	●			●	●	●	●			●	●		●	●	●					●	
PORTER'S SENECA PARK MAR. Middle River/Seneca Creek (301)335-6563	8′	●	●										●			●		●	●	●			
RIVER WATCH RESTAURANT & MARINA Middle R./Hopkins Cr. (301)687-1422	8′	●	●	●		●	●	●	●			●	●	●		●						●	
RILEY'S MARINA Middle River (301)686-0771	8′	▶	●	▶	▶	●	●	▶	▶	▶	▶	▶	▶	▶	▶	●	▶	●	●	●	▶	Exxon VISA MC	All Boat Repairs New Boat Sales & Brokerage
STANSBURY YACHT BASIN Middle River/Dark Head (301)686-3909	12′	●	●		▶	●	●		▶	▶			●	▶	▶	●		●	●	●	●	VISA	
Back River																							
LYNHURST MARINE Back River (301)477-1910	8′	●				●			▶				▶	▶	▶	▶	▶	●	●	●			
MAKO YACHT BASIN Back River (301)686-6998	5′	●	●	▶	▶	●	●	▶	▶	▶			●	▶	▶	●	▶	●	●	●	▶	None	
RUDY'S MARINA Back River (301)477-3276	6′	●	●			●	●		▶				●	▶		●		●	●	●	●	Exxon	Fiberglass Repair 8-Ton Travel Lift/Fork Lift up to 24′
WEAVER BROS. BOATYARD Back River (301)686-4944	6′		●	●		●	●		▶				●	▶		●		●	●	●	▶	M/C VISA	Woodwork
Worton and Fairlee Creeks and Tolchester Beach																							
GREAT OAK LANDING MARINA Fairlee Creek (301)778-2100	6½′	●	●	●	▶	●	●	●	●	●	●	●	●	●	●	●	●	●	●			VISA M/C AMEX	

MARINAS

● ON PREMISES
▶ NEARBY

	Water Depth MLW	Overnight Slips	Gas	Diesel	Propane	Electric	Showers	Laundromat	Restaurant	Motel	Pool	Holding Tank Pumpout	Ice	Beer	Groceries	Marine Supplies	Bait	Engine Repairs	Hull Repairs	Haul-Out Services	Launch Ramp	*Credit Cards	*Other
GREEN POINT MARINA Worton Creek (301)778-1615	6′	●	●	●		●	●		▶			●	●	▶	●	●	●	●		●	▶	VISA M/C Mobil	
TOLCHESTER MARINA Chesapeake Bay/Buoy #20 (301)778-1400	6′	●	●	●		●	●	●	▶				●	●	●	●	●	●	●	●		VISA M/C	
WORTON CREEK MARINA Worton Creek (301)778-3282	6′	●	●	●		●	●	●	●			●	●	●	●	●	●	●	●	●		Gulf VISA	
Swan Creek, Gratitude and Rock Hall																							
GRATITUDE BOAT SALES, INC. Chesapeake Bay/Swan Creek (301)639-7111 or 7112	4′	●				●	●		▶				●										Yacht Sales & Charters
GRATITUDE MARINA Chesapeake Bay/Swan Creek (301)639-7011	6′	●	●	●		●	●	▶	▶	▶			●	▶	●	●		●	●	●			
HAVEN HARBOUR Off Swan Creek (301)639-7251	5½′	●	●	●		●	●	●	▶	▶	●		●	▶	▶	●	▶	●	●	●		VISA M/C	Gift Shop Snack Bar
SPRING COVE MARINA Swan Creek/The Haven (301)639-2110	6′		▶	▶		●	●		▶		●								▶	▶			
SWAN CREEK MARINA Swan Creek (301)639-7813	7′	●	●	▶	▶	●	●	▶	▶	▶	▶	▶	●	▶	▶	●	▶	●	●	●	▶		Yacht Carpentry Inside Mast Storage
HUBBARD'S PIER AND SEAFOOD Rock Hall Harbor (301)778-4700	10′	●	●	●	▶	▶	▶	▶	●	▶			●	●	▶	▶	●	▶	▶	▶	▶		
KENDALL'S MARINA Rock Hall Harbor (301)639-7377	6′	●	●	●		●	●	●					●		●	●	●	●	●			●	Yacht Sales & Chartering
NORTH SIDE MARINA, INC. Rock Hall Harbor (301)639-2263	6′	●	●	●		●	●	●	▶	▶			●	●	▶	●	▶	●	▶	▶	▶	VISA M/C Shell	
PELORUS SAILING MARINA Rock Hall Harbor (301)639-2151	6′	●	▶	▶		●	●	▶	▶	▶			●	▶	▶	▶	▶	●	●	●			
ROCK HALL MARINE RAILWAY Rock Hall Harbor (301)639-2263	5′	●	●	●		●	●		●	●			●	▶	▶	●		●	●	●	▶	Gulf	
THE SAILING EMPORIUM Rock Hall Harbor (301)778-1342	7′	●	●	●	●	●	●	●	▶	▶	●		●	●	▶	●		●	●	●	●	M/C VISA	CNG Yacht Sales Charter Service Trans. to Rest.
Patapsco River																							
ANCHORAGE MARINA Baltimore Harbor (301)522-4007	9′	●	▶	▶	▶	●	●	●	▶	▶		●	●	▶	▶	▶	▶	●	●	●	▶	None	

● ON PREMISES
▶ NEARBY

Marina	Water Depth MLW	Overnight Slips	Gas	Diesel	Propane	Electric	Showers	Laundromat	Restaurant	Motel	Pool	Holding Tank Pumpout	Ice	Beer	Groceries	Marine Supplies	Bait	Engine Repairs	Hull Repairs	Haul-Out Services	Launch Ramp	*Credit Cards	*Other
BAR HARBOR MARINA Patapsco R./Rock Creek (301)255-5500	10′		●	●		●	●						▶	▶	▶	●		●	●	●			
BEAR CREEK MARINA Patapsco R./Bear Creek (301)284-1044	8′	●	●	▶	▶	●	▶	▶	▶	▶	▶	▶	●	▶	▶	●	▶	●	●	●	●	Exxon	▶
CARBACK'S MARINA Patapsco R./Bodkin Creek (301)437-3400	6′	2	●			●	●		▶				▶	▶	▶	●	▶	●	●	●	●		
FAIRVIEW MARINE CORP. Patapsco R./Rock Creek (301)437-3400	8′	●	●	●	▶	●	●		▶				●			Lmtd.	▶	●	●	●			
GREEN HAVEN MARINA Patapsco R./Stony Creek (301)255-4422			●			●							●					▶	▶	●			
HAMMOCK ISLAND MARINA Patapsco R./Bodkin Creek (301)437-1870	7′	●				●	●						●					▶	▶	▶	▶		
HENDERSON'S WHARF Patapsco R./Inner Harbor (301)522-7900	10′	●	▶	▶	▶	●	●	●	●	●	●	●	●	●	●	●	▶	●	●	▶	▶	●	Boat Sales Charters Floating Piers
IMAN'S YARD Patapsco R./North Point Creek (301)477-4430	4′	4				●							●			▶		●	●	●			
INNER HARBOR MARINA Baltimore Inner Harbor (301)837-5339	24′	80	●	●		●	●	●	●	▶	▶	●	●	●	●	●	▶	▶	▶	▶	▶	Fuel Only	MD Science Ctr. Harbor Place Six Flags Top of the World
KEY BRIDGE MARINA Patapsco R./Bear Creek (301)285-3122	18′	●	▶	●	▶	●	●	▶					▶	▶	▶	●		●	●	●			Snacks Refrigeration Repair
LYNCH COVE MARINA Patapsco R./Lynch Cove (301)228-1332	10′	2	●		▶	●	●	▶	▶														
MARKEL'S BOAT YARD Patapsco R./North Point Creek (301)477-3445	5′	●	●		●								●			●	▶		●	●		Exxon VISA M/C	Rowboat Rentals
MAURGALE MARINA Patapsco R./Stony Creek (301)437-0402	10′	●				●	●						●	▶	▶	●		●	●	●			
NAUTICO MARINE CENTER Baltimore Inner Harbor at Rusty Scupper (301)962-1172													●	●	●	●		●	●			●	
NORTH POINT MARINA Patapsco R./Old Road Bay (301)477-2446		●	▶			●							▶	▶	▶	▶	▶	▶	▶	●	●		Balto. County Police Boat Station
OAK HARBOR YACHT YARD Patapsco R./Rock Creek (301)255-4070	10′	●				●	●		▶				●			●		●	●	●		None	
PASADENA YACHT YARD Patapsco R./Rock Creek (301)255-1771	12′	●	●	●	▶	●	●		▶	▶						●		●	●	●			

MARINAS

● ON PREMISES
▶ NEARBY

	Water Depth MLW	Overnight Slips	Gas	Diesel	Propane	Electric	Showers	Laundromat	Restaurant	Motel	Pool	Holding Tank Pumpout	Ice	Beer	Groceries	Marine Supplies	Bait	Engine Repairs	Hull Repairs	Haul-Out Services	Launch Ramp	* Credit Cards	* Other
STONEY CREEK BOAT WORKS Patapsco River/Stony Creek (301)522-4987	12′	●	●		▶	●		▶	▶				●	▶	▶	●	▶	●	●	●			
THOMAS POINT MARINA Patapsco R./Baltimore Harbor (301)522-4987	9′-13′		●	●		●																	
VENTNOR MARINE Patapsco R./Bodkin Creek (301)255-4100	10′	●	●	●		●			●				●	▶	▶	●	▶	●	●	●	●	Exxon M/C VISA	Stern Drive Service
WHITE ROCKS YACHTING CENTER Patapsco R./Rock Creek (301)255-3800	14′	●	●	●		●	●	●	●				●	●		●		●	●	●		M/C VISA Amoco	
YOUNG'S BOAT YARD Patapsco R./Old Road Bay/Jones Cr. (301)477-0915	5′	●	●			●	●									●				●			
Magothy River																							
CAPT. CLYDE'S MARINA Magothy R./Deep Creek (301)757-4045	8′	●	●	●		●			●				●	●		●		●	●	●	●	VISA M/C	
CYPRESS MARINE Magothy R. (301) 647-7940	12′	●	▶	▶	▶	110 220	●	●	▶	▶			▶	▶	▶	●	▶	●	●	●	▶	Cash Only	Emerg. haulout Welding Rigging Fiberglass work
FAIRWINDS MARINA Magothy R./Deep Creek (301)974-0758/261-1548			●			●	●						●			●		●	●	●	●	Exxon VISA M/C	25 Ton Open End Travel Lift
FERRY POINT YACHT BASIN Magothy R./Mill Creek (301)647-9793	12′		●		▶	●	●												▶	●	●	Exxon	
GIBSON ISLAND YACHT BASIN Magothy River (301)255-3488	10′	●	●	●		●	●		▶				●					●	●	●		●	
MAGOTHY MARINA Magothy R./Crystal Beach (301)647-2356	6′	●	●	●		●	●	●			●		●					●			●		
MAGOTHY YACHT YARD Magothy R./Boundary Stone (301)647-0733	13′		●	●		●							●			●		●	●	●	●	M/C VISA Amoco	
Chester River/Kent Narrows/Kent Island																							
CASTLE MARINA, LTD. Chester River (301)643-6300	6′	●	●	●		●	●	●	●		●	Possible	●			●		●	●	●		Most	Chris Craft Dealer
KENNERSLEY POINTE MARINA Chester R./Island Creek (301)758-2394	6′	●	●	▶	▶	●	●	●	▶	▶	●		●	▶	▶	●	▶	●	●	●			
KIBLER'S MARINA Chester R./Chestertown (301)778-3616	5′	●	●	●		●	●	●	▶				●	●		●		●	●	●	●	Gulf	Chevron

NATIONAL WEATHER SERVICE COASTAL WARNING DISPLAYS

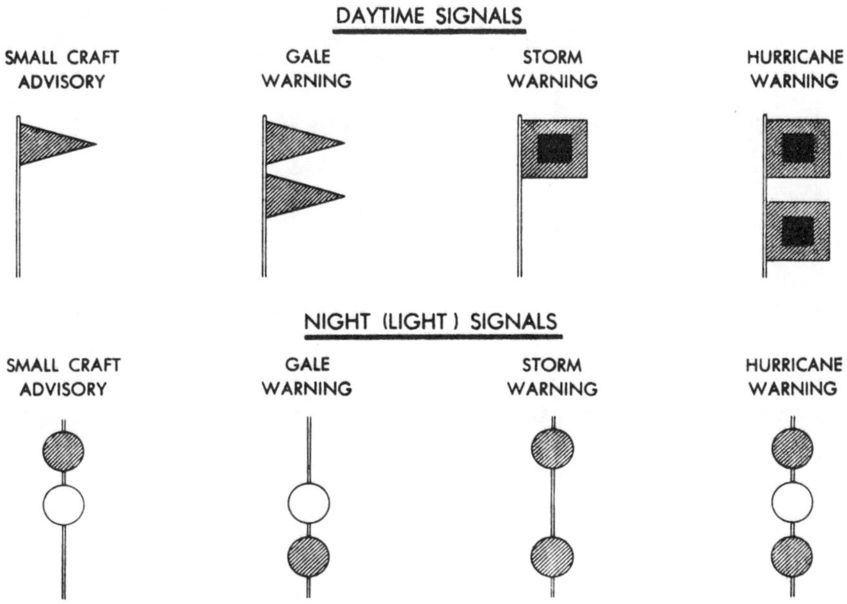

Note: Shaded area represents the color RED on flags and lights.

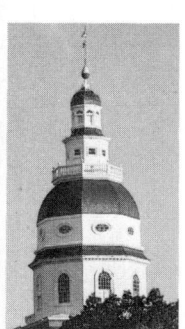

● ON PREMISES
▶ NEARBY

Marina	WATER DEPTH MLW	OVERNIGHT SLIPS	GAS	DIESEL	PROPANE	ELECTRIC	SHOWERS	LAUNDROMAT	RESTAURANT	MOTEL	POOL	HOLDING TANK PUMPOUT	ICE	BEER	GROCERIES	MARINE SUPPLIES	BAIT	ENGINE REPAIRS	HULL REPAIRS	HAUL-OUT SERVICES	LAUNCH RAMP	*CREDIT CARDS	*OTHER
LANKFORD BAY MARINA Chester R./Lankford Bay (301)778-1414	6′	●	●	●		●	●						●	●	●	●	●	●	●	●		●	
SCOTTS POINT MARINA Chester R./Chestertown (301)778-2959	12′	●				●	●						●										4 Blocks From Down-town Chestertown
CAPT. ALEX'S MARINA Kent Narrows (301)827-6340	8′	●	●	●	▶	●			●	▶		▶	●	●	●	▶	●	▶	▶	▶	▶	●	
CEDAR POINT-LIPPINCOTT Southside of Kent Narrows (301)822-6939	6′	●		●	▶	●	●	●	▶	▶			●			●		●	●	●	●		Charter Fleet Sailing School
EAST SHORE MARINA Kent Narrows (301)827-8441	6′	4	●	●	▶	●	●	▶	▶	▶			●	▶	▶	●	▶	●	●	50T	▶	VISA M/C Choice Oil	
MEARS POINT MARINA Kent Narrows (301)827-8888	8′	●	●	●	▶	●	●	●	●	▶	●	▶	●	●	▶	●	▶	●	●	●	▶	VISA M/C AMEX Amoco	
PINEY NARROWS YACHT HAVEN Kent Narrows (301)643-6601	7′	●	●	●	▶	●	●	●	▶	▶	●		●	▶	▶	●	▶	●	●	●	●	Texaco VISA M/C	Yacht Brokerage
W.A. THOMAS & SON Kent Narrows (301)827-8011	8′	●	●	●		●			●	▶	▶	▶	●	●	●	▶	●	▶	▶	▶	▶	●	
KENTMORR HARBOUR Kent Island, Brick House Bar (301)643-4201	6′	●	●	●		●	●		●		●		●	●				●	●	●		M/C VISA Shell	
PIER I MARINA Kent Island, East end of Bridge (301)643-3162	5′		●	●		●	●	▶	●				●					●	●	●		VISA M/C Amoco	
QUEEN ANNE MARINA Kent Island/Price Creek (301)643-5065	4′	6	●	●		110	●		●				●	●	●	●	●			●	●	M/C VISA	Live Hard & Soft Crabs
Chesapeake Bay Bridge Area																							
PLEASURE COVE YACHT & BEACH CLUB On the Bay, Western Shore near Bridge (301)757-8000 261-2529	6′	●	▶	▶		●	●	●	▶	▶	●		●	▶	▶	▶				●	▶		
SANDY POINT BOATING Sandy Point State Park (301)974-0772	8′		●	●					▶	▶		●	●	▶	▶	▶	●				●	VISA M/C Gas Co. Cards	
Severn River Whitehall Bay																							
ALOHA YACHT SALES Severn R./Back Creek (301)267-9243	12′					●	●	▶	▶						▶			●	●	●			Full Service Boatyard
ANNAPOLIS CITY DOCK Severn R./Annapolis Harbor (301)263-7973	10′	18	▶	▶	▶	●	●	▶	▶	▶			▶	▶	▶	▶	▶	▶	▶	▶	▶		Bulkhead Docking 10 Boats

MARINAS

● ON PREMISE
▶ NEARB

Marina	Water Depth MLW	Overnight Slips	Gas	Diesel	*Propane	Electric	Showers	Laundromat	Restaurant	Motel	Pool	Holding Tank Pumpout	Ice	Beer	Groceries	Marine Supplies	Bait	Engine Repairs	Hull Repairs	Haul-Out Services	Launch Ramp	*Credit Cards	*Other
ANNAPOLIS CITY MARINA Severn R./Spa Creek/Annapolis (301)268-0660	6′	●	●	●		●	●	●	▶				●	●	▶	●		▶	▶	▶		VISA M/C AMEX Texaco	
ANNAPOLIS HARBOR BOATYARD Severn R./Spa Creek/Annapolis (301)267-9050	5′					●		▶	▶				▶	▶	▶			●	●	●			
ANNAPOLIS HILTON INN Severn R./Annapolis Harbor (301)268-7555	5′	●	▶	▶	▶	●	●	▶	●	●	●	▶	●	●	▶	▶	▶	▶	▶	▶	▶	●	
ANNAPOLIS YACHT BASIN Severn R./Spa Creek/Annapolis (301)263-3544	9½′	●	●	●		●	●	●	▶	▶	●		●									VISA Gulf M/C Chevron	
HORN PT. MARINA Severn R./Back Creek (301)263-0550	14′	●	▶	▶	▶	●	●	▶	▶	▶			▶	▶	▶	▶	▶	▶	▶	▶	▶		
CHESAPEAKE HARBOUR MARINA North of Lake Ogleton · (301)261-1050/(301)269-5180	8′	20				●	●				●		●			▶		▶	▶			VISA M/C	Tennis
SEVERN R./HORN PT. MARINA Severn R./Back Creek (301)263-0550	7′	6				●	●													●			
JONES MARINA Severn R./Back Creek (301)268-2050	7′	●	▶	▶		●	●						▶		▶	▶		▶	▶	▶			
BURT JABIN'S YACHT YARD Severn R./Back Cr. (301)268-9667/(301)269-0821	9′	●				●	●						●			●		●	●	●		VISA MC	Complete Yacht Repair & Maint.
MARINER'S WHARF Severn R./at Old Bridge (301)757-2424	10′-12′	●				●		●	●				●	●	●	▶		●				VISA M/C AMEX	
MEARS MARINA Severn R./Back Creek (301)268-8282	8′	●	▶	▶	▶	●	●	●	▶	▶	●		●	▶	▶	▶	▶	●	●	●	▶		
PETRINI YACHT YARD & MARINA Severn R./Spa Creek (301)263-4278	10′	●	▶	▶		●	●	▶	▶	▶			▶	▶	▶	●		●	●	●	▶		50 Ton Lift Full Service
PIER 4 MARINA Severn R./Spa Creek (301)268-2987	12′	●	▶	▶	▶	30A	●	▶	▶	▶	▶		▶	▶	▶	▶	▶	▶	▶	▶	▶		
PLEASURE COVE MARINA Severn R./Spa Creek (301)757-8000	12′	●				●	●	●	●			●	●	●	●	●		●	●	●		All Major Ones	
PORT ANNAPOLIS MARINA Severn R./Back Creek (301)268-2212	10′	●	●	●		●	●	●			●		●			●		●	●	●		M/C VISA Choice	35 Ton Travel Lift
SARLES BOAT & ENGINE SHOP Severn R./Spa Creek/Annapolis (301)263-3661	12′		●	●		●	●						●			●		●	●	●	●	●	
SMITH'S MARINA Severn R./Brown Cove (301)923-3444/987-9370	4′		●			●	●						●	▶	▶	●		●	●	●	●		Amoco

FULL SERVICE MARINA

250 DEEP WATER SLIPS TO 100'LOA

150 HIGH & DRY SPACES

The Newest, Brightest Yacht Club & Marina On The Chesapeake Bay

Conveniently located on the Bay side of the new South River Bridge within walking distance of convenience stores, restaurants, etc...

- Ships Store
- Laundromat
- Club House
- Swimming Pool
- Lounge
- Restaurant
- Snack Bar

LIBERTY YACHT CLUB

ON THE SOUTH RIVER

64 Old South River Road   Edgewater, Maryland 21037

Annapolis-266-5633 • Baltimore-841-5040
Washington, D.C.-261-8595

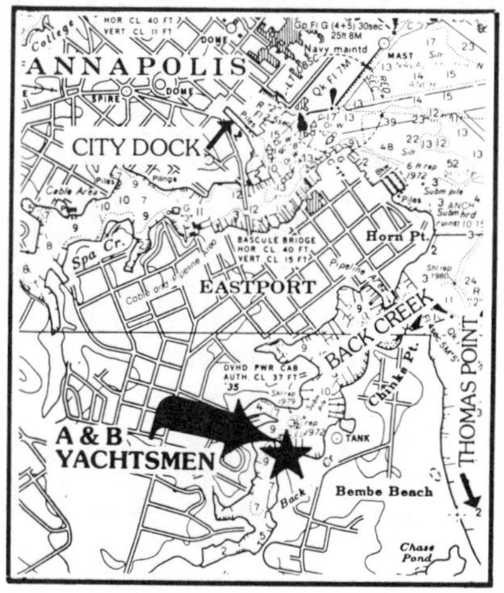

FULL SERVICE

REPAIRS

SLIPS

A&B YACHTSMEN, INC.

7310 EDGEWOOD RD. • ANNAPOLIS • MD 21403

Located On Back Creek, Annapolis, MD At Bert Jabins Yacht Yard

- 2 20 Ton Travelifts
- Deep Water Slips/ Dry Storage
- Fiberglass/Gelcoat Repairs
- Year Round Awlgrip/ Imron Spray Painting
- Carpentry
- Electrical
- Rigging
- Mechanical
- Overland Boat Transport
- Brokerage Boats Displayed

Call Tom Aga, Service Manager, for information, reservations and prices. Free estimates. Open year round, Mon.-Fri., 8AM to 5PM. Supermarket, restaurant, laundry, sailmakers within walking distance. Local taxi service to downtown.

301/263-9073

MARINAS

● ON PREMISES
▶ NEARBY

	WATER DEPTH MLW	OVERNIGHT SLIPS	GAS	DIESEL	PROPANE	ELECTRIC	SHOWERS	LAUNDROMAT	RESTAURANT	MOTEL	POOL	HOLDING TANK PUMPOUT	ICE	BEER	GROCERIES	MARINE SUPPLIES	BAIT	ENGINE REPAIRS	HULL REPAIRS	HAUL-OUT SERVICES	LAUNCH RAMP	*CREDIT CARDS	*OTHER
SCOTT MARINE SERVICE Whitehall Bay (301)974-0545	12′						●		▶	▶			▶	▶	▶	●		●	●	●			
WHITEHALL MARINA & CONDO Whitehall Bay (301)757-2050	10′	●	▶	▶		●	●		▶	▶			●	▶	▶	●	▶	●	●	●	▶		Condo Slip Sales
South River																							
BAY VIEW MARINA South R./Ramsey Bay (301)798-1850																							
LIBERTY YACHT CLUB South R./NE side at bridge (301)266-5633	7′ 6″		●	●		●	●	●	●		●		●	●	●	●		●	●	●		MC VISA	
HOLIDAY POINT MARINA South R./Selby Bay (301)956-5077	6′	5	▶	▶		●	●		▶				▶	▶	▶	Lmtd.		●	●	●			
LONDON TOWNE MARINA South R./Glebe Creek (301)956-5077	6′		●			●	●						●			●		●	●	●	●	●	
MIKE'S REST./CRABHOUSE South River (301)956-2784	20′	●				●			●	▶	▶		●	●	●	●	●				▶	M/C VISA AMEX	
OAK GROVE MARINE CENTER At South River Bridge (301)266-6696	13′	●	●	●		●	●		●				●	●		●		●				Amoco	
PIER 7 At South River Bridge (301)956-2288	8′-12′	●	●	●		●	●		●				●	●		●					●	AMEX M/C VISA Mobil	
SELBY BAY YACHT BASIN South R./Selby Bay (301)798-0232	8′	●	●	●		●	●		▶				●			●		●				●	Boat Sales
TURKEY PT. MARINA South R./Ramsey Bay (301)798-1369	4′	●	●	▶		●	●		▶	▶			●	▶	▶	●	▶	●	▶	●	●	M/C VISA Amoco	
WILKINS YACHT SALES South R./Gingerville Cr. (301)266-8585	5′																	●	●	●		VISA M/C	Hatteras Dealer
Rhode and West Rivers																							
CASA RIO MARINA Rhode R./Cadle Cr. (301)798-4731	5′		▶	▶		●			▶				●			●		●	●	●	●		Boat Sales & Do it Yourself
RHODE RIVER MARINA Rhode R./Bear Neck Creek (301)798-1658	4½′		●	●		●							●			●		●	●	●	●	Mobil M/C VISA	Snacks

● ON PREMISES
▶ NEARBY

Marina	Water Depth MLW	Overnight Slips	Gas	Diesel	Propane	Electric	Showers	Laundromat	Restaurant	Motel	Pool	Holding Tank Pumpout	Ice	Beer	Groceries	Marine Supplies	Bait	Engine Repairs	Hull Repairs	Haul-Out Services	Launch Ramp	*Credit Cards	*Other
BACKYARD BOATS West R./Parish Cr. (301)261-5115	4′		●			●			▶				●	▶	▶	●		●	●	●	●	●	
CADLE CREEK MARINA West River (301)798-1915	6′	●	●	●		●							●		▶	●		▶	●	●		VISA M/C Exxon	
HARTGE YACHT YARD West R./Lerch Cr. (301)867-2188	8′	●	●	●	▶	●	●		▶				●	▶	▶	●		●	●	●			
PIRATE'S COVE West R./Galesville (301)867-2300	12′	●	▶	▶	▶	●	●	▶	●	●	▶	▶	●	●	▶	▶	▶	▶	▶	▶	▶	VISA M/C AMEX	
SHADY OAKS MARINA West River (301)867-0977	5′					●	●	●								●		●	●	●			
SHADY SIDE BOAT YARD West R./Parish Cr. (301)261-5736	4′	●				●										●			●	●	●	VISA M/C	
Herring Bay to Long Beach																							
BERLITZ MARINE Herring Bay/Rockhold Cr. (301)867-2121	5′	●	●			●	●						●			●		●	●	●	●	Gulf VISA M/C	
DEALE MARINA Herring Bay, Rockhold Cr. (301)261-5220	3′		●			●	●		▶									●			●	VISA M/C	
GATES MARINA Herring Bay/Rockhold Cr. (301)867-2157	4′	●	●			●	●	▶	●	●			●	▶	▶	●	▶	●	●	●	●	M/C Phillips 66	Full Service Marina
HERRINGTON HARBOUR Herring Bay (301)741-5100	7′	●	●	●		●	●	●	●	●	●		●	●	●	●		▶				VISA M/C AMEX	Tennis Courts Beach
HERRINGTON HARBOUR NORTH Herring Bay/Rockhold Cr. (301)867-4343	7′	●	●	●		●	●		●				●			●		●	●	●	●	VISA M/C	
MCMASTERS MARINA Herring Bay/Rockhold Cr. (301)261-5257	5′	●	▶	▶		●	●		▶	▶				▶	▶								
SHERMAN'S MARINA Herring Bay/Rockhold Cr. (301)261-5013	8′	●	●	●	▶	●	●	▶	▶				●	▶	▶	●	●	▶	▶	▶	●	VISA M/C Choice	
SHIPWRIGHT HARBOR Herring Bay/Rockhold Cr. (301)867-7686/261-5632	3′	●	▶	▶		●	●	▶	▶				▶	▶	▶		▶	●	●	●		VISA M/C Choice	
FISHING CREEK MARINA Chesapeake Beach (301)855-8351	5½′	●	●	●		●	●		●				●	●	▶	▶	●	▶	▶	▶	▶	VISA M/C	
KELLAM'S MARINA Chesapeake Bay/West Beach (301)257-2701	10′	●	●					▶	▶				●	▶	▶	●	▶	●		●	●		Fishing Tackle

● ON PREMISES
▶ NEARBY

Marina	Water Depth MLW	Overnight Slips	Gas	Diesel	Propane	Electric	Showers	Laundromat	Restaurant	Motel	Pool	Holding Tank Pumpout	Ice	Beer	Groceries	Marine Supplies	Bait	Engine Repairs	Hull Repairs	Haul-Out Services	Launch Ramp	*Credit Cards	*Other
ROD 'N REEL Chesapeake Beach (301)257-2191/855-8351	6′	●	●	●	▶	●	●	▶	●	▶			●	●	▶	▶	●	▶	▶	▶	▶	VISA M/C	
BREEZY POINT Chesapeake Bay/Plum Pt. (301)855-1844	3½′	●	●			●	●		●	●		●	●	●	●	●	●	●	▶		●	Mobil	Netted Swimming Area
FLAG HARBOR MARINA Chesapeake Bay/Long Beach (301)586-0070	7′	●	●	●		●	●	●			●							●	●	●			Tennis Cookout Pavillion
Eastern Bay																							
CRAB ALLEY MARINA Crab Alley Bay/Crab Alley Cr. (301)643-5588	42″					●										●	●	●			●		Rowboat Rental
ISLAND VIEW MARINA Crab Alley Creek (301)643-2842	10′	●	▶		▶	●	●	●	▶	▶			●	▶	▶	▶		●	●	●	●		
Miles River																							
HIGGINS YACHT YARD Miles R./St. Michaels (301)745-9303	9′	●	●	●		●	●						●			●		●	●	●		Exxon	30 Ton Travel Lift
ST. MICHAELS HARBOUR MARINA Miles R./St. Michaels (301)745-9001	3′-10′	●	▶	▶	▶	●	●	●	●	●	●	▶	●	●	●	▶	▶	▶	▶	▶	▶	M/C VISA Choice AMEX	
ST. MICHAELS TOWN DOCK MARINA Miles R./St. Michaels (301)745-2400	9′	●	●	●	▶	●	●	▶	●	▶		●	●	●	▶	▶	▶	●	▶	▶	▶	VISA M/C Choice AMEX	Charters Runabouts Bicycles
Knapps Narrows																							
BAY HUNDRED AT KNAPPS NARROWS MARINA Knapps Narrows (301)886-2622	6′	●	●	●		●			●	▶			●	●	▶	●	●	▶				M/C VISA	
HARRISON'S CHESAPEAKE HOUSE Knapps Narrows (301)886-2123		●	▶	▶	▶	●	▶	▶	●	●	●		●	●	▶	▶	▶	●	●	●	●	M/C VISA Choice	
REESER'S BOATYARD Knapps Narrows (301)886-2166	7′-8′					●			▶	▶	▶		▶	▶	▶	●	▶	●	●	●			
TILGHMAN INN & LODGING Knapps Narrows (301)886-2644		●	●	●		●	●		●	●	●		●	●								Mobil AMEX VISA M/C	Tennis Court Bicycle Rental
Tred Avon River																							
APPLEGARTH'S MARINE YARD Tred Avon R./Oxford (301)226-5170	5′	●				●		▶	▶							●		●	●	●			

● ON PREMISES
▶ NEARBY

Marina	Water Depth MLW	Overnight Slips	Gas	Diesel	Propane	Electric	Showers	Laundromat	Restaurant	Motel	Pool	Holding Tank Pumpout	Ice	Beer	Groceries	Marine Supplies	Bait	Engine Repairs	Hull Repairs	Haul-Out Services	Launch Ramp	*Credit Cards	*Other
BATES MARINE BASIN Tred Avon R./Oxford (301)226-5105	7′	●	●	●	▶	●	●	●	▶	▶			●	▶	▶	●		●	●	●		Texaco M/C VISA AMEX Major Oil	Dockage to 70′/Bicycles
CROCKETT BROS. BOATYARD Tred Avon R./Oxford (301)226-5113	6+′	●	▶	▶	●	●	●	●	▶	▶			●	▶	▶	●		●	●	●		VISA Bank Am. AMEX	CNG
CUTTS AND CASE, WILEY SHIPYARD Tred Avon R./Oxford (301)226-5416	6½′	●				●												●	●	●			
EASTON POINT MARINA Tred Avon R./Easton Pt. (301)822-1201	5′	3	●	●		15 30	●		Carryout	●			●	●	Some	●	●	●	●	●	●		Weaver's Inn Open 7 Days Good Water all the way up
MEARS YACHT HAVEN Tred Avon R./Oxford (301)226-5450	6′	Var.	●	●		●	●	●			●		●									M/C VISA Texaco	Picnic Area
OXFORD BOAT YARD Tred Avon R./Oxford (301)226-5101	12′	●				●	●	●	▶				●		▶	●		●	●	●		M/C VISA	
PIER ST. MARINA Tred Avon R./Oxford (301)226-5411	6′	●	●	●		●	●		●				●	●								●	
TOWN CREEK REST. & MARINA Tred Avon R./Town Cr./Oxford (301)226-5131	8′	●				●			●				●	●								●	
Choptank River																							
CAMBRIDGE MUNICIPAL YACHT BASIN Choptank R./Cambridge (301)228-4031	7′	●	▶			●	●	●	▶				▶	▶	▶			▶	▶	▶	2		Travelers Checks Personal Checks
CAMBRIDGE YACHT CLUB Choptank R./Cambridge (301)228-2141	4′-9′	●	●			●	●	▶	●	▶			●	●	▶	▶	▶	▶	▶	●	●	VISA M/C Choice	Cocktail Lounge
CLAYTON'S Choptank R./Cambridge Cr. (301)228-7200	6′		▶	▶			▶	▶	●				●	●	▶	▶	▶	▶	▶	▶	▶	●	Seafood Mkt. Carry Out
DICKERSON BOATBUILDERS Choptank R./La Trappe Cr. (301)822-8556	6′	●	●	●									●		▶			●	●	●	●		
PHILLIPS HARDWARE & OIL Choptank R./Cambridge (301)228-0690	14′		●	●		●				▶			●	●		●						Choice M/C VISA	
SUICIDE BRIDGE RESTAURANT Choptank R./Cabin Cr. (301)943-4689	4′	●	●			●			●				●	●							●		
YACHT MAINTENANCE CO. Choptank R./Cambridge Cr. (301)228-8878	10′	●	▶	●	▶	●	▶	▶	▶	▶	▶		▶	▶	▶	●	▶	●	●	●		M/C	

MARINAS

● ON PREMISES
▶ NEARBY

Marina	Water Depth MLW	Overnight Slips	Gas	Diesel	Propane	Electric	Showers	Laundromat	Restaurant	Motel	Pool	Holding Tank Pumpout	Ice	Beer	Groceries	Marine Supplies	Bait	Engine Repairs	Hull Repairs	Haul-Out Services	Launch Ramp	* Credit Cards	* Other
Little Choptank River																							
TAYLORS ISLAND MARINA Little Choptank R./Slaughter Cr. (301)397-3454	10′	●	●	●		●	●	●	▶				●	●	▶	●				●		Shell	
Wicomico River																							
PORT OF SALISBURY MARINA Wicomico R./Salisbury (301)548-3176	8′	●	●	●		●	●	●	▶	▶	▶	●	●	▶	▶			▶			▶	M/C VISA AMEX	Shopping Plaza Nearby
Patuxent River																							
BALCO SHELTERED HARBOR MARINE Patuxent R./Lynch Cove (301)288-4100	15′		▶	▶	▶	●	●	▶	▶				●		▶	●		●	●	●		MC VISA	
BENEDICT MARINA Patuxent R./Mill Cr. (301)274-4429	4′	●	●				●		●				●	●		●					●	M/C VISA	
BLACKSTONE MARINA Patuxent R./Cuckhold Creek (301)373-2015	14′		●	●		●	●						●			●		●	●	●			
BOWEN'S INN & MARINA Patuxent R./Back Cr. (301)326-2214		6	●	●		●	●		▶	●			●	●	▶	▶							
BROOMES ISLAND MARINA Patuxent R./Island Creek (301)586-2437	6′					●			●	▶			●		▶	▶	●				●		Boat Storage
CALVERT MARINA Patuxent R./Back Cr. (301)326-4251	12′	●	●	●	▶	●	●	●	●	▶			●	●		●		●	●	●		M/C VISA	
CAPE ST. MARY'S MARINA Patuxent R./Queen Tree Landing (301)373-2001	4½′	●	●	●		●	●		●			●	●	●		●	●	●	●	●	●	Gulf VISA M/C	
DE SOTO'S LANDING MARINA Patuxent R./Benedict (301)274-4301	4′		●						▶				●	▶	▶	●	●	●			●		Evinrude Johnson Outboard
DOCKSIDE Patuxent R./Solomons (301)328-3837	14′	●	●	●	▶	●	●	▶	▶	▶	▶	▶	●	●	●	●	●	▶	▶	▶	●		Liquor
HOME PORT MARINA Patuxent R./Town Creek (703)560-2098	7′					●	●	●															
HARBOR ISLAND MARINA Patuxent R./Solomons (301)326-3441	12′	25	●	●		●	●	▶	●	▶			●	●	▶	●	▶	●	●	●	▶	Gulf VISA M/C	Machine Shop Services
PINE COVE MARINA Patuxent R./Head of Mill Cr./Solomons (301)326-2817	5′	●	●	▶	▶	●	●	▶	▶	▶		▶	●	●	▶	●	▶	●	●	●	●		

● ON PREMISES
▶ NEARBY

Marina	Water Depth MLW	Overnight Slips	Gas	Diesel	Propane	Electric	Showers	Laundromat	Restaurant	Motel	Pool	Holding Tank Pumpout	Ice	Beer	Groceries	Marine Supplies	Bait	Engine Repairs	Hull Repairs	Haul-Out Services	Launch Ramp	*Credit Cards	*Other
SHEPERD'S YACHT YARD Patuxent R./Back Cr./Solomons (301)326-3939	10′	▶	▶	▶	▶	●	▶	▶	▶	▶	▶	▶	▶	▶	▶	●	▶	●	●	●	●	VISA M/C	
SOLOMONS BEACON INN & MARINA Patuxent R./Solomons (301)326-3807	12′	●	▶	▶		●	●	●	●	●	●	▶	●	▶	▶	●	▶	●	●	●	●	M/C VISA	VHF-16 Crane Sail Charter
SOLOMONS MARINE Patuxent R./Solomons (301)326-4258		●	●	●		●	●	▶	▶	▶			●			●		●	●	●		M/C VISA Exxon	
SOLOMONS YACHTING CENTER Patuxent R./Solomons (301)326-2401	12′	●	●	●	▶	●	●	▶	▶	▶	▶	●	●	●	▶	●	●	●	●	●	▶	M/C VISA Amoco Diners	VHF 16 Towing Emer. Repair
SPRING COVE MARINA Patuxent R./Solomons (301)326-2101	12′	20	●	●	▶	●	●	●	●	▶	●	▶	●	▶	●	●	▶	●	●	●	▶	VISA M/C Choice	Picnic Ground/Play Ground
TOWN CREEK MARINA Patuxent R./Town Cr. (301)862-3553		●	●			●			●				●	●			●				●		
WHITE SANDS REST. & MARINA Patuxent R./St. Leonard Cr. (301)586-1182	12′	●	●	●		●	●		●		●		●								●	For Fuel Only	
ZAHNISER'S SAILING CENTER Patuxent R./Solomons (301)326-3311	12′	●	▶	▶	●	●	●	●	●	▶	●	●	●	●	▶	●	▶	●	●	●	▶	M/C VISA Check	Bicycles Charters
Chesapeake Bay St. Jerome Creek																							
DEANS RAILWAY & BOAT RAMP St. Jerome Creek (301)872-5887	4′		●	●		●			▶	▶			●		▶		●	●	●	●	●		200 Boat Storage on Trailer
TROSSBACH MARINE St. Jerome Creek (301)872-5321	5′		●			●	●						●								2		
Potomac River Md. Shore																							
LAKE CONOY SMALL BOAT FACILITY Point Lookout State Park (301)872-5688	7′		●	●								●	●		●	●	●				●		
PT. LOOKOUT MARINA Potomac R./Smith Cr. (301)872-5145	9′	●	●	●	▶	●	●	●	●	▶	●	●	●	●	●	●	▶	●	●	●	▶	MC VISA AMEX Texaco	
AQUA LAND MARINA Potomac R./at 301 Bridge (301)259-2123	5′	●	●	●		●							●	●	●	●	●	●	●	●	●	●	
BRUCE'S MARINA Potomac R./Cobb Neck (301)259-2221		●	●	●		●			●				●	●	●	●	●	●	●	●	●	Texaco MC VISA	
CAPT. JOHN'S CRABHOUSE Potomac R./Neale Sound (301)259-2315	8′	●	●	●		●			●				●	●	●	●	●	▶	▶	▶	●	MC VISA Texaco	

MARINAS

● ON PREMISES
▶ NEARBY

Marina	Water Depth MLW	Overnight Slips	Gas	Diesel	Propane	Electric	Showers	Laundromat	Restaurant	Motel	Pool	Holding Tank Pumpout	Ice	Beer	Groceries	Marine Supplies	Bait	Engine Repairs	Hull Repairs	Haul-Out Services	Launch Ramp	* Credit Cards	* Other
CATHER MARINE Potomac R./St. Patricks Cr. (301)769-3335	6′	●	●	▶		●	●		▶				●	▶	▶	●	●	●	●	●	●	Exxon	VHF Chan. 16
COBB ISLAND MARINA Potomac R./Neale Sound (301)259-2780	12′	●	●	●	●	●	●		●				●	●	●	●	●		●	●		●	
COMB'S CREEK MARINA Potomac R./Breton Bay/Combs Cr. (301)475-2017	9′	●	●			●			▶				●	▶	▶		▶	●	●	●	●	Shell	
DENNIS POINT MARINA Potomac R./St. Mary's/Carthagena Cr. (301)994-2288	11′	5	●	●		●	●	●	●		●	●	●	●	●	●	●	●	●	●	●	●	Campground
DOCK 'O THE BAY MARINA Potomac R./Breton Bay (301)475-3129		●	●	▶	▶	●		▶		▶			●	●	▶	▶	▶	▶	▶	▶	●		
FT. WASHINGTON MARINA Potomac R./Piscataway Cr. (301)292-6200	4.5′	●	●	●	▶	●	▶	▶	●	▶	▶	●	●	●	●	●	●	●	●	●	●	M/C VISA Choice	Sailboat Rental Lessons Boardsail
GOOSE BAY MARINA Potomac R./Port Tobacco/Goose Cr. (301)934-3812	3½′-4′	●	●				●					●	●		●	●	●	●	●	●	●	Texaco	
HARBOR VIEW INN Potomac R./Breton Bay (301)475-9432	8′-10′	●	●			●			●				●	●			▶	▶	▶	▶			
KOPEL'S MARINA Potomac R./Colton Pt. (301)769-3121	5′	●	●	●	●	●	●						●	●	●	●	●	●	●	●	●	●	
OAKWOOD LODGE Potomac R./Piney Pt. (301)994-2271	6′	8				●			●				●	●									Rooms W/Bath
PORT TOBACCO CAMPGROUND Potomac R./Port Tobacco R. (301)934-9707	5′		●			●	●	▶	▶	▶		●	●	▶	▶	▶	●			●	●		
PORT TOBACCO MARINA Potomac R./Port Tobacco R. (301)932-1407	4½′		●	●	●	●	●	●	●	●			●	●	●	●	●	●	●	●	●	●	
QUADE'S STORE Potomac R./Wicomico R. (301)769-3903			●						●				●	●	●		●				●		
ROBERTSON CRABHOUSE Potomac R./Popes Cr. (301)934-9236	4′								●				●	●									
SAUNDERS MARINE Potomac R./Cobb Neck (301)259-2309	4′	●				●			▶						▶			●	●	●	●		
SCHEIBLE FISHING CENTER Potomac R./Smith Cr. (301)872-5185	6′	▶	●	●					●	●			●	●	●		●						
SWANN'S PIER Potomac R./St. George Cr. (301)994-0774	8′	●	●	●	●	●							●	●	●	●	●					Texaco	

● ON PREMISES
▶ NEARBY

Marina	WATER DEPTH MLW	OVERNIGHT SLIPS	GAS	DIESEL	PROPANE	ELECTRIC	SHOWERS	LAUNDROMAT	RESTAURANT	MOTEL	POOL	HOLDING TANK PUMPOUT	ICE	BEER	GROCERIES	MARINE SUPPLIES	BAIT	ENGINE REPAIRS	HULL REPAIRS	HAUL-OUT SERVICES	LAUNCH RAMP	*CREDIT CARDS	*OTHER
TALL TIMBERS VACATION CLUB Potomac R./Herring Cr. (301)994-1508	6′	●	●	●		●	●		●		●		●	●	●	●		●	●	●	●	VISA M/C Gulf	
Washington Area																							
ANACOSTIA MARINA Anacostia R. (202)544-5191	6′	●	▶	▶		●	●	▶	▶	▶	▶		▶	●	▶	●		●	●	●	▶	VISA M/C	
CAPITAL YACHT CLUB Potomac R./Washington, D.C. (202)554-3059	25′	●	▶	▶	▶	●	●	●	▶	▶	▶		▶	▶	▶	▶	▶	▶	▶	▶	▶	●	
COLUMBIA ISLAND MARINA Potomac R./Pentagon Lagoon (202)347-0173	5′	●	●			●	●		●			●	●	●		●	●				●	●	
FT. MCNAIR YACHT BASIN Anacostia River (202)554-8844	9′	●	▶	▶	▶	●	●	▶	▶	▶	▶	▶	●	▶	▶	▶	▶	▶	▶	●	●		
GANGPLANK MARINA Washington Channel (202)554-5000		●		▶		●	●	●	●	●		●	●	▶	▶	▶		▶	▶	▶	▶	●	
SAFFORD MARINE Anacostia River (301)779-4133	3′		●													●		●	●	●	●	●	
WASHINGTON MARINA Potomac R./Washington, D.C. (202)554-0222	10′			●		●	●	▶	▶	▶				▶	▶	●		●	●	●	●	VISA M/C Choice	Elevator
Potomac River Va. Shore & Little Wicomico River																							
AQUIA CREEK MARINA Potomac R./Aquia Cr. (703)659-2745	4′ -8′	●	●	●		●	●	▶	▶			●	●	▶	▶	●	●	●	●	●	●		
BAY YACHT CENTER Potomac R./Monroe Bay/Colonial Bch. (804)224-7230	10′	●	●	●		●	●		▶	▶		●	●	●	●	●	●		●	●	●	M/C VISA Major Oil Co.	
BRANSON'S COVE MARINA Potomac R./Lower Machodoc Cr. (804)472-3866	8′	●	●	●		●	●		▶				●	●	●	●	●		▶	▶	●	Major Cards For Petro Prod.	
COAN RIVER MARINA Potomac R./Coan R. (804)529-6767	7′		●	●								●	●						●	●	●	M/C VISA	
COLES PT. MARINA Potomac R./Coles Neck (804)472-2240	5′	●	▶	▶	▶	●	●	●	▶	▶	▶	▶	●	●	●	●	●	▶	▶	●	●		Clubhouse
E-Z CRUZ, INC. Potomac R./Neabsco Cr. (703)670-8115	2½′	●	●			●	●		▶			▶	●	▶		●		●	●	●	●	M/C VISA	Service w/a smile
HOFFMASTER'S MARINA Potomac R./Occoquan River (703)494-7161	12′		●	●		●	●					●	●	●	●	●		●	●	●		●	

MARINAS

● ON PREMISES
▶ NEARBY

	WATER DEPTH MLW	OVERNIGHT SLIPS	GAS	DIESEL	PROPANE	ELECTRIC	SHOWERS	LAUNDROMAT	RESTAURANT	MOTEL	POOL	HOLDING TANK PUMPOUT	ICE	BEER	GROCERIES	MARINE SUPPLIES	BAIT	ENGINE REPAIRS	HULL REPAIRS	HAUL-OUT SERVICES	LAUNCH RAMP	*CREDIT CARDS	*OTHER
KINSALE HARBOR MARINA Potomac R./W. Yeocomico R. (804)472-2514	11′	15	●	●	▶	●	●	●	●	●	●	●	●	●	●	●	●	●	●		●	VISA	Tennis/Golf NB-Sail & Power Charter Available
KRENTZ MARINE RAILWAY Potomac R./Yeocomico River (804)529-6800	10′	●	●	●	●	●	●		▶	▶			●	▶	▶			●	●	●		Texaco	Trans. to Supermarket 3 mi.
LEWISETTA MARINA Potomac R./Travis Pt. (804)529-6267	8′	2	●	●		●							●	●	●		●				●		Snackbar
NIGHTINGALE MARINA Potomac R./Monroe Cr./Colonial Bch. (804)224-7956	6′	●	▶	▶	▶	●		▶	▶	●	▶	▶	▶	▶	▶	▶	▶	▶	▶	▶	▶		
OLVERSON'S MARINE INC. Potomac R./Yeocomico/Lodge Cr. (804)529-6868	10′	●	●	●	▶	●	●	▶	▶	▶	▶	▶	●	▶	▶	▶	▶	▶	▶	▶	●	●	150 slips
OUTDOOR WORLD/HARBOR VIEW YACHT CLUB Potomac R./Mattox Creek (804)224-8164	6′	●	●	●	●	●	●	●			●	●	●	●	●	●	●				●	AMEX M/C VISA Texaco	Tennis Courts
PILOT HOUSE REST. & MARINA Potomac R./Neabsco Cr. (703)221-1010	5′	●	●			●	●		●				●	●				●	●	●	●	All	
RAGGED PT. HARBOR Potomac R./Ragged Point (804)472-3955	4′-4½′	●	●	●	●	●	●	●	●	●	●	●	●	●	●	●	●	●			●	Shell M/C	
SANDY POINT MARINA Potomac R./Yeocomico/NW Branch (804)472-3237	6′		●	●		●			5 mi.			●	●	●	▶		●		▶	●	●		
STANFORD MARINE RLWY. Potomac R./Monroe Bay/Colonial Bch. (804)224-7644	7′	●	●	●		●	●						●			●		●	●	●		Gulf	
WAUGH PT. MARINE BASIN Potomac R./Potomac Cr. (703)775-7121	2½′		●						▶				●			●		●	●	●	●	Shell	
WHITE POINT MARINA Potomac R./Yeocomico/White Pt. Cr. (804)472-2977	9′	●	●	●	▶	●	●	▶	▶	▶	●		●	▶	▶	●	▶	●	●	●	▶	VISA M/C Shell	Tennis Courts Ch. 16
YEOCOMICO MARINA Potomac R./Yeocomico River (804)472-2971	7′	20	●	●	●	●	●	●	●	●	●	●	●	●	●	●	●	●	●	●	●	Texaco All Major	
COCKRELL'S MARINE RLWY. Little Wicomico River (804)453-3560	5′	●	●			●										●		●	●	●	●		
SMITH POINT MARINA Little Wicomico River (804)453-4077	5′	●	●	●	●	●	●	●	▶	▶		●	●	●	▶	▶	●	●	●	●	●	●	Campground
Smith and Tangier Crisfield and Onancock																							
ESSEX SEAFOOD INC. Tangier Sound/Deal Island (301)651-0282	6′	●	●	●		●							●		●	●	●	●			▶		

● ON PREMISES
▶ NEARBY

	WATER DEPTH MLW	OVERNIGHT SLIPS	GAS	DIESEL	PROPANE	ELECTRIC	SHOWERS	LAUNDROMAT	RESTAURANT	MOTEL	POOL	HOLDING TANK PUMPOUT	ICE	BEER	GROCERIES	MARINE SUPPLIES	BAIT	ENGINE REPAIRS	HULL REPAIRS	HAUL-OUT SERVICES	LAUNCH RAMP	*CREDIT CARDS	*OTHER
SCOTTS COVE MARINA Tangier Sound (301)784-2363	3½′		●	●		●							●			●		●		●			
SOMERS COVE MARINA Little Annemessex River (301)968-0925	10′	●	●	●	▶	●	●	●	▶	▶	●	●	●	▶	▶	▶	▶	▶	▶	▶	●	Oil Co. Cards VISA M/C	
Pocomoke River																							
SHAD LANDING MARINA Pocomoke R. (301)632-2566	7′	●	●		▶	●	●	▶	▶	▶	●	●	●	▶	●	▶	▶				●	Exxon	
Great Wicomico and Va.'s Northern Neck																							
CHESAPEAKE BOAT BASIN Northern Neck/Indian Creek (804)435-3110	13′	4	●	●	▶	●	●	▶	▶	▶	▶		●	●	●	●	▶	●	●	●	●	M/C VISA Exxon	
RAPPAHANNOCK OYSTER CO. Northern Neck/Indian Cr. (804)435-1605	8′	●	●	●		●							●	●	●	●	●					M/C VISA	
BUZZARD'S POINT MARINA Great Wicomico R./Cockrell Cr. (804)453-3545	10′	●	●	●		●	●		▶	▶			●			●	●	●	Small Boats			Texaco	
GREAT WICOMICO MARINA Great Wicomico River (804)453-3351	10′	●	●		●	●	●	●	●				●	●			●				●		
INGRAM BAY MARINA Great Wicomico R./Ingram Bay (804)580-7292	7′	●	●	●	▶	●	●	●	▶	▶		●	●	▶	▶	●	▶	●	▶	▶	●	Citco For Gas	Sailboat Rentals Sailing School Camping
JENNINGS BOATYARD Great Wicomico R./Cockrell Cr. (804)453-7181	15′	●				●	●									●		●	●	●	●		
TIFFANY YACHTS Great Wicomico River (804)453-3464	12′	●	●	●		●							●		▶	●	▶	●	●	●	▶	Texaco	
Rappahannock and Corrotoman Rivers																							
BURRELL'S MARINA Rappahannock R./Robinson Cr. (804)758-5016	4′		●			●			●				●		●	●	●	●	●	●	●	M/C VISA	
CHESAPEAKE COVE MARINA Rappahannock R./Broad Cr. (804)776-6855	5′	●	●	●	▶	●	●	▶	▶	▶	▶	●	●	▶	●	●	●	●	●	●	▶		New Owners
DELTAVILLE DOCKSIDE INN Rappahannock R./Broad Creek (804)776-9224	6′	●	▶	▶	▶	●	●	●	▶	●	●	●	●	▶	▶	▶	▶	▶	▶	▶	●	VISA M/C	
DOZIER'S DOCKYARD Rappahannock R./Broad Creek (804)776-6711	6′	10	●		●	30	●	●	▶	▶	●		●			●		●	●	●		M/C VISA	Full Service Marina

● ON PREMISES
▶ NEARBY

Marina	Water Depth MLW	Overnight Slips	Gas	Diesel	Propane	Electric	Showers	Laundromat	Restaurant	Motel	Pool	Holding Tank Pumpout	Ice	Beer	Groceries	Marine Supplies	Bait	Engine Repairs	Hull Repairs	Haul-Out Services	Launch Ramp	*Credit Cards	*Other
GARRETT'S MARINA Rappahannock R./Bowlers Wharf (804)443-2573		●	●			●	●						●		●	●	●	●	Lmtd.	●	●	●	
GREENVALE CREEK MARINA Rappahannock R./Greenvale (804)462-7350	8′		●	●		●							●	●	●	●	●	●		●	●	●	
THE HAVEN MARINA Rappahannock R./Tappahannock (804)443-3738	7′	●	●	▶	▶	●		▶	●	●			▶	▶	▶		▶						
IRVINGTON MARINA Rappahannock R./Carter Creek (804)438-5113	10′	3	●	●		●	●	▶	▶	▶			●	▶	▶	●		●	●	●	●	Gulf	
J&M MARINA Rappahannock R./Broad Creek (804)776-6751	6′	3	●	▶	▶	●	●	▶	▶	▶	▶	●	●	▶	▶	●	●	●	●	●	▶	Exxon M/C VISA	Courtesy Car
JAMISON'S COVE MARINA Rappahannock R./Locklies Creek (804)758-4502	12′	5	▶	▶	▶	●	●	▶	●	▶	▶	▶	▶	▶	▶	▶	▶		▶	▶	▶	M/C VISA	
LOCKLIES MARINA Rappahannock R./Locklies Creek (804)758-2871	6′	●	●	●		●				▶		●	●	●	●	●	●				●		
MILLER'S MARINE RAILWAY Rappahannock R./Broad Creek (804)776-9662	6′					●												●	●	●	●		
NORTON'S MARINA Rappahannock R./Broad Creek (804)776-9211	6′	●	●	●		●	●					●	●			●		●	●	●	●	VISA M/C	
NORVIEW MARINA Rappahannock R./Broad Creek (804)776-6463	6′	15	●	●		●	●	●	▶	▶		●				●	●	●	●	●	●	VISA Amoco M/C	
RAPPAHANNOCK YACHTS Rappahannock R./Carter Creek (804)438-5353	6′		●	●		●	●		▶	▶		●	●			●		●	●	●		●	
REGENT POINT MARINA Rappahannock R./Locklies Creek (804)758-4457	6′	●				●	●					●											
REMLIK MARINE SERVICE Rappahannock R./La Grange Creek (804)758-5450	3′		●			●	●						●		▶	●		●	●	●	●		
SOUTHERN CHESAPEAKE YACHT SERVICES Rappahannock R./Carter Creek (804)438-5150	7′					●						●				●		●	●	●		All Major & Choice	
SOUTHSIDE MARINE SERVICE Rappahannock R./Urbanna Creek (804)758-2331	9′	●	▶	▶	▶	●	●	▶	▶	▶		▶	▶	▶	▶	●	▶	●	●	●	▶		
THE TIDES INN Rappahannock R./Carter Creek (804)438-5000	10′	20	●	●	▶	110 & 220	●	●	●	●	●	●	●	●	▶	▶	▶	▶	▶	▶	▶	VISA Exxon M/C	Golf
THE TIDES LODGE Rappahannock R./Carter Creek (804)438-6000	6′	●	●	●	▶	220	●	●	●	●	●	●	●	●	●	●	▶	▶	▶	▶	▶	Exxon	Resort

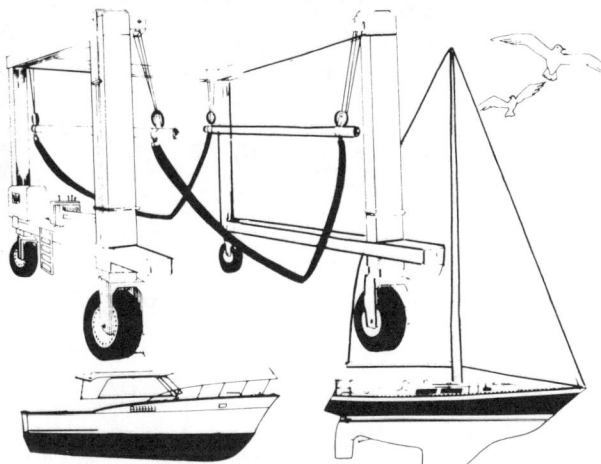

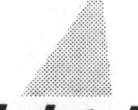

Deltaville Diesel Co., Inc.

Authorized Dealer For:

VOLVO PENTA

DETROIT DIESEL ALLISON

Onan GENERATORS

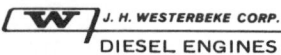

J. H. WESTERBEKE CORP. DIESEL ENGINES

FACTORY TRAINED PERSONNEL WILL SERVE YOU AT ALL AREA MARINE FACILITIES.

(804)776-6331

HENRY LACKEY DELTAVILLE, VIRGINIA 23043

Irvington Marina, Inc.

on Carter's Creek (next to the Tides Inn)

VOLVO PENTA

merCruiser

PERKINS DIESEL

• Full Service Marina • Repairs • Travelift • Marine Supplies • Covered Slips • NOS Charts • Mercruiser & Volvo Sales & Service • New & Used Sail & Motor Boats

MASTS & RIGGING

MEMBER

A. Wylie, Irvington,Va. 22480 804/438-5113

Norton's Marina, Inc.

Broad Creek, Deltaville, Va.

AWLGRIP & IMRON PAINTING

CHRYSLER Marine — Chrysler Marine Engines

a full service marina

Complete hull repairs for power & sail yachts up to 65′

EXXON GAS & DIESEL

PARTS & SERVICE FOR CHRYSLER & WESTERBEKE MARINE ENGINES

40 TON MARINE LIFT

50 TON MARINE RAILWAY

HUNTER

call: 804/776-9211

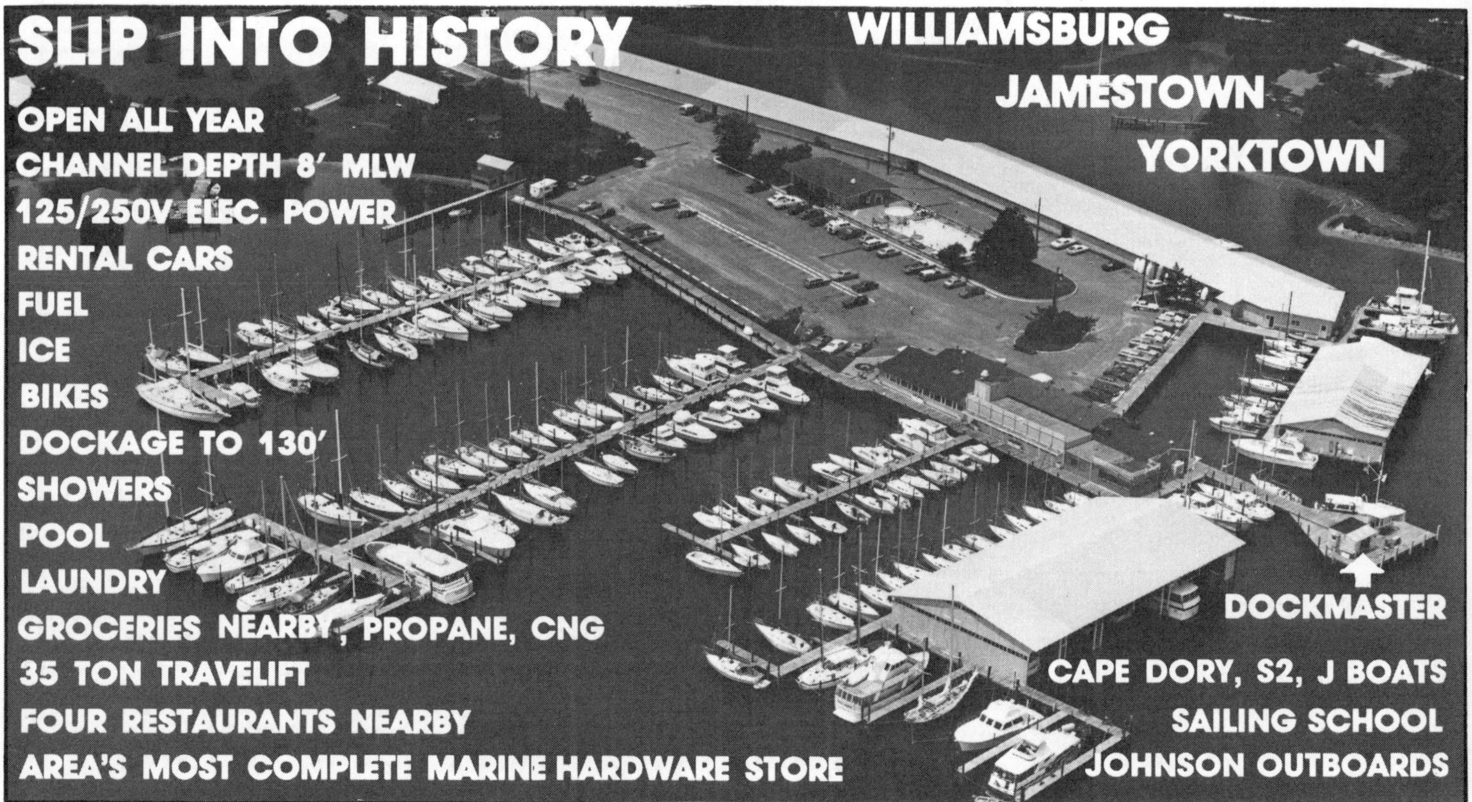

york river yacht haven

BOX 296 • GLOUCESTER POINT, VIRGINIA • 23062
VHF CHANNEL 16 • RESERVATIONS • (804) 642-2156

● ON PREMISES
▶ NEARBY

	WATER DEPTH MLW	OVERNIGHT SLIPS	GAS	DIESEL	PROPANE	ELECTRIC	SHOWERS	LAUNDROMAT	RESTAURANT	MOTEL	POOL	HOLDING TANK PUMPOUT	ICE	BEER	GROCERIES	MARINE SUPPLIES	BAIT	ENGINE REPAIRS	HULL REPAIRS	HAUL-OUT SERVICES	LAUNCH RAMP	*CREDIT CARDS	*OTHER
URBANNA MARINE CORPS. Rappahannock R./Urbanna Creek (804)758-4180	12′	5	●	●	▶	●	●	▶	▶	▶		●	●	▶	▶	●	▶	▶	●	●	●	M/C VISA	
WALDENS MARINA Rappahannock R./Broad Creek (804)776-9440	10′	●	●	●	▶	●	●	▶	▶	▶	▶	●	●	●	●	●	●	●	●	●	●	●	
WINDMILL POINT RESORT Mouth of Rappahannock River (804)435-1166	7′	●	●	●		●	●	●	●	●	●	●	●	●	▶	●		▶	▶	▶	●	●	Golf Tennis
YANKEE PT. SAILBOAT MARINA Rappahannock R./Corrotoman R./ Myer Creek (804)462-5627/462-7018	8′	●	●	●		●	●						●			●		●	●	●		●	
Piankatank River and Horn Harbor																							
DEAGLES MARINA Piankatank R./Fishing Bay (804)776-6911/776-9535	9′	●	●	●		●	●	▶	▶				●	●	●	●		●	●	●		VISA M/C Exxon	Trans. Avail. to Rest. & Motel
DELTAVILLE MARINA Piankatank R./Fishing Bay (804)776-9633	8′	●	●	●	▶	●	●	●	▶	▶		●	●	●	●	●	▶	●	●	●	▶	●	
GINNEY POINT MARINA Piankatank R./Cobbs Creek (804)725-4040	6′					●	●													●			
NARROWS MARINA Piankatank R./Gwynn's Island (804)725-2151	6′	●	●	●		●	●	●	●	●	●		●	●	▶	●	▶	●	●	●	▶	●	Tennis Courts Play Yard
PORPOISE COVE MARINA Entrance to Piankatank R. (804)776-7606	6′	●	●	▶	▶	●	●	▶	▶	▶	●	●	●	▶	▶	▶	▶	●	●	●		Exxon	
RUARK MARINA Piankatank R./Fishing Bay (804)776-9776	4′-16′	●				●	●						●										
HORN HARBOR MARINA & BOATYARD-Horn Harbor, North of Mobjack Bay-(804)725-3223	6′	●	●	●	▶	●	●	●	▶				●			●		●	●	●	●	Major Gas	
Mobjack Bay																							
GLASS MARINE, INC., Mobjack Bay/SW Branch of Severn R. (804)642-2800	6′	●	●	●		●							●			●		●	●	●			Boat Builder
HOLIDAY MARINA Mobjack Bay/Severn R. (804)642-2528	6′	2	●	●	▶	●	●	▶	▶	▶			●		▶	●	●	●	●	●	●	VISA M/C Mobil	
MOBJACK BAY MARINA Mobjack Bay/North River (804)725-7559	6′	●	●	●		●	●						●			●				●	●		
ZIMMERMAN MARINE Mobjack Bay/East River (804)725-3440	4′																	●	●	●			Repair Yard

MARINAS

● ON PREMISES
▶ NEARBY

	WATER DEPTH MLW	OVERNIGHT SLIPS	GAS	DIESEL	PROPANE	ELECTRIC	SHOWERS	LAUNDROMAT	RESTAURANT	MOTEL	POOL	HOLDING TANK PUMPOUT	ICE	BEER	GROCERIES	MARINE SUPPLIES	BAIT	ENGINE REPAIRS	HULL REPAIRS	HAUL-OUT SERVICES	LAUNCH RAMP	*CREDIT CARDS	*OTHER
York River																							
COOK'S LANDING MARINA York R./Perrin River (804)877-3104/604-6177	7′	●	●	●	▶	●	●	▶	▶	▶	●	●	●	●	●	●		●	●	●	●	VISA M/C	Playground
GLOUCESTER POINT MARINA York R./Sarah Creek (804)642-6156	4′	●	●			●	●						●			●	●	●		●	●	M/C VISA	
WORMLEY CREEK MARINA York R./Wormley Creek (804)898-5060	6′	●	●	●		●	●					●	●			●			●	●			
YORK RIVER YACHT HAVEN York R./Sarah Creek (804)642-2156	8′	●	●	●	▶	●	●	●	▶	▶	●	●	●	●	▶	●	▶	●	●	●	▶	M/C VISA AMEX	Courtesy Car & Rental Cars
Poquoson River																							
AL HARTZ MARINA Poquoson R./White House Cove (804)868-6821	5′	●	▶	▶		●	●					▶	●		▶		●		▶	▶	▶		
MILLS MARINA Poquoson R./Tue Pt./Goodwin Island Back Cr. (804)898-4411	6′	●	●	●		●							●	●	●	●					●		
POQUOSON MARINA INC. Poquoson R./Bennett Creek (804)868-6171	6′	●	●	●	▶	●	●	▶	●	▶	▶	▶	●	●	▶	▶	●	▶	▶	▶	●		
YORK HAVEN MARINA, INC. Poquoson R./Bennett Creek (804)808-7829	9′	●	▶	▶	▶	●			▶			●	▶	▶	▶	●	▶	●	●	●	▶		
SMITH'S MARINE RAILWAY Poquoson R./Chisman Creek (804)898-8736	10′					●	●									●			●	●			
THOMAS MARINA Poquoson R./Chisman Creek (804)898-6839	3′	●	▶			●			▶			▶	▶	▶		▶	▶	▶	▶	▶	●		
Hampton																							
BLUEWATER YACHT SALES Hampton Rds./Hampton Creek (804)723-0795	6′	4				50										●		●	●	●	●	●	
HAMPTON ROADS MARINA Hampton R./Sunset Creek (804)723-6517	6½′	●	▶	▶	▶	●	●	▶	▶			●	●	▶	▶	●	▶	●	●	●			
JOYS MARINA Hampton Roads/Hampton Creek (804)851-1550	6′	●	▶	▶	▶	●	●						▶	▶	▶								
SUNSET YACHTING CENTER Hampton R./Sunset Creek (804)722-3325			●	●					▶				●	●	●	●	●	●	●	●	▶	●	

● ON PREMISES
▶ NEARBY

Marina	WATER DEPTH MLW	OVERNIGHT SLIPS	GAS	DIESEL	PROPANE	ELECTRIC	SHOWERS	LAUNDROMAT	RESTAURANT	MOTEL	POOL	HOLDING TANK PUMPOUT	ICE	BEER	GROCERIES	MARINE SUPPLIES	BAIT	ENGINE REPAIRS	HULL REPAIRS	HAUL-OUT SERVICES	LAUNCH RAMP	*CREDIT CARDS	*OTHER
Back River																							
DANDY HAVEN MARINA Back River (804)851-1573	5½'		●															●	●	●		●	
FOXHILL MARINA Back R./Wallace Creek (804)850-2772	5'	●	●			●	●	▶	▶	▶			●	●	●	●	●	●			Free	Cash	Fish House Next Door Fresh Seafood
Willoughby Bay																							
REBEL MARINE SERVICE NW Corner Willoughby Bay (804)588-6022	7'	2	▶	▶		●	●	▶	▶	▶	▶	▶	●	▶	▶	▶	▶	▶	▶	▶	▶	●	Library
WILLOUGHBY BAY MARINA Willoughby Spit (804)588-2663	8'	●	●	●		●	●	▶	▶	▶			●	●	▶	●	●	●	●	●	●	M/C VISA Major Gas Co.	
WILLOUGHBY HARBOR MARINA Willoughby Bay (804)583-4150	8'	●				●	●	●	▶	▶	▶		●										
Elizabeth River Western Branch																							
LEE'S YACHT HARBOR Elizabeth R./Western Branch (804)484-2652	14'	●	●	●		●	●		▶				●			●	●	●	●	●		●	
PRITCHARD MARINE RAILWAY Elizabeth R./Scott's Creek (804)393-2632	5'	●				●			●					●				●	●	●			
TIDEWATER YACHT MARINA, INC. Elizabeth R./Buoy #1 (804)393-2525	6'	●	●	●		●	●	●	●	●		●	●	●	●	●		●	●	●		M/C VISA AMEX Texaco	
VIRGINIA BOAT & YACHT SERVICE Elizabeth R./Western Branch (804)484-0308	12'	●			●	●	●	●	●			●	●					●	●	●			
WATERSIDE MARINA Norfolk (804)441-2222	18'	45				●			●			●	▶	▶	▶							VISA M/C	
James River																							
COLONIAL HARBOR James R./Chickahominy R. (804)966-5523	8'	5	●										●	●	●	●		●	●	●	●	Philips M/C Bank Am	
JAMES RIVER MARINA James R./Deep Creek (804)599-5921	8'	5	●	●		●	●		●			▶	●	●		●	●	●	●		●		
JAMESTOWN YACHT BASIN James R./Deep Creek (804)599-5921	14'	●	●	●		●	●		●			▶	●			●	●	●	●	●			

MARINAS

● ON PREMISES
▶ NEARBY

Marina	Water Depth MLW	Overnight Slips	Gas	Diesel	Propane	Electric	Showers	Laundromat	Restaurant	Motel	Pool	Holding Tank Pumpout	Ice	Beer	Groceries	Marine Supplies	Bait	Engine Repairs	Hull Repairs	Haul-Out Services	Launch Ramp	*Credit Cards	*Other
JORDON POINT YACHT HAVEN James R./Jordon Point (804)458-3398	5½′	●	●	●		●	●	●	▶				●	●	●	●		●			●	Texaco	
KINGSMILL REST. & MARINA James River (below Jamestown Is.) (804)253-3919	6′	●	▶	▶	▶	●	●	▶	●	●		●	●	▶	▶	▶	▶	▶	▶		●	VISA AMEX M/C	36 Holes of Golf 12 Tennis Courts Busch Gardens Theme
MENCHVILLE MARINE SUPPLY James R./Deep Creek (804)877-0207	11′	▶						▶	▶	▶	▶	●	●	●	●	●	●	▶	▶	▶	●	Texaco VISA M/C AMEX	
RESCUE MARINA James R./Jones Creek (804)357-4842			●	●					●				●	●		●	●				●	Gulf	
SMITHFIELD STATION James R./Pagan River (804)357-7700/357-3176	7′	●	▶	▶	▶	●	●	●	●	●		●	●	●	▶	▶	▶	▶	▶	▶	▶	Major	
Lynnhaven Inlet and Little Creek																							
LYNNHAVEN MUNICIPAL MARINA Lynnhaven Bay (804)481-7137	8′	●	●	●		●			▶	▶		●	●	●	●	●	●					M/C VISA Choice	
BAY MARINA INC. Chesapeake Channel/Little Creek (804)583-9502	6′	●	●	●	▶	●	●	▶	▶	▶			●	●	●	●	●	●	●	●	▶	●	
COBBS MARINA Chesapeake Channel/Little Creek (804)588-5401	8′	●	●	●	▶	●	●	▶	▶	▶		▶	●	●	▶	●	●	●	●	●	●	Philips 66 VISA M/C	
CUTTY SARK MARINA, INC. Chesapeake Channel/Little Creek (804)480-2942	5′	●	●	●		●	●		●	▶			●	●	▶	●	●	▶	●	●	▶	VISA Choice M/C	
TAYLOR'S LANDING MARINA Chesapeake Channel/Little Creek (804)587-3480	7′	●	●	●	▶	●	●	▶	●	▶	●	●	●	▶	▶	▶	▶	▶	▶	▶	▶		
Cape Charles Kings Creek																							
CAPE CHARLES CITY MARINA Cape Charles (804)331-3789		●	●			●																	
KINGS CREEK MARINA Kings Creek/Cape Charles (804)331-2058		●	●	●		●	●	▶	▶	▶			●	●	▶	●	●			●	●	●	

INDEX

Rivers, Creeks, Anchorages, Towns and Points of Interest

TIDAL DIFFERENCES

Apply the following averaged corrections to the **Baltimore** tide tables:

	hr.	min.
Point Lookout	-5	31
Patuxent River, Solomons	-4	48
Cove Point	-4	16
Sharps Island Light	-3	49
Choptank R., Cambridge	-2	42
Choptank R. Light	-3	10
Herring Bay, Rose Haven	-2	48
West R., Galesville	-1	43
Thomas Point Light	-2	10
Kent Is. Narrows	-1	34
Severn R., Annapolis	-1	43
Sandy Point	-1	23
Bloody Pt. Bar Light	-2	43
Chester R., Love Point	-0	28
Swan Cr., Deep Lndg.	-0	08
Fairlee Cr. Entrance	+0	52
Worton Cr. Entrance	+1	12
Sassafras R., Betterton	+2	24
Gunpowder R. Battery Pt.	+1	07
Elk R. Town Pt. Wharf	+3	08
Havre de Grace	+3	21

Apply the following corrections to the **Washington** tide tables (Potomac River):

	hr.	min.
Cornfield Harbor, Md.	-6	59
Yeocomico River, Kinsale Virginia	-6	25
St. Mary's R., Kitt Pt.	-6	56
Coltons Point, Md.	-6	05
Colonial Beach, Va.	-5	54
Port Tobacco R., Goose Bay	4	40
Aquia Creek, Va.	2	06
Mattawoman Cr., Md., Deep Point	-1	25
Occoquan Bay, Va., High Pt.	1	15
Fort Washington, Md.	-0	19

All times given are Eastern Standard Time; add one hour for Daylight Savings Time.

To find actual depth of water at a given time, add the height of the tide to the charted depth. If the height of the tide is negative—has a (-) sign before the tabular height—it should be subtracted from the charted depth.

Apply the following corrections to the **Hampton Roads** tide tables:

	hr.	min.
Stingray Pt.	+1	16
Windmill Pt. Light	+1	57
Tangier Sound Light	+2	54
Great Wicomico R. Lt.	+3	02
Smith Pt. Light	+3	30
Little Annemessex, Crisfield	+3	55
Smith Is., Ewell	+4	13
Corrotoman R., Millenbeck	+2	46
Rappahannock River, Urbanna	+2	54
Rappahannock River, Bowlers Rock	+4	06
Tappahannock	+4	54
Onancock, Onancock Cr.	+3	05
Piankatank River, Jackson Creek	+1	45
Wolftrap Light H	-0	07
Wolftrap Light L	+0	27
York Spit Lt.	0	13
Pagan R., Smithfield	+1	26

TIDE TABLES

BALTIMORE, MD., 1987

Times and Heights of High and Low Waters

MAY

Day	Time h m	Height ft	Height m	Day	Time h m	Height ft	Height m
1	0203	0.0	0.0	16	0148	0.0	0.0
F	0908	1.5	0.5	Sa	0858	1.8	0.5
	1601	0.3	0.1		1556	0.2	0.1
	2103	0.7	0.2		2106	0.8	0.2
2	0242	0.1	0.0	17	0243	0.0	0.0
Sa	0950	1.4	0.4	Su	0949	1.7	0.5
	1643	0.3	0.1		1648	0.2	0.1
	2148	0.7	0.2		2211	0.8	0.2
3	0330	0.2	0.1	18	0345	0.1	0.0
Su	1036	1.3	0.4	M	1045	1.6	0.5
	1726	0.3	0.1		1742	0.2	0.1
	2243	0.8	0.2		2321	0.9	0.3
4	0424	0.3	0.1	19	0456	0.2	0.1
M	1122	1.2	0.4	Tu	1148	1.5	0.5
	1814	0.3	0.1		1835	0.2	0.1
	2350	0.8	0.2				
5	0528	0.3	0.1	20	0034	1.0	0.3
Tu	1215	1.1	0.3	W	0620	0.3	0.1
	1859	0.3	0.1		1249	1.3	0.4
					1924	0.2	0.1
6	0054	0.9	0.3	21	0143	1.2	0.4
W	0642	0.4	0.1	Th	0743	0.3	0.1
	1311	1.1	0.3		1348	1.2	0.4
	1945	0.3	0.1		2013	0.2	0.1
7	0157	1.0	0.3	22	0245	1.3	0.4
Th	0756	0.4	0.1	F	0904	0.3	0.1
	1404	1.0	0.3		1451	1.1	0.3
	2025	0.2	0.1		2058	0.1	0.0
8	0254	1.1	0.3	23	0341	1.5	0.5
F	0903	0.4	0.1	Sa	1016	0.3	0.1
	1454	1.0	0.3		1546	1.0	0.3
	2107	0.2	0.1		2138	0.1	0.0
9	0341	1.2	0.4	24	0433	1.6	0.5
Sa	1003	0.3	0.1	Su	1121	0.3	0.1
	1543	1.0	0.3		1635	0.9	0.3
	2143	0.1	0.0		2215	0.1	0.0
10	0426	1.4	0.4	25	0522	1.7	0.5
Su	1056	0.3	0.1	M	1215	0.3	0.1
	1625	0.9	0.3		1721	0.8	0.2
	2215	0.1	0.0		2256	0.1	0.0
11	0509	1.5	0.5	26	0604	1.7	0.5
M	1145	0.2	0.1	Tu	1301	0.3	0.1
	1711	0.9	0.3		1759	0.8	0.2
	2252	0.0	0.0		2335	0.1	0.0
12	0551	1.6	0.5	27	0646	1.8	0.5
Tu	1236	0.2	0.1	W	1346	0.3	0.1
	1753	0.9	0.3		1839	0.8	0.2
	2333	0.0	0.0				
13	0636	1.7	0.5	28	0010	0.1	0.0
W	1322	0.2	0.1	Th	0725	1.7	0.5
	1835	0.8	0.2		1427	0.3	0.1
					1921	0.8	0.2
14	0015	0.0	0.0	29	0049	0.1	0.0
Th	0721	1.8	0.5	F	0804	1.7	0.5
	1413	0.2	0.1		1505	0.4	0.1
	1923	0.8	0.2		1958	0.8	0.2
15	0057	-0.1	0.0	30	0130	0.2	0.1
F	0807	1.8	0.5	Sa	0842	1.6	0.5
	1503	0.2	0.1		1539	0.4	0.1
	2012	0.8	0.2		2044	0.8	0.2
				31	0212	0.3	0.1
				Su	0919	1.5	0.5
					1614	0.4	0.1
					2132	0.9	0.3

JUNE

Day	Time h m	Height ft	Height m	Day	Time h m	Height ft	Height m
1	0301	0.3	0.1	16	0343	0.3	0.1
M	0956	1.4	0.4	Tu	1026	1.7	0.5
	1651	0.4	0.1		1711	0.2	0.1
	2227	0.9	0.3		2310	1.2	0.4
2	0353	0.4	0.1	17	0456	0.4	0.1
Tu	1040	1.4	0.4	W	1121	1.5	0.5
	1728	0.4	0.1		1758	0.2	0.1
	2327	1.0	0.3				
3	0456	0.5	0.2	18	0018	1.3	0.4
W	1121	1.3	0.4	Th	0613	0.4	0.1
	1807	0.3	0.1		1214	1.3	0.4
					1845	0.2	0.1
4	0027	1.1	0.3	19	0124	1.4	0.4
Th	0605	0.5	0.2	F	0737	0.5	0.2
	1207	1.2	0.4		1310	1.2	0.4
	1847	0.3	0.1		1928	0.2	0.1
5	0123	1.2	0.4	20	0228	1.6	0.5
F	0718	0.6	0.2	Sa	0859	0.5	0.2
	1256	1.1	0.3		1409	1.0	0.3
	1926	0.3	0.1		2014	0.2	0.1
6	0216	1.3	0.4	21	0324	1.7	0.5
Sa	0828	0.6	0.2	Su	1011	0.5	0.2
	1348	1.0	0.3		1500	0.9	0.3
	2008	0.2	0.1		2059	0.2	0.1
7	0309	1.5	0.5	22	0418	1.8	0.5
Su	0935	0.5	0.2	M	1118	0.5	0.2
	1440	1.0	0.3		1556	0.8	0.2
	2048	0.1	0.0		2141	0.2	0.1
8	0357	1.6	0.5	23	0506	1.8	0.5
M	1038	0.5	0.2	Tu	1212	0.5	0.2
	1532	0.9	0.3		1642	0.8	0.2
	2130	0.1	0.0		2223	0.2	0.1
9	0443	1.7	0.5	24	0549	1.8	0.5
Tu	1135	0.4	0.1	W	1300	0.5	0.2
	1622	0.9	0.3		1730	0.8	0.2
	2213	0.0	0.0		2304	0.2	0.1
10	0532	1.9	0.6	25	0631	1.8	0.5
W	1225	0.3	0.1	Th	1337	0.5	0.2
	1717	0.9	0.3		1812	0.8	0.2
	2300	0.0	0.0		2348	0.2	0.1
11	0617	2.0	0.6	26	0710	1.8	0.5
Th	1317	0.3	0.1	F	1413	0.5	0.2
	1809	0.9	0.3		1855	0.9	0.3
	2348	0.0	0.0				
12	0707	2.0	0.6	27	0029	0.2	0.1
F	1405	0.3	0.1	Sa	0744	1.7	0.5
	1904	0.9	0.3		1441	0.4	0.1
					1941	0.9	0.3
13	0041	0.0	0.0	28	0111	0.3	0.1
Sa	0753	2.0	0.6	Su	0820	1.7	0.5
	1451	0.2	0.1		1510	0.4	0.1
	2001	0.9	0.3		2024	0.9	0.3
14	0136	0.1	0.0	29	0157	0.4	0.1
Su	0842	1.9	0.6	M	0851	1.6	0.5
	1540	0.2	0.1		1542	0.4	0.1
	2101	1.0	0.3		2113	1.0	0.3
15	0237	0.1	0.0	30	0242	0.4	0.1
M	0935	1.8	0.5	Tu	0924	1.5	0.5
	1626	0.2	0.1		1610	0.4	0.1
	2204	1.1	0.3		2202	1.1	0.3

JULY

Day	Time h m	Height ft	Height m	Day	Time h m	Height ft	Height m
1	0331	0.5	0.2	16	0447	0.5	0.2
W	0957	1.4	0.4	Th	1047	1.4	0.4
	1641	0.4	0.1		1715	0.2	0.1
	2254	1.1	0.3		2353	1.5	0.5
2	0427	0.6	0.2	17	0600	0.6	0.2
Th	1033	1.3	0.4	F	1136	1.3	0.4
	1715	0.3	0.1		1757	0.2	0.1
	2349	1.2	0.4				
3	0530	0.7	0.2	18	0058	1.6	0.5
F	1111	1.3	0.4	Sa	0721	0.6	0.2
	1748	0.3	0.1		1223	1.1	0.3
					1843	0.2	0.1
4	0045	1.4	0.4	19	0201	1.7	0.5
Sa	0640	0.7	0.2	Su	0844	0.7	0.2
	1156	1.2	0.4		1319	1.0	0.3
	1831	0.2	0.1		1929	0.2	0.1
5	0141	1.5	0.5	20	0300	1.7	0.5
Su	0757	0.7	0.2	M	1002	0.7	0.2
	1245	1.1	0.3		1415	0.9	0.3
	1913	0.2	0.1		2020	0.2	0.1
6	0237	1.6	0.5	21	0356	1.8	0.5
M	0912	0.7	0.2	Tu	1108	0.6	0.2
	1341	1.0	0.3		1514	0.9	0.3
	2001	0.1	0.0		2107	0.2	0.1
7	0330	1.8	0.5	22	0447	1.8	0.5
Tu	1021	0.6	0.2	W	1201	0.6	0.2
	1443	0.9	0.3		1613	0.8	0.2
	2049	0.1	0.0		2159	0.3	0.1
8	0421	1.9	0.6	23	0531	1.8	0.5
W	1121	0.5	0.2	Th	1239	0.6	0.2
	1549	0.9	0.3		1708	0.9	0.3
	2144	0.1	0.0		2246	0.3	0.1
9	0512	2.0	0.6	24	0612	1.8	0.5
Th	1215	0.5	0.2	F	1312	0.5	0.2
	1651	0.9	0.3		1756	0.9	0.3
	2240	0.0	0.0		2335	0.3	0.1
10	0603	2.0	0.6	25	0647	1.8	0.5
F	1302	0.4	0.1	Sa	1344	0.5	0.2
	1754	0.9	0.3		1842	1.0	0.3
	2335	0.1	0.0				
11	0651	2.1	0.6	26	0017	0.3	0.1
Sa	1347	0.3	0.1	Su	0720	1.7	0.5
	1854	1.0	0.3		1409	0.5	0.2
					1924	1.1	0.3
12	0034	0.1	0.0	27	0059	0.4	0.1
Su	0739	2.0	0.6	M	0750	1.7	0.5
	1429	0.3	0.1		1434	0.5	0.2
	1954	1.1	0.3		2007	1.1	0.3
13	0134	0.1	0.0	28	0141	0.4	0.1
M	0826	1.9	0.6	Tu	0821	1.6	0.5
	1511	0.2	0.1		1459	0.4	0.1
	2053	1.2	0.4		2048	1.2	0.4
14	0236	0.2	0.1	29	0227	0.5	0.2
Tu	0914	1.8	0.5	W	0850	1.5	0.5
	1553	0.2	0.1		1524	0.4	0.1
	2152	1.3	0.4		2132	1.3	0.4
15	0339	0.3	0.1	30	0313	0.6	0.2
W	1000	1.6	0.5	Th	0921	1.5	0.5
	1632	0.2	0.1		1556	0.3	0.1
	2254	1.4	0.4		2218	1.3	0.4
				31	0404	0.6	0.2
				F	0953	1.4	0.4
					1624	0.3	0.1
					2309	1.4	0.4

AUGUST

Day	Time h m	Height ft	Height m	Day	Time h m	Height ft	Height m
1	0504	0.7	0.2	16	0026	1.7	0.5
Sa	1025	1.3	0.4	Su	0659	0.7	0.2
	1700	0.3	0.1		1138	1.1	0.3
					1758	0.2	0.1
2	0003	1.5	0.5	17	0129	1.7	0.5
Su	0613	0.8	0.2	M	0821	0.8	0.2
	1107	1.2	0.4		1230	1.0	0.3
	1742	0.2	0.1		1850	0.3	0.1
3	0102	1.6	0.5	18	0231	1.7	0.5
M	0733	0.8	0.2	Tu	0941	0.7	0.2
	1156	1.1	0.3		1335	0.9	0.3
	1828	0.2	0.1		1944	0.3	0.1
4	0204	1.7	0.5	19	0329	1.7	0.5
Tu	0854	0.8	0.2	W	1040	0.7	0.2
	1259	1.0	0.3		1445	0.9	0.3
	1924	0.2	0.1		2043	0.3	0.1
5	0303	1.8	0.5	20	0420	1.7	0.5
W	1006	0.7	0.2	Th	1125	0.7	0.2
	1414	0.9	0.3		1552	0.9	0.3
	2023	0.1	0.0		2142	0.4	0.1
6	0402	1.9	0.6	21	0505	1.7	0.5
Th	1105	0.6	0.2	F	1201	0.6	0.2
	1530	0.9	0.3		1648	1.0	0.3
	2128	0.1	0.0		2234	0.4	0.1
7	0455	2.0	0.6	22	0544	1.7	0.5
F	1154	0.5	0.2	Sa	1231	0.6	0.2
	1641	1.0	0.3		1739	1.1	0.3
	2231	0.1	0.0		2323	0.4	0.1
8	0546	2.0	0.6	23	0620	1.7	0.5
Sa	1236	0.4	0.1	Su	1257	0.5	0.2
	1747	1.1	0.3		1823	1.1	0.3
	2333	0.1	0.0				
9	0636	2.0	0.6	24	0009	0.4	0.1
Su	1315	0.3	0.1	M	0649	1.6	0.5
	1844	1.2	0.4		1323	0.5	0.2
					1903	1.2	0.4
10	0033	0.2	0.1	25	0051	0.4	0.1
M	0719	1.9	0.6	Tu	0721	1.6	0.5
	1357	0.3	0.1		1348	0.4	0.1
	1940	1.4	0.4		1943	1.3	0.4
11	0135	0.2	0.1	26	0131	0.5	0.2
Tu	0804	1.8	0.5	W	0749	1.5	0.5
	1434	0.2	0.1		1413	0.4	0.1
	2036	1.5	0.5		2021	1.4	0.4
12	0232	0.3	0.1	27	0213	0.5	0.2
W	0850	1.7	0.5	Th	0815	1.5	0.5
	1511	0.2	0.1		1439	0.3	0.1
	2130	1.6	0.5		2101	1.5	0.5
13	0332	0.4	0.1	28	0259	0.6	0.2
Th	0931	1.5	0.5	F	0845	1.4	0.4
	1550	0.2	0.1		1506	0.3	0.1
	2225	1.6	0.5		2145	1.5	0.5
14	0436	0.5	0.2	29	0349	0.6	0.2
F	1013	1.3	0.4	Sa	0917	1.3	0.4
	1632	0.2	0.1		1539	0.2	0.1
	2324	1.7	0.5		2235	1.6	0.5
15	0542	0.6	0.2	30	0449	0.7	0.2
Sa	1054	1.2	0.4	Su	0953	1.2	0.4
	1712	0.2	0.1		1615	0.2	0.1
					2330	1.7	0.5
				31	0559	0.8	0.2
				M	1035	1.1	0.3
					1701	0.2	0.1

SEPTEMBER

Day	Time h m	Height ft	Height m	Day	Time h m	Height ft	Height m
1	0032	1.7	0.5	16	0152	1.6	0.5
Tu	0716	0.8	0.2	W	0859	0.7	0.2
	1127	1.0	0.3		1307	0.9	0.3
	1754	0.2	0.1		1915	0.4	0.1
2	0134	1.8	0.5	17	0249	1.6	0.5
W	0837	0.7	0.2	Th	0954	0.7	0.2
	1239	0.9	0.3		1425	0.9	0.3
	1858	0.2	0.1		2024	0.4	0.1
3	0240	1.8	0.5	18	0341	1.6	0.5
Th	0944	0.7	0.2	F	1034	0.6	0.2
	1409	0.9	0.3		1534	1.0	0.3
	2011	0.2	0.1		2123	0.4	0.1
4	0340	1.9	0.6	19	0427	1.5	0.5
F	1039	0.6	0.2	Sa	1108	0.6	0.2
	1531	1.0	0.3		1631	1.1	0.3
	2123	0.2	0.1		2219	0.4	0.1
5	0437	1.9	0.6	20	0505	1.5	0.5
Sa	1122	0.5	0.2	Su	1137	0.5	0.2
	1639	1.1	0.3		1718	1.2	0.4
	2231	0.2	0.1		2311	0.4	0.1
6	0529	1.9	0.6	21	0540	1.5	0.5
Su	1202	0.4	0.1	M	1208	0.4	0.1
	1737	1.3	0.4		1757	1.3	0.4
	2335	0.2	0.1		2356	0.4	0.1
7	0615	1.8	0.5	22	0614	1.5	0.5
M	1239	0.3	0.1	Tu	1230	0.4	0.1
	1831	1.4	0.4		1836	1.4	0.4
8	0035	0.2	0.1	23	0038	0.4	0.1
Tu	0658	1.7	0.5	W	0644	1.4	0.4
	1317	0.2	0.1		1257	0.3	0.1
	1926	1.6	0.5		1915	1.4	0.4
9	0132	0.3	0.1	24	0121	0.4	0.1
W	0740	1.6	0.5	Th	0713	1.3	0.4
	1353	0.2	0.1		1324	0.2	0.1
	2015	1.7	0.5		1953	1.5	0.5
10	0229	0.3	0.1	25	0205	0.5	0.2
Th	0820	1.4	0.4	F	0741	1.3	0.4
	1430	0.2	0.1		1353	0.2	0.1
	2106	1.7	0.5		2034	1.6	0.5
11	0325	0.4	0.1	26	0251	0.5	0.2
F	0858	1.3	0.4	Sa	0813	1.2	0.4
	1508	0.2	0.1		1425	0.1	0.0
	2158	1.7	0.5		2119	1.6	0.5
12	0422	0.5	0.2	27	0342	0.6	0.2
Sa	0935	1.2	0.4	Su	0848	1.1	0.3
	1547	0.2	0.1		1458	0.1	0.0
	2251	1.7	0.5		2209	1.7	0.5
13	0521	0.6	0.2	28	0442	0.6	0.2
Su	1014	1.1	0.3	M	0927	1.0	0.3
	1630	0.2	0.1		1543	0.1	0.0
	2350	1.7	0.5		2305	1.7	0.5
14	0635	0.7	0.2	29	0550	0.6	0.2
M	1058	1.0	0.3	Tu	1018	0.9	0.3
	1716	0.3	0.1		1633	0.1	0.0
15	0050	1.6	0.5	30	0006	1.7	0.5
Tu	0746	0.7	0.2	W	0703	0.6	0.2
	1154	0.9	0.3		1125	0.9	0.3
	1813	0.3	0.1		1738	0.2	0.1

OCTOBER

Day	Time h m	Height ft	Height m	Day	Time h m	Height ft	Height m
1	0110	1.7	0.5	16	0200	1.3	0.4
Th	0813	0.6	0.2	F	0853	0.5	0.2
	1249	0.9	0.3		1403	0.9	0.3
	1850	0.2	0.1		1955	0.3	0.1
2	0216	1.7	0.5	17	0249	1.3	0.4
F	0913	0.5	0.2	Sa	0930	0.4	0.1
	1416	1.0	0.3		1508	0.9	0.3
	2010	0.2	0.1		2101	0.3	0.1
3	0316	1.6	0.5	18	0337	1.3	0.4
Sa	1000	0.4	0.1	Su	1007	0.3	0.1
	1531	1.1	0.3		1601	1.0	0.3
	2125	0.2	0.1		2159	0.3	0.1
4	0412	1.6	0.5	19	0416	1.2	0.4
Su	1044	0.3	0.1	M	1039	0.3	0.1
	1634	1.2	0.4		1646	1.2	0.4
	2237	0.2	0.1		2252	0.3	0.1
5	0503	1.5	0.5	20	0454	1.2	0.4
M	1124	0.2	0.1	Tu	1109	0.2	0.1
	1727	1.4	0.4		1731	1.3	0.4
	2337	0.2	0.1		2338	0.3	0.1
6	0549	1.4	0.4	21	0530	1.1	0.3
Tu	1200	0.1	0.0	W	1139	0.1	0.0
	1819	1.5	0.5		1810	1.4	0.4
7	0036	0.2	0.1	22	0024	0.3	0.1
W	0631	1.3	0.4	Th	0602	1.1	0.3
	1237	0.1	0.0		1207	0.0	0.0
	1908	1.6	0.5		1849	1.5	0.5
8	0129	0.2	0.1	23	0110	0.3	0.1
Th	0709	1.2	0.4	F	0634	1.0	0.3
	1313	0.0	0.0		1239	0.0	0.0
	1956	1.7	0.5		1930	1.5	0.5
9	0222	0.3	0.1	24	0157	0.3	0.1
F	0748	1.1	0.3	Sa	0709	0.9	0.3
	1348	0.0	0.0		1312	-0.1	0.0
	2042	1.7	0.5		2013	1.6	0.5
10	0315	0.4	0.1	25	0249	0.3	0.1
Sa	0823	1.0	0.3	Su	0748	0.9	0.3
	1426	0.0	0.0		1348	-0.1	0.0
	2131	1.7	0.5		2058	1.6	0.5
11	0406	0.5	0.2	26	0340	0.3	0.1
Su	0900	0.9	0.3	M	0830	0.8	0.2
	1505	0.1	0.0		1432	-0.1	0.0
	2219	1.6	0.5		2150	1.6	0.5
12	0505	0.5	0.2	27	0436	0.3	0.1
M	0941	0.9	0.3	Tu	0919	0.8	0.2
	1549	0.1	0.0		1521	-0.1	0.0
	2312	1.5	0.5		2243	1.6	0.5
13	0600	0.6	0.2	28	0539	0.3	0.1
Tu	1030	0.8	0.2	W	1022	0.7	0.2
	1638	0.2	0.1		1619	0.0	0.0
					2343	1.5	0.5
14	0006	1.5	0.5	29	0645	0.3	0.1
W	0700	0.6	0.2	Th	1136	0.7	0.2
	1133	0.8	0.2		1729	0.0	0.0
	1739	0.2	0.1				
15	0104	1.4	0.4	30	0048	1.4	0.4
Th	0802	0.5	0.2	F	0740	0.3	0.1
	1247	0.8	0.2		1300	0.8	0.2
	1843	0.3	0.1		1851	0.1	0.0
				31	0148	1.4	0.4
				Sa	0833	0.2	0.1
					1417	0.9	0.3
					2014	0.1	0.0

Time meridian 75° W. 0000 is midnight. 1200 is noon.
Heights are referred to mean low water which is the chart datum of soundings.

All times given are Eastern Standard Time; add one hour for Daylight Savings Time.

To find actual depths of water at a given time, add the height of the tide to the charted depth. If the height of the tide is negative—has (-) sign before the tabular height—it should be subtracted from the charted depth.

For tidal differences see page 358.

WASHINGTON, D.C., 1987

Times and Heights of High and Low Waters

MAY

Day	Time h m	Height ft	Height m	Day	Time h m	Height ft	Height m
1	0417	0.3	0.1	16	0412	0.3	0.1
F	0944	3.1	0.9	Sa	0928	3.6	1.1
	1718	0.2	0.1		1718	0.1	0.0
	2235	2.6	0.8		2216	2.9	0.9
2	0456	0.4	0.1	17	0509	0.3	0.1
Sa	1024	3.0	0.9	Su	1022	3.4	1.0
	1800	0.3	0.1		1812	0.1	0.0
	2322	2.5	0.8		2313	2.8	0.9
3	0536	0.5	0.2	18	0610	0.3	0.1
Su	1107	2.9	0.9	M	1119	3.2	1.0
	1842	0.3	0.1		1906	0.1	0.0
4	0013	2.5	0.8	19	0019	2.7	0.8
M	0624	0.5	0.2	Tu	0713	0.3	0.1
	1155	2.8	0.9		1226	3.0	0.9
	1929	0.4	0.1		2003	0.1	0.0
5	0109	2.5	0.8	20	0125	2.7	0.8
Tu	0717	0.6	0.2	W	0819	0.2	0.1
	1250	2.7	0.8		1340	2.8	0.9
	2013	0.5	0.2		2059	0.0	0.0
6	0205	2.5	0.8	21	0233	2.8	0.9
W	0817	0.7	0.2	Th	0926	0.2	0.1
	1353	2.7	0.8		1453	2.7	0.8
	2104	0.5	0.2		2155	0.0	0.0
7	0257	2.6	0.8	22	0333	2.8	0.9
Th	0918	0.7	0.2	F	1032	0.1	0.0
	1456	2.7	0.8		1558	2.6	0.8
	2152	0.5	0.2		2248	0.0	0.0
8	0345	2.7	0.8	23	0430	2.9	0.9
F	1020	0.6	0.2	Sa	1131	0.0	0.0
	1557	2.7	0.8		1655	2.6	0.8
	2239	0.5	0.2		2339	0.0	0.0
9	0427	2.9	0.9	24	0519	3.0	0.9
Sa	1118	0.5	0.2	Su	1228	0.0	0.0
	1648	2.7	0.8		1748	2.6	0.8
	2324	0.4	0.1				
10	0506	3.1	0.9	25	0026	0.0	0.0
Su	1213	0.4	0.1	M	0606	3.1	0.9
	1732	2.8	0.9		1320	-0.1	0.0
					1835	2.6	0.8
11	0009	0.4	0.1	26	0111	0.1	0.0
M	0545	3.3	1.0	Tu	0647	3.1	0.9
	1305	0.4	0.1		1408	0.0	0.0
	1817	2.9	0.9		1921	2.6	0.8
12	0054	0.4	0.1	27	0153	0.2	0.1
Tu	0625	3.5	1.1	W	0725	3.1	0.9
	1356	0.3	0.1		1453	0.0	0.0
	1901	2.9	0.9		2005	2.5	0.8
13	0139	0.3	0.1	28	0233	0.3	0.1
W	0707	3.6	1.1	Th	0804	3.1	0.9
	1445	0.2	0.1		1535	0.1	0.0
	1948	3.0	0.9		2047	2.5	0.8
14	0228	0.3	0.1	29	0311	0.3	0.1
Th	0752	3.7	1.1	F	0839	3.1	0.9
	1535	0.2	0.1		1617	0.1	0.0
	2034	3.0	0.9		2129	2.5	0.8
15	0317	0.3	0.1	30	0349	0.4	0.1
F	0839	3.7	1.1	Sa	0916	3.1	0.9
	1626	0.1	0.0		1654	0.2	0.1
	2124	2.9	0.9		2211	2.5	0.8
				31	0431	0.5	0.2
				Su	0956	3.0	0.9
					1733	0.3	0.1
					2253	2.5	0.8

JUNE

Day	Time h m	Height ft	Height m	Day	Time h m	Height ft	Height m
1	0515	0.5	0.2	16	0602	0.1	0.0
M	1038	3.0	0.9	Tu	1113	3.2	1.0
	1810	0.3	0.1		1843	-0.2	-0.1
	2338	2.5	0.8				
2	0602	0.6	0.2	17	0003	2.9	0.9
Tu	1123	2.9	0.9	W	0701	0.1	0.0
	1850	0.4	0.1		1219	2.9	0.9
					1935	-0.2	-0.1
3	0022	2.6	0.8	18	0106	2.9	0.9
W	0650	0.6	0.2	Th	0803	0.1	0.0
	1212	2.8	0.9		1325	2.7	0.8
	1929	0.4	0.1		2028	-0.1	0.0
4	0109	2.6	0.8	19	0209	2.9	0.9
Th	0745	0.7	0.2	F	0906	0.1	0.0
	1304	2.7	0.8		1430	2.6	0.8
	2013	0.4	0.1		2120	-0.1	0.0
5	0154	2.7	0.8	20	0307	2.9	0.9
F	0841	0.7	0.2	Sa	1009	0.1	0.0
	1403	2.7	0.8		1533	2.5	0.8
	2055	0.4	0.1		2213	0.0	0.0
6	0240	2.9	0.9	21	0402	2.9	0.9
Sa	0942	0.6	0.2	Su	1109	0.1	0.0
	1502	2.6	0.8		1631	2.4	0.7
	2141	0.4	0.1		2303	0.1	0.0
7	0328	3.0	0.9	22	0451	2.9	0.9
Su	1042	0.6	0.2	M	1206	0.0	0.0
	1559	2.7	0.8		1723	2.4	0.7
	2228	0.4	0.1		2353	0.1	0.0
8	0415	3.2	1.0	23	0537	2.9	0.9
M	1143	0.5	0.2	Tu	1259	0.0	0.0
	1651	2.7	0.8		1814	2.4	0.7
	2319	0.4	0.1				
9	0504	3.4	1.0	24	0039	0.2	0.1
Tu	1238	0.4	0.1	W	0623	3.0	0.9
	1743	2.7	0.8		1350	0.1	0.0
					1900	2.4	0.7
10	0014	0.3	0.1	25	0124	0.3	0.1
W	0551	3.5	1.1	Th	0703	3.0	0.9
	1334	0.3	0.1		1431	0.1	0.0
	1834	2.8	0.9		1945	2.4	0.7
11	0109	0.3	0.1	26	0208	0.3	0.1
Th	0641	3.6	1.1	F	0742	3.0	0.9
	1427	0.1	0.0		1513	0.1	0.0
	1926	2.9	0.9		2028	2.5	0.8
12	0206	0.2	0.1	27	0250	0.4	0.1
F	0732	3.7	1.1	Sa	0819	3.0	0.9
	1519	0.0	0.0		1552	0.2	0.1
	2018	2.9	0.9		2108	2.5	0.8
13	0305	0.2	0.1	28	0331	0.4	0.1
Sa	0824	3.7	1.1	Su	0857	3.0	0.9
	1610	-0.1	0.0		1628	0.2	0.1
	2110	2.9	0.9		2145	2.5	0.8
14	0402	0.1	0.0	29	0412	0.5	0.2
Su	0918	3.5	1.1	M	0934	3.0	0.9
	1701	-0.1	0.0		1704	0.2	0.1
	2206	2.9	0.9		2222	2.6	0.8
15	0501	0.1	0.0	30	0454	0.5	0.2
M	1014	3.4	1.0	Tu	1012	3.0	0.9
	1752	-0.2	-0.1		1739	0.3	0.1
	2304	2.9	0.9		2257	2.7	0.8

JULY

Day	Time h m	Height ft	Height m	Day	Time h m	Height ft	Height m
1	0539	0.6	0.2	16	0642	-0.1	0.0
W	1054	2.9	0.9	Th	1200	2.9	0.9
	1811	0.3	0.1		1903	-0.3	-0.1
	2333	2.7	0.8				
2	0623	0.6	0.2	17	0037	3.0	0.9
Th	1138	2.8	0.9	F	0740	0.0	0.0
	1846	0.3	0.1		1302	2.7	0.8
					1952	-0.2	-0.1
3	0013	2.8	0.9	18	0135	2.9	0.9
F	0712	0.6	0.2	Sa	0840	0.1	0.0
	1224	2.7	0.8		1402	2.5	0.8
	1922	0.4	0.1		2040	-0.1	0.0
4	0055	2.9	0.9	19	0233	2.8	0.9
Sa	0805	0.7	0.2	Su	0940	0.1	0.0
	1317	2.7	0.8		1503	2.4	0.7
	2003	0.4	0.1		2133	0.1	0.0
5	0147	3.0	0.9	20	0330	2.8	0.9
Su	0904	0.7	0.2	M	1042	0.2	0.1
	1413	2.6	0.8		1603	2.3	0.7
	2049	0.4	0.1		2226	0.2	0.1
6	0239	3.1	0.9	21	0423	2.8	0.9
M	1008	0.6	0.2	Tu	1140	0.2	0.1
	1515	2.6	0.8		1658	2.3	0.7
	2141	0.4	0.1		2317	0.2	0.1
7	0334	3.2	1.0	22	0515	2.8	0.9
Tu	1112	0.5	0.2	W	1233	0.2	0.1
	1616	2.6	0.8		1751	2.3	0.7
	2239	0.3	0.1				
8	0431	3.3	1.0	23	0010	0.3	0.1
W	1217	0.4	0.1	Th	0601	2.9	0.9
	1715	2.6	0.8		1322	0.2	0.1
	2346	0.3	0.1		1840	2.4	0.7
9	0527	3.5	1.1	24	0058	0.4	0.1
Th	1313	0.3	0.1	F	0645	2.9	0.9
	1812	2.7	0.8		1406	0.2	0.1
					1924	2.5	0.8
10	0051	0.2	0.1	25	0145	0.4	0.1
F	0623	3.5	1.1	Sa	0725	3.0	0.9
	1409	0.1	0.0		1445	0.2	0.1
	1907	2.8	0.9		2006	2.5	0.8
11	0154	0.1	0.0	26	0229	0.4	0.1
Sa	0719	3.6	1.1	Su	0803	3.0	0.9
	1501	-0.1	0.0		1522	0.2	0.1
	2003	2.9	0.9		2044	2.6	0.8
12	0255	0.0	0.0	27	0312	0.4	0.1
Su	0814	3.6	1.1	M	0839	3.1	0.9
	1550	-0.2	-0.1		1557	0.2	0.1
	2056	3.0	0.9		2116	2.7	0.8
13	0354	-0.1	0.0	28	0353	0.5	0.2
M	0910	3.5	1.1	Tu	0913	3.1	0.9
	1640	-0.3	-0.1		1630	0.3	0.1
	2150	3.0	0.9		2145	2.8	0.9
14	0449	-0.1	0.0	29	0434	0.5	0.2
Tu	1005	3.3	1.0	W	0947	3.0	0.9
	1728	-0.3	-0.1		1700	0.3	0.1
	2245	3.1	0.9		2216	2.9	0.9
15	0545	-0.1	0.0	30	0515	0.5	0.2
W	1102	3.1	0.9	Th	1025	3.0	0.9
	1816	-0.3	-0.1		1732	0.3	0.1
	2341	3.0	0.9		2248	3.0	0.9
				31	0557	0.6	0.2
				F	1105	2.9	0.9
					1805	0.4	0.1
					2327	3.0	0.9

AUGUST

Day	Time h m	Height ft	Height m	Day	Time h m	Height ft	Height m
1	0643	0.7	0.2	16	0056	2.9	0.9
Sa	1150	2.8	0.9	Su	0810	0.2	0.1
	1840	0.4	0.1		1332	2.5	0.8
					2001	0.1	0.0
2	0013	3.1	0.9	17	0151	2.8	0.9
Su	0732	0.7	0.2	M	0911	0.3	0.1
	1241	2.7	0.8		1433	2.4	0.7
	1919	0.4	0.1		2052	0.2	0.1
3	0104	3.1	0.9	18	0253	2.8	0.9
M	0835	0.7	0.2	Tu	1011	0.4	0.1
	1337	2.6	0.8		1535	2.3	0.7
	2009	0.4	0.1		2149	0.3	0.1
4	0159	3.2	1.0	19	0352	2.8	0.9
Tu	0943	0.7	0.2	W	1109	0.4	0.1
	1440	2.5	0.8		1633	2.3	0.7
	2108	0.4	0.1		2247	0.4	0.1
5	0302	3.2	1.0	20	0447	2.8	0.9
W	1052	0.6	0.2	Th	1201	0.3	0.1
	1548	2.5	0.8		1727	2.4	0.7
	2218	0.4	0.1		2343	0.4	0.1
6	0407	3.3	1.0	21	0538	2.9	0.9
Th	1159	0.5	0.2	F	1251	0.3	0.1
	1655	2.6	0.8		1815	2.5	0.8
	2335	0.3	0.1				
7	0511	3.3	1.0	22	0034	0.4	0.1
F	1257	0.3	0.1	Sa	0625	3.0	0.9
	1756	2.8	0.9		1332	0.3	0.1
					1901	2.6	0.8
8	0044	0.2	0.1	23	0123	0.4	0.1
Sa	0614	3.4	1.0	Su	0705	3.0	0.9
	1349	0.1	0.0		1411	0.3	0.1
	1854	2.9	0.9		1939	2.8	0.9
9	0147	0.0	0.0	24	0208	0.4	0.1
Su	0710	3.5	1.1	M	0742	3.1	0.9
	1438	-0.1	0.0		1447	0.3	0.1
	1947	3.1	0.9		2011	2.9	0.9
10	0245	-0.1	0.0	25	0250	0.4	0.1
M	0804	3.5	1.1	Tu	0817	3.1	0.9
	1527	-0.3	-0.1		1521	0.3	0.1
	2039	3.2	1.0		2039	3.0	0.9
11	0339	-0.2	-0.1	26	0331	0.5	0.2
Tu	0858	3.4	1.0	W	0849	3.1	0.9
	1613	-0.3	-0.1		1552	0.4	0.1
	2131	3.2	1.0		2106	3.1	0.9
12	0432	-0.2	-0.1	27	0412	0.5	0.2
W	0950	3.3	1.0	Th	0921	3.1	0.9
	1657	-0.3	-0.1		1625	0.4	0.1
	2220	3.2	1.0		2136	3.2	1.0
13	0526	-0.2	-0.1	28	0453	0.6	0.2
Th	1042	3.1	0.9	F	0959	3.1	0.9
	1742	-0.3	-0.1		1654	0.4	0.1
	2309	3.2	1.0		2212	3.3	1.0
14	0619	-0.1	0.0	29	0533	0.6	0.2
F	1136	2.9	0.9	Sa	1038	3.0	0.9
	1827	-0.2	-0.1		1727	0.4	0.1
					2253	3.3	1.0
15	0000	3.1	0.9	30	0618	0.7	0.2
Sa	0713	0.1	0.0	Su	1120	2.9	0.9
	1231	2.7	0.8		1803	0.5	0.2
	1914	0.0	0.0		2339	3.3	1.0
				31	0712	0.8	0.2
				M	1211	2.7	0.8
					1850	0.5	0.2

SEPTEMBER

Day	Time h m	Height ft	Height m	Day	Time h m	Height ft	Height m
1	0032	3.3	1.0	16	0212	2.7	0.8
Tu	0818	0.8	0.2	W	0932	0.5	0.2
	1311	2.6	0.8		1507	2.4	0.7
	1948	0.5	0.2		2113	0.5	0.2
2	0130	3.2	1.0	17	0317	2.7	0.8
W	0928	0.8	0.2	Th	1030	0.5	0.2
	1418	2.5	0.8		1605	2.4	0.7
	2058	0.5	0.2		2213	0.5	0.2
3	0241	3.1	0.9	18	0419	2.8	0.9
Th	1036	0.6	0.2	F	1122	0.5	0.2
	1533	2.6	0.8		1658	2.5	0.8
	2218	0.5	0.2		2311	0.5	0.2
4	0353	3.1	0.9	19	0511	2.9	0.9
F	1138	0.5	0.2	Sa	1209	0.4	0.1
	1644	2.7	0.8		1746	2.7	0.8
	2332	0.3	0.1				
5	0501	3.2	1.0	20	0006	0.5	0.2
Sa	1236	0.2	0.1	Su	0559	3.0	0.9
	1743	2.9	0.9		1251	0.4	0.1
					1828	2.8	0.9
6	0038	0.1	0.0	21	0057	0.4	0.1
Su	0604	3.3	1.0	M	0641	3.1	0.9
	1326	0.0	0.0		1330	0.4	0.1
	1838	3.1	0.9		1902	3.0	0.9
7	0136	0.0	0.0	22	0142	0.4	0.1
M	0659	3.4	1.0	Tu	0716	3.1	0.9
	1414	-0.1	0.0		1406	0.4	0.1
	1929	3.2	1.0		1933	3.1	0.9
8	0232	-0.2	-0.1	23	0226	0.4	0.1
Tu	0753	3.4	1.0	W	0749	3.1	0.9
	1459	-0.2	-0.1		1440	0.4	0.1
	2017	3.3	1.0		2000	3.2	1.0
9	0324	-0.2	-0.1	24	0308	0.4	0.1
W	0842	3.3	1.0	Th	0823	3.1	0.9
	1544	-0.2	-0.1		1514	0.4	0.1
	2104	3.4	1.0		2028	3.3	1.0
10	0414	-0.2	-0.1	25	0350	0.5	0.2
Th	0929	3.2	1.0	F	0855	3.1	0.9
	1627	-0.2	-0.1		1548	0.4	0.1
	2149	3.3	1.0		2102	3.4	1.0
11	0503	-0.1	0.0	26	0431	0.5	0.2
F	1018	3.1	0.9	Sa	0932	3.1	0.9
	1709	-0.1	0.0		1621	0.4	0.1
	2235	3.3	1.0		2142	3.5	1.1
12	0553	0.0	0.0	27	0515	0.6	0.2
Sa	1107	2.9	0.9	Su	1014	3.0	0.9
	1751	0.0	0.0		1659	0.5	0.2
	2321	3.1	0.9		2225	3.4	1.0
13	0645	0.2	0.1	28	0605	0.6	0.2
Su	1200	2.7	0.8	M	1059	2.8	0.9
	1835	0.1	0.0		1744	0.5	0.2
					2315	3.4	1.0
14	0012	3.0	0.9	29	0701	0.7	0.2
M	0739	0.3	0.1	Tu	1153	2.7	0.8
	1258	2.5	0.8		1837	0.5	0.2
	1922	0.3	0.1				
15	0109	2.8	0.9	30	0010	3.2	1.0
Tu	0835	0.4	0.1	W	0806	0.7	0.2
	1402	2.4	0.7		1256	2.6	0.8
	2014	0.4	0.1		1948	0.5	0.2

OCTOBER

Day	Time h m	Height ft	Height m	Day	Time h m	Height ft	Height m
1	0114	3.1	0.9	16	0236	2.6	0.8
Th	0912	0.6	0.2	F	0943	0.4	0.1
	1409	2.5	0.8		1530	2.4	0.7
	2102	0.5	0.2		2139	0.5	0.2
2	0230	3.0	0.9	17	0341	2.6	0.8
F	1018	0.5	0.2	Sa	1032	0.4	0.1
	1525	2.6	0.8		1622	2.6	0.8
	2218	0.4	0.1		2239	0.5	0.2
3	0346	2.9	0.9	18	0434	2.7	0.8
Sa	1116	0.3	0.1	Su	1119	0.4	0.1
	1631	2.8	0.9		1708	2.7	0.8
	2327	0.2	0.1		2335	0.4	0.1
4	0455	3.0	0.9	19	0523	2.8	0.9
Su	1210	0.1	0.0	M	1203	0.3	0.1
	1729	2.9	0.9		1746	2.8	0.9
5	0028	0.0	0.0	20	0025	0.3	0.1
M	0554	3.1	0.9	Tu	0604	2.9	0.9
	1300	0.0	0.0		1242	0.3	0.1
	1820	3.1	0.9		1818	3.0	0.9
6	0125	-0.1	0.0	21	0115	0.3	0.1
Tu	0646	3.1	0.9	W	0641	2.9	0.9
	1347	-0.1	0.0		1323	0.3	0.1
	1909	3.3	1.0		1850	3.2	1.0
7	0217	-0.2	-0.1	22	0200	0.3	0.1
W	0736	3.1	0.9	Th	0718	3.0	0.9
	1431	-0.2	-0.1		1359	0.3	0.1
	1954	3.3	1.0		1921	3.3	1.0
8	0307	-0.2	-0.1	23	0245	0.3	0.1
Th	0822	3.1	0.9	F	0753	3.0	0.9
	1513	-0.2	-0.1		1437	0.3	0.1
	2036	3.3	1.0		1956	3.4	1.0
9	0355	-0.2	-0.1	24	0328	0.3	0.1
F	0907	3.0	0.9	Sa	0831	2.9	0.9
	1556	-0.1	0.0		1517	0.3	0.1
	2119	3.3	1.0		2035	3.5	1.1
10	0441	-0.1	0.0	25	0413	0.3	0.1
Sa	0951	2.9	0.9	Su	0912	2.9	0.9
	1635	0.0	0.0		1556	0.3	0.1
	2200	3.2	1.0		2118	3.5	1.1
11	0528	0.1	0.0	26	0502	0.3	0.1
Su	1041	2.7	0.8	M	0955	2.8	0.9
	1715	0.1	0.0		1644	0.3	0.1
	2245	3.0	0.9		2206	3.4	1.0
12	0616	0.2	0.1	27	0554	0.4	0.1
M	1131	2.5	0.8	Tu	1046	2.7	0.8
	1758	0.2	0.1		1739	0.3	0.1
	2331	2.9	0.9		2258	3.2	1.0
13	0706	0.3	0.1	28	0652	0.4	0.1
Tu	1226	2.4	0.7	W	1142	2.6	0.8
	1846	0.3	0.1		1841	0.3	0.1
					2358	3.0	0.9
14	0024	2.7	0.8	29	0751	0.3	0.1
W	0757	0.4	0.1	Th	1248	2.5	0.8
	1328	2.4	0.7		1950	0.3	0.1
	1938	0.4	0.1				
15	0128	2.6	0.8	30	0106	2.8	0.9
Th	0848	0.4	0.1	F	0852	0.3	0.1
	1431	2.4	0.7		1401	2.5	0.8
	2038	0.5	0.2		2103	0.2	0.1
				31	0221	2.7	0.8
				Sa	0953	0.2	0.1
					1511	2.6	0.8
					2211	0.1	0.0

Time meridian 75° W. 0000 is midnight. 1200 is noon.
Heights are referred to mean low water which is the chart datum of soundings.

All times given are Eastern Standard Time; add one hour for Daylight Savings Time.

To find actual depth of water at a given time, add the height of the tide to the charted depth. If the height of the tide is negative—has (-) sign before the tabular height—it should be subtracted from the charted depth.

For tidal differences see page 358.

HAMPTON ROADS (Sewells Pt.), VA., 1987

Times and Heights of High and Low Waters

MAY

Day	Time h m	Height ft	Height m	Day	Time h m	Height ft	Height m
1	0528	0.1	0.0	16	0513	-0.1	0.0
F	1122	2.1	0.6	Sa	1112	2.4	0.7
	1717	0.2	0.1		1711	0.0	0.0
	2341	2.6	0.8		2341	3.1	0.9
2	0610	0.2	0.1	17	0607	0.1	0.0
Sa	1205	2.0	0.6	Su	1210	2.4	0.7
	1757	0.3	0.1		1808	0.2	0.1
3	0023	2.5	0.8	18	0039	3.0	0.9
Su	0655	0.3	0.1	M	0707	0.2	0.1
	1252	1.9	0.6		1311	2.4	0.7
	1844	0.4	0.1		1913	0.3	0.1
4	0111	2.3	0.7	19	0140	2.8	0.9
M	0745	0.4	0.1	Tu	0806	0.3	0.1
	1343	1.8	0.5		1418	2.5	0.8
	1935	0.5	0.2		2025	0.4	0.1
5	0202	2.2	0.7	20	0246	2.7	0.8
Tu	0833	0.4	0.1	W	0909	0.3	0.1
	1438	1.8	0.5		1524	2.6	0.8
	2035	0.5	0.2		2138	0.4	0.1
6	0254	2.1	0.6	21	0350	2.6	0.8
W	0925	0.4	0.1	Th	1009	0.3	0.1
	1534	1.9	0.6		1630	2.7	0.8
	2135	0.5	0.2		2246	0.4	0.1
7	0350	2.1	0.6	22	0453	2.5	0.8
Th	1013	0.3	0.1	F	1106	0.2	0.1
	1627	2.0	0.6		1727	2.8	0.9
	2235	0.4	0.1		2347	0.3	0.1
8	0445	2.1	0.6	23	0550	2.4	0.7
F	1059	0.2	0.1	Sa	1158	0.2	0.1
	1718	2.2	0.7		1821	2.8	0.9
	2331	0.2	0.1				
9	0536	2.1	0.6	24	0044	0.2	0.1
Sa	1145	0.1	0.0	Su	0643	2.4	0.7
	1804	2.3	0.7		1245	0.1	0.0
					1909	2.9	0.9
10	0022	0.0	0.0	25	0134	0.1	0.0
Su	0624	2.1	0.6	M	0731	2.3	0.7
	1229	-0.1	0.0		1328	0.0	0.0
	1849	2.6	0.8		1955	2.9	0.9
11	0109	-0.1	0.0	26	0218	0.0	0.0
M	0709	2.2	0.7	Tu	0814	2.2	0.7
	1309	-0.2	-0.1		1410	0.0	0.0
	1933	2.7	0.8		2036	2.8	0.9
12	0157	-0.2	-0.1	27	0303	-0.1	0.0
Tu	0755	2.2	0.7	W	0858	2.1	0.6
	1354	-0.3	-0.1		1451	0.0	0.0
	2019	2.9	0.9		2117	2.8	0.9
13	0243	-0.3	-0.1	28	0345	-0.1	0.0
W	0842	2.3	0.7	Th	0937	2.0	0.6
	1439	-0.3	-0.1		1530	0.0	0.0
	2106	3.0	0.9		2155	2.7	0.8
14	0331	-0.3	-0.1	29	0424	0.0	0.0
Th	0928	2.3	0.7	F	1018	2.0	0.6
	1527	-0.3	-0.1		1610	0.0	0.0
	2155	3.1	0.9		2235	2.6	0.8
15	0422	-0.2	-0.1	30	0503	0.0	0.0
F	1018	2.4	0.7	Sa	1100	1.9	0.6
	1616	-0.2	-0.1		1650	0.1	0.0
	2246	3.1	0.9		2314	2.5	0.8
				31	0545	0.1	0.0
				Su	1141	1.9	0.6
					1733	0.2	0.1
					2354	2.4	0.7

JUNE

Day	Time h m	Height ft	Height m	Day	Time h m	Height ft	Height m
1	0623	0.1	0.0	16	0026	3.0	0.9
M	1226	1.9	0.6	Tu	0650	0.0	0.0
	1815	0.3	0.1		1300	2.6	0.8
					1906	0.2	0.1
2	0036	2.3	0.7	17	0124	2.8	0.9
Tu	0705	0.2	0.1	W	0745	0.1	0.0
	1311	1.9	0.6		1401	2.6	0.8
	1905	0.4	0.1		2012	0.3	0.1
3	0121	2.2	0.7	18	0222	2.6	0.8
W	0747	0.2	0.1	Th	0841	0.2	0.1
	1358	1.9	0.6		1502	2.7	0.8
	1956	0.4	0.1		2120	0.4	0.1
4	0208	2.1	0.6	19	0324	2.5	0.8
Th	0830	0.2	0.1	F	0937	0.2	0.1
	1448	2.0	0.6		1601	2.7	0.8
	2051	0.4	0.1		2224	0.4	0.1
5	0257	2.0	0.6	20	0423	2.3	0.7
F	0915	0.2	0.1	Sa	1031	0.2	0.1
	1538	2.1	0.6		1701	2.7	0.8
	2151	0.3	0.1		2326	0.3	0.1
6	0353	2.0	0.6	21	0520	2.2	0.7
Sa	1003	0.1	0.0	Su	1124	0.2	0.1
	1630	2.3	0.7		1755	2.7	0.8
	2249	0.2	0.1				
7	0445	2.0	0.6	22	0024	0.3	0.1
Su	1052	0.0	0.0	M	0614	2.1	0.6
	1721	2.4	0.7		1214	0.1	0.0
	2347	0.1	0.0		1843	2.7	0.8
8	0540	2.0	0.6	23	0114	0.1	0.0
M	1142	-0.1	0.0	Tu	0704	2.0	0.6
	1814	2.6	0.8		1259	0.1	0.0
					1930	2.7	0.8
9	0040	-0.1	0.0	24	0202	0.0	0.0
Tu	0633	2.0	0.6	W	0751	1.9	0.6
	1233	-0.2	-0.1		1344	0.0	0.0
	1906	2.8	0.9		2012	2.6	0.8
10	0133	-0.2	-0.1	25	0244	0.0	0.0
W	0726	2.1	0.6	Th	0835	1.9	0.6
	1325	-0.3	-0.1		1426	0.0	0.0
	1957	3.0	0.9		2054	2.6	0.8
11	0226	-0.3	-0.1	26	0324	-0.1	0.0
Th	0821	2.2	0.7	F	0919	1.9	0.6
	1417	-0.3	-0.1		1508	0.0	0.0
	2048	3.1	0.9		2133	2.5	0.8
12	0316	-0.3	-0.1	27	0402	-0.1	0.0
F	0915	2.3	0.7	Sa	0957	1.9	0.6
	1511	-0.3	-0.1		1547	0.0	0.0
	2143	3.1	0.9		2211	2.5	0.8
13	0409	-0.3	-0.1	28	0439	-0.1	0.0
Sa	1009	2.4	0.7	Su	1037	1.9	0.6
	1607	-0.2	-0.1		1629	0.0	0.0
	2235	3.1	0.9		2249	2.4	0.7
14	0501	-0.2	-0.1	29	0515	-0.1	0.0
Su	1104	2.5	0.8	M	1117	1.9	0.6
	1704	-0.1	0.0		1708	0.1	0.0
	2330	3.1	0.9		2326	2.3	0.7
15	0554	-0.1	0.0	30	0549	0.0	0.0
M	1202	2.6	0.8	Tu	1154	2.0	0.6
	1805	0.0	0.0		1749	0.2	0.1

JULY

Day	Time h m	Height ft	Height m	Day	Time h m	Height ft	Height m
1	0005	2.2	0.7	16	0101	2.8	0.9
W	0626	0.1	0.0	Th	0716	0.1	0.0
	1235	2.0	0.6		1337	2.8	0.9
	1832	0.2	0.1		1950	0.3	0.1
2	0044	2.2	0.7	17	0155	2.6	0.8
Th	0658	0.1	0.0	F	0808	0.2	0.1
	1315	2.1	0.6		1433	2.8	0.9
	1919	0.3	0.1		2052	0.4	0.1
3	0122	2.1	0.6	18	0250	2.4	0.7
F	0740	0.1	0.0	Sa	0900	0.3	0.1
	1401	2.2	0.7		1532	2.7	0.8
	2012	0.3	0.1		2155	0.5	0.2
4	0212	2.0	0.6	19	0351	2.2	0.7
Sa	0822	0.1	0.0	Su	0954	0.3	0.1
	1451	2.3	0.7		1630	2.7	0.8
	2109	0.3	0.1		2300	0.5	0.2
5	0303	1.9	0.6	20	0451	2.0	0.6
Su	0912	0.1	0.0	M	1050	0.3	0.1
	1546	2.4	0.7		1726	2.6	0.8
	2210	0.3	0.1		2359	0.4	0.1
6	0402	1.9	0.6	21	0546	1.9	0.6
M	1008	0.0	0.0	Tu	1144	0.3	0.1
	1645	2.6	0.8		1819	2.6	0.8
	2313	0.2	0.1				
7	0503	1.9	0.6	22	0051	0.3	0.1
Tu	1105	-0.1	0.0	W	0640	1.9	0.6
	1745	2.7	0.8		1236	0.2	0.1
					1906	2.6	0.8
8	0014	0.1	0.0	23	0138	0.2	0.1
W	0606	2.0	0.6	Th	0728	1.9	0.6
	1206	-0.2	-0.1		1321	0.1	0.0
	1843	2.9	0.9		1949	2.6	0.8
9	0113	-0.1	0.0	24	0219	0.0	0.0
Th	0706	2.1	0.6	F	0814	1.9	0.6
	1306	-0.3	-0.1		1405	0.0	0.0
	1941	3.0	0.9		2031	2.5	0.8
10	0209	-0.2	-0.1	25	0300	-0.1	0.0
F	0804	2.3	0.7	Sa	0855	1.9	0.6
	1405	-0.3	-0.1		1447	0.0	0.0
	2037	3.1	0.9		2109	2.5	0.8
11	0300	-0.3	-0.1	26	0333	-0.1	0.0
Sa	0900	2.5	0.8	Su	0933	2.0	0.6
	1503	-0.3	-0.1		1528	0.0	0.0
	2130	3.2	1.0		2147	2.5	0.8
12	0353	-0.3	-0.1	27	0408	-0.1	0.0
Su	0955	2.6	0.8	M	1010	2.1	0.6
	1558	-0.3	-0.1		1607	0.0	0.0
	2222	3.2	1.0		2222	2.4	0.7
13	0445	-0.3	-0.1	28	0440	-0.1	0.0
M	1050	2.7	0.8	Tu	1045	2.1	0.6
	1656	-0.2	-0.1		1643	0.0	0.0
	2315	3.1	0.9		2256	2.4	0.7
14	0535	-0.2	-0.1	29	0511	0.0	0.0
Tu	1146	2.8	0.9	W	1120	2.2	0.7
	1753	-0.1	0.0		1722	0.1	0.0
					2330	2.3	0.7
15	0008	3.0	0.9	30	0543	0.0	0.0
W	0625	-0.1	0.0	Th	1156	2.3	0.7
	1239	2.8	0.9		1801	0.2	0.1
	1850	0.1	0.0				
				31	0005	2.2	0.7
				F	0615	0.1	0.0
					1234	2.4	0.7
					1844	0.3	0.1

AUGUST

Day	Time h m	Height ft	Height m	Day	Time h m	Height ft	Height m
1	0044	2.2	0.7	16	0216	2.3	0.7
Sa	0654	0.2	0.1	Su	0821	0.5	0.2
	1319	2.5	0.8		1453	2.8	0.9
	1935	0.4	0.1		2126	0.7	0.2
2	0129	2.1	0.6	17	0314	2.2	0.7
Su	0738	0.2	0.1	M	0918	0.6	0.2
	1412	2.5	0.8		1553	2.7	0.8
	2033	0.5	0.2		2228	0.7	0.2
3	0224	2.0	0.6	18	0420	2.0	0.6
M	0833	0.2	0.1	Tu	1016	0.6	0.2
	1512	2.6	0.8		1654	2.6	0.8
	2139	0.5	0.2		2329	0.6	0.2
4	0329	2.0	0.6	19	0521	2.0	0.6
Tu	0933	0.2	0.1	W	1116	0.5	0.2
	1617	2.7	0.8		1749	2.6	0.8
	2249	0.4	0.1				
5	0438	2.1	0.6	20	0022	0.5	0.2
W	1041	0.2	0.1	Th	0616	2.0	0.6
	1723	2.8	0.9		1211	0.4	0.1
	2355	0.3	0.1		1838	2.6	0.8
6	0548	2.2	0.7	21	0108	0.3	0.1
Th	1150	0.1	0.0	F	0703	2.0	0.6
	1827	3.0	0.9		1301	0.3	0.1
					1922	2.6	0.8
7	0056	0.1	0.0	22	0149	0.2	0.1
F	0653	2.4	0.7	Sa	0749	2.1	0.6
	1256	-0.1	0.0		1344	0.2	0.1
	1926	3.1	0.9		2003	2.6	0.8
8	0152	0.0	0.0	23	0225	0.1	0.0
Sa	0752	2.6	0.8	Su	0827	2.2	0.7
	1356	-0.2	-0.1		1425	0.1	0.0
	2021	3.2	1.0		2041	2.6	0.8
9	0245	-0.1	0.0	24	0300	0.0	0.0
Su	0848	2.8	0.9	M	0903	2.3	0.7
	1453	-0.2	-0.1		1504	0.0	0.0
	2114	3.3	1.0		2118	2.6	0.8
10	0334	-0.2	-0.1	25	0332	0.0	0.0
M	0940	3.0	0.9	Tu	0937	2.4	0.7
	1548	-0.2	-0.1		1541	0.0	0.0
	2205	3.2	1.0		2151	2.5	0.8
11	0421	-0.2	-0.1	26	0402	0.0	0.0
Tu	1032	3.1	0.9	W	1010	2.5	0.8
	1642	-0.1	0.0		1618	0.1	0.0
	2255	3.1	0.9		2225	2.5	0.8
12	0509	-0.1	0.0	27	0432	0.1	0.0
W	1122	3.1	0.9	Th	1045	2.6	0.8
	1734	0.0	0.0		1655	0.2	0.1
	2343	3.0	0.9		2259	2.5	0.8
13	0554	0.0	0.0	28	0503	0.1	0.0
Th	1213	3.1	0.9	F	1122	2.7	0.8
	1828	0.2	0.1		1733	0.3	0.1
					2333	2.4	0.7
14	0032	2.8	0.9	29	0536	0.2	0.1
F	0642	0.2	0.1	Sa	1202	2.8	0.9
	1305	3.0	0.9		1818	0.4	0.1
	1923	0.4	0.1				
15	0124	2.6	0.8	30	0013	2.3	0.7
Sa	0729	0.3	0.1	Su	0618	0.3	0.1
	1359	2.9	0.9		1247	2.8	0.9
	2020	0.6	0.2		1908	0.6	0.2
				31	0100	2.3	0.7
				M	0705	0.4	0.1
					1343	2.8	0.9
					2009	0.7	0.2

SEPTEMBER

Day	Time h m	Height ft	Height m	Day	Time h m	Height ft	Height m
1	0159	2.2	0.7	16	0347	2.1	0.6
Tu	0804	0.5	0.2	W	0942	0.8	0.2
	1446	2.8	0.9		1617	2.6	0.8
	2118	0.7	0.2		2251	0.8	0.2
2	0309	2.2	0.7	17	0449	2.1	0.6
W	0913	0.5	0.2	Th	1046	0.8	0.2
	1557	2.9	0.9		1715	2.6	0.8
	2231	0.7	0.2		2347	0.6	0.2
3	0425	2.3	0.7	18	0545	2.1	0.6
Th	1029	0.4	0.1	F	1142	0.6	0.2
	1710	3.0	0.9		1804	2.6	0.8
	2339	0.5	0.2				
4	0538	2.5	0.8	19	0029	0.5	0.2
F	1144	0.3	0.1	Sa	0633	2.2	0.7
	1814	3.1	0.9		1233	0.4	0.1
					1848	2.6	0.8
5	0040	0.3	0.1	20	0110	0.3	0.1
Sa	0641	2.7	0.8	Su	0714	2.4	0.7
	1249	0.2	0.1		1317	0.3	0.1
	1914	3.2	1.0		1930	2.6	0.8
6	0133	0.2	0.1	21	0146	0.2	0.1
Su	0738	3.0	0.9	M	0751	2.5	0.8
	1348	0.0	0.0		1359	0.2	0.1
	2007	3.3	1.0		2008	2.6	0.8
7	0223	0.0	0.0	22	0220	0.1	0.0
M	0831	3.2	1.0	Tu	0827	2.6	0.8
	1443	-0.1	0.0		1436	0.1	0.0
	2056	3.3	1.0		2044	2.6	0.8
8	0309	-0.1	0.0	23	0251	0.1	0.0
Tu	0921	3.3	1.0	W	0903	2.7	0.8
	1533	-0.1	0.0		1514	0.0	0.0
	2145	3.2	1.0		2120	2.6	0.8
9	0355	0.0	0.0	24	0323	0.1	0.0
W	1009	3.4	1.0	Th	0939	2.8	0.9
	1623	0.0	0.0		1552	0.1	0.0
	2232	3.1	0.9		2153	2.6	0.8
10	0437	0.0	0.0	25	0355	0.1	0.0
Th	1055	3.3	1.0	F	1013	2.9	0.9
	1712	0.2	0.1		1629	0.2	0.1
	2317	2.9	0.9		2229	2.5	0.8
11	0522	0.2	0.1	26	0429	0.2	0.1
F	1141	3.3	1.0	Sa	1052	3.0	0.9
	1802	0.3	0.1		1712	0.3	0.1
					2309	2.5	0.8
12	0003	2.7	0.8	27	0506	0.3	0.1
Sa	0605	0.4	0.1	Su	1135	3.0	0.9
	1231	3.1	0.9		1758	0.5	0.2
	1852	0.6	0.2		2353	2.4	0.7
13	0050	2.5	0.8	28	0552	0.4	0.1
Su	0651	0.5	0.2	M	1225	3.0	0.9
	1321	2.9	0.9		1851	0.6	0.2
	1947	0.7	0.2				
14	0142	2.3	0.7	29	0044	2.4	0.7
M	0741	0.7	0.2	Tu	0646	0.5	0.2
	1417	2.8	0.9		1323	3.0	0.9
	2049	0.8	0.2		1954	0.8	0.2
15	0241	2.2	0.7	30	0148	2.4	0.7
Tu	0841	0.8	0.2	W	0752	0.7	0.2
	1517	2.7	0.8		1432	2.9	0.9
	2152	0.8	0.2		2103	0.8	0.2

OCTOBER

Day	Time h m	Height ft	Height m	Day	Time h m	Height ft	Height m
1	0302	2.4	0.7	16	0411	2.1	0.6
Th	0909	0.7	0.2	F	1010	0.8	0.2
	1546	2.9	0.9		1630	2.4	0.7
	2215	0.7	0.2		2257	0.6	0.2
2	0418	2.5	0.8	17	0505	2.2	0.7
F	1028	0.6	0.2	Sa	1108	0.6	0.2
	1656	3.0	0.9		1722	2.4	0.7
	2321	0.6	0.2		2342	0.4	0.1
3	0527	2.8	0.9	18	0552	2.3	0.7
Sa	1139	0.5	0.2	Su	1200	0.5	0.2
	1800	3.1	0.9		1808	2.4	0.7
4	0020	0.4	0.1	19	0024	0.3	0.1
Su	0629	3.0	0.9	M	0634	2.4	0.7
	1242	0.3	0.1		1246	0.3	0.1
	1856	3.1	0.9		1851	2.4	0.7
5	0110	0.2	0.1	20	0101	0.2	0.1
M	0724	3.2	1.0	Tu	0714	2.6	0.8
	1338	0.1	0.0		1328	0.1	0.0
	1949	3.2	1.0		1931	2.4	0.7
6	0159	0.1	0.0	21	0136	0.1	0.0
Tu	0813	3.3	1.0	W	0751	2.7	0.8
	1429	0.0	0.0		1409	0.0	0.0
	2035	3.1	0.9		2010	2.4	0.7
7	0242	0.0	0.0	22	0210	0.0	0.0
W	0859	3.4	1.0	Th	0830	2.9	0.9
	1516	0.0	0.0		1447	0.0	0.0
	2121	3.0	0.9		2048	2.4	0.7
8	0325	0.0	0.0	23	0247	0.0	0.0
Th	0944	3.4	1.0	F	0908	3.0	0.9
	1603	0.1	0.0		1529	0.0	0.0
	2207	2.9	0.9		2127	2.4	0.7
9	0407	0.1	0.0	24	0323	0.0	0.0
F	1029	3.4	1.0	Sa	0950	3.1	0.9
	1649	0.2	0.1		1610	0.1	0.0
	2249	2.7	0.8		2207	2.4	0.7
10	0448	0.3	0.1	25	0404	0.1	0.0
Sa	1112	3.2	1.0	Su	1032	3.1	0.9
	1737	0.4	0.1		1655	0.2	0.1
	2333	2.6	0.8		2251	2.4	0.7
11	0532	0.4	0.1	26	0448	0.2	0.1
Su	1157	3.1	0.9	M	1119	3.1	0.9
	1823	0.5	0.2		1746	0.3	0.1
					2341	2.4	0.7
12	0020	2.4	0.7	27	0541	0.3	0.1
M	0615	0.6	0.2	Tu	1212	3.1	0.9
	1244	2.9	0.9		1842	0.5	0.2
	1915	0.7	0.2				
13	0111	2.2	0.7	28	0039	2.4	0.7
Tu	0707	0.7	0.2	W	0639	0.5	0.2
	1335	2.7	0.8		1312	3.0	0.9
	2011	0.8	0.2		1942	0.6	0.2
14	0206	2.1	0.6	29	0143	2.4	0.7
W	0803	0.8	0.2	Th	0748	0.6	0.2
	1433	2.6	0.8		1419	2.9	0.9
	2108	0.8	0.2		2051	0.6	0.2
15	0310	2.1	0.6	30	0259	2.5	0.8
Th	0905	0.8	0.2	F	0906	0.6	0.2
	1531	2.5	0.8		1532	2.8	0.9
	2205	0.7	0.2		2156	0.6	0.2
				31	0410	2.7	0.8
				Sa	1022	0.6	0.2
					1641	2.8	0.9
					2259	0.5	0.2

Time meridian 75° W. 0000 is midnight. 1200 is noon.
Heights are referred to mean low water which is the chart datum of soundings.

All times given are Eastern Standard Time; add one hour for Daylight Savings Time.

To find actual depth of water at a given time, add the height of the tide to the charted depth. If the height of the tide is negative—has a (-) sign before the tabular height—it should be subtracted from the charted depth.

For tidal differences see page 358.

PLANNING CHART OF THE CHESAPEAKE BAY

With an approximate five mile grid,
to be used for estimating distances only,
and not to be used for navigational purposes.

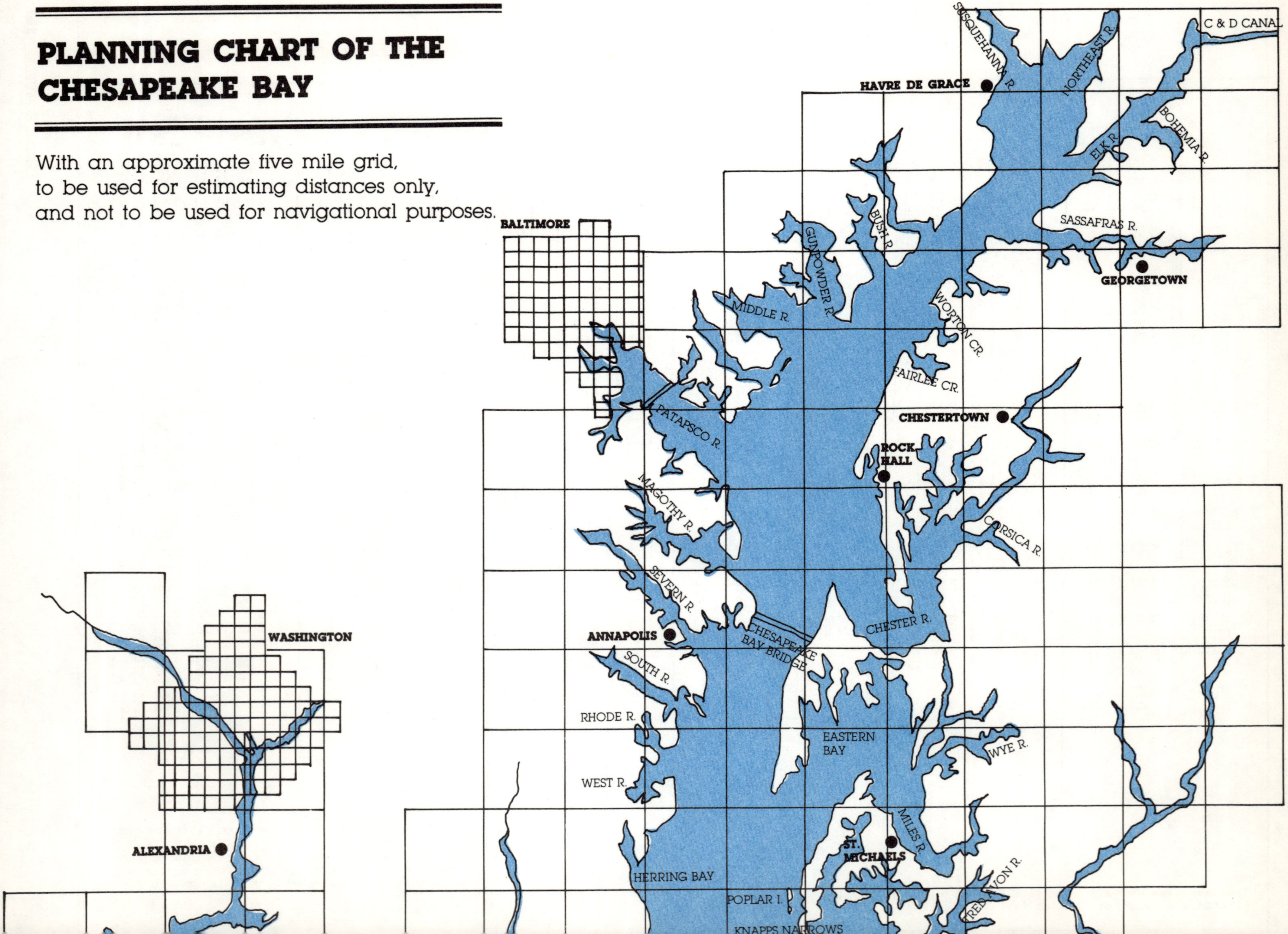

ADVERTISER'S INDEX

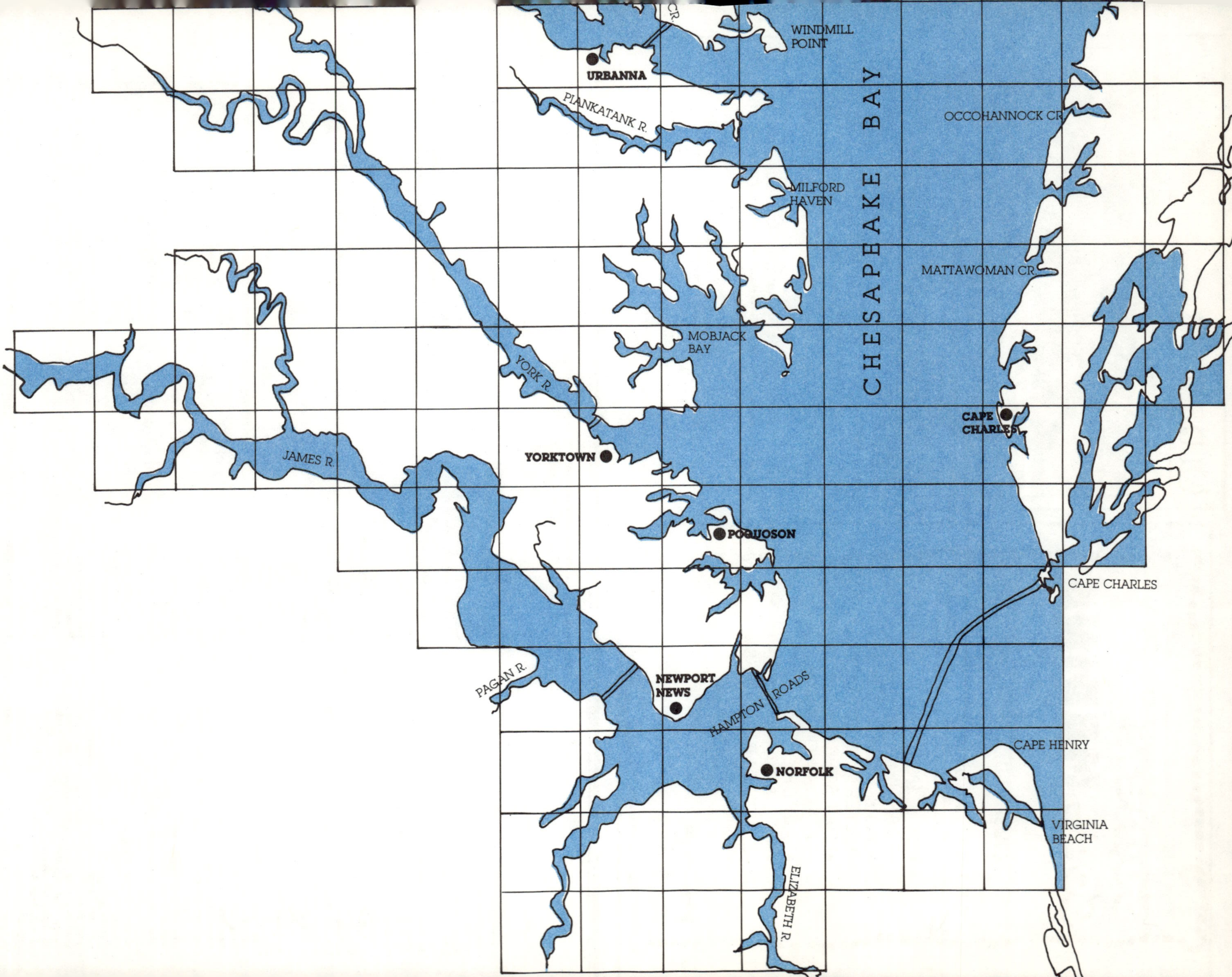

CR.
WINDMILL POINT
URBANNA
PIANKATANK R.
CHESAPEAKE BAY
OCCOHANNOCK CR.
MILFORD HAVEN
MATTAWOMAN CR.
MOBJACK BAY
YORK R.
CAPE CHARLES
JAMES R.
YORKTOWN
POQUOSON
CAPE CHARLES
PAGAN R.
NEWPORT NEWS
HAMPTON ROADS
CAPE HENRY
NORFOLK
VIRGINIA BEACH
ELIZABETH R.

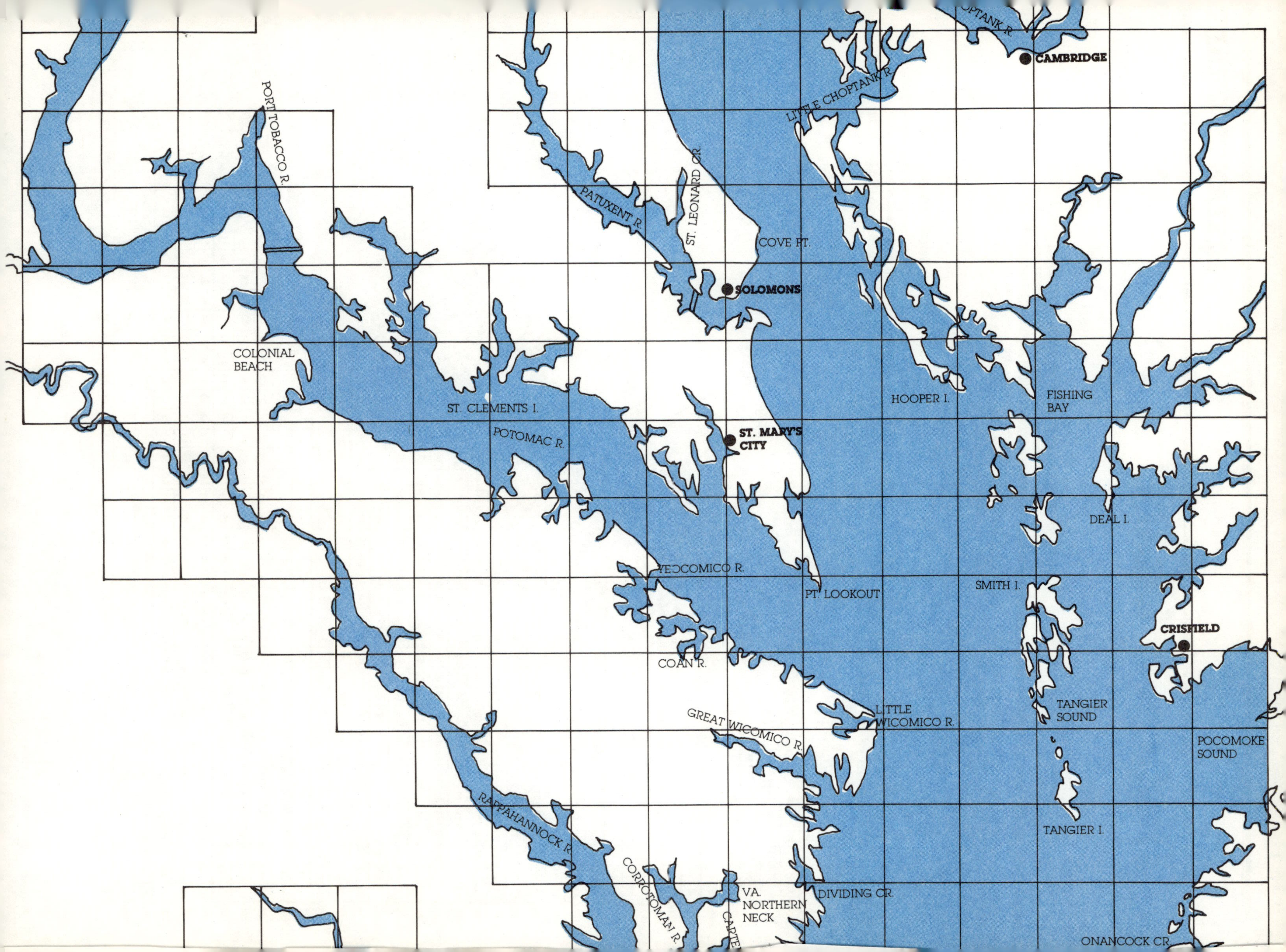
CAMBRIDGE
CHOPTANK R.
LITTLE CHOPTANK R.
PORT TOBACCO R.
PATUXENT R.
ST. LEONARD CR.
COVE PT.
SOLOMONS
COLONIAL BEACH
ST. CLEMENTS I.
POTOMAC R.
ST. MARY'S CITY
HOOPER I.
FISHING BAY
DEAL I.
SMITH I.
YEOCOMICO R.
PT. LOOKOUT
CRISFIELD
COAN R.
LITTLE WICOMICO R.
GREAT WICOMICO R.
TANGIER SOUND
POCOMOKE SOUND
TANGIER I.
RAPPAHANNOCK R.
CORROTOMAN R.
VA. NORTHERN NECK
DIVIDING CR.
ONANCOCK CR.

Distance Chart

To utilize distance chart, note the black numbers opposite your two destination points. Follow the first vertically to its intersection horizontally with the second. The point of intersection indicates the distance between the two points. Example: the distance from Annapolis (#9) to Solomons (#21) is 49 nautical miles. (approx.)

DISTANCE TABLE

Approximate Nautical Mileage between Major Cruise Points by direct courses for small craft (less than 5 ft. draft)

1 Nautical Mile = 1.15 Statute Miles (6,076 feet approx.)

1. Chesapeake City 39° - 31.7' N Lat., 75° - 48.7' W Long.
2. Georgetown 39° - 21.7' N Lat., 75° - 53.1' W Long.
3. Howell Point 39° - 22.3' N Lat., 76° - 06.8' W Long.
4. Worton Creek Entrance, Qk Fl R "2" 39° - 17.4' N Lat., 76° - 10.3' W Long.
5. Middle River Entrance, Qk Fl R "4" 39° - 17.6' N Lat., 76° - 23.1' W Long.
6. Baltimore Ft. McHenry, Qk Fl G "1" 39° - 15.7' N Lat., 76° - 34.5' W Long.
7. Swan Creek Entrance 39° - 08.7' N Lat., 76° - 15.8' W Long.
8. Chesapeake Bay Bridge Main Channel 38° - 59.6' N Lat., 76° - 22.9' W Long.
9. Annapolis Harbor 38° - 58.5' N Lat., 76° - 29' W Long.
10. Bloody Point Light Fl 6 sec 38° - 50' N Lat., 76° - 23.5' W Long.
11. Thomas Point Light Fl 6 sec 38° - 53.9' N Lat., 76° - 26.2' W Long.
12. West & Rhode Rv. Entrance Fl R 2½ sec 38° - 51.9' N. Lat., 76° - 29.5' W Long.
13. Herring Bay Parkers Shoal Fl 4 sec "2" 38° - 44.4' N. Lat., 76° - 32.6' W Long.
14. St. Michaels Harbor 38° - 47.2' N Lat., 76° - 13.1' W Long.
15. Knapps Narrows Bridge 38° - 43.2' N Lat., 76° - 20' W Long.
16. Oxford Harbor Town Creek 38° - 41.6' N Lat., 76° - 10' W Long.
17. Cambridge Harbor 38° - 34.4' N Lat., 76° - 04.2' W Long.
18. Sharps Island Light Fl 6 sec 38° - 38.3' N Lat., 76° - 22.5' W Long.
19. Little Choptank River Entrance Fl G 2½ sec "1" 38° - 33.3' N Lat., 76° - 19.3' W Long.
20. Cove Point Light Fl 10 sec 38° - 23.1' N Lat., 76° - 22.9' W Long.
21. Solomons Harbor 38° - 19.3' N Lat., 76° - 27.3' W Long.
22. Point Lookout Light I Qk Fl 38° - 01.6' N Lat., 76° - 19.3' W Long.
23. St. Mary's River Entrance RB I Qk Fl R 38° - 04.5' N Lat., 76° - 26.1' W Long.
24. Smith Island West Entrance 38° - 0' N Lat., 76° - 03.4' W Long.
25. Crisfield Harbor 37° - 58.6' N Lat., 75° - 51.9' W Long.
26. Tangier Island West Entrance 37° - 49.9' N Lat., 76° - 00.2' W Long.
27. Smith Point Light Fl 10 sec 37° - 52.8' N Lat., 76° - 11' W Long.
28. Great Wicomico River Light Fl 6 sec 37° - 48.3' N Lat., 76° - 16.1' W Long.
29. Onancock Creek Entrance Fl 4 sec "1" 37° - 43.5' N Lat., 75° - 51.1' W Long.
30. Windmill Point Light Fl 6 sec 37° - 35.8' N Lat., 76° - 14.2' W Long.
31. Corrotoman River Entrance Fl R "2" 37° - 40' N Lat., 76° - 29' W Long.
32. Stingray Point Light Fl 4 sec 37° - 33.7' N Lat., 76° - 16.2' W Long.
33. Wolftrap Light Fl 15 sec 37° - 23.4' N Lat., 76° - 11.4' W Long.
34. New Point Comfort Light Fl R 2½ sec "2" 37° - 17.8' N Lat., 76° - 15.7' W Long.
35. Sarah Creek Entrance Fl R 4 sec "2" 37° - 14.7' N Lat., 76° - 29.1' W Long.
36. Cape Charles Harbor 37° - 15.9' N Lat., 76° - 01.4' W Long.
37. York River Spit Fl G 4 sec "3" 37° - 15.7' N Lat., 76° - 20' W Long.
38. Thimble Shoal Light Fl 10 sec 37° - 0.9' N Lat., 76° - 14.4' W Long.
39. Willoughby Spit Fl G 4 sec "9" 36° - 57.9' N Lat., 76° - 18' W Long.
40. Newport News Bridge Main Channel 37° - 0.2' N Lat., 76° - 28.1' W Long.

	1	2	3	4	5	6	7	8	9	10	11	12	13	14	15	16	17	18	19	20	21	22	23	24	25	26	27	28	29	30	31	32	33	34	35	36	37	38	39	40
1	**1**																																							
2	25	**2**																																						
3	18	12	**3**																																					
4	26	20	8	**4**																																				
5	34	28	16	11	**5**																																			
6	47	41	29	23	17	**6**																																		
7	44	38	26	21	20	24	**7**																																	
8	45	39	27	22	20	22	12	**8**																																
9	52	46	34	29	27	29	19	7	**9**																															
10	55	4	37	32	30	32	22	10	11	**10**																														
11	52	46	34	29	27	29	19	7	7	5	**11**																													
12	56	50	38	33	31	33	23	11	11	6	4	**12**																												
13	63	57	45	40	38	40	30	18	19	9	12	11	**13**																											
14	71	65	53	48	46	48	38	26	27	16	21	22	25	**14**																										
15	64	58	46	41	39	41	31	19	20	9	14	15	10	19	**15**																									
16	76	70	58	53	51	53	43	31	32	21	26	27	22	31	12	**16**																								
17	81	75	63	58	56	58	48	36	37	26	31	32	27	36	17	12	**17**																							
18	67	61	49	44	42	44	34	22	22	12	17	17	10	24	7	12	18	**18**																						
19	74	68	56	51	49	51	41	29	29	19	24	24	17	31	11	15	21	7	**19**																					
20	84	78	66	61	59	61	51	39	40	29	33	31	24	40	22	26	30	16	12	**20**																				
21	93	87	7	70	68	70	60	48	49	38	42	40	33	49	31	35	39	25	21	9	**21**																			
22	108	102	90	85	83	85	75	63	64	53	57	55	48	64	46	50	54	40	36	24	25	**22**																		
23	115	109	97	92	90	92	82	70	71	60	64	62	55	71	53	57	61	47	43	31	32	7	**23**																	
24	113	107	95	90	88	90	80	68	69	58	62	60	53	69	51	55	59	45	41	29	30	13	20	**24**																
25	123	117	105	100	98	100	90	78	79	68	72	70	63	79	61	65	69	55	51	39	40	27	34	19	**25**															
26	124	118	106	101	99	101	91	79	80	69	73	71	64	80	62	66	70	56	52	40	41	19	26	13	13	**26**														
27	117	111	99	94	92	94	84	72	73	62	66	64	57	73	55	59	63	49	45	33	34	12	19	9	26	9	**27**													
28	124	118	106	101	99	101	91	79	80	69	73	71	64	80	62	66	70	56	52	40	41	18	25	16	28	13	7	**28**												
29	135	129	117	112	110	112	102	90	91	80	84	82	75	91	73	77	81	67	63	51	52	31	38	22	21	11	19	21	**29**											
30	134	128	116	111	109	111	101	89	90	79	83	81	74	90	72	76	80	66	62	50	51	29	36	26	31	18	17	13	20	**30**										
31	148	142	130	125	123	125	115	103	104	93	97	95	88	104	86	90	94	80	76	64	65	43	50	40	45	32	31	27	34	14	**31**									
32	137	131	119	114	112	114	104	92	93	82	86	84	77	93	75	79	83	69	65	53	54	32	39	29	34	21	20	16	23	3	13	**32**								
33	146	140	128	123	121	123	113	101	102	91	95	93	86	102	84	88	92	78	74	62	64	41	48	38	40	27	29	26	27	13	24	11	**33**							
34	153	147	135	130	128	130	120	108	109	98	102	100	93	109	91	95	99	85	81	69	71	48	55	45	47	34	36	33	34	20	31	18	7	**34**						
35	164	158	146	141	139	141	131	119	120	109	113	111	104	120	102	106	110	96	92	80	82	59	66	56	58	45	47	44	45	31	42	29	18	11	**35**					
36	161	155	143	138	136	138	128	116	117	106	110	108	101	117	99	103	107	93	89	77	78	56	63	51	52	40	44	40	39	28	40	27	16	15	24	**36**				
37	157	151	139	134	132	134	124	112	113	102	106	104	97	113	95	99	103	89	85	73	75	52	59	49	51	38	40	37	38	24	35	22	11	4	7	17	**37**			
38	169	163	151	146	144	146	136	124	125	114	118	116	109	125	107	111	115	101	97	85	87	64	71	61	63	50	52	49	48	36	47	34	23	17	21	19	16	**38**		
39	174	168	156	151	149	151	141	129	130	119	123	121	114	130	112	116	120	106	102	90	92	69	76	66	68	55	57	54	53	41	52	39	28	22	26	24	21	5	**39**	
40	183	177	165	160	158	160	150	138	139	128	132	130	123	139	121	125	129	115	111	99	101	78	85	75	77	64	66	63	62	50	61	48	37	31	35	33	30	14	11	**40**